THE
ACTIVE READER

THE
ACTIVE READER

Strategies for Academic Reading and Writing

Third Edition | *Eric Henderson*

OXFORD
UNIVERSITY PRESS

OXFORD
UNIVERSITY PRESS

Oxford University Press is a department of the University of Oxford.
It furthers the University's objective of excellence in research, scholarship,
and education by publishing worldwide. Oxford is a registered trade mark of
Oxford University Press in the UK and in certain other countries.

Published in Canada by
Oxford University Press
8 Sampson Mews, Suite 204,
Don Mills, Ontario M3C 0H5 Canada

www.oupcanada.com

Library and Archives Canada Cataloguing in Publication
Henderson, Eric, author
The active reader : strategies for academic reading and
writing / Eric Henderson. — Third edition.

Includes bibliographical references and index.
ISBN 978-0-19-901245-9 (pbk.)

1. English language—Rhetoric—Textbooks. 2. Academic
writing—Textbooks. 3. Report writing—Textbooks. 4. Reading
comprehension—Textbooks. 5. College readers. I. Title.

PE1408.H385 2015   808'.042   C2015-900354-7

Cover image: Rene Mansi/Getty Images

Printed and bound in Canada

3 4 — 16 15

CONTENTS

PART II | Academic Writing   63

PART III | The Reader   159

The Active Voice

PREFACE

Academic Writing and the New Realists

The future turns out to be a work-in-progress, not a set of map coordinates but the product of a never-ending argument between the inertia as things-as-they-are and the energy inherent in the hope of things-as-they-might-become.

Lewis Lapham, Editor, *Harper's Magazine*
Convocation Address, Queen's University

All life is problem-solving. All organisms are inventors and technicians, good or not so good, successful or not so successful, in solving technical problems. This is how it is among animals—spiders, for example. Human technology solves human problems such as sewage disposal, or the storage and supply of food and water, as, for example, bees already have to do.

Philosopher Karl Popper

More than a decade ago, I watched first-year students tapping hesitantly on keyboards in a computer lab at my university, completing a simple early-term assignment: a short essay on what they considered the major challenge humans face today. Predictably, I read about dwindling oil supplies, overpopulation, pollution, the Middle East battleground, and terrorism. While many of the problems remain the same, the students' responses today are different: more thoughtful, paradoxically less concrete. Typical problems identified include "our lack of concern for the world around us," "lack of co-operation," "loss of faith in our ability to act," "problems communicating," "flawed human perception," "hatred," "evasion of important issues," "intolerance," "humanity itself," "*we* are the problem."

If this does, indeed, suggest a trend, these students could be called the "new realists" for their willingness to confront underlying causes and acknowledge human responsibility. Certainly, most students today are well aware of the challenges that their generation and future ones face. They also understand the role that communication, especially written communication, will play in meeting these challenges. This book was designed in response to the need both for problem-solvers and for good communicators, the two faces of today's (and tomorrow's) realists.

One of the reasons for studying the conventions of academic reading and writing is to direct the human need to explore and learn, to express and create, to discuss and debate, in writing, into useful and fulfilling channels. Although the immediate result might be a level of competence that will help students in their other courses and lead to improved grades, the acquisition of writing and reading skills serves many long-term goals. Language is one of the most powerful tools—possibly the most powerful—for ensuring our survival as individuals, as a society, and as a species. Through the medium of language, we can read about contemporary problems, ask a range of pertinent questions, and propose practical solutions to these problems. *The Active Reader: Strategies for Academic Reading and Writing* seeks to provide student readers, writers, and researchers with the training to question, investigate, analyze, and communicate.

For the Third Edition

The words above, written for the first edition, resound even more urgently seven years later in a world increasingly beset by challenges both to the quality of life and to sustaining the diversity of life in the generations to come. It is for the "new realists" mentioned above—students and instructors—that the third edition has been prepared.

This edition includes several necessary adaptations of the first and second, although selection criteria have remained the same: essays of high interest, relevance, and accessibility to today's student have been chosen.

While popular academic essays have been retained from the second edition, the updated selections give prominence to the academic review essay and the editorial/argumentative essay, both highly suitable formats for study. The academic review essay affords an apt model for the research essay, in which students investigate sources on a topic, organize them logically, and evaluate their contribution, forming conclusions or answering questions posed in their introductions. Like student writers, academic writers often have opinions on the topics they investigate, and may make recommendations based on their findings. By studying the essays in Part III, students should find assurance that scholarly writing is a place for informed discussion and enlivened debate, thus providing an efficacious model for argumentation.

The 34 readings, all published in journals or books, are divided into six categories of interest to today's students: "University Issues," "Canada in the World," "Voices within Canada," "Media and Image," "Aggression and Society," and "Intersections with Science." They embrace diverse disciplines, from economics to environmental studies, history to health sciences. The essays are integrated with a well-developed rhetoric—10 chapters covering the conventions of academic writing and reading, critical thinking, summarizing, argumentation, and writing rhetorical analyses and research papers. Plentiful examples from student writing, many of which include explanatory comments, illustrate material covered.

Using many resources to assist in comprehension, *The Active Reader* actively challenges the stereotype that academic writing is dry and inaccessible to students today. The focus remains squarely on academic writing, but, recognizing that students will encounter various kinds of essays and a multitude of styles and formats in their studies and beyond, several non-academic essays in a variety of disciplines have been included in the third edition. The pages that follow will fully equip students to successfully read and write about challenging texts, the kinds of texts they will often be called on to read, understand, and model in many of their assignments.

Additional Highlights

- More than half of the essays in Part III: The Reader are new to this edition, reflecting the need for topical content in a fast-changing world. These readings continue to be accompanied by pre- and post-reading questions, vocabulary lists, useful web links, and suggested readings.
- Many of the new academic essays are high-interest, offering a diversity of subjects and formats, and are shorter in length than in the previous edition.
- The new non-academic essays engage students while illustrating conventions of non-academic prose.
- More sample essays with annotations appear throughout the chapters, helping students to improve their analytical and writing skills.
- Content has been reorganized so that there are now separate chapters on writing summaries (Chapter 7), using critical thinking to analyze essays (Chapter 8), and writing argumentative essays (Chapter 9).
- New "Active Voice" essays include "Brave New Words: Technology and the Future of Writing" and "Rhetorical Analysis: What, Why, and How." The essays on digital research, Google and the Internet, and writing for the disciplines have been updated.
- Coverage of APA, MLA, CMS, and CSE formats has been updated and expanded.
- Key terms and concepts are defined in the margins and compiled in a glossary at the end of the book.
- A new index of academic essay types helps students recognize the readings by their academic conventions.

As in previous editions, "The Active Voice" boxes provide informative essays by instructors, writing professionals, and students (see below) that alert readers to issues of practical concern today—from developing research skills to the challenges of report and online writing. Some of these essays flow seamlessly from the text, while others elaborate on or demonstrate the application of a point mentioned in the text. Many can be treated as mini-essays that can be discussed and analyzed.

The Active Voice

Homelessness 101

In a busy city, many people become so immersed in their daily routines and problems that they are unaware of their own surroundings. Most do not notice the many homeless people living on the streets and simply carry on with their day as if they didn't exist. In my final year of high school, I was able to participate in a unique and truly meaningful experience that allowed me to spend a day with the homeless people of Vancouver. My class-mates and I set up a "free-market" at Oppenheimer Park, an area inhabited by many of the homeless. We handed out donated clothing, toiletries, and house-hold items, as well as holding a free barbeque where we served hot dogs. The most memorable experience, however, was playing soccer against a team of homeless people. Through the experience I learned that not all the homeless are "druggies" and that they are not scary or intimidating. Mostly, I learned the importance of acceptance and of giving back.

The term "homeless" instantly evokes many stereotypes, the most common of which is that homeless people all suffer from addictions or drug-related problems. Through my experience at the free-market, I learned that this is not true. Although many of them, unfortunately, have serious addictions, I met others who were homeless for different reasons. For instance, Devon is a woman in her twenties who ran away from an abusive family. She didn't have a job and was temporarily forced to live on her own on the streets. Luis came from Mexico with very little money and no place to live. Not everyone understands that drugs do not play a role in all their lives—many have never even done drugs before.

Second, I learned that the homeless are not scary or hard to approach. When playing soccer with the homeless team, we all had a great time. Not only were they much better than we were at the game, but they were also extremely friendly and fun to compete against. After the game, I struck up a conversation with a member of the victorious team. He told me he was an ex-Hell's Angel, which initially made me somewhat timid; however, during our conversation, I became aware how intelligent he was

and how easy he was to talk to. I learned that it really is worth striking up a conversation with people living on the streets and hearing their stories.

Last, I learned the importance of giving back. It was an amazing feeling to see somebody pick up one of the shirts I donated and the smile on her face as she tried it on. Seeing the homeless competing as a team and showing off their considerable skills also showed me that we all have hidden talents that can be put to good use, that we are really all one community. Many people pass homeless people downtown on their way to work, trying to avoid eye contact or acknowledging them in any way. It is important to remember how lucky we are to live in a warm house with food and to remember to give back to the less fortunate—even if it means just giving them a smile to show you know they are there.

That day gave me an entirely new perspective on homeless people. By talking and engaging in a game with them, it became evident that there is nothing wrong with them; they just need our support. I found them approachable and their stories interesting. Mostly, I learned how important it is to help those in need. It was a unique and rewarding experience that opened me to a new world.

Ilona Mihalik, 1st-year student

Acknowledgements

I wish to gratefully acknowledge the editorial staff at Oxford University Press Canada for their enthusiasm and expertise. I would particularly like to thank Leah-Ann Lymer, my helpful and patient developmental editor, for charting the course of the new edition; Dave Ward and Eric Sinkins for their ongoing support; and Michelle Welsh for making the proofing and production stages virtually frustration free.

I much appreciate the help of my colleagues at the University of Victoria. I am especially indebted to Monika Rydygier Smith who has contributed to all editions in numberless ways. I am grateful to suggestions and other input from Richard Pickard, Brian Day, Celeste Derksen, Rebecca Gagan, Joseph Grossi, Sean Henry, Andrew Murray, Harb Sanghara, and Madeline Walker.

I am indebted to the generosity of those individuals who took the time to write new essays or update their original contributions for the third edition: John Archibald, Jim Henderson, Erin Kelly, David Leach, and Christine Walde. All "Active Voice" contributors have enlarged the scope of this book significantly, imbuing it with their knowledge of and passion for their subject.

I would like to thank the named and anonymous reviewers who offered valuable feedback that helped to shape this edition:

- Karin Collins, University of Winnipeg
- Theresa Hyland, Huron University College
- Dennis R. Nighswonger, Lakehead University
- Abdollah Zahiri, Seneca College

From its inception to the completion of the third edition, *The Active Reader: Strategies for Academic Reading and Writing* has been rooted in my teaching life at UVic, particularly the teaching of academic reading and writing to first-year students. I am indebted to the many students who allowed their writing to be represented in this book.

Above all, Madeline Sonik has been a constant and sustaining presence in my life, in which the aspirations for and planning of this book occupy a small—but vital—part.

Eric Henderson
January 2015

PART I

Academic Reading: An Introduction

As students, you will be introduced to many different kinds of writing during your post-secondary education. Your goal usually is to interact with these texts in various ways, such as the following:

- discuss the issues they raise with your classmates
- respond to them in writing, agreeing or disagreeing with the argument
- learn the ways they are put together and/or the rhetorical strategies used
- acquire the specialized knowledge they contain or become familiar with the procedures through which this knowledge can be acquired
- refer to their findings as part of a research project
- use them as models for your own writing, perhaps in preparation for other undergraduate courses

As you proceed in your program of study, the nature of this interaction will likely increase in complexity. New skill acquisition invites new challenges. By rising to these challenges early in your university career, you will be better prepared for the discipline-specific reading and writing challenges that lie ahead. Inevitably, some of these challenges will present themselves as academic readings, researched and documented essays by experts who seek to advance knowledge in their discipline. Part I is designed to help you interact with these essays.

Chapters 1 and 2 introduce the kinds of reading tasks you perform at the post-secondary level. They attempt to answer the questions, What can you expect when you read academic essays? Who are they written for and how are they written? In what ways is academic writing a distinct genre with its own rules and procedures? What do academic readings across the disciplines have in common?

In chapter 3 we consider three distinct formats of academic essays. What can you look for when you read a humanities essay? How does an essay in the humanities differ from one in the social sciences or the sciences?

Of course, reading academic prose involves much more than identifying its main features and where to find them. Chapters 4 and 5 highlight the unique engagement between writers and readers of academic texts and the strategies that can enhance this engagement. Chapter 4 focuses on applying critical-thinking skills to academic reading. Although we exercise critical thinking in many everyday activities, the complex and diverse nature of academic writing requires us to be conscious of critical thinking before, during, and after reading academic texts. Chapter 5 is designed to help you understand challenging essays: to become familiar with their rules and procedures and to use them in practical ways throughout your university career. Questions addressed include, What kinds of thinking does academic reading require of you? What kinds of reading skills are required? What specific strategies can you use to make the reading process easier, increase comprehension, and develop the skills to analyze the text?

1

An Introduction to Academic Prose

What Is Academic Writing?

For some people, *academic writing* is a euphemism for dense, abstract writing, so highly specialized as to be virtually impenetrable to non-specialists. However, successful academic writing is not intended to baffle the reader but is customized for an audience familiar with a given discipline's conventions and modes of discourse, its central ideas, and its ways of presenting and analyzing them.

What is meant by *academic writing?* The answer depends on who is doing the writing (and the reading).

1. Academic writing can refer to the practices of scholars and researchers, the nature of the texts that you will be asked to read in many of your classes.
2. For students, academic writing could be considered writing at a level that demonstrates your literacy through clear, precise, and grammatical prose and that successfully conveys your ideas through appropriate structures and the use of critical thinking—in short, writing at the university level.

In part I, we will be addressing the first definition, while in part II, we will be addressing the second.

Collaborative Exercise 1.1
Defining Academic Writing

In groups of three, expand on the first definition of academic writing, incorporating any other features you believe are important. Your completed definition should be two sentences. Compare your group's definition with that of other groups.

Roadblocks to Reading

Like most other writing, academic writing has a distinct purpose, in this case, to advance knowledge in a discipline. It is also intended for a specific audience: knowledgeable and interested readers. In most kinds of writing, including the kinds you will do in many of your courses, purpose and audience are two key variables that you must consider before you begin.

However, language and/or problems with discipline-specific concepts can be barriers to understanding for the uninitiated reader. To become a competent academic reader, then, might require working to understand vocabulary, including specialized terms, and establishing a firmer grounding in key concepts and their uses.

In order to be prepared for the kinds of sophisticated reading tasks that lie ahead, you need to become acquainted with academic discourse: its conventions and vocabulary, as well as the critical-thinking skills that enable you to respond fully to its challenges.

What Are Conventions?

You can think of conventions (the word means "come together") as a set of instructions. Conventions are recurrent patterns that direct and organize the behaviour of specific groups of people. One reason we follow conventions is to help us communicate with one another. For example, it is a convention in some cultures to bow respectfully when being introduced to a stranger or simple acquaintance. In formal letter-writing, it is conventional to use a form of salutation like *Dear Sir/Madam*; however, in email a more appropriate salutation might be *Hello* or *Hi*. A convention must continue to serve a purpose; otherwise, it may be replaced by a newer, more useful convention.

Academic writing also has its conventions, which help direct the reader and organize the essay. They help the reader respond appropriately and knowledgeably. They also open up an effective channel of communication between writer and reader. The next section focuses on general information applicable to most academic writing as well as several of the conventions. We will discuss the conventions of academic writing in more detail in chapter 2.

---

purpose
Why you are writing; variables affecting purpose include your topic and your audience.

audience
Whom you are writing to; includes one or more readers with common interests, knowledge level, and/or expectations.

conventions
Recurrent patterns that direct and organize the behaviour of specific groups of people and that, applied appropriately, help us communicate with our audience.

General Features of Academic Writing

Knowledge Across the Disciplines

Although academic writing is generally written for knowledgeable readers, knowledge itself differs somewhat across the disciplines, as the following definitions suggest. (See chapter 9 for more information on which research methods and procedures are best suited to the various disciplines.)

- *Humanities:* The branch of knowledge concerned with examining the cultural tools that humans use to express and represent themselves. Humanities writing focuses on how ideas and values are used to interpret human experience, analyzing primary sources to draw conclusions about their literary themes, language, art and culture, historical significance, theoretical basis, or universality. Typical humanities disciplines are classical studies, history, linguistics, literature, modern languages, Native studies, philosophy, and religious studies, among others.
- *Social sciences:* The branch of knowledge concerned with the study of human behaviour within a well-defined order or system (e.g., society, human mind, economics, political system). Social science disciplines include anthropology, economics, geography, political science, psychology, and sociology, among others.
- *Sciences:* The branch of knowledge concerned with the study of natural phenomena using empirical methods to determine or validate their laws. The natural and applied sciences include biology, chemistry, engineering, environmental sciences, health sciences, mathematics, and many more.

The Active Voice

Why Study the Humanities?

Today's students are under a lot of pressure from many sources to attain a "useful" post-secondary degree. According to many media commentators, and some governments, the so-called useful areas of study could include science, technology, engineering, and mathematics (the STEM fields). Government funding often goes to enhance these programs so that more students can study them. But it is a mistake to ignore the value of the humanities—which traditionally includes languages (modern, classical, and linguistics), literature, philosophy, and history. There are two arguments I want to present.

The first is that studying in the humanities results in a knowledge and skill set that is valuable in many ways. Students will acquire the so-called soft skills of analytical reading, writing, and thinking which, as it turns out, are valued by many employers. John Manley (former deputy prime minister of Canada, and now leader of the Canadian Council of Chief Executives) reports on the results of a survey of 100 leading companies which indicate the skills employers are looking for in new hires: (1) people skills, (2) communication, (3) problem-solving, (4) analytic abilities, (5) leadership, and, clocking in at (6), industry-specific skills. And these are the skills which will get you promoted in a job as well. These humanities skills, then, are good both for your job and for broader life satisfaction. We need to remember that so much of our life is outside of our jobs. In order to be an engaged citizen in today's complex world, we need to know the historical, cultural, and social contexts of current events. It is a reality that students today are much more likely to have multiple careers than youth in past generations. The key to success in such a world is flexibility. And that is where the notion of utility which I referred to earlier comes in. There is a temptation to assume that specific skills are useful: computer-assisted drafting, arc welding. But any skill not properly taught runs the risk of becoming obsolete: 35-mm film projection, carburetor repair. In the humanities, you learn how to learn, how to solve problems, how to analyze data, and how to work in teams. These are skills which are useful in many contexts. Utility is a slippery notion, indeed.

It's true that our graduates probably will not get jobs with titles like historian or philosopher, but if that was the logic behind our actions, why would we go to the gym or take a yoga class? We are unlikely to become professional lifters or stretchers. Nonetheless, the activity will enhance the quality of our lives. Similarly, humanities students will get jobs that draw on their knowledge and skills and allow them to acquire new knowledge and new skills which will, in turn, advance them up the job ladder while enriching them materially, cognitively, and spiritually.

My second argument is that the students themselves actually speak to the value of humanities: they vote with their feet and with their words. Over the past 50 years, the proportion of people studying the humanities as a percentage of population has remained quite constant (about 4 per cent of the population). Demand is not falling. At time of writing, the humanities students at my university have the highest high-school admission average of any faculty (that is to say, they have lots of choices but choose us), our first-year course enrolments are up, and our student body is the size of a small city—about the size of many small universities or colleges in North America. These are not members of some lost generation who slip thought the cracks and end up in the safety net of humanities. About 90 per cent of our fourth-year students say that if they had it all to do over again, they would choose the same program. So, students are coming, they like what they get, and they would do it all again. Who are we not to listen to the voices of our students?

By studying the humanities, you will discover the person you can become. The person you become will determine the world you live in.

References

Manley, John. "Jobs, skills and opportunities: strengthening Canada's human capital advantage." Notes for remarks by the Honourable John Manley, President and CEO Canadian Council of Chief Executives. Presented at the Canadian Club of Toronto. 28 November 2013.

—**Dr. John Archibald**, Dean of Humanities, University of Victoria

Audience: Who Reads Academic Writing?

It will come as no surprise that the largest audience for academic writing is scholars, people with knowledge about and interest in the discipline or subject area. However, not all writing in academic books and journals is intended for the same audience. The expert in cell biology will not necessarily speak the same language as the expert in theoretical physics. The biologist may read the academic journal *Cell* while the physicist may read every issue of *Communications in Mathematical Physics*. Yet both may faithfully subscribe to scientific journals like *Nature* or *Science* that publish articles of interest in the broad field of science and the social sciences, as well as the results of research. Academic journals and many academic presses vary in their readership, from highly knowledgeable readers to those with a general knowledge.

One way of gauging the intended audience is to note what criteria are used to determine the suitability of an article for publication. The most reliable academic journals are peer-reviewed (refereed). (See below, Where Academic Writing Is Found, for

peer-reviewed
A type of journal in which submissions are reviewed by experts before publication; indicates an authoritative source for scholarly research.

different categories of journals and magazines.) The aims of academic publications are well summarized by John Fraser, a well-known journalist and educator:

> [T]he best academic publications extend our understanding of who we are in ways that trade publications and magazines and newspapers have largely abandoned. Canada's collective memory, our understanding of our social and economic conditions, aboriginal challenges to national complacency, the actual consequences of de-linking ourselves from the realities of our past . . . all find provocative and highly useful resonances from our academic publishers.
>
> —J. Fraser, "Academic publishers teach mainstream ones a lesson,"
> *The Globe and Mail* 4 June 2005: F9.

In non–peer-reviewed journals, authors may summarize and rewrite technical prose for interested but not highly knowledgeable readers. Such journals are not usually considered academic: their stress is less on original research and more on making this research accessible to the literate non-specialist. However, they are different from consumer-type magazines in which writers must often adopt strategies to attract and maintain the interest of a general reader.

The Purposes of Academic Writing

The most obvious function of academic journals, particularly those in the social sciences and sciences, is to publish the results of experiments. However, not all articles in journals are concerned with original research. Many articles in humanities journals refer to previous studies and interpret them in light of a specific theory or framework. Depending on the purpose of the author(s), the focus may be on generating new knowledge through experimentation or on modifying the way future researchers interpret this knowledge. Still others review what is currently known about a particular topic, summarizing what has been written to date and its significance.

These distinctions suggest three basic kinds of academic texts:

1. those that present the results of original research
2. those that build on existing research, offering new interpretations
3. those that review and analyze the current state of knowledge about a topic (see chapter 3)

original research
Research in which the author(s) conducts an experiment to generate raw data or uses available data to prove/ disprove a hypothesis or answer a research question. Such research includes the method, results, and discussion of results.

An Exchange of Ideas

Academic writing operates as a shared or "open" system, *a medium for the exchange of ideas among informed and interested experts*, in order to explore an idea, concept, or text; to answer an important question; to test a hypothesis; or to solve a problem. In spite of the occasional inconsistencies in results and disagreements among experts, it is this common objective—to help us better understand ourselves and our world—that unites those working in specialized fields. This objective undermines the stereotype of the "isolated scholar." Scholars, especially those involved in experimentation, seldom work alone. More often, they work in collaborative teams in which a breakdown in communication or a lack of co-operation could endanger the experiment's validity and damage their own credibility.

Analysis, Synthesis, and Academic Writing

Analysis

Another basic feature of academic writing is the emphasis on analysis. When you analyze, you "loosen [something] up." Analysis can be applied to all the disciplines: an earth scientist may literally "loosen up," or break down, the constituents of a soil sample to determine the concentration of its elements, while a nuclear physicist may study the behaviour of sub-atomic particles in a particle accelerator as they reach very high speeds and begin to break down into smaller units. A literary analysis could involve breaking down a poem's stanzas or a novel's narrative to study smaller units, such as metre (in a poem) or point of view (in fiction).

Analysis can serve several functions. Thus, there are various ways that an analysis can proceed:

- by attention to detail (description)
- by applying a timeline to events (chronology)
- by comparing and contrasting
- by dividing and perhaps subdividing a whole (division and classification)
- by looking at the pros and cons of something

There are many other methods as well (see Rhetorical Patterns and Paragraph Development, page 79).

Synthesis

Just as in the academic essays of experts, in most research essays you write, you do not just break down; you also synthesize. Synthesis is the act of "putting together." The writer(s) of a scientific experiment presents the raw data that emerged in the study of a particular phenomenon. However, the data alone are not meaningful or relevant until they are placed within a larger context—the hypothesis that the experiment was intended to test, for example, or results from similar experiments. In the final section of the write-up, the writer attempts to synthesize his or her findings by connecting them with the hypothesis and/or the results of similar studies.

When you organize the sources you have used in your research essays, you, too, will be synthesizing, combining the results of your research to reflect your purpose and approach to your topic. Part of the synthesizing process will involve decisions about whether to quote your sources directly, summarize the findings, or paraphrase important passages. Synthesis can also take place on two levels: the ideas you use and the language you use to express them (see chapter 9).

Where Academic Writing Is Found

Academic writing is published in academic journals and in books published by academic (university) presses. When searching for research sources, you should pay particular attention to *who* publishes the work.

University presses are generally run by non-profit, university-affiliated organizations that disseminate the research of scholars. Although the decision to publish usually rests with the editors, they are guided by the comments of "readers," or peer-reviewers,

analysis

In analysis, you break up a whole in order to (1) closely examine each part individually and/or (2) investigate the relationships among the parts.

synthesis

Writing in which elements of a work or other studies about a work are brought together, usually in order to draw a conclusion or interpret a claim you wish to assert about the work.

university press

A university-affiliated publisher, usually of books or journals; they are authoritative sources for scholarly research.

experts in the same subject as the work's author, who evaluate the manuscript; they recommend its publication or rejection. Although the work may be controversial—for example, if it challenges previous findings or interpretations—you can be confident that it is a credible source. University presses also produce monographs, the term for highly specialized scholarly works or treatises in book form.

Trade books, published for profit and usually to appeal to a wider audience than books published by academic presses, may also be reliable sources, particularly if they have been received favourably by authorities. The best way to assess their reliability is by looking for reviews from independent sources. Many journals regularly include book reviews relevant to their subject area.

Academic (scholarly) journals are subscribed to by university libraries and made available to faculty and students in hard-copy versions and/or through electronic databases and indexes. (Do not assume, however, that every article you locate in your library's database is an academic source. Databases often include both scholarly and non-scholarly material.) They are often more current sources than book-length studies because most journals publish several times a year, and the pre-publication process is quicker than with longer works; thus, journals can provide "leading-edge" research in rapidly developing fields.

An increasing number of academic journals publish only in online formats. Open-access journals permit free access by users. The publishers of such journals may wish to promote the use of their studies' findings in the interests of a more informed and knowledgeable public. As with everything you encounter online, however, you should scrutinize such sources for their reliability before using them in your essay. (The Directory of Open Access Journals lists more than 5,000 international open-access journals, many of them peer-reviewed: www.doaj.org.)

For complete information about source reliability, see pp. 137–139.

Figure 1.1 summarizes some of the different classifications of academic and non-academic writing. However, the categories are not always clear-cut; for example, some academic journals include material intended for a more general audience. (Note that periodical is a general term for the kind of publication that is issued periodically, at regular or semi-regular intervals.)

In this text, essays written for a prospective audience comprising scholars, researchers, and professors are referred to as academic or scholarly essays, whether they are in book or journal format, while essays written for an audience comprising non-specialists who share certain interests, beliefs, or ideologies are referred to as journalistic essays. Articles in mass-circulation magazines or newspapers are usually written for an audience with varied knowledge and interest levels.

Although the essays in this text are primarily scholarly, a few are written for a literate audience of non-specialists and do not conform in all respects to the conventions of scholarly writing. Furthermore, not all your assignments may be modelled on scholarly conventions or require you to use scholarly discourse. For example, you may be asked to respond online with other class members to an essay and be permitted to write more informally. In some of your assignments, your instructor may ask you to begin with a *hook*, a deliberate strategy to engage a reader, such as a catchy phrase, question, or brief narrative, a technique less used in scholarly writing. Understanding the strategies professional writers use to "spice up" their prose or make it more concise when space is at a premium will give you more options when scholarly conventions are less crucial.

---

monograph
A highly specialized scholarly work or treatise in book form.

trade books
Books published by non-academic presses for general readers about topics of interest to them.

academic (scholarly) journal
A type of periodical containing scholarly content (articles, reviews, and commentaries) by experts for a knowledgeable audience in related fields of study.

open-access journal
A kind of journal (usually scholarly) that is available online without a fee.

periodical
A kind of publication that is issued periodically, at regular or semi-regular intervals; academic journals and magazines are examples of periodicals.

Peer-reviewed journals have the most authority, but non–peer-reviewed journals could still be good scholarly sources. Most databases let you search for peer-reviewed articles only, excluding magazines, newspapers, and non–peer-reviewed scholarly sources.

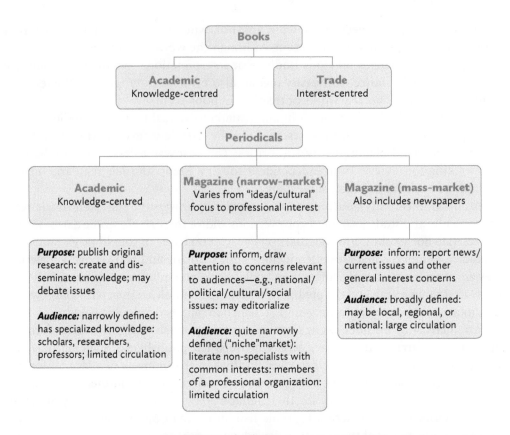

FIGURE 1.1   Published texts can be divided into categories depending on their purpose and audience.

The Influence of the Academic Community

While some students may interact with the academic community throughout their careers, most eventually leave school and the academy behind. What have the "isolated" interests of the scholarly community to do with those outside this community, whose everyday lives may be focused on the struggle to get or keep a job?

In fact, the academy and the world outside it benefit from one another in unmistakable ways. The rigour of academia provides training for those who take the skills they acquired in university out into the world. They are better equipped to confront problems, both in their personal lives and in dealing with the larger concerns of our society and world because of their exposure to the specialized skills, along with the general reading, writing, and critical-thinking skills that the academy seeks to instill.

In less obvious ways, the influence of academic research is far-reaching and consequential. For one thing, the results of major academic studies often help shape our future by influencing government policies. Government agencies and independent think tanks may consult scholars or commission scholarly research before recommending a particular action; they may even provide the funds for research in areas of interest or concern.

Since 1990, governments and scientists, including many with connections to universities, have joined forces to produce four assessment reports and many special reports on climate change through the agency of the Intergovernmental Panel on Climate Change (IPCC). The creation of these non-binding but highly influential reports on "the current state of knowledge on climate change" suggests that, notwithstanding the tensions that can exist between governments and researchers, the relationship between them is symbiotic. Furthermore, the role of the media in publicizing the content of these reports underscores its vital relationship with the academic community.

A Self-Regulating Community

There is another important fact about the academic community that helps to make it a true community: academic writing, by its very nature, is self-regulating. Researchers are always questioning, testing, retesting, and, in some cases, criticizing one another's work. Recently, a major British medical journal, *The Lancet*, retracted a study published a dozen years before that linked a common vaccine with an increased incidence of autism, finding flaws in the study's methodology as follow-up studies found no such link. Three of the study's thirteen authors continued to endorse the study and, consequently, found their careers as physicians in jeopardy.

Academic writers often anticipate criticism or, at least, challenges to their methods or findings. To assure readers that they are aware of a study's possible weaknesses, authors often include a section at the end of the article that addresses limitations. For example, they could note that the study used a small sample, which might mean that the findings cannot be generalized. Doing so extends an invitation to future researchers to conduct similar studies using a larger sample size in order to make the results more reliable, more applicable to larger or more diverse groups.

academic writer

A specialist in his or her subject area who is familiar with what has been written and is able to assess the strengths as well as the limitations of others' work. He or she can discriminate between a study that satisfies its objectives and one that does not, and between one whose methods are consistent with its aims and one whose methods are not. In other words, self-criticism is built into the model of research-oriented scholarship.

The Active Voice

Although self-criticism is fundamental to the scientific model, ensuring that only well-tested and reliable results are presented to the public and governments, the scientific community has sometimes reacted to criticism from those outside that community. In 2010, 255 scientists, including at least 11 Nobel laureates, wrote an open letter that was published in a prominent academic journal. In it, they explained how scientific theories become facts, how the attacks of "climate deniers" on scientists distort these facts, and why it is vital to act now against the consequences of global warming.

Climate Change and the Integrity of Science

Gleick, P.H. et al.

1   We are deeply disturbed by the recent escalation of political assaults on scientists in general and on climate scientists in particular. All citizens should understand some basic scientific facts. There is always some uncertainty associated with scientific conclusions; science never absolutely proves anything. When someone says that society should wait until scientists are absolutely certain before taking any action, it is the same as saying society should never take action. For a problem as potentially catastrophic as climate change, taking no action poses a dangerous risk for our planet.

2   Scientific conclusions derive from an understanding of basic laws supported by laboratory experiments, observations of nature, and mathematical and computer modeling. Like all human beings, scientists make mistakes, but the scientific process is designed to find and correct them. This process is inherently adversarial—scientists build reputations and gain recognition not only for supporting conventional wisdom, but even more so for demonstrating that the scientific consensus is wrong and that there is a

better explanation. That's what Galileo, Pasteur, Darwin, and Einstein did. But when some conclusions have been thoroughly and deeply tested, questioned, and examined, they gain the status of "well-established theories" and are often spoken of as "facts."

3   For instance, there is compelling scientific evidence that our planet is about 4.5 billion years old (the theory of the origin of Earth), that our universe was born from a single event about 14 billion years ago (the Big Bang theory), and that today's organisms evolved from ones living in the past (the theory of evolution). Even as these are overwhelmingly accepted by the scientific community, fame still awaits anyone who could show these theories to be wrong. Climate change now falls into this category: There is compelling, comprehensive, and consistent objective evidence that humans are changing the climate in ways that threaten our societies and the ecosystems on which we depend.

4   Many recent assaults on climate science and, more disturbingly, on climate scientists by climate change deniers are typically driven by special interests or dogma, not by an honest effort to provide an alternative theory that credibly satisfies the evidence. The Intergovernmental Panel on Climate Change (IPCC) and other scientific assessments of climate change, which involve thousands of scientists producing massive and comprehensive reports, have, quite expectedly and normally, made some mistakes. When errors are pointed out, they are corrected. But there is nothing remotely identified in the recent events that changes the fundamental conclusions about climate change:

i.   The planet is warming due to increased concentrations of heat-trapping gases in our atmosphere. A snowy winter in Washington does not alter this fact.

ii.   Most of the increase in the concentration of these gases over the last century is due to human activities, especially the burning of fossil fuels and deforestation.

iii.   Natural causes always play a role in changing Earth's climate, but are now being overwhelmed by human-induced changes.

iv.   Warming the planet will cause many other climatic patterns to change at speeds unprecedented in modern times, including increasing rates of sea-level rise and alterations in the hydrologic cycle. Rising concentrations of carbon dioxide are making the oceans more acidic.

v.   The combination of these complex climate changes threatens coastal communities and cities, our food and water supplies, marine and freshwater ecosystems, forests, high mountain environments, and far more.

5   Much more can be, and has been, said by the world's scientific societies, national academies, and individuals, but these conclusions should be enough to indicate why scientists are concerned about what future generations will face from business-as-usual practices. We urge our policy-makers and the public to move forward immediately to address the causes of climate change, including the unrestrained burning of fossil fuels.

6   We also call for an end to McCarthy-like threats of criminal prosecution against our colleagues based on innuendo and guilt by association, the harassment of scientists by politicians seeking distractions to avoid taking action, and the outright lies being spread about them. Society has two choices: We can ignore the science and hide our heads in the sand and hope we are lucky, or we can act in the public interest to reduce the threat of global climate change quickly and substantively. The good news is that smart and effective actions are possible. But delay must not be an option.

Questions to Consider

1.   In your own words, explain what is meant by the statement, "When someone says that society should wait until scientists are absolutely certain before taking any action, it is the same as saying society should never take action" (paragraph 1).

2.   What is the difference between a theory and a fact? (paragraph 2)

3.   According to the authors, what is the fundamental difference between those who "gain recognition . . . for demonstrating that the scientific consensus is wrong" (paragraph 2) and those who believe that the theory of climate change is wrong?

4.   Among the opponents of the climate change theory, to whom do you believe the authors are referring in paragraph 6? What shows you this?

5.   Do you think the authors produced a strong argument in the letter? Why or why not? (For more information about argumentative strategies, see pp. 113–116.)

2

Conventions of Academic Writing

Some of the conventions of academic writing described below apply more to scholarly journals than to books. However, academic essays on a related topic are often collected in edited volumes and follow formats similar to those described. Although essays in edited books are not preceded by abstracts (see Abstracts, page 16), an editor may summarize the purpose and content of each essay in a book's introduction and indicate how it contributes to the field of study.

Authors

Collaborative research is very common in the sciences and social sciences. This is due to the nature of empirically based study, such as experimentation, which relies on direct observation under controlled conditions. Many people may be needed to observe the data or perform statistical operations on it; members of the research team contribute their expertise, as well as having input in the final version. For example, in "Author Contributions" at the end of "Trends in North American Newspaper Reporting of Brain Injury in Ice Hockey," the responsibilities of the authors are outlined (see page 328 in part III, The Reader).

In some studies, it is necessary to sample varied populations, so the authors may work in different provinces or countries. For example, a 2005 study on national stereotypes published in the journal *Science* lists 65 authors from 43 different countries; interestingly, the complete article is only five pages long! Most academic writing could be considered collaborative, in a sense, because the authors draw heavily on the work of their predecessors in the field.

empirically based study

Data or information based on an experiment or on observation; it can be verified.

Length

Academic essays vary in length. It is a truism, however, that good science writing is straightforward and concise. Scientific studies, in particular, may be as short as two or three pages; others are longer (see Academic Language and the Challenge of Reading for Learning about Science, page 160). Writing in some humanities disciplines, such as philosophy, history, and English, is more **discursive** (i.e., covers a wide area), partly because of the way that knowledge is defined in these disciplines: many fundamental ideas and concepts have been debated for generations, and writers continue to explore new subtleties in and variations on them.

Length is often a function of the depth and detail expected in academic writing. Many science and social science essays use tables, graphs, charts, and other illustrations to simplify content. In other essays, authors summarize the work of other researchers and integrate it with their own analysis. In addition, writers in the humanities often make extensive use of primary sources, quoting from these texts to support their points.

Research

Research Sources

The most authoritative research sources for an academic writer are previously published studies on the topic. Academic writers depend on the writing of scholars in their fields; however, not all academic writing is concerned only with what has been written previously in academic journals or books. Nor does academic writing consist mostly of summaries of other scholars' work. Thus, when you are asked to write a research paper, you too must do more than summarize.

Most research, whether conducted by scholars or by scholars-in-training—students—involves analysis, which is often centred on first-hand or **primary sources**, *original material in a field of study.* Much research begins with primary source material; for example, it would be logical to study a literary work (primary source) before you looked at what other people had to say about it (secondary source). *Primary,* then, means "first in order," not necessarily first in importance. **Secondary sources,** by contrast, *comprise commentary on or interpretation of primary material.*

Kinds of primary sources vary from discipline to discipline. Here are a few examples from various disciplines:

- *Anthropology and archaeology:* artifacts, fossils, original field notes, reports resulting from direct observations
- *Literature:* poems, plays, fiction, diaries/letters of writers
- *Fine arts:* sheet music, recordings, photographs, sketches, paintings, sculpture, films
- *History:* contemporary documents from the period being studied—e.g., newspaper accounts, letters, speeches, photographs, treaties, diaries, autobiographies
- *Natural sciences:* data from experimentation, field/laboratory notes, original research reports
- *Sociology:* interviews, questionnaires, surveys, the raw data from these sources

Of course, it is not just *writers of scholarly articles* who use research. Magazine writers, including journalists writing for a "niche" market or for the mass market, may

---

discursive

Expansive, or covering a wide area.

primary sources

Original material in a field of study; examples include literary texts, historical documents, and interviews.

secondary sources

Commentary on or interpretation of primary material; examples include academic studies, reports, and presentations.

Academic writers seek to add to the store of knowledge in their discipline; to do so, they analyze the findings of previous studies. In turn, future researchers will attempt to use the findings of these current studies to help answer a question, test a hypothesis, or solve a problem of their own. It would be very difficult to locate important studies if the writer failed to say where they appeared. Thus, the writer provides a bibliographic "trail" that future researchers can follow to the source.

conduct extensive research. But a journalist, unlike a scholarly writer, does not cite sources. *Using citations is a feature of academic writing.*

Documenting Sources

An academic publication usually employs one documentation method consistently, using a set of established standards (conventions) for citing sources. The method varies from publisher to publisher, and academic journals in similar disciplines may not always use identical documentation. However, there are four basic formats preferred by most book and journal publishers, which are described in detail in the major manuals published by university presses and research organizations:

- *MLA Style Manual and Guide to Scholarly Publishing*, 3rd ed. Published by the Modern Language Association of America (MLA). The MLA also publishes a manual designed for student writers and researchers: *MLA Handbook for Writers of Research Papers*, 7th ed.
- *Publication Manual of the American Psychological Association*, 6th ed.
- *The Chicago Manual of Style*, 16th ed. Published by the University of Chicago Press.
- *Scientific Style and Format: The CSE Manual for Authors, Editors, and Publishers*, 7th ed. Published by the Council of Science Editors.

See pages 148–154 for a summary of major documentation methods and formats. See also The Active Voice: The Historian's Critical Apparatus on page 21 for a discussion of documentation in history papers.

Voice and Style

The voice in academic essays is generally objective and analytical, avoiding the expression of personal views. In this sense, academic writing can be considered expository rather than argumentative, since most academic writers do not usually try to persuade their audience of the rightness of a system of values or of a course of action.

On the other hand, academic studies often set out to investigate a real-life problem, and their authors may propose solutions to the problem at the end of the study. This may take the form of recommendations or areas that future research should focus on.

Furthermore, academic writing can be considered persuasive in that it seeks to convince its reader of the validity of the findings. And, of course, academic writers do have opinions and a stake in what they are investigating. Objectivity, then, is not synonymous with a lack of involvement but refers to the degree of detachment that ensures the writer will not be swayed by contrary or faulty evidence or by imprecise reasoning. Such a guarantee is necessary if the author is to be seen as reliable and the findings as credible.

Objectivity and Style

As observers and recorders of natural phenomena, scientists must assume a distance from the object of study to avoid influencing the results or raising the perception of bias. Thus, they may use voice in specific ways to convey distance. For example, writers may use passive constructions, in which the subject of the sentence is acted upon, rather than acting itself.

passive construction (passive voice)
A way of constructing a sentence to show that the subject is being acted upon.

The Passive Voice and Other Common Constructions in Academic Writing

Student writers may be told to avoid the passive voice in their writing—for good reason, because it often results in a weaker sentence. However, if the purpose is to de-emphasize the subject, such as the researcher, or to stress the object (receiver of the action), such as that which is being studied, then a passive construction may be preferred to an active one. Note the difference between passive and active in the following examples:

Active voice: Researchers have carried out several studies to assess psychiatric risk factors in motor vehicle accidents.

Researchers is the active subject, but in this case, the *studies* (object of the verb) that assess risk factors are more important than the generic subject, *researchers*. By changing the construction of this sentence to the passive, the writer can replace an active but unimportant subject with a passive but more important subject. Note that in passive constructions, the active subject may not appear in the sentence. Below, the original, unimportant subject is indicated by the use of brackets.

Passive voice: Several studies have been carried out [by researchers] to assess psychiatric risk factors in motor vehicle accidents.

If an active construction is used, writers may either use the first person, *I, we, our*, etc., or substitute *this study shows* or *the research confirmed*.

abstract

A condensed summary used in an empirical study; it is placed before the essay begins and includes at a minimum purpose, methods, and results.

Abstracts, which precede many journal articles in the natural and social sciences, typically use passive constructions to convey detachment and objectivity. In the abstract below, from the journal *Child Development*, the writer uses the passive voice and displaces the authors of the study. The passive voice is italicized and the substituted subject is bolded:

Using a genetic design of 234 six-year-old twins, **this study examined** (a) the contribution of genes and environment to social versus physical aggression, and (b) whether *the correlation between social and physical aggression can be explained by* similar genetic or environmental factors or by a directional link between the phenotypes. For social aggression, *substantial (shared and unique) environmental effects but only weak genetic effects were found.* For physical aggression, *significant effects of genes and unique environment were found.* . . .

—M. Brendgen, G. Dionne, A. Girard, M. Boivin, F. Vitaro, & D. Pérusse (2005), "Examining genetic and environmental effects on social aggression: a study of 6-year-old twins." *Child Development, 76*: 930–46.

Language and Academic Writing

Many readers can identify scholarly writing simply by the level of the language itself. Academic writers may also use specialized diction, or jargon. Compared to literary writing, however, academic writing is characterized by a lack of ornamentation. Writing in the sciences, in particular, is marked by direct, straightforward prose with few modifiers (adjectives and adverbs). Academic writers are also much less likely to use figurative language, such as metaphors, similes, personification, and the like, than literary writers. They may, however, use analogies to help explain a point. An analogy is a systematic comparison between the topic item and another one that is like it in the relevant point but is otherwise unlike the first one. The analogy can be used to make the first item more easily understood. The authors of "The More You Play, the More Aggressive You Become" (p. 313 in Part III: The Reader) compare the effects of smoking to those of video game playing.

In spite of a lack of ornamentation, academic writing may strike ordinary readers as hard to follow. Although jargon and language level can be obstacles to understanding, other elements of style, such as complex sentence and paragraph structure, and intrusive documentation, can hinder comprehension. Many of these obstacles can be overcome, though, by frequent exposure to this kind of writing and by learning the conventions of the various disciplines. However, inexperienced readers must read more closely, more slowly, and more consciously than they have to do when presented with simpler material. New reading habits can be cultivated by adopting specific strategies, such as learning to differentiate more important ideas from less important ones and using context to identify crucial words and concepts. Fortunately, clarity is a major aim of all successful academic writers, as it should be for writers in general, and academic writers employ deliberate techniques to make this goal attainable. Inexperienced readers, with practice, can overcome most difficulties.

The three-pronged approach to reading challenging essays is summarized below:

- learn the conventions of academic writing and of your discipline (chapters 2 and 3)
- develop an effective large-scale reading strategy based on the conventions and reading purpose (chapter 5, pp. 49–60)
- learn to recognize words by their context; look up jargon and other words essential to meaning (chapter 5, pp. 58–60)

See also Academic Language and the Challenge of Reading for Learning about Science, page 160.

Strategies for Approaching Academic Essays

Previewing Content

True to their purpose as "knowledge-based" rather than "interest-based" writing, academic texts usually provide a "preview" of the article's content through an informative, often lengthy, title and an abstract. In addition, many include structural markers such as headings.

analogy

A systematic comparison between the topic item and another one that is like it in the relevant point but is otherwise unlike the first one; it can be used to make the first item more easily understood.

Academic studies, particularly in the sciences, may use various strategies to convey objectivity, such as passive constructions and displaced subjects. They may also include direct references to the authors. Such strategies are usually not appropriate in student essays.

Titles

Academic titles are often

- lengthy and informative
- divided into two parts with a colon separating them
- composed mostly of nouns, many of them specific to the discipline

The title of a scholarly article is designed to give the reader information about content at a glance. This is helpful not only for experts but also for student researchers because it enables them to gauge an article's potential usefulness by a scan of a journal issue's contents. Typically, key terms in the article appear in the title; thus, searching by keyword in an electronic database often yields useful entries.

Many scholarly titles include two parts separated by a colon. In this example from the *Journal of Clinical Child and Adolescent Psychology*, the first part summarizes the study's finding while the second part reveals the method:

> School Connectedness is an Underemphasized Parameter in Adolescent Mental Health: Results of a Community Prediction Study

If you turn to this book's table of contents and look at the titles in part III, The Reader, you will often be able to predict an essay's topic and perhaps its findings or conclusion by looking at the detail included in the title.

Abstracts

An abstract is a kind of summary. Abstracts precede most journal articles, giving a preview of content by focusing on the study's purpose, method, results, and conclusion. They may also briefly explain background (for example, the need for the study) or consider the findings' significance. They often include keywords, which enable a researcher to find the article electronically when searching for words and phrases related to the topic. Abstracts are usually written by the study's author(s) and range in length from 100 to 250 words but can be longer.

> The function of the abstract is not to introduce the essay but to provide a concise overview so that readers can determine whether they should read the entire article.

Section Markers

Section markers can be used to *review* or to *preview* content. Because of the complex organizational scheme of many academic essays, writers may use markers throughout the essay, including in the introductory section where they preview the essay's organizational scheme (see Thesis Statements below for information on the essay plan). They may also review what the writer has already covered. Section markers, in effect, indicate specific places in an essay where readers can get their bearings. Used after complex material, they summarize content before the writer moves on to a new area. The following is a brief summary late in "Social Norms of Alcohol, Smoking, and Marijuana Use within a Canadian University Setting" that acts as a reminder about the purpose of the study (see page 185 in Part III: The Reader):

> The primary objective of this study was to determine the relationship between perceived and actual substance use in a sample of Canadian university students.

The following is the first sentence of a paragraph that follows a detailed discussion on a government paper on the digital economy: it summarizes the main content before the author proceeds to her next point (see "Missing in Action" on page 251 in Part III: The Reader):

> As is clear from the submissions and government paper on the digital economy, digital policy frames skill as the ability to participate in the labor force and to purchase and consume products and services. . . .

Writers often announce upcoming content by using headings. In empirical studies, these markers serve a *formal function* by dividing the essay into conventional categories, each having a particular purpose: for example, "Introduction," "Methods," "Results," "Discussion," and "Conclusion." Writers may include subsection markers as well.

In other kinds of academic writing, the markers serve a *descriptive function*, enabling readers to preview content. Descriptive headings are one way that writers can make essay structure clearer to their readers. They orient the readers of long academic essays or those that deal with complex material. Because the essays students write for class are usually much shorter, headings are seldom necessary. However, if you are writing a scientific, engineering, or business report, you may be required to use formal headings to designate the sections of your report (see The Active Voice: Report Writing—Aims and Goals, page 85).

> Empirical studies use formal headings: "Introduction," "Methods," "Results," and "Discussion." Authors of other kinds of studies may use descriptive or content headings, which make it easy for readers to determine the essay's main points or areas of discussion.

> *descriptive headings*
> Headings usually consist of a phrase summarizing the content of the section that follows.

Activity 2.1

A good way to prepare for reading academic essays is to look at specific articles and see how they make use of the general academic conventions discussed so far. Access a periodical index or electronic database and evaluate a sample issue of three different journals—one each from the humanities, social sciences, and natural sciences—noting some of the differences among them. You can answer the following questions by scanning the table of contents and a representative number of essays—say, three or four.

1. What kinds of articles does the journal contain? How long are they? What are some typical titles?

2. Were most articles written by a single author or by multiple authors?
3. Do the articles include abstracts?
4. How many articles are there per issue?
5. Are book reviews included? Are there editorials?
6. How are the essays laid out (for example, note the use of formal/standardized or content/descriptive headings or other markers)?
7. Typically, how many sources are used per article (you can determine this by looking at the last pages of the article where references are listed alphabetically)?
8. Is specialized language used? Is the level of language difficult?

Features of Introductions in Academic Writing

This section discusses some common characteristics of introductions of academic essays, usually the first part of the essay you read after you preview or "pre-read" the whole essay for content. In the order you are likely to encounter them in academic writing, they include the literature review, the justification, and the hypothesis or essay plan.

Like virtually all essays, academic essays begin with an introductory section. It may be titled "Introduction" or "Background" or have no heading, but its purpose is to prepare the reader for the body of the essay by introducing important concepts or summarizing previous studies on the topic. If the purpose is primarily to summarize scholarship, the essay might begin with a review of relevant literature.

Literature Review

By summarizing related studies on the topic, the author prepares the way for the unique contribution of his or her own study through a literature review. Studies may be ordered chronologically and end either with the most recent study or with that most closely related to the author's approach. Having a clear structure is vital because, typically, the literature review summarizes many studies concisely in a short space, perhaps only one or two paragraphs.

The following literature review begins with general facts concerning the prevalence of concussions. In the second paragraph of the introduction, shown below, the authors mention consequences of concussions, especially as they apply to hockey players. As the review continues, it becomes more specific (see "Trends in North American Newspaper Reporting of Brain Injury in Ice Hockey" on page 320 of Part III: The Reader):

> Repeated concussions and TBI are of particular concern as they may cause life-lasting cognitive and psychosocial deficits [5,6]. These injuries are common in all contact sports, but those who play ice hockey are at particular injury risk [7,8,9,10]. The potential long-lasting effects of TBI suggest that these injuries are an important threat to public health [11]. Prevention of sport-related TBIs requires multifaceted approaches that consider issues related to the nature of play and the culture existent within ice hockey [12,13].

Justification

While students generally write essays to become more proficient planners, researchers, and writers (as well as to satisfy a course requirement and receive a grade, of course), academic authors need to convince their peers that their essay is worth consideration through a justification. Thus, they usually need to go one step further than student writers and announce how, specifically, their work will contribute to the field of study. The justification answers questions like:

- Why is the study important?
- How will it advance knowledge about the topic?
- What gap will it fill?

Like many justifications, the following clearly states the gap that the study will attempt to fill:

> We have scholarly studies on technical improvements during the nineteenth century, on social interest in the microscope, and on its use by literary figures. But we have little on how the microscopic world itself was perceived. . . .

—"The Microscopic World": page 363 in Part III: The Reader.

literature review
A condensed survey of articles on the topic arranged in a logical order, usually ending with the article most relevant to the author's study. *Literature* here carries the broad meaning of something written; it does not refer only to literary works.

Some citation styles use numbers to refer to sources; they are keyed to entries at the end of the essay that give publication details.

Literature reviews with parenthetical names and years or a succession of numbers can be hard to read. A good strategy is to ignore the parentheses and pay attention to studies mentioned near the end of the introduction: they will likely be directly relevant to the review.

justification
Announces reason for undertaking the study; it may focus on what it will add to previous research or what gap in the research it will fill.

The literature review and the justification together demonstrate the writer's credibility, showing what others have written and where the author's own study fits in. After the literature review and the justification, typically, comes the thesis, which can take one of several forms, such as the hypothesis or the essay plan. (The thesis could also take the form of questions that the author will answer.)

Thesis Statements

Student writers are familiar with the common practice of including a thesis statement in the introduction. Academic writers refer to their thesis near the end of the introduction, but the form that the thesis takes can vary.

In experiments, the thesis may consist of a hypothesis or prediction. The experiment is designed to test the hypothesis, and the conclusion will announce whether it was proven or disproven. Another common form is an essay plan, a statement of intent. An essay plan outlines the areas to be explored in the order they will appear. Authors may refer to the plan throughout the essay to orient the reader as he or she is conducted through the different stages of the essay's development.

The following three-part hypothesis predicts the experiment's outcomes (see "Social Norms of Alcohol, Smoking, and Marijuana Use within a Canadian University Setting," page 180 in Part III: The Reader):

> It was hypothesized that (1) the Canadian students surveyed would perceive more frequent alcohol, cigarette, and marijuana use among their peers than actually reported; (2) perceived use would predict actual use for all 3 substances assessed; and (3) actual use and perceived norms would be lower for Canadian post-secondary students than their US peers.

The following two-part essay plan clearly sets out the author's argument (see "Doping Is a Threat to Sporting Excellence" on page 358 in Part III: The Reader):

> In the first section, I argue that sporting competition should be understood as an excellence-based activity, that is, as an activity organised at least in part around the purpose of encouraging competitors to display certain kinds of excellence. In the second section, I contend that doping threatens to obscure the display of at least some relevant sporting excellences.

For more on thesis statements in student essays, see page 65.

hypothesis
A prediction about an outcome; it is used in essays in which an experiment is set up to prove/disprove the prediction.

essay plan
A form of a thesis in which main points are outlined in the order they will occur in the essay.

The Active Voice

Although it is not unusual for scholarly bibliographies (the alphabetical list of sources at the end of the essay) to be many pages long, articles in the field of history typically include extensive notes as well, either at the foot of the page (footnotes) or at the end of the essay (endnotes), suggesting the unique engagement of the historical researcher with other scholars in the field. The following essay focuses on academic historical writing, although some of the comments about using research sources apply across the disciplines.

The Historian's Critical Apparatus

1   The heart of most academic writing in a field such as history lies not in the text on the page but is hidden away either at the bottom of the page or at the end of the book in the references. Here, the whole story is told about the writer, the audience, the subject, and the standards of the discipline. Certainly references serve to document sources: to provide the origin of a quote, to substantiate a fact that might otherwise be disputed, to guide readers

to find their place in the original source material. So much more than that is being revealed, however, and that is why many historians prefer notes to the more abbreviated in-text reference system that is favoured in some social science and science disciplines.

2   A text with no notes (or what we might also call a critical apparatus) has been written with a particular audience in mind. The author has assumed a position of absolute authority on the subject being discussed and is saying to the reader that he or she is to be trusted as a source. Such writing is often deemed "popular" in academic circles. It suggests that the historical "facts" are known for certain and that there are accepted ways of understanding the flow of history that need no debate.

3   A few footnotes or endnotes providing direct sources of information or quotes do not indicate much about the writer's imagined audience, but they do reflect honesty on the part of the researcher in disclosing his or her debts to other scholars. For the reader, they give a few hints of a different nature: they tell you about other relevant sources for this topic of discussion, names of authoritative writers in the field, and sometimes the theoretical perspective that is implicit in the essay being read. Academics tend to work within a single intellectual trend of their discipline. The sources indicated in authors' notes give the first hint of the genealogy of their ideas and perspective. History is being revealed to be more complex; these notes suggest that writing history is not just a recounting of data but an intellectual reconstruction through a framework built upon theoretical generalizations.

4   It is in the essay with an elaborate note apparatus that a scholar's full range is displayed. Not only will you find a bibliography on the topic and its related aspects packed into these notes, but you will also find the traces of the debates that the discipline of history engenders and the methodological issues that produce divergent perspectives. Such documentation tells the reader—especially one who is approaching a field for the first

time—a good deal about the extent to which the essay has a particular perspective or even bias that needs to be taken account of in using it as a source.

5   The full experience of scholarly reading incorporates the aptly called footnote: it is the foundation and the support of the entire endeavour, the key to decoding the values of the writer and the value of the writing. That said, a question lingers. What is the best way for the reader to tackle an essay laden with notes, whether the latter be brief, long, or a combination of the two? As surprising as it may seem, one way is to skim the notes first. For this to be a fully meaningful exercise, it is necessary for you to know something of the subject about which you are reading first. If you do, then the notes can reveal quite quickly all the hidden secrets that are their very purpose. By reading the notes first, you can make an initial and rapid assessment of whether the essay is relevant to your research topic. If it is, then you can turn to the text and read it through, ignoring most of the notes except where a quick glance might suggest that the note has something relevant to tell. That completed, your critical reflection upon the whole essay is possible. Certainly this is a process which takes practice. It also does not work as well if you are learning a subject for the first time. In that situation, there is little alternative to the opposite strategy of reading the text without the notes first and then reviewing them subsequently for their hints for further reading and the like. With practice and some immersion in your topic of research, however, that initial quick skim of the notes will prove rewarding.

6   Such are the joys of historical writing. The same set of data is repeated in different essays, but the picture that emerges varies in the hands of different writers. The notes can frequently be the key to understanding the hows, whys, and wherefores of the discipline.

—Andrew Rippin, Professor, Department of History, University of Victoria

3

Three Common Kinds of Academic Essays

Although academic writing shares many characteristics, most academic essays can be divided into one of three categories. You can think of them as Type A (for "*arts*," often referred to as the humanities), Type B (for "*biology*," an example of a discipline within the natural sciences), and Type C (for "*critical* review"). Since formats and other conventions vary among these different kinds of essays, being able to identify their type will enable you to access information more efficiently.

Type A: Qualitative Essays

Type A is common in the arts/humanities disciplines and in other disciplines in which the methodology is *qualitative*, concerned with ideas, values, or theories, rather than with data that can be measured and quantified. Typically, a Type A essay includes a thesis, an essay plan, or questions that the writer will attempt to answer. Descriptive headings may be used to summarize section content. See Characteristics of Type A, Type B, and Type C Essays in appendix B, and the excerpt from a Type A essay, page 26, for more details.

Type B: Quantitative Essays

In Type B essays, the writer's research design involves an experiment or some other empirical process through which primary sources, such as raw data, are generated. Research of this kind is sometimes called original research to distinguish it from the kind of research that depends heavily on underlying theories and perspectives.

In addition to using quantitative methods, these essays use standardized divisions that replicate the chronological stages of the experiment, beginning with "Introduction,"

Authors of Type A essays use a qualitative methodology, concerned with the interpretation of ideas, values, or theories, which they may apply to specific primary sources.

Authors of Type B essays use quantitative data, often generated through an experiment, or qualitative data to prove a hypothesis or answer a question.

followed by "Methods," "Results," and "Discussion" and/or "Conclusion." The divisions may then be subdivided. For example, "Methods" may be divided into "Subjects," "Participants," "Measures," "Procedures," "Statistical Analyses Used," and so on. See Characteristics of Type A, Type B, and Type C Essays in appendix B, and the sample Type B essay, page 27, for more details.

Type B Subgenre: Qualitative Methodologies

Some essays use conventional Type B formats while employing qualitative methods to analyze evidence gathered from unstructured interviews, focus groups, forums, or written texts like print media. As contrasted with the sometimes artificial setting of the psychology lab, qualitative methods enable the researcher to examine human motivations and interactions within naturally occurring contexts. For example, Healey et al. analyze the results of collaborative research on climate change in northern Inuit communities by recording community perspectives and capturing everyday life experiences through photography (p. 388 in Part III: The Reader). In spite of the advantages of qualitative studies, data generated through these methods may be harder to generalize to larger populations than data generated through quantitative methods. In addition, data analysis requires careful and skilled interpretation to avoid researcher bias.

Type C: Synthesis and Critical Evaluation

> Authors of Type C essays synthesize and critically evaluate published studies to reveal the progress toward solving a problem.

Common in the social sciences—especially psychology—and in the sciences, Type C essays synthesize and critically evaluate relevant texts, such as scholarly articles. Type C essays reveal the progress toward solving a problem; they may also draw attention to inconsistencies or gaps in the research. In this sense, they look back to see how far social scientists have come and look ahead to future directions for research; their authors may conclude by making recommendations. Review essays may be occasioned by a specific phenomenon, such as the prevalence of online gaming among adolescents (see page 313), or a significant social concern, such as "Addressing Driver Aggression," page 330 in Part III: The Reader. In format, Type C essays resemble Type A essays with a thesis/essay plan and content divisions. See Characteristics of Type A, Type B, and Type C Essays in appendix B, and the sample Type C essay, page 31, for more details.

Although not all academic essays conform precisely to the characteristics outlined here and in appendix B, the majority closely resemble Type A, Type B, or Type C. Works published in books generally follow the formats of Type A or Type C, whereas experimental results (Type B) typically appear in journals. As well as much scientific writing, several kinds of public writing, such as case studies, proposals, and business and other kinds of formal reports, commonly use the methodology and structure of Type B essays.

Argumentative essays, such as editorials and commentaries, are discussed in chapter 9.

Tables, Graphs, and Other Visuals

> *table*
> Presents detailed information in matrix format, in columns and rows that are easily scanned.
>
> *graph*
> Represents relationships between two variables.

A table presents detailed information in matrix format, in columns and rows that are easily scanned. Graphs represent relationships between two variables. *Line graphs* show a relationship over time while *bar graphs* show values or trends within the data.

Writers may use tables, graphs, and charts (the last two are often represented by the abbreviation "Fig.," for "Figure") to present their raw data. They are especially common in the "Results" section of Type B essays where their primary function is to concisely summarize the quantitative results of the experiment. Writers may explain the most significant results in the text of the essay, reserving detail for the table to which the reader will be directed in the explanatory text.

Reading Tables and Graphs

- Read the text material first to understand specific terms and/or abbreviations used in the table/figure.
- If there is a heading, read it carefully; headings are sometimes given above the figure and explanatory material below it. At other times, the information is all in one place, and the first sentence summarizes the table's/figure's purpose, the following sentence(s) giving further explanation.
- If the table/figure is particularly detailed or complex, reread the relevant section(s) in the text. Text material will often direct you to specific parts of the table/figure deemed significant by the author(s).
- Read labels carefully, but do not be distracted by superscript numbers, letters, or symbols, which often refer to statistical significance of specific items.

Activity 3.1

It can be helpful to be able to identify types of academic essays in order to determine your approach and the reading strategies most applicable to your assigned reading. Choose two essays of different types identified on page 412 as A, B, or C. (Do not choose other types—for example, argumentative—though they may be similar in some ways to the kinds of essays discussed in this chapter.) Identify three features of each essay type as discussed in this chapter; if they apply to individual paragraphs, identify them by paragraph number. Note: For more detailed information about Type A, B, and C essays, see appendix B.

Academic Essay Formats

In your career as a student, you will be asked to write essays and reports that conform to one or another of the essay types discussed. For example, you may be asked to write a lab report as a result of a specific experiment you performed. Such empirically based reports resemble the Type B academic essay. For information on how to write reports, see The Active Voice: Report Writing—Aims and Goals, page 85.

Inevitably, you will write essays in several of your classes in which you generate a position about a literary text, historical event, or philosophical system and defend that position, citing from primary sources, as authors of Type A essays also do.

The use of research, synthesis, summarizing, and critical evaluation makes the student research essay much like the Type C essay. The following samples demonstrate key features of the types of essays discussed in this chapter.

Type A

The introduction of the essay on page 290 in Part III: The Reader is excerpted here in order to illustrate some of the conventions of Type A essays.

▶ # Excerpt from "Post-Princess Models of Gender: The New Man in Disney/Pixar"

> Type A essays often have a two-part title that includes key words from the essay. The phrase *the new man* recurs throughout the essay and is a heading.

1   Lisping over the Steve McQueen allusion in Pixar's *Cars* (2006), our two-year-old son, Oscar, inadvertently directed us to the definition(s) of masculinity that might be embedded in a children's animated film about NASCAR. The film overtly praises the "good woman" proverbially behind every successful man: the champion car, voiced by Richard Petty, tells his wife, "I wouldn't be nothin' without you, honey." But gender in this twenty-first-century *bildungsroman* is rather more complex, and Oscar's mispronunciation held the first clue. To him, a member of the film's target audience, the character closing in on the title long held by "The King" is not "Lightning McQueen" but "Lightning the queen"; his chief rival, the always-a-bridesmaid runner-up "Chick" Hicks.

> Humanities essays may begin with a brief narrative or, occasionally, a personal experience that introduces the subject. Another common pattern is to begin by referring to a key study. The author may then expand on, qualify, or disagree with this study.

2   Does this nominal feminizing of male also-rans (and the simultaneous gendering of success) constitute a meaningful pattern? Piqued, we began examining the construction of masculinity in major feature films released by Disney's Pixar studios over the past thirteen years. Indeed, as we argue here, Pixar consistently promotes a new model of masculinity, one that matures into acceptance of its more traditionally "feminine" aspects.

3   Cultural critics have long been interested in Disney's cinematic products, but the gender critics examining the texts most enthusiastically gobbled up by the under-six set have so

> Type A essays do not always include a thorough review of the literature. In this paragraph, only one critic is mentioned; however, several more are referred to in the notes (see page 297).

far generally focused on their retrograde representations of women. As Elizabeth Bell argues, the animated Disney features through *Beauty and the Beast* feature a "teenaged heroine at the idealized height of puberty's graceful promenade, [f]emale wickedness . . . rendered as middle-aged beauty at its peak of sexuality and authority [and] [f]eminine sacrifice and nurturing . . . drawn in pear-shaped, old women past menopause" (108). Some have noted the models of masculinity in the classic animated films, primarily the contrast between the uber-macho Gaston and the sensitive, misunderstood Beast in *Beauty and the Beast*,[1] but the male protagonist of the animated classics, at least through *The Little Mermaid*, remains largely uninterrogated.[2] For most of the early films, this critical omission seems generally appropriate, the various versions of Prince Charming being often too two-dimensional to do more than inadvertently shape the definition of the protagonists' femininity. But if the feminist thought that has shaped our cultural texts for three decades now has been somewhat disappointing in its ability to actually rewrite the princess trope (the spunkiest of the "princesses," Ariel, Belle, Jasmine, and, arguably, even Mulan, remain thin, beautiful, kind, obedient or punished for disobedience, and headed for the altar), it has been surprisingly effective in rewriting the type of masculine power promoted by Disney's products.[3]

> The justification of this study is the absence of critical studies focusing on male protagonists in Disney films. The rest of this paragraph elaborates on this statement, explaining the reason for the gap.

> This lengthy sentence illustrates several stylistic features of humanities writing. For example, the sentence is balanced by repeated verb phrases (*has been*; *to rewrite/in rewriting*). It includes an example of jargon, *trope*, and a parenthetical independent clause with balanced descriptive words and phrases: "thin, beautiful, kind, obedient or punished for disobedience, and headed for the altar." It is a rhetorically effective sentence that is not difficult to follow in spite of its length and complexity.

4   Disney's new face, Pixar studios, has released nine films—*Toy Story* (1995) and *Toy Story 2* (1999); *A Bug's Life* (1998); *Finding Nemo* (2003); *Monsters, Inc.* (2001); *The Incredibles* (2004); *Cars* (2006); *Ratatouille* (2007); and now *WALL•E* (2008)—all of which feature interesting male figures in leading positions. Unlike many of the princesses, who remain relatively static even through their own adventures, these male leads are actual protagonists; their characters develop and change over the course of the film, rendering the plot. Ultimately these various developing characters—particularly Buzz and Woody from *Toy Story*, Mr. Incredible from *The Incredibles*, and Lightning McQueen from *Cars*—experience a common narrative trajectory, culminating in a common "New Man" model[4]: they all strive for an alpha-male identity; they face emasculating failures; they find themselves, in large part, through what Eve Sedgwick refers to as "homosocial desire" and a triangulation of this desire with a feminized object (and/or a set of "feminine" values); and, finally, they achieve (and teach) a kinder, gentler understanding of what it means to be a man.

> The three-part essay plan begins here. The order of points is repeated in the section headings (see pages 292–295).

> At the end of their introduction, the authors refer to gender studies critic Eve Sedgwick. Type A essays often draw on theory. The terms mentioned here are amplified in the section "Homosociality, Intimacy, and Emotion," p. 294.

Type B

The following is a short example of a Type B essay, illustrating some of the conventions of this kind of essay.

Adaptive Responses to Social Exclusion: Social Rejection Improves Detection of Real and Fake Smiles

by **Michael J. Bernstein, Steven G. Young, Christina M. Brown, Donald F. Sacco, and Heather M. Claypool**

> As is often the case in Type B essays, the two-part title includes the result of the study (following the colon). The first part of the title identifies the area studied. Unlike most Type B essays, there is no abstract. The literature review is a major focus in the introductions of most Type B essays. Here it begins in the first sentence and continues for much of the introduction.

1   Being excluded from social relationships poses numerous immediate and long-term threats (e.g., Baumeister & Leary, 1995). Consequently, it is not surprising that people are sensitive to cues that indicate potential rejection (Pickett & Gardner, 2005). For example, individuals who are dispositionally high in need to belong are better than others at identifying facial expressions and vocal tones (Pickett, Gardner, & Knowles, 2004), and ostracized participants have better memory for socially relevant information than do nonostracized participants (Gardner, Pickett, & Brewer, 2000). In both cases, individuals either fearing rejection or suffering actual rejection show increased attention to social cues.

2   Facial expressions of emotion can act as such social cues. A Duchenne smile, for example, involves the automatic activation of two facial muscles in response to the experience of pleasure and is generally considered a "true" smile (Ekman, Davidson, & Friesen, 1990), indicative of cooperation and affiliation (Brown & Moore, 2002). In contrast, non-Duchenne, or "masking," smiles can conceal the experience of negative emotions (Ekman, Friesen, & O'Sullivan, 1988). Knowing whether a facial expression is conveying an honest affiliation signal should help rejected individuals identify targets who are likely to offer the greatest opportunity for reconnection.

> Typically, the last study mentioned by the authors in the literature review is the one most relevant to their own research. In this sentence, the dependent clause summarizes the results of an important study while the independent clause suggests a gap in the research. The complete sentence justifies the need for the current study.

3   Although research has shown that individuals with greater belongingness needs (Pickett et al., 2004) are more accurate at discriminating among true, diagnostic facial-expression signals (e.g., discriminating between expressions of anger and happiness), no research has examined the extent to which rejected individuals are able to determine whether the expression being identified is genuine in the first place. Although being able to identify the qualitative emotional category of a facial display is of value to socially excluded individuals, distinguishing real from fake emotions seems especially important to ensure that reaffiliation efforts are maximally distributed toward people displaying genuine affiliative cues. Indeed, directing resources toward an individual faking an affiliative display would likely be a costly error for socially rejected individuals, who already find themselves in a perilous situation. Accordingly, we hypothesized that rejected individuals would show an enhanced ability to discriminate between real and fake smiles, presumably because they are more attuned than others to subtle social cues, including those present in Duchenne smiles (involuntary signals of cooperation) as opposed to non-Duchenne smiles (controllable and unreliable indicators of cooperation).

> The hypothesis (prediction) occurs at the end of the introduction in most Type B essays. It arises out of previous research and the attempt to extend or refine the results of earlier studies in order to explain a phenomenon or solve a problem.

Method

4   Participants were randomly assigned to social-inclusion, social-exclusion, or control conditions. They were then shown faces exhibiting Duchenne or non-Duchenne smiles and were asked to decide whether each was "real" or "fake."

> The "Method" section is divided into three short subsections, "Participants" (who took part), "Materials," (what was used), and "Procedure," (how the experiment was done). The precise detail is needed so that future researchers can replicate the study or build on it by varying the research methods.

Participants

5   Thirty-two undergraduates (17 females, 15 males) participated in the study for course credit.

Materials

6   The facial stimuli were located on the BBC Science & Nature Web site (BBC, n.d.).[1] Respondents were asked to watch 20 color videos (approximately 4 s each) one at a time. Each depicted an individual who had an initially neutral expression and then smiled before returning to a neutral expression. Which faces exhibited real/fake smiles remained constant for all participants. Thus, there were 20 faces, 10 of which were always exhibiting real smiles and 10 of which were always exhibiting fake smiles. Thirteen men and seven women were depicted in the videos.[2]

> The result of the manipulation check confirms that the manipulation worked as it was designed to do. If it had failed to confirm the validity of the social status manipulation, the researchers would probably have had to redesign their experiment. The check, then, acted as a backup, confirming the validity of the methodology.

Procedure

7   Participants were informed that they were to perform two ostensibly unrelated tasks concerning memory and face perception. The first was an essay task that constituted the manipulation of social status. Participants, having been randomly assigned, wrote about a time they felt "rejected or excluded," a time they felt "accepted or included," or their morning the day before the study (control condition). This manipulation has been used previously with success (e.g., Gardner et al., 2000). As a manipulation check, participants responded to a scale assessing the degree to which they felt a threat to their sense of belonging, a

---

1 The faces were pretested for equivalency of attractiveness and positivity. Ratings of neutral expressions of targets showing Duchenne smiles versus neutral expressions of targets showing non-Duchenne smiles revealed no differences ($p > .2$).

2 The stimuli included three minority-group individuals. Removing data for these targets from analyses did not change any findings.

common measure used to confirm the effectiveness of rejection manipulations (Williams, Cheung, & Choi, 2000).

The citation underscores the reliance of researchers on prior studies. By using an established procedure, the authors add to their credibility.

8   Finally, participants watched each video and indicated, on a response sheet next to the computer, whether the smile was "genuine" or "fake." Upon completion of this task, participants responded to demographic questions before being probed for suspicion, thanked, and debriefed.

Results

Manipulation Check

9   To examine whether the manipulation of social rejection was successful, we conducted a one-way between-subjects analysis of variance (ANOVA) on the belongingness measure.

10   Results indicated that the manipulation had the intended effect (prep > .99); rejected participants experienced a greater threat to their sense of belonging.

Discrimination Scores

11   We calculated d', a signal detection measure examining the ability to discriminate stimuli—in this case, the ability to discriminate Duchenne smiles from non-Duchenne smiles. This measure simultaneously considers hits (correctly identifying a Duchenne smile as genuine) and false alarms (incorrectly identifying a non-Duchenne smile as genuine) in the calculation. The one-way ANOVA on these scores was significant, $F_{(2, 29)} = 5.63$, $p_{rep} = .97$; compared with control participants ($M = 1.05$, $SD = 0.56$) and included participants ($M = 1.34$, $SD = 0.56$), rejected participants ($M = 1.88$, $SD = 0.62$) exhibited greater discriminability, $t(29) = 3.33$, $p_{rep} = .98$, $d = 1.35$, and $t(29) = 2.12$, $p_{rep} = .92$, $d = 0.87$, respectively. Discrimination ability did not differ between included and control participants ($p > .25$; see Fig. 1).

Researchers often present their data by referring to complex statistical methods, and the "Results" section may be written by a specialist in statistics. Non-specialists, including students, can learn to read such sections carefully to extract the most important information while ignoring unneeded detail. The key finding, which is discussed more fully in the next section, is highlighted here. For more information about statistics, see Appendix A, A Note on Statistics p. 403.

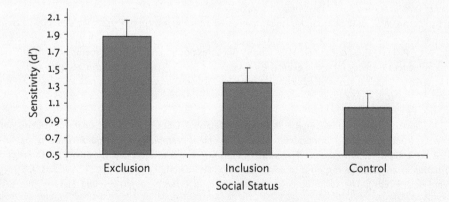

FIGURE 1   Mean ability to discriminate (sensitivity, d') Duchenne and non-Duchenne smiles as a function of social-status condition. Error bars indicate standard errors.

Most Type B essays are accompanied by tables, graphs, or charts that summarize the study's results. In this case, a bar graph shows the relationship between social status and the ability to tell fake from genuine smiles. Note the clear labelling of both axes and the brief explanation below the graphic.

12   There was no effect of target or participant sex. Thus, these variables are not discussed further.

Discussion

In the first sentence, the authors indicate that the hypothesis was proven. The next sentence discusses the significance of the results.

13   We found that socially rejected individuals have enhanced ability to determine whether the "happy" facial expression of a target individual is genuine (a true indication of an affiliative opportunity) or deceptive (feigning the appearance of positive affect). This suggests that motivation to reaffiliate increases rejected individuals' sensitivity to other social cues indicating belongingness opportunities—specifically, facial displays that are honest signals of cooperation and affiliation.

14   Although the results of the current study are congruent with some of the rejection literature showing reaffiliative responses to social exclusion (Lakin & Chartrand, 2005; Maner, DeWall, Baumeister, & Schaller, 2007), these results are among the first to show that rejection can lead to increases in performance at a perceptual level, provided that the performance supports opportunities for affiliation. Once rejected, people are left with a strong desire to be accepted, which leads them toward interaction partners with whom they might affiliate. Therefore, it seems essential to detect legitimate signs of positivity that indicate possible reaffiliation with other people. Otherwise, rejected individuals could miss out on new chances for acceptance or "waste" affiliation efforts on people who are not receptive. Future research should examine whether other faked emotions can be differentiated from true emotions, as well as how these perceptual skills may guide subsequent behavioral choices.

After discussing the significance of the findings in the larger, "real-world" context, the authors suggest areas for future research, in effect extending an invitation to others to build on their conclusions. Researchers often discuss possible limitations of their study in the "Discussion" section. Bernstein et al. do not do so, possibly because of the study's brevity.

References

Baumeister, R.F., & Leary, M.R. (1995). The need to belong: Desire for interpersonal attachments as a fundamental human motivation. *Psychological Bulletin*, 117, 497–529.

BBC. (n.d.). Spot the fake smile. Retrieved October 1, 2007, from http://www.bbc.co.uk/science/humanbody/mind/surveys/smiles

Brown, W.M., & Moore, C. (2002). Smile asymmetries and reputation as reliable indicators of likelihood to cooperate: An evolutionary analysis. In S.P. Shohov (Ed.), *Advances in psychology research* (Vol. 11, pp. 59–78). Huntington, NY: Nova Science Publishers.

Ekman, P., Davidson, R.J., & Friesen, W.V. (1990). The Duchenne smile: Emotional expression and brain physiology II. *Journal of Personality and Social Psychology*, 58, 342–353.

Ekman, P., Friesen, W.V., & O'Sullivan, M. (1988). Smiles when lying. *Journal of Personality and Social Psychology*, 54, 414–420.

Gardner, W.L., Pickett, C.L., & Brewer, M.B. (2000). Social exclusion and selective memory: How the need to belong influences memory for social events. *Personality and Social Psychology Bulletin*, 26, 486–496.

Lakin, J.L., & Chartrand, T.L. (2005). Exclusion and nonconscious behavioral mimicry. In K.D. Williams, J.P. Forgas, & W. von Hippel (Eds.), *The social outcast: Ostracism, social exclusion, rejection, and bullying* (pp. 279–296). New York: Psychology Press.

Maner, J.K., DeWall, C.N., Baumeister, R.F., & Schaller, M. (2007). Does social exclusion motivate interpersonal reconnection? Resolving the "porcupine problem." *Journal of Personality and Social Psychology*, 92, 42–55.

Pickett, C.L., & Gardner, W.L. (2005). The social monitoring system: Enhanced sensitivity to social cues and information as an adaptive response to social exclusion and belonging need. In K.D. Williams, J.P. Forgas, & W. von Hippel (Eds.), *The social outcast: Ostracism, social exclusion, rejection, and bullying* (pp. 213–226). New York: Psychology Press.

Pickett, C.L., Gardner, W.L., & Knowles, M. (2004). Getting a cue: The need to belong and enhanced sensitivity to social cues. *Personality and Social Psychology Bulletin*, 30, 1095–1107.

Williams, K.D., Cheung, C.K.T., & Choi, W. (2000). Cyberostracism: Effects of being ignored over the Internet. *Journal of Personality and Social Psychology*, 79, 748–762.

Type C

The following is a short example of a Type C essay.

Why Ordinary People Torture Enemy Prisoners

by Susan T. Fiske, Lasana T. Harris, and Amy J.C. Cuddy

1 As official investigations and courts-martial continue, we are all taking stock of the events at Abu Ghraib last year. Initial reactions were shock and disgust. How could Americans be doing this to anyone, even Iraqi prisoners of war? Some observers immediately blamed "the few bad apples" presumably responsible for the abuse. However, many social psychologists knew that it was not that simple. Society holds individuals responsible for their actions, as the military court-martial recognizes, but social psychology suggests we should also hold responsible peers and superiors who control the social context.

2 Social psychological evidence emphasizes the power of social context; in other words, the power of the interpersonal situation. Social psychology has accumulated a century of knowledge about how people influence each other for good or ill [1]. Meta-analysis, the quantitative summary of findings across a variety of studies, reveals the size and consistency of such empirical results. Recent meta-analyses document reliable experimental evidence of social context effects across 25,000 studies of 8 million participants [2]. Abu Ghraib resulted in part from ordinary social processes, not just extraordinary individual evil. This Policy Forum cites meta-analyses to describe how the right (or wrong) social context can make almost anyone aggress, oppress, conform, and obey.

3 Virtually anyone can be aggressive if sufficiently provoked, stressed, disgruntled, or hot [3–6]. The situation of the 800th Military Police Brigade guarding Abu Ghraib prisoners fit all the social conditions known to cause aggression. The soldiers were certainly provoked and stressed: at war, in constant danger, taunted and harassed by some of the very citizens they were sent to save, and their comrades were dying daily and unpredictably. Their morale suffered, they were untrained for the job, their command climate was lax, their return home was a year overdue, their identity as disciplined soldiers was gone, and their own amenities were scant [7]. Heat and discomfort also doubtless contributed.

4 The fact that the prisoners were part of a group encountered as enemies would only exaggerate the tendency to feel spontaneous prejudice against outgroups. In this context, oppression and discrimination are synonymous. One of the most basic principles of social psychology is that people prefer their own group [8] and attribute bad behavior to outgroups [9]. Prejudice especially festers if people see the outgroup as threatening cherished values [10–12]. This would have certainly applied to the guards viewing their prisoners at Abu Ghraib, but it also applies in more "normal" situations. A recent sample of U.S. citizens on average viewed Muslims and Arabs as not sharing their interests and stereotyped them as not especially sincere, honest, friendly, or warm [13–15].

Titles of Type C essays are often shorter than those of other types, containing a statement of the problem under investigation.

The authors of this study introduce the problem in the first paragraph, understanding the behaviour of American troops at an Iraqi prison. In the next paragraph, they explain how social psychology can help us understand the complexities of the factors involved.

The paragraph begins by briefly outlining the study's methodology and concludes with the simple thesis.

The review is divided into four categories or sub-topics. Typically, categories in Type C essays include content headings; however, because three of the categories are only one paragraph long, the authors probably thought headings were unnecessary.

The Council of Science Editors (CSE) documentation method, used here, consists of numbers in the text, which correspond to a list of sources at the end of the essay arranged by their order in the text.

Review essays contain a large number of concise summaries.

The category or sub-topic of outgroups is analyzed in paragraphs 4–6.

5   Even more potent predictors of discrimination are the emotional prejudices ("hot" affective feelings such as disgust or contempt) that operate in parallel with cognitive processes [16–18]. Such emotional reactions appear rapidly, even in neuroimaging of brain activations to outgroups [19,20]. But even they can be affected by social context. Categorization of people as interchangeable members of an outgroup promotes an amygdala response characteristic of vigilance and alarm and an insula response characteristic of disgust or arousal, depending on social context; these effects dissipate when the same people are encountered as unique individuals [21,22].

6   According to our survey data [13,14], the contemptible, disgusting kind of outgroup—low-status opponents—elicits a mix of active and passive harm: attacking and fighting, as well as excluding and demeaning. This certainly describes the Abu Ghraib abuse of captured enemies. It also fits our national sample of Americans [14] who reported that allegedly contemptible outgroups such as homeless people, welfare recipients, Turks, and Arabs often are attacked or excluded [14].

In this paragraph, the authors introduce two important research areas to help explain the prevalence of prisoner mistreatment. The first, "conformity to peers," is analyzed in this paragraph; the second, "obedience to authority," is discussed in the following one. Clear organization is vital in Type C essays.

7   Given an environment conducive to aggression and prisoners deemed disgusting and subhuman [23], well-established principles of conformity to peers [24,25] and obedience to authority [26] may account for the widespread nature of the abuse. In combat, conformity to one's unit means survival, and ostracism is death. The social context apparently reflected the phenomenon of people trying to make sense of a complex, confusing, ambiguous situation by relying on their immediate social group [27]. People rioted at St. Paul's Church, Bristol UK, in 1980, for example, in conformity to events they saw occurring in their immediate proximity [28]. Guards abuse prisoners in conformity with what other guards do, in order to fulfill a potent role; this is illustrated by the Stanford Prison Study, in which ordinary college students, randomly assigned to be full-time guards and prisoners in a temporary prison, nevertheless behaved respectively as abusers and victims [29]. Social psychology shows that, whatever their own good or bad choices, most people believe that others would do whatever they personally chose to do, a phenomenon termed false consensus [30,31]. Conformity to the perceived reactions of one's peers can be defined as good or bad, depending on how well the local norms fit those of larger society.

8   As every graduate of introductory psychology should know from the Milgram studies [32], ordinary people can engage in incredibly destructive behavior if so ordered by legitimate authority. In those studies, participants acting as teachers frequently followed an experimenter's orders to punish a supposed learner (actually a confederate) with electric shock, all the way to administering lethal levels. Obedience to authority sustains every culture [33]. Firefighters heroically rushing into the flaming World Trade Center were partly obeying their superiors, partly conforming to extraordinary group loyalty, and partly showing incredibly brave self-sacrifice. But obedience and conformity also motivated the terrorist hijackers and the Abu Ghraib guards, however much one might abhor their (vastly different) actions. Social conformity and obedience themselves are neutral, but their consequences can be heroic or evil. Torture is partly a crime of socialized obedience [34]. Subordinates not only do what they are ordered to do, but what they think their superiors would order them to do, given their understanding of the authority's overall goals. For example, lynching represented ordinary people going beyond the law to enact their view of the community's will.

Compare and contrast, a common pattern of development in Type C essays, is used in this paragraph.

9   Social influence starts with small, apparently trivial actions (in this case, insulting epithets), followed by more serious actions (humiliation and abuse) [35–37], as novices overcome their hesitancy and learn by doing [38]. The actions are always intentional, although the perpetrator may not be aware that those actions constitute evil. In fact, perpetrators may see themselves as doing a great service by punishing and or eliminating a group that they perceive as deserving ill treatment [39].

10   In short, ordinary individuals under the influence of complex social forces may commit evil acts [40]. Such actions are human behaviors that can and should be studied scientifically [41,42]. We need to understand more about the contexts that will promote aggression. We also need to understand the basis for exceptions—why, in the face of these social contexts, not all individuals succumb [43]. Thus, although lay-observers may believe that explaining evil amounts to excusing it and absolving people of responsibility for their actions [44], in fact, explaining evils such as Abu Ghraib demonstrates scientific principles that could help to avert them.

> The focus of this paragraph is on research needed in specific areas. Identifying gaps in the literature is a common feature of Type C essay conclusions.

11   Even one dissenting peer can undermine conformity [24]. For example, whistle-blowers not only alert the authorities but also prevent their peers from continuing in unethical behavior. Authorities can restructure situations to allow communication. For example, CEOs can either welcome or discourage a diversity of opinions. Contexts can undermine prejudice [1]. Individual, extended, equal-status, constructive, cooperative, contact between mutual outgroups (whether American blacks and whites in the military or American soldiers and Iraqi civilians) can improve mutual respect and even liking. It would be harder to dehumanize and abuse imprisoned Iraqis if one had friends among ordinary Iraqis. A difficult objective in wartime, but as some Iraqis work alongside their American counterparts, future abuse is less likely. The slippery slope to abuse can be avoided. The same social contexts that provoke and permit abuse can be harnessed to prevent it. To quote another report [(45), p. 94]: "All personnel who may be engaged in detention operations, from point of capture to final disposition, should participate in a professional ethics program that would equip them with a sharp moral compass for guidance in situations often riven with conflicting moral obligations."

> Type C essays usually have a clear practical focus on the progress of research in clarifying and solving a problem. Authors may address possible research applications at the end of specific sections or at the end of the essay, as Fiske et al. do here.

References and Notes

1.   S.T. Fiske, Social Beings (Wiley, New York, 2004).
2.   F.D. Richard, C.F. Bond, J.J. Stokes-Zoota, Rev. Gen. Psychol. 7, 331 (2003).
3.   B.A. Bettencourt, N. Miller, Psychol. Bull. 119, 422 (1996).
4.   M. Carlson, N. Miller, Sociol. Soc. Res. 72, 155 (1988).
5.   M. Carlson, A. Marcus-Newhall, N. Miller, Pers. Soc. Psychol. Bull. 15, 377 (1989).
6.   C.A. Anderson, B.J. Bushman, Rev. Gen. Psychol. 1, 19 (1997).
7.   A. Taguba, "Article 15–6. Investigation of the 800th Military Police Brigade," accessed 30 June 2004 from www.npr.org/iraq/2004/prison%5fabuse%5freport.pdf
8.   B. Mullen, R. Brown, C. Smith, fur. J. Soc. Psychol. 22, 103 (1992).
9.   B. Mullen, C. Johnson, Br. J. Soc. Psychol. 29, 11 (1990).
10. J. Duckitt, in Advances in Experimental Social Psychology, M.P. Zanna, Ed. (Academic Press, New York, 2001).
11. When their own mortality is salient, as in wartime, people particularly punish those from outgroups seen to threaten basic values (12).
12. S. Solomon, J. Creenberg, T. Pyszczynski, Curr. Dir. Psychol. Sci. 9. 200 (2000).
13. S.T. Fiske, A.J. Cuddy, P. Click, J. Xu, J. Person. Soc. Psychol. 82. 878 (2002).
14. A.J. Cuddy, S.T. Fiske, P. Click, "The BIAS map: Behaviors from intergroup affect and stereotypes," unpublished manuscript (Princeton University, Princeton, NJ, 2004).
15. L.J. Heller, thesis. Princeton University, 2002.
16. H. Schütz, B. Six, Int. J. Intercuit. Relat. 20, 441 (1996).
17. J.F. Dovidio et al., in Stereotypes and Stereotyping, C.N. Macrae, C. Stangor, M. Hewstone, Ed. (Guilford, New York, 1996).
18. C.A. Talaska, S.T. Fiske, S. Chaiken, "Predicting discrimination: A meta-analysis of the racial attitudes—behavior literature," unpublished manuscript (Princeton University, Princeton, NJ, 2004).
19. A.J. Hart et al., Neuroreport 11, 2351 (2000).
20. E.A. Phelps et al., J. Cogn. Neurosci. 12, 729 (2000).

> Typically, Type C essays include more sources than other types, as the purpose is to critically analyze all studies in the field in order to fully show how researchers have investigated a problem.

21. Neuroimaging data represent college student reactions to photographs of outgroup members. These data should not be interpreted to mean that such reactions are innate or "wired in"; they result from long-term social context [9] and vary depending on short-term social context [46].

22. M.E. Wheeler. S.T. Fiske, Psychol. Sci., in press.

23. J.P. Leyens et at., Eur. J, Soc. Psychol. 33, 703 (2003).

24. R. Bond, P.B. Smith, Psychol. Bull. 119, 111 (1996).

25. S. Tanford, S. Penrod, Psychol. Bull. 95, 189 (1984).

26. J. Tata et al., J. Soc. Behav. Pers. 11, 739 (1996).

27. J.C. Turner, Social Influence (Brooks/Cole, Pacific Grove, CA, 1991).

28. S.D. Reicher, Eur. J. Soc. Psychol. 14, 1 (1984).

29. C. Haney, C. Banks, P. Zimbardo, Int. J. Criminol. Penol. 1, 69 (1973).

30. B. Mullen et at., J. Exp. Soc. Psychol. 21, 262 (1985).

31. B. Mullen, L. Hu, Br. J. Soc. Psychol. 27, 333 (1988).

32. S. Milgram, Obedience to Authority (Harper & Row, New York, 1974).

33. T. Blass, J. Appl. Soc. Psychol. 29, 955 (1999).

34. H.C. Kelman, in The Politics of Pain: Torturers and Their Masters, R.D. Crelinsten, A.P. Schmidt, Eds. (Univ. of Leiden, Leiden, NL, 1991).

35. A.L. Beaman et al., Pers. Soc. Psychol. Bull. 9, 181 (1983).

36. A.L. Dillard, J.E. Hunter, M. Burgoon, Hum. Commun. Res. 10, 461 (1984).

37. E.F. Fern, K.B. Monroe, R.A. Avila, J. Mark. Res. 23, 144 (1986).

38. E. Staub, Pers. Soc. Psychol. Rev. 3, 179 (1999).

39. A. Bandura, Pers. Soc. Psychol. Rev. 3, 193 (1999).

40. L. Berkowitz, Pers. Soc. Psychol. Rev. 3, 246 (1999).

41. J.M. Darley. Pers. Soc. Psychol. Rev. 3, 269 (1999).

42. A.G. Miller, Ed., The Social Psychology of Good and Evil (Guilford, New York, 2004).

43. Although social context matters more than most people think, individual personality also matters, in accord with most people's intuitions: Social Dominance Orientation (SDO) describes a tough-minded view that it is a zero-sum, dog-eat-dog world, where some groups justifiably dominate other groups. People who score low on SDO tend to join helping professions, be more tolerant, and endorse less aggression: they might be less inclined to abuse. People choosing to join hierarchical institutions such as the military tend to score high on SDO, in contrast [47]. Right-Wing Authoritarianism (RWA) entails conforming to conventional values, submitting to authority, and aggressing as sanctioned by authority. People who score low on RWA would be less prone to abuse. [48] High SDO and RWA both predict intolerance of outgroups social groups outside one's own.

44. A.G. Miller, A.K. Gordon, A.M. Buddie, Pers. Soc. Psychol. Rev. 3. 254 (1999).

45. J.R. Schlesinger, H. Brown, T.K. Fowler, C.A. Homer, J.A. Blackwell Jr., Final Report of the Independent Panel to Review DoD Detention Operations, accessed 8 November 2004, from www.informationclearinghouse.info/article6785.htm

46. L.T. Harris, S.T. Fiske, unpublished data.

47. J. Sidanius. F. Pratto, Social Dominance: An Intergroup Theory of Social Hierarchy and Oppression (Cambridge Univ. Press, New York, 1999).

48. B. Altemeyer, Enemies of Freedom: Understanding Right-Wing Authoritarianism (Jossey-Bass, San Francisco, 1988).

Critical Thinking

You can apply the thinking and reading strategies discussed in chapters 4 and 5 both to the essays in *The Active Reader* and to many of the other readings you will undertake as part of your education. They will make you a more conscious and active reader and, in the end, make reading less a matter of overcoming challenges and more a matter of personal satisfaction.

Academic essays call on the reader's use of critical-thinking skills. Other kinds of writing, such as literary works, do this as well, but exercising the range of critical-thinking skills is crucial when you read academic prose because academic arguments are frequently based on tight logic or a series of claims that increase in complexity. Questioning and testing these claims is at the heart of critical thinking.

Writing at the post-secondary level also requires readers to make inferences, to draw valid conclusions based on evidence. What is common to all forms of interactive reading is a reliance on critical thinking, which can involve any of the following:

> Critical thinking
> Is a process of
> engagement. It
> consists of a series
> of logical mental
> processes that lead to a
> conclusion.

- analyzing
- questioning
- hypothesizing
- evaluating
- comparing
- judging
- reconsidering
- synthesizing
- weighing the evidence
- drawing a conclusion

If you look up the words *critical*, *critic*, and *criticism* in a dictionary, you will see that each word has several meanings, including making a negative judgment, or criticizing.

However, the root of *critical* comes from a Greek word that means "to judge or discern," to weigh and evaluate evidence. It is this meaning that is implied in the term *critical thinking.*

Much of what we do today is done quickly. This is true not only of video games, text messages, Twitter, and email but also in leadership roles where "instant" decisions are valued (especially if they turn out to be good decisions!). However, because critical thinking involves many related activities, speed is not usually an asset. Leaders may sometimes need to make quick decisions, but more often, their decisions arise after carefully weighing an issue and receiving input from diverse sources. Since critical thinking is a process, the best way to succeed is to slow down, to be more deliberate in your thinking so you can complete each stage of the process.

When Do You Use Critical Thinking?

In many of your assignments you will have to form conclusions about what you have read. You might employ critical thinking to decide whether to use a secondary source in your research essay. Then, you will need to judge the reliability of the sources and the validity of the findings—critical thinking, again.

Critical-thinking skills are also triggered whenever you read a work in order to comment on it; this could be in the form of a classroom discussion or a written assignment, such as a review or critical analysis. When you use research, you will have to assess the reliability and usefulness of your sources, compare their claims, and organize them logically in your essay.

> Reviews, critical analyses, research, and many everyday activities involve critical thinking.

Critical skills are also used in many everyday situations, like those described below (Inferences and Critical Thinking), and in fieldwork projects, like those discussed in The Active Voice: Silent Witnesses to the Past (p. 42) in which the fieldworker observes phenomena in his or her surroundings and draws conclusions from these observations.

For a writer, critical thinking is stimulated whenever analysis is involved, as it is in most kinds of problem-solving. A writer asks a question about a relevant topic in his or her discipline and uses the methods and processes of the discipline to answer it. For example, Douglas C. Nord questions the "traditional" perception of the Canadian–American relationship. He uses critical thinking, political theory, and relevant primary sources to explore the "other" side of the dialogue from the US perspective ("Discourse and Dialogue between Americans and Canadians," page 206 in Part III: The Reader). Using critical thinking in an argument, as Joel Lexchin does in "Pharmaceutical Innovation: Can We Live Forever? A commentary on Schnittker and Karandinos" (p. 354 in Part III: The Reader), involves challenging the conclusions of a scholarly study; he uses questioning, evaluating, comparing, and weighing the evidence to help him reach his conclusion.

Although critical thinking involves typical activities, they vary somewhat from discipline to discipline:

- Empirical studies in the natural and social sciences often identify problems, generate hypotheses, predict occurrences, create raw data, analyze using cause and effect, and attempt to generalize from their findings.

- Studies in the arts/humanities often identify problems, ask questions, propose a thesis, interpret primary and secondary sources, and analyze using definitions, examples, comparison and contrast, and other patterns.

Inferences and Critical Thinking

Context clues can be used to infer the meaning of an unfamiliar word (see Word Meanings, page 58). More broadly, inferences apply to ideas and the way we use them to form conclusions. Writers do not always explicitly state their points but may leave it to the reader to infer meaning.

Many research methods rely on inferences: astronomers, for example, study the phenomenon of black holes by observing the behaviour of the matter that surrounds them. They know that before gas is swallowed up by a black hole, it is heated to extreme temperatures and accelerates. In the process, X-rays are created, which escape the black hole and reveal its presence. Scientists cannot actually *see* black holes, but they can *infer* their existence through the emission of X-rays.

We practise critical thinking every day, inferring causes or consequences from what we observe—the evidence. For example, say you are jogging while wearing headphones. Another jogger catches your eye and points to her wrist. What is the probable reason (cause)? You might infer that she is asking for the time. Other inferences are possible too, but *the most valid inference is the one with the greatest probability of being correct.* If you shouted out the time and she looked puzzled, you might then infer that your original inference was incorrect.

If you are impatiently waiting for a bus and someone at the bus stop tells you that the buses are running 15 minutes late, you might be more interested in inferring the consequence than the cause: you will be late for class. However, if the bus immediately arrives, you might revise your original conclusion, which was based on the testimony of the person at the bus stop. You might also infer that this person is not a reliable source.

You use critical thinking as you read whenever you evaluate evidence and draw conclusions about claims (assertions) or the writer. Although critical thinking can involve all the activities mentioned above, there are three general activities that will promote critical-thinking skills as you read a text: reading closely and objectively, asking questions, and drawing logical conclusions. However, although most texts are linear (that is, we read them from beginning to end), our engagement with them is not always linear. It is important to remember that critical thinking is a *process of rigorous but flexible engagement* with a text (or a non-textual situation) that may change as you read (or learn more about the non-textual situation).

More than one inference might be possible in a given situation—that is, an inference could be a *possible* conclusion, but not the *most probable* one, such as in the examples above about the jogger and the person at the bus stop. A more probable inference is said to be a better one. However, an incorrect inference could occur if you drew a hasty conclusion without thinking something through or if you had a bias (for example, if you prejudged someone based on appearance). In reading, you might make an incorrect inference if you failed to read the instructions for an assignment or read them too quickly. Making correct inferences is essential in responding to everyday situations and to the reading challenges of your university career.

inference
A conclusion based on what the evidence shows or points to. More than one inference might be possible in a given situation, but the most probable one is said to be the best inference.

Activity 4.1

When students move away from home to live with room-mates, the new environment promotes critical thinking, and making correct inferences can be a key to survival. In groups, evaluate the evidence and discuss the best of the possible conclusions (inferences); try to make specific inferences based on the evidence rather than general ones. Share your group's conclusions with those of other groups.

1.   Evidence:

   a.   I noticed bottles of iron and Vitamin C pills beside my roommate's bed.

   b.   She had complained of being tired and had talked about visiting the campus medical centre.

   Conclusion: _____

2.   Evidence:

   a.   When I came home from classes, I noticed that the fridge was nearly empty.

   b.   The reusable grocery bags were gone.

   c.   The grocery list was still on the fridge door.

   Conclusion: _____

3.   Evidence

   a.   My roommate and I were planning to see a movie if he finished his essay by 3 pm.

   b.   At 1:30 pm, he texted me to say that he was working on his last paragraph.

   c.   At 3 pm, I still had not received another text from him.

   Conclusion: _____

4.   Evidence:

   a.   My roommate is hard-working and often complains about the noise on our floor of the rez.

   b.   She told me as I left for classes that she had an important exam coming up.

   c.   When I returned home after class, she was not there, and her laptop was gone.

   Conclusion: _____

5.   Evidence:

   a.   My roommate works long hours at a restaurant after his last class and on weekends, so I do not see him until late at night.

   b.   He has always taken a bus to work, and if it is behind schedule, he occasionally arrives late for work, which causes him much anxiety.

   c.   Last night he came back, smiling, earlier than usual and told me to look in the driveway.

   Conclusion: _____

Activity 4.2

The two passages below contain specific statements from which readers may be able to make inferences about the writer's belief or attitude concerning his or her subject. Choose the most valid (most probable) conclusion:

1.   Binkley paid for all the travel and expenses, and what was only 12 months ago a very new and controversial transaction has today left Binkley a healthy man—and the first of 16 people who have successfully received organs through MatchingDonors.com. (Desai, J, 2006. "Google yourself an organ donor." *Science & Spirit,* 17(1) 46–52)

   a.   The author believes that this method of soliciting donors is wrong.

   b.   The author believes that this method of soliciting donors is, at the very least, ethically questionable.

c. The author sees nothing wrong with this method of soliciting donors.

d. No inference is possible about the author's beliefs; he/she is just reporting the facts.

2. They're the impulse buys piled up next to the cash register. They're the books stocked by Urban Outfitters and hipster gift stores. They're the books you pick up, laugh at, and figure would be just about right for that co-worker who's into sci-fi (*The Space Tourist's Handbook*) [or] the friend who watches too much TV (*Hey! It's That Guy!: the Fametracker.com Guide to Character Actors*). . . .

Pop-culture-inspired handbooks for situations you're never going to face featuring information you're never going to need, these gimmicky, kooky, sometimes just plain stupid books have at least one thing in common: There are more and more of them out there, because they sell. (Hal Niedzviecki. 2005. "Publishers feel smart about selling people stupid books." *The Globe and Mail*, 17 Dec.: R1.)

a. The writer's attitude to his subject is one of respect.

b. The writer's attitude to his subject is one of amusement.

c. The writer's attitude to his subject is one of contempt.

d. No inference is possible about the writer's attitude.

Collaborative Exercise 4.1
Reading for Meaning

After reading the passage below, discuss the author's use of linguistic strategies (such as word choice), exaggeration, and similar cues to suggest that he does not actually believe what he says. Some areas for discussion are underlined, but other parts of the paragraph may also be relevant:

When I was a youngster, I spent the bulk of my Saturday mornings in front of the television, entertained by the hand-drawn shenanigans of a host of animated cartoon characters. I remember so many of them fondly, like family members or good friends: Bugs Bunny, Tweety Bird, Scrooge McDuck, Ronald Reagan. It's only now, armed with the wisdom and hindsight that comes with age, that I realize how dangerous an indulgence this may have been. For this, I have the good Dr. James Dobson, founder of Focus on the Family, to thank. He noticed the effete tendencies of a pant-wearing sponge on a video entitled *We Are Family: A Musical Message For All*. (The video bears the name of the infamous disco song that hinted at the indiscriminate inclusiveness of vice-ridden dens such as Studio 54.) *We Are Family* is a video that was distributed to school groups all over the United States and, by all accounts (no, I have not seen it), it can make people either tolerant, open-minded and/or homosexual. . . . Dobson, with characteristic sharpness of mind and tongue, has opened up a Pandora's box, and the torrent subsequently unleashed will change the face of popular entertainment. Forever.

Or, at the very least, for several weeks.

—Richard Poplak (2005), "Fear and Loathing in Toontown." *This* May/June: 39–40. © Richard Poplak

Critical Thinking and Skepticism

Focused reading is a systematic method that can be used in reading for content (see Focused Reading, page 51). By reading a text very closely, by attending objectively to its claims, to the details that support these claims, and to the writer's language and tone, you will be in a position to go beyond simple comprehension and apply critical-thinking skills.

Reading closely, then, means becoming conscious not only of content but also of how you interact with a text—for example, being open to challenges to your own ways of thinking but not being swayed by other views unless they stand up to the tests of logic and consistency. One attitude often used to describe this state of readiness is *skepticism*. Adopting an attitude of healthy skepticism does not mean you should mistrust everything you read or are told. It is different from being a cynic, as explained in the philosophical statement of the Skeptics Society, a group of scholars who publish the quarterly magazine *Skeptic*:

> Some people believe that skepticism is the rejection of new ideas, or worse, they confuse "skeptic" with "cynic" and think that skeptics are a bunch of grumpy curmudgeons unwilling to accept any claim that challenges the status quo. This is wrong. *Skepticism is a provisional approach to claims.* It is the application of reason to any and all ideas—no sacred cows allowed. In other words, skepticism is a method, not a position. Ideally, skeptics do not go into an investigation closed to the possibility that a phenomenon might be real or that a claim might be true. When we say we are "skeptical," we mean that we must see compelling evidence before we believe.
>
> —www.skeptic.com/about_us/

In critical thinking, you constantly test and assess the evidence presented, considering how it is being used and where the writer is going with it. Key activities in a close reading of a text are questioning, evaluating, and reconsidering.

The Spirit of Inquiry

The popular tabloid *National Enquirer* promotes itself as a magazine "for enquiring minds." In fact, a typical tabloid reader believes anything he or she is told or, at least, finds humour in improbable claims.

A truly inquiring mind analyzes what it reads and does not take everything at face value. The critical thinker questions assumptions, tests the evidence, and accepts (or rejects) conclusions after careful analysis. When questions arise, the critical thinker first seeks for answers within the text itself but may also consider relevant knowledge from outside sources or from personal experience.

In analyzing arguments, the critical thinker should ask, Does the writer reason consistently? Does he or she do justice to the argument's complexity? Are there inconsistencies or oversimplifications? (See Failures in Reasoning, chapter 9, page 112). The critical thinker should also be aware of the counter-arguments, especially those unacknowledged by the writer. Is the writer avoiding certain issues by not mentioning them? By considering all sides and angles and by questioning all easy answers, the critical thinker sets logical boundaries within which the text can be understood.

Critical Factors in Critical Thinking

A writer might make a claim that directly contradicts what our knowledge or common sense tells us—for example, that cats are more intelligent than humans. More commonly, a writer might make a claim about an often debated topic—for example, that cats are smarter than dogs. Such a claim would probably cause you to use critical thinking to evaluate the following:

- *The writer's credibility:* Is the writer an expert? A researcher into animal behaviour? A veterinarian? An animal trainer? Someone who has owned dogs and cats? Someone who has owned cats only? Could the writer have a bias? Are there any logical fallacies in the argument? Has fact been carefully distinguished from opinion?

> Logical fallacies are failures or distortions in reason or logic. See chapter 9.

- *The writer's audience:* In other words, who is his or her audience? How might the audience affect the claim? Is he or she addressing pet owners? Just dog owners? Animal behaviour experts?
- *Nature of the claim (assertion):* Specific claims are stronger than general ones and often easier to prove. Since there are many varieties of dog breeds, it would be difficult to generalize about the intelligence of *all* dogs.
- *Basis of the claim:* A claim may depend on an underlying assumption, such as a definition. Intelligence can be defined or measured in different ways: physiologically (e.g., the weight of the brain in proportion to the weight of the body) and behaviourally (e.g., trainability, adaptability, independence). Advocates of a dog's superior intelligence may point to trainability as the intelligence factor, while advocates of cat intelligence may point to adaptability or independence.
- *Method:* How does the writer attempt to prove the claim? A method that sought to measure intelligence scientifically would be more credible than one that relied only on personal observation. However, not all valid arguments make use of scientific evidence. Deductive methods are based on general statements, such as beliefs or values, which are then applied to specific cases. Does the statement seem reasonable/logical? (See chapter 9, page 110, for more about deductive reasoning.)
- *Support:* In critical thinking, you must evaluate the nature of the evidence and the way the writer uses it. Typical questions might include the following: What kind of evidence did the writer use? Has the writer relied too much on one kind of evidence? How many sources were used? Were they current ones? Did the writer ignore or minimize some sources (e.g., those that found dogs more intelligent than cats)?

Drawing Conclusions

Drawing a conclusion about a work you have read usually involves more than making one inference; it results from the *incremental process of reading critically*. In arriving at a conclusion, you weigh the factors involved in your analysis of the text. As you complete your reading, you will synthesize the evidence you analyzed in order to say something definitive about it, about its presentation, and/or about the writer.

In the end, *your goal is to determine whether the accumulated weight of evidence supports the writer's claim*, or, as members of the Skeptics Society would ask, Is the weight of evidence "compelling"? You might consider how weaker points affect the validity of the findings. Were there any gaps or inconsistencies in reasoning? Was the writer's conclusion logically prepared for? Did the writer's findings/conclusion reflect what he or she set out to investigate? Was the original hypothesis proved or disproved? Was the original question answered?

If you have been using your critical-thinking skills to write a critical analysis of a work, you will need to show how critical thinking led you to your conclusions (see page 94). For a critical-thinking assignment involving research, see chapter 10, page 137.

The essay in the Active Voice feature demonstrates how critical thinking can be used to "reconstruct" the past. The questions that follow stress the application of critical thinking to the essay itself.

Clearly, the effects of critical thinking, whether applied to small practical problems or to controversial social issues (see "Pipeline Debate Shaping Up as Propaganda War" below), allow us to better understand our past and radically transform our future.

The Active Voice

Silent Witnesses to the Past

1   No academic subject can claim a greater longevity in the Western educational system than the study of Greek and Latin. From the Renaissance on, it was thought that the mastery of these two difficult languages would provide a mental training without equal. The consequences of this belief were still apparent until quite recently. During the Second World War, for instance, classicists came second only to mathematicians in the recruitment of code-breakers, having intellectual capabilities, it was believed, perfectly honed to tackle complex problems. That said, despite their formidable reputation, classical languages have of late suffered an astonishingly rapid decline. Dominant for some 500 years, the study of Latin all but disappeared from schools in a single generation, while Greek is in an even more perilous state.

2   University departments of classics (now usually called something along the lines of "Greek and Roman Studies") have generally shown themselves to be highly adept at adjusting to the changing circumstances. Their new mission is to introduce students to classical civilization through non-linguistic media. None has proved more successful than archaeology.

3   Classical archaeology is, of course, much more than an inferior substitute for the ancient languages.

It is a highly effective way for students to gain a direct and tangible connection with antiquity, in many ways far more direct than they ever could from the written text. I might illustrate this from my own experience with a training excavation conducted on behalf of the University of British Columbia. The practicum, conducted for academic credit at the Lunt Roman Fort, near Coventry, England, from 1985 to 2002, was in each of those years attended by 35 or so students from UBC and elsewhere in North America.

4   The Lunt Fort was first built in the early sixties AD (during the reign of Nero) and remained under occupation for about 30 years. Our work concentrated on its defensive system, in the form of a turf rampart fronted by a series of ditches. In the course of excavation, the students brought to light objects that had remained untouched since they were discarded nearly 2,000 years ago by the fort's original occupants. The term *discarded* is deliberate, since most of the material was there because its owners had thrown it away: pieces of pot, old nails, a belt buckle, a broken brooch, and the like. For students sensitive to the spirit of history, the thrill of gaining this direct physical contact with the ancient Romans proved to be a life-transforming experience.

5   Archaeology is not, of course, a mere treasure hunt. The students, usually from faculties of arts, were obliged to acquire a whole new set of skills. They were given thorough training in the techniques required of the modern archaeologist. They learned to plan, to survey, to enter items into a systematic database. They were taught to date fragments of pottery, to identify different types of corroded metal, to distinguish between natural strata in sandy soil and deposited material compacted over hundreds of years. This last is not an easy task but a crucial one on a site like ours, where no stone construction was used and the residual material is often detectable only through variations in the colour of the soil.

6   More importantly, however, beyond these essentially technical skills, the students developed crucial expertise in applying logical thought processes to the investigation of complex evidence. Archaeological remains are silent witnesses to the past. Like other witnesses, they surrender their testimony only under skilful cross-examination. Let me illustrate this with a concrete example. The most useful features on any Roman fort are the "v"-shaped defensive ditches. When forts were demolished to give way to civilian settlements, the ditches were filled, and the material deposited in them came primarily from the fort's upper structures. In the ensuing centuries, the surface area would almost invariably be subject to human activity, usually plowing. The evidence at ground level would thus often be destroyed or damaged. But the fill of the ditches would survive intact, and much of the history of the site can be recovered from it. Students noticed when they drew a plan of a section of a ditch that there was, at the bottom, at the point of the "v," a roughly square-shaped slot. What had caused this? They soon learned to dismiss such fanciful ideas such as "ankle-breakers" by observing what happened in the newly excavated ditches when it rained: they filled with silt.

7   The slots were clearly made by Roman soldiers dragging buckets along the ditch-bottom to remove the silt. Students were then told to observe whether the excavated slot was silt-free or full of silt. What could that observation tell us? We made the students try to think in Roman terms. In the case of a silted-up ditch, why would the Romans have stopped removing silt from the bottom of the ditch? Almost certainly, it means that the occupants anticipated that they would be abandoning the fort at some point in the near future and saw no need to keep the ditch clean. In other words, it suggests an orderly redeployment. Conversely, a meticulously cleaned ditch suggests that the fort was abandoned and the ditches filled in as the immediate result of an order to move, perhaps because of some military crisis.

8   Archaeology thus involves not only the collection of material from which evidence is derived but, most importantly, the interpretation of that evidence by a series of logical mental sequences. It is a never-ending process. Examination of surviving material will reveal the size and nature of wall foundations. Foundations of a certain size token walls of a certain size. Why do walls have to be so high, so thick? Would that size have been needed for storage? If not, it presumably means that the walls were needed for defence. But, let us suppose, the period was peaceful and the region settled, at least according to Tacitus and the like. Does the evidence on the ground suggest that we have to question the literary evidence (written, after all, in Rome, usually by historians who never set foot in a military camp and almost certainly had never been to Britain)? There are numerous permutations of this kind of questioning.

9   Interestingly, the very mental discipline that the detailed knowledge of the ancient languages reputedly bestowed on previous generations is now well matched by what archaeology offers the students of today. The vast majority will not become professional archaeologists. But after their training, they see their world differently and will have developed considerable proficiency as problems-solvers, acquiring broad skills that stand them in excellent stead in their chosen future careers.

—**Anthony Barrett**, Professor, Department of Classical, Near Eastern and Religious Studies, University of British Columbia

Questions to Consider

1. Why do you think that the study of classical languages was considered "a mental training without equal"? Can you infer reasons for its decline after the Second World War?

2. Explain how the specialized skills mentioned in paragraph 5 equip students to draw more accurate conclusions about the objects they will be studying. How do the skills described in paragraph 6 differ from those in paragraph 5?

3. What are "ankle-breakers," and why does the writer dismiss them as "fanciful"?

4. What is the function of the questions in paragraph 8? Does the writer answer the last question in this paragraph? Why or why not?

5. Paraphrase (put in your own words) the last sentence, in which the writer summarizes the value of the skills students gain through the experience at the excavation of the Lunt Fort.

In the following essay, the writer uses critical thinking to challenge the argument of another writer. Before reading Stephen Hume's essay, below, you could read the essay to which he is responding (see Kenneth Green, "A Northern Gateway to ongoing conflict; Pipeline: Failure to allow project tells world our political process is broken," *The Vancouver Sun*, 27 December 2013, p. A12.) The annotations focus on the use of critical thinking—for example, on the way that the author questions the basis and nature of his opponent's statements. However, this essay could also be used as an example of a critical analysis and to illustrate the use of argumentative strategies (see chapter 9, Writing Argumentative Essays).

Pipeline Debate Shaping Up as Propaganda War

by Stephen Hume

Hume is responding to an article published in the same newspaper for which he writes, following approval of the Northern Gateway project by the National Energy Board. More importantly, he is invoking the long-standing debate over the contentious issue of the pipeline.

Hume is questioning and analyzing the basis of his opponent's claim (see "Basis of the claim" under Critical Factors in Critical Thinking, above). By attacking those who oppose the pipeline, the validity of their objections are sidestepped, a fallacy in reasoning, according to Hume. See Failures in Reasoning, p. 113, "Emotional fallacies."

1   Well, that didn't take long. The New Year isn't even here yet and the Northern Gateway pipeline debate already begins to polarize.

2   First, an argument that non-governmental organizations vowing to stop the proposed project following its approval by the National Energy Board—subject to more than 200 conditions—are somehow undermining the democratic process through intimidation, threats of violent protest, political sabotage, slander and disinformation.

3   This is all code. It is intended to define a category to which those who think the pipeline is a bad idea can be routinely consigned. Thus, opposition may be dismissed without assessing the merits of the objections—simply opposing the pipeline invites automatic framing of that protest as the work of enemies of the Canadian way of life.

4   British Columbians have heard all this rhetoric before. It is a propaganda strategy devised by giant public relations firms. It was first deployed here more than 20 years ago by the forest industry in response to protest and civil disobedience aimed at preventing the denuding of great swaths of the province with vast industrial clearcuts.

Critical thinking may involve comparing. Here, Hume recalls the controversy over clearcutting, which created a similar opposition between corporations and environmental activists. In the next paragraphs, Hume reasons that the "propaganda strategy" didn't work then and isn't likely to work in the present situation. See Kinds of Evidence in Argumentative Essays, p. 109 "Precedents."

5   For those who need a refresher course on this strategy (and a handy antidote to its use in many other arenas), I recommend *The War Against the Greens* by indie journalist David Helvarg; *The Age of Propaganda: The Everyday Use and Abuse of Persuasion* by communications scholars Anthony Pratkanis and Elliot Aronson; and *The Sultans of Sleaze: Public Relations and the Media* by social analyst Joyce Nelson.

> The author shows his credibility by referring to three books on the uses of propaganda.

6   A word to the enthusiasts for this approach: It didn't work in the early 1990s; it won't work now.

7   As it turned out, the protests—even civil disobedience—didn't result in the collapse of the economy. What did happen was that the forest industry modified its approach. Today, although there is still protest at the margins and over specifics of policy, industry has found that building consensus, engaging with critics and consultation is far more effective than confrontation.

8   Instead of seeking to polarize the issue into "them" versus "us," advocates of such projects might think about the idea that "we" are "them," in the sense that democracy accommodates dissent and the right of citizens to protest what their governments—and government proxies—want to do.

> Recalling his opening paragraph, Hume questions the method of his opponent, who, he says, is "seeking to polarize the issue." This claim leads him to affirm the basis of his own claim by defining "civil disobedience" as an inherent right of citizens.

9   And that accommodation extends to civil disobedience, which can't and shouldn't be equated with criminal violence. Very few sympathize with criminal acts, but civil disobedience is another matter. If it weren't for civil disobedience we would still be run by the Family Compact, would still have slavery and indentured labour instead of trade unions and labour codes, and women wouldn't have the vote.

10   The inherent assumption in the demonization of opposition to the Northern Gateway pipeline proposal—please note, it's a proposal that hasn't yet addressed its ability to meet even the most basic conditions imposed by the NEB, let alone B.C.—is that the economic interests of giant corporations represent the Canadian way of life.

> Hume reasons that civil disobedience is sometimes beneficial as it helps create a more equal society. If we then agree that protesting the pipeline is an example of civil disobedience, Hume, through the deductive reasoning process, concludes that it is beneficial and a citizen's right.

11   It is common for proponents of industrial mega-projects to portray their expectations of profit as vital to the economic interests of the nation. But the economic interests of Canada—or the province, or communities, or First Nations, or workers—are not what motivate corporations. They seek to do what is in their own immediate economic interests. This is fine. It's called business. But it doesn't follow that business interests and other interests automatically coincide.

12   Corporate interests can certainly be congruent with other interests, and they can be modified to complement one another. However, just because a trans-national corporation sees profit in a particular enterprise, it doesn't follow that its interests are everyone's.

> Hume questions the assumption of his opponents that the economic interests of corporations represent Canadian interests in general.

13   So, as the "eco-terrorism" balloon is once again inflated, let us please keep in mind this fact.

14   Among those objecting to the Northern Gateway pipeline project as proposed are

> Hume refutes the claim that opposition to the pipeline comes from radical groups that do not represent the Canadian way of life.

> 1. The official Opposition in the House of Commons; 2. The province of British Columbia; 3. The Union of B.C. Municipalities; 4. First Nations governments through whose territories the pipeline and tankers will pass; 5. Major trade unions, including Canada's largest; 6. The municipal governments of Terrace, Prince Rupert, Victoria and the Regional District of Queen Charlotte; 7. The B.C. Wilderness Tourism Association; 8. Various non-governmental environmental organizations— they range from those who will employ direct action to those who reject it.

15   This opposition does not look like radical green eco-terrorists out to destroy business or the Canadian way of life. It looks like a broad cross-section of serious citizens with concerns to express. And they have the democratic right to do so.

5

Reading Strategies

Interacting with Texts

Reading is not just a passive process. It is an *interactive* one involving a relationship *between* you and the text you are reading (*inter-* is a prefix meaning "between"), which often changes as you read and apply critical-thinking skills. That is why when you read a text for the second time, you uncover new meanings and make new inferences.

Each reader approaches a text in a different way: your ideas, beliefs, and specific knowledge about the topic reflect who you are and your unique experiences. You will therefore interact with the text in a unique way.

In addition, the nature of the text itself, the purpose of the author in writing, the audience it was intended to reach, and the reason for reading it all play a role in the way you interact with it, as do the author's own ideas, beliefs, background, and the specific choices—in diction, style, and tone—that he or she makes.

Consider, for example, what you might find yourself thinking about as you began reading an essay by David Suzuki on wind farms as an alternative energy source:

> Off the coast of British Columbia in Canada is an island called Quadra, where I have a cabin that is as close to my heart as you can imagine. From my porch on a good day you can see clear across the waters of Georgia Strait to the snowy peaks of the rugged Coast Mountains. It is one of the most beautiful views I have seen. And I would gladly share it with a wind farm.
>
> But sometimes it seems like I'm in the minority. All across Europe and North America, environmentalists are locking horns with the wind industry over the location of wind farms.
>
> —D. Suzuki (2005), "The beauty of wind farms." *New Scientist, 186* (2495): 20–21.

Questions about the subject itself: What do I know about wind farms? Where did my knowledge come from (the media, teachers or textbooks, conversations with friends, my own observation)? Have I any personal experience that might affect my reading? Do I have opinions about the topic? What might change them?

Questions about the writer: Is the author's name familiar? What do I associate with him and his writing? Where did these associations come from (previous work by the author or by another author, something mentioned in class or in general conversation)? Is he an authority? How would the average Canadian respond to an essay written by this writer?

While many readers have different knowledge and opinions about wind farms, most know something about the author, a noted Canadian scientist and environmentalist. The following comments on his essay illustrate the different ways that reader and writer can interact based on prior knowledge and experience. What they reveal is that each reader's point of view is shaped, at least somewhat, by his or her experience with the subject of wind farms and, in one case, with the author. Each reader, therefore, has likely approached the essay in a different way. Reflecting on your knowledge of the subject and author(s) is a practical pre-reading activity that will make you more conscious of the background, opinions, and possible biases that could come into play as you read.

Student Comments

Katherine W.: I was not very knowledgeable about the "windmill issue" before I read this article, but by the end, I was pretty much convinced that it is an important issue. Of course, my viewpoint might have been a little biased because I have always been a fan of windmills (no practical reason) and have a lot of respect for David Suzuki. I guess that is the main reason I was convinced.

Tristan H.: Since I grew up in southern Alberta, I am no stranger to windmills, but I never imagined they were an issue with certain groups. Whenever we talked about windmills, it was not to say how ugly or unpleasant they were. They were more of an accent to the background. Without reading this essay, I would never have thought they were an environmental issue at all.

Andrew M.: In the first paragraph, David Suzuki speaks of his cabin on Quadra Island and the fact he would "gladly share it with a wind farm." I have flown over and around Quadra Island numerous times as well as across the Georgia Strait to the Coastal Mountains referred to in his article. The island is covered by forest, as are the mountains across the strait. I have seen wind farms in various parts of Alberta, all of them in non-forested areas. I don't see his point as credible, as it is impractical to set up wind farms in forested areas.

As you continue to read an essay, of course, many other factors arise. Your initial impressions may intensify or weaken through the evidence the writer presents. A simple issue may begin to appear more complex, or the level of detail may make it difficult to follow; more likely, points could become clearer. Whatever the case, some general reading strategies can make the reading process more manageable, ensuring that you remain in control of the reading situation.

Annotating Texts

annotation (verb annotate)

A note that explains, expands on, or comments on a written text.

One simple way of responding to an essay is to reflect on what the author has written. If your purpose for reading is to prepare for a general discussion of a topic for the next class, this might be adequate preparation. On the other hand, if you are to write a critical analysis of the essay, simply thinking about it is probably not sufficient. You will need to jot your ideas down, to annotate the essay (*ad* = to + *nota* = note).

Making annotations about the text you are reading is an important (perhaps the *most* important) reading strategy, not just because it enables you to return to the essay later and have your questions and other responses fresh in your mind but also because when you annotate an essay, you are *beginning your actual work on the assignment*: you are translating abstract ideas and impressions into concrete language, solidifying those ideas.

Pre-reading Strategies: Reading Purpose

It is important to know why you are reading a text; the reason affects the way you respond to it. There are many different reasons for reading—beyond the obvious one of satisfying a course requirement. Are you reading it to determine whether the essay is related to your topic? To extract the main ideas? To use the text as a secondary source in your essay? To write a critical analysis of it? Each of these questions affects the way you respond to the essay and the reading strategies to adopt.

Reading to Determine Whether the Essay Is Related to Your Topic (to explore)

When you search for potential sources for a research essay, you look for essays that seem promising, perhaps from their titles or the fact that they are listed in bibliographies of general works such as textbooks or in encyclopedias, indexes, or subject directories. If you are using an online resource, you might search for articles or books by keywords related to your topic. Since you are reading for exploratory purposes, you do not want to waste time by closely reading each text, so a different strategy is essential.

Once you find a potentially useful essay, you can read the abstract, if available, the introduction, and headings. If it still looks promising, turn your attention to the main parts of the essay, scanning for topic sentences and other content clues (see Reading Paragraphs: Locating Main Ideas, page 53). Finally, read the concluding section. Scanning prevents wasting time on what might not be useful, giving you more time to scan other potential sources. Underlining and annotation can be minimal at this stage since you are evaluating the essay's usefulness.

It is vital, however, that you record all relevant bibliographic information for every potential source—title, author, journal or book title (and include names of editors if the source is an edited book), journal volume and issue numbers, and page range, or website details. This information will enable you to access the source quickly when you are ready. It often happens that you end up using some information you recall from a source you were not planning to use. Having the bibliographic information at hand can be a life-saver for late-stage additions to your essay.

Reading to Extract Main Ideas (to summarize)

You might read an essay in order to write a formal summary, or précis (see page 89). In this case, you identify the important points, perhaps by underlining them, after you have thoroughly read the text, as you will not know which are the main and which the sub-points until you have completed your first reading. This practice applies to other reading purposes too: do the underlining in a later reading—after you have become familiar with the entire contents of the essay, its purpose, its tone, and so on.

Reading to Use the Text as a Secondary Source in Your Essay (to synthesize)

After you have explored to determine the best sources, you need to flesh out the general areas of each article that you identified as potentially useful. Thus, you must now read closely, take careful notes, and think of how each point relates to your thesis. How much you annotate depends on the importance of the source, so your initial task is to attempt to answer this question. After scanning the entire essay, you might decide that only one section directly pertains to your topic. You may then wish to summarize this section to use in your essay. If a phrase or sentence is particularly significant or expressed in a memorable way, you can record its wording exactly for future use (see Integrating Your Sources, page 142). Make sure that you record the page numbers of every potential source whether you are quoting directly, summarizing, or making a brief reference.

> Record page numbers (or paragraph numbers if they are given in an electronic source) for future reference. Direct quotations, paraphrases, and most summaries require citations that include page numbers.

Reading to Analyze

Although simply responding to a work may or may not be an assignment at the university level, rhetorical analyses are common because they reveal how an essay is put together, making them useful as models for your own writing. In an analysis you are concerned with breaking down the text to determine the author's premises, to test the validity of the claims and conclusion, and to examine the author's methods and strategies. Thus, your interaction with the text will involve such activities as identifying and evaluating; it will involve critical thinking and objective analysis. (See Critical Thinking, page 35, and The Rhetorical Analysis: Explaining the How and Why, page 94).

> **rhetorical analysis**
> A writing activity concerned with breaking down a text to examine its structure, reasoning, rhetorical strategies, significance, and other features.

Of course, there are other reasons for reading: to write a review of a book or film, to prepare an informational or evaluative report, to compare and contrast two essays, to study for an exam, to see whether an essay topic interests you, for pure pleasure, and many more. Asking "How am I going to use the text?" before you begin can orient you appropriately and help you select the most useful strategies of those discussed below.

Reading Strategies: The Big Picture

People often assess their own strengths by saying, "I like to look at the big picture" or "I'm a detail person." Many of us do seem to have an aptitude—or at least a preference—for one or the other. In order to complete many tasks, both skills are required. In much scientific research, a professor or senior researcher will oversee an experiment; the success of the experiment, however, depends just as much on the painstaking work of graduate students or junior researchers. Successful essay writing, too, requires attention to the large and the small: while large-scale concerns relating to essay organization and paragraph structure (sometimes referred to as *macro-composing*) tend to occur in the early and middle stages, by the final-draft stage, the focus will be on detail-oriented tasks (*micro-composing*), such as sentence construction, word choice, grammar, and source integration. These details increasingly become the focus throughout the revision process. This general pattern applies to reading as well, with some significant differences.

Selective Reading: Scanning and Focused Reading

In **selective reading**, your reading strategy is determined by your pre-reading choices, which can depend on what you are reading (for example, an introduction, a book chapter, an academic essay, or a book review) and your purpose for reading, as discussed above. It is therefore very different from simply sitting down with a book or essay and closely reading every word from beginning to end. Unlike reading for pleasure, selective reading, then, is planned, conscious reading.

Scanning

Scanning is a form of selective reading. In a *general scan*, you read to get the gist of a text. You read efficiently, keeping an eye out for content markers, such as headings and places in which the author summarizes material (this summary could include tables, graphs, and other visual representations used to condense textual explanation). You try to identify main ideas in the essay by locating topic sentences within major paragraphs; topic sentences are often, but not always, the first sentence of the paragraph. Thesis statements, plans, or hypotheses are found in academic essays at the end of the introductory section. You proceed to skim, skipping detail such as examples. General scanning is a good way to start reading a text since it gives you an overview of content. From a general scan, you might then move on to another selective reading method.

In a specific scan, or *targeted scan*, you look for specific content, for words and phrases related to your topic. If you are looking for information in a book, you are likely able to locate it by referring to the **subject index** (or author index) found at the back of the book after any appendices or bibliographies. These indexes may give you many page references, so you may have to scan several pages to access the information you seek.

If your source is a journal article involving original research, you may not need to target scan the whole article—only the appropriate sections. But if your potential source is a journal article that is not divided into formal sections, you may have to scan the entire text. If you are accessing a text online, however, you can use your browser's Find function to locate significant words or phrases.

A *general scan* is helpful if you know you will be using the whole text—for example, if you are going to summarize a work or refer to it often in your essay—since it can give you an overview of content. A *targeted scan* is helpful if you want to assess the usefulness of a text; if you decide that it does contain relevant content, you can then apply another method of selective reading, such as focused reading.

selective reading

A reading strategy designed to meet a specific objective, such as scanning for main points or reading for detail.

scanning

A form of selective reading in which you skim sections or an entire text. In a general scan, you try to determine the gist of a text—for example, by locating main ideas; in a targeted scan, you look for specific concepts or topics by key words or phrases. In research, a targeted scan typically occurs after you have narrowed your general topic.

subject index

A list of important words in a printed text, ordered alphabetically and usually placed at the end of the text.

In order to successfully scan academic essays, you must be familiar with their conventions—in particular, where to find important information (see chapter 2).

Reading Hypothesis

After scanning an essay's title, abstract, headings, list of sources, and introduction, one strategy is to construct a reading hypothesis that can guide you throughout a first reading of an essay. In essence, a reading hypothesis is a prediction about the essay's content or other elements, such as the writer's style or tone. Its main purpose is to solidify your expectations about the essay and shape the way you approach your reading of it.

It can be useful to make the hypothesis concrete by writing it up as a short paragraph of, perhaps, three to four sentences. Essentially, the reading hypothesis answers questions like, What is the essay about? What is the author trying to prove and how does he or she accomplish this? How might the essay be similar to or different from others on the same topic? Of course, your hypothesis is a starting point and may well change as you read more closely.

A reading hypothesis could also list the specific strategies you will use to read the text, such as those discussed in the next few pages.

Focused Reading

Because focused reading is time-consuming, it is best to scan a text beforehand to find the most relevant portions, which you then read in detail. University-level reading across the disciplines often involves both scanning and focused reading.

Activity 5.1

Below are several reading situations with two variables for each—reading purpose and kind of text. Consider how the variables would help you decide on the most appropriate reading strategy(ies) to use in each situation.

Reading Purpose	Kind of Text	Reading Strategy(ies)?
to provide an overview or a general summary	journalistic essay	
to see whether the topic interests you sufficiently to write an essay on it	informative essay	
to summarize results	journal study that describes original research (an experiment)	
to write a character or thematic analysis	novel	
to prepare for an exam question with a topic assigned in advance	essay you have never read	
to study for a final exam	your class notes	
to write a critical response to an essay about a recent controversial topic (e.g., face transplants)	journalistic essay accessed online	
to compare/contrast two essays (e.g., two tax systems)	edited collection of essays with differing points of view published by an academic press	
to write a critical analysis	argumentative essay	
to pass the time before your dentist appointment	popular magazine	
to check the accuracy of a direct quotation you used in your essay	academic essay	

As the term focused reading implies, you read the text closely line by line and word by word. You may want to analyze the text's rhetorical strategies, tone, or stylistic elements. You may want to subject it to a critical analysis by testing the author's premises or questioning the conclusions he or she draws from the evidence, or you may simply want to determine the main ideas. Many of the strategies for focused reading are discussed below under Dividing the Whole and Reading Strategies: The Detail Work.

In a focused reading, you often concentrate on one or more short or medium-length passages and relate them to a main idea or to other sections of the text. For example, if you are writing an essay for a history class, you might concentrate on specific passages from a primary text, such as a historical document, in order to connect key ideas in the passage to a historical event or other historical element. The purpose of analyzing the specific passage(s) is to support your thesis about the significance or interpretation of the event.

Dividing the Whole

Information is more easily grasped if it is separated into logical divisions. Experiments may be divided into formal sections, each labelled according to convention; formal reports also use standardized headings. Such predictable categories tell you where specific information can be found; for example, in the "Methods" section, the writer describes how the study was set up, the number of participants, how they were chosen, what measurements were applied, and similar details. If you are interested in whether the author proved a hypothesis, you would read the abstract or the introduction and then read the "Discussion" section.

However, not all academic essays clearly indicate how they are broken down. In Type A and Type C essays, descriptive headings may be used, but you might want to subdivide the essay further to create more manageable content subcategories.

One way to figure out an academic essay's structure is to return to the introduction and reread the thesis or essay plan in which the author announces the essay's organization. Fortunately, most academic writers are aware of the importance of structure and organize content in the body of their essays logically. In the absence of an essay plan, headings, additional spacing, or similar aids, your job is to determine that logic and use it to create manageable subdivisions. As well as making the essay easier to read, when you do this you are also familiarizing yourself with the parts of the essay that are going to be useful to you.

Information can often be organized by rhetorical patterns. Identifying these patterns makes the text easier to follow. For example, in the chronological method, the writer traces a development over time, usually from old to new. In the spatial method, the writer describes an object or scene in a systematic way, from top to bottom, for example, or from one side to another. In enumeration, points are listed in a numbered sequence (see Rhetorical Patterns and Paragraph Development, page 79).

In addition, the relationship between ideas is often shown through transitional words and phrases. These transitions can indicate whether an idea is going to be expanded or whether there will be a shift in ideas. Transitions can occur between one paragraph and the next (as shown below) or between parts of a paragraph, linking smaller parts of the text (for examples, see pp. 55 and 77). Paying attention to organizational patterns and transitions can help you break down an essay into smaller and more manageable units. In the passage below, the writers use enumeration to indicate the beginning of a new point after a statement that divides the topic into four parts (ellipses show that sentences in between have been omitted):

---

focused reading

A reading strategy in which close attention is paid to sentences and words in order to extract detail, tone, style, relevance, etc.

---

rhetorical pattern

A method of organizing and presenting information in essays and paragraphs; examples include cause–effect, chronology, comparison and contrast, and definition.

transitional words and phrases

Words and phrases that connect ideas in a sentence or paragraph, or between paragraphs.

The average American tends to see Canada and Canadians along four dimensions. *The first* of these relates to being a "neighbor" of the United States. . . ."

The second dimension along which most Americans see Canada relates very much to the latter point. . . .

A *third* dimension of the American image of Canada . . . .

—Nord, "Discourse and dialogue between Americans and Canadians": page 207 in Part III: The Reader.

Reading Paragraphs: Locating Main Ideas

Scanning paragraphs for important information is not a mechanical process. The paragraphs in much academic writing may be long and detailed; sentences may also be long and complex. Furthermore, in academic or journalistic prose, the topic sentence is not always the first sentence of the paragraph. A topic sentence states the main idea of the paragraph, which can be developed by examples or analysis throughout the rest of the paragraph. Although it is less common in academic writing, a writer may build *toward* the central idea, in which case the topic sentence may be a middle or even the last sentence in the paragraph. The function of the topic sentence is partly structural— providing a foundation for the paragraph; this anchoring can occur in different places in the paragraph.

The following paragraphs illustrate different methods of paragraph construction. In the first, the opening sentence announces the paragraph's main idea, that Canadians have much to be proud of but are often unaware of their heroes; it is the topic sentence, which is developed through examples. This paragraph can be said to have been developed *deductively*: the topic sentence makes a general statement after which more specific statements are used for support:

> *Canadians have lots to celebrate, aside from hockey and Medicare, though we tend not to celebrate very loudly.* How many Canadians even know that Nancy Huston, a Calgarian by origin but writing in French, won France's prestigious Prix Fémina, or that Canadian composer Howard Shore has won three Oscars, three Golden Globes and four Grammies for his film scores?. . . .

—Toope, "Of hockey, Medicare and Canadian dreams": page 224 in Part III: The Reader.

In contrast to the first example, the paragraph below begins with a quotation from a Canadian senator on the Chinese Head Tax proposal. After a second quotation by another senator, a general statement follows, the topic sentence, which reflects the main idea in the paragraph as a whole. The paragraph can be said to have been developed *inductively*: the topic sentence is a general statement arrived at after specific "evidence" has been considered:

> Even George W. Allan, who introduced the amendments in the Senate for the government, said that he had "no special leaning towards this Chinese legislation." Given the level of agreement against the proposals, it would be, Richard W. Scott averred, "a service to the empire if we allow this question to stand over another year." By that time, he hoped, passions in British Columbia might have calmed somewhat and a more reasonable examination of the question might be assayed. *Thus, the same Senate that had seemed to sanction the 1885 Chinese Immigration Act now let the debate on its amendment*

topic sentence
A sentence that contains the main idea in the paragraph.

stand for six months, thereby signaling an unwillingness to allow the law to be changed in a more restrictive manner.

—Anderson, "The Senate and the fight against the 1885 Chinese Immigration Act":
page 243 in Part III: The Reader.

In the final example, the topic sentence is neither the first nor the last sentence. It can be determined by asking which sentence best describes what the paragraph is about. The first sentence states the year that the story was written. However, the main idea is the effect of technology on life at that time. Succeeding sentences expand on this idea:

"The Story of an Hour" was first published in Vogue in 1894. More than a century later, now in the midst of our own technological revolution, *it is difficult to grasp how fundamentally nineteenth-century technologies were altering the world in Chopin's time.* Before the railroad, traveling was extremely difficult and dangerous. In the 1850s, it took an average of 128 days to traverse the Oregon Trail (Unruh 403), with a mortality rate of 4% to 6% (408). . . .

—Foote, "Speed that kills": page 371 in Part III: The Reader.

Activity 5.2

Identify the topic sentences in the following paragraphs. If you wish to get a sense of paragraph context, page numbers where the full essays are found have been given.

1. Many people do resist the temptation to engage in self-serving behaviours that contribute to climate change. Yet, admittedly, many do yield to the temptation. What will it take to change these people's behaviour? As a start—but only a start—understanding environment-related motivations, attitudes, social and organizational perceptions, rationales, biases, habits, barriers to change, life-context, and trust in government will help. Certainly, psychologists are already engaged in the effort on their own. For example, some have investigated the psychological dimensions of global warming (e.g., Dresner, 1989–90; Heath & Gifford, 2006; Nilsson, von Borgstede, & Biel, 2004). However, the major thesis of the present article is that we psychologists must do more.

   —Gifford, "Psychology's essential role in alleviating the impacts of climate change": page 378 in Part III: The Reader.

2. The underlying contradiction in purpose and method between the market's private exchanges for money and the university's public commitment to advanced learning is not yet realized, even as low-paid sessional teachers replacing normal faculty carry more and more of university teaching loads and as salaries for corporate management escalate. University presidents now conceive themselves as corporate CEOs; research is increasingly only possible with outside money backing it; campuses are ever more pervasively occupied by corporate ads, brands and products; multinational corporations control the academic journal and textbook system across borders; and students are cumulatively made into debt-slaves to banks.

   —McMurtry, "University wars: The corporate administration vs. the vocation of learning": page 166 in Part III: The Reader.

3. Does this nominal feminizing of male also-rans (and the simultaneous gendering of success) constitute a meaningful pattern? Piqued, we began examining the construction of masculinity in major feature films released by Disney's Pixar studios over the past thirteen years. Indeed, as we argue here, Pixar consistently promotes a new model of masculinity, one that matures into acceptance of its more traditionally "feminine" aspects.

   —Gillam and Wood, "Post-princess models of gender: The new man in Disney/Pixar": page 291 in Part III: The Reader.

Using Transitions and Repetitions in Reading

Not every paragraph needs to be closely read to determine its main idea. It is useful to scan a paragraph's first sentence, which may contain the main idea and may also suggest the paragraph's development. Also, important words and phrases tend to recur throughout related paragraphs, and since topic sentences anchor the thought in the paragraph, they often contain these recurring words. The first place to look, then, is the first sentence of the paragraph.

Rhetorical patterns, transitions, repetitions, and topic sentences give structural and content cues about where important information can be found. Prompts are another kind of cue that direct readers to important content in the next sentence or paragraph. Thus, brief summaries and questions can act as prompts to what lies ahead.

In the following paragraph excerpt, the first sentence refers to a "myth" about cyberbullying: it acts as a prompt for the main idea, the "reality," discussed in the second sentence, the topic sentence:

> Many individuals may believe that they already fully understand and can recognize what cyberbullying is. *The reality, however, is that there exists much variability in the way cyberbullying is defined and considered—even among cyberbullying.*

> —Sabella, Patchin, and Hinduja, "Cyberbullying myths and realities": page 339 in Part III: The Reader.

In the following excerpt, the authors provide cues through the use of comparison as a rhetorical pattern, a topic sentence, transitions and a repeated phrase to guide the reader to the main idea in the paragraph:

> The United States and Canada are 2 countries that have many shared values. <u>However,</u> there are important differences between these 2 countries that may be reflected in different normative beliefs about health behaviors. <u>For example</u>, the legal drinking age in Canada is much younger (18–19 years) than in the United States (21 years). <u>In terms of drug control policies</u>, the United States has a greater conservatism towards legalizing drugs such as marijuana than Canada. Under current Canadian legislation, possession of small amounts of marijuana for personal use (i.e., ≤15 g) will not typically result in a criminal record. <u>In terms of smoking</u>, such differences may inevitably be reflected in cross-cultural differences in postsecondary students' use of alcohol and drugs and normative beliefs regarding such health behaviors. . . .

> —Arbour-Nicitopoulos et al., "Social norms of alcohol, smoking, and marijuana use within a Canadian university setting": page 181 in Part III: The Reader.

The first sentence introduces the rhetorical pattern used in the paragraph: comparison. The second sentence, the topic sentence, announces the paragraph's focus on contrasts. Transitions (underlined in the excerpt) are used to qualify and give an example. A repeated phrase (underlined) suggests specific contrasts between the two countries.

It is important to realize that the hints above serve as rough guides to where the main ideas in any text can be found. The best way to become familiar with the reading process is to read frequently and to be conscious of both the author's attempts to create coherence through specific strategies and your own attempts to find coherence by being aware of these strategies.

When you scan an essay, a section, or a paragraph, try to identify the topic sentence(s)—often, but not always, the first sentence of paragraphs.

prompt
A word, phrase, or clause that directs readers to important content rather than containing important content itself.

Thinking of transitions, repeated words, prompts, and other strategies for reading reinforces the importance of using them to create coherence in your own writing. Although they are usually discussed as *writing* rather than as *reading* strategies, thinking of them as *reading* strategies highlights the essential relationship between writing and reading. Writing consciously by using strategies for coherence helps conscious readers to decode a difficult text. See Writing Middle Paragraphs (p. 75), which discusses strategies for coherent writing.

Activity 5.3

Analyze the following paragraphs, identifying comprehension strategies such as rhetorical patterns, topic sentences, transitions, repetitions, and prompts.

1. Given all of this research, one might ask: Why is it a myth that "cyberbullying causes suicide?" The answer to this question lies in the important difference between the nature of correlation and causation. While it is true that there exists a relationship between bullying and suicide (a connection or correlation), no conclusive statistical evidence has shown that a cyberbullying experience directly "leads to" or causes suicide. As previously stated, most youth who are cyberbullied do not take their own lives. So, the best that we can confidently say is that, among some young people, cyberbullying and suicide may be co-occurring (or are "co-related") with at least one of many other factors such as depression, social withdrawal, disability, social hopelessness, or other psychiatric morbidity (Skapinakis et al., 2011). That is, cyberbullying may aggravate the victim's already existing vulnerabilities.

    —Sabella, Patchin, and Hinduja, "Cyberbullying Myths and Realities": page 341 in Part III: The Reader.

2. A working definition of *alpha male* may be unnecessary; although more traditionally associated with the animal kingdom than the Magic Kingdom, it familiarly evokes ideas of dominance, leadership, and power in human social organizations as well. The phrase "alpha male" may stand for all things stereotypically patriarchal: unquestioned authority, physical power and social dominance, competitiveness for positions of status and leadership, lack of visible or shared emotion, social isolation. An alpha male, like Vann in *Cars*, does not ask for directions. . . . These models have worked in Disney for decades. The worst storm at sea is no match for *The Little Mermaid*'s uncomplicated Prince Eric—indeed, any charming prince need only ride in on his steed to save his respective princess. But the post-feminist world is a different place for men, and the post-princess Pixar is a different place for male protagonists.

    — Gillam and Wood, "Post-princess models of gender: The new man in Disney/Pixar": page 292 in Part III: The Reader.

Reading Strategies: The Detail Work

Sooner or later readers find themselves grappling with the elements of the sentence—words, phrases, and clauses. When you look more closely at a text, you may be confronted with problems in any of the three areas listed below, but the last two typically present most of the challenges for student readers:

1. The relationships among words and the other syntactical units in a sentence, phrases and clauses (grammar and sentence structure).
2. The author's stylistic and linguistic choices.
3. Word meanings (vocabulary).

Grammar and Sentence Structure

> Syntax refers to the order of words, phrases, and clauses in a sentence.

Knowing the meaning of words is not going to help with comprehension unless you are familiar with the conventions that govern the arrangement of these words in a sentence—that determine the order of words and other relationships among the syntactical units in a sentence. Fortunately, most English speakers entering university have been practising these conventions for years, albeit unconsciously, in their daily speech and writing.

English sentence structure and rules of grammar are governed largely by these syntactical relationships, and when you write in English, it is necessary to know them well. Poor grammar or sentence structure undermines your credibility as a writer.

Connotations and Denotations

All readers need to know *how* a writer is using words before they can make assumptions about meaning. Individual words carry connotations, or implications, beyond those of their dictionary meanings, or denotations. Paying careful attention to context—the surrounding words—can help you determine a word's connotation and help you figure out its meaning. Sometimes dictionaries suggest a word's connotations, although often, when you look up a word in a dictionary, you find one or more of its common definitions and have to look at the passage itself to know exactly how it is being used (its connotation). Dictionaries are often not the "final word" on meaning but necessary starting places.

A word can acquire different connotations through its use over time or by a specific group. In some cases, positive or negative values have become associated with the word. Many common words have several connotations. Consider, for example, the implications of the words *slender, slim, lean, thin, skinny, underweight, scrawny,* and *emaciated,* which suggest a progression from positive (graceful, athletic . . .) to negative (. . . weak, sickly). Sometimes only context will make a word's connotation clear.

> **connotation (verb connote)**
>
> The implications or additional meanings of a word; a word's context may suggest its connotations.
>
> **denotation (verb denote)**
>
> The meaning of a word, for example, as defined in a dictionary.

Activity 5.4

In groups or individually, make a list of 10 common adjectives. Then, for each word, come up with five words similar but not identical in meaning to the original word and use them in sentences. The sentences should reveal the word's connotation, so ensure that you provide adequate context for each word's exact meaning in the sentence. This exercise could also be done after reading Word Meanings, below.

Linguistic Resources

Writers may indirectly signal their intended meaning to their readers, and if readers fail to pick up the signals, they will fail to "read" the work correctly. Thus, reading an essay might involve more than figuring out contextual clues: it might involve asking questions like, What response is the author looking for from me? Does the author want me to read literally, or does the surface level of the words hide another meaning? Although these kinds of questions relate to the author's purpose, their answers are inevitably embedded in the language of the text. Therefore, the author's use of language is the place to find answers.

Such questions are especially relevant to essays written to persuade. Thus, writers might adopt an ironic tone to make the reader question a commonly accepted or simplistic perspective. In irony, you look beyond the literal meaning of words to their deeper or "true" meaning. The object might be to make you aware of another perspective, to poke fun at a perspective, or to advocate change.

> **irony**
>
> The existence in a text of two levels of meaning, one surface and literal, the other deeper and non-literal.

allusion

An indirect reference to an outside source in order to clarify a point or get the reader to look at it in a new light.

Authors whose primary purpose is to entertain may do so by using humour. Although some humour engages us directly, other kinds of humour rely on subtle linguistic techniques revealed through implication or through devices like word play or *allusion*; many essays, of course, use humour not just to entertain but to criticize people or institutions, employing irony as well. Literary works present yet another way in which writers seek to encode multiple meanings beyond those of literal representation.

Word Meanings

Dictionaries are an indispensable part of the writing life whether you are a professional writer or a student writer. They are also an essential part of the reading life. But while a good dictionary is part of the key to understanding challenging texts, it is not the only one—sometimes it is not even the best one.

This is because the texts you read at the post-secondary level may be more challenging than what you are used to. To look up every unclear word would require too much time; as well, if you interrupt your reading too often, it will be hard to maintain continuity, reducing your understanding. Thankfully, you do not need to know the precise meaning of every word you read; you need to know the exact meanings of the most important words but only approximate meanings for many of the others.

We all have three vocabularies: a speaking vocabulary, a writing vocabulary, and a reading, or *recognition*, vocabulary. The speaking vocabulary is the smallest, and 2,000 words can be considered sufficient for most conversations. Our recognition vocabulary is the largest, but it includes words we would not use in our writing. That is why, if you are asked the meaning of a word from your recognition vocabulary, you might struggle to define it, even though you might *think* you know what it means; you probably know it only within the contexts of your reading.

Since relying *only* on a dictionary is both inefficient and unreliable, you should cultivate reading practices that minimize—not maximize—the use of a dictionary. Use a dictionary if you have to, but first try to determine meanings by utilizing context clues, as discussed below.

Context Clues

Important nouns, verbs, adjectives, and adverbs are also often revealed through context—the words around them. Writers may define difficult words or may use synonyms or rephrasing to make their meanings easy to grasp; such strategies are used if the author thinks the typical reader may not know them. On the other hand, authors may use an unfamiliar word in such a way that the meanings of the surrounding words clarify the meaning and connotation of the unfamiliar word. There are various ways of using these context clues, as we see in the examples below.

Specialized words, such as words borrowed from another language or culture, are defined for general audiences:

> *Shikata ga nai,* as the saying goes—what's done is done.

> —Miyagawa, "A sorry state": page 234 in Part III: The Reader.

Even in highly specialized writing, the writer may define terms the reader might not know:

Young female larvae of bees, wasps, and ants are usually *totipotent*, that is, they have the potential to develop into either a queen or a worker.

—F.L.W. Ratnieks & T. Wenseleers (2005), "Policing insect societies." *Science 307*(5706): 54.

Rather than being stated directly in a clause or phrase that follows, a word's meaning may be inferred from a word or phrase elsewhere in the sentence:

Minoxidil has some benefit in male pattern *alopecia*, but baldness is not a fatal disease.

—Lexchin, "Pharmaceutical innovation: Can we live forever? A commentary on Schnittker and Karandinos": page 354 in Part III: The Reader.

When a writer does not define a word, you may be able to infer its meaning by determining the idea the writer is trying to express. In the following example, the preceding word, *parts*, and the following word, *whole*, help reveal the word's meaning as "touching" or "adjoining." The previous part of the sentence also suggests something stronger than *linked*:

Since at least the end of the 19th century, cartoonists in Canada . . . have depicted North America as a collection of territories whose identities are linked, and sometimes even as parts of a *contiguous* whole.

—A.J. Green (2007), "Mapping North America: Visual representation of Canada and the United States in recent academic work and editorial cartoons." *The American Review of Canadian Studies* 37(2): 134.

In addition to looking at nearby words to guide you to meaning, you can often look at relationships expressed in the sentence or a previous one, like those showing contrasts. In the sentence below, a contrastive relationship can help you infer the meaning of the italicized word:

The availability of pornographic material at the library . . . represents the *defilement* of something regarded by Mali'hah as "pure."

—T.F. Ruby (2006), "Listening to the voices of *hijab*." *Women's Studies International Forum* 29 (2006): 54–66.

Similarly, if a writer uses examples, they can sometimes be used to infer the meaning of a previous word. In this sentence, the author gives the example of *dressmaker* used as a substitute for *prostitute*; a *euphemism* is a kind of substitution:

When prostitutes were recorded on nominal census schedules, the space beside their names for "occupation, trade or calling" was left blank, or some innocuous term or *euphemism*—such as dressmaker—was entered in the space.

—P.A. Dunae (2009), "Sex, charades and census records: Locating female sex trade workers in a Victorian city." *Histoire sociale/Social History* 42: 267–97.

What follows *innocuous* could also help define that word, especially if it occurs to you that *innocuous* has the same first five letters as the word *innocent* (see Family Resemblances, below).

In the passage below, examples of *changes across* the spectrum of light are given (it also helps to look at the etymology of the word; *trans* = across + *mutare* = change):

> [N]atural philosophers assumed that coloured rays of light were *transmutable*. To change blue into red, white into yellow, or orange into violet, they reckoned that one simply had to find a way to quicken or retard the speed at which the pulses moved through the aether.
>
> —J. Waller (2004), *Leaps in the Dark: The Forging of Scientific Reputations*. Oxford: Oxford University Press.

Family Resemblances

If context does not help you determine a word's meaning, you can look for resemblances, recalling words that look similar and whose meanings you know. A "family" of words may arise from the same Latin or Greek root. (Most English words of more than one syllable are derived from Latin; others come from Greek.) Thus, you may be able to infer the meaning of a new word by recalling a known word with the same word element. For example, you can easily see a family resemblance between the word *meritocracy* and the familiar word *merit*. You can take this a step further by looking at the second element and recalling that *meritocracy* and *democracy* contain a common element. In a *democracy*, the *people* determine who will govern them. In a *meritocracy*, then, *merit* determines who governs.

Specialized Language

The strategies discussed above for understanding unfamiliar words apply to all kinds of writing. However, the academic disciplines have their own specialized vocabularies that scholars use to communicate with each other. This language is known as jargon, and even the jargon of two subdisciplines, such as plant sciences and zoology, can vary. When you take undergraduate courses in a discipline, you begin to acquire this specialized vocabulary, which has developed along with the discipline itself. To acquire knowledge about a subject is to simultaneously acquire its language, in addition to the other conventions of the discipline.

Although some highly technical articles may use jargon that is beyond the reach of the undergraduate, both novice and more experienced readers can make use of the variety of discipline-specific dictionaries, encyclopedias, and research guides that can be accessed through many libraries. For example, Oxford University Press publishes a series of subject dictionaries in art and architecture, the biological sciences, classical studies, computing, earth and environmental sciences, and many other disciplines.

jargon

Discipline-specific language used to communicate among members of the discipline.

Activity 5.5

Using contextual or word resemblance strategies whenever necessary, determine the meanings of the italicized words in the following passages, all of which are taken from readings in part III of this book:

1. Frequencies were calculated in the demographic characteristics, which were subsequently *dichotomized* into the following categories. (p. 182)
2. These influences [on a person's decisions] are presumed to determine the different strategies or *heuristics* that individuals as decision-makers actually employ. (p. 380)
3. Although industry and government describe the tar sands as "Canada's new economic engine," the project has in reality given Canada a bad case of the Dutch Disease. This economic *malaise* . . . takes its name from a 1977 article that detailed how a natural gas boom hollowed out the manufacturing base of the Netherlands. (p. 190)
4. As Louisa Lane Clark emphasized in *Origins for the Microscope* (1858), the microscope was to be used to *edify*, not just to entertain. (p. 364)
5. The BBC, for example, helped pioneer the *hybridization* of documentary and entertainment. (p. 285)
6. If one takes an *unflinching* look at Canadian conduct in the world, the evidence permits no conclusion other than that the country has lately been engaged in a *liquidation* of its internationalism. (p. 192)
7. At first, the reception of the Chinese was relatively *cordial*: "Colonial British Columbians were initially remarkably tolerant of the thousands of Chinese who came." (p. 240)
8. Responsive action to these effects must *transpire* at multiple socio-ecological levels. (p. 397).
9. Often Canada is seen by Americans as a "societal laboratory" where significant public policy options are *incubated* and evaluated. (p. 207)
10. Conventional wisdom would have us believe that since technology has *proliferated* over the last decade and stories of cyberbullying are frequently mentioned in the news, it is likely more *prevalent* than traditional, schoolyard bullying. (p. 341)

PART II
Academic Writing

Academic discourse can be thought of as *a set of oral and written procedures used to generate and disseminate ideas within the academic community*. Most of the classes you take in university focus on written discourse: by writing down your thoughts, you are recording them to be analyzed by others (and, yes, usually graded). Familiarity with the conventions of written discourse will be valuable to you throughout your academic career and beyond because, in spite of the uses of modern technology, it is primarily through writing that knowledge is transmitted. (See The Active Voice: Brave New Words, page 78.)

You will probably be writing essays and reports in most of your courses, which, while they share similarities, may be markedly different. To write a lab report for a chemistry class, for example, you use different procedures, or conventions, from those you use in a literary analysis for an English class, which, in turn, are different from those you use to write a marketing plan for a business class or a feasibility study for an engineering class.

Despite these differences, there are two relatively distinct forms that academic writing can take: the essay and the report. You will be required to write essays in many of your undergraduate courses. Writing reports may be limited to your science courses, some of your social sciences courses, along with business, engineering, or health sciences courses. Chapter 6 reviews the fundamentals of writing academic essays, followed by an overview of report writing (The Active Voice: Report Writing—Aims and Goals, page 85).

Chapters 7–9 discuss specific kinds of writing assignments. Learning summarization skills (chapter 7) enables you to represent in your essays the ideas and words of other writers. When you summarize, then, you focus more on *re-presenting* than on analyzing. When you write a rhetorical analysis—discussed in chapter 8—you use your critical-thinking skills to "break down" one or more specific texts.

In chapter 9, you will learn about applying general academic writing skills to the mode of argument: in argumentative essays, you assert and defend a claim. When you try to convince someone that something is good or bad or to adopt a particular action, you consider the use of specific strategies in order to support your claim; outside sources may also strengthen your claim.

Research papers, discussed in chapter 10, display the fullest range of skills for student readers and writers because they combine various skills, including summarizing, analysis, synthesis, and critical thinking. They call on what is for many students one of the most challenging of skills at the post-secondary level: research—locating, evaluating, and integrating outside sources.

6

An Overview of the Essay

The Stages in Writing

Essays, like most projects, are written in chronological stages. Although academic writing may emphasize revising and editing the rough draft or research more than you are used to, students approach academic writing with the knowledge that it is a chronological process that usually begins with a broad topic.

The stages in writing an essay are

- formulating a thesis
- finding support for the thesis
- relating parts and discovering structure (outlining)
- composing the essay
- revising

Formulating a Thesis

Using pre-writing techniques, you explore the topic, asking what you know and what you want to find out about it. The objective is to narrow the topic to express your specific focus or approach in a thesis statement. (See pages 72-3.)

Many different methods can be used to narrow a topic. These include association techniques, such as freewriting, brainstorming, and clustering, or mapping. A good beginning point is to use the "subject test" and consider how the topic would apply to various disciplines: for example, dance is considered a subject or subdiscipline within

> **thesis statement**
> A statement that includes the main point of your essay or what you will attempt to prove; it is placed at the end of your introduction.

the fine or performing arts, yet this subject could be explored from a number of different angles within other disciplines:

- dance as self-expression (humanities—fine arts)
- dance as entertainment (humanities—fine arts)
- the history of dance (humanities—history)
- the function of dance in other cultures (humanities—cultural studies; social sciences—anthropology)
- dance as the expression of a collective identity (social sciences—sociology)
- dance as therapy (social sciences—psychology)
- dance as physical movement (science—kinesiology)
- dance as an area of skill acquisition and study (education)

Each of these approaches suggests a way of narrowing the broad subject of dance in order to write on it for different classes or as an assignment for your English class. In fact, the approaches could already be considered topics, but they are, as yet, undeveloped. *What would you like to know about it?* Let us say that you are planning to major in psychology. Therefore, the topic of dance as therapy is something you would like to know more about. One option is to begin your research now by finding out what has been written about this topic. Accordingly, you could check out your library's databases, such as *Humanities Index* or *Periodical Contents Index*, which cover journals focusing on the performing arts. However, there are other techniques you can use to narrow your topic further before you commit yourself to research. These techniques can also be used when you have only a broad subject (such as dance) and want to make it more specific.

Once you have narrowed your topic, you can try one of the pre-writing strategies, such as brainstorming, to narrow it further. Eventually, you should be able to sum up your specific approach in a thesis statement.

Pre-writing Techniques

freewriting
A pre-writing technique in which you write on a subject without stopping to edit.

questioning
A pre-writing technique in which you ask relevant questions about the topic.

Freewriting utilizes your associations with something. To freewrite, begin with a blank piece of paper or a blank screen and start recording your associations with a subject. Do not stop to reflect on your next thought or polish your writing: simply write continuously for a predetermined time—such as five or ten minutes. A good starting point is a sentence that includes the subject you want to find out more about, such as a tentative definition: "Dance as therapy is. . . ."

In the questioning technique, you ask questions pertinent to the topic. Initially, these questions could be the basic *What?*, *Who?*, *Where?*, *When?*, *Why?*, and *How?*

- What is dance therapy? What are its basic elements/divisions/stages? What are its goals?
- Who would use dance as therapy? Who would benefit from it?
- Where can you go to study dance therapy? Where is it practised?
- When did dance therapy begin? Why?
- How does it work? How is it similar to/different from other kinds of creative healing techniques?

Each question suggests a different approach to the topic and a different rhetorical pattern. For example, the first question might lead you to the definition pattern; the second question might lead you to divide dance therapy into different types or other subcategories (division/classification). The last question could lead you to focus on comparison and contrast (e.g., dance therapy versus music therapy) or to analyze the costs and benefits of different creative healing techniques (see Rhetorical Patterns and Paragraph Development, page 79).

In brainstorming, which can be done either collaboratively or individually, you list your associations with a topic, writing down words and phrases until you feel you have covered the topic thoroughly. Although you do not intentionally look for connections when you generate your list, you can later look back to explore possible connections between the items.

Clustering is a spatial technique that generates associations and seeks connections among them. You begin by writing a word or phrase in the middle of a blank page and circling it. As associations occur to you, you write them down and circle them, connecting them by a line to the word/phrase that gave rise to the association. As you continue this process beyond the first layer of connections, you will develop larger clusters in some places than in others. The well-developed clusters may suggest the most promising ways to develop your topic.

Whatever method you use, the thesis statement you come up with should reflect your purpose in writing. For example, if you were writing a personal essay on dance as part of your application to a performing arts program, it would be very different from what you would write for a research essay. In Thesis Statements (below, page 72) you will learn more about incorporating the statement into the introduction of your essay.

brainstorming
A pre-writing technique in which you list your associations with a subject in the order they occur to you.

clustering
A pre-writing technique that works spatially to generate associations with a subject and connections among them.

Activity 6.1

Three sample thesis statements on dance follow. Determine which one would be applicable to

a. a personal essay
b. an argumentative essay that attempts to persuade the reader to take a particular course of action
c. a research essay concerned with the historical development of dance therapy

1. With its roots in modern dance and its stress on self-expression over performance, dance therapy has evolved into a vibrant profession that today serves such diverse groups as disabled people and employees of large corporations.

2. One of my earliest memories is of pulling myself up close to the TV so I could follow the intricate moving shapes before my eyes, trying to make sense of the patterns they formed. Now, at 18, I want to personally explore what it is like to be a part of the visual pattern called dance.

3. Cuts to the operating budgets of performing arts programs at this university must be curtailed so these students can feel the security they need to succeed in their studies and the university community can experience the benefits of the performing arts on campus.

Finding Support

In the next stage, you attempt to back up your thesis. Thesis statements are claims of some kind. A claim must have support. For example, although you could claim that the dog ate your homework, your instructor is not likely to take such a claim seriously.

support
Evidence to help prove a claim.

But if you produced your vet bill, the claim would at least have some support and may merit your instructor's consideration. If you were writing a critical analysis of a poem, the support would need to come from the poem itself (a primary source). If you were writing a research paper, you would need to find out what other people have discovered about your topic (secondary sources).

See Kinds of Evidence, page 83; see also Kinds of Evidence in Argumentative Essays, page 109, and Selecting Resources for Your Research Topic in The Active Voice: A Beginner's Guide to Researching in the Academic Library, page 132.

Relating Parts and Discovering Structure

When you have found enough support, it is time to begin thinking about how you will use it in your essay. Thus, you begin organizing claims and support in a logical and consistent way, one that clearly expresses the relationship between each claim and its support. One way to clarify these relationships is to construct an outline, a diagrammatic representation of the essay and a plan you can use in the composing stage so you stay on-track.

An outline can be a brief listing of your main points, a *scratch* or *sketch outline*, often used for in-class or exam essays when you do not have time for detailed planning. With longer essays, an outline can be extensively developed to include levels of sub-points (developments of main points) along with details and examples. The *formal outline* uses a number/letter scheme to represent the essay's complete structure. The conventional scheme goes like this:

> I. First main point (topic sentence of paragraph)
>   A. First sub-point (development of main point)
>   1. first sub-sub-point (development of sub-point: detail or example)
>   2. second sub-sub-point
>   B. Second sub-point
>   1. first sub-sub-point
>   2. second sub-sub-point

This example represents a paragraph with a three-level outline—that is, one main point and two sub-points. Some paragraphs may be less developed, while overly long paragraphs can be subdivided in the most logical place.

When you are considering your outline, especially if it is a formal outline, remember that it serves as the blueprint for the essay itself. Therefore, to construct a useful outline, you should ask questions like the following:

- How do the main points in my outline relate to my thesis statement?
- How do the sub-points relate to my main points?
- Do I have enough main points to support my thesis and enough sub-points to support each topic sentence?
- Do any points seem irrelevant or out of place? (If the latter, where do they belong?)
- What is the most effective order for my points? (In argumentative essays, you should order points according to their persuasiveness—for example, least to most persuasive, the climax order. In expository essays, you often order them

outline

A linear or graphic representation of main and sub-points, showing an essay's structure.

The topic sentence states the topic or the main point of the paragraph. It is often the paragraph's first sentence.

according to a consistent organizational method—for example, comparison and contrast, cause–effect, chronology.)

- Are my points logically related to each other (i.e., each one should naturally follow from the previous point)?
- Can points be expanded? Have I covered everything my reader would expect me to cover?

Composing

Making the commitment to the first draft is difficult for many people—students and non-students alike. It is important to realize that a first draft is inevitably "drafty"— in need of revising. But this should not hold you back from fully recording your thoughts—imperfectly expressed as they may be. When you compose an essay, you draft the introduction, middle paragraphs, and conclusion. Techniques and strategies for these tasks are described in detail in The Structure of the Essay (below).

Revising

Although in composing the first "rough" drafts your focus is on getting ideas down, during the revision stage you should not expect to be simply dotting i's and crossing t's. The word *revise* means to "see again." First, you should take a hard, objective look at your essay's purpose and audience, its structure, support, and clarity. Review these areas as if you are seeing them for the first time. Waiting at least several hours after you have completed a rough draft before revising is sensible. Ask the kinds of questions you originally asked when you were creating an outline (see above, page 68), and see if you are satisfied with the results.

Next, check for grammatical correctness and concision. *Then*, it will be time to dot the i's and cross the t's—checking for spelling errors and typos and ensuring that the essay conforms to the required format.

The importance of these end-stage activities cannot be underestimated, although they sometimes are. After all, when you have finished the rough draft, the paper looks physically complete. But try to see your essay through the eyes of your instructor. What often strikes a reader first are the very things you may have glossed over as your dead-line approached: grammatical errors, lack of coherence, faulty word choice, wordiness, typos, and mechanical errors that are simple to fix.

Though nothing will replace careful attention to every detail, here is a checklist that will help you "re-see" your essay.

Content and Structure

- Is the essay's purpose clear from the introduction? Is it consistent throughout the essay?
- Is it written for a specific audience? What would show a reader this (for example, level of language, voice or tone, kinds of evidence, citations)?
- Is the thesis statement consistent with the focus of the essay and its main points? If not, consider adjusting the thesis so that it is.
- Are all paragraphs adequately developed and focused on one main idea?
- Are any paragraphs noticeably shorter or longer than others? If so, can you effectively combine short paragraphs or break up longer ones?

❑   Have different kinds of evidence been used for support? Does any part of the essay seem less well supported than other parts?

❑   Would an example, illustration, or analogy make an abstract point more concrete or a general point more specific?

❑   Could a reader misunderstand any point? If so, would this be due to the way it is expressed? If your draft has been commented on/edited by a peer, pay particular attention to passages noted as unclear. If one reader has difficulties in comprehension, others will too.

Grammar and Style

- Are there sentence fragments (i.e., "sentences" missing a subject or predicate), run-on sentences (two "sentences," or independent clauses, with no punctuation between them), or comma splices (two "sentences" separated only by a comma)?

- Is punctuation used correctly? For example, are commas used (1) to separate independent clauses with a coordinating conjunction (*and, or, but, for, nor, yet, so*) and to separate an introductory word, phrase, or clause from a following independent clause; (2) to separate items in a list or series; (3) to separate non-essential information from essential information? Are semicolons and colons used correctly? Are dashes and parentheses used correctly and sparingly (dashes for emphasis, parentheses for asides)?

- Are apostrophes used correctly to indicate possession and similar relationships in nouns and indefinite pronouns (e.g., *the book's author*—one book; *the books' authors*—more than one book; *anyone's opinion*—indefinite pronoun)?

- Do verbs agree in number with their subjects and pronouns with their antecedents (the noun they replace)?

- Is the relationship between a noun and its antecedent clear (i.e., every pronoun should refer back to a specific noun)?

- Has the principle of pronoun consistency been maintained (i.e., pronouns should not arbitrarily change from third person [*he/she, they/them*] to first or second person [*I/me, we/us, you*])?

- Is parallelism present in sentences with elements that must be parallel (lists, compounds, correlative conjunctions, and comparisons)?

- Are there any misplaced or dangling modifiers, confusing sentence meaning?

- Are you satisfied that every word you have used is the best word and expresses precisely what you want to say? Is the level of language appropriate and have you avoided contractions and slang?

- Have you avoided repetition? Have you managed to eliminate unnecessary words and phrases?

Mechanics

- Have all outside references been cited correctly? Have you used the documentation style favoured by your instructor or by your discipline?

- Have you met word count, essay/page format, and other specific requirements?

- Have you proofread the essay at least twice (once for content and flow, once for minor errors such as typos—breaking each word into syllables and reading syllabically throughout is the best way to catch minor errors)?

The Process-Reflective Method

Although most essays are written in stages, most writers do not engage with their topic mechanically but by moving back and forth—from composing to outline, for example, if they need to rethink their structure, or from composing back to the research stage to check on a source or find more support for a point. Some writers, in fact, do not follow a linear process but begin composing without any firm plan in place, trusting to their instincts and realizing that it is sometimes only by writing something down and taking the risk of going off-topic occasionally that they can discover what they really want to say. In the exploratory model, your intentions and goals are revealed through the act of writing itself, and an outline is less important than in the linear approach. Below, Frans de Waal, primatologist and author of *Our Inner Ape*, describes his personal process. It illustrates the importance of revising and the necessity of finding the approach that works best for you:

> I write my books without much of an outline except for the chapter titles. My main strategy is to just start writing and see what happens. From one topic follows another, and before you know it I have a dozen pages filled with stories and thoughts. . . . I have a very visual memory, and remember events in great detail. When I write, my desk fills up with ever higher piles of papers and books used for reference, until it is a big mess, which is something I cannot stand. I am very neat. So, at some point I put all that stuff away, print out the text I've written, and sit down comfortably with a red pen. By that time I have already gone over the text multiple times. With pen in hand, I do a very rigorous rereading and again change things around.
>
> —http://www.emory.edu/LIVING_LINKS/OurInnerApe/book.html

When de Waal reveals, above, that he has "gone over the text multiple times" before he considers large-scale changes, he is revealing his preference for a writing process in which he pauses to reflect, re-examine, and change, if necessary, before continuing—a kind of revision on the fly, or paragraph-by-paragraph approach. As with the traditional-linear approach, however, you should not be concerned with mechanical correctness as you write.

Typical activities in process-reflective drafts are rephrasing, clarifying, expanding, and connecting: you concern yourself with making logical transitions from one thought to the next and checking to see that your developing points are consistent with your general plan. You should begin with a few rough points and "reminders," such as important authors or quotations you want to use, but you do not need to have a detailed plan. Rather, the plan evolves as you write. Process-reflective writing can also be used for in-class and exam essays in which there is seldom time to outline your points in detail.

process-reflective draft

A draft that emerges from a flexible engagement with what you are writing, one that reflects the connections between thinking and writing.

The Structure of the Essay

Most essays are divided into an introduction, middle or body paragraphs, and a conclusion. Each part contributes in a different way to the essay. In this section you will learn techniques and strategies for drafting each part.

Writing Introductions

The introduction is more than just a starting place. Its primary function is to inform the reader about the essay's purpose, topic, and approach to the topic (usually through the thesis statement); it may include the essay's main points. As well, the introduction may indicate the primary organizational pattern for the essay. In all these ways, the introduction previews what is forthcoming.

A good introduction is persuasive: it must sufficiently interest the reader, encouraging him or her to read on, perhaps by conveying the importance of the topic. The introduction not only introduces the essay but also introduces its writer; therefore, you must come across as credible and reliable. Otherwise, your essay may not be read. (See Issues of Credibility, page 83.)

Student writers are often advised to write the introduction last because they will not know precisely how the topic will develop until the body of the essay is written. On the other hand, many writers like to have a concrete starting point. If the latter describes you best, you should return to the introduction after you have written your middle paragraphs to ensure that it fits well with them.

Writing Thesis Statements

The Greek word *thesis* refers to the act of placing or setting down. *A thesis statement, then, is a formal assertion, a generalization that is applicable to the entire essay.* However, this generalization can take different forms depending on purpose and audience. Student and academic writers usually place the thesis statement in the introduction; journalistic writers often do not. For kinds of theses in academic essays, see chapter 2 (p. 21).

Thesis statements vary in what they include:

- A *simple thesis statement* announces the topic and includes a comment about it.
- An *expanded thesis statement*, or essay plan, includes the main points in the order they will appear in the essay.

  Simple thesis: Xenotransplantation, the transplantation of organs across a species barrier, is emerging as a possible alternative to transplants from human donors.

  Expanded thesis: In order to understand the extent of bullying today, we must consider who is affected by bullying, what are its impacts, and how we can prevent it.

claim

An assertion about the topic appearing in the thesis statement and topic sentences.

The thesis statement usually embodies a claim, the nature of which depends on the essay's purpose:

- Claims of *fact* are common in expository essays in the sciences and social sciences in which reliable studies and factual information are used for support.

- Claims of *value* or *policy* are common in argumentative essays. Such claims argue that something, such as a law, is good or bad or that it needs to change.
- *Interpretive* claims are common in humanities essays in which the writer sets out to analyze one or more primary sources by using a specific frame of reference, such as a critical theory. For example, a poem could be analyzed through its literary motifs or through the lens of feminist theory. When you write a rhetorical or critical analysis, you will also use an interpretive claim (the essay you analyze is your primary source).

> Fact-based claims are common in exposition. Claims of value or policy are common in argument. Interpretive claims are common in the humanities, in which primary sources are analyzed.

The following statements demonstrate different kinds of claims:

Thesis with factual claim: Cultural, psychological, and economic factors are contributing to an increasingly prevalent phenomenon, hikikomori, or the withdrawal from society by extreme isolation.

Thesis with policy claim: More sustainable, shade-grown coffee plantations need to be established in order to counter the effects of habitat destruction and help maintain the planet's diversity.

Thesis from a rhetorical analysis with interpretive claim: In his essay, Robidoux presents a strong argument through the use of historical documentation, examples, and appeals to ethos.

The thesis you write must not just state your topic but also show the reader how the essay will be developed. Once you have narrowed your topic, you should work on your thesis to ensure it is

- informative
- well-focused
- clearly expressed

Creating Reader Interest

Readers need to be convinced at the outset that your essay is worth reading. The most traditional way to generate interest and persuade your reader of the topic's importance is to use a logical opening: to begin with a universal statement that becomes more specific and ends with the most specific claim, the thesis itself; this method is called the inverted triangle method.

One risk in this approach is that in making the first sentence too broad or familiar, it fails to interest the reader. Therefore, student writers are often encouraged to use dramatic opening. Examples of dramatic openings include the use of personal experience, description, or narration, or asking a pertinent question that intrigues the reader. An opening could also make an emotional appeal; however, use these appeals cautiously because you cannot always assume that a typical reader will respond in the way you wish. The following examples illustrate two different ways of attracting reader interest. Note that, in both cases, the last sentence is the thesis statement.

> *logical opening*
> A technique for creating reader interest by beginning with a generalization and narrowing to the thesis.
>
> *dramatic opening*
> A technique for creating reader interest by beginning with a question, illustration, anecdote, quotation, description, or other attention-grabbing technique.

Logical opening: The writer begins with a statement about her subject area, health and nutrition. In sentence 3, she mentions the importance of reliable research. Her specific topic is addressed in sentence 4, and her thesis is her final sentence:

> The field of health and nutrition is evolving fast, which can make it confusing as experts often disagree on what is healthy and what is not. The average citizen is easily influenced by media claims, which may be part truth and part "hype." *A good way to ensure that what is being consumed is beneficial to health is to research exactly what it is and how its constituents affect the human body; this research enables educated health decisions and personalized diets. Coffee is an example of a controversial health topic today.* Millions of people drink coffee every day, yet few know its true effect on health. In Canada alone, 14 billion cups of coffee are consumed each year (Hales & Lauzon, 2008). Despite old studies which show coffee as detrimental to health, new research on the health benefits of coffee have begun to emerge. *While certain health concerns still exist based primarily on quantity of consumption and any pre-existing health conditions, new evidence suggests that caffeine as well as other compounds present in coffee offer surprising health benefits.*
>
> —student writer Clara Buttemer

Dramatic opening (questions): The writer begins with two questions, referring to the popular connotation of perfectionism. Using the reversal strategy, she then cites the definition of experts. Her final sentence makes it clear that her essay will focus on the problems of the "maladaptive perfectionist":

> What does it mean to say that one is a perfectionist? Does it mean that one does everything perfectly? In common language, the term "perfectionist" carries the connotation that the perfectionistic individual does everything perfectly, but according to perfectionism experts in social psychology, perfectionism is a term referring to a mentality, or set of cognitions, that are characteristic of certain people. According to Hollender (as cited in Slade & Owens, 1998), perfectionism refers to "the practice of demanding of oneself or others a higher quality of performance than is required by the situation" (p. 384). Although the name suggests to the layperson that perfectionism would be a desirable trait, this quality is in fact often unrecognized for its detrimental effects on the lives of people who are maladaptively perfectionistic. *Perfectionism is associated with mental illness and can contribute to problems in areas of life such as academic success and intimate relationships.*
>
> —student writer Erin Walker

Activity 6.2

In the following paragraphs

a. identify the method for creating interest
b. discuss how the writer establishes his or her credibility
c. identify the thesis statement and whether it is a simple thesis or an expanded one

You can also pre-read Rhetorical Patterns and Paragraph Development, page 79, to determine the essay's main organizational method.

1. Women in society have come a long way, from earning the right to vote to becoming political leaders, and from riding horses side saddle to riding motorcycles. Today, with more dual income families and an increasing number of wives whose salaries are more than their husbands, the gender wage gap has improved significantly. However, women are still not treated equally in the workplace, and women's salaries remain a very relevant issue as, on average, women make only seventy-two cents for every dollar that men make (Drolet, "Why has the gender wage gap narrowed?"). In a society that has promoted gender

pay equality since 1956 by implementing the *Female Employees Equal Pay Act* (Canadian Human Rights Commission "Federal Government adopts the *Female Employees Equal Pay Act*"), how can such a large disparity still exist? By examining the gender wage gap and its causes, the problem is clear, but what are the solutions? Action must be taken to overcome this disparity by an extensive education program that informs society about the gender wage gap and its contributing factors.

—student writer Jacqueline Greenard

2. On April 6, 1994, the plane transporting Rwandan President Juvenal Habyarimana was shot down, killing everyone on board. This tragedy was only the beginning; the death of President Habyarimana set in motion a violent genocide that had been brewing for more than a century. The dominant Hutus feared an uprising of the oppressed Tutsis and sought to avoid the threat by exterminating them. The Rwandan capital of Kigali was engulfed in violence within minutes of the president's death, and the presidential guard embarked on a "campaign of retribution." A massive Hutu civilian mob known as the Interahamwe, meaning "those who attack together," rampaged across the country for the next three months as anti-Tutsi propaganda pumped through the airwaves. The Rwanda Patriotic Front (RPF) eventually launched an organized counter-attack in July and regained control of Kigali, but by the time the last shot was fired, nearly 800,000 Tutsis had lost their lives. In the aftermath of this mass murder, experts began analyzing how a tragedy of this magnitude could have happened and have isolated three main factors: the long-standing Rwandan struggle for racial dominance, the ineffective pre-emptive mediation during the years preceding the genocide, and the absence of foreign aid and intervention once the massacre had begun (Walker & Zajtman, 2004).

—student writer Alec Page

Writing Middle Paragraphs

The structure of middle paragraphs is often said to mirror that of the essay itself: the paragraph begins with a generalization that is supported by the sentences that follow. In its structure and function, the essay's thesis statement is equivalent to the topic sentence of a paragraph, which announces the main idea (topic) of that paragraph. This analogy is useful because it stresses the importance of a predictable order for both essays and paragraphs. But not all paragraphs are constructed this way.

When a writer uses a topic sentence to announce the central idea, the rest of the paragraph provides support, such as examples, reasons, statistical data, or other kinds of evidence. It illustrates, expands on, or reinforces the topic sentence. In the following paragraph, student writer Leslie Nelson expands on the main idea, first by explaining the function of talking therapies and then by dividing them into three different subcategories and explaining the function of each (the topic sentence is italicized):

> *Talking therapies—especially when combined with medication—are common to treatment of adolescent depression.* There are several kinds of talking therapies, including cognitive and humanistic approaches, and family and group sessions. Each of these therapy types confronts depression in a different way, and each is useful to adolescent treatment. Cognitive therapies confront illogical thought patterns that accompany depression; humanistic therapies provide support to the patient, stressing unconditional acceptance. Group therapies, on the other hand, encourage depressed patients to talk about their feelings in a setting with other people who are undergoing treatment for similar problems. This therapy can inspire different coping strategies, and it allows people to realize that they are not alone in their problems.

However, in the following paragraph, the writer uses his first sentence to set up a common opinion with which he disagrees. His own position is not

topic sentence
A sentence that states the main idea in the paragraph; it is usually the first sentence.

fully explained until the final sentence, the paragraph's topic sentence, italicized below:

> Some suggest that we should actively limit our reliance on technological props and aids, not just to protect our privacy but to control our own destinies and preserve our essential humanity. Here, the title of the book gives me away. Human-machine symbiosis, I believe, is simply what comes naturally. It lies on a direct continuum with clothes, cooking, bricklaying, and writing. *The capacity to creatively distribute labour between biology and the designed environment is the very signature of our species, and it implies no real loss of control on our part, for who we are is in large part a function of the webs of surrounding structure in which the conscious mind exercises at best a kind of gentle, indirect control.*
>
> —A. Clark (2004), *Natural-born Cyborgs: Minds, Technologies, and the Future of Human Intelligence.* New York: Oxford University Press.

You can experiment by trying different placements for your topic sentences. The common placement as the first sentence tends to make for a coherent paragraph, while similarly structured paragraphs contribute to a readable, coherent essay, but students should choose the order that best reflects the paragraph's purpose. For example, in the first paragraph above, the writer is dividing a general category into subcategories, while in the second paragraph, the writer is raising a point in order to counter it with his own point. These purposes require contrastive approaches to paragraph construction.

Writing Strong Paragraphs

Effective paragraphs are unified, coherent, and well-developed. A unified paragraph focuses on only one main idea; when you move to another main idea, you begin a new paragraph. If, however, a paragraph is long, you should consider dividing it into two paragraphs even if each contains the same idea. Look for the most logical place to make the division. For example, you could divide the paragraph where you begin an important sub-point.

A coherent paragraph is easy to follow. Coherent paragraphs are both clear and carefully arranged to place the emphasis where you want it to be. Compositional theorists use the term reader-based prose to suggest a focus on the concerns of the reader. In reader-based prose, the writer carefully designs the paragraph for a specific audience by using understandable and well-organized prose, stressing what is most important and omitting what is irrelevant, and clarifying the relationships among the points and sub-points. Coherence can be achieved by considering the following points.

Strategies for Coherent Writing

1. *Logical sentence order:* In logical sentence order, one sentence follows naturally from the preceding one, and there are no sentences out of order or off-topic. (An off-topic sentence would not result in a unified paragraph). There are no gaps in thought that the reader has to fill.
2. *Organizational patterns:* You can order the paragraph according to specific patterns (see Rhetorical Patterns and Paragraph Development, below).
3. *Precise language:* When you consider what words to use, remember that it is not always a case of the right word versus the wrong word. Always choose the *best word for the given context*. Whenever you use a word that is not part of your everyday vocabulary, you should confirm its meaning by looking it up in a dictionary.

unity

A principle of paragraph construction in which only one idea is developed throughout the paragraph.

coherence

A principle of paragraph construction in which ideas are logically laid out with clear connections between them.

reader-based prose

Clear, accessible writing designed for an intended reader.

4. *Appropriate adverbial transitions:* Transitional words and phrases enable you to convey precise relationships between one idea and the next.

5. *Selective rephrasing and reiteration:* Knowing the knowledge level of your audience will determine whether and when you should rephrase in order to clarify difficult concepts.

6. *Repetition of key words/phrases or the use of synonyms:* Repetition can be used to emphasize important ideas. Of course, *needless* repetition should always be avoided.

7. *Parallel/balanced structures:* Employing parallel/balanced structures creates coherence, in part, through the use of familiar syntactic patterns. Writers and politicians alike know the virtue of balanced structures: they are pleasing to the audience and often easy to recall.

Being aware of these strategies will make you a more conscious writer, focused on the needs of your readers. In the excerpt below, after defining the term *nanotechnology,* student writer Jeff Proctor makes effective use of transitions (noted by italics) to help explain a difficult concept to general readers. He uses a balanced structure in sentence 4 to make a comparison understandable and repeats the key word *precision* at strategic points in the paragraph (the beginning, middle, and end). Other words, too, can be considered near-synonyms for *precision* (synonyms and repetition are underlined):

> Nanotechnology will allow the construction of compounds at nanometre <u>precision</u>. *Essentially,* this capability would allow scientists to form a substance one atom at a time and to put each atom <u>exactly</u> where it needs to be. *Consequently,* any chemical structure that is stable under normal conditions could theoretically be produced.[4] In comparison to semiconductor lithography, which <u>could be imagined</u> as the formation of electrical circuits by joining large heaps of molecules, the techniques of nanotechnology <u>could be imagined</u> as the <u>careful</u> arrangement of molecules with a pair of tweezers. With this incredible degree of <u>precision</u>, electrical circuits could be designed to be smaller than ever before. *Currently,* each component in a computer is the size of thousands of atoms; *however,* if nanotechnological processes were used to produce it, one component could be on the scale of several atoms. This fact alone emphasizes the potential efficiency of next-generation computer circuits, for smaller components are closer together and, *thus,* able to communicate with each other in less time. *Furthermore,* it could be guaranteed that products are reproducible and reliable as a result of the absolute <u>precision</u> of these formation processes.

Transitions in the paragraph above convey various relationships:

- summary: *essentially*
- cause–effect: *consequently, thus*
- time: *currently*
- contrast: *however*
- addition: *furthermore*

Other relationships include

- concession or limit (e.g., *admittedly, although, though, it is true that, of course*)
- illustration (e.g., *for example, for instance, such as*)
- sequence (e.g., *first, second . . .; then, next*)
- emphasis (e.g., *certainly, especially, in fact, indeed, undoubtedly*)

For more information on paragraphs, see Dividing the Whole, page 52, and Reading Paragraphs: Locating Main Ideas, page 53.

Striving for coherence throughout the writing process should not just enable a reader to follow you but also assist you in clarifying your thoughts as you write. Therefore, it is useful to consciously rephrase ideas and specific passages as you write. Without crossing out what you wrote, follow it with transitions like *in other words, in short, in summary, to reiterate, that is* and a paraphrase or expansion of the original. If your second attempt is clearer—and it often is—you can then consider crossing out the original to avoid needless repetition.

The Active Voice

Brave New Words: Technology and the Future of Writing

by David Leach

1   Google is making us stupid! Text messages ruin our spelling! Facebook and Twitter turn students into illiterate zombies!

2   Every month, a new report sounds the alarm that digital tools are reducing, not improving, our ability to communicate. Should we believe the gloomy headlines? Is the Internet really the enemy of good writing?

3   The truth is, teachers have always fretted that technology will corrupt our minds—ever since the dawn of writing itself. We don't usually think of the alphabet as a "technology," but when humans first devised systems to transcribe oral language onto physical media (from stone tablets to papyrus, paperbacks to e-readers), it had a profound effect on our civilization. And not everyone welcomed it.

4   The Greek philosopher Socrates preferred oral questioning to teach critical thinking. (It is what we now call the "Socratic Method.") Writing down facts and ideas, he argued, would turn the keen memories of his fellow citizens into mush. (Of course, we know Socrates' opinion only because Plato, his famous pupil, recorded his words for posterity.) Still, Socrates was probably right. Most people can't recite a 1,000-line epic poem by heart. Some of us need a list to remember which five ingredients to buy at the corner store.

5   Still, the benefits of writing outweighed the unintended consequences. Storing information in written records, rather than human memory, allowed us to transfer greater knowledge between generations. Manuscripts were the original form of ROM or "Read-Only Memory"—data preserved via a special code only a special few people could interpret.

6   Around 1493, when Johannes Gutenberg unveiled his movable-type printing press, his device—a combination of several pre-existing technologies—reduced the time and cost of duplicating manuscripts by hand and extended the power of the written word. Kings, popes and other authority figures quickly regulated what got published. They were right to worry. The rise of literacy spread political revolution, democratic reform and a scientific worldview throughout Europe and beyond.

7   Not everyone benefitted equally from the right to write and the power to publish. In the mid-20th-century, American journalist A.J. Liebling quipped: "Freedom of the press is limited to those who own one." The printing press may have ushered in modern democracy, but it was never a truly "democratic" technology. In the 1970s and 1980s, copy machines and desktop publishing lowered duplication costs and opened the potential of self-publishing to everyone from dissidents in Soviet-era Russia (who secretly distributed samizdat literature) to punk-rock fans (who produced music "zines").

8   Then along came the Internet—and everything changed.

9   The original ARPANET was designed by the U.S. military to withstand a nuclear attack. Who could have predicted the explosion of creativity unleashed when this global computer network was opened to public access? Since the 1990s, the Internet has evolved into a wide-reaching platform to share writing (and other media) via websites, blogs, and social media by removing middle managers from the publication process. "That's not a job anymore," observed New York University professor Clay Shirky of the skills needed to publish in the 21st century. "That's a button."

10   Thanks to the Internet, students today write more than ever. But do they write better?

Teachers have always complained that their current crop of pupils can't compose as well as previous generations. (We also think the music was better back in our day.) Before, comic books or TV rotted their grammar. Now, the taint of "text-lish"—digital slang and acronyms, like LOL or OMG! —creeps into their prose from Instant Messaging, SMS texting or emails punctuated with emoticons.

11   In fact, so-called "digital natives" of the "millennial generation" can write as well as their great-grandparents, who composed in longhand or on touch typewriters. Andrea Lunsford, a scholar of writing at Stanford University, compared first-year composition papers from 2006, 1986, 1930, and 1917. She found no meaningful change in the error rate over the past 90 years.

12   Sali Tagliamonte and Derek Denis, linguists at the University of Toronto, analyzed a million words of instant messages written by 72 teenagers. They concluded the students' online writing reflects the "same dynamic, ongoing processes of linguistic change that are currently under way

on contemporary varieties of English." Our language is constantly evolving, and new additions to our vocabulary, taken from digital culture, are a natural part of that evolution.

13   Computers might have an impact, though, on how we read. Studies suggest that students comprehend longer texts better when read on paper versus an LCD screen. Journalist Nicholas Carr has argued the Internet has created a cultural "shallows" in which we're constantly surfing from fact to fact, across a surface of hypertext, without the deep understanding of immersing ourselves in a book.

14   We certainly aren't helped by the temptations to multi-task while writing on a Net-connected device. Rather than focus on the assignment at hand, we often scroll through news feeds, glance at Facebook updates, and click tempting links that catch our eye. Inevitably, our writing gets caught in this crossfire of shifting contexts. Some people hopefully claim the Internet is "rewiring" our brains for the digital age, but psychological research suggests we remain clumsy at such cognitive juggling acts.

15   Finally, the power of instantaneous publication also comes with great responsibility. Writers on the Internet must think carefully before they press "Send" or "Post." (Unfortunately, most don't.) Our online "global village" is built on a paradox: What might feel like a casual exchange (or argument) between friends (or strangers) is often broadcast around the world to a potential audience far wider than a typical newspaper. Your words are preserved as a digital breadcrumb trail that can be traced back to your name long after you close your laptop.

16   Students have lost scholarships or faced discipline for posting inappropriate or offensive content online. Professors have had tweets or blog posts come back to haunt them. Hitting "Reply All" by mistake has been a career-limiting move for careless communicators. Authors have always needed to master spelling and grammar, style and content, research and rhetoric. Now we must mind our "digital footprint," too. Writing, Socrates worried, would ruin our memories. But the Internet, it seems, never forgets. It is hard to know what's worse.

17   It would be foolish to speculate on what technological change might come next. Will Google still dominate our quest for information? Will we continue to compress thoughts into 140-character "micro-blogs"? Or will the very act of writing be transformed as we compose on holographic virtual keyboards or even blink messages (or whole novels!) using augmented-reality eyewear?

18   In the end, it won't make a big difference. The skills of effective written communication will remain universal, whatever the medium: The right words, in the right order, for the right reasons, to the right reader. We must still learn to focus on the vision—and revision—necessary to make our sentences as meaningful as possible, even as we accelerate into the future.

Works Cited

Lunsford, Andrea A., and Karen J. Lunsford. "Mistakes Are a Fact of Life: A National Comparative Study." *College Composition and Communication* 59.4 (2008): 781–806.

Shirky, Clay. "How We Will Read: Clay Shirky." *Findings Blog*. Findings. com., 5 Apr. 2012. Web. 15 Sep. 2014.

Tagliamonte, Sali A., and Derek Denis. "Linguistic Ruin? Lol! Instant Messaging and Teen Language." *American Speech* 83.2 (2008): 3–34.

—David Leach is the Director of the Interdisciplinary Minor in Technology & Society at the University of Victoria.

Rhetorical Patterns and Paragraph Development

Rhetorical patterns are systematic ways to organize and present information. They apply both to the essay itself and to individual paragraphs. That is, while a writer may focus on the benefits of coffee throughout the essay, he or she might begin by defining caffeine and develop another paragraph by contrasting the new research stressing benefits with older research stressing costs.

Thus writers also use rhetorical patterns to help organize and develop individual paragraphs, supporting the specific claims in the topic sentences. Part of an essay's success lies in choosing the most appropriate rhetorical pattern(s) to develop a claim.

rhetorical pattern

A method for organizing and presenting information in essays and paragraphs; examples include cause–effect, classification, comparison and contrast, cost–benefit, and definition.

One way to help narrow down a general topic is to think of different ways it can be developed by using rhetorical patterns.

Most topics can be developed by using one or more of the methods listed in Table 6.1 or the two methods discussed below. For example, if you were looking for ways to develop the topic "fighting in hockey," you could use description or narration to convey the excitement of a hockey brawl. Conversely, you could use either method to convey it as an unseemly spectacle. You could use the process analysis pattern to depict the step-by-step procedures officials use to break up a fight, the chronological pattern to trace the history of rules governing fighting, or the pattern by example to call attention to notorious fighting incidents in recent years.

Table 6.1	Rhetorical Patterns	
Purpose	**Rhetorical Pattern**	**Description/Explanation**
	definition	• see page 81 for a detailed explanation of definition
	comparison and contrast	• see page 81 for a detailed explanation of comparison and contrast
to create an image or picture of something	description	• uses images related to sight or the other senses to create immediacy and involve the reader • uses modifiers (adjectives and adverbs) to add detail • may systematically focus on a scene, using a logical method such as from left to right, top to bottom, etc.
to tell a story	narration	• relates an occurrence, usually in chronological order • stresses action through the use of strong verbs • provides anecdotes—brief narratives that introduce or illustrate a point
to show how something works or is done	process analysis	• breaks down a (usually) complex process into a sequence of successive steps, making it more understandable • provides instructions or directions
to show the way something changed/ developed	chronology	• uses time order to trace something, often from its beginning to the present day • can be applied to people, objects (like inventions), or situations
to particularize the general or concretize the abstract	example	• gives particular instances of a larger category, enabling readers to better understand the larger category • gives immediacy and concreteness to what can seem otherwise broad or abstract
to analyze why something happened or a result/ outcome	cause–effect	• uses inductive methods to draw conclusions • works from causes to effects or from effects to causes, for example, to determine whether smoking leads to (causes) heart disease or to determine whether heart disease results from (is an effect of) smoking
to account for or justify something	reasons	• uses deductive methods that draw on one's knowledge or experience (which may ultimately be derived from inductive findings), for example, you should not smoke because it often leads to heart disease (reason derived via empirical evidence)
to analyze by dividing into subcategories	classification/division	• Classification: groups items according to shared characteristics (e.g., types of bottled water: purified, mineral, sparkling) • Division: separates large category into constituent parts (e.g., the essay into introduction, middle paragraphs, conclusion)
to look at two sides/views of something	cost–benefit analysis	• weighs the pros and cons of an issue, question, or action, usually to decide which is stronger • in argument, is used to support a value or policy claim and/or refute an opposing claim
to identify a problem or solve/ resolve it	problem–solution	• analyzes or explains a problem or proposes a solution • may incorporate other methods, such as reasons, cause–effect, or cost–benefit analysis.
to better understand something	analogy	• shows how one subject is similar to another to clarify the nature or a feature of the first subject

Definition

Using definition as a rhetorical pattern is common in expository essays written for a general audience who would be unfamiliar with specialized terms. Thus, definitions often precede large sections that focus on explaining or analyzing, as in this introduction to an essay on the effects of trans fat on human health:

> In the early 1900s, William Normann invented the hydrogenation process in which trans fat, short for trans-fatty acid, is the by-product. A tiny amount of trans fat is found naturally, usually in animal fat; however, the majority of trans fats are made when hydrogen is added to vegetable oil in a process called hydrogenation. Hydrogenation is the modification of vegetable oil to allow it to be a solid at room temperature. The way the atoms of the fatty acids are bonded shows whether the fat is saturated or unsaturated: saturated fats have only single bonds while unsaturated fats have double bonds. A trans fat is a fat that was once an unsaturated fat but has had its double bonds weakened through the process of hydrogenation.
>
> —student writer Kim Snyder

Using definition can also be an effective strategy in argument. Value claims, in particular, often rely on definition: after explaining what you mean by something, you can link the definition to your evidence. For example, if you were arguing that gymnastics should or should not be considered a sport, you would need to state what you meant by a *sport*. Ensuring that this was a definition with which most readers would agree, you could then use the definition as a springboard into your claim and main points by showing how gymnastics does or does not fit this definition.

Comparison and Contrast

When you compare, you look at how two items are similar; when you contrast, you consider their differences. However, the term *compare* is generally used to refer to both similarities and differences. You can compare ideas, issues, people, places, objects, or events—as long as bases of comparison exist to make such comparisons valid. For example, you can compare two jobs by looking at their salaries, workweeks, levels of responsibility, and so on. However, if you were comparing two things in order to evaluate them, you would have to ensure that the same evaluation standards could be fairly applied to each. For example, you could not evaluate two universities that were vastly different in size. That is why the compilers of *Maclean's Guide to Canadian Universities* categorize universities by their size before applying their performance measures, such as student body, classroom size, and calibre of faculty, which serve as the bases of comparison.

Organizing a comparison and contrast essay can be more complicated than organizing essays that use another primary rhetorical pattern. Consider using the three-step organizational approach:

1. Determine whether the two items you want to compare *can* logically be compared. The health-care system in the US cannot be compared to the education system in Canada. Although the health-care systems in the two countries are comparable, such a large undertaking might prove unmanageable. More reasonable would be a comparison between two provincial health-care or education systems.

2. Carefully select the bases of comparison, or criteria for comparing (choosing at least three should help make the comparison valid). Each basis can serve as a main point in your essay.

3. Choose one of two possible methods for organizing your main points: the *subject-by-subject (block)* method or the *point-by-point (topics)* method. In the first, you begin with the first subject of comparison and apply your bases of comparison to it; you then do the same for the second subject, keeping your points (criteria) in the identical order. In the more commonly used point-by-point method, you begin with a basis of comparison and apply it to the first, then the second subject. You continue to do this until you have represented all your bases of comparison.

Which is the better method? The block method stresses the subjects themselves, while the point-by-point method stresses the criteria for comparison. If there seems no compelling reason to prefer one over the other, consider that the point-by-point method can be easier to follow because in the block method, the reader needs to keep in mind each basis of comparison as it has been applied to the first subject while it is being raised for the second subject. For this reason, essays that use the block method can be more challenging to write and to read.

The following paragraphs use one basis of comparison, human health benefits, as part of an essay that compares organic and locally grown foods to determine which is better for human and ecosystem health. The paragraph that discusses the benefits of organic food is longer because more studies have been done on this. Nevertheless, the second paragraph on locally grown foods is well-developed through logical reasoning. Notice that both paragraphs present different contrasts: the first between organic and non-organic food and the second between locally grown and imported foods. Thus, the essay's main organizational method is comparison and contrast, while individual paragraphs are also developed through this pattern:

The demand for organically produced food in supermarkets across North America has steadily increased over the past decade (USDA, 2008). A big reason for this is the widely held belief that organic food is better for our health than "conventional" food, largely based on differences in how the food is grown. Organic food is produced naturally and has no contact with synthetic inputs, such as pesticides, chemical food additives, or chemical fertilizers. "Conventional" food, by contrast, is grown in conditions where synthetic chemicals are used. Naturally, this has led many people to believe that there is more nutritional value in organic than in non-organic food (Williams, 2002). However, a critical review of past research shows an inconsistency in data regarding the relationship between organic food and increased nutrients (Magkos, Arvaniti, Zampelas, 2006). Short-term studies have shown mixed results regarding the health benefits of conventional and organic food; long-term studies, due to time and money constraints, have been too difficult to undertake. It remains unclear if organic is indeed more nutritious than conventionally grown food.

There have been substantially fewer scientific studies on the health effects of eating local food, but it has garnered no shortage of public awareness. In a wave of new food initiatives, regimens that stress eating locally, like the 100-mile diet, have become extremely popular. Although people tend to buy local food for political reasons, it can be argued that it is actually better for your health than exotic food. Fruits and vegetables that travel a great distance before being consumed are harvested early to allow time to ripen during transportation. Local food travels a very short distance before being consumed, which allows for it to ripen in its natural environment. With shortened food chains (Feagen, 2007), produce that is ripened by the sun and consumed soon after harvest will not only taste better but also retain more nutrients than produce grown at a distance.

—student writer Stephen Littleford

For examples of essays in *The Active Reader* that employ different rhetorical patterns, including definition and comparison and contrast, see Classification of Readings by Rhetorical Mode/Pattern, (inside back cover).

Kinds of Evidence

Although it is good to use various kinds of evidence in your essay, some are likely going to be more important than others. The choices you make depend on your purpose, audience, topic and claim, and the type of essay you are writing. For example, if you are writing a rhetorical or critical analysis, it will focus on the essay you are analyzing as a primary source; if you are writing a research essay, your focus will likely be on secondary sources. For kinds of evidence typically used in argumentative essays, see page 109.

Some kinds of evidence can be more authoritative than others. In fact-based writing, "hard" evidence—facts, statistics, and the findings of empirical research—provides the strongest grounds for support. "Soft" evidence, such as expert opinion, examples, illustrations, and analogies, may also be important to help explain a concept but will likely be less important than "hard" evidence. Argumentative essays may use analogies, precedents, expert opinion, and even, perhaps, personal experience.

One kind of example that is often pertinent to fact-based social sciences writing, as well as writing in business and education, is the case study, a detailed exploration of one particular case, such as a real-life situation, in order to gain a depth of understanding of the issue being investigated. Case studies use empirical methods of observing and recording, although typically the data produced and then analyzed is qualitative rather than quantitative, based, for example, on interviews, questionnaires, and personal observation. Because of their systematic methodology and the wealth of detail that is analyzed, the findings from case studies can often be generalized, while ordinary examples cannot.

Issues of Credibility

Credibility factors include *knowledge*, *reliability*, and *fairness*. You exhibit your knowledge by appearing well informed about your topic and supporting each claim with solid and substantial evidence. You convey reliability in several ways:

- by using the accepted conventions of the discipline in which you are writing; this includes using the appropriate citation style, being aware of the specialized language of the discipline, and following format requirements, such as the use of an abstract and formal sections (report writing)
- by writing effectively and following the rules of grammar, punctuation, syntax, sentence structure, and spelling

Common kinds of evidence may vary from discipline to discipline. Humanities writing often uses extensive direct quotation from primary sources. Social sciences writing tends to focus on statistics, interviews, questionnaires, case studies, and interpersonal observation. The sciences rely on direct methods that involve experimentation.

case study
A carefully selected example that is analyzed in detail in order to support a writer's claim.

credibility
Credibility can be demonstrated by an author's knowledge, reliability, and fairness.

- by writing efficiently, using words that express exactly what you want them to
- by using credible and authoritative sources (research essays)
- by reasoning logically and avoiding logical fallacies (argumentative essays)

Although fairness applies particularly to argumentative essays, it can also be important in research essays, since synthesis could involve acknowledging sources whose findings contradict your claim or hypothesis; this means explaining contrary evidence. The following criteria, however, apply mostly to argument. You convey fairness in several ways:

- by using an objective voice and not showing bias
- by acknowledging and accurately representing the opposing view
- by looking for common ground
- by avoiding slanted language and emotional fallacies

Writing Conclusions

conclusion
The last paragraph or section of an essay whose function is to summarize the thesis and/or main points in the body of the essay.

circular conclusion
Reinforces the thesis.

Like introductions, conclusions can vary depending on the kind of essay and other factors. While conclusions are always a vital part of essays, their functions differ. They may refer back to the thesis statement, reasserting its importance and usually rephrasing it. They may also look ahead by considering a way that the thesis can be applied or the ways that it could be further explored.

Although the essay conclusion may both look back to the thesis statement and look ahead to the thesis's implications, the stress often falls on one or the other. A circular conclusion is primarily concerned with reminding the reader of your thesis and with reinforcing it. Even so, if you want to emphasize these functions, you should not repeat the thesis word for word, nor should you simply summarize what you have already said in your introduction. You should draw attention to the significance of the paragraphs that follow your introduction and precede your conclusion—after all, they are probably the most substantial part of the essay. One way you can do this is to summarize the most important point, connecting it to your thesis.

spiral conclusion
Suggests applications or further research.

A spiral conclusion refers to the thesis but is more concerned with considering its larger importance. In argumentative essays, you may want to make an emotional or ethical appeal or, especially if your purpose is to reach a compromise, to suggest common ground between your view and the opposing one. Other strategies in spiral conclusions include ending with a relevant anecdote or personal experience (informal essays) or a question or hypothesis that extends from your research (formal essays or reports). If your focus has been on a problem, you could suggest solutions by making recommendations. If your topic was applicable to a small number of people, you can suggest how it could be generalized to a larger group, one that would include the reader.

The paragraph below uses the circular pattern. Although it repeats some information from the introduction, it uses different words and introduces a new term, *adaptive perfectionism*, from the middle paragraphs of the essay. In the final sentence, the writer advocates further research in the field to benefit people who are maladaptive perfectionists. You can compare the conclusion to the introduction, above on page 74:

As an infiltrating personality characteristic, perfectionism is often deleterious and psychologically harmful. Although adaptive perfectionism has been associated with positive elements such as a proclivity for excellence, it has also been associated with increased levels of depression as compared to non-perfectionists. Maladaptive perfectionism is that much more detrimental to an individual's life in that it is associated with more elements of mental illness and with difficulty in academics and intimate relationships. Since, as Costa and McCrae (1986) point out, personality is relatively stable, research on perfectionism is a warranted endeavour to better understand, and to better help people suffering from, this quality.

—Student writer Erin Walker

The Active Voice

The following essay gives guidelines relevant to students writing reports in the sciences, social sciences, engineering, and other disciplines in which an adaptation of the Type B essay is required. Note the emphasis on clear, direct, and active writing.

Report Writing—Aims and Goals

1   Of all types of writing, report writing is the most categorically active. It is built on *doing something*, then writing about what was discovered as a result of doing it—a lab experiment, for instance, or a survey, or a site visit. *Planned, designed, measured, saw, researched, interviewed, calculated, analyzed, evaluated, solved*: verbs—dynamic action or "doing" words—lie at the heart of all report writing. That is because reports record the results of a study undertaken to *find out something specific*: answer a question, clarify an issue, solve a problem, analyze a policy, establish a cause or consequence, decide on a course of action, evaluate possible outcomes, make a recommendation, or give an update on a project. In all these cases, reports "write up" the results of a study conducted to yield specific, concrete information that is otherwise missing, unknown, or incomplete.

2   Original findings based on original research—that is what reports typically deal with. In fact, "report of original research" is a common name for this type of writing in the science and social science disciplines, where the principal goal is to expand the field of knowledge— to fill gaps in the current state of research. The audience for such reports is typically other scientists or scholars. The report writer's job is to convince experts in the field that the findings are valid, making an original contribution to knowledge.

3   In other situations, however, report writing may answer more practical goals. Engineers, for example, may write investigative reports, recommendation reports, feasibility reports, or progress reports. The information compiled in these types of reports is usually intended to promote a specific course of action—for example, to implement (or scrap) a policy, develop a community program, approve an expansion of medical facilities, upgrade a highway, purchase new educational software, build a new gas line, or restore polluted waterways. As a result, they tend to be written for a mixed audience—other engineers as well as managers, policy-makers, public administrators, budgeting personnel, or company clients. Consequently, while they are generally technical in scope, they are often written so as to make sense to non-experts as well, with the goal of persuading them to act on the findings.

Organizing Reports

4   We have said that the goal of report writing is to provide specialized, concrete information, based on empirical research, in response to a question, problem, or project. At the same time, to ensure the report is sufficiently persuasive—allowing important decisions to be made on the information presented—reports also record *how* the information was compiled. They provide a methodology. This is a key way in which science and much social science writing differs from humanities writing. It explains not only the facts but how the facts were derived. This is important because knowing *how* the data was compiled means readers can gauge its trustworthiness for themselves.

5   Report writers therefore organize reports with an eye to showing *how* the information was found so they

can demonstrate its reliability. Luckily, organizational *templates* make this a relatively easy task. Formal reports have a rigidly defined structure that report writers are expected to follow to meet disciplinary demands for clarity and accountability. The American Psychological Association (APA), the disciplinary body that regulates report writing in the social sciences and some of the sciences, requires an IMRAD style of organization: introduction, methods, results, and discussion, with each section clearly signalled by headings.

Introduction

6 Introductions provide context and needed background, explaining topic and purpose, and describing what the study was intended to find out and why. In the academic disciplines, this usually involves giving an opening literature review, an overview of current research in the field. A research question that the study is designed to answer may also be stipulated.

7 The introduction often ends with a hypothesis, a "prediction" about expected results that the study is designed to test.

Methodology

8 This section explains *how* the study was conducted. It outlines steps taken to compile the data, giving details about *where*, *when*, and *how*. In many cases, this section may also explain *why* the study was designed the way it was. The methodology section, in short, stipulates the techniques used to gather information:

- lab experiment
- fieldwork
- "on-site" observations
- tests, surveys, or questionnaires
- primary and secondary sources (print and electronic)
- interviews
- technical descriptions or specifications

- mathematical formulas or calculations
- computer modelling

Results

9 This section objectively describes the findings yielded by the study. The focus is on presenting the "raw data": no discussion of its significance takes place yet. What the data *means* (interpretation and evaluation) is reserved for the next section.

Discussion

10 The *APA Publication Manual* is very specific about key functions of a conclusion (usually called "Discussion") of an APA report. Primarily, this is where the study's findings are evaluated or interpreted. Their significance is explained. This section answers the questions, What do the results mean? What conclusions can we derive from them? If a hypothesis has been presented, the discussion should likewise state whether it is been confirmed or not, always bearing in mind that a negative result can be as valuable as a positive one. In either case, something new has been discovered.

11 Finally, a discussion usually ends with a closing peroration, a final "heightened appeal" for the significance or worth of the study. The goal here is to avoid a "so what?" response. The *APA Manual* suggests that report writers should aim to answer the following questions:

- What have I contributed here?
- What has my study helped resolve?
- What broader theoretical implications can I draw from my study?
- Can meaningful generalizations be drawn?
- Does further research need to be done to clarify any remaining uncertainties?

—Monika Rydygier Smith is Instructor of Technical Writing in the Department of English, University of Victoria.

7

Writing Summaries

Student researchers are often told that when they use secondary sources in their research essays, they must do more than simply summarize them. Similarly, when students analyze literature, they may be advised to "avoid plot summary." From these examples, it might seem that summarization should play a minor role in academic discourse. Nothing could be further from the truth: although there are specific times and places for summaries, they are a major part of research-related writing.

Times and Places for Summaries

Summarization is concerned with representing the ideas of a writer in a condensed form, using mostly your own words. The key words in this definition are *representing*—"*re*-presenting"—and *condensed*—"concentrated." A summary does not interpret or analyze but presents again the essence of the original. The summary is more concentrated than the work being summarized because it contains only the main ideas, and sometimes only *the* main idea, of the original.

If you are reviewing a novel, you will typically summarize its plot or characters before you begin your analysis. If you are critiquing a text in order to argue against the author's position, you might begin by summarizing the author's arguments before replying with your own points. Similarly, in a critical analysis, you will likely briefly summarize a point before applying your critical-thinking skills to it. (There is an example of a student critical analysis in chapter 9, page 123; a student rhetorical analysis can be found in chapter 8, page 100.) The following are specialized summaries; their functions are discussed below:

- abstract
- literature review
- annotated bibliography

summarization

A broadly inclusive term for representing the ideas of a writer in a condensed form, using mostly your own words.

abstract

A condensed summary used in an empirical study; it is placed before the essay begins and includes at a minimum purpose, methods, and results.

literature review

A condensed survey of articles on the topic arranged in a logical order, usually ending with the article most relevant to the author's study.

annotated bibliography

An expanded bibliography that includes not only the information of standard bibliographies but also highly condensed summaries of related works.

In many academic essays, a concentrated summary called an abstract precedes the essay, giving an overview of what follows (see page 18). Another form of summary is the literature review, in which the author concisely summarizes relevant studies before stating his or her own thesis or hypothesis (see page 20).

Another kind of summary is the annotated bibliography, an expanded bibliography that includes the information of both standard bibliographies and condensed summaries of works. These include studies referred to in the text, but they may also include significant studies not cited there. Typically, each entry in the bibliography includes the main point, or thesis, and a comment on what it contributes to the field as a whole—where it fits in. Annotated bibliographies may form appendices to book-length studies.

Some authorities in a subject compile such bibliographies as independent projects. For example, *The World Shakespeare Bibliography Online* is a massive compilation of annotated entries for "all important books, articles, book reviews, dissertations, theatrical productions, reviews of productions, audiovisual materials, electronic media, and other scholarly and popular materials related to Shakespeare" created in the last 40 years. It includes more than 135,000 annotated entries in many languages. Students may be assigned a more modest annotated bibliography as part of a research project or as an independent project. In either case, the purpose will be to demonstrate your ability to research and summarize relevant works on a topic.

The following is an example of an entry in an annotated bibliography by the student writer whose completed essay appears on page 155. Lorinda Fraser summarizes one of the studies she used in her research essay and provides a brief assessment of its value:

> Sublette and Mullan analyzed 471 studies on Massively Multiplayer Online Games (MMOGS) addiction or "problematic game play," narrowing themselves down to only 16 studies that they felt met their criteria for unbiased data to evaluate the reliability of the evidence. These studies were then combined, compared, and discussed; recommendations for future research directions were proposed. In their review, Sublette and Mullan satisfy an important need by providing an extensive, objective review of current evidence-based research removed from the fear-based hype and sensationalism frequently offered in this field today.

Summarizing and Research

Summary is an important feature of scholarly discourse, whether practised by students or academics, because it enables writers to situate their own points relative to those of others. By presenting the main idea(s) of your sources and synthesizing them with your own ideas, you are developing and supporting your thesis. Writers of academic essays rely on this form of development. Academic writers summarize the ideas of other writers

- to support their own point
- to disagree with a relevant study
- to explain a concept or theory relevant to their topic
- to compare/contrast a study's findings with those of other studies

The amount of space you devote to a summary depends on how you want to use it and on its importance to your thesis. If you are summarizing an author's position with which you disagree, you probably will do no more than briefly mention the main arguments on the other side. If one source is particularly important to your research essay, your summary should be longer than those of less important sources. Summaries, then, can range greatly in length, as well as in purpose.

The Stand-Alone Summary: The Précis

Summaries can also serve as ends in themselves. A stand-alone summary, sometimes called a précis (meaning something precise), represents all the main points in a complete work or section(s) of a work. In effect, it is a miniature version of the original, following the same order of points as the original but omitting detail and less important sub-points. The specific guidelines that apply to stand-alone summaries do not apply to all types of summaries, but learning these guidelines and practising them is the best way to master summary writing. The important skills required in précis writing include the following:

Comprehension skills: Because summaries require you to change the wording of the original, you focus more closely on comprehension than if you quoted the words of the source directly: you must be clear on content in order to write a successful summary. This could mean using contextual clues to determine a word's meaning or looking it up in a dictionary. It could also mean understanding relevant concepts. You cannot express another's ideas clearly if you are not clear on their meaning.

Prioritizing skills (establishing a hierarchy): Distinguishing the main ideas from the less important ideas is a fundamental part of the reading process. In précis writing, you often have to go further than this: if you are assigned to write a summary that is 20 to 25 per cent the length of the original, you may have to include one or more important sub-points or a key example in addition to the main points to meet the word quota; on the other hand, if your summary is too long, you may have to omit a main point or important sub-point. In effect, you need to think about the importance of a point relative to other points, the importance of a sub-point relative to other sub-points, and so on.

Concision skills: A crucial principle applies to précis writing: the more economical your writing, the more content you can include and the more informed your reader will be. Therefore, you should strive for concise writing. Wherever possible, too, you should try to tighten up the writing of the original without sacrificing clarity. Focusing on conciseness will serve you well in any writing you do, making you a more disciplined writer.

> Stand-alone summaries help develop three main skills basic to reading and writing at the university level: comprehension, prioritizing, and concision skills.

Ten Pointers for Précis Writing

When writing précis-style summaries, you should keep the following guidelines in mind:

1. Be accurate. Use focused reading strategies to ensure you do not misrepresent a fact, idea, or opinion.
2. Follow the order of the original. Begin the summary with the thesis or first main point.
3. Include only the most important points. You may include the most important sub-point(s) as well, depending on space. Most sub-points develop a main point.

4. Avoid detail. If a reader wants detail, he or she can read the original. Do not include examples unless they are very important.

5. Avoid repetition. However, writers may emphasize a point by repeating it. Ideas stressed in the original should be stressed in your summary too, but without creating redundancy.

6. Do not repeat the author's name or the work's title any more than necessary.

7. Do not add your own opinions. Do not analyze or interpret. Summaries require you to be objectively represent, not to respond to the writer or his/her views.

8. Use your own words, minimizing direct quotations. If a brief passage cannot be easily paraphrased, you may quote it directly, but *ensure that you use quotation marks to show the reader that those exact words occurred in the source.* You can also use direct quotation if a word/phrase is significant or memorably expressed. Common everyday words from the original do not have to be placed in quotation marks unless they occur in longer phrases (for the number of consecutive words that can be used without quotation marks, check with your instructor).

9. Write economically. Use no more words than you must, stressing basic words—nouns and verbs, adjectives and adverbs if they are important and can be expressed concisely, and transitions (sparingly) to create a logical flow between one idea and the next.

10. Ensure that the verbs you use reflect the author's rhetorical purpose. For example, if the writer is arguing rather than explaining a point, use a verb that reflects this: The author *argues . . . claims . . . criticizes . . .* (argument); the author *states . . . explains . . . discusses . . .* (exposition).

When summarizing, space is at a premium, so remember to be SPACE conscious. Be

- **Specific**
- **Precise**
- **Accurate**
- **Clear**
- **Efficient**

A How-To of Précis Writing

Reading strategies: Reading to summarize means you should use the forms of selective reading appropriate for this activity. Begin by scanning the text to get its gist—its thesis—and to determine its structure—that is, how the author has divided the text. When you have determined this, focused reading is required. You can use one of these methods to construct your summary:

1. *Outline method:* Identify main ideas by double underlining them. In *paragraphs*, for important ideas, look for topic sentences (often, but not always, the first sentence of the paragraph). In *sentences*, look for independent clauses, which contain the main idea. Identify the most important sub-points (developments) by single underlining. For information about using contextual cues, such as transitions and prompts, to lead you to main ideas, see Reading Paragraphs: Locating Main Ideas, page 53.

Next, prepare an outline with all main points and important sub-points. You can indent sub-points as in a formal outline. Then write your summary from the outline, using your own words as much as possible and adding transitions for coherence. If the summary exceeds the allowable length, omit the least important sub-point(s). *This method is particularly useful for shorter summaries.*

2. *Section summary method:* Prepare a section-by-section breakdown. Sections can be determined by headings or additional spacing between paragraphs. If there are none, try to determine where the writer has shifted focus or introduced a new concept. Summarize each section in your own words. Aim for one sentence for short sections, two sentences for mid-length sections, and two or three sentences for longer sections. As in the outline method, look for main ideas in topic sentences. However, since you are dividing the text differently from the way you would in the outline method, pay strict attention to the opening paragraph of each section, where the main idea(s) in the section may be introduced. Then combine your section sentences to write your summary, adding transitions for coherence. If the summary exceeds the allowable length, omit the least important sub-point(s). *This method is particularly useful for longer summaries.*

Some Summary Writing Strategies

In addition to the guidelines discussed above, consider the following strategies:

- Read through the essay at least twice before beginning to identify main points and important sub-points.
- To help identify main points, ask whether or how they connect with or contribute to the thesis. Main points usually provide support for the thesis. If you are summarizing part of a complete work and not all of it, you may not find a thesis, but every section should contain a controlling idea.
- It might be easier to identify main ideas after you have first put parentheses around non-essential details and examples.
- For longer works, pay particular attention to the writer's own summaries, which may occur in the introduction, in the conclusion, or toward the end of lengthy sections.
- All paragraphs are not equally important; some may even not contain a topic sentence. Introductory paragraph(s) will not necessarily contain important information. In journalistic writing, for example, opening paragraphs may serve to attract the reader's interest; they may contain little of substance and should, in that case, be omitted.

The following is a section from an essay in Part III: The Reader. In the essay's previous section, "So Why Then Has Psychology Not Been a Climate-Change Player?" Robert Gifford lists his answers to the question in clear topic sentences. In the section shown below, it may be more difficult to identify main ideas. However, by using the reading strategies discussed on pp. 53–54, a reader can determine main points. The section is 732 words; a 150-word summary would represent approximately 20 per cent of the original, a typical length for a précis summary.

The Basis for Psychology's Role

by Robert Gifford

Although they will not
be part of your actual
summary, headings can help
you determine the topic
or controlling idea of the
section that follows. Thus,
the heading suggests that
the first two paragraphs,
focusing on the role of
the individual rather than
psychology, will not be too
important. They should,
therefore, not play an
important role in a summary.

The author uses a
transition—*in short*—to
summarize content. Such
cues direct the reader to
concisely phrased and
important information.

In this paragraph, the
author begins with prompts,
then poses a question to
draw attention to the topic
of the paragraph.

When you are summarizing
a section from an essay, you
need to ask whether a point
applies to the section or to
the essay as a whole. If the
latter, you may not want
to include it in the section
summary. Of course, to
successfully summarize a
section of an essay, you
should be familiar with the
entire essay.

The transition suggests
that an important point will
follow.

1   Each person, whether an average citizen or a CEO, has some level of choice and control over sustainability-related behaviours and actions. As Paul Stern (2005) has pointed out, these choices often are heavily constrained by contextual factors and one's own habits. Stern posits a hierarchical set of forces in which structural factors above or external to the individual usually are much more powerful influences on behaviour than individual-level influences.

2   Although one must acknowledge the power of context, and that Stern's hierarchy often accurately describes environmental behaviour choices, I maintain that individuals truly are the ultimate key to climate-change amelioration: policies, programmes, and regulations themselves do not change anything. For one thing, to be acceptable and efficacious to individuals, policies must be "bought into" by individuals. In short, policy beckons or even commands, but persons accept or refuse its demands. Behavioural change does not occur until this happens.

3   Many people do resist the temptation to engage in self-serving behaviours that contribute to climate change. Yet, admittedly, many do yield to the temptation. What will it take to change these people's behaviour? As a start—but only a start—understanding environment-related motivations, attitudes, social and organisational perceptions, rationales, biases, habits, barriers to change, life-context, and trust in government will help. Certainly, psychologists are already engaged in the effort on their own. For example, some have investigated the psychological dimensions of global warming (e.g., Dresner, 1989–90; Heath & Gifford, 2006; Nilsson, von Borgstede, & Biel, 2004). However, the major thesis of the present article is that we psychologists must do more.

4   I do not wish to argue that environmental psychology is, or even could be, a stand-alone panacea. For example, Schmuck and Vlek (2003) advocate that we work more closely with environmental scientists. However, I believe that we must work with at least four other groups to be effective: natural scientists, technical experts, policy experts, and local citizens' committees.

5   Fortunately, environmental psychologists have a history of interdisciplinary collaboration, beginning with geography and architecture, embodied in the collaborations between Robert Sommer, Humphry Osmond, and Kiyo Izumi in 1950s Saskatchewan (Sommer, 1983), or between Raymond Studer and David Stea in the United States (1966). More recently, and more pertinent to current concerns, fruitful collaborative work is being done in sustainability research (e.g., Schoot Uiterkamp & Vlek, 2007), including some collaborations that represent new bridges. Schoot Uiterkamp and Vlek (2007) describe five instances of collaborations, and their account is particularly valuable for its advice about the practicalities of engaging in multidisciplinary studies. This collaboration trend has been influenced, one suspects, by policies at national and international grant agencies that, for better or worse, virtually require interdisciplinary collaboration. In terms of influencing policy, collaborative efforts not only have "face credibility" based on the very breadth of their approach, but also success that is legitimately based on the increased validity of policy suggestions that emerge from studying a given problem with multiple valuable perspectives.

6   Gattig and Hendrickx (2007) bring perspectives from economics and behavioural decision theory into the mix. Discounting, the tendency to reduce the importance of an outcome
with greater "distance" (temporally, socially, geographically, and probabilistically), is seen to
be an important component of thinking about sustainability-related thinking. Fortunately,
environmental problems appear to be less subject to discounting than some other matters.
Although they incorporate some concepts from economics, Gattig and Hendrickx demonstrate why using those concepts in the same way that traditional economists do could lead
to ineffective policies (cf. Stern, 1986). "Rational" discount rates are not the same as those of
the public which, to its credit, seems to discount environmental impacts less than in other
domains. This helps to illustrate why other disciplines need psychology as much as psychology needs them.

7   Turning the policy issue upside down, some psychologists are examining the effects
of policy strategies, as opposed to conducting studies that they hope will inform policy.
Jager and Mosler (2007) are amongst those who use modeling to understand the outcomes
of different policy choices. This form of active modeling offers the attractive advantage of
trying out various policies before they are implemented and understanding why they might
or might not work, thereby potentially avoiding expensive mistakes in policy-making. As
Jager and Mosler point out, modeling can also be used to train policy-makers. The very act
of modeling encourages the idea that many policy alternatives exist, when often only a few
may occur to a policymaker.

> The author uses many examples throughout his essay. If you include an example in your summary, it must be an important one. Key examples may be repeated, be expanded on, or appear in topic sentences. Most detail, however, should be omitted from summaries.

Collaborative Exercise 7.1

Using the marginal comments and your own focused reading, write a summary of
approximately 150 words of "The Basis for Psychology's Role."

Or

Write a summary of another section in "Psychology's Essential Role in Alleviating the
Impacts of Climate Change," page 376 in Part III: The Reader. Aim for a summary 20 to
25 per cent as long as the original. Individual students or student groups should compare
their summaries, rewriting them if necessary.

8

Using Critical Thinking to Analyze Essays

The Rhetorical Analysis: Explaining the How and Why

In a *rhetorical analysis*, you use critical thinking and your knowledge of texts to break down a work in order to examine its parts and the author's rhetorical strategies.

In a *critical analysis*, you analyze the writer's argument for its effectiveness. For more on critical analyses and the language of argument, see chapter 9, page 121. For an example of a critical analysis, see chapter 9, page 123.

A rhetorical analysis is usually focused on one text. When you analyze a work, you break it down in order to examine its parts and the author's rhetorical strategies, using your critical-thinking skills and your knowledge of texts. The rhetorical analysis assumes you are familiar with how such texts are written and capable of evaluating the author's success in achieving his or her objectives. The main purposes of rhetorical analyses are (1) to explain and (2) to evaluate/critique the text. They should be objective in both content and voice.

Analyses need careful planning; for example, it is a good idea to outline your points before beginning your draft. The reader of your analysis should not get the impression that spontaneity has been your organizing principle.

Writing a rhetorical analysis makes you more conscious of the way that texts written by academics and other professionals are put together, as well as the kinds of strategies you can use to make content clear and accessible. In this sense, you critically analyze a text to see what works—and why—in order to use some of its features as models for your own writing. Of course, the text under consideration could serve as a negative model too.

The Active Voice

Rhetorical Analysis: What, Why, and How

What Is Rhetoric?

1   Many people now use the term *rhetoric* to mean empty language or even as a synonym for *lying*. The long history of rhetorical studies, however, suggests that we should give this word more respect. Among the earliest formal education one could receive in ancient Greece was training in rhetoric, defined as persuasive speech. All participation in that society's civic institutions—such as defence of oneself in a court of law or engagement in a public debate about whether to erect a new statue—required public speaking, so the ability to deliver stirring arguments was highly valued. By the fifth century BCE, schools of rhetoric existed, and their instructors wrote manuals on the art of rhetoric. Rhetoric remained central to the training of educated people across Europe from the medieval period well into the eighteenth century. Twentieth- and twenty-first-century scholars of rhetoric debate how arguments work in a variety of contexts ranging from political speeches to scientific studies to pop songs.

2   Perhaps the most influential of the ancient rhetorical theorists was Aristotle (384 BCE–322 BCE), a student at Plato's academy who himself served as tutor to Alexander the Great. He wrote on a wide range of subjects, including imaginative literature (*Poetics*), logic (*Organon*), and philosophy (*Nicomachean Ethics*, *Metaphysics*). Still foundational to the work of contemporary rhetoric studies is his treatise *On Rhetoric*. Responding to already existing rhetorical handbooks, Aristotle defined the goal of rhetoric not merely as persuasion itself but as the discovery and consideration of all available means of persuasion. Rhetoric thus included not just style, the arrangement of points, and emotional impacts—the topics stressed by other writers on the subject. It also involved consideration of audiences, speakers, subject matter, occasions for speaking, logic, and the character of the speaker. With his discussion of rhetoric, Aristotle did not invent a new field or discover new concepts. Rather, he described in a systematic way what effective speakers already did and, in the process, created a set of specialized terminology on which rhetorical theory still relies.

Rhetorical Appeals

3   If we agree with Aristotle that rhetoric involves all available means of persuasion, then a rhetorical analysis could take into account anything that has an impact on persuasiveness. Argumentative patterns used to shape each paragraph, types of introductions, lengths of sentences, and qualities of word choices—all of these are rhetorical elements that could be described and analyzed. But for a discussion of every persuasive aspect, even a very short argument would be too long and wide-ranging to be easily understood. By focusing on the key means of persuasion identified by Aristotle, we can develop more focused and coherent evaluations of arguments.

4   According to Aristotle, an individual making an argument has three basic means of persuasion at his or her disposal. We usually refer to these means of persuasion as the three rhetorical appeals since they comprise different ways of appealing to, winning over, an audience of listeners or readers. A particular argument might stress one more than the others, but all three are always present and having some effect. We use Greek terms for these appeals not in order to complicate matters unnecessarily: relying on Aristotle's specialized terminology allows an analysis to convey complex ideas concisely to any reader familiar with basic rhetorical theory.

5   Most readily understood is the appeal to logos, the persuasive impact of logical argumentation. Logos includes claims that an audience will perceive as probable as well as the reasons, examples, and evidence that support these claims. In the field of rhetoric, logical argumentation differs from that found in formal logic—as far as rhetoricians are concerned, it is sufficient for an audience to perceive a point as logical, not necessary for that point to be perfectly valid or true in all cases. As such, logos includes most of what we think of as the content of an argument such as the points it presents and the supporting statistics, cases, or testimonies it offers.

6   Aristotle recognized, however, that there were other factors than content that could lead an audience to find an argument persuasive. The emotional state of those listening to or reading a set of points could influence the likelihood of their agreeing with the claims being defended.

Speakers or writers who could invoke particular feelings in their audiences, therefore, had a useful tool at their disposal. Vivid description or even emotionally charged language might lead an audience to feel anger, grief, or pity and thus be moved to act in a particular way. More subtle emotions like friendliness or a general sense of belonging to a group could be created through the way a speaker addressed an assembled crowd. Influencing emotions as a means of persuasion is called the appeal to pathos, and emotionally charged arguments are said to be pathetic.

7   Finally, the extent to which an argument might persuade an audience depends upon who delivers that argument. Aristotle recognized that listeners were much more likely to believe a wise, virtuous, and well-meaning speaker than one who seemed ignorant or ruthless. He called the appeal based on the character of a speaker or writer ethos, the elements of a speech that established character ethical appeals.

8   The treatise *On Rhetoric* is particularly concerned with how a speaker can make effective ethical appeals within the argument itself. One can create the impression of being an expert by talking about personal experience of a field or simply by showing mastery of complex ideas; one can seem a moral person by speaking about having done good deeds; and one can appear open-minded and rational being respectful towards opposing arguments. The character of the speaker or writer created within the argument is known as intrinsic ethos.

9   Aristotle recognized, though, that the impression an audience had of the speaker before the speech began could have an impact on its persuasiveness. A very old man might have difficulty convincing an audience that he would fight in the war for which he was advocating, but he could convince the same group of listeners that he had extensive experience of previous wars and thus authority to speak to this issue that no young soldier could possess. A jury might not accept the same argument about having mistakenly taken a bracelet from a shop without paying for it from someone they knew as an already-convicted thief that they would find very persuasive from a pious priest. Extrinsic ethos, what is known about the speaker outside the argument itself, can powerfully alter the effectiveness of that argument.

Rhetorical Appeals and Argument

10   Aristotle was most concerned with public speeches, but many of the examples of arguments we encounter today, and most of the ones we analyze, come in other forms, either as broadcasts of speeches on radio, television, or online or, more commonly, in writing. Even so, the three appeals can be identified in all arguments we might wish to analyze.

11   Advertising regularly uses all available means of persuasion to convince an audience that a product is worth buying. A television advertisement introducing a new hybrid car might appeal to logos by arguing the car is good because of its gas mileage. Simultaneously, the same ad could appeal to pathos by using bright colours and bouncy music, thus implying the audience should associate the car with happiness. It could also make an extrinsic ethical appeal by mentioning the name of the well-regarded company that makes this new car and an intrinsic ethical appeal by presenting the new car's name in an attractive script and having it read by a smooth-voiced announcer.

12   Academic arguments employ appeals for more limited audiences. Indeed, it might seem at first glance that a document like an article in a peer-reviewed sociology journal relies on only one appeal, offering logical arguments in the form of data and statistics generated by a study to persuade readers that its results are accurate and that its conclusions are true. Certainly logos is the primary appeal of most academic writing, but other appeals are present. The prestige of the journal in which the article appears can help establish strong extrinsic ethos. The quality of the writing in the article itself and the extent to which the authors have mastered the conventions of scientific discourse creates intrinsic ethos. Pathos is likely subtle in such an argument, but the extent to which an article's choice to define certain terms or explain particular points makes an audience feel either confidently well informed or anxiously confused will determine the extent to which that group of readers is persuaded.

Why Study Rhetoric?

13   In addition to using the three appeals to analyze advertisements, speeches, blog posts, newspaper editorials, or academic articles, you can use these concepts to generate arguments that will effectively persuade those listening to or reading them. To create a new argument, it is important that you start not with a choice of which appeal to emphasize but rather with consideration of your audience. Rhetoric emphasizes practical, utilitarian considerations of what will be effective in the real world, not abstract thought about what would be best in an ideal situation. Begin by thinking about how each appeal might affect your actual audience in relation to a particular case, being sure to take into account what values,

attitudes, and knowledge members of that group share. Then decide which appeals would be most appropriate to use.

14   It is because rhetoric is a tool that can be applied in a variety of situations to almost any subject matter that it remains helpful to those of us living in a complex, media-saturated culture. Understanding the rhetorical appeals enables one to analyze existing arguments and to consider why they are or are not effective for a particular audience—and to think critically about whether one should be persuaded by the writer's or speaker's ideas. These same concepts can serve as prompts for generating effective arguments. One can also consider the appeals when attempting what is perhaps the most ancient rhetorical exercise of all, writing a highly persuasive argument with which you disagree, a practice Aristotle recommends not just to hone skills but also to put strain on and thus test the limits of one's convictions. Learning about rhetoric places you into an ancient and enduring Western educational tradition while simultaneously preparing you to succeed in crafting effective personal, popular, and academic arguments.

—**Erin E. Kelly** is Assistant Professor in the Department of English, University of Victoria

Key Terms

appeal to ethos   The strategic use of ethics or morality in order to help convince a reader. Intrinsic ethos demonstrates the writer's credibility, for example, through knowledge or fairness; extrinsic ethos is shown by the writer's character or abilities as perceived by others.

appeal to logos   The strategic use of reason and logic in order to help convince a reader.

appeal to pathos   The strategic use of emotion in order to help convince a reader.

Activity 8.1

Find an advertisement (it could be a current example or one from another era) in the media and bring it to class or access it on your computer for others in your group to see. Analyze its effectiveness, referring specifically to the logical, emotional, or ethical appeals discussed in this section.

Rhetorical analyses can be approached in different ways, depending on the nature of the source text. One kind of analysis applies to literary works. The literary analysis breaks down the elements of the text—in the case of fiction, such elements might include plot, character, setting, point of view, or language—showing how they relate to one another. Literary works contain no thesis but rather themes, which can be inferred from the interconnections among these elements. Like other kinds of texts, literary texts can be analyzed according to their conventions, which vary by genre (poetry, drama, fiction, creative non-fiction) and by subgenre (lyric, dramatic, and narrative poetry, for example).

> For more on logical, emotional, and ethical appeals as they can be used in argument, see chapter 9.

Because these and other humanities essays usually make interpretive rather than fact-based claims, they are often assigned for a rhetorical analysis. Although students may believe that they lack the expertise to address the writers on their own terms, it is helpful to remember that rhetorical analyses do not necessarily involve a negative critique of the author or his or her methods. For example, they could focus on why an author organizes his or her material in a certain way or on the variety of evidence used for support.

Organizing a Rhetorical Analysis

A typical rhetorical analysis begins with an introduction that includes a generalization about the essay and/or the topic, such as its importance or relevance in today's world.

It must also include a summary of the author's thesis or what questions he or she tried to answer. If a reader of your analysis might be unfamiliar with the source text, you should briefly summarize the essay or at least give enough detail so that your reader will understand its essence. Summarization can be a part of a rhetorical analysis, but rhetorical analyses are much more than simple summaries.

At the end of your introduction, include your thesis statement, which should address whether the text successfully fulfills its purpose and supports its claims. An effective thesis statement goes further than just stating whether the text is successful but also explain why; thus, it is advisable to use an expanded thesis statement.

In the body paragraphs, your analysis should break down the most relevant features of the essay, explaining how these features, such as the author's organization or rhetorical strategies, reflect his or her purpose, objectives, and audience. The aim is to explain and evaluate the how and the why of the source text: How does the author explore the subject and support the claims? Why are those particular methods and strategies used and not other ones? How effective is the support? What are the essay's strengths and weaknesses? How could the text be improved?

In any analysis, being specific is vital. Support all claims you make about a text by referring specifically to examples that illustrate your point. As in literary analyses, use direct quotations for important examples, remembering to provide citations. The best critical analyses proceed from a close and detailed reading of the source text (see Focused Reading, page 51).

The questions below, organized according to purpose, can be used to help generate points for a rhetorical analysis. The author's thesis, type of essay, purpose, and intended audience, along with other factors, will help determine which questions are the most relevant to your analysis.

For information on critical analyses, which analyze a writer's argument, see chapter 9, page 121.

> An *expanded thesis statement*, or essay plan, includes the main points in the order they will appear in the essay.

> For citations formats, see chapter 10, page 149–154.

Explaining

- When was the essay written? Is it current?
- Why was it written? Is it intended to inform, explain, persuade?
- Who is the intended audience? How do you know this?
- What do you know about the author(s)? Does he or she appear to be an expert in his or her field or otherwise qualified to write on the topic? How is this apparent (if it is)? What makes the author credible (or not)?
- Is there an identifiable introduction? What is the writer's thesis or central question? What is the justification for the study? In what way(s) does the author propose to add to his or her field of knowledge? Is a literature review included?
- How does the author convey essay structure? Essay plan? Questions?
- What are the essay's main points?
- What format does the essay follow? How does the text reflect the conventions of the discipline for which it was written? Does it follow these conventions exactly, or does it depart from them in any way?
- What kinds of evidence does the author use? Which are used most extensively? Are primary and secondary sources included?
- Is there a stress on either analysis or synthesis in the essay? On both equally?
- How is the essay organized? Is there a primary rhetorical pattern? What other kinds of patterns are used? (See chapter 6, page 80.)

- What level of language is used? Does the author include any particular stylistic features (e.g., analogies, metaphors, imagery, unusual/unconventional sentence structure)?
- Is there a conclusion? What is its primary purpose?

Evaluating/Critiquing

- Does the author manage to create interest in the topic? How is this done?
- Main points: Are they identifiable (in topic sentences, for example)? Are they well supported? Is supporting detail specific and relevant?
- If secondary sources are used, are there an adequate number? Are most of them current references?
- What kinds of sources were used? Books? Journal articles? Websites? Have the author(s) published related works in the field of study?
- Are some sources more important than others—for example, are they used more often? Is there an overreliance on a particular source or kind of source?
- Does the author adequately respond to findings that are at odds with his or her own? How does he or she do this?
- Are the kinds of evidence used relevant to the topic, audience, and discipline? Are examples and illustrations used to make points more concrete?
- What kinds of strategies and techniques does the author use to facilitate understanding? Are they effective? Are there other ways that organization or content could have been made clearer?
- Is the voice or tone appropriate, given the kind of essay and the audience? Does the author make it clear that he or she is using a distinctive voice/tone for a specific purpose?
- Does the conclusion answer the question that the author sets out to investigate? Does it explain the relevance of the study, what it contributes to the field?
- Does the author appear reasonable? Has he or she used reason effectively, establishing a chain of logic throughout?
- Does the author succeed in making the issue relevant to the reader? Does he or she appeal to the reader's concerns and values?
- Is the order of points appropriate? Do points progress from weakest to strongest (climax order) or strongest to weakest (reverse climax)?

Activity 8.2

Preparing to Write a Rhetorical Analysis

1. After reading one of the Type A or Type C essays in part III (see page 412 for essay types), choose at least five questions under Explaining and five questions under Evaluating/Critiquing that would be relevant to a rhetorical analysis of the chosen essay.

2. Use these 10 questions to outline an analysis, identifying and answering other relevant questions to fill out your outline.

3. Determine the best order of points for your outline (see Relating Parts and Discovering Structure, page 68).

Sample Rhetorical Analysis

A rhetorical analysis, like the one below on "Imagining a Canadian Identity through Sport," by Michael Robidoux (p. 300 in Part III: The Reader), highlights some of the main features of the source text, using summary, explanation, and evaluation. The annotations refer to some of the points discussed above.

He Refutes, He Scores: A Rhetorical Analysis of "Imagining a Canadian Identity through Sport"

by Kathleen Ruby Hopkins

Hopkins's first sentence attracts interest but also leads effectively to her claim concerning the importance of hockey to the Canadian identity.

1   In 2010, 80 percent of Canadians watched the gold medal Men's Hockey game during the Winter Olympics ("Oh Canada!"). It is safe to say that hockey has become a recognizable aspect of Canada's national identity. The origins of hockey in Canada and its aggressive characteristics have become cause for discussion and debate, and all these discussions must be carefully analyzed and evaluated. The need for critical thinking becomes crucial when validating claims. Michael A. Robidoux's article in *Journal of American Folklore*, "Imagining a Canadian Identity through Sport: A Historical Interpretation of Lacrosse and Hockey," uses specific development patterns, especially cost-benefit, cause and effect, and chronology to add to the debate about hockey's significance. Robidoux claims that the key to understanding our modern attitudes and feelings about hockey and how the game came to symbolize a Canadian culture lies in the exploration of early forms of the sport and the way that the game's traits maintained themselves (209). Through the use of well-supported counter-arguments, cause and effect discussions, and representative examples of general claims, Robidoux presents a convincing case.

An expanded thesis outlines the main points the writer will use to analyze the essay.

2   In his article, Robidoux acknowledges the faults as well as the validity of the opposing points, then proceeds to present his own claims, resulting in a well-supported counter argument. Using this cost/benefit form of analysis is useful, as it successfully weighs the pros and cons of an issue and then refutes an opposing claim. Robidoux implements this strategy when he acknowledges sports historian Don Morrow's claims concerning the expulsion of Aboriginal origins from lacrosse by nineteenth-century promoters (276). In rebuttal, Robidoux asserts that while religious components were erased from the game, "there were native/vernacular elements of the game that remained," and it is "incorrect to claim, as Morrow does," that these elements were cast out. Similarly, in response to Gruneau and Whitson's comments on the irrelevance of hockey to Canada's history (278), Robidoux reasons that some of their sentiments concerning the social struggles surrounding hockey are valid, but others that separate hockey from Canada's pertinent history are untrue. Robidoux successfully locates points that authors have made and counters them with his own claims, thus acknowledging and answering the questions and doubts that might arise about his reasoning.

Hopkins supports her claim by two examples from the essay, successfully integrating a direct quotation to support her first example (Morrow).

3   Furthermore, Robidoux implements cause–effect discussions that not only support his claims but utilize chronology to precisely depict the sequence of events. Such discussions

employ inductive reasoning to draw conclusions, tracing significant events in hockey's development. In his discussion of the development of organized sport, Robidoux mentions that the sudden need for a national Canadian identity was rooted in the stirrings of excessive British influence in Canada. As a result, the adoption of the indigenous game of *baggataway* was an attempt to manufacture a truly unique identity. In his discussion, Robidoux successfully showcases the origins of and ensuing events that shaped the beginning of Canadian nationalism found through hockey. Robidoux also states that the National Lacrosse Association's deliberate restriction of undesirable participants in order to cleanse and purify the game of lacrosse "forced potential lacrosse players to pursue alternative sporting options." Robidoux correctly and accurately pinpoints exact causes and events and follows them up with his explanations of results, or consequences. Through the cause–effect rhetorical pattern, then, Robidoux makes clear connections between modern day Canadian hockey conventions and their origins.

4   Finally, Robidoux expertly represents his claims with concrete instances and specific historical events, making effective use of primary sources. For example, in order to illustrate how *baggataway* embodied the earliest forms of the aggression and violence that eventually became a trademark of Canadian hockey, Robidoux refers to a late eighteenth-century account that comments, "the Chippewas play with such vehemence that they frequently wound each other, and sometimes a bone is broken . . . " (274). From this contemporary example, the reader can conclude that early indigenous sport included forms of aggression and violence. In a more recent example, the 1972 U.S.–Soviet "Summit Series," he is able to link hockey with not only the nation of Canada but also the distinctly aggressive way that Canadians played the game, which was approved by many Canadian fans: Robidoux refers to specific incidents, including one in which a Canadian player broke the ankle of a Soviet player (281). By presenting these documented occasions in distinct historical contexts and linking them to his thesis, Robidoux successfully connects specific claims to supporting evidence, showing how violence in hockey has remained a surprising but integral part of the Canadian identity. This leaves the reader satisfied that general claims have been adequately supported and contribute to a thorough argument overall.

5   Robidoux expertly establishes a persuasive argument with the assistance of counterarguments, chronological and cause–effect patterns, and concrete examples from primary sources. Robidoux's insights into the connections between modern Canadian nationality and early forms of hockey present an alternative yet compelling outlook on the social stigma of hockey-loving-Canadians. Although it had been widely accepted that the Canadian identity is rooted in hockey, Robidoux supports his thesis that the specific way Canadians play the game is a direct result of the early versions that were pioneered by the indigenous people of Canada. As we see from a focused reading of Robidoux's article, the implementation of rebuttals, developmental patterns, and concrete examples can be used effectively to support an author's claims. As readers, it is always crucial to actively acknowledge and evaluate these strategies.

A paragraph wrap reinforces the topic of the paragraph. Clear structure is crucial to successful rhetorical analyses.

Hopkins announces her points in the topic sentence, indicating by the transition *finally* that this is her last body paragraph. Again, Hopkins thoroughly develops the paragraph by analyzing two examples.

Hopkins begins her conclusion by summarizing her main points. In the next two sentences, she explains what Robidoux's essay contributes to the study of hockey and Canadian identity. She concludes by acknowledging the importance of critical thinking and focused reading.

Works Cited

Robidoux, Michael. "Imagining a Canadian Identity through Sport: A Historical Interpretation of Lacrosse and Hockey." *The Active Reader: Strategies for Academic Reading and Writing*. Third Edition. Ed. Eric Henderson. Don Mills: Oxford UP, 2015. 300–12. Print.

"Oh Canada! 80 Percent of Canadians Watch Gold Game." TSN.ca, 1 March 2010. Web.

9

Writing Argumentative Essays

Argumentative Purpose

Although argument today reflects its origins in classical thought and the theories of Aristotle, its contemporary uses are diverse. For example, today argument can serve several purposes:

- to defend a point of view
- to make a proposal, such as a better way to do something
- to interpret or critique a text
- to expose or raise awareness of a problem
- to promote affiliation
- to reach a compromise

The most straightforward kind of argument is one in which you take a position on an arguable topic and defend it. However, argumentative purpose can extend beyond this. For example, you can analyze both sides to reach a compromise, finding common ground. Thus, in her essay on a section of the Criminal Code that permits corporal punishment under specific circumstances, student writer Danielle Gudgeon steers a middle ground between those who want the law upheld and those who want it abolished. Her middle position makes it likely that an audience on both sides will consider her points, making her argumentative goal more attainable:

Section 43 of the Criminal Code has a social utility for both teachers and parents, but it is an old law that must be amended to reflect society's progression. The addition of clear guidelines to the law regarding the severity of discipline and the use of objects as weapons will create a distinction between abuse and discipline. This will prevent subjectivity within the courts and discourage future abuse, while affording parents the option of disciplining their children.

The kinds of evidence and the argumentative strategies you use depend on your purpose in arguing, your audience, and the topic itself. It is useful to look at three diverse forms that written argument can take in the media in order to see how these elements interact: the letter to the editor/blog, the review, and the editorial (see the table on page 104). Each has a different purpose, which is reflected in its structure, voice, language, kinds of evidence, and typical reader/viewer. The letter to the editor is the most subjective, in which writers can "have their say," whereas the voice of the editorial writer is usually objective and formal. Within these categories, there can be much variation; for example, although many reviewers are experts in their field, many forums exist online today for non-experts who may be less objective in their critiques.

Like the old letter-to-the-editor writer, "bloggers" range from opinionated novices to informed experts. Unlike letters to the editor, blogs often take the form of entries and are not restricted by length requirements. Another obvious difference is that bloggers can incorporate interactive elements in the design of their site, including direct feedback. Blogs have become a major part of many online publications, as well as print publications that want to extend their online presence.

Everyday Arguments

Consider the following scenario: you have moved into a residence at your university only to find the rules and regulations there particularly unfair (a 10 p.m. curfew for weekday social functions, for example). You might well discuss your disagreement with other residents and write a petition that argues for more reasonable rules—you are arguing your case, rather than engaging in conflict. The impulse to argue can easily arise if we perceive our values or beliefs challenged; similarly, we may argue to defend our self-interest or that of a group with which we identify, such as our family, school, or community.

Whenever you send a resumé to a prospective employer, you are implicitly arguing that you are the best person for the job and supporting your claim by facts about your knowledge and experience. If you are asked during the interview why you believe you should be hired, you will have to marshal your strongest persuasive skills in response. Argument in its myriad forms is ingrained not only in our society—in our legal and legislative systems, for example—but also in our daily lives.

Facts versus Opinions

An *opinion* is not the same as a *fact*, which can be verified by observation or research; opinions are challengeable. Of course, facts can be interpreted differently and used for different purposes. Facts, therefore, can be used to support the thesis of an argumentative essay. However, effective arguers are always clear about when they are using facts and when they are using opinion. In reading, use your critical-thinking skills to ask if the writer always clearly separates facts from opinion. If not, he or she might be guilty of faulty reasoning (see page 112).

See The Active Voice: Climate Change and the Integrity of Science, page 11 in chapter 1, on the distinction between scientific fact and opinion.

Table 9.1	Argument in Different Kinds of Writing		
	Letter to the Editor/Blog	**Book/Film Review**	**Editorial**
Purpose	to sound off, state your viewpoint; other purposes are possible as well	to critique a text, film, or some other type of material	to critique a position, expose a problem, reach a compromise, or promote affiliation
Writer	any interested reader	is knowledgeable in the field; professional reviewers are named in bylines	member of an editorial board; writer's name is not given; represents the views of the publication
Audience	those with similar values and views	book readers, film-goers, readers with an interest in the subject matter, etc.	educated readers, often the politically informed
Structure	usually short; might be edited for length and for style	usually follows conventional structure of argument: generalization with value claim followed by supporting evidence from the film/book	usually short; tight structure: focused on one issue
Claim	value or policy; argument may present only one side	value; will consider the pros and cons but will come down on one side or the other—"thumbs up" or down	policy; will carefully weigh both sides; may argue for one side, but argument characterized by careful reasoning
Voice	subjective—*I*	sometimes uses first person—*I*	objective—the "editorial *we*"
Language/tone	may be colourful, emotional, or volatile: "I'm appalled by our political leaders"; conversational, informal	may use some specialized words and terms; may be ironic or sarcastic, direct or evocative	elevated, sophisticated; formal, detached
Evidence	personal opinion may predominate	mostly expert opinion on primary source (text); may use comparison; evaluates according to established standards	facts and figures; precedents; reason-based evidence

Fact: The moon averages 384,400 kilometres from earth's equator.

Now consider the following two pairs of statements, each consisting of a fact and a related opinion:

Fact: According to moon-landing conspiracy theories, the 1969 Apollo moon landing was faked.

Opinion: The Apollo moon landing didn't actually take place; it was all a hoax.

Fact: On 13 November 2009, NASA announced that water had been found on the moon.

Opinion: Now that water has been found on the moon, humans should set up colonies at the moon's poles by 2050.

Collaborative Exercise 9.1

Consider the two pairs of statements above on the topic of humans on the moon. Discuss the ways that fact differs from opinion in each case. Come up with two other topics and write two statements for each, one of which represents a fact and the other of which represents an opinion.

Claims in Argument

The term claim is particularly appropriate to argument: when you set up your position in the introduction of your argumentative essay, you are doing more than *stating* a thesis: you are *actively asserting* one. When you claim something, you assert your right to it. The claim is the assertion that you will actively attempt to prove through valid evidence and logical reasoning in the body of your essay.

An argumentative claim is usually one of value or policy. In a value claim, you would argue that something is good or bad, right or wrong, fair or unfair, and so on. A policy claim proposes an action. In this sense, a policy claim goes further than a value claim on which it often rests. However, value claims may be appropriate if you wish to make your audience consider something in a more positive light. For example, if you argue in favour of euthanasia to a general or unreceptive audience, you might not want to use a policy claim, one that proposes a change in the law. A value claim instead would focus on changing attitudes, getting the reader to see, as a first step, perhaps, that euthanasia relieves the suffering of a terminally ill patient.

Sometimes, a writer begins with a value claim in the introduction before recommending specific action in the conclusion. See Sample Argumentative Essay with Annotations, page 124.

For the purposes of an academic essay—outside of formal arguments, of course, people can and will debate anything—successful argumentative claims must be *arguable*, *specific*, and *realistic*.

Arguable Claims

Most factual claims are not arguable because, as mentioned, a fact is different from an opinion. Facts can be questioned, and their interpretation is sometimes open to debate, but it is difficult for facts themselves to serve as the basis of an argumentative claim, though they may help support it. For example, you could not easily argue against the fact that the closest star to Earth is 4.2 light years away. However, you could use this fact as evidence to support a policy claim, say, for allocating more (or fewer) financial resources to the space program.

In addition, a belief—for example, that God exists—is not arguable in a formal way, although you could argue for the interpretation of a passage from the Koran or other religious text. Similarly, you could not logically argue that one religion is better than another since there are no clear and objective standards that reasonable members of your audience could agree on (and on which to base your claim; see Connecting Claim to Evidence, page 107). *Arguable claims must be supported through objective evidence, not just opinion.*

---

claim

An assertion that you will attempt to prove through evidence and reason. Claims occur in thesis statements; many topic sentences also assert a claim about the topic of the paragraph.

value claim

An assertion about a topic that appeals to its ethical nature (e.g., good/bad or fair/unfair).

policy claim

An assertion about a topic that advocates an action (e.g., to fix a problem or improve a situation).

Essays that set out to extol the benefits of something, for example, exercise, a clean environment, or a good diet, can also be difficult to present as an argument. You do not have a meaningful claim if your audience accepts an idea as obvious. *If you cannot think of a strong opposing view to the one you want to argue, consider revising the topic so that it is arguable, or choose another topic.*

Cost–Benefit Essays

When you set out to argue that one method or system is better than another—for example, that the flat tax system is better than the progressive tax system—you may find yourself considering the pros and cons of each in a point-by-point rebuttal, although your purpose at the outset would be to argue in favour of one side. You could also write a comparison and contrast *expository* essay on this topic, but in that case, you would set the essay up as a question to be considered (e.g., which system most benefits taxpayers in the middle-income bracket?) and use factual evidence to evaluate the question. There can be a fine line between an argumentative and an expository cost–benefit essay; therefore, it is necessary to clearly announce your purpose—argumentative/persuasive or investigating/explaining—in your claim.

Specific Claims

An overly broad or vague claim can be hard to support: "We need to change our attitude toward the environment"; "We need to do something about bullying." One way to make a broad claim more specific is to think about how it might apply to a subject you are knowledgeable about. For example, if you wanted to argue that the media promotes unhealthy weight loss in teenagers, a very big topic, and you were an athlete, you could consider what rules or procedures can lead to unhealthy weight loss in your sport. Many sports, such as rowing, have weight categories. In some provinces, the junior female lightweight category is 135 pounds and under. As a rower, you may be aware of unhealthy eating habits that can develop in rowers seeking to remain in a lower weight category in order to be competitive. Your thesis statement might take this specific form: *To help prevent unhealthy and dangerous eating habits in young rowers, junior lightweight categories should be eliminated from provincial regattas.*

A broad claim can also be made more specific (and manageable) if you can apply it to a particular group. It might be unwieldy to apply an anti-smoking claim to Canada or even to an entire province, since municipalities may have their own smoking bylaws; you might therefore restrict the focus to your city or even your campus.

Realistic Claims

Unrealistic claims are usually policy claims that have little chance of being implemented. One could argue for almost anything that would make life easier or that would fulfill a need, but if it is not realistic, the argument becomes moot. You may be able to muster some points in favour of a return to Prohibition or the legalization of all currently illegal drugs, but since such arguments would not take account of social conditions today, the claim would not be realistic. Unenforceable policy claims are also unrealistic.

Activity 9.1

In discussion groups, evaluate the 10 claims below, determining whether they would make good thesis statements for an argumentative essay. Are the claims arguable, specific, and realistic? If not, consider what changes would make them arguable. Revise them accordingly.

1. Cloning should be prohibited because it is wrong for humans to "play God."
2. In order to represent the interests of voters more accurately, give voters a wider selection of candidates, and provide a stronger voice for minority issues, the government should adopt the single transferable vote (STV) electoral model.
3. *The Simpsons* is a much funnier sitcom than *Family Guy*.
4. Having a Twitter account today is essential if you want to be successful in business.
5. The Wii is a more popular gaming system than the Xbox 360 or PlayStation 4.
6. Fighting should be banned from all levels of hockey.
7. Internet dating services are an innovative, convenient, and affordable alternative to the singles scene.
8. The culture of consumerism is responsible for many of the problems that our world faces today.
9. There need to be legal guidelines for genetic testing because it may threaten our privacy, lead to harmful gene therapy, and have dangerous social costs.
10. Because of the dangerousness of the sport utility vehicle, people should have to prove that they really need an SUV before being permitted to purchase one.

Connecting Claim to Evidence

Strong arguments do not simply consist of an arguable claim and supporting evidence: there needs to be a link between claim and evidence, showing why the evidence is relevant to or supports the claim. Philosopher Stephen Toulmin called this the warrant.

One way to test the logical connection between a claim and its support, then, is through the rationale for the claim, the warrant. If the warrant is self-evident to the reader, it does not have to be announced. The following warrant is clear without being stated:

> *Claim:* I have to buy a new watch.

> *Evidence:* My current watch says the same time as it did 30 minutes ago.

> *Warrant:* My watch is broken.

The evidence is sufficient support for the claim because the reader would infer the link ("My watch is broken"). On the other hand, if someone used the same claim and offered as evidence "I just bought a new outfit to attend a wedding," a reader or listener might ask what that had to do with buying a new watch. The speaker might then reply,

warrant

A link between claim and evidence, showing how the evidence is relevant to or supports the claim.

"I could never show up at a wedding with an accessory that didn't match the rest of my outfit!" which would be an attempt to link the claim to the evidence.

A warrant can arise from various sources, including physical laws, human laws, assumptions, premises, common knowledge, ethical principles, or, in the case of the fashionable wedding guest, above, aesthetic values. For an argument to be successful, the reader must agree with the warrant, whether stated or implied.

An underlying assumption of Daniel J. Dutton et al. in "A Ban on the Marketing of Foods/Beverages to Children" (p. 279 in Part III: The Reader) is expressed in the first sentence in which the authors claim that interventions are needed to improve human health outcomes. Clearly, the essay is not written for those who would disagree with the warrant—market-forces advocates, for example.

Consider the warrants in the following example in which the same evidence is used to support different claims. It is the underlying assumption, the warrant, which links evidence to the claim in each case.

Claim #1: More resources should be allocated to boost the survival rate of lung transplant recipients.

Warrant: The survival rate could be improved if we allocate more resources. (An assumption, it could be based on the economic principle that allocating more resources is likely to improve a result.)

Evidence: Just over 50 per cent of lung transplant recipients have a five-year survival rate.

Claim #2: Fewer resources should be allocated to lung transplants since the result is less promising than for other kinds of transplants in Canada.

Warrants: The survival rate does not justify the allocation of the present level of resources for this procedure. (This is an ethical principle.) The resources could be better allocated to help more people. (This is an economic principle.)

Evidence: Just over 50 per cent of lung transplant recipients have a five-year survival rate.

Activity 9.2

What warrant(s) could be used to connect the following claim to the evidence?

Claim #3: The allocation of resources for lung transplant recipients should be maintained at its present level.

Warrant(s): _____

_____

Evidence: Just over 50 per cent of lung transplant recipients have a five-year survival rate.

Kinds of Evidence in Argumentative Essays

Although an effective argument can be built around reasonable points with logical connections between them, specific kinds of evidence can bolster a claim. Some are more common to argument than to exposition, but most can be used in both.

For other kinds of evidence, some of which can be used in argument, see chapter 6, page 83.

Experts and Authorities

Experts are directly involved in the issue you are arguing. You will usually use expert testimony to support your claim; however, the occasional use of experts with whom you disagree can make your argument more balanced. One way to stress experts who agree with you is to cite them directly (direct quotation), while putting the ideas of opposing experts in your own words (summarization or paraphrase), ensuring that you do so accurately and fairly. Because academic writers are often experts in their chosen field, they may refer to their own studies throughout their papers. Doing so gives them credibility.

Authorities can also lend credibility by virtue of who they are and what they say: even if they do not have direct experience in the issue you are arguing, they may make the reader pay more attention to it. Citing Robert Louis Stevenson's comment that "politics is the only occupation for which no preparation is thought to be necessary" (p. 247) draws the reader's attention to the claim, which the author then refutes.

Examples and Illustrations

Using examples can make a general claim more concrete and understandable, enabling the reader to relate to it. An illustration could take the form of an *anecdote* (a brief informal story) or other expanded example. In his essay "The Ugly Canadian" (p. 192 in Part III: The Reader), Amir Attaran begins by relating the story of two kidnapped Canadian diplomats; the expanded example leads directly to his thesis concerning Canada's international reputation. John Ralston Saul uses examples in the body paragraphs of his essay "Listen to the North," (p. 216), developing them extensively to help support his claim (see paragraphs 16–24).

Precedents

In law, a precedent is an important kind of example: to *set a precedent* means to establish a procedure for dealing with future cases. In argument, appealing to precedents—the way something was done in the past—can be particularly effective in policy claims. To use a precedent, you must show (1) that the current situation (what you are arguing) is similar to that of the precedent, and (2) that following the precedent will be beneficial. (Of course, you can use a precedent as a negative example as well, showing that it was not beneficial.)

Precedents can be used to argue controversial issues, such as decriminalizing marijuana or prostitution or providing universal access to post-secondary education. Timothy Krahn ("Where Are We Going with Preimplantation Genetic Diagnosis?," page 366 in Part III: The Reader) makes it clear in his first paragraph why he intends to use the precedent of British policy on preimplantation genetic diagnosis.

precedent
A kind of example that refers to the way a situation was dealt with in the past in order to argue for its similar use in the present.

Personal Experience

The selective use of personal experience in argumentative essays can involve your reader and can increase your credibility; for example, if you have worked with street people, you may be seen as better qualified to argue a claim about homelessness. Personal experience could take the form of direct experience, of observing something first-hand, or of reporting on something that happened to a friend.

However, some kinds of personal experience are less successful. Simply announcing that you experienced something and benefited by it does not necessarily make your argument stronger; for example, saying that you enjoyed physical education classes in high school is not going to convince many people that it should be a required subject in schools.

Facts, Statistics, and Scientific Studies

Policy claims can often benefit from factual support. Use the most current statistics available from the most reliable sources. Be especially wary of sources that do not reveal where they obtained their facts. Sources need to be acknowledged in your essay; your citations will reveal both the currency and the reliability of the source. Referring to a fact, statistic, or study that is outdated or otherwise lacking authority can damage your credibility (see "Issues of Credibility," page 83).

Two Kinds of Reasoning

inductive reasoning
Reasoning that relies on facts, details, and observations to draw a conclusion.

deductive reasoning
Reasoning based on a generalization, which is applied to a specific instance to draw a conclusion.

syllogism
A logical three-part structure that can be used to illustrate how deductive conclusions are made.

Two methods of reasoning are inductive and deductive reasoning. In inductive reasoning, you arrive at a probable truth by observing and recording specific occurrences. Flaws in inductive reasoning can occur if not enough observations have been made—that is, the evidence is insufficient to make a generalization—or if the method for gathering the evidence is faulty. Thus, researchers try to include as large a sample as possible within the population they draw from; this makes their findings more reliable (see Appendix A, "A Note on Statistics" page 403). Similarly, researchers reveal the details of their experiment's methodology. They need to show that their evidence-gathering methods are logical and unbiased.

While inductive reasoning works from detail to generalization, deductive reasoning begins with a major premise, which can be summed up by a general statement assumed to be true. A second premise, which is a subset or instance of the major premise, is then applied to the major premise. If both statements are, in fact, true and logically related, the conclusion follows as true. The way deductive reasoning works can be shown by the syllogism, a three-part structure in which a conclusion is valid because both premises are true and are logically related:

Major premise: All students who wish to apply for admission to the university must submit their grade transcripts.

Minor premise: Deanna wishes to apply for admission to the university.

Conclusion: Deanna must submit her grade transcripts.

Using Reason in Arguments

Most arguments will require you to reason both inductively and deductively. Inductive reasoning could involve the following:

- using factual and statistical evidence
- ensuring that your sources are credible, such as peer-reviewed articles
- providing an adequate number of supporting points

Deductive reasoning could involve the following:

- making appropriate and valid generalizations
- ensuring that your audience would agree with them
- ensuring that generalizations are logically connected to your specific points

Whatever the purpose in arguing—whether to settle an issue, expose a problem, or reach a compromise—it is vital that the reader believes you have presented enough evidence and that your claims are valid. Although using specific argumentative strategies is important (see page 113), *most successful arguments begin and end with your effective use of reason* or what Aristotle called appeals to logic, logos (see chapter 8, "The Active Voice: Rhetorical Analysis: What, Why, and How").

However, reason can also be misused in arguments. Consider the following statements. The first illustrates the misuse of inductive reasoning because there is inadequate evidence to justify the conclusion; the second illustrates the misuse of deductive reasoning because a false premise has resulted in a faulty conclusion. Avoiding logical fallacies (failures in reasoning) in your own essays and pointing them out in the arguments of others will make your arguments stronger and more credible.

> The premier broke a promise he made during his election campaign. He is a liar, and his word can no longer be trusted.

It is not reasonable to distrust a politician because he broke one promise. If the premier broke several promises, there would be much stronger grounds for the conclusion. Thus, in most people's minds, there is not enough inductive evidence to support the claim. Furthermore, politicians do not always deliver on their pre-election promises (this could almost be considered a generalization peculiar to campaigning politicians!); thus, the statement also shows faulty deductive reasoning.

> Eduardo is the only one in our family who has a PhD. He is obviously the one who inherited all the brains.

Major premise: Possessing a PhD means you are very intelligent.

Minor premise: Eduardo possesses a PhD.

Conclusion: Eduardo is very intelligent.

Possessing an advanced degree could be partly a measure of intelligence; it could also indicate persistence, a fascination with a particular subject, a love of learning, inspiring teachers, an ambitious nature, strong financial and/or familial support, and so on.

Failures in Reasoning

logical fallacies
Categories of faulty reasoning.

Errors in reasoning fall into several categories, termed logical fallacies. To argue effectively and to recognize weak arguments when you read them, it is not necessary to be able to categorize every failure in logic. Most errors are the result of sloppy or simplistic thinking—the failure to do justice to the complexity of an issue (sometimes deliberate in the case of conscious distortions, but often unconscious). Developing your critical-thinking skills will make you alert to errors of logic. A few examples of fallacious reasoning follow:

- *Oversimplification:* An arguer may consider only two possibilities, one of which may be clearly unacceptable (*either/or fallacy*):

  If you do not get a university degree, you might as well resign yourself to low-paying jobs.

- *Cause–effect fallacy:* Among the many cause–effect fallacies is the one that argues a claim on the basis of a coincidental (non-causal) relationship between two occurrences:

  Re-elect your prime minister; the economy grew by 4 per cent while she was in office.

- *Slippery slope fallacy:* The arguer claims that a challenge to the status quo will lead to a breakdown of social order or of human values; it has been used as an argument against such practices as euthanasia, legalizing marijuana, and the screening of embryos. Of course, arguments can be made against these issues, but using "slippery slope" logic does not make for a sound argument:

  If gay marriage is legalized, the next thing people will want to do is marry their pets!

- *Circular reasoning:* An arguer may assume something is true simply by citing the premise as if it validated the claim, for example by appealing to a premise that has yet to be proven:

  I'm an "A" student. How can the teacher give me a B– on the assignment?

- *Irrelevance:* One type of fallacy of irrelevance is a non sequitur—literally, "it does not follow"—as the "evidence" (supposed questionable personal conduct) has no logical connection with the claim (trustworthiness as a public official); it does not *follow from* the claim:

He can't be trusted for public office. After all, he admitted to an extramarital affair.

Another fallacy of irrelevance is *name-dropping*, citing a famous person as if his or her personal opinion can have the strength of evidence; in the *guilt by association fallacy*, the arguer uses the fact that some allegedly disreputable person or group supports a view as an argument against it (or opposes it as an argument in its favour).

- *False analogy:* In a false analogy, you make a comparison between two things that are not comparable because they are, in fact, not alike or they differ greatly in one respect. In the heat of the moment (see "Emotional fallacies" below), people sometimes compare a perpetrator of a minor crime to Adolf Hitler or another bona fide tyrant. In the example below, the writer compares animals in zoos to those in people's homes. Calling pet owners "hypocrites" is also an example of slanted language (see below):

People who complain about zoo animals but who also own pets are nothing but hypocrites.

- *Slanted language:* An arguer may use highly charged language to dismiss an opponent's claims. Simply characterizing an opponent as "ignorant" or "greedy" serves no constructive purpose. Of course, you may be able to show through unbiased evidence that the opponent has demonstrated these characteristics.

- *Emotional fallacies:* These statements appeal to the emotions of a reader in a manipulative or unfair way, such as a partisan appeal, guilt by association, name-calling (*ad hominem*), or dogmatism (simply asserting something without offering proof—often, over and over). They are very different from legitimate appeals to emotion:

Don't believe the claims of those neo-liberals. They just want to take your hard-earned money away from you. (partisan appeal)

A common emotional fallacy is the *bandwagon*, which asserts that because something is popular, it has value:

All my friends' parents give them unrestricted curfews on Friday nights.

Giving Life to Logic: Strategies for Argument

Although effective arguments depend heavily on the use of reasonable claims supported by convincing evidence, logic alone will not necessarily convince readers to change their minds or adopt the writer's point of view. Student writers should consider using the following strategies, depending on topic, purpose, and audience, to shape a logical and appealing argument, one that will make readers more responsive to the claim.

Dramatic introductions: Dramatic introductions are used more often in argument than in exposition, because they may enable the reader to relate to a human situation or to set a scene. For example, the first-person introductory paragraph by Mitch Miyagawa in "A Sorry State" (page 231 in part III, The Reader) introduces the author's family conflicts, appropriate in an essay that shows how racist decisions can disrupt families' lives. For a dramatic opening in "Doping Is a Threat to Sporting Excellence" (page 358 in part III, The Reader), John William Devine uses a direct quotation which concisely summarizes the main point of the argument to which he is responding.

Establishing common ground: Getting your readers to see that you share many of their values enables you to come across as open and approachable, making them potentially more receptive to your argument. Although familiarity with your audience is important in knowing where your values and those of your audience intersect, you can assume that most readers will respond favourably to universal qualities like generosity, decency, security, and a healthy and peaceful environment. The common ground strategy can be considered a form of ethical appeal.

Making concessions: In granting concessions, you acknowledge the validity of an opposing point, demonstrating your fairness and willingness to accept other views, at least in part. After conceding a point, you should follow with a strong point of your own. In effect, you are giving some ground in an effort to get the reader to do the same. The concession can be made in a dependent clause and your own point in the independent clause that follows: "Although it is valid to say. . . [concession is made], the fact is . . . [your point]."

Concessions can be vital in cases in which there is a strong opposition or in which you wish to reach a compromise. Simon N. Young makes a concession in the first paragraph of his essay "Universities, Governments and Industry: Can the Essential Nature of Universities Survive the Drive to Commercialize?" (p. 171), acknowledging a positive change in the direction that universities are taking before mentioning what he sees as a recent, more damaging change.

Appeal to reader interests: When you appeal to the interests of your readers, you show how they might be affected by your claim. For example, in a policy claim, you might show how they could benefit by the implementation of a particular policy—how it will be good for them—or what costs might result if it is not implemented—how it will be bad for them. Arguing in favour of a costly social program may be a hard sell to those whose approval and support are vital, such as business leaders. Therefore, you could explain how the program could benefit these leaders—for example, by helping to prevent a bigger problem, such as increased health-care costs or taxes. If you know the values and motivations of your readers, you may be able to use this knowledge to make your points directly relevant to them.

Emotional and ethical appeals: While dramatic openings can be successful in many argumentative essays, the success of an opening that includes an appeal to emotion depends greatly on your audience. Beginning an essay on animal testing by describing a scene of caged animals at a slaughterhouse may alienate neutral readers. If you do use such an opening, you need to ensure that a typical reader will respond in the way you wish. Emotional and ethical appeals, however, are commonly used in conclusions. They provide an effective coda, a final way that the audience can reflect on the topic. In the following conclusion, student writer Mary McQueen appeals

common ground

An argumentative strategy in which you show readers that you share many of their values, making you appear open and approachable.

concession

An argumentative strategy in which you concede or qualify a point, acknowledging its validity, in order to come across as fair and reasonable.

Appeals are designed to evoke emotional or ethical (morally grounded) responses from your reader.

For more about Aristotle's three appeals, see chapter 8, pages 95–97.

to landlords in order to subtly reinforce her claim advocating a more open policy toward pets in apartments:

> The human/animal bond is special and worth preserving and promoting. Landlords who allow pets make an important, generous contribution towards the solution of the pet-friendly housing problem and have the opportunity to make the partnerships of landlords, tenants, and companion animals so successful that they become role models to inspire others around the community, the province, and the country.

In the cases of neutral or opposing viewpoints, emotional and ethical appeals work best when they are subtle, not overstated. In the example above, the writer indirectly evokes the emotional bond that many owners have with their pets, showing how landlords can contribute to this bond. Ethical appeals focus on issues like fairness, equality, responsibility, and the like. Thus, the example also demonstrates a subtle ethical appeal since it evokes a hierarchical relationship (landlord and tenant) based on the demonstration of ethical qualities like respect. For examples of argumentative strategies in practice, see Sample Argumentative Essay with Annotations, page 124.

Refutation Strategies

In a refutation, or *rebuttal*, you show the weaknesses or limitations of opposing claims. Here are three general strategies to consider. Which one you use depends on the three factors that you need to take into account when planning your argumentative essay: your topic, purpose, and audience. There may be additional factors involved too, such as essay length.

refutation
An argumentative strategy of raising opposing points in order to counter them with your own points.

Acknowledgement

You may need to do no more than simply acknowledge the opposing view, for example if the argument on the other side is straightforward or obvious. In the case of arguing for more open policies toward pets (above), the position of landlords is simple: allowing pets increases the potential for property damage. After acknowledging the competing claim, the writer would go on to raise strong points that counter this claim without necessarily referring to it again.

If your argumentative purpose is to raise awareness of an important issue, as Robert Gifford does in "Psychology's Essential Role in Alleviating the Impacts of Climate Change" (p. 376 in Part III: The Reader), there may be no clear opposing view to refute. In his introduction, Gifford clearly states his thesis that psychology "has an important role to play in easing the pain caused by climate change" and that his essay is necessary because "the thesis is not broadly acknowledged." In most arguments, however, one of the two strategies below can be used.

Refutations can range from simply acknowledging the opposing viewpoint to focusing on one or two main opposing points to a systematic point-by-point critique. The refutation strategy you choose depends on your topic, your purpose in arguing, and your audience.

Limited Rebuttal

In a limited rebuttal, you raise and respond to the major point(s) on the other side, then follow with your own points without mentioning minor competing claims. One obvious reason for using a limited rebuttal is that in a short essay, you will not have space to respond to all the competing claims. This strategy may also be appropriate if the strength of the opposing view is anchored by one or perhaps two very significant claims. You would not want to give strength to the other side by raising and refuting less important issues unless you are trying to reach a compromise when both strengths and weaknesses might be considered. When you are analyzing the main argument on the other side, however, it is important to represent that position fairly, for example, by using concessions.

Whether you adopt the limited rebuttal strategy can depend on your audience and purpose for arguing. For example, if your audience is only generally knowledgeable about an issue, mentioning less important points on the other side might be counter-productive since they might not have been aware of them.

Full Rebuttal

There are two ways to organize a full rebuttal. You may systematically raise competing claims and respond to them one at a time (*point-by-point rebuttal*). Although concessions could be involved, especially if your purpose is to arrive at a compromise, usually you point out the flaws in each before responding with your counterclaim. Alternatively, you could summarize the competing claims before you present the support for your claim, right after your introduction or after you have presented that support, just before your conclusion (*block rebuttal*).

Point-by-point rebuttals can be very effective if the competing claims of an argument are well known, if there is strong opposition to your claim, or if you are critiquing a text, as is Joel Lexchin in "Pharmaceutical Innovation: Can We Live Forever? A Commentary on Schnittker and Karandinos" (p. 354 in Part III: The Reader). If your argumentative purpose is to reach a compromise, you might also choose to use the point-by-point strategy. Here, however, you would be attempting to reach out to the other side (or both sides), showing that you understand the points that define their position. This strategy would demonstrate your knowledge and fairness.

The paragraph below illustrates the effective use of the point-by-point strategy in an essay on mandatory physical education classes in high school. Notice how student writer Meghan Cannon skilfully uses a concession (second sentence, italicized) to help turn a competing claim into a point in her favour:

> Some individuals argue against mandatory physical education because they believe that many teenagers feel self-conscious about their bodies and, therefore, self-conscious about physical activity. *While the initiation of physical activity may be difficult for one suffering from body image issues, the long-term effect is invariably one of satisfaction.* Students learn to appreciate what they can do with their bodies instead of being completely concerned with how it looks. Physical activity promotes self-awareness and acceptance. Self-confidence soars from participation in sport and the social interaction induced by sport.

Organizing Your Argument

order of points
The way in which points are presented in an essay. Climax order is the order of points that proceeds from the weakest to the strongest; other orders include inverted climax order and mixed order.

For most argumentative essays, deciding on your order of points will mean choosing between two options: the *climax order* or a *mixed order*. In the first, you begin with the weakest point and build toward the strongest; in the second, you could begin with a strong point—but not the strongest—follow with weaker points, and conclude with the strongest. It may not be advisable to begin with the weakest point if your audience opposes your claim, since an initial weak point may make your readers believe your entire argument is weak. Other orders are also possible. For example, if you are arguing to reach a compromise, you might need to focus the first part of your essay on one side of the debate, the second part on the opposite side, and the third on your compromise solution.

There is nothing wrong in ending with your weakest point either (*inverted climax order*), although some advise against it. If you have presented a strong argument, a weaker concluding point is not necessarily going to undo your work. The last point could contain something humorous, anecdotal, or personal, for example, and serve as a fitting transition to a strong conclusion. If you use an expanded thesis statement, follow the same order of points in your body paragraphs.

Whichever rebuttal strategy you use, you should consider outlining the points on the other side before writing the essay. Consider how someone who disagreed with your claim might respond to your main points. This could reveal the strengths on the other side and any weaknesses in your own argument. More important, perhaps, it should serve to keep the opposing view in focus as you write, causing you to reflect carefully on what you are saying and how you say it.

Collaborative Exercise 9.2
The Audience Plan

Taking the audience factor into account is very important as you prepare to write an argumentative essay. Constructing an audience plan will enable you to consider your approach to the essay, including the kinds of strategies to use. Team up with two other students and interview the other members of your group to determine their knowledge level, their interest level, and their orientation toward your position (agree, disagree, neutral, or mixed); they will serve as your "audience," the basis for an audience profile. Then, use this information to construct an audience plan based on your specific audience, your topic, and argumentative purpose. Discuss strategies you would use to persuade this audience. Include your topic and your writing purpose in the plan.

Readers could agree with your argumentative claim, disagree with it, be neutral, or be composed of some who agree and some who disagree. The makeup of your audience will help determine which argumentative strategies are the most effective ones for your essay.

Sample Student Argumentative Essay (APA Citation Style)

Consider the following questions while reading Simone Chiang's argumentative essay on rape culture.

1. After reading the introduction, consider Chiang's argumentative purpose and her audience.
2. In her introduction, identify (a) a concession; (b) her thesis and the form it takes.
3. How does defining rape (par. 5) help her argument? Why does she not accept the definition verbatim?
4. Consider the kinds of evidence and/or rhetorical patterns used in paragraph 6.
5. What argumentative strategies does Chiang use in her conclusion? Are they effective?

Rape Culture: Its Manifestation in Fraternities and Similar Micro-level Environments in Universities

by Simone Chiang

1   In recent events, the topic of rape within fraternities has come to prominence. Although not all fraternities should be stigmatized, news stories and studies have shown rape's prevalence within these micro-societies. Bohmer and Parrot (1993) boldly express that "the men who are most likely to rape in college are fraternity pledges" (p. 21). Even though rape occurs throughout society, what factors specifically give fraternities such a reputation? Exploring the facets of rape culture can help us determine why it seems especially prevalent in fraternities and similar "brotherhood" communities. The essay will present two recent rape-related cases that exemplify the problem in question. The terms "rape" and "rape culture" will then be clarified to provide context for the investigation of rape culture's perpetuation in the psychology of fraternity members, and the ways in which universities, indeed all of society, should respond to such incidents. By becoming aware of the cultural factors, we can take steps to educate the perpetrators and the general public, reducing these troubling occurrences among youth.

2   In 2010, a rape case from Connecticut, known as the "Wesleyan University Rape Factory," became national news. A female freshman, referred to as Jane Doe, was raped at a Beta Theta Pi fraternity Halloween party. Doe is now pressing charges against her sexual offender, as well as Wesleyan University itself. The reason behind Doe's legal action against Wesleyan does not lie in its association with the Beta Theta Pi fraternity, allegedly known as the "rape factory" on campus; rather, it lies in the university's failure to prevent, sympathize, or assist. Before her entrance to Wesleyan, an email was sent to the student body warning them that their safety could not be ensured in the vicinities of the Beta Theta Pi fraternity house. However, Jane Doe enrolled the following semester and never received such a notification. Then, when she reported the rape to her Resident Advisor (R.A.), the R.A. did not report the case to the police nor refer Doe to any type of counseling considered appropriate in such traumatic events. Finally, when Doe's true identity was leaked onto campus after pressing charges, other students harassed her for getting Beta Theta Pi in trouble while Wesleyan did little more than spectate (Kingkade, 2013).

3   Unfortunately, this incident is just one of the many rape-related occurrences that take place at colleges and universities annually. Canada has had similar occurrences as well. In September 2013, there was public uproar when a disturbing, rape-promoting chant leaked onto social media during a University of British Columbia (UBC) Sauder School of Business Frosh event. Variations of this chant, with lyrics such as "UBC boys we like them young. Y is for your sister. O is for oh-so-tight. U is for underage. N is for no consent. G is for grab that ass," also caused controversy at Halifax's University of Saint Mary where it was also recited (CBC News, 2013, para. 19). Despite acknowledging the chant's offensive nature, the UBC Fact Finding Report (as cited in Strapageil, 2013) reveals that frosh leaders encouraged first-years to take part in the chant to "take [them] out of their comfort zone and bring them together" (par. 11). A Sauder student stated the chant was a "brotherhood type of thing" (para. 10).

4   Though there are large variations between the Wesleyan University "rape factory" case and the UBC rape chant scandal, these stories bear two fundamental similarities. First, both rape-related events took place at universities within micro-level environments—one a fraternity, the other a similar "brotherhood" setting. Moreover, while one directly involved

rape, and the other did not, both stories contain attitudes or components that perpetuate a rape culture.

5   Although "rape" is a common term, it is in need of clarification to provide context for the discussion of rape culture in fraternities. Most people identify rape as "unwanted penetration by force or threat of force" (Cullen, Fisher, & Turner, 2006, p. 8). While accurate, this definition's simplicity reduces rape's magnitude and neglects its less obvious forms. The law states that any sexual activity with a woman who is incapable of giving consent is legally rape (Fisher, Krebs, Lindquist, Martin, & Warner, 2007, p. ix). Penetration can be obtained through physical force and threats of physical harm, but also through emotional manipulation and incapacitation through alcohol or drug use (Peterson & Strang, 2013, p. 3370). In fraternity rape scenarios, victims are more often incapacitated than coerced with force (Krebs et al., 2007, p. vii). While rape can be performed by both genders and on each gender, this essay examines rape in fraternities by focusing on male attacker and female victim relationships.

6   The term "rape culture" is even harder to define. If culture is identified as the ways that a society operates based on attitudes, beliefs, customs and rituals that its members perceive as the norm, then rape culture is the complex set of values and beliefs that provide an environment conductive to rape and present them as a norm. These sets of values and beliefs are sometimes nestled into the subconscious of society, and many do not notice or refuse to recognize its presence (Fletcher, 2010, p. 1). Some examples of rape culture involve the glorification of violence, the trivialization of rape, victim blaming, the degradation of women, the insinuation that rape is a compliment, as well as making a victim feel tainted or ashamed after an assault. Ernhart and Sandler (as cited in Sanday, 1990, p. 3) reported multiple stories of rape in fraternities where few of the perpetrators were prosecuted; the victim was blamed for placing herself in compromising social situations, implying that the male adolescents had no control over their hormones. Both Sanday and Fletcher (2010) emphasize that male sexual aggression is not human nature, but a product of social ideologies: if a girl is dressed provocatively and incapacitated, it should not be "expected" that men will take advantage of her. The attitude of "boys will be boys," "she deserved it," or "she wanted it" exemplify the essence of rape culture. In the Wesleyan University case, the R.A. and the university trivialized rape in their failure to treat Doe's rape with urgency and sympathy while fellow students ridiculed and shamed the victim for coming forward. Likewise, the UBC rape chant glorified rape and trivialized the serious subject matter by treating it as a joke.

7   Although rape culture is woven throughout society, recent events and past studies show its concentration in fraternities. Several studies have examined the psychology behind fraternity behaviour to explain its spike in rape and rape-conducive activity. Hummer and Martin (1989) found that the social construction of fraternities emphasizes a narrow idea of masculinity and an equally stereotypical view of femininity (p. 469). In their interviews with various fraternity members, they found these constricted views lead to the commodification of women; members admitted to intentionally "[using] women as bait for new members, as servers of brothers' needs, and as sexual prey" (p. 466). Sanday (1990) found that these narrow-minded ideals pervert the inherent human longing to fit in. Like most human beings, a prevalent factor in fraternity members' psyches is the desire to belong and feel accepted; however, she asserted that men use the sharing of exaggerated sexual boasting to feel accepted and included by brothers (p. 18). In addition to the macho perception of masculinity, Hall and LaFrance's (2007) study noted that extreme homophobia is commonly found in fraternities; therefore, excessive displays of sexual intercourse are used to prove

heterosexuality as a measure of manhood. In a later study, they explain that "the desire to be accepted by a masculine group manifests itself in a fear of being perceived as gay" (Hall & LaFrance, 2012, p. 44). Finally, Sanday (1990) observed that members sometimes watch gang-bang pornography in a group setting as a means to brotherhood bonding. She condemned this communal activity as it not only causes desensitization to violent sexual interactions but also skews their view of reality and implies that such acts are normal sexual experiences. "Pulling train," a fraternity practice of "men lining up like train cars to take turns having sex with the same woman" (p. 1), are notable products of such ways of thinking. Thus, the warped model of masculinity, paired with the need for belonging and the desensitization to reality's morals, appears to be main reasons for the manifestation of rape culture in fraternities.

8   The way in which universities deal with such inappropriate discourses could also play a role in perpetuating rape culture. Like Wesleyan, many universities have been reported to virtually ignore rape reports to protect their image (Sanday, 1990, p. 14; DeKeseredy & Schwartz, 1997, p. 6), and waive fraternities and athletic teams of student violation penalties (Cullen, Fisher, & Karjane, 2002, p. xiii). Sanday (1990) found fraternities monopolize their privileged status, as university administrators do not want to oppose the many wealthy and politically important alumni who commonly support these communities (p. 27). Two main implications lie in a university's decision to spectate instead of take action: empowerment of the attacker and belittlement of the victim. Without reprimanding the perpetrator for his actions, it allows him, as well as others, to deem such actions acceptable or even normal. In addition, when such lack of empathy is shown, the victim's feelings of violation are belittled; she subconsciously receives the message to ignore her feelings, and the wrongdoings are trivialized. Essentially, when a university ignores a victim or undermines the magnitude of the situation, the attacker's actions are inadvertently encouraged, and victim shaming resonates.

9   While rape is not exclusive to fraternities, nor are most fraternity members rapists, rape culture is magnified in such "brotherhood" environments. Fraternities provide micro-level societies in which members can be removed from reality and its morals, resulting in skewed views of masculinity and commodification of women. When a university turns a blind eye to such inappropriate behaviour, it can feed the attacker's distorted sense of morals and inadvertently shift blame onto the victim. Educators, including university administrators, have a constructive role to play by helping to provide an environment in which all genders are respected: they can send the message that such behaviour, whether directly or indirectly expressed, will not be tolerated. Perhaps with a better understanding of rape culture and its manifestation in fraternities, studies and programs can be put into place to reduce, if not stop, the outflow of stories like the Wesleyan rape factory and the UBC rape chant. Universities are expected to provide model for social progress and enlightened thinking. By responding quickly and decisively to the "culture of rape" when it declares itself, universities will show commitment to this ideal.

References

Bohmer, C., & Parrot, A. (1993). *Sexual assault on campus: The problem and the solution*. New York, NY: Lexington.

CBC News. (2013, September 18). UBC promises "lasting change" following rape chant. *CBC News*. Retrieved from http://www.cbc.ca/news/canada/british-columbia/ubc-promises-lasting-change-following-rape-chant-1.1859234

Cullen, F.T., Fisher, B.S., & Karjane, H.M. (2002). Campus sexual assault: Institutions of higher education respond. Washington, DC: [funded and made available by] U.S. Department of Justice.

Cullen, F.T., Fisher, B.S., & Turner, M.G. (2006). *The sexual victimization of college women*. Washington, DC: National Institute of Justice, U.S. Department of Justice.

DeKeseredy, W.S., Schwartz, M.D. (1997). *Sexual assault on the college campus: The role of male peer support*. Thousand Oaks, CA: SAGE Publications.

Fisher, B.S., Krebs, P., Lindquist, C.H., Martin, S.L., & Warner, T.D. (2007). *The campus sexual assault (CSA) study*. Washington, DC: [funded and made available but not published by] U.S. Department of Justice.

Fletcher, P. (2010). Dismantling rape culture around the world: A social justice imperative. *Forum on Public Policy Online, 2010* (4), 1–14. Retrieved from http://forumonpublicpolicy.com/vol2010.no4/archive.vol2010.no4/fletcher.pdf

Hall, J., & LaFrance, B. (2007). Attitudes and communication of homophobia in fraternities: Separating the impact of social adjustment function from hetero-identity concern. *Communication Quarterly, 55*(1), 39–60. doi: 10.1080/01463370600998673

Hall, J., & LaFrance, B. (2012). "That's gay": Sexual prejudice, gender identity, norms, and homophobic communication. *Communication Quarterly, 60*(1), 35–58. doi: 10.1080/01463373.2012.641833

Hummer, R., & Martin, P. (1989). Fraternities and rape on campus. *Gender and Society, 3*(4), 457–473. doi: 10.1177/089124389003004004

Kingkade, T. (2013, September 11). Wesleyan, fraternity settle 'rape factory' lawsuit on undisclosed terms. The Huffington Post. Retrieved from http://www.huffingtonpost.com/2013/09/11/wesleyan-rape-lawsuit-settlement_n_3908416.html

Peterson, Z., & Strang, E. (2013). The relationship among perceived peer acceptance of sexual aggression, punishment certainty, and sexually aggressive behavior. *Journal of Interpersonal Violence, 28*(18), 3369–3385. doi: 10.1177/0886260513502126

Sanday, P. (1990). *Fraternity gang rape: Sex, brotherhood, and privilege on campus*. New York, NY: New York University Press.

Strapageil, L. (2013, September 18). UBC frosh rape chant report released. *Canada.com*. Retrieved from http://o.canada.com/news/ubc-frosh-rape-chant-report-released/

For examples of essays in *The Active Reader* that use argument, see Classification of Readings by Rhetorical Mode/Pattern (inside back cover).

Using Critical Thinking to Analyze Arguments

Analyzing an argument involves a similar approach to that of analyzing an essay, as discussed in Chapter 8. However, while a rhetorical analysis breaks down an essay to look at its rhetorical features, which *may* include Aristotle's three appeals—logos, pathos, and ethos—a critical analysis breaks down the argument; in writing a critical analysis, you determine whether the argument is successful (or not) and why. A critical analysis of an argumentative essay, then, should focus on the hows and whys of the author's argument. It should not be used as a forum for expressing your personal agreement or disagreement with the author's opinions.

Literary writers do not necessarily stop to think about specific techniques, such as imagery or metaphors, as they write. Similarly, the techniques of argument are ingrained in experienced writers, and they are not always conscious of their persuasive strategies. However, student writers, like student arguers, benefit the most if they are consciously aware of the techniques used by successful writers (arguers). To produce a thorough and effective argument, then, it is necessary to be familiar with the *language* of argument. This also applies when you analyze someone's argument.

The Language of Argument

The following terms relevant to argument have been discussed in this or previous chapters. Using them, where appropriate, in analyzing an argument will not only enable you to explain your points clearly but also add to your credibility as an analyzer:

General Terms

claim (value, policy, and interpretation), page 105
credibility, page 83
deductive reasoning, page 110
inductive reasoning, page 110
purpose (argumentative), page 102

Kinds of Evidence

analogy, page 17
anecdotal evidence, page 109
authorities/expert opinion, page 109
examples/illustrations, page 109
precedent, page 109

Strategies

appeal to reader interests, page 114
common ground, page 114
comparison, page 81
concession, page 114
definition, page 81
emotional appeal, page 114
ethical appeal, page 114
rebuttal (acknowledgement, limited, full), page 115

Fallacies

logical and emotional fallacies, page 112
slanted language, page 113

The kind of critical analysis that breaks down an argument is structured like the rhetorical analysis, discussed in chapter 8 (see "Organizing a Rhetorical Analysis," page 97).

The following is a student critical analysis of "Universities, Governments and Industry: Can the Essential Nature of Universities Survive the Drive to Commercialize?" by Simon Young (p. 171 in Part III: The Reader). The writer uses MLA style (see chapter 10).

A Critical Analysis of "Universities, Governments and Industry: Can the Essential Nature of Universities Survive the Drive to Commercialize?" by Simon N. Young

by Taylor Lingl

1   In "Universities, Governments and Industry," Simon Young exposes the pressure to commercialize in post-secondary education. Young mentions many of the changes and trends in the nature of universities, both good and bad. However, he focuses on what he considers the most threatening: the government use of universities for short-term economic gain (197). To his audience of educators, administrators, and students, Young explains how the university grants have become favorably distributed to those researching matters of economic worth. With his strong opinion against this commercialization, he proposes the idea that the average university teacher is changing from creative researcher to commercial entrepreneur (198). His ideas form a very effective critique, which is strengthened by the use of definitions, strong ethical appeal, credibility, and effective reasoning.

2   Young opens his essay with the *Oxford English Dictionary* definition of the word "university" which consists, in part, of a "whole body of teachers and scholars engaged in the higher branches of learning" (197). Though "university" is a familiar word, Young uses this definition to his advantage by setting up the image of an ideal university, and prepares the reader for its use throughout the essay. In his closing paragraphs, Young proposes a new definition based on the changing values of these universities. The definition that he finds suitable is "a whole body of teachers and scholars engaged in turning ideas into profit" (200). The sense of sarcasm is quite apparent, which can create an inappropriate or combative tone, depending on the reader. However, by using such contrasting definitions, he develops strength for his argument, which triumphs over a questionable tone.

3   Throughout the essay, Young makes good use of ethical appeals by providing a strong basis to evoke morally grounded responses from the reader. One application of this moral consciousness can be seen when he states that "curiosity-driven research will always tend to serve the best interests of patients," and concludes by saying that "the biggest losers from the pressure to commercialize will be psychiatric patients" (199). This universal quality of decency establishes common ground, and enables Young to come across to the reader as open and approachable.

4   Young proves his credibility by promoting his knowledge and by displaying fairness in his argument. He opens the article by stating that he has spent 40 years in universities. He goes on in the first paragraph to make concessions to the other side, stating that many changes in the nature of universities are actually commendable, such as the raise in proportion of the population attending (196). By granting this concession he is able to demonstrate his willingness to accept other views, while following with a statement that reveals his own view about today's universities as the more damaging change. To add to his credibility, Young uses sources effectively and backs up claims with proper substantiation. Throughout the essay he uses reputable authorities such as the Association of Universities and Colleges of Canada, the Canadian Association of University Teachers, and the Society for Neuroscience to support his argument.

Lingl uses an abbreviated form of the title. However, a better practice is to use the full title on first reference and an abbreviated title on successive ones; ask your instructor if you're uncertain. She uses many specific references to the text she is analyzing. As she has named the author in her first sentence, she doesn't need to repeat the name in her citation.

The student efficiently combines concerns with the audience, topic, and Young's stance in one sentence before her detailed yet concise thesis statement (last sentence).

Lingl draws attention to Young's use of definition as a basis for his argument.

Being aware of audience is important in analyses.

The next two paragraphs focus on analysis, not summary. They also demonstrate the writer's familiarity with various argumentative strategies: ethical appeals, common ground, concessions, and authorities.

Rather than touch briefly on several features, the writer selects only a few *representative* ones and uses critical thinking to analyze them. Here she explains the use of deductive reasoning in a specific paragraph. She makes it clear that her example is *representative* of Young's argument throughout.

5   Young's method of development and use of effective reasoning are strongly demonstrated in paragraph 9. In this paragraph, he uses deductive reasoning by beginning with a generalization and applying a concrete example. He opens with a quote from the Canadian Association of University Teachers stating, "the future of academic medicine is in danger" (198). From here, he incorporates a specific example of the treatment and prevention of depression, and proves that the unprofitable natural products and strategies receive little attention (199). He succeeds in producing a reasonable and valid generalization.

Young's inconclusive ending could just as easily be seen as a weakness. However, the writer explains why she sees it as a strength.

6   In the final paragraph, Young strongly reiterates his concern for the problem but expresses little hope for a positive ending. He makes reference to charitable organizations, one of the only sources of funding that maintain the sole purpose of providing benefits to society. However, he goes on to admit that though they are able to avoid the move to commercialization, they will have little effect on combatting it (200). By finishing up without a concrete solution, Young succeeds at making the problem even more paramount.

7   In conclusion, Young's essay presents an interesting view into the changing nature of universities. He succeeds in exposing the problems that have developed due to commercialization. Young combines strongly supported evidence and credibility with definitions and moral reasoning to construct a very convincing essay.

Sample Argumentative Essay with Annotations

The following argument appeared in a journal for medical professionals. Not surprisingly, therefore, the authors make extensive use of inductive reasoning. However, specific strategies strengthen the argument, increasing the likelihood their essay will reach a wider audience comprised of those who might reconsider the value of Bill C-65 after reading the essay. Italicized words in the notes refer to specific kinds of evidence and strategies mentioned in this or previous chapters. They could be used as a basis for a critical analysis of "Supervised Injection Sites."

Supervised Injection Sites:
Prejudice Should Not Trump Evidence of Benefit

by Maria Zlotorzynska PhD, Evan Wood MD PhD, Julio S. Montaner MD, Thomas Kerr PhD

A value-based thesis is used. A *policy claim*, however, is implied (i.e., the government should not pass this bill).

1   In 2011, the Supreme Court of Canada issued a unanimous ruling granting Insite, Canada's first government-sanctioned supervised injection facility for people who use illicit drugs, an extended exemption to operate, stating "Insite saves lives. Its benefits have been proven."[1] This decision marked a triumph for evidence-based medicine and public health, and presented opportunities to extend this form of intervention to other jurisdictions in Canada. However, with the recent tabling of Bill C-65, this opportunity may be under threat.

2   Bill C-65, known as the Respect for Communities Act, introduces new requirements to be fulfilled by supervised injection facilities before they can be granted an exemption from the Controlled Drugs and Substances Act. Without this legal exemption, people who use

an injection facility risk criminal prosecution for drug possession. It appears that the federal government would see Canada's drug policy continue to follow a strategy that has proven both costly and ineffective at combatting problematic drug use.

3   The proposed legislation would give the federal Minister of Health sole authority in deciding whether to approve a facility's application for exemption. Special emphasis is placed on the need for broad community and police support as part of the application process, and the bill empowers the Minister to seek input directly from the general public regarding any proposed supervised injection facility.

4   Many of Canada's leading health bodies, including the Canadian Medical Association and the Canadian Nurses Association, have expressed concern that this legislation places such onerous burdens on applicants that it is doubtful any new facilities will be approved. Furthermore, the passing of the bill could potentially result in Insite's closure, given that the facility would thus be required to reapply for an exemption in 2014.

5   Although community consultation is important in ensuring that public health and public safety interests are balanced, this bill appears to be structured in such a way that the voices of opponents to harm reduction, however ill-informed, are privileged above others who speak to the robust evidence showing that supervised injection facilities save lives. The result is that Bill C-65 may prioritize the opinions of people who find intravenous drug users distasteful over the need to use effective measures to limit the spread of disease and save lives. This proposed legislation seems to ignore evidence from a decade of experience in Vancouver and, in so doing, jeopardizes the expansion of these services to other Canadian cities where a need for them has been identified.[2]

6   Insite opened in Vancouver in 2003 as a response to devastating twin epidemics of HIV[3] and drug overdoses.[4] A large body of peer-reviewed research, published in leading medical journals, has documented the various benefits of the program, including reductions in syringe sharing and fatal overdoses, and increased uptake of addiction treatment.[5] Three separate studies have found Insite to be cost-effective.[6-8] Meanwhile, the feared negative consequences of opening Insite have failed to materialize. Although concerns persist that supervised injection facilities attract crime and increase drug use, research undertaken in Vancouver has shown that such fears are unfounded. The results of several studies suggest that disorder associated with public injecting has declined.[5] The rigorous scientific evaluation of Insite, as well as the evidence derived from the 90 other supervised injection facilities internationally,[9] support increasing these services as part of a comprehensive response to drug use and its associated harms.

7   The opposition to supervised injection in Canada ultimately comes down to a question of values. The central arguments offered by opponents of facilities like Insite may be summarized as follows: such facilities enable drug use and send a message to drug users that society has given up on their ability to stop using drugs; money should be spent on abstinence-based treatments, not programs that accommodate active drug use; and drug use constitutes a moral failing that is best dealt with through punishment and control.

8   These arguments are easily countered with evidence. A large body of scientific research shows that addiction is a chronic relapsing condition and that many people cycle in and out of active use.[10] Thus, although there is a role for abstinence-based programs, harm-reduction models serve to decrease risk during phases of active use. Moreover, attempts to control addiction through criminal justice measures have proven neither effective nor economical. The criminalization of drug users has also been shown to increase high-risk behaviours and elevate the risk of acquiring infectious disease.[11]

Marginal annotations:

In the topic sentence of this body paragraph, the authors use *expert opinion* as evidence.

The authors begin with a *concession* but follow with a strong claim of their own: "[T]his bill appears to be structured in such a way that the voices of opponents to harm reduction, however ill-informed, are privileged above others."

The references to sound conclusions made through evidence-based (inductive) methods are key to their argument throughout.

An *ethical appeal* is made as readers are asked to choose between personal "taste" and saving lives.

The authors rebut an important claim, using the study named in note 5 for support.

The authors raise the main arguments on the other side. Although they address all the criticisms briefly in paragraph 8, they save their main rebuttal for paragraph 9; thus, they use a *limited rebuttal strategy*.

Here, the authors refer to two studies but do not include all the details. Interested readers could read the studies for more information.

The authors make a *concession*.

9   Supervised injection facilities and other harm-reduction initiatives are not antithetical to abstinence-based programs and their associated values. Insite operates within the same building as a detox centre and transitional housing for people seeking to cease drug use altogether. Indeed, research has found that supervised injection services can play a role in facilitating uptake of addiction treatment services and promoting cessation from drug use.[12] Other studies have shown injection facilities have no adverse effects on drug use in the broader community, such as increasing rates of initiation into injecting among vulnerable populations.[13] Ultimately, these facilities appear to help advance the very goals that their opponents espouse.

10   We must focus on how to facilitate the implementation of new supervised injection facilities in Canada, not on whether such facilities should be opened. The passage of Bill C-65 into law could further entrench an agenda set by the National Anti-Drug Strategy that appears to ignore harm reduction in the face of overwhelming scientific evidence of its benefits. The bill was not debated by Parliament before the summer recess. We believe it should not be reintroduced when the House of Commons reconvenes, unless it is dramatically altered to promote evidence-based drug policy that emphasizes the health and human rights of drug users. Local health officials should be empowered to make evidence-based decisions about what interventions are offered to people who inject drugs. These decisions should only consider concerns about public safety for which there is robust evidence. Concerns that arise out of prejudice and ignorance, for which there are no sound arguments, should be set aside. It is rare that a government is given the opportunity to build policy that is simultaneously fiscally sound, compassionate and backed by high-quality scientific research. We should not allow the opportunity to do the right thing to pass by again.

References

1. *Canada (Attorney General) v. PHS Community Services Society*, 2011 SCC 44, [2011] 3 S.C.R. 134.
2. Bayoumi AM, Strike C, Jairam J, et al. *Report of the Toronto and Ottawa Supervised Consumption Assessment study.* Toronto (ON): St. Michael's Hospital and the Dalla Lana School of Public Health, University of Toronto; 2012.
3. Patrick DM, Strathdee SA, Archibald CP, et al. Determinants of HIV seroconversion in injection drug users during a period of rising prevalence in Vancouver. *Int J STD AIDS* 1997;8:437–45.
4. Tyndall M, Johnston C, Craib K, et al. HIV incidence and mortality among injection drug users in Vancouver—1996–2000 [abstract]. *Can J Infect Dis Med Microbiol* 2001;12:69B.
5. Wood E, Tyndall MW, Montaner JS, et al. Summary of findings from the evaluation of a pilot medically supervised safer injecting facility. *CMAJ* 2006;175:1399–404.
6. Bayoumi AM, Zaric G. The cost-effectiveness of Vancouver's supervised injection facility. *CMAJ* 2008;179:1143–51.
7. *Vancouver's Insite service and other supervised injection sites: What has been learned from research?* Final report of the Expert Advisory Committee. Ottawa (ON): Expert Advisory Committee of Supervised Injection Site Research; 2008.
8. Andresen MA, Boyd N. A cost-benefit and cost-effectiveness analysis of Vancouver's supervised injection facility. *Int J Drug Policy* 2010;21:70–6.
9. Bravo MJ, Royuela L, De la Fuente L, et al. Use of supervised injection facilities and injection risk behaviours among young drug injectors. *Addiction* 2009;104:614–9.
10. Camí J, Farre M. Drug addiction. *N Engl J Med* 2003;349:975–86.
11. Small W, Kerr T, Charette J, et al. Impacts of intensified police activity on injection drug users: evidence from an ethnographic investigation. *Int J Drug Policy* 2006;17:85–95.
12. Wood E, Tyndall MW, Zhang R, et al. Attendance at supervised injecting facilities and use of detoxification services. *N Engl J Med* 2006;354:2512–4.
13. Kerr T, Tyndall M, Zhang R, et al. Circumstances of first injection among illicit drug users accessing a medically supervised safer injection facility. *Am J Public Health* 2007;27:1228–30.

Affiliations: British Columbia Centre for Excellence in HIV/AIDS (Zlotorzynska, Wood, Montaner, Kerr), St. Paul's Hospital; Department of Medicine (Wood, Montaner, Kerr), University of British Columbia, St. Paul's Hospital, Vancouver, BC.

Margin annotations:

A clear topic sentence sets up the authors' strongest point. Using their knowledge of Insite, the results of credible research, and an example, they end by a surprising *appeal to reader interests*: "Ultimately, these facilities appear to help advance the very goals that their opponents espouse."

The authors argue that the success of Insite should be used as a *precedent* to establish more such facilities in Canada.

Note the careful phrasing as the authors refrain from calling opponents "prejudiced" and "ignorant." Instead, they use deductive reasoning to make their point indirectly:

Major premise: Concerns that arise out of prejudice and ignorance should be set aside.

Minor premise (unstated but implied by their argument): Bill C-65 arises out of ignorance.

Conclusion: Bill C-65 should be set aside.

The authors end with an *emotional appeal*, evoking the reader's "compassion" and an ethical appeal, referring to the need to seize the opportunity and act morally. In their use of the phrase *fiscally sound* they also appeal to *reader interests*. Finally, by using *we*, they appeal to *common ground*.

10

Writing Research Papers

Research essays call on various kinds of reading and writing skills, many of which have been discussed in this text. The usual formats for academic research writing are the essay and the report, discussed in chapter 6. Since research requires you to read your sources closely, it is wise to adopt specific strategies to make the most of your reading, as discussed in chapter 5. Further, comprehension of the material depends on your use of critical thinking, as discussed in chapter 4. Responding to texts in writing involves such processes as evaluating and comparing sources. In addition, identifying which ideas from a source are the most relevant to your topic and integrating them into your own essay are key research skills essential in summarization. These kinds of activities were discussed in chapters 7 and 8.

However, the fundamentals of research extend beyond these skills. In this chapter, we focus on

- locating sources in the modern library
- assessing the reliability of sources, particularly electronic ones
- integrating ideas and giving credit to your sources

We begin with some brief comments on the nature of the research process.

Coming Up with a Topic

For many students, finding a topic to write on is the first challenge to overcome. Here are some questions to consider when you need to come up with a topic from scratch:

- Where do your interests lie (hobbies, leisure pursuits, reading interests, extra-curricular activities)?
- What would you like to learn more about? Curiosity is a good motivator. A topic you are familiar with does not always make a good one for a research essay.

- What topic do you think readers might like to learn about? Thinking of *other* people's interests can guide you to a worthwhile topic. What topic could benefit society or a specific group (for example, students at your university)?
- Can you think of a new angle on an old topic? Neglected areas of older topics can be new opportunities for exploration.

Preparing for Research

Research often begins after you have come up with a research question or a statement of the problem to be investigated.

However, your research question or thesis will likely not be clear until you have conducted preliminary research. Typically, this begins with narrowing a general topic. If you began with a topic like "energy sources in today's world," you will soon find that the topic is much too large; the information available would be overwhelming. However, you can use any of the pre-writing strategies mentioned on pages 66–67 to make the topic more manageable.

One way to narrow the topic of energy sources is to focus on alternatives to fossil fuels, for example nuclear power, with its safety and environmental concerns, or thermo-mechanical energy, which is often considered a less viable long-term energy source. This research can be done either in the library or online using your library's electronic resources.

Your reading will narrow the topic further. It could lead you to three specific energy sources: bio-diesel, solar energy, and hydrogen. However, writing on all three sources in one essay would probably prevent you from going into detail about any of them. Although one option might be simply to randomly select one of the three alternative sources, a better option would be to ask what you or your potential readers might want to know about these energy sources: *Why are these sources important? Who would be interested in knowing about them, and what more do you need to find out about them in order to inform others? Whom could they benefit? What are the potential benefits? What are the potential costs?* Posing these kinds of questions may lead you directly to a research question or thesis statement.

In this case, all these energy sources offer a potential global solution to the energy crisis. *Which of the three offers the best potential?* With this last question in mind, you can recall what you have read about each or continue to browse general works for more background information—in particular, information concerning the costs and benefits of these three energy sources. In the end, you might decide that the most promising is hydrogen. Your thesis might take this form:

> Current research into the development of alternative fuels provides hope for an oil- and nuclear-free future, but of the different types of alternative fuels, hydrogen is the most promising because it satisfies the requirements for a long-term energy plan.

It could also be phrased as a research question:

> Among the various alternative fuels being promoted today, does hydrogen live up to the claims of its proponents by being able to satisfy the requirements for a long-term energy plan?

You could begin your research into alternative energy sources by consulting general reference works, such as textbooks, encyclopedias, or dictionaries, along with indexes and guides in the fields of applied science, engineering, and technology.

Now, with a tentative thesis and organizational pattern (cost/benefit analysis), you can conduct further research by turning to specific journals, especially peer-reviewed journals in which academics, scientists, and researchers publish their findings. This is where library search skills enter the picture. Knowing how the modern library works will save you a lot of time and help you find high-quality sources. By following the guidelines in "The Active Voice: A Beginner's Guide to Researching in the Academic Library," below, you will be able to locate specific sources directly relevant to a topic like energy sources.

As with most projects involving a combination of skills that develop through *doing them*, doubts, false starts, and occasional frustrations are inevitable. The information that follows on research methods and sources is designed to make this process a more comprehensible and satisfying experience.

> **peer-reviewed journal**
>
> A type of journal in which submissions are reviewed by experts before publication; it is an authoritative source for scholarly research.

Research Proposals

Research proposals are a part of the professional world. For the student researcher, a proposal is usually written before your major research, but it can also be written after it and may include an essay outline. The main purpose of a *proposal*, whether for your instructor or for a potential employer, is to convince a reader that the project you propose is worth doing and that you are the right person to do it. For you, a successful proposal will persuade your instructor that you have done adequate preparation and are on the right track to a successful research paper.

At a minimum, research proposals need two parts: (1) a description of what you are undertaking and (2) your methodology. In the first part, you include your thesis and main points. You could also include your reason for wanting to research the topic; thus, you could mention your interest in the area or summarize the importance of research in this field to others. You will not be held to the specific terms of your proposal if you discover on further research that you need to amend your thesis or your main points. The proposal represents a *probable* plan: your thesis and main points can be revised if necessary.

In the second part of the proposal, you should include the sources you have found useful so far and the kinds of sources that you will be looking at as your research continues. Be as specific as possible, naming books, journals, websites, and so on, along with article titles. If you are planning other kinds of research, such as interviews or questionnaires, mention them too. The more detail you provide, the more your reader will be convinced. Being specific makes your proposal credible.

A final function of the research proposal is that it gives you a preliminary plan to follow; it solidifies your topic and your approach to the topic in your own mind.

A proposal may even include projected dates, such as the date you plan to begin your major research and the date you plan to complete it.

> The main purpose of a research proposal is to convince a reader that the project you propose is worth doing and that you are the right person to do it. At a bare minimum, research proposals need two parts: (1) a description of what you are undertaking, including your thesis and main points and (2) your methodology, including the kinds of sources you will be using.

Sample Proposal

The sample student proposal below uses main points in the form of questions, which can be used to generate possible research directions.

Proposal for Research Essay on the Effects of Implementing Prison-Based Needle Exchange Programs in Canadian Federal Prisons

by Kate Newcombe

Topic: The benefits that introducing needle exchange programs into the Canadian federal prison system will have on inmates and employees.

Purpose: To investigate prison-based needle exchange programs and argue the benefits of implementing such a system in Canadian federal prisons.

Description: With the recent introduction of the safe injection site in downtown Vancouver, a growing interest in these sites has developed throughout the community, health services programs, and governments. Although it is a controversial topic, evidence from the Vancouver needle exchange site demonstrates the benefits of these programs. This issue is worth exploring because drug use continues to be widespread in Canadian prisons, and the increased health risks to intravenous drug users due to lack of proper injecting equipment are growing rapidly. Currently, no such programs exist in Canadian prisons. I am interested in discovering more about prison-based needle exchange programs and arguing for the benefits they provide to inmates as well as prison workers. The main organizational methods will be problem–solution and cause–effect.

Tentative Thesis Statement and Central Questions: Prison-based needle exchange programs are an effective, cost-efficient, and beneficial safety tool for public health officials to implement in Canadian prisons in efforts to control drug-related problems and the spread of HIV/AIDS.

- What are the health benefits to intravenous drug users by introducing a system such as this into Canadian prisons?
- Will the introduction of needle exchange systems increase drug use by inmates?
- How will its introduction affect prison employees? (i.e., will there be a physical threat to the health and safety of workers?)
- Have other countries implemented this system into their prisons? If so, what are the results?
- How, if at all, will the introduction of this system help control the spread of HIV/AIDS in the prison population?
- How has the Canadian government dealt with groups and individuals who argue for implementation?
- Is this truly a cost-effective system?

Methodology: In my preliminary research through my university database, I have found several reliable scholarly articles and reviews of prison-based needle exchange programs. They are peer-reviewed and diverse, from such journals as *Addiction, CMAJ, The Lancet,* and *The New England Journal of Medicine.* Tentative articles include Dolan, Rutter, and Wodak (2002), "Prison-Based Syringe Exchange Programmes: A Review of International Research and Development", and Bayoumi and Zaric (2008), "The Cost-Effectiveness of Vancouver's Supervised Injection Facility"; other studies available also evaluate the success of the

Vancouver program. The researchers' findings support the argument that the introduction of prison-based needle exchange programs is beneficial to inmates and employees, while it does not appear that the health benefits of clean syringes and needles increase intravenous drug use within prisons. Davies' "Prison's Second Death Row" (2004) also looks promising as the author accounts for the reluctance of some governments to institute harm reduction programs.

Recording Important Information

Keeping methodical and accurate records during the research phase of the essay-writing process allows you to read material efficiently as well as save time (and your sanity) when you write your paper. You should record notes as you research, ensuring that they include the following information:

- a direct quotation, a summary, or a paraphrase of the writer's idea (if it is a direct quotation, make sure you put quotation marks around it)
- the complete name(s) of the author(s), ensuring correct spelling
- the complete name(s) of any editors or translators
- the complete name of the book, journal, magazine, newspaper, or website
- the title of the specific article, chapter, section, or webpage
- full publication details, including date, edition, and translation (if appropriate)
- the name of the publisher and the company's location (including province or state) for books
- in the case of an article accessed electronically, the day you viewed the page and either the URL or the digital object identifier (DOI); the date of the site or its most recent update should also be recorded
- the call number of a library book or bound journal (to help you find it again if necessary)
- the page numbers you consulted, both those from which specific ideas came and the full page range of the work (or some other marker, such as section headings and paragraph numbers, for unnumbered Internet documents)

Organizing Research Notes

There are many ways to organize information from your research in order to use it later, including the manual method—for example, notecards, which are portable and practical. Many software programs are designed to help with planning and organization. For example, *RefWorks* (www.refworks.com) is an Internet-based "citation manager" that allows you to import references from popular databases like *Academic Search Complete*, *MLA Bibliography*, and *EconLit*. Others are databases, such as *EndNote* (www.endnote. com), *Bibliographix* (www.bibliographix.com), and *Nota Bene* (www.notabene.com). Students can usually take a tutorial for these programs on the websites or even through their own institution if it has purchased licences allowing students to use them. These programs offer many benefits, such as automatic formatting for a great variety of citation and bibliographic systems.

Ensure that you keep your research notes, such as summaries and direct quotations, separate from your personal annotations. Use a method that clearly distinguishes between the two; otherwise, you could end up plagiarizing by failing to attribute the idea or words of a source, thinking they were your own.

digital object identifier (DOI)
A number-letter sequence that begins with the number 10 often found on journal articles; it serves as a persistent link for digital material.

The Active Voice

A Beginner's Guide to Research in the Academic Library

1   The twenty-first-century academic library can seem overwhelming to the undergraduate researcher. In addition to the traditional materials found in the library's online catalogue, there are numerous other electronic resources available, including databases, journals, and e-books, as well as other digital formats and media. The sheer volume of information resources in today's academic library need not be intimidating. On the contrary, an effective research strategy will enable you to take full advantage of all the wealth of print and electronic information resources available to you.

2   An effective strategy should include three important considerations:

1.   Your *research topic*
2.   The *information resources* most relevant to your topic
3.   The *search strategy* you will use to obtain and retain information from those resources

3   When you understand how to choose a well-defined research topic, where to look for information on that topic, and how to construct an effective search in an academic library catalogue or database, you will have the basic tools required for most research projects at the first-year level. As you become a more confident researcher, you can expand on these basic skills and strategies by exploring more specialized resources and experimenting with advanced search methods.

The Research Topic

4   The starting point for your research will be your topic. When choosing your own topic, make sure to select one that is neither too broad nor too narrow. If your topic is too broad, you will have difficulty focusing your research and writing. Alternatively, if your topic is too narrow or obscure, you may not be able to find enough relevant information to support your research question.

5   For instance, you may want to write about *homelessness* or *the homeless*. It would be difficult to write a focused paper on such a broad topic. To narrow your focus, you might want to research homelessness in a particular age group, such as teenagers. However, this would probably still be too broad. You could narrow your focus further by looking at particular health problems of homeless teens or risk factors associated with homelessness in teens, such as poverty, addiction, or abuse.

Selecting Resources for Your Research Topic

6   **Subject or Research Guides:** Once you have decided on a research topic, you must choose your resources. The academic library is your ultimate destination for a diversity of scholarly and non-scholarly sources. Most academic libraries provide subject or research guides on their website. These guides are prepared by subject librarians with specialized knowledge in the information resources of their particular subject areas. Most subject guides provide direct links to relevant online databases, scholarly websites, and primary source materials for the subject, as well as valuable information on reference resources such as dictionaries, encyclopedias, biographies, and bibliographies, including subject headings and call number ranges.

7   **Primary and Secondary Sources:** Your research may require that you investigate both primary and secondary source information. The meaning of primary and secondary sources can vary across the disciplines, but in the humanities and social sciences, primary sources generally provide *first-hand* information or data. This may include original works such as autobiographies, interviews, speeches, letters, diaries, unpublished manuscripts, data sources, government records, newspapers, and government policy papers, among others. Secondary sources are works that analyze or provide criticism or interpretation of a primary work, source, or experience from a *second-hand* perspective. These can include scholarly journal articles, textbooks, collections of critical essays, biographies, historical articles, and films, to name a few examples.

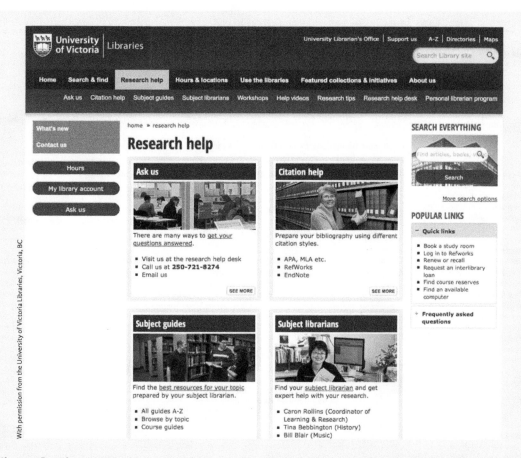

8   The Library Catalogue: The library catalogue is the most important tool for finding secondary print sources like books, encyclopedias, dictionaries, and journals in your library, as well as any electronic versions of these materials that are available. Unlike an Internet search engine such as Google, the library's catalogue is a bibliographic index and provides a comprehensive list of the most relevant scholarly and non-scholarly sources related to your research topic through its combined use of subject headings and descriptors. For concise, general information on your topic, the academic library can also provide you with encyclopedias and dictionaries, which are more scholarly sources of information than Wikipedia, and can help you to narrow your focus by highlighting key academic issues and concepts, as well as providing suggestions for further research. Scholarly books relevant to your topic are also important sources for you to explore. In addition to covering a subject in more depth than a journal article, they often provide important historical, biographical, literary, or cultural context that may not be available elsewhere. Books also feature images or tables of contents that can help you to identify important aspects of the subject that you may want to explore further and bibliographies to help you locate other resources. E-books are especially useful for browsing tables of contents and bibliographies and for keyword searching within the full text of a book.

9   Online Databases: Scholarly journal articles are a key secondary source for your research. Journal articles review what other scholars have said about your topic and often provide important supportive or alternative perspectives relevant to your thesis. Online databases and indexes are your main tools for finding journal articles in both print and online formats. Your library's home page may provide a discovery search tool, such as *Summon*, for searching for information sources. In a single unified search box, the system retrieves a number of relevant articles from your library's catalogue and journal subscriptions, and allows you to limit your search, save or export your results, or link to the full text. This method is useful for quickly finding information on your topic, and can be further refined by using the additional filters and limiters available.

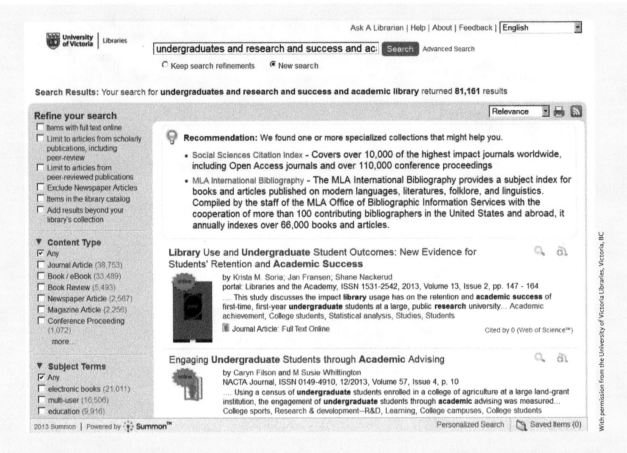

10   A good multidisciplinary online database like *Academic Search Complete* provides relevant information on most topics at the undergraduate level. However, you may also want to take advantage of the many subject and specialized databases available. Most subject areas feature a core database that indexes the key journals for that discipline, such as ERIC for Education, *Sociological Abstracts* for sociology, or the *MLA International Bibliography* for language and literature. It is important to get to know the core databases in your subject area. If your library has subject guides, these will list the core databases or "best bets" for each subject. Most libraries will also allow you to select databases by subject in addition to providing an A–Z list. This can be helpful, particularly if the database indicates it includes full text, coverage dates available, authenticated links for mobile access, and anything else that may be pertinent.

11   You should also consider the type of information you require. For example, it is unlikely that you will find complex data or statistical information unless you search a statistical database. Historical government information, too, will require different search strategies, and may include specialized use of websites such as the Internet Archive. Again, the specialized subject guides, as well as consultation with your subject librarian, will help you in determining the right information resources you need for your research topic.

Search Strategies

12   **Determining Keywords:** Once you have chosen some relevant resources, the next step will be to identify the key concepts from your topic to use as keywords or search terms. For instance, if you want to search for information on risk factors associated with homelessness in youth, you will want to identify keywords that embody the concepts *risk factors*, *homelessness*, *youth*. Some risk factors might be *poverty*, *addiction*, or *abuse*. Using *risk* or *factors* as search terms would be too broad and would not provide good search results. Similarly, using *"risk factors"* as a single term would not find results unless the books or articles used this exact term.

13   **Boolean Operators:** To be effective, the actual search process should employ some form of Boolean strategy. The most common Boolean operators, AND, OR, and NOT, are

used to combine, expand, or eliminate keywords in your search. For instance, AND combines the two different terms *homelessness* AND *youth*. A search conducted using AND will also narrow your results. This is more effective than searching for each of the keywords separately, since any sources retrieved must include both terms. The OR operator is used to expand your search results by including other concepts. These may be the same concepts or different aspects of a broader concept. In this example, you might want to search for results that include the keywords *youth* OR *teens* OR *adolescents*, which are synonymous concepts. Or you may want to search for *poverty* OR *abuse* OR *addiction* as different aspects of the risk factors. The NOT operator is used to eliminate results with that given keyword, such as *children* if you do not want results that discuss young children. The NOT operator should be used judiciously, however, because you may eliminate an article that discusses both children and teens, which may be relevant to your topic.

14   The Boolean terms are capitalized here for readability but this is not necessary in most databases. Also, many databases will now allow you to combine your keywords without using the Boolean operators at all. You simply enter your terms and choose the correct search mode. Using Basic Search in *Academic Search Complete* as an example, the search mode *Find all of my search terms* is equivalent to AND, and the search mode *Find any of my search terms* is equivalent to OR. Many other databases and

catalogues now work similarly, including *Google Scholar*, which can be an important resource to consult either when you are in the beginning stages of your research or when you are looking for a specific article you are unable to locate elsewhere. When using *Google Scholar*, however, remember to access it through your academic library website, so that you can directly link to online resources in your library's catalogue, including open-access journals. Keep in mind that *Google Scholar* is a search engine, and although it may be extensive, it is certainly not exhaustive (see The Active Voice: Google and the Invisible Web, page 140). Your library's catalogue or discovery tool is still the best choice for scholarly academic sources related to your research topic.

15   **Truncation and Wildcards:** Boolean search strategy is often used with truncation and/or wildcard symbols. Truncation symbols enable you to include all variants of a search term. Using the asterisk as the truncation symbol in *teen** will ensure that your search results include all the terms *teen*, *teens*, and *teenager*. Wildcards are used within a word, for instance in *colo#r* to search for an alternative spelling (*colour* and *color*) or *wom?n* to search for any unknown characters (*woman* and *women*). Most databases and catalogues use the asterisk (*) or a question mark (?) for the truncation or wildcard symbol. Some databases may also use the pound sign (#) or another symbol.

16 Basic or Advanced Search: Online catalogues and databases usually feature simple or basic search and advanced search options. The basic search field can be used to enter single terms, as described above, or more complex search statements using Boolean operators. However, to construct a search statement using Boolean strategy in a basic search field, you must use parentheses to separate the OR terms from the AND terms as indicated below. The database will search for the terms in parentheses first, then from left to right.

> (*Homeless** OR *runaway**) AND (*teen** OR *adolescen** OR *youth*) AND (*poverty* OR *abuse* OR *addict**)

17 Also, if you want to use a combined term such as "*risk factors,*" you must use quotation marks unless the field provides the option to search two or more words as a phrase.

18 The Advanced Search option allows you to insert your terms and then select AND, OR, or NOT to combine the fields and to add additional fields, if necessary. Advanced search also allows you to search for terms in various fields, such as *All Text, Abstract, Author, Title,* or *Subject Terms.* By selecting a specific field, you limit the search to that field alone. It is often best to try a search in the default field initially and then try other advanced strategies to refine your results, if necessary.

19 Subject Headings or Descriptors: Subject headings or descriptors are very useful for refining your search strategy. In an academic library, under the Library of Congress classification system, subject headings have been applied to each bibliographic entry to describe what it is about. A subject heading is not merely a keyword found in the article or abstract, and some online databases enable you to search the subject directly to show related subject headings. Sometimes, subject headings within the results list are linked, so you can either expand or narrow the results of your current search to all of the related records in the database with that subject term.

20 Another strategy is to take note of the subject headings in your initial keyword searches. Combining these terms again in the *Subject Terms* field will often yield more relevant results. Most online library catalogues will also provide related subject headings to other resources with the same heading. Additionally, there may also be a link to other items in the same immediate call number range. This will enable you to easily browse the collection for other relevant materials.

21 Limiters: Another search strategy is using the limiters available to you in a particular database. This strategy is generally used to limit your results if there are too many, or to limit to a particular date range, article type, format, or publication. One very useful limiter found in many databases is the scholarly or peer-reviewed limiter. Peer-reviewed articles are scholarly articles that have been reviewed by a board or panel of scholars from the same discipline for publication in academic journals. They are a more reliable source of information for your research than popular sources that are intended for a general audience. Some databases will limit to scholarly sources automatically and return the results under a *peer-reviewed* link or tab. *Academic Search Complete* provides a *Scholarly (Peer Reviewed) Journals* check box to the right of your search results list, or you can check the *Scholarly (Peer Reviewed) Journals* box in the *Limit your results* field before you execute your search, and the database will only retrieve scholarly articles.

22 Marking and Saving: Most online databases and library catalogues provide a marking and saving feature. You can select your most relevant results, mark them by checking a box or adding them to a folder, and then choose from several options—usually print, email, save, or export. Export often includes an option to download or export to the bibliographic management software of your choice, such as *RefWorks* or *EndNote.* These citation management tools allow you to create a customized personal account so that you can store and organize your citations, as well as create a bibliography conforming to a particular citation style, such as APA, MLA, or Chicago. Citation management tools can help you keep track of your search history, as well as store links to previously searched databases and full-text articles, and often include areas where you can write your own comments. As you scan abstracts and articles, and later during your readings, be sure to note the points and ideas you wish to quote and paraphrase. Remember, crediting sources is an essential part of academic writing.

23 Refining Your Strategy: One final consideration for effective academic library research is refining your strategy throughout the process. It may be necessary to re-evaluate your topic, choice of resources, or search strategy if your initial search efforts are unsuccessful.

Do not feel frustrated: this is not an indication that your strategy is not a good one or that you have failed. On the contrary, conducting academic research is a naturally evolving process, and knowing how to access the resources at your academic library is a part of the learning experience. In the end, your goal is a strong research topic with thoughtful, meaningful research accompanied by accurate citations to scholarly resources. Therefore, it is important to start your library research early. This will allow you enough time to determine a manageable topic, consult your subject librarian, explore as many resources as possible, refine your search strategy as necessary, and obtain any materials that are not readily available online or in your academic library.

—Based on original text by Danielle Forster, Subject Librarian, and updated by Justin Harrison, Caron Rollins, and Christine Walde, University of Victoria Libraries

Activity 10.1

Using one of your library's search engines or a general/science database, such as *Academic Search Complete* or *Medline*, answer the questions below. To make your search more efficient, you can use the search limiters *journal article only* and *peer-reviewed journals only*; you can also set the publication date to 2004 and/or enter the main author's name "Tatem" in the Search window.

Access the academic journal *Nature* volume 432, issue 7014. Referring to the letter "Biology Students Find Holes in Gap Study" on page 147, answer the questions below, all of which stress the critical-thinking skills discussed in chapter 4:

1. How do these students establish their credibility to critique a study in an academic journal?

2. How do the students use the study by Whipp and Ward?

3. What year did Tatem et al. begin studying women's times? How can you infer this?

4. How many points do the students use to support their claim? Which do you consider the strongest? Why?

5. Following the letters, the authors of the study responded to the criticisms (see "Mind the Gap: Women Racers Are Falling Behind," page 147). After reading all the letters on the page, along with the authors' response, consider whether the authors effectively answered the charges. What tone did they use in their response? Note: It is not necessary to be familiar with the models mentioned by the authors.

Using Credible Sources

In determining whether to use a source in your research essay, bear in mind the four "Re's" of research sources: reputable, reliable, recent, and relevant.

- *Re*putable: Reputable sources are usually associated with well-known organizations or acknowledged experts in their field.
- *Re*liable: Information from reliable sources can be trusted as accurate and free of bias.
- *Re*cent: Although currency is more important to some topics than others, recent information is generally superior to older information.
- *Re*levant: The information in relevant sources is directly related to your thesis and/or main points.

Credibility Issues in Online Sources

Of the four qualities mentioned above, the first two—reputable and reliable—are especially pertinent to online searches. The explosion of information via the Internet has made it more difficult to assess the authority of written information today. Because the boundaries are sometimes blurred between knowledge and speculation and between fact and opinion, those who surf the net, reading indiscriminately, may not be able to tell reliable from unreliable information. (See The Active Voice: Google and the Invisible Web—Using Library Resources for Deeper and Broader Research, page 140.) Today's student researcher must read carefully and ask questions about the source's sponsor(s) and/or author(s), along with the accuracy, currency, objectivity, and scope of the information.

The criteria below apply particularly to open-access resources, from Google Scholar to the array of commercial, governmental, and personal websites that anyone sitting in front of a computer screen can view. In contrast to these are the more authoritative resources accessed through your institution's library home page. The way you use open-access resources, or *if* you use them in your research, depends on what kind of information you are looking for.

You should first consider your purpose for seeking out a source. Is it for reliable information from an objective source with evidence-gathering methods beyond reproach (Statistics Canada, for example), or is it to learn about a particular viewpoint? If the latter, it might be acceptable to use a website that advocates a position or supports a cause. If you were writing an essay on animal rights, you might want to access People for the Ethical Treatment of Animals (PETA) or Animal Rights Canada, since their advocacy of animal rights is clear and above board—which is not to say that their information is always factual or accurate.

Not all websites, however, are forthcoming in acknowledging their true stake in an issue, nor do all websites use quality control to ensure accurate content. Even seemingly reliable and objective websites, such as government-affiliated ones, may contain misleading or outdated information. The questions below are therefore relevant to most sources you access via the Internet.

Sponsors and Authors

- What group or individual has created the site or is responsible for its content? If the organization/individual is unfamiliar, try to find (a) its parent organization, (b) affiliated organizations, or (c) a mission statement concerning the organization's and/or website's purpose. This information could be on the home page, or accessible from it. You should be suspicious of websites lacking self-identification.
- Who are the authors of the material on the site? Are names and affiliations given? Biographies? Is contact information provided? Mailing address, telephone number, email address? Note the domain of the website or email address: the most common ones in North America for educational institutions are ".edu" (US) and ".ca" (Canada), preceded by an abbreviated form of the school's name; ".gov" (a government source); ".org" (a non-profit organization); and ".com" (a commercial site).

Accuracy and Currency

- What is the source of the content? Are informational sources identified—by author, title, date? How has statistical information been calculated (e.g., through censuses, surveys, questionnaires by reliable organizations)? How are statistical information and other factual data being used? Does the use seem consistent with the website's purpose?
- Are all claims and other statements reasonable and well supported?
- What is the original date of the site? Has it been updated recently? Does factual information appear verifiable? Can it be verified by checking a reliable and unaffiliated website?

Objectivity

- Does the content seem presented without bias? Is it politicized? Does it seem to address a specific reader (e.g., is the voice familiar and informal?) or directed more toward a general reader? Do statements seem provocative? Is the tone neutral? Can you identify any slanted language or bias?
- If opinion exists, is it clearly differentiated from fact? Are other points of view besides those of the author/organization represented? How are they treated?
- Is there advertising on the site?

Scope and Comprehensiveness

- Does the site appear to include different views of and approaches to issues?
- Is there a menu or site map that provides an overview of content? (You could get an indication of scope from that.)
- Are there links to other sites? Do these sites appear reliable?
- Does content primarily consist of text? What is the approximate proportion of text to graphics (for research purposes, text should outweigh graphics)? Are there accompanying charts, graphs, or other illustrative material? If so, do they seem designed to explain and summarize (as opposed to being merely decorative)?

Other Issues

- Is the information on the website easy to access? Does it appear well organized? What specific resources are designed to enhance accessibility or navigation?
- Is the site appealing and attractive rather than just glitzy?

In the following essay, the writer uses the techniques referred to in The Active Voice: A Beginner's Guide to Researching in the Academic Library, above, to compare the effectiveness of the search engine Google with that of the resources of the "deep" web, such as bibliographic databases that can be accessed through your institution's library.

The Active Voice

Google and the Invisible Web:
Using Library Resources for Deeper and Broader Research

1   The Internet is a window on many worlds. A few words in Google can lead to more than enough information on almost any topic. But is Google a door to the "best" information? How complete is a Google search? Much of the "best," more scholarly information is not accessible, either hidden in private sources behind search forms or available only for a fee.[1] These commercial and private sources represent much of the "deep" or "invisible" web,[2] the huge part of the Internet not reached comprehensively by the spiders of search engines. This essay argues that Google and similar tools open only some of the worlds accessible via the Internet. It draws attention to the commercial bibliographic databases indexing the literature of specific subjects and providing retrieval tools more appropriate for these subjects than Google. Libraries license these databases for their clientele, opening up the "deep" web and the information inaccessible on the surface of the web through search engines.

2   The web is indiscriminate, with no restrictions on what may be put up by whom. Web search engines rate and list sites using various criteria. Google uses word frequency counts and gives priority to sites that are linked on many others. In the scholarly literature, books and articles more highly cited are considered better, but this basic principle does not always apply in Google. Because the web includes commercial, popular, and self-published as well as scholarly sites, all rated by popularity, much of the best scholarly material—especially on topics of wide interest—is not given priority because it is less popular than the material on non-scholarly sites. Google recognized this issue and created Google Scholar to search only sites identified as more scholarly. A number of academic publishers are opening their sites to be indexed by Google. In addition, Google is digitizing a huge number of books. So, Google Scholar now searches the full text of articles and books as well as scholarly sites. However, access to full text is limited. Books still under copyright display with some pages missing. Articles are increasingly made accessible through the push to "open access" but, still, many are available only to users covered by the licenses purchased by libraries on behalf of these users. The free-for-all that is the Internet is pushing publishers to open more material, presenting issues for searching that Google has begun to address.

3   Even though the Internet is undergoing rapid change and more information is becoming easily accessible, two unvarying features of information mean that a Google search may never be enough. First is the need in searching for information to bring together similar items, even if they do not use the same words for the same concepts. For example, computers do not recognize terms from their context, not able to tell if a hedge is a row of plants or a type of fund. Humans recognize that information on Shakespeare and Chekhov would be relevant to a search on playwrights, but all terms, general and specific, must be input into Google to ensure a comprehensive search, the names of individual playwrights as well as the term *playwrights*. Second is the need for critical appraisal, bringing out qualities other than word frequency or popularity. The availability of tools for extracting the best items (peer reviewed, in more important journals) and selection of what is indexed based on quality address this need. While Google pulls *more* information, these other features lead to a focus on the *best* information.

4   Bibliographic databases licensed by libraries for their users offer these features, bringing together and indexing items, print and electronic, from the literatures on particular topics. They give structure to this literature by using standard vocabulary and, often, concepts. Examples are *PsycInfo* for psychology and the *MLA (Modern Language Association) Bibliography* for literary criticism. As a health librarian, I use *Medline* daily, which indexes 23 million citations and gives structure to the literature of health sciences from research to clinical practice.

5   Comparing search results on Google vs. bibliographic databases makes the differences apparent. For example, a search[3] on "seasonal affective disorder" on *PsycInfo* led to 883 articles focusing on that topic (focused subject heading or with the phrase in the title). The particular interface I used, *Ovid*, allows limits to be applied, including to literature reviews as a methodology, leading to 39 articles, for many of which my university offered direct connections

to the full text.[4] Google did provide useful information, mostly for patients, including an article with numerous academic citations in Wikipedia, the co-operatively developed online encyclopedia.

6   Google Scholar did not work well for this topic, leading to older scholarly articles unless the date limit was used (I searched back to 2010), and then the articles were too specialized and less useful. One link led to the full text of a book chapter—great, except two key pages were not accessible. Interestingly, my library's catalogue also provided good, recent printed books on this topic, which neither source retrieved. In summary, Google and *PsycInfo* both led to quality articles on seasonal affective disorder, the difference being the purpose, with Google providing information at a more basic level understandable to patients and *PsycInfo* giving access to more scholarly material.

7   I also tried a search on the portrayal of music in eighteenth-century literature using Google and the *MLA Bibliography*. This search proved treacherous, particularly for Google, with retrieval including sites and articles discussing music *and* literature, not music *in* literature, in the eighteenth century. I tried the Advanced Search with "music in literature" as a phrase in Google. Although references to music in the work of specific authors were not included, a few hits looked useful, leading me to repeat in *Google Scholar*. It performed well enough, providing useful citations from the books digitized by Google although few journal articles. A basic search in *MLA Bibliography* pulled some good hits but also much dross. Using Advanced Search here allows searches to be entered using Period—I used "1700–1799"—and Literature Topic—I used simply "music." All hits were relevant, 84 when I refined my search to English only. More specific topics—music in the writing of Rousseau and Goethe—suggested themselves. In this example, I found Google generated mostly irrelevant links and Google Scholar useful links to books, while *MLA Bibliography* enabled me to find information specific to the topic in both journals and books.

8   Four similar examples were examined more carefully in a 2005 article.[5] The authors found that "Google is superior for coverage and accessibility. Library systems are superior for quality of results. . . . Improving the skills of the searcher is likely to give better results from the library systems, but not from Google."

9   There are hundreds of bibliographic databases, large and small, general and specific, reflecting the structure and communication patterns of the literatures of many subjects. While some interfaces are better than others, such databases can generally be searched using techniques and vocabulary which suit the particular discipline indexed. Precise searches can be executed on specific topics. Databases collecting together and organizing the information of a discipline and made accessible with effective retrieval tools represent powerful adjuncts to the wide-ranging, indiscriminant search engines of the Internet.

10   So, Google away. But, are Google and friends good enough? As a librarian, I say "No!" Using Google or other search engines, you will find much useful information, much of high quality, even *some* of the "best" available. Google Scholar continues to improve and offer more sophisticated tools. It is used increasing by researchers for keeping up-to-date and for determining the impact of their work.[6] As well, some studies indicate that Google Scholar is useful in specialized fields, perhaps through increased indexing of the full text of articles.[7] But for complete and more precise searches, you will need to augment Google with the databases of the deep web that index the literature on the topic you are exploring. How scholars communicate, even who are "scholars," is being changed by the web and the free flow of information. Google will turn up items available outside the controlled world of scholarly communication. While Google continues to index more and more scholarly content, databases indexing the published literature point to items not covered by Google and use more varied concepts via interfaces adapted to the topic of the literature. As a librarian, I am pleased that a variety of tools is making information more accessible. I am thrilled that the value placed on using information, applying what is known, has increased. With the surface of the web readily accessible via Google and friends, and with increased understanding of the value of databases provided by libraries, more of the best information is going to reach and address the needs of more people.

Notes

1.   Since the 2006 first version of this article, Google has recognized the "deep web"—see Madhavan J et al. Google's deep web crawl. *Proceedings of the VLDB Endowment* (2008): 1241–1252. However, their efforts do not broaden access significantly.

2. For a bibliography, see Egger-Sider F, Devine J. Beyond Google: the invisible web. May 2003, revised August 2013. http://library.laguardia.edu/invisibleweb/webography (accessed 9 January 2014). It includes the key paper, Bergman MK. White Paper: The Deep Web: surfacing hidden value. *Journal of electronic publishing* 7(1) 2001. http://dx.doi.org/10.3998/3336451.0007.104 (accessed 8 January 2014).

3. All searches tested January 2014.

4. Many libraries have set up links via Google to full-text content they purchase on behalf of their users.

5. Brophy J, Bawden D. Is Google enough? Comparison of an Internet search engine with academic library resources. *Aslib Proceedings: New Information Perspectives* 57(6) 2005: 498–512.

6. Bohannon J. Google Scholar Wins Raves—But Can It Be Trusted? *Science* 343(6166) 2014: 14.

7. Shariff SZ et al. Retrieving clinical evidence: a comparison of PubMed and Google Scholar for quick clinical searches. *J Med Internet Res* 15(8) 2013:e164.

—Jim Henderson, Librarian (Retired), McGill University

Integrating and Documenting Sources

When you integrate your research into your essay, you can use one or more of several methods to combine the source material with your own words. When you document these sources, you use a standardized format to show your readers where you obtained this material. Typically, you integrate, or synthesize, your sources as part of the composing process. Documenting your sources is often the final stage in the composing process. The value in documenting as early as possible in the process, however, is that it will give you time to check and double-check the accuracy of your information.

Integrating Your Sources: Summary versus Paraphrase

summary

A method of extracting the main idea (or ideas) from an original source, expressing it in your own words.

paraphrase

A method of source integration in which you put someone else's ideas in your own words, keeping the length of the original.

When you summarize a source, you extract an idea (ideas) from the source that is directly relevant to your essay, expressing it in your own words. If you wanted to summarize a large portion of the original, you would follow the guidelines for précis summaries (see page 89). What distinguishes a summary from a paraphrase is that summaries are selective: they focus on main ideas. When you paraphrase, you include *all of the original, putting it in your own words*. You could paraphrase anything from a part of a sentence to one or two paragraphs. Paraphrasing is reserved for very important information.

Whereas a summary condenses and is thus an efficient method for synthesizing material, a paraphrased passage is not usually shorter than the original—in fact, it may be longer. Because you include so much in a paraphrase, you must be careful to use completely different wording or you may unknowingly be plagiarizing. Changing the order of the original will also help you avoid plagiarism (see Plagiarism, below).

Direct Quotation and Mixed Format

Like a paraphrase, a direct quotation applies to specific content. When you represent a source by direct quotation, you use exactly the same words as the original, enclosing them within quotation marks. Authors of empirical studies make sparing use of direct quotations, but they are often used by authors of humanities essays, which analyze primary sources, such as literary or historical texts, and may depend on direct quotations for support. Researchers in the social sciences who use a qualitative methodology, such as interviews or focus groups, may also rely on direct quotations.

As a general guideline, prefer summary or paraphrase to direct quotation. When you summarize or paraphrase, you show your comprehension of a source by "translating" it into your own words.

> *Direct quotation unnecessary or inappropriate:* "Pilot error accounted for 34 per cent of major airline crashes between 1990 and 1996, compared with 43 per cent from 1983 to 1989." [Statistical detail does not need be quoted directly.]

> *Paraphrase:* In the six-year period between 1990 and 1996, 34 per cent of major airline crashes were due to pilot error, a decrease of 9 per cent over the previous six-year period.

If factual material can be easily put in your own words, prefer summary or paraphrase to direct quotation.

> *Direct quotation unnecessary:* "Students often find ways to compensate for their symptoms of ADD in their earlier years so that the disorder reveals itself only with the increased intellectual and organizational demands of university."

> *Summary:* Because of the greater demands of university, compared to earlier schooling, students with ADD may not have to confront their disorder until university.

In a mixed format, you combine summary or paraphrase with direct quotation. Effective use of mixed format demonstrates both your understanding and your polished writing skills since it requires you to seamlessly integrate the language of the source with your own language. You can use this format when you want to cite part of an important passage in which key words or phrases occur, carefully choosing the significant words and excluding the less important parts.

Specific contexts for using direct and mixed quotations: You can use direct or mixed quotations if you want to define something or if the exact wording is important for another reason—for example, to lend authority to your point or if the wording of the source is significant or memorable:

> The Yerkes-Dodson law "predicts an inverted U relationship between arousal and performance and that the optimal level of arousal for a beginner is considerably less than that for an expert performing the same task" ("Yerkes-Dodson Law," 2002b, *The Oxford Dictionary of Sports Science and Medicine*).

The definition of a specialized term makes direct quotation a good choice:

> But how do we define our Canadian democracy? "The genius of a free and democratic people is manifested in its capacity and willingness to devise

If there is no compelling reason to use direct quotation, use summary, paraphrase, or a mixed format instead.

mixed format
A method of source integration in which you combine significant words of the source, placed in quotation marks, with your own words.

institutions and laws that secure fairness and equitable opportunities for citizens to influence democratic governance" (Royal Commission on Electoral Reform and Party Financing).

Using direct quotation is appropriate when the writer wants to stress the authority of the source:

> According to Sir Clifford Sifton, Prime Minister Wilfrid Laurier's interior minister, Canada was to be "a nation of good farmers," meaning Asian immigration was discouraged (Royal Commission 24).

Mixed format is useful here, quoting a significant phrase to reveal discrimination against Asians in the first decade of the twentieth century in Canada.

Integrating Quotations

When you incorporate direct quotations into your essay, you must do so grammatically and smoothly; you must also provide adequate context for your reader. The following shows a poorly integrated quotation and its well-integrated alternative:

> An unloving parent–child relationship can be characterized as "unaccepted, unacknowledged, or unloved" (Haworth-Hoeppner 216).

> *Well-integrated:* An unloving parent–child relationship exists when the child feels "unaccepted, unacknowledged, or unloved" (Haworth-Hoeppner 216).

Omitting, Adding, or Changing Material

You may omit quoted material in the interests of efficiency or add material in the interests of completeness or clarity, making minor changes, if needed, for grammatical or stylistic reasons. Whenever you alter a direct quotation, you must indicate these changes to the reader.

Omitting: You may omit part of a sentence if it is irrelevant or unimportant for your purposes. To indicate an omission of one or more words in the middle of a sentence, use an ellipsis, which consists of three spaced dots. If you leave out all the words to the end of the sentence—and if you leave out the following sentence(s) as well—add a fourth dot, which represents the period at the end of the sentence:

> *Original:* The present thesis is that psychology, in concert with other disciplines, has an important role to play in easing the pain caused by climate change. Were this thesis widely recognised, the present article would be unnecessary. Unfortunately, the thesis is not broadly acknowledged. (Gifford, "Psychology's essential role in alleviating the impacts of climate change," page 455).

ellipsis

Three or four spaced dots in a direct quotation, indicating that one or more words have been omitted.

Words omitted in the middle of the first sentence: The present thesis is that psychology . . . has an important role to play in easing the pain caused by climate change.

The second sentence omitted: The present thesis is that psychology, in concert with other disciplines, has an important role to play in easing the pain caused by climate change. . . . Unfortunately, the thesis is not broadly acknowledged.

Adding and changing: If you add or change material, you need to indicate this by using *brackets* (brackets are square; parentheses are rounded). Changes can be made for grammatical, stylistic, or clarification/explanation purposes. The following examples illustrate some of the different reasons for using brackets to add or change words:

Grammatical (provide a needed verb): Researchers categorically state that we cannot "[become] tolerant to steroids" (student writer Pritpal Mann).

Stylistic (upper case "T" to begin a sentence): As Benjamin Barber argued in 1995, "[T]he true tutors of our children are not schoolteachers or university professors but filmmakers, advertising executives and pop culture purveyors" (Gillam and Wooden, "Post-princess Models of Gender: The New Man in Disney/Pixar," page 290 in Part III: The Reader).

Clarification (to indicate words added to original): The Federal Plan for Gender Equality stated that "the absence of equity and access-related research [regarding the information infrastructure] is of growing concern" (Status of Women Canada 1995, par. 270) (Shade, "Missing in Action," page 251 in Part III: The Reader).

In addition to the uses of brackets within quotations, they can also be used to indicate parentheses within parentheses, similar to the use of single quotation marks to show quotations within quotations:

"[T]he need for population-level intervention (i.e., intervention [policy or program] operating within or outside the health sector . . .) is increasingly recognized." (Dutton et al., "A Ban on Marketing of Foods/Beverages to Children," page 279 in Part III: The Reader).

To understand the reason for the changes to the sentence above, see page 279 (the direct quotation is taken from the first sentence of "A Ban on Marketing of Foods/ Beverages to Children").

Table 10.1 summarizes some of the main features of the four integration methods discussed above. Note that whatever method you use, documentation is usually required. See below, "Seven Common Questions about Source Citation."

Table 10.1 Integration Methods

Method	What It Includes	When and How to Use It
summary	only main ideas or most important points; is in your words	when you want to refer to main idea in a paragraph, findings of a study, and similar uses; you can summarize as little as part of a sentence, as much as an entire article
paraphrase	all of the original in your own words, often with the structure changed	when you want to refer to important material directly relevant to your point; paraphrases are used for small but significant passages
direct quotation	words and punctuation taken directly from the source; put in quotation marks	when material is both important to your point and memorably phrased, or is difficult to paraphrase; must be integrated grammatically and smoothly
mixed format	significant words from source with your own words (i.e., summary or paraphrase)	when you want to include only the most significant or memorable words, omitting the inessential; integrate words from the source grammatically and smoothly with your own prose, using brackets and ellipses as required

Documenting Your Sources

Documenting sources serves several practical purposes: it enables a reader to distinguish between your ideas and someone else's, and it makes it possible for any reader to access the source itself to ensure its accuracy or focus on its content. Documentation formats (called documentation styles) provide a coherent and consistent way for scholars to communicate with other scholars (and also with student researchers, who must learn the fundamentals of documentation formats in order to use them in their essays).

Plagiarism

Plagiarism is an extremely serious academic offence. Many students approaching post-secondary study believe that plagiarism is limited to cases in which they use direct quotations and fail to cite their sources. In fact, plagiarism encompasses much more than this: you *plagiarize* if you use any material that is not your own—whether you quote directly, summarize, paraphrase, or refer to it in passing in your essay—without acknowledging it.

But it is not only lack of acknowledgement that constitutes plagiarism: you plagiarize if you use the exact words of the source and do not put them in quotation marks. Finally, you plagiarize if you follow the structure of the original too closely.

Specifically, what kind of information must be acknowledged and what does not need to be? Two principles can guide you as you consider the question. You do not need to cite anything that falls under the category of *general knowledge*. If a typical reader is likely to know something, a citation may be unnecessary. Further, if a fact or idea is *easily obtainable*, a citation may also be unnecessary. (You may be told a specific number of sources that satisfies the "easily obtainable" criterion—often three.)

Both these categories depend on your audience; for example, if you were writing for an audience that is knowledgeable about the topic, your essay would probably contain fewer citations than if you were writing for a general audience that is less knowledgeable and would probably find it difficult to trace the information. If in doubt, err on the side of caution and make the citation.

The questions in the box below about citation are often asked by students beginning research projects at university.

documentation style
Guidelines for documenting sources put forth in style manuals and handbooks for researchers and other academic writers.

Other common forms of plagiarism include using the exact words of a source without putting them in quotation marks and following the structure of the original too closely.

Seven Common Questions about Source Citation

Q: Do you need to cite information that you do not quote directly in your essay?

A: Yes. Specific content requires a citation, whether you use direct quotation, paraphrase, or summary to integrate it into your essay. Even general information may necessitate a citation.

Q: If you already knew a fact and you encounter it in a secondary source, does it need to be cited?

A: Probably. The issue is not whether you know something but whether your reader would know it. If you are writing for an audience familiar with your topic, you may not need to cite "common knowledge," that is, knowledge that all or almost all readers would be expected to know. If you are uncertain about the common knowledge factor, make the citation.

Q: What about specific information, such as a date, that is easy to look up, though it may not be common knowledge?

A: A fact that is easily obtained from a number of different sources (even if a typical reader would not know it) may not need to be cited. Other factors could be involved (for example, would a typical reader know where to look?). Your instructor may be able to tell you how many sources constitute "easily obtainable" information; a minimum number often given is three (i.e., at least three common, easily accessible sources).

Q: If you use a source that you have already used earlier in the same paragraph, do you need to cite it a second time?

A: Yes, you do if another source, or your own point, has intervened. If all the content of the paragraph is from one source, you may not have to cite it until the end of the paragraph. However, always make it clear to the reader what is taken from a source.

Q: Is it necessary to cite "popular" quotations, for example, the kind that appear in dictionaries of quotations? What about dictionary definitions?

A: Yes, these kinds of quotations should be cited unless the quotation has entered everyday use. For example, the first quotation would not need a citation, though the second would—even though it is unlikely a reader would know either source: "When the going gets tough, the tough get going"; "Making your mark on the world is hard. If it were easy, everybody would do it." (Joan W. Donaldson is the author of the first quotation; Barack Obama is the author of the second). Dictionary definitions should be cited.

(Continued)

Q: Does a list of your sources on the final page of your essay mean that you do not have to cite the sources within the essay itself?

A: No. All major documentation methods require both in-text and final-page citations. (In some formats, the in-text citations consist only of numbers.)

Q: What can you do to guarantee that the question of plagiarism never arises in your essay?

A: Honesty alone may not be enough, but it is a good start. Knowledge about what needs to be and what may not need to be cited is also essential and can be learned. Finally, being conscious of "grey areas" and checking with your instructor or another expert, such as a librarian, should almost guarantee that this serious issue doesn't arise.

Note: A good strategy for avoiding plagiarism (and consciously integrating the information) is to carefully study the passage you want to use; then, close the text and write the passage from memory completely in your own words. Finally, look at the passage again, ensuring that it is different in its structure as well as in its language—and that you have accurately restated the thought behind it. Don't forget to include the citation.

Major Documentation Styles

There are four major documentation styles but many variants on these styles. The Modern Language Association (MLA) style is widely used in the humanities, including English literature. The American Psychological Association (APA) style is used in many social science disciplines and some science disciplines, as well as in education and business. Both are parenthetical styles, meaning that a brief citation including the author's name and page number (MLA) or name and publication year (APA) follows the reference in the text of an essay.

Both the Chicago Manual of Style (CMS), used in history, and the Council of Science Editors (CSE) style, used in mathematics, biology, health sciences, and some other science disciplines, follow a number/note method. Superscript (raised) numbers are placed after the in-text references; they correspond to the numbers at the end of the document where full bibliographical information is given (in the Chicago style, these notes can also be placed at the foot of the page). MLA, APA, and CMS styles also require a final-page listing of sources alphabetically by last name. CSE style requires a listing of sources that follows the order they were used in the text.

Some book publishers use a distinct "house" style, and different departments at your institution may publish their own set of guidelines applicable to students in that discipline. The major manuals are also constantly changing as new editions are brought out. Fortunately, there are an increasing number of online resources for the various documentation styles; university library sources are the most reliable. Each organization that produces the manuals also maintains websites with recent updates. Further, when you decide on an area of study, you will become familiar with the style prominent in your discipline.

Many of the distinguishing features of the styles are given below. Examples of the most common bibliographic formats are then provided.

Note: A signal phrase names the author before the reference is given; thus, in MLA and APA styles, the parenthetical citation will not include the author's name if a signal phrase precedes it.

Electronic formats in all styles should include as much information as is available. If an author's name is not given, use the name of the organization or sponsoring group in its place. If there is no sponsor, use the work's title alphabetized by the first major word. MLA and CSE styles require you to include date of access for Internet citations; APA and CMS style do not. Paragraph number or section heading can sometimes be used to identify location, if necessary, if page numbers are absent.

signal phrase
Introduces a reference by naming the author(s) and usually includes a "signal verb" (e.g., *states*, *argues*, *explains*).

MLA (Modern Language Association) Style

- MLA uses an "author/number" referencing format. The basic parenthetical format includes author's last name and page number with no punctuation in between:

(Slotkin 75)

(Rusel and Wilson 122)

- If a signal phrase is used, only the page number will be in parentheses:

Slotkin states, " . . ." (75)

- Block quotations should be used for important passages at least four typed lines long. They are indented 10 spaces from the left margin, double-spaced, and do not include quotation marks. The end period precedes the parenthetical citation.

- The final page, titled "Works Cited," alphabetically lists by author's last name all works used in the essay. Entries are double-spaced with the first line flush left and successive lines indented one-half inch (1.25 cm). All major words in titles begin with a capital letter. Names of books and journals are italicized, and the medium of publication is included at the end of most entries.

MLA Sample Formats

Book (one author)

Berger, Arthur Asa. *Video Games: A Popular Culture Phenomenon*. New Brunswick: Transaction, 2002. Print.

Book/Journal (multiple authors)

Bolaria, B. Singh, and Peter S. Li. *Racial Oppression in Canada*. 2nd edn. Toronto: Garamond Press, 1988. Print. (second author's name is not reversed)

More than three authors: Give the name of the first author, followed by a comma and "et al."

Selection in Edited Work

Wright, Austin M. "On Defining the Short Story: The Genre Question." *Short Story Theory at a Crossroads*. Ed. Susan Lohafer and Jo Ellyn Clarey. Baton Rouge: Louisiana State UP, 1989. 46–63. Print. (UP is the abbreviation for *University Press*)

Journal Article

Fetterley, Judith. "*Little Women:* Alcott's Civil War." *Feminist Studies* 5.2 (1979): 369–83. Print.

Include both volume and issue number. For electronic articles in a database, include database name in italics before "Web."

Internet Source

Environment Canada. "10 Things You Should Know about Climate Change." 12 Aug. 2012. Web. 15 Aug. 2013. <www.ec.gc.ca/cc/default.asp?lang=En&n=2F049262-1>.

The first date is that of the site; access date follows with the publication medium between. Angle brackets enclose the website address if the source would be hard to locate without it or if your instructor requires it.

APA (American Psychological Association) Style

- APA uses an author–year referencing format. One basic format includes author's last name and year of publication (general references and summaries); the other basic format also includes page number (direct quotations and paraphrases).
- Commas separate author's name from year and year from page number (if required); "p." or "pp." (for more than one page) precedes page number(s):

  (Hasan et al., 2012, p. 224)

  (Bryson & de Castell, 1998, pp. 542–544)

- If a signal phrase is used, the year will follow the author's name in parentheses:

  Hasan et al. (2012) explain, . . .

- If a page number is required, it will be placed in parentheses after the reference:

  Hasan et al. explain, "Contrary to what Calvin thinks, experimental studies do allow for causal inferences (p. 224)"

- Works by the same author(s) from the same year are assigned different letters—e.g., 2004a, 2004b. They are listed this way in "References" alphabetically by title.

- Block quotations should be used for important passages more than 40 words long. They are indented five spaces from the left margin, double-spaced, and do not include quotation marks. The end period precedes the parenthetical citation.
- The final page, titled "References," alphabetically lists by author's last name all works used in the essay; authors' initials are used, not given names. Entries are double-spaced with the first line flush left and successive lines indented five spaces. In article and book titles, only the first letter of first words, first words following colons, and proper nouns, along with all letters in acronyms, are capitalized.

APA Sample Formats

Book (one author)

Heyd, D. (1992). *Genetics: Moral issues in the creation of people.* Berkeley, CA: University of California Press.

Book/Journal (multiple authors)

Sahalein, R., & Tuttle, D. (1997). *Creatine: Nature's muscle builder.* Garden City Park, NY: Avery Publishing Group. (Second author's name is reversed.)

Three to seven authors: give all names; *more than seven:* list first six names followed by three points of ellipsis and the last author's name.

Selection in Edited Work

Chesney-Lind, M. & Brown, M. (1999). Girls and violence: An overview. In D. Flannery & C. R. Huff (Eds.), *Youth violence: Prevention, intervention and social policy* (pp. 171–199). Washington, D.C.: American Psychiatric Press.

Journal Article

Clegg, S., Mayfield, W., & Trayhurn, D. (1999). Disciplinary discourses: A case study of gender in information technology and design courses. *Gender and Education, 11*(1), 43–55.

The volume number is italicized; the issue number (required if each issue begins with page number 1) is not italicized. If it is available for print and electronic articles, include the DOI (digital object identifier) as last item; it is not followed by a period.

Internet Source

Statistics Canada (2010, March 26). Gasoline and fuel oil, price by urban centre. Retrieved from www40.Statcan.ca/101/cst01/econ154a.htm.

CMS (Chicago Manual of Style) Style

- CMS uses the "note" referencing format with numbered footnotes (at the bottom of the page) or endnotes (at the end of the text) corresponding to superscript numbers in the text of the essay. Each entry is single-spaced with the first line indented five spaces and successive lines flush left.

- Full bibliographic details are given for first references, beginning with author's first name(s), followed by surname, work's title, and (in parentheses) place of publication, publisher, and date, and ending with page number(s).

  e.g., "As is well known, the sociobiologist E.O. Wilson has entitled one of his books *Consilience*."[15]

The note would look like this:

> 15. Edward O. Wilson, *Consilience: The Unity of Knowledge* (New York: Alfred A. Knopf, 1998).

Successive references are condensed forms of the first citation:

> 18. Wilson, *Consilience*, 55.

Consecutive references to the same work:

> 19. Ibid.

(the page number would follow if different from preceding note)

- Block quotations should be used for important passages at least four typed lines long. They are indented five spaces from the left margin, double-spaced, and do not include quotation marks. The end period precedes the parenthetical citation.
- On the final page, titled "Bibliography," entries are listed alphabetically by author's last name. Entries are single-spaced with double-spacing between them; the first line is flush left, and successive lines are indented five spaces.

CMS Sample Formats

Book (one author)

Note:

> 1. Keith D. McFarland, The Korean War: An Annotated Bibliography (New York: Garland, 1986), 91.

Bibliography:

> McFarland, Keith D. The Korean War: An Annotated Bibliography. New York: Garland, 1986.

Book/Journal (multiple authors)

Note:

> 2. Bob Beal and Rod Macleod, *Prairie Fire: The 1885 North-West Rebellion* (Edmonton: Hurtig Publishers, 1984), 104.

More than three authors: The name of the first author is given, followed by "and others."

Bibliography:

Beal, Bob, and Rod Macleod. *Prairie Fire: The 1885 North-West Rebellion.* Edmonton: Hurtig Publishers, 1984.

More than three authors: All authors are named (the second author's name is not reversed).

Selection in Edited Work

3. Marcia K. Lieberman, "'Some Day My Prince Will Come': Female Acculturation through the Fairy Tale," in *Don't Bet on the Prince*, ed. Jack Zipes and Ingrid Svendsen (New York: Routledge, 1987), 185–200.

Bibliography:

Lieberman, Marcia K. "'Some Day My Prince Will Come': Female Acculturation through the Fairy Tale." In *Don't Bet on the Prince*, edited by Jack Zipes and Ingrid Svendsen, 185–200. New York: Routledge, 1987.

Journal Article

Note:

4. Robert Garner, "Political Ideologies and the Moral Status of Animals," *Journal of Political Ideologies* 8 (2003): 235.

If it is available for an electronic article, include the DOI as last item, followed by a period for both note and bibliographic entry. If there is no DOI, include a URL. The access date is optional for an online article.

The issue number is required if each issue begins with page number 1: 8, no. 1 (2003).

Bibliography:

Smith, John Maynard. "The Origin of Altruism." *Nature* 393 (1998): 639–40.

Internet Source

Note:

5. The Internet Encyclopedia of Philosophy, "Deductive and Inductive Arguments," www.iep.utm.edu/d/ded-ind.htm.

Bibliography entries are listed alphabetically by the first major word of each entry; if the access date is required, it can be placed in parentheses: (accessed March 21, 2014).

CSE (Council of Science Editors) Style

- CSE uses a citation–sequence referencing format with superscript or bracketed numbers corresponding to numbered sources at the end of the text in a separate section.

- To cite more than one source for a specific reference, each source number is included, followed by a comma with no space between; a dash is used to indicate consecutive sources (e.g., 2–5).

  There is increasing evidence for the efficacy of exercise [10,11] and fish oils [12,13] in the treatment and prevention of depression.

- For references to a source for a second time or more, the number first assigned to the source continues to be used.
- On the final page, titled "References" or "Cited References," authors are listed beginning with the author's last name followed by initial(s) with no spaces or periods between initials. The order of entries is based on their sequence in the text (i.e., the first cited source is assigned the number 1, the second one the number 2, etc.). Entries are single-spaced with double-spacing between them.

CSE Sample Formats

Book (one author)

> 1. Fleiss JL. The design and analysis of clinical experiments. New York (NY): John Wiley and Sons; 1986.

Book/Journal (multiple authors)

> 2. Thursby, JG, Thursby, MC. Intellectual property: university licensing and the Bayh-Dole Act. Science 2003; 301:1052.

More than 10 authors: The names of the first 10 authors are listed, followed by *and others.*

Selection in Edited Work

> 3. Saper CB, Iversen S, Frackowiak R. Integration of sensory and motor function: the association areas of the cerebral cortex and the cognitive capabilities of the brain. In: Kandel ER, Schwartz JH, Jessell TM, editors. Principles of neural science. 4th ed. New York (NY): McGraw-Hill; 2000. p. 349–380.

Journal Article

> 4. Bayer R, Fairchild AL. The genesis of public health ethics. Bioethics. 2004;18(6):473–492.

CSE uses abbreviations for most journal titles; for example, Can J Psychiatry is the abbreviation for *Canadian Journal of Psychiatry.*

Internet Source

> 5. Health Canada. A report on mental illnesses in Canada [Internet]. Ottawa (ON): Health Canada; 2002. [modified 2002 Oct 15; cited 2006 Nov 28], Available from: www.phac-aspe.gc.ea/publicat/miic-mmae/.

Sample Student Research Essay

The essay below uses MLA documentation style.

The Price of Play? Social, Physical, and Mental Consequences of Video Game Addiction among Adults

by Lorinda Fraser

1   As the sophistication of technology and our dependency on computers increase so too does the amount of time spent on the Internet, and for some, playing computer video games. But how much game play is too much? Video games are no longer relegated to video arcades, and with the recent proliferation of mobile devices, games are accessible at any time and anywhere. While video game addiction is not currently a formally recognized term or disorder, concern about the amount of time spent on these pursuits is growing. Research and alarming reports regarding the addiction of children and adolescents appear to be readily available; however, much less research has been conducted on the impact of video game addiction on adults. "The video gaming world has been established, but the actual physical and psychosocial effects of video gaming [on adults] have not" (Sublette and Mullan). Despite the lack of consensus on whether the act of video game playing qualifies as a clinical addiction and a shortage of "[e]pidemiological surveys and clinical studies" (Flisher 559), there seems to be no debate that excessive video gaming by adult players can lead to addictive behaviour, resulting in adverse social, physical, and mental consequences.

2   Psychiatrist Dr van Goldberg was the first to use the term "Internet Addiction" (IA) in 1995 (Flisher 557). While the term "IA," or its sub-component "video game addiction," waits to be formally recognized by "reputable organization[s] responsible for defining disorders of the mind or body" (Wood 169), many experts have already begun establishing criteria for describing excessive video game playing based on existing criteria for gambling addiction. According to these experts, for video game playing to be considered an addiction, it would need to meet a minimum of three of the Diagnostic and Statistical Manual of Mental Disorders (DSM IV) and International Statistical Classification of Diseases (ICD-10) criteria for gambling addiction: "tolerance, salience, withdrawal symptoms, difficulty controlling use, continued use despite negative consequences, neglecting other activities, desire to cut down" (Flisher 557). Kimberly Young further adapted the criteria specifically for IA, and subsequently, video game addiction:

> preoccupation with use of the computer, thinking about previous online activity/ anticipation of next online session; craving more and more time at the computer; making efforts to cut back on computer use or stop, and failing repeatedly; feelings of emptiness, depression, and irritation when not at the computer or when attempting to cut down; staying online longer than originally intended; jeopardizing significant relationships, job, career, or education because of the Internet; hiding the extent of computer/Internet use to family and friends; use of the Internet as a way of escaping from problems or of relieving a dysphoric mood (e.g. feelings of helplessness, guilt, anxiety, depression). (qtd. in Flisher 557)

Leading up to her thesis, Fraser justifies her approach to the topic, explaining, as the writers of scholarly essays often do, that the topic has not been adequately explored.

As this source appeared in pre-publication form without page numbers, they cannot be included in the citation. Use of current sources, however, is critical in an essay on such a recent topic.

Fraser's clear thesis states that she will be investigating three effects of "addictive behaviour" in adult video gamers.

MLA documentation style includes the author's name and page number with a space between. Later in the essay, Fraser names the author before the reference; the citation does not then repeat the author's name.

This quotation is set up in the block format— indented, double-spaced, and without quotation marks. This format should be reserved for lengthy and important content.

In the next two paragraphs, Fraser mediates the debate between Wood, who believes that excessive video gaming is not an addiction, and Turner, who believes that it is. Considering contradictory findings and viewpoints and drawing conclusions about their respective merits through the use of critical thinking can be an important part of research.

3   Those labelling excessive video game playing as addictive have their challengers. Wood writes, "If people cannot deal with their problems, and choose instead to immerse themselves in a game, then surely their gaming behaviour is actually a symptom rather than the specific cause of their problem" (172). He lists four factors he feels need to be considered before video game playing can be labelled an "addiction":

1. That some people are labelled "addicts" . . . when they have no problems with their game playing behaviour.
2. That some people who have underlying problems may choose to play games to avoid dealing with those problems.
3. That some people who are concerned about their own behaviour because of either 1 or 2 above end up labelling themselves as video game "addicts."
4. That some people are not very good at managing how much time they spend playing video games. (176)

4   However, Turner argues that alcohol and gambling, among other addictions, could also meet these criteria. Furthermore, he questions Wood's assertion that if video games were "inherently addictive . . . a large[r] proportion of the population would be seriously addicted" to them (Turner 186). Again, if such an argument were applied to alcoholism and gambling, they too would no longer be considered addictions. However, Wood's contention that excessive game playing is a symptom of other problems rather than their cause also loses its validity when applied to addictions such as drug abuse, alcoholism, and gambling. Typically, well adjusted, stable people without underlying problems do not turn to addictive substances or avoidance activities in the first place. As Turner asks, "do happy people inject heroin?" (188).

5   The social consequences of video game addiction on adults' lives are numerous. Reports of an overall decrease in "the quality of interpersonal relationships" have led to social withdrawal, marital problems, and divorce (qtd. in Sublette and Mullan). Disturbed sleep patterns, physical ailments, and increased mental-health sick days can all negatively impact work performance resulting in job loss (Flisher 558). An international survey found that online video game players sacrificed "another hobby or pastime" (25 per cent), "socializing with friends, family and/or partner" (20 per cent), "sleep" (20 per cent), and/or "work and/or education" (less than 10 per cent) (Weaver et al. 300) in order to play their game of choice. As with other addictions, the effects on a video game addict's children would also likely show significant impact on their development and relationship with the addicted parent.

6   The physical repercussions of a sedentary pastime affect both male and female players; these can range from troublesome to life threatening. Flisher lists relatively mild complaints such as repetitive strain injury and back ache which can progress to more serious issues such as the development of deep vein thrombosis and pulmonary embolus (558). "Differences are [also] evident for three of the five measures in the health-assessment domain . . . [where] video game players report lower health status, a higher frequency of poor-mental-days, and higher BMI [body mass index]" (Weaver et al. 302) than non-players. Video game players also report poor sleep quality due to disturbed sleep schedules and the effects of withdrawal symptoms and cravings (qtd. in Sublette and Mullan) when video games are stopped. In a few alarmingly extreme cases, at least 10 Korean and Chinese video game players have collapsed and died as a result of multiple days of continuous video game playing (Flisher 558).

The writer uses brackets and an ellipsis to indicate changes to a direct quotation. However, it might have been more effective if she had paraphrased this passage instead as overuse of brackets and ellipses can be distracting.

7   In contrast to the physical and social repercussions associated with excessive video game playing, mental-health issues effect male and female players differently. While both sexes experience depression, anger problems, anxiety disorders (Flisher 558), and reduced health status (Weaver et al. 303), male players experience more negative ramifications than their female counterparts with higher addiction scores, along with greater aggressive attitudes and reduced empathy (qtd. in Sublette and Mullan). Also, female players seem to use video games as a form of "digital self-medication," using their games to "take their minds off their worries" whereas male players "prefer video games that provide an impetus [stimulant] for socializing" (Weaver et al. 303–04). Noar, Benac, and Harris (qtd. in Weaver et al. 304) suggest "gender-based tailoring" for treatment options of the social effects of video game addiction.

8   Currently, no standardized test for identifying video game addiction exists. The development of a "theory-based clinical instrument" for measuring all addictions to technology (King, Delfabbro, and Zajac 74) would be beneficial to the study, treatment, and prevention of video game addiction. Previously, 30 hours of video game playing a week was considered "unhealthy." Today, video game playing for more than 50 hours per week is now considered a "highly prevalent activity" (75), but no definitive benchmark has been established (73). The Problem Video Game Playing Test (PVGT) was developed to identify the "core components" of addiction and investigate the negative personal and social consequences of extreme playing (76) and has shown initial success for gauging problem video game playing (85). Nevertheless, effective treatment options need to be established and standardized. Currently, in the US, psychological treatment programs, telephone counselling services, and treatment clinics using the 12-step program along with CBT [Cognitive Behavioural Therapy], family therapy, group therapy, social skills training, and addiction counselling have been offered. Chinese treatment clinics take a stricter approach, implementing regimented timetables, discipline, medication, and electric shock treatment (Flisher 558). Young proposes implementing "behavioural strategies" such as "practising the opposite, . . . external stoppers , . . . setting clear goals, reminder cards, . . . personal inventory, . . . [and] abstinence" (Flisher 558). Due to the relatively new proliferation of technological addictions, long-term research on the effectiveness of these treatments needs to be conducted before any can be considered a success (559).

9   While moderate online video game play seems to have few negative consequences (Sublette and Mullan), it is reasonable to assume that any activity engaged in for prolonged periods of time will eventually affect one's social, physical, and mental health. Family and friends of avid video game players may experience the negative effects of game playing first-hand. As relationships develop and lifestyle choices become increasingly important beyond the adolescent years, concern for the player's physical and mental health proportionally escalates. As the popularity and accessibility of immersive environments increase, the need for evidence-based research becomes crucial to ensure an emphasis on prevention, education, and treatment of the negative costs of gaming. Future research needs to include consistency in data collection, inclusion and expansion of demographic information, and alternate forms of testing; research also must consider socio-economic implications (Sublette and Mullan). "[I]t is time for . . . standardized treatment protocols, [v]alidation of diagnostic instruments, and the establishment of a set of standard criteria . . . " (Flisher 559) to determine how much play is too much and when the consequences outweigh the entertainment.

As the phrases in the last two sentences are memorable, use of a mixed format with direct quotation was a good choice. Notice the precise placement of citations throughout this paragraph to ensure that the sources are unambiguous.

In her final paragraph, Fraser draws conclusions based on her synthesis of the major studies on her topic. Like the writers of scholarly essays, she applies these findings to society and families, and ends by suggesting further research.

In the interests of efficiency in her last sentence, Fraser combines two sentences from the same page of her source. The original reads, "Arguably, it is time for the World Health Organization and health departments around the world to develop effective health polices to increase public awareness of IA and produce standardized treatment protocols. Validation of diagnostic instruments and the establishment of a set of standard criteria for IA will aid swift and accurate diagnosis."

Fraser has accessed her sources electronically so has followed the MLA guidelines for electronic sources from a database. See page 150.

For articles published online rather than in a database, MLA advises that as many publication details as possible should be given. In this case, neither page numbers nor volume/issue is available. Note the abbreviation for "no pagination."

When a work has more than three authors, all authors' names can be given or the first author only followed by *et al.* ("and others").

Works Cited

Flisher, Caroline. "Getting Plugged in: An Overview of Internet Addiction." *Journal of Paediatrics and Child Health* 46.10 (2010): 557–59. *Academic Search Complete*. Web. 10 Mar. 2011.

King, Daniel L., Paul H. Delfabbro, and Ian T. Zajac. "Preliminary Validation of a New Clinical Tool for Identifying Problem Video Game Playing." *International Journal of Mental Health and Addiction* 9.1 (2011): 72–87. *Academic Search Complete*. Web. 10 Mar. 2011.

Sublette, Victoria, and Barbara Mullan. "Consequences of Play: A Systematic Review of the Effects of Online Gaming." *International Journal of Mental Health and Addiction* (2010): n. pag. Web. 10 Mar. 2011.

Turner, Nigel. "A Comment on 'Problems with the Concept of Video Game 'Addiction': Some Case Study Examples.'" *International Journal of Mental Health and Addiction* 6.2 (2008): 186–90. *Academic Search Complete*. Web. 10 Mar. 2011.

Weaver, James B., Darren Mays, Stephanie Sargent Weaver, Wendi Kannenberg, Gary L. Hopkins, Doğan Eroğlu, and Jay M. Bernhardt. "Health-Risk Correlates of Video-Game Playing Among Adults." *American Journal of Preventative Medicine* 37.4 (2009): 299–305. *Medline*. Web. 10 Mar. 2011.

Wood, Richard. "Problems with the Concept of Video Game 'Addiction': Some Case Study Examples." *International Journal of Mental Health and Addiction* 6.2 (2008): 169–78. *Academic Search Complete*. Web. 10 Mar. 2011.

PART III
The Reader

UNIVERSITY ISSUES

Academic language and the challenge of reading for learning about science

Catherine E. Snow

(2,409 words)

Pre-reading

1. What are your perceptions of or associations with "academic language" or "academic reading"? Write down some of these perceptions in point or bulleted form. Where do your perceptions come from (e.g., high school classes, university instructors, textbooks, general knowledge)? As a pre-reading activity, you could exchange your list with another person's and discuss some of the similarities and differences.

1   A major challenge to students learning science is the academic language in which science is written. Academic language is designed to be concise, precise, and authoritative. To achieve these goals, it uses sophisticated words and complex grammatical constructions that can disrupt reading comprehension and block learning. Students need help in learning academic vocabulary and how to process academic language if they are to become independent learners of science.

2   Literacy scholars and secondary teachers alike are puzzled by the frequency with which students who read words accurately and fluently have trouble comprehending text (*1, 2*). Such students have mastered what was traditionally considered the major obstacle to reading success: the depth and complexity of the English spelling system. But many middle- and high-school students are less able to convert their word-reading skills into comprehension when confronted with texts in science (or math or social studies) than they are when confronted with texts of fiction or discursive essays. The greater difficulty of science, math, and social studies texts than of texts encountered in English language arts (mostly narratives) suggests that the comprehension of "academic language" may be one source of the challenge. So what is academic language?

3   Academic language is one of the terms [others include language of education (*3*), language of schooling (*4*), scientific language (*5*), and academic English

(*6, 7*)] used to refer to the form of language expected in contexts such as the exposition of topics in the school curriculum, making arguments, defending propositions, and synthesizing information. There is no exact boundary when defining academic language; it falls toward one end of a continuum (defined by formality of tone, complexity of content, and degree of impersonality of stance), with informal, casual, conversational language at the other extreme. There is also no single academic language, just as there is no single variety of educated American English. Academic language features vary as a function of discipline, topic, and mode (written versus oral, for example), but there are certain common characteristics that distinguish highly academic from less academic or more conversational language and that make academic language—even well-written, carefully constructed, and professionally edited academic language—difficult to comprehend and even harder to produce (*8*).

4   Among the most commonly noted features of academic language are conciseness, achieved by avoiding redundancy; using a high density of information-bearing words, ensuring precision of expression; and relying on grammatical processes to compress complex ideas into few words (*8, 9*). Less academic language, on the other hand, such as that used in emails, resembles oral language forms more closely: Most sentences begin with pronouns or animate subjects; verbs refer to actions rather than relations; and long sentences are characterized by sequencing of information

rather than embeddings. The two excerpts in Fig. 1, both about torque (a topic included in many state standards for seventh grade science), display the difference between a nonacademic text (from the website www.lowrider.com) and an academic text (from the website www.tutorvista.com).

5 A striking difference between more informal and more academic language exemplified in the Lowrider/TutorVista text comparison is the greater presence of expressive, involved, interpersonal stance markers in the first Lowrider posting (". . .guys get caught up. . .," "I frequently get asked. . .," "Most of us. . .,") and in the response ("Jason you are right on bro"). Though both the Lowrider authors are writing to inform, they are not assuming the impersonal authoritative voice that is characteristic of academic language. They claim their authority to provide information about the advantage of torque over horsepower adjustments on the basis of personal experience. The scientist's authoritative stance, on the other hand, derives from membership in a community committed to a shared epistemology; this stance is expressed through a reduction in the use of personal pronouns, a preference for epistemically warranted evaluations (such as "rigorous study" and "questionable analysis") over personally expressive evaluations (such as "great study" and "funky analysis"), and a focus on general rather than specific claims. Maintaining the impersonal authoritative stance creates a distanced tone that is often puzzling to adolescent readers and is extremely difficult for adolescents to emulate in writing.

6 Perhaps the simplest basis for comparing the Lowrider and TutorVista texts is to consider how rare in other contexts are the words they use most frequently. The rarest words used in the Lowrider text are the special term "lolo" and its alternative form "lowrider," "upgrade," "carb," "HP," "exhaust," "spin," and "torque." Only two words from the Academic Word List (*10*), a list of words used frequently across academic texts of different disciplines, appear in this passage. The TutorVista text rare words include "magnitude," "perpendicular," "lever," "pivot," "hinge," "fulcrum," and "torque," and it uses the academic words "task," "maximum," "significance," and "illustration." The difference in word selection reflects the convention in the more academic text of presenting precise information in a dense, concise manner.

7 Nominalizations are a grammatical process of converting entire sentences (such as "Gutenberg invented the printing press") into phrases that can then be embedded in other sentences (such as "Gutenberg's invention of the printing press revolutionized the dissemination of information"). Nominalizations are crucial to the conciseness expected in academic language. In the TutorVista sentence "We may increase the turning effect of the force by changing the point of application of force and by changing the direction of force," "application" and "direction" are nominalizations representing entire propositions. "Application" is shorthand for "where we apply," and "direction" is shorthand for "how we direct." Thus, although this sentence has the same apparent structure as "We can get a smile from a baby by changing his diaper and by patting his back," the processing load is much higher. "Increase" in the original sentence is a verb referring to a relation between two quantities, whereas "get" in the baby-sentence adaptation refers to an action or effect in the real world. "Diaper" and "back" are physical entities subjected to actions, whereas "application" and "direction" are themselves actions that have been turned into nouns. Part of the complexity of academic language derives from the fact that we use the syntactic structures acquired for talking about agents and actions to talk about entities and relations, without recognizing the challenge that that transition poses to the reader. In particular, in science classes we may expect students to process these sentences without explicit instruction in their structure.

8 Science teachers are not generally well prepared to help their students penetrate the linguistic puzzles that science texts present. They of course recognize that teaching vocabulary is key, but typically focus on the science vocabulary (the bolded words in the text), often without recognizing that those bolded words are defined with general-purpose academic words that students also do not know. Consider the TutorVista definition of torque: "Torque is the product of the magnitude of the force and the lever arm of the force." Many seventh graders are unfamiliar with the terms "magnitude" and "lever"; and some proportion will think they understand "product," "force," and "arm" without realizing that those terms are being used in technical, academic ways here, with meanings quite different from those of daily life. Yet this definition,

From www.lowrider.com/forums/10-Under-the-Hood/topics/183-HP-vs-torque/posts (spelling as in the original posting)

Often times guys get caught up in the hype of having a big HP motor in their lolo. I frequently get asked whats the best way to get big numbers out of their small block. The answer is not HP, but torque. "You sell HP, you feel torque" as the old saying goes. Most of us are running 155/80/13 tires on our lolo's. Even if you had big HP numbers, you will *never* get that power to the ground, at least off the line. I have a 64 Impala SS 409, that i built the motor in. While it is a completely restored original (I drive it rolling on 14" 72 spoke cross laced Zeniths), the motor internals are not. It now displaces 420 CI, with forged pistons and blalanced rotating assembly. The intake, carb and exhaust had to remain OEM for originality's sake, and that greatly reduces the motors potential. Anyway, even with the original 2 speed powerglide, it spins those tires with alarming ease, up to 50 miles per hour!

In my 62, I built a nice 383 out of an 86 Corvette. I built it for good bottom end pull, since it is a lowrider with 8 batteries. And since it rides on the obligitory 13's, torque is what that car needs. It pulls like an ox right from idle, all the way up to its modest 5500 redline. But I never take it that high, as all the best power is from 1100 to 2700 RPM.

So when considering an engine upgrade, look for modifications that improve torque. That is what your lolo needs!

© iStockphoto.com/Steve Bower

Posted by Jason Dave, Sept 2009

Jason you are right on bro. I have always found an increase in torque placement has not only provided better top end performance but also improved gas mileage in this expensive gas times.

Posted by Gabriel Salazar, Nov 2009

FIGURE 1 Examples of nonacademic text (Lowrider, above) and academic text (TutorVista, right).

with its sophisticated and unfamiliar word meanings, is the basis for all the rest of the TutorVista exposition: the trade-off between magnitude and direction of force.

9   Efforts to help students understand science cannot ignore their need to understand the words used to write and talk about science: the all-purpose academic words as well as the discipline-specific ones. Of course some students acquire academic vocabulary on their own, if they read widely and if their comprehension skills are strong enough to support inferences about the meaning of unknown words (*11*). The fact that many adolescents prefer reading Web sites to books (*12*), however, somewhat decreases access to good models

of academic language even for those interested in technical topics. Thus, they have few opportunities to learn the academic vocabulary that is crucial across their content-area learning. It is also possible to explicitly teach academic vocabulary to middle-school students. Word Generation is a middle-school program developed by the Strategic Education Research Partnership that embeds all-purpose academic words in interesting topics and provides activities for use in math, science, and social studies as well as English language arts classes in which the target words are used (see the website for examples) (*13*). Among the academic words taught in Word Generation are those used to make, assess, and defend claims, such as "data," "hypothesis," "affirm,"

From www.tutorvista.com/content/physics/physics-iii/rigid-body/torque.php

Torque is the product of the magnitude of the force and the lever arm of the force.

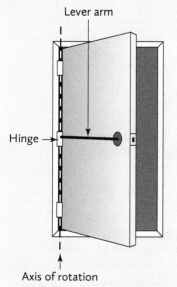

Lever arm

Hinge →

Axis of rotation

What is the significance of this concept in our everyday life?

Dependence of torque on lever arm

To increase the turning effect of force, it is not necessary to increase the magnitude of the force itself. We may increase the turning effect of the force by changing the point of application of force and by changing the direction of force.

Let us take the case of a heavy door. If a force is applied at a point, which is close to the hinges of the door, we may find it quite difficult to open or close the door. However, if the same force is applied at a point, which is at the maximum distance from hinges, we can easily close or open the door. The task is made easier if the force is applied at right angles to the plane of the door.

When we apply the force the door turns on its hinges. Thus a turning effect is produced when we try to open the door. Have you ever tried to do so by applying the force near the hinge? In the first case, we are able to open the door with ease. In the second case, we have to apply much more force to cause the same turning effect. What is the reason?

The turning effect produced by a force on a rigid body about a point, pivot or fulcrum is called the moment of a force or torque. It is measured by the product of the force and the perpendicular distance of the pivot from the line of action of the force.

Moment of a force = Force x Perpendicular distance of the pivot from the force.

The unit of moment of force is newton metre (N m). In the above example, in the first case the perpendicular distance of the line of action of the force from the hinge is much more than that in the second case. Hence, in the second case to open the door, we have to apply greater force.

"convince," "disprove," and "interpret." We designed Word Generation to focus on dilemmas, because these promote discussion and debate and provide motivating contexts for students and teachers to use the target words. For example, one week is devoted to the topic of whether junk food should be banned from schools, and another to whether physician-assisted suicide should be legal. Discussion is in itself a key contributor to science learning (*14*) and to reading comprehension (*15, 16*). Words learned through explicit teaching are unlikely to be retained if they are taught in lists rather than embedded in meaningful texts and if opportunities to use them in discussion, debate, and writing are not provided.

10   It is unrealistic to expect all middle- or high-school students to become proficient producers of academic language. Many graduate students still struggle to manage the authoritative stance, and the self-presentation as an expert that justifies it, in their writing. And it is important to note that not all features associated with the academic writing style (such as the use of passive voice, impenetrability of prose constructions, and indifference to literary niceties) are desirable. But the central features of academic language—grammatical embeddings, sophisticated and abstract vocabulary, precision of word choice, and use of nominalizations to refer to complex processes—reflect the need to present complicated ideas in efficient

ways. Students must be able to read texts that use these features if they are to become independent learners of science or social studies. They must have access to the all-purpose academic vocabulary that is used to talk about knowledge and that they will need to use in making their own arguments and evaluating others' arguments. Mechanisms for teaching those words and the ways that scientists use them should be a part of the science curriculum. Collaborations between designers of science curricula and literacy scholars are needed to develop and evaluate methods for helping students master the language of science at the undergraduate and high-school levels as well as at the middle-school level that Word Generation is currently serving.

Science. 2010. 328 (450).

References and Notes

1. Carnegie Council on Advancing Adolescent Literacy, *Time to Act: An Agenda for Advancing Adolescent Literacy for College and Career Success* (Carnegie Corporation of New York, New York, 2010); http://carnegie.org/fileadmin/Media/Publications/PDF/tta_Main.pdf.
2. J. Johnson, L. Martin-Hansen, Sci. Scope **28**, 12 (2005).
3. M.A.K. Halliday, paper presented at the Annual International Language in Education Conference, Hong Kong, December 1993.
4. M.J. Schleppegrell, *Linguist. Educ.* **12**, 431 (2001).
5. M.A.K. Halliday, J.R. Martin, *Writing Science: Literacy and Discursive Power* (Univ. of Pittsburgh Press, Pittsburgh, PA, 1993).
6. A. Bailey, *The Language Demands of School: Putting Academic English to the Test* (Yale Univ. Press, New Haven, CT, 2007).
7. R. Scarcella, *Academic English: A Conceptual Framework* (Technical Report 2003-1, Univ. of California Linguistic Minority Research Institute, Irvine, CA, 2003).
8. C. Snow, P. Uccelli, in *The Cambridge Handbook of Literacy*, D. Olson, N. Torrance, Eds. (Cambridge Univ. Press, New York, 2008), pp. 112–133.
9. Z. Fang, *Int. J. Sci. Educ.* **28**, 491 (2006).
10. A. Coxhead, *TESOL Q.* **34**, 213 (2000).
11. J. Lawrence, *Read. Psychol.* **30**, 445 (2009).
12. E.B. Moje, M. Overby, N. Tysvaer, K. Morris, *Harv. Educ. Rev.* **78**, 107 (2008).
13. C. Snow, J. Lawrence, C. White, J. *Res. Educ. Effectiveness* **2**, 325 (2009); www.wordgeneration.org.
14. J. Osborne, *Science* **328**, 463 (2010).
15. J. Lawrence, C. Snow, in *Handbook of Reading Research IV*, P.D. Pearson, M. Kamil., E. Moje, P. Afflerbach, Eds. (Routledge Education, London, 2010).
16. P.K. Murphy, I.A.G. Wilkinson, A.O. Soter, M.N. Hennessey, J.F. Alexander, J. *Educ. Psychol.* **62**, 387 (2009).
17. Preparation of this paper was made possible by collaborations supported by the Strategic Education Research Partnership and research funded by the Spencer Foundation, the William and Flora Hewlett Foundation, the Carnegie Corporation of New York, and the Institute for Education Sciences through the Council of Great City Schools. Thanks also to www.TutorVista.com for permission to reprint their lesson on torque.

Key and challenging words

discursive, proposition, redundancy, animate (adj), epistemology, emulate, syntactic, proficient, impenetrability

Questions

1. In your own words, explain the problem discussed in paragraph 1.
2. a) Why do you think the author believes that narrative texts are less difficult for high school students to understand than those in the sciences or social studies? b) Are narratives, such as novels, the only kinds of texts studied in English language arts?

3. How does academic language differ from non-academic (informal) language? Give two examples of everyday writing situations in which you would use non-academic language.

4. What is the function of the two excerpts in Fig. 1? How would you describe a typical reader of each excerpt? How could audience and purpose affect the way both excerpts are written?

5. Several phrases in this article demonstrate "a high density of information-bearing words" (paragraph 4). Using a dictionary, if necessary, explain in your own words the meaning of one of the following phrases from paragraph 5: "epistemically warranted evaluations"; "impersonal authoritative stance."

6. a) In your own words, define *nominalization* (paragraph 7); b) Change the following verbs into nouns that could be embedded in a sentence (e.g., *classify* (verb) → *classification* (noun: how we classify): associate, combine, observe.

7. Explain why putting all your effort into learning the meanings of bolded terms in textbooks might be of limited usefulness. What else can be done to make comprehension of academic language easier?

8. Why might it be particularly important to address the issue of academic language at the middle-school level?

Post-reading

1. Find an encyclopedia entry of at least 200 words on one topic and a comparable entry from the Internet, ensuring that the Internet entry is not from an educational or similar authoritative source. Using the same criteria as discussed in "Academic language and the challenge of reading for learning about science," compare the entries, noting the kinds of detail referred to in paragraphs 4–5.

2. Write a paragraph in informal (non-academic) prose that explains a topic you're knowledgeable about. Rewrite the paragraph in academic language. Use the guidelines given in paragraph 3. For example, you can use a "chatty" tone and 1st- and 2nd-person pronouns in the non-academic example but an impersonal tone and nouns originating as verbs (nominalizations) in the academic example.

3. The following are verbs from the Academic Word List (see paragraph 6). Change five verbs below into corresponding nouns and use each in a sentence on a topic you're interested in (e.g., identify → *identification*. The use of DNA identification to establish guilt in a criminal case has been subjected to recent legal challenges.).

   acquire
   assume
   compute
   conclude
   define
   estimate
   interpret
   regulate
   specify
   vary

Related website of interest

Oxford Advanced Learner's Dictionary (Academic Word List):
www.oxfordadvancedlearnersdictionary.com/academic/

Additional library reading

Krajcik, J.S., & Sutherland, L.M. (2010). Supporting students in developing literacy in science. *Science, 328,* 456–459.

Osborne, J. (2010). Arguing to learn in science: The role of collaborative, critical discourse. *Science, 328,* 463–466.

Schleicher, A. (2010). Assessing literacy across a changing world. *Science, 328,* 433–434.

van den Broek, P. (2010). Using texts in science education: Cognitive process and knowledge representation. *Science, 328,* 453–456.

University wars: The corporate administration vs. the vocation of learning

John McMurtry
(2,561 words)

Pre-reading

1. Unlike most of the other readings in this textbook, this essay is from a periodical published by an independent research institute. After scanning the article, write a brief paragraph considering at least two ways it differs from other readings, such as the one before and after it. Go to the institute's home page and read the brief introduction at www.policyalternatives. ca/offices; then, summarize this information in a couple of sentences.

1   For over 20 years, the academy has undergone a cumulative subordination of the university to corporate-market methods and appropriation of educational funds by central administrations overriding academic standards. This "internal assault on academic freedom" warned of by the Canadian Association of University Teachers (CAUT) has deepened and widened in both visible and invisible ways.

2   The occupation of the academy by a corporate agenda forwarded by university central administrations themselves has been analyzed by Howard Woodhouse in his forthcoming book, *Selling Out: Academic Freedom and the Corporate Market*. Yet tracking of this corporate invasion of the academy leads back to what is not yet confronted: the unaccountable right of central administrations to spend public money on their own growth, privileges, and salaries instead of the constitutional objectives of the university: the advancement of learning and the dissemination of knowledge. University presidents who once received a faculty member's salary with a modest stipend now arrange with their business-dominated boards to have incomes exceeding the prime minister's, while raising tuition fees for students to unaffordable levels.

3   In historical fact, university presidents deliberately planned with corporate executives to defund the universities *"to provide a greater incentive in the university community to seek out corporate partners,"* as Howard Buchbinder and Janice Newson put it in their 1991 paper, "Social Knowledge and Market Knowledge." This early strategy was planned by the Corporate Higher Education Forum (CHEF), founded in 1983 to join 25 university presidents to 25 senior executives of major corporations in setting the "new direction" for universities. Most academics were and are so caught up in their career microworlds that they did not recognize what was going on.

4   "Bring your knowledge to market" is the master slogan of the corporate occupation. As one professor promoted to deputy minister of education, and then to head of a major national research granting council declared: "I contend that the one global object of education must be for the people of Ontario to develop new services which we can offer in trade in the world market." To this Paul Martin, our next Prime Minister, added that "tripling of the commercialization of university research is not nearly fast enough."

5   The underlying contradiction in purpose and method between the market's private exchanges for money and the university's public commitment to advanced learning is not yet realized, even as low-paid sessional teachers replacing normal faculty carry more and more of university teaching loads and as salaries for corporate management escalate. University presidents now conceive themselves as corporate CEOs; research is increasingly only possible with outside money backing it; campuses are ever more pervasively occupied by corporate ads, brands and products; multinational corporations control the academic journal and textbook system across borders; and students are cumulatively made into debt-slaves to banks.

6   Few seem to observe that the ongoing financial marketization has led the rest of the world to ecological, social, and economic collapse; nor the coincidence of this profile with the academy as its knowledge servant. Even less do corporate administrations notice

the contradiction of values between the academy's purpose of critical search for truth and the university's stripping down to a commercial venture. As Ursula Franklin has memorably said from her own experience of the 1930s era of Nazi Germany in Europe and the corporatizing academy today: "They had their collaborators, and we have ours."

*

7 The control of all knowledge that corporations can copyright or patent is a given of the global market, but it systematically contradicts the university's freedom of dissemination of knowledge. Consider how academic journals have become copyright-controlled by private corporations' buying up the journals, and then multiplying the prices for their purchase and use by university libraries, whose own faculties have created the material for no cost to the corporations. Indeed, there is a standard copyright form required to be signed by faculty authors whose work is produced and refereed free for these corporately-owned journals, which demand exclusive world copyright in perpetuity for no returns to the university or the author.

8 Thus the public, the students, and the universities pay for faculties to research and publish and for all the university resources to support them, while private corporations buy the vehicles of publication to sell them back to the university communities that have created them at staggering prices that beggar libraries themselves. The academy's freedom of knowledge dissemination is thus reversed, but university administrators and funders increasingly press for still more commercialization of university knowledge creation.

9 In the global market as a whole, the inner logic of value adding is to turn money into more money for money managers and possessors, appropriating ever more money command for themselves. Corporate university administrations have been an unidentified fifth column of imposing this meta-program on universities. They lead privatization of the knowledge commons, the casualization and low pay of teaching positions, escalation of student costs, commodification of university spaces and functions, and—in general—streaming ever more university income into their corporate hierarchy of pay, privileges and positions performing no teaching or research functions.

10 There are five properties by which we can recognize corporate administrations:

1. They have exclusive hierarchical signing control of all financial expenditures, their ultimate lever of control mystified as their "leadership."
2. They do not perform the constitutional goals and primary functions of the academy: to advance learning and disseminate knowledge.
3. They draw off ever more of the academy's financial and physical resources to multiply their positions and incomes.
4. They call themselves "the university" although they perform no function of advancing or disseminating learning.
5. They selectively gang-attack faculty members for anti-academic reasons (as Professor Ken Westhues valuably describes in his book, *The Envy of Excellence: Administrative Mobbing of High-achieving Professors*).

11 At present, we may most deeply understand the university wars of corporate administration versus the learning vocation by laying bare their opposite structures of rationality, method, and purpose. Corporate administrators and their retinues follow the global market program of *i)* self-maximizing strategies in *ii)* conditions of scarcity, or conflict over *iii)* desired payoffs at *iv)* minimum costs for the self to *v)* appropriate ever more for the self with no productive contribution.

12 In direct opposition, those in the learning vocation follow an opposite inner value code: *i)* to maximize learning advancement and dissemination by *ii)* knowledge sharing without limit for *iii)* understanding and truth as ultimate value in itself at *iv)* any cost of difficulty to *v)* develop humanity's more inclusive comprehension of natural and human phenomena.

13 We can directly see corporate administrations warring against the learning vocation by an onslaught of anti-learning practices. Corporate research displaces independent science; knowledge sharing is prohibited by contract and specialty lock-in; research is made dependent on external money received by faculty; every decision is increasingly financialized with money gain the supreme value; and, to fortify the powers to impose marketization, those who follow the

search for truth where it leads against the ruling value program are besieged by bureaucratic campaigns of anti-educative isolation and destruction of academic freedom—for example, inciting students to formal complaint, publishing personal attacks, closing off academic resources, and perhaps, as in the case of Professor Denis Rancourt of the University of Ottawa, CEO banning from campus, handcuffing and firing.

*

14   To get a sense of the academy's increasing submergence in corporate-market values, consider the words of the past Harvard President, Larry Summers, now chief economic adviser to the Obama administration. He was interviewed by the *Globe and Mail* in glowing admiration after a lecture in 2003 at University of Toronto. "The essential truth," he declared, is that all "basic value"—including "literacy"—is "linked to market growth."

15   We may formalize the equation of the paradigmatic corporate president as follows: More/less money-value sales = more/less market growth = more/less "basic values" for the world. No substantiation of the given equations is deemed necessary. No explanation of contra-indicative evidence is conceived. Yet mind-numbing implications follow. Whatever is without a market price is therefore without any value—the world's biodiversity of species, for example. Life itself is of no value except as it sells for a market price. So, too, research and knowledge. If they are not marketable, they do not exist.

16   *The New York Times* recently gave much page and blog space to Stanley Fish, an academic servant to money and power as Allan Bloom before him. In his tirade against academics following "the inner light," Fish defended the use of coercive force against them. Indeed, he said that coercion was required. Professors need to be reduced to a master–servant relationship with "their employer," the same as all other employees: that is, with university CEOs and designates who hire and fire by unilateral control of the purse-strings with no ultimate accountability to academic standards.

17   When it is believed that academics' work is at the leading edge of the "global knowledge economy," none ask what the criterion of "knowledge" is. There is none, except what reduces money costs and increases money revenues for money managers and possessors. That is

what "accountability" means in this value system. Thus teaching comes to mean only what produces graduates who make more money in the global market than they would without their degree, with ever higher tuition fees as the cost of acquiring and selling their skills at a higher price. At the same time, selling campus grounds as marketing sites follows from the same money-value program: corporate ads, junk foods, and market franchises invading space and sightlines across university schools, buildings, lecture halls, and courses.

18   Consider corporate-partner research. Here university researchers must find projects that corporations are willing to fund. Independent research in the public interest that is most urgently required is thus silently selected out—for example, in the agricultural sciences, integrated pest management, organic farming for productive efficiency, management-intensive grazing, small-scale producer cooperatives, and alternatives to factory-processed livestock and avoidance of ecological contamination by genetically-engineered commodities. According to organic farming research leader Professor Ann Clark, who has long been persecuted and ostracized by factory-farm colleagues and agribusiness administrators at the University of Guelph, "the end of the historical role of governments in supporting impartial agricultural science was brought about by corporate-partnerships [because] non-proprietary research of the sort that benefits everyone is of no interest to industry sponsors."

19   In the humanities, too, corporate administrations require that professors bring in money from outside the university to defray the costs of their student's graduate education, or they cannot have graduate students. Educational costs are thus downloaded onto faculty themselves, who are forced to become funding entrepreneurs. Those not competing successfully at getting grants have no graduate students, and may lose their jobs. Faculty are generally so wound up in getting the grant money that they do not think about the structural undermining of independent research and academic freedom in the university, as well as in their own work. The result is more effective than direct censorship control. Either faculty get money committed from private corporations which are structured to repel any finding against their interests, or they lose their lab space. Either they bring money into administrations' revenues from a government or private

funding body, or their research and graduate students are shut off. A silent rule of gagging prevails. *Nothing that does not payoff in more money to administrations is supported within the corporate university.*

20   The ultimate assault on the university's vocation lies at the level of truth-seeking itself. The university is constitutionally committed to critically reasoned inquiry which goes wherever the quest for truth leads it. The truth is not an end state, but an open process in which partialities are continually exposed by thinking through deep assumptions, evidence, and connections. This thinking through is the nature of learning and knowledge. Reason's movement is always by a more inclusive taking into coherent account open to counterevidence and argument, the inner logic of all disciplines—from the problem of self and other in philosophy, to the nature of tropes in literature, to the hypotheses of subatomic waves and particles in physics. In one way or another, the critical search for more comprehensively coherent understanding leads the academy in every domain and the human condition itself. Deprived of the freedom to pursue truth independent of external money added to administration funds, the academy's learning vocation is systematically blocked. Academic excellence now means what gets more money coming in.

21   The known standard of research to guard against conflict of interest and cooked results is straightforward. *Any research in which the funder has a financial stake in the outcome is a conflict of interest which must be ruled out.* Yet this standard of research independence and validity has been usurped by the centre. For example, when a "research integrity" clause was explicitly specified on two occasions by decision of the Medical Research Council of Canada, it was annulled with no justification. If universities are not to be so subordinated to such political control, a research integrity condition must be instituted on campuses to protect higher research from conflicts of interest and corporately cooked science. Just as research biased by conflict of interest must be stopped, so too must be making graduate student supervision dependent on external revenues captured by faculty. Faculty dependency on outside money determines the topics and direction of faculty research. Thus, solicitous grantmanship and academic fads supplant original and critical inquiry. This structural violation of academic freedom, however, is taboo to discuss for fear of offending the granting authorities. Yet one has to wonder: why have the most self-evident defences of the academy's research integrity been so easily overridden by corporate administrations? Why have faculty and faculty organizations submitted to these assaults on academic integrity and freedom? The answer is that a collective academic presence on campus has been lacking. This is why an independent Faculty Board of Academic Review (or Academic Freedom) needs to bring active scholars across disciplines into one independent body on every university campus to review all administrative decisions so as to ensure against financially-led distortions and depredations of research and teaching—including by arbitrary administrative cuts of courses to claw back money to inflated executive revenue siphons serving no academic function.

22   Cuts must begin at the top, and campus-based faculty associations and unions must in the end be willing to strike for protection of the university's learning objectives against their system-wide violations by corporate administrations. At the same time, such a faculty academic review body needs to institute policy-by-policy identification and ranking of the performance of local central administrations, including so-called academic senates and like bodies whose terms of reference are financially dictated from the centre and vote-loaded by ex-officio members.

23   A Faculty Board of Academic Review needs also to press hard specifically for ceilings on ballooned salaries as an item of faculty negotiations: for starter norms, no administrative salary higher than the provincial premier's, and no faculty salary more than $120,000 to bring balance back into the gross money-class divisions which have grown ever deeper in the corporate university. Once the facts on the systematic misallocation of public education funds on anti-educative salaries, privileges and offices are flushed into the open, they will not be accepted by the public. Those in the university who follow more money as their ruling goal are then free to leave the academy where they do not belong. The vocation of the academy is the advancement of higher learning by academic freedom, but the mission has been usurped.

CCPA Monitor. 2009. July/August 16 (3).

Key and challenging words

fifth column, casualization, hierarchical, substantiation, unilateral, solicitous

Questions

1. Identify three words or phrases in the first paragraph that reveal the writer's argumentative tone. What audience is this essay written for?
2. Identify the thesis statement. What is the writer's argumentative purpose?
3. Although citations aren't given, as they are in scholarly journal articles, the essay does include specific names of professors, politicians, and writers. Choose one of the following names and use a reliable source to find out about the individual and his/her importance to the essay itself: Ursula Franklin (paragraph 6); Ken Westhues (paragraph 10); Stanley Fish (paragraph 16).
4. In paragraph 11, the writer outlines the "opposite structures of rationality, method, and purpose" that characterize "corporate administration versus the learning vocation." Paraphrase the sentences that contrast the two positions, according to McMurtry. (You could set it up in chart form in which two columns represent the two sides and the rows represent the corresponding points.)
5. McMurtry includes direct quotation from several people with whom he disagrees. In general, do you think this is an effective strategy? Using one such quotation, analyze its effectiveness.
6. Who does the author primarily blame for the situation he criticizes at universities? Does he believe others are also accountable to some degree? Refer to specific passages.
7. In a brief paragraph, explain what you consider the author's strongest, most effective point. In another brief paragraph, explain what you consider his least effective point.

Post-reading

1. *Collaborative activity:* a) In groups, discuss the accuracy or validity of McMurtry's thesis; b) Consider how corporate relationships between university administrators and business could affect or have affected you as a student.
2. Do you think the money for research derived through corporate sponsorship is essentially a bad thing or a good thing? Defend your point of view.

Related website of interest

Higher Education Public Forum:
http://www.highereducationforum.net/

Additional library reading

Caulfield, Timothy, Shawn Harmon, and Yann Joly. "Open Science versus Commercialization: A Modern Research Conflict?" *Genome Medicine* 4.2 (2012): 1–11. Print.

Newson, Janice, Claire Polster, and Howard Woodhouse. "Toward an Alternative Future for Canada's Corporatized Universities." *English Studies in Canada* 38.1 (2012): 51–70. Print.

Polster, Claire, and Janice Newson. "Open for Business? What's Wrong with Corporatizing Canada's Universities? Plenty!" *CCPA Monitor* 15.8 (2009): 32–35. Print.

Universities, governments and industry: Can the essential nature of universities survive the drive to commercialize?

Simon N. Young
(2,622 words)

Pre-reading

1. Based on the essay's title, come up with a reading hypothesis of two sentences that includes a) the kind of essay to follow (i.e., argumentative or expository) and b) the author's thesis. Do not use any major words from the title.

1   Having spent 40 years in universities, I have had sufficient time to consider some of the idiosyncrasies, foibles, and problems of these academic institutions. The purpose of this editorial is to discuss the current state of university research and explain why I find some aspects of the current situation disturbing. Changes that started during the second half of the twentieth century and that have continued into the twenty-first threaten to bring about fundamental changes in the nature of universities. Some of the changes are commendable, for example, the large expansion in the proportion of the population attending universities, at least in the richer nations. Other trends are disturbing, especially the increasing tendency of governments and industry to view universities as engines for short-term economic gain. While universities certainly cannot ignore the context in which they function and the needs of society, responding purely to short-term economic considerations threatens to subvert the very nature of universities and some of the benefits they provide to society.

2   So what exactly is a university, and what is its purpose? I much prefer the *Oxford English Dictionary* definition of the word "university" to some of the more utilitarian definitions in other dictionaries. The Oxford definition reads, in part, "whole body of teachers and scholars engaged in the higher branches of learning." Thus, it is the community of faculty and students that is the essence of a university. The higher branches of learning in which teachers and scholars engage have two important products: the educated minds that are essential for the well-being of society and new knowledge and ideas. Some of that new knowledge will enrich society by producing economic growth, directly or indirectly, but the benefits of new knowledge go far beyond economic gain.

3   Universities have always been subjected to outside influences. The oldest European university, the University of Bologna, has existed at least since the 1080s. Some time before 1222, about 1,000 students left Bologna and founded a new university in Padua because of "the grievous offence that was brought to bear on their academic liberties and the failure to acknowledge the privileges solemnly granted to teachers and students."[1] The outside interference came from the Roman Catholic Church, and for several centuries, Padua was home to the only university in Europe where non-Catholics could get a university education. Both Bologna and Padua were student-controlled universities with students electing the professors and fixing their salaries. However, in spite of marked differences, there are similarities between what happened then and what is happening today, with important outside influences—then the dogma of religion, now the dogma of business—threatening to change the activities of the community of teachers and scholars.

4   The seeds of what is happening now were sown in the years following World War II. Before the war, the most important influence on a faculty member was probably the departmental chair, who in those days had power to influence in an important way what went on in the department. Nonetheless, a faculty member would have had access to departmental resources and would not necessarily have required outside research funding (although such funding was sometimes available from private foundations). The

mechanism of funding research, and the amount of money available for research, changed greatly in the postwar years. In 1945, Vannevar Bush's landmark report to President Harry Truman, *Science the endless frontier,*[2] had an important influence on university research. In this report, Bush stated, "The publicly and privately supported colleges, universities, and research institutes are the centres of basic research. They are the wellsprings of knowledge and understanding. As long as they are vigorous and healthy and their scientists are free to pursue the truth wherever it may lead, there will be a flow of new scientific knowledge to those who can apply it to practical problems in Government, in industry, or elsewhere." Bush supported the idea that the US government should provide strong financial support for university research but also supported the idea that the individual investigator should be the main determinant of the topics for investigation, with statements such as "Scientific progress on a broad front results from the free play of free intellects, working on subjects of their own choice, in the manner dictated by their curiosity for exploration of the unknown."[2]

5   In the latter half of the last century, many countries adopted the model of granting councils, which used a system based on peer review to distribute money for investigator-initiated research. This model has been a great success, but it has also contributed to important changes in universities. Much more money has been available to support medical research, basic science research, and engineering research than has been available for the social sciences or arts. Thus, decisions about support for different disciplines devolved from the universities to governments, who decided on the budgets of their various grant-giving bodies. Also, individual researchers who were successful in obtaining grants no longer depended as much on departmental facilities. In my opinion, this not only weakened the power of departmental chairs but also decreased collegiality within departments.

6   With increased enrolments, as a university education became accessible to a greater proportion of the population, and an increased need for infrastructure for the larger student population and for complex research equipment, administrators became more concerned about sources of funding and consequently more detached from the faculty. There is always a tendency for senior academic administrators to speak and behave as though they *were* the university (when of course they are there to serve the community of teachers and scholars). This is of course a normal human trait, no different from the tendency of politicians to forget that they are elected to serve the people. However, this increasing detachment of senior university administrators from the faculty has facilitated the erosion of collegiality within departments and universities. The individual personalities of university faculty probably also facilitated this change. I learned recently, when looking at the literature on personality, that an inverse correlation between intelligence and conscientiousness has been demonstrated in a number of studies (see, for example, Moutafi et al[3]). Thus, it might be more than just my paranoia leading me to believe that the small proportion of university faculty who lack conscientiousness and collegiality is larger than in some other walks of life. The erosion of collegiality is not a matter of great significance, except that it probably played a role in making researchers more open to the efforts of governments to transform them into entrepreneurs.

7   The most recent and possibly the most important change in university research resulted from the push by governments to commercialize the results of such research. In the United States, the Bayh-Dole Act of 1980 encouraged universities to license to private industry discoveries made with federal funds.[4] The push by governments for commercialization of new knowledge grew during the 1980s and 1990s and continues to have an important influence on universities. Recently, Lord Sainsbury, the science and innovation minister in the United Kingdom, boasted that there had been a cultural change in universities there, which has resulted in a substantial increase in university spin-offs.[5] In 2002 the Association of Universities and Colleges of Canada entered an agreement with the government to double the amount of research performed by these institutions and to triple their commercialization performance by 2010.[6] Although this agreement was reached in the absence of any broad consultation with the faculty who are supposed to commercialize their work, the universities seem to be well on track to achieve this objective, with a 126 per cent increase in revenues from licence royalties between 1999 and 2001.[7] Most major universities now have a technology transfer office, and at many universities success in

commercialization is taken into account when faculty are considered for tenure. Will there come a time when success in commercialization carries the same weight as (or more weight than) teaching and research in the awarding of tenure?

8   The end result of all the changes discussed above is that individual faculty members have become much more like entrepreneurs whose main allegiance is to the maintenance or growth of their own research programs and not infrequently to the commercialization of their research. The researcher exploring Vannevar Bush's "endless frontier" could be considered the modern equivalent of the homesteader taming the seemingly endless frontier of the nineteenth-century American West.[8] This is not necessarily detrimental if a new generation of university research entrepreneurs provides the new knowledge that will benefit patients and society. However, the change in culture that made university faculty more like entrepreneurs also made them more open to the desire of governments to make them entrepreneurs in the economic sense. Although the nature of universities has been changing, there was no threat to the fundamental nature of universities until the drive for commercialization began.

9   A recent report of the Canadian Association of University Teachers[9] states that university administrators have been "building increasingly hierarchical management structures" that "place the future of academic medicine in danger." The report's main concern is that "incentives to create commercializable products push economic concerns, rather than scientific and ethical considerations, to the forefront."[9] In the fields of biologic psychiatry and behavioural neuroscience, the emphasis on commercial applications has already, to some extent, moved research priorities away from an emphasis on mental well-being to an emphasis on commercial products. There are many examples of this shift. For example, more research is being carried out on antidepressant drugs than on psychotherapy, even though in mild to moderate depression (the majority of cases) drugs and psychotherapy are approximately equal in efficacy. There is increasing evidence for the efficacy of exercise[10,11] and fish oils[12,13] in the treatment and prevention of depression. However, these strategies receive much less attention than antidepressant drugs. Even an established antidepressant treatment such as S-adenosylmethionine (SAMe)[14] receives little

attention. Searching the abstracts of the 2004 meeting of the Society for Neuroscience, I found 179 with the keyword "antidepressant" and only four with the keyword "S-adenosylmethionine," and none of those four was concerned with the antidepressant action of SAMe. SAMe is a major methyl donor and seems to work in a fundamentally different way from any product being investigated by drug companies. Surely we could expect that an antidepressant acting through a different mechanism would be a popular topic of investigation. However, SAMe is a natural product and not of commercial interest. Similarly, insights into what exercise or fish oils do to the brain may provide important insights into the pathophysiology of depression and its treatment, but these subjects receive little attention.

10   Many basic science researchers investigating the mechanisms of antidepressants produced by drug companies do not receive funding from those companies. However, enough are lured by drug company research funds into working on topics of interest to the companies to significantly influence what are fashionable topics of research. Laboratories with funding from industry can often afford more trainees, who may then adopt a more industry-centred approach in their own research. While the availability of funds from industry has certainly influenced research, the pressure on university faculty to commercialize the results of their research will undoubtedly cause even greater distortion in the areas of research that are most popular.

11   Granting agencies have increasingly tried to foster research in neglected areas by allocating funds to specific areas of research and requesting applications in those areas. Although this approach is certainly necessary, it has not done much to alter the effects of drug company money on research output. Also, in some ways it moves research even further away from the ideal in Vannevar Bush's report that "Scientific progress on a broad front results from the free play of free intellects, working on subjects of their own choice, in the manner dictated by their curiosity for exploration of the unknown."[2] This model was notably successful in the last half of the twentieth century, but it may not survive the pressure to commercialize. While there is still much scope for curiosity-driven research, the curiosity of researchers is likely to be aligned increasingly with the interests of drug companies. As mentioned above, a cultural change has

accompanied the increasing commercialization of university research. The pressure to commercialize has been critiqued in some quarters, but many university faculty have nonetheless embraced commercialization or at least remained unconcerned about it. Are we far from a time when a researcher without a patent that is being commercialized will be regarded in the same way as those who do not publish regularly in the top journals? And how long will it be before governments make commercialization a mandate of granting councils and a requirement for the majority of grants?

12 A fascination with the workings of the brain and how it can malfunction in mental illness is the usual motivator for researchers in neuroscience and psychiatry research. As a result, curiosity-driven research will always tend to serve the best interests of patients. Although research driven by commercial interests will certainly benefit psychiatric patients in some ways, it cannot serve their overall needs, as it is much too narrowly focused. The designation of funds by granting agencies for specific neglected topics will help but is unlikely to produce any large changes in the direction of research. Thus, the biggest losers from the pressure to commercialize will be psychiatric patients. In addition, I am concerned whether students who are trained to focus on the short-term commercial implications of their research will be able to maintain the breadth of vision that is a characteristic of the majority of creative researchers.

13 Changes due to pressure from governments to commercialize are not limited to researchers. The increased emphasis on commercialization in universities has in some ways distorted the perceptions of senior university administrators about the purpose of the institutions. For example, there seems to be a lack of concern about some of the sources of funds that universities receive. Universities now hold patents on many life-saving drugs. These patents sometimes limit access to the drugs, particularly in low-income countries.[15] In Canada, one-quarter of the faculties of medicine receive funding from the tobacco industry.[16] Perhaps a suitable future definition of a university will be a "whole body of teachers and scholars engaged in turning ideas into profit."

14 In thirteenth-century Italy, the response to interference by the Roman Catholic Church in the work of scholars was a move to another location to escape the interference. In the twenty-first century, that option is not available even to the minority who are concerned about the drive to commercialize. However, the picture is not entirely bleak. Charitable foundations will remain immune to commercial interests. In addition, even though charitable foundations will probably remain relatively small players in the funding of research, there are promising signs. For example, the Bill and Melinda Gates Foundation, created in 2000, has an endowment of about US$27 billion and is striving to use its money for the benefit of humankind in areas neglected by governments. This foundation is not involved in psychiatric research, but its focus on preventive approaches may help to direct interest to that important area. Research on prevention in psychiatry is still in its infancy and will certainly remain that way if short-term commercial considerations stay paramount. However, charitable foundations cannot be expected to have any large effect on the change in university culture brought about by the drive to commercialize. Although I would like to be able to end this editorial on a more hopeful note, I am concerned about these cultural changes, and I do not see any solution. Still, one lesson from history is that the communities of teachers and scholars making up universities have adapted to many changes over the centuries without changing the fundamental nature of universities, and they will surely continue to do so. I am just not sure how.

Journal of Psychiatry & Neuroscience. 2005. 30 (3).

References

1. *History.* Padua (Italy): Università Degli Studi di Padova. Available: www.unipd.it/en/university/history.htm (accessed 2004 Dec 13).

2. Bush V. *Science the endless frontier. A report to the President by Vannevar Bush, Director of the Office of Scientific Research and Development, July 1945.* Washington: US Government Printing Office; 1945. Available: www.nsf.gov/od/lpa/nsf50/vbush1945.htm (accessed 2004 Dec 13).

3. Moutafi J, Furnham A, Paltiel L. Why is conscientiousness negatively correlated with intelligence? *Pers Individ Differ* 2004;37:1013–22.

4. Thursby JG, Thursby MC. Intellectual property. University licensing and the Bayh-Dole Act. Science 2003;301:1052.

5. Sainsbury L. A cultural change in UK universities [editorial]. *Science* 2002;296:1929.

6. Allan Rock welcomes framework on federally funded university research [press release]. Toronto: Industry Canada; 2002 Nov 19[modified 2003 Jun 16]. Available: www.ic.gc.ca/cmb/welcomeic.nsf/558d63659099294285256488005215 5b/85256-a220056c2a485256c76004c7d44 (accessed 2004 Dec 13).

7. Berkowitz P. Spinning off research: AUCC sets new tool to measure universities' commercialization performance. *Univ Aff* [serial on-line] 2004;June/July. Available: www.universityaffairs.ca/issues/2004/junejuly/print/spinning-off.html (accessed 2004 Dec 13).

8. Kennedy D. Enclosing the research commons [editorial]. *Science* 2001;294:2249.

9. Welch P, Cass CE, Guyatt G, Jackson AC, Smith D. *Defending medicine: clinical faculty and academic freedom.* Report of the Canadian Association of University Teachers (CAUT) Task Force on Academic Freedom for Faculty at University-Affiliated Health Care Institutions. Ottawa: Canadian Association of University Teachers; 2004 Nov. Available: www.caut.ca/en/issues/academicfreedom/DefendingMedicine.pdf (accessed 2004 Dec 21).

10. Salmon P. Effects of physical exercise on anxiety, depression, and sensitivity to stress: a unifying theory. *Clin Psychol Rev* 2001; 21:33–61.

11. *Depression: management of depression in primary and secondary care.* Clinical guideline 23. London (UK): National Institute for Clinical Excellence; 2004 Dec. Available: www.nice.org.uk/pdf/CG023NICEguideline.pdf (accessed 2005 Mar 8).

12. Nemets B, Stahl Z, Belmaker RH. Addition of omega-3 fatty acid to maintenance medication treatment for recurrent unipolar depressive disorder. *Am J Psychiatry* 2002; 159:477–9.

13. Su KP, Huang SY, Chiu CC, Shen WW. Omega-3 fatty acids in major depressive disorder. A preliminary double-blind, placebo controlled trial. *Eur Neuropsychopharmacol* 2003;13:267–71.

14. Papakostas GI, Alpert JE, Fava M. S-Adenosylmethionine in depression: a comprehensive review of the literature. *Curr Psychiatry Rep* 2003;5:460–6.

15. Kapczynski A, Crone ET, Merson M. Global health and university patents [editorial]. *Science* 2003;301:1629.

16. Kaufman PE, Cohen JE, Ashley MJ, Ferrence R, Halyak AI, Turcotte F, et al. Tobacco industry links to faculties of medicine in Canada. *Can J Public Health* 2004; 95:205–8.

Key and challenging words

dogma, collegiality, infrastructure

Questions

1. Explain why it is important for Young to define the common word "university" in paragraph 2.

2. Do you believe that the comparison in paragraph 3 between what happened at Italian universities before 1222 and what is occurring at today's universities is valid? Why or why not?

3. Name two negative consequences that resulted from adoption of the "model of granting councils" in the second half of the twentieth century.

4. Analyze paragraph 9. Among the factors you could consider are the method(s) of development (rhetorical patterns), the kinds of support, and the writer's credibility.

5. Who does Young believe will ultimately be most affected if research in neuroscience and psychiatry research continues to be "driven by commercial interests?"

6. Comment on the author's use of *two* argumentative strategies in the essay (see pp. 124–125): a) establishing common ground with the reader; b) making concessions to the other side; c) using an emotional appeal; or d) appealing to reader interests.

7. Could Young have ended his editorial more positively or assertively than he did? Does the concluding paragraph add or detract from the strength of the essay?

8. Would you say that Young's main purpose is (a) to expose a problem, (b) to change a situation, (c) to critique a position, or (d) to reach a compromise? How might his audience affect his purpose?

Post-reading

1. *Collaborative activity:* As students who may be going on to intensive undergraduate work or perhaps graduate school, are you concerned about the increasing ties of university research to commercial interests? How do you think it could affect you or students like you in the next few years?

2. *Collaborative activity:* It is well known that substantially more money is given today to research in science, engineering, and medicine than to research in the arts. Do you think this allocation is inevitable? Do you think it is fair? Do you believe that students, administrators, or society should be concerned about the possible consequences to arts programs throughout the country?

3. Reflect on the idea of a "student-controlled university" (see paragraph 3). Write up a one- to two-page proposal in which you urge your government to finance such a university. In your proposal, you should outline the need for the project, along with goals and objectives, and provide a few specific features of such a university.

4. Write a rhetorical analysis in which you compare this essay with John McMurtry, "University wars: The corporate administration vs. the vocation of learning," p. 166. Establish two or three bases of comparison (see p. 81), at least one of which pertains to the effectiveness of each author's argument.

See the Related Websites and Additional Library Readings on page 170.

Intellectuals and democracy

Mark Kingwell
(2,238 words)

Pre-reading

1. Reflect on your own assumptions about why you are in university: to get a well-paying job, acquire general knowledge, or achieve some other goal? Where do these assumptions come from—for example, parents, teachers, friends? In a paragraph or two, record your thoughts. (See Post-reading question 1 for a follow-up question.)

2. Who is Mark Kingwell? Using at least two reliable sources, summarize his background, career, publications, and the like in one or two paragraphs.

1   You might think judges would make diverting dinner companions, but I can tell you that on the whole they don't. The judge sitting next to me, who shall go nameless, condemned all modern art as overpraised child's play. She railed against graduated income tax. She told me I would outgrow my socialist tendencies (I was 48 at the time). She left without contributing to the bill.

2   So I was not surprised when, after hearing what I did for a living, she said, "But what will your students *do* with that?"

3   There is a special intonation to this use of the verb 'do', familiar to anyone who has studied classics or considered a graduate degree in mathematics, with its long vowel of contempt honeyed over by apparent

concern. When I was in my second postgraduate year, a woman in an Edinburgh bus queue delivered the best version I have so far encountered: "Philosophy! Really! Do you have any idea what you'll *do* with that?" (Poor sod: useless *and* out to lunch!)

4   I could have told the judge something she ought to have known already, which is that *philosophy students usually rock the LSAT.* They get into prestigious law schools, even sometimes make it onto the bench. Statistically speaking, there is no better preparation for success in law than an undergraduate degree spent thinking about the nature of knowledge, the meaning of being and, especially, what makes a valid argument.

5   But even though this is itself a valid argument, it is not a good one. I mean that the success of the argument actually conceded a greater failure; it gives away the game of justification to a base value. A degree in philosophy, or humane study more generally, does not require validation in the court of do-with usefulness. It is a convenient reality that such validation is sometimes gained, but the victory is really a surrender performed on the enemy's ground.

6   What's surprising is how many of today's university administrators are rushing to do just this, hyping the 'competitiveness' and 'pragmatism' of higher education. The annual higher education supplement published by *Maclean's*, the Canadian weekly magazine, is ground zero for the transactional reduction of learning. The latest version of the supplement included this representative claim from Robert Campbell, president of Mount Allison University in Sackville, New Brunswick. Parents of prospective students, he told a reporter, "are looking for a return on investment" in their child's tuition.

7   And so professors are told that they need to justify their activities according to a market model of 'research effectiveness', where quantifiable 'impact indicators' and 'external research use values' can be totted up and scanned. Students respond by assuming a consumer stance to their own education, swapping tuition dollars not for the chance to interact with other minds but to acquire a postgraduate market advantage. When a 2010 survey of 12,500 students asked, "What was the single most important reason in your decision to attend university," just 9% picked "a good general education" as their answer, while almost 70% had enrolled to "get a good job" or "train for a specific career."

8   Historically, median earning power for university graduates is indeed higher than that of college or high school grads, and over their lifetimes university graduates earn substantially more—75% by some estimates—than non-graduates. And yet, paradoxically, recent years have witnessed an avalanche of over-qualification. "[M]ore than a quarter of a million Canadian university students are about to graduate into the workforce this spring," *Maclean's* noted. "Yet studies show that fifty percent of Canadian arts and science grads are working in jobs that don't require a university credential two years after graduation."

9   All is not lost, however. "As the knowledge economy continues to grow—and manufacturing jobs disappear—there's more demand for university grads in the workforce than ever." Rest easy, parents. Pony up, students. There's still reason to get an education! It's just not anything to do with education.

10   Call this familiar mixture of doom and market optimism the *standard position*. It can be summarized this way: university education must be judged according to its ultimate usefulness. That usefulness will be understood as career success of one sort or another, especially as measured by wealth. The position then adds the *soft option*: get a degree because the "knowledge economy" will otherwise crush you.

11   The soft option is favoured by presidents as well as university presidents. Barack Obama, giving a speech at a college in 2011, noted that America's need to 'remain competitive' was an argument for higher education: "If we want more good news on the jobs front then we've got to make more investments in education." He offered no other arguments in its favour.

———

12   For all its currency, the standard position strikes me as wrong-headed, if not dangerous. It is a philistine position, obviously; it works to hollow out the critical possibilities of education. Holders of this position regard real humanistic educations as a dispensable luxury of idiosyncratic and purely personal value, and that makes them, in turn, dangerous.

13   They are correct, however, that the standard position is now so deeply presupposed that even calling attention to it can be enough to brand one an ivory-tower whackjob, tilting at windmills. The 2011 *Maclean's* authors noted with some satisfaction that

nobody would nowadays express the indignation that greeted similar reductive accounts of education a decade ago, not apparently aware of the role *Maclean's* and its consumer-style surveys have played in that reduction.

14 As far as I'm concerned the judge and all those in the standard-position camp are the enemy. They are not enemies of philosophy, or me, or my students; they are enemies of democracy, and insofar as we refuse to admit that—insofar as we soft-pedal the value of the humanities when confronted by a scale of value keyed only to wealth—we are not being serious about what democracy means. As with the democratic narratives discussed in relation to Francis Fukuyama (see "The Tomist," in this collection) and the electoral system (see "Throwing Dice"), we are witnessing nothing less than the regulatory capture of universities under the general influence of a market model that can only be challenged by arguments rooted in another, human code of value.

15 Most defences of the humanities fall back on preaching to the choir: they assume the value of the very thing they need to defend, namely the cultivation of self and world that marks genuine study, what Aristotle called *skholé*, or leisure (hence the word 'school'). At that point, there is usually a predictable spinoff into denunciations of elitism and counter-denunciations of its reverse-snobbery evil twin, anti-intellectualism. The net result is either an impasse or a trail into absurdity: witness the 2006 *National Post* reader poll which concluded that bombastic hockey commentator Don Cherry was the nation's "most important public intellectual". . . .

16 But there's not need to go through any of that, because the standard position is actually self-defeating.

———

17 Let's do a little casual philosophical analysis. What are the unspoken premises of the standard position?

18 Most obviously, it assumes (1) that we know what *use* is. Something is useful when it has instrumental value. Things of instrumental value serve needs other than their own, either some higher instrumental value or an intrinsic value. And yet, in practice 'use' almost always comes down to money, which is itself a perfect example of a *lower* instrumental value. Money is just a tool, but we talk and act as if it were an end in itself.

19 So the position likewise assumes (2) that we know how to value things that contribute to use. We can convert any activity or human possibility into some quantified assessment, and thus dispose of the question of whether it is worth doing. Not only does this make a mockery of human action, quickly narrowing the scope of what is considered worth doing, but it simultaneously narrows the scope of argument about the nature of worth. This leads to a market monopoly on the notion of the 'real': anything that is not in play in a market is irrelevant or imaginary.

20 The position in turn presupposes (3) that education is in thrall to this 'real world' of market value—actually a massive collective delusion as abstract as anything in Hegel's *Phenomenology*—because according to (2) all human activities are. The market's monopoly on reality reinforces the dominant value of competition and selfishness, incidentally converting education into a credential-race that can (and rationally should) be gamed rather than enjoyed itself.

21 Lurking nearby are two other implicit ideas about life after graduation: (4) education must be intimately linked to work; and (5) doing work while 'over-qualified' is a bad thing. This link between education and work is a nifty piece of legerdemain which preys on the uncertainties all humans have about the future, even as it leaves untouched the general presumption that one must have a job to be human. Parents and children alike fall for it.

22 Finally, at least in the soft option, there is (6): the assumption that education can find its match in white-collar work of the knowledge economy, and so justify doing a degree after all. This completes the regulatory capture of education. What was once considered a site of challenge to received ideas and bad argument, even to entrenched power and pooled wealth, is now a not particularly successful adjunct to the pursuit of that power and wealth.

23 Unfortunately the facts do not bear this out, and this is where the entire arrangement collapses.

24 While the number of jobs asking for a degree has increased over the past two decades, the fact is that, since 1990 or so, the North American job market has not been characterized by a smooth rise in demand for cognitive skills to match growth in technology. Instead, there has been a hollowing out of the market's middle, such that top-level jobs (creating

technologies, playing markets, scoring touchdowns) have risen in overall wealth but not numbers, while low-end jobs (fixing pipes, driving semi-trailers, pouring lattes) have remained steady or grown slightly. In between, there is a significant depression of the very middle-class occupations that most university graduates imagine will be their return on investment.

25   The consequences of this economic reality are twofold. First, it explodes the assessment of education in terms of economic reality. There is no prospect of the competitive 'knowledge economy' future to underwrite a decision to go to university. The soft option is gone.

26   Second, and more profoundly, the standard position now exhibits its full contradictions. If you cannot value education in terms of money, then education has no value. That means that, if you decide to pursue such an education, it has to be for reasons other than value. But that would mean doing something that has no use, and surely that is silly.

27   There is an ironic benefit to this collapse. Sure, some people will conclude that university is not for them: it doesn't confer the market benefit it used to, so to hell with it. For others, though, the land beyond use might continue to beckon, a place where there is no easy decline into the disengagement of merely personal interests.

28   The standard position was founded on a paradox: university graduates are overqualified for the jobs they do; but you should still go because there is a statistical link between a degree and higher income. This is now replaced with a new paradox, the paradox of philosophy in the general sense: there is no use in pursuing a university education; but you should pursue it anyway because it's the only way to see any use beyond what is everywhere assumed.

29   What does any of this have to do with democracy? Again, a twofold conclusion. First, wider university admission isn't going to result in prosperity for everyone. If we want to have more equitable distributions of wealth and opportunity, we can't rely on markets to do it, even or especially markets flooded with dazed graduates looking for work in a depression created, in part, by high-flyers gaming the abstract markets. And no, more business schools are not the answer.

30   Second, though, we actually need graduates more than ever precisely because democracy depends on a population of engaged, critical thinkers who have general humane knowledge of history, politics, culture, economics, and science, citizens and not consumers who see that there exist shared interests beyond their own desires. Once the link between higher education and work has been broken, the value of the humanities and non-applied sciences becomes clear. Education is not there to be converted into market value; it is there to make us better and more engaged citizens, maybe even better and more virtuous people. There, I said it! The entailed benefit is that these citizens are ones who will challenge the reduction of all consideration to the price of everything and the value of nothing.

31   Aristotle again: usefulness is not virtue. He meant to ask us each to consider how and why we come to value things, to consider them relevant, to think them worth doing. "What are you going to do with that?" asks the concerned fellow diner or transit passenger.

32   But as Socrates said, philosophy concerns no small thing, just the tricky matter of *wondering how best to live*. So the answer is: I'm already doing it. And you should be too.

Unruly Voices: Essays on Democracy, Civility, and the Human Imagination. 2012.

———

Key and challenging words

philistine, idiosyncratic, intrinsic, legerdemain, paradox, equitable

Questions

1. (a) Using your own words, explain what Kingwell means in paragraph 5; (b) explain what Kingwell means by the "regulatory capture of universities" (see paragraphs 14 and 22).

2. Identify, then paraphrase, Kingwell's thesis.
3. Analyze the essay's introduction (paragraphs 1–11) to determine the purpose of his essay and intended audience. Factors you could consider include language level, diction, tone, use of anecdotes and dialogue, and other rhetorical strategies.
4. Explain Kingwell's extensive use of *Maclean's* as a source on pages 177–178. Do you think he believes its annual university rankings serve a useful purpose? Support your answer by specific references to Kingwell's essay.

5. Identify at least one example of (a) humour and (b) irony in the essay. Discuss what either humour or irony contributes to the essay.
6. In the third section of the essay, identify a paragraph in which Kingwell uses deductive reasoning and one in which he uses inductive reasoning. (See chapter 9, Writing Argumentative Essays, for the differences between deductive and inductive reasoning.)
7. Discuss the function and effectiveness of the concluding section. In your discussion, consider how it is connected to the introduction and to the essay as a whole.

Post-reading

1. Look back at how you answered pre-reading question 1. Has your response changed after studying the essay? Depending on your response to the essay, write one or two paragraphs that consider (a) how or why the essay made you question or change your original assumptions or (b) why the essay did not change your original assumptions. What would Kingwell need to do to make his argument more convincing to you?
2. Analyze Kingwell's use of ethical appeals in his essay. (See Chapter 8, The Active Voice: Rhetorical Analysis: What, Why, and How.)

Additional library reading

Coates, Ken, and Bill Morrison. "The Uses and Abuses of University." *Walrus* Oct. 2012: 34–39. Print.

Social norms of alcohol, smoking, and marijuana use within a Canadian university setting

Kelly P. Arbour-Nicitopoulos, Matthew Y.W. Kwan, David Lowe, Sara Taman, and Guy E.J. Faulkner
(2,496 words)

Pre-reading

1. *Collaborative activity:* (a) Reflect on the problems of alcohol and drug consumption on your university campus. Do they affect you or people you know? (b) Does your university have a policy on drinking or drug use? Do you believe it is a good policy? How could it be improved in order to help reduce alcohol and drug consumption?

Abstract

Objective: To study actual and perceived substance use in Canadian university students and to compare these rates with US peers. **Participants**: Students (*N*= 1,203) from a large Canadian university. **Methods**: Participants were surveyed using items from the National College Health (NCHA) Assessment of the American College Health Association questionnaire. **Results**: Alcohol was the most common substance used (65.8%), followed by marijuana (13.5%) and cigarettes (13.5%). Substance use and norms were significantly less than the NCHA US data. Overall, respondents generally perceived the typical Canadian student to have used all 3 substances. Perceived norms significantly predicted use, with students more likely to use alcohol, cigarettes, or marijuana if they perceived the typical student to use these substances. **Conclusions**: Similar to their US peers, Canadian university students have inaccurate perceptions of peer substance use. These misperceptions may have potentially negative influences on actual substance use and could be a target for intervention. Further research examining the cross-cultural differences for substance abuse is warranted.

———

1   Excessive alcohol consumption, smoking, and drug use are all identified as modifiable risk factors associated with heart and liver diseases, and cancer.[1] However, young adults, specifically college students, do not attribute such health-risk behaviors to the development and progression of these diseases.[2] Transition from late adolescence to young adulthood is often associated with greater autonomy and independence. It is conceivable that previous inhibitions to some health-risk behaviors, such as smoking and alcohol consumption, may weaken due to reductions in parent–guardian influence, and the perception that these behaviors become socially "normal" and "acceptable" within the campus setting.[3]

2   Group norms are characterized as the attitudes, expectations, and behaviors within regular group members, and are seen as a powerful agent that can often account for, and even determine, an individual's behavior.[4] Peer norms may be particularly salient within a collegiate population, as students find themselves situated within a peer-dominated environment, with less

frequent contact with parents, siblings, or other previous reference groups. Moreover, college students generally tend to overestimate the degree to which their peers are engaging in normative behaviors. For example, Perkins and colleagues[5] found nearly 75% of US college students overestimated the amount of alcohol being consumed by their peers at social events. These misperceptions are consistent with the findings from 2 review papers that examined student norms of alcohol consumption,[4,6] as well as findings from a nationwide survey, which found most students from each of the US colleges surveyed perceiving more frequent alcohol consumption among their peers than actually reported.[7]

3   The United States and Canada are 2 countries that have many shared values. However, there are important differences between these 2 countries that may be reflected in different normative beliefs about health behaviors. For example, the legal drinking age in Canada is much younger (18–19 years) than in the United States (21 years). In terms of drug control policies, the United States has a greater conservatism towards legalizing drugs such as marijuana than Canada. Under current Canadian legislation, possession of small amounts of marijuana for personal use (i.e., ≤ 15 g) will not typically result in a criminal record.[8] In terms of smoking, such differences may inevitably be reflected in cross-cultural differences in postsecondary students' use of alcohol and drugs and normative beliefs regarding such health behaviors. National data on the usage of alcohol and drugs among Canadian[9] and US[10] postsecondary students indicate substantially lower cigarette, marijuana, and alcohol use among Canadian students (12.7%, 16.7%, and 77.1%, respectively) than their US peers (39.8%, 38.2%, and 84.8%, respectively). However, no study has compared peer norms for substance use among Canadian and US postsecondary students. Understanding misperceptions of peer norms is particularly important because they may have strong implications towards students' engagement in health-risk behaviors.

4   Most of the research on health-risk behavior norms within the campus setting has been conducted in the United States,[5,7,11–14] with the primary focus on alcohol use.[6] The purpose of this study was to extend the findings on substance use norms to a Canadian sample of university students by (1) examining the relationship between Canadian postsecondary students' actual

and perceived use of alcohol, cigarettes, and marijuana; and (2) comparing substance use and perceived norms between Canadian and US postsecondary students. It was hypothesized that (1) the Canadian students surveyed would perceive more frequent alcohol, cigarette, and marijuana use among their peers than actually reported[7]; (2) perceived use would predict actual use for all 3 substances assessed[7,12-14]; and (3) actual use and perceived norms would be lower for Canadian postsecondary students than their US peers.[9,10]

Methods

Design and Sample

5   Data were collected during the Spring of 2006 using the National College Health Assessment of the American College Health Association (NCHA-ACHA; for further information, see ACHA 2006[10]). The NCHA-ACHA consists of 58 questions and approximately 300 items primarily assessing student health status and health behaviors, access to health information, impediments to academic performance, and perceived norms across a variety of health risk behaviors such as alcohol, tobacco, and other drug use.[10] It has been evaluated extensively for reliability and validity in US college students.[15,16] To the best of our knowledge, this is the first study to use the NCHA-ACHA in a sample of Canadian university students.

6   Five thousand students (from a student body of approximately 50,000) at the largest campus of the University of Toronto, Ontario, Canada, were randomly chosen to receive an invitation by e-mail to participate in the survey. Over a period of 1 month, each potential participant received 3 such invitations to go to a secure Web site, maintained by the ACHA, to complete the NCHA-ACHA Web version of the survey. Participants were also entered into a draw to receive bookstore coupons as an incentive. Approval for the research protocol was granted by the university research ethics board.

Measures

Demographics

7   Participants provided demographic information, including age, sex, living situation, relationship status, ethnicity, body mass index (BMI; determined from self-reported weight [kg] and height [m]), and student status (i.e., undergraduate versus graduate/ full-time versus part-time).

Self-reported Substance Use

8   Participants were asked to respond to the following question: *"Within the last 30 days, on how many days did you use the following. . ."* In line with our research objectives, data were extracted for cigarettes, alcohol, and marijuana use. Response options ranged from *never used* and *have used but not in the last 30 days* to *used all 30 days*.[10]

Perceived Substance Use Norm

9   Perceived substance use was assessed by the question, *"Within the last 30 days, how often do you think the typical student at your school used. . ."* Consistent with our research objectives, data were extracted for perceived cigarettes, alcohol, and marijuana use. Response categories were *never used, used one or more days, used daily*.[10]

Statistical Analyses

10   Frequencies were calculated in the demographic characteristics, which were subsequently dichotomized into the following categories: *sex*—male versus female; *residence*—living at home (parental/guardian's home) versus away from home (college residence, fraternity or sorority, off campus housing); *relationship status*—single (not in a relationship) versus other (married, divorced, engaged or in a committed relationship); *student status*—undergraduate versus graduate student; *full-time status*—full-time versus part-time; and *ethnicity*—white versus other (aboriginal, Arab, black, Chinese, Filipino, Japanese, Korean, Latin American, South Asian, Southeast Asian, West Asian, multiracial, other).

11   Logistic regression was conducted to examine the relationship between perceived and self-reported substance use. Hence, responses to the 2 substance use variables were recoded into 2 categories: *not used in the past 30 days* versus *used in the past 30 days*. Demographic variables (age, BMI, sex, relationship status, student status, residence, full-time status, ethnicity) were entered first (Block 1) as covariates, whereas perceived substance use was entered second (Block 2).

All models showed nonsignificant Hosmer-Lemeshow statistics, and significant omnibus chi-squares, indicating good model fit.[17]

Results

Demographics

12   A total of 1,203 students were surveyed, representing a 24% response rate. This response rate is slightly lower than the 31% to 35% response rate reported in other college studies that have used the NCHA.[10,15] Median age of the sample was 22 years (range 18–45). Participants were primarily white (60%), female (60%), single (51%), full-time (60%) undergraduate (65%) students, who were living away from home (68%). Mean BMI was 22.73 kg/m², which is indicative of a healthy body weight.

Actual and Perceived Substance Use in Past 30 Days

13   Data on self-reported and perceived substance use are shown in Figure 1. In the past 30 days, alcohol was the most commonly used substance (65.8%), followed by marijuana (13.5%) and cigarettes (13.5%; Figure 1a). National data on the usage of alcohol, cigarettes, and marijuana among 54,111 US college students drawn from 71 institutes (ACHA)[10] is also shown in Figure 1a. In comparison to the US data, cigarette, alcohol, and marijuana use in the current sample were lower.

14   Perceived substance norms are presented in Figure 1b. Despite the lower substance use, the majority of respondents in the present study had indicated that the typical student on their campus had used alcohol (95.6%), cigarettes (86.6%), or marijuana (76.7%) in the past 30 days (see Figure 1b). However, these perceptions were slightly lower than those reported previously for alcohol, cigarettes, and marijuana in the US data (i.e., 99%, 96%, and 94%, respectively).[10]

Do Substance Norms Predict Self-reported Substance Use?

15   Results from the logistic regression predicting self-reported cigarette, alcohol, and marijuana use are presented in Tables 1 to 3, respectively. For all 3 substances, ethnicity was a common predictor of actual 30-day use. Students of a white ethnicity were twice as likely to use cigarettes and alcohol, and were over 3 times as likely to use marijuana in the past 30 days, than students of a nonwhite ethnicity. For alcohol use, residence and relationship status were also found to be significant predictors, such that actual 30-day use was one-half times as likely for students currently in

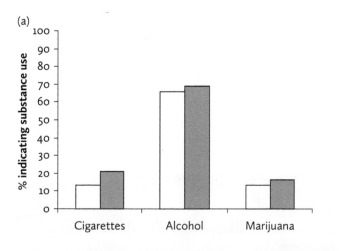

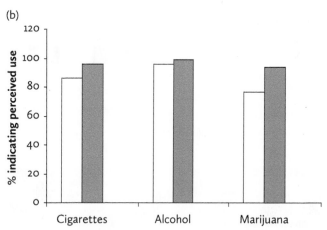

FIGURE 1   Reported (a) versus perceived (b) alcohol, cigarette, and marijuana use in the past 30 days. Actual substance use is based on respondents' self-reported use of cigarettes, alcohol, and marijuana within the past 30 days. Perceived substance use is based on respondents' perceptions of the *typical students'* use of the 3 substances within the past 30 days. *n* = 54,111 for the US[10] sample. ■ Current sample; □ US data.

a relationship and almost twice as likely for students living away from their parents' or guardians' home. After controlling for demographic characteristics, perceived substance use remained a significant predictor of actual 30-day substance use. Students were twice as likely to use cigarettes, over 3 times as likely to use marijuana, and 7 times as likely to consume alcohol in the past 30 days if they perceived the typical student to have used these substances in the past 30 days (see Tables 1, 2, 3).

Table 1	Logistic Regression Predicting Self-reported Cigarette Use					95.0% CI (OR)	
Predictor	B	SE	Wald	Significance	OR	Lower	Upper
Ethnicity	.89	.21	17.49	< .001			
White					2.44	1.61	3.72
Other					1.00		
Smoking norm	.66	.33	3.93	< .05			
Perceived use					1.93	1.01	3.69
Perceived nonuse					1.00		

Note. OR indicates the likelihood of using cigarettes in the past 30 days. Data only shown for significant predictors ($p < .05$).

Table 2	Logistic Regression Predicting Self-reported Alcohol Use					95.0% CI (OR)	
Predictor	B	SE	Wald	Significance	OR	Lower	Upper
Relationship status	0.38	.14	7.02	< .01			
In a relationship					1.46	0.52	0.91
Single					1.00		
Residence	0.56	.15	14.48	< .001			
Away from home					1.75	0.43	0.76
Parents'/Guardian's home					1.00		
Ethnicity	0.64	.14	21.87	< .001			
White					1.90	1.45	2.49
Other					1.00		
Alcohol norm	1.96	.37	28.73	< .001			
Perceived use					7.12	3.47	14.60
Perceived nonuse					1.00		

Note. OR indicates the likelihood of using alcohol in the past 30 days. Data only shown for significant predictors ($p < .05$).

Table 3	Logistic Regression Predicting Self-reported Marijuana Use					95.0% CI (OR)	
Predictor	B	SE	Wald	Significance	OR	Lower	Upper
Ethnicity	1.36	.24	31.01	< .001			
White					3.89	2.41	6.27
Other					1.00		
Marijuana norm	1.30	.34	14.48	< .001			
Perceived use					3.68	1.88	7.21
Perceived nonuse					1.00		

Note. OR indicates the likelihood of using marijuana in the past 30 days. Data only shown for significant predictors ($p < .05$).

Comment

16   The primary objective of this study was to determine the relationship between perceived and actual substance use in a sample of Canadian university students. Similar to previous research,[4-7,10] students overestimated the use of substances on campus, specifically cigarettes, alcohol, and marijuana, relative to their own self-reported use. Perceived substance use was found to be a significant predictor of actual use for all 3 substances measured, with the strongest relationships shown for alcohol and marijuana. In addition to perceived substance use, ethnicity was a common predictor of actual use, with students of a white ethnicity at a greater risk of using cigarettes, alcohol, and marijuana than their nonwhite peers. For the alcohol model, being in a relationship and living away from home were also associated with greater alcohol use.

17   A secondary objective was to compare substance use and norms between Canadian and US postsecondary students. As hypothesized, substance use and norms were much higher in the US data[10] in comparison to data from the present study. Earlier research has shown greater cigarette use among US versus Canadian postsecondary students.[18] The current study findings suggest that, in addition to cigarette use, Canadian university students also use alcohol and marijuana less so than their US peers. Similar to the US data,[4-6,10] students in the current study had overestimated the use of all 3 measured substances, with the greatest discrepancies seen amongst cigarette and marijuana use. As shown in Figure 1, over 75% of students perceived the "typical" student to use cigarettes or marijuana, whereas only 13.5% actually reported using these substances. Although the discrepancy was smaller for alcohol consumption (~30%), it still remains noteworthy. Together, these findings suggest that Canadian university students, similar to their US peers, have a bias towards overestimating the prevalence of cigarette, alcohol, and marijuana use on campus. Future research should examine the factors underlying students' misperceptions of peer substance use as well as the cross-cultural differences for substance use and normative beliefs between Canadian and US postsecondary students.

18   As hypothesized, perceived use was a common predictor of actual use for all 3 substances assessed.

These results parallel what has been found in previous research on campus substance use norms in both the United States[7,12,13] and Canada.[14] However, our findings also suggest that perceived norms may have a stronger influence, and therefore act as a moderator, on students' use of some substances (e.g., alcohol, marijuana) over other substances (e.g., cigarettes). One implication of this moderating effect is that future substance use interventions should consider the relationship between social norms and the targeted substance. For substances where the social norm–substance use relationship is strong (e.g., alcohol), social norms campaigns may be an effective strategy for changing students' actual substance use. Meanwhile, social norm interventions may be less effective for preventing and/or treating postsecondary students' use of other substances (e.g., smoking) where this relationship is small.

Limitations

19   As with other studies, our study has some limitations that warrant mention. First, the use of survey invitations to a random group of students influences the generalizability of the results to the larger Canadian university population. In particular, the current sample was predominately white so the findings regarding ethnicity must be interpreted with caution. Second, measures of actual and perceived use were self-report, and therefore may be influenced by response biases. Furthermore, these measures only focused on a 30-day period, which may not be representative of students' actual behavior. However, the substance use rates reported in the current sample are similar to those reported in a previous national data set,[9] which used data from over 6,000 Canadian university students. Lastly, the study design was cross-sectional, hence causation cannot be inferred.

Conclusions

20   These results contribute to the student norm research by examining the relationship between actual and perceived use across a variety of substances, within a Canadian sample of university students. The findings suggest that Canadian university students, similar to their US peers, have inaccurate perceptions of substance use by their campus peers. Moreover, these misperceptions may have potentially negative influences on students' actual substance use, although this needs confirmation through experimental research. These findings are particularly relevant to campus health services, as they suggest incorporating social norms in future interventions or campaigns that focus on altering students' engagement in health-risk behaviors. For example, campaigns that highlight the discrepancies between actual and perceived student health behaviors (e.g., cigarette use, incidences of binge drinking) may help to alter students' perceptions and possibly their own engagements in those behaviors. Future research should examine the feasibility of social norms campaigns for different health-risk behaviors, as well as the possibility of a "synergistic effect" of targeting one substance norm, specifically alcohol, on other related health-risk behaviors.

Journal of American College Health. 2010. 59 (3).

Acknowledgements

The research was supported by a Postdoctoral Fellowship (to K.A.-N.) and a Doctoral Scholarship (to M.K.) from the Social Sciences and Humanities Research Council of Canada.

References

1. World Health Organization. *The World Health Report: Reducing Risks, Promoting Healthy Life*. Geneva, Switzerland: World Health Organization; 2002.

2. Poortinga W. The prevalence and clustering of four major lifestyle risk factors in an English adult population. *Prev Med.* 2007;44:124–128.

3. Colder CR, Flay BR, Segawa E, Hedeker D, TERN members. Trajectories of smoking among freshmen college students with prior smoking history and risk for future smoking: data from the University Project Tobacco Etiology Research Network (UpTERN) study. *Addiction.* 2008;103:1534–1543.

4. Perkins HW. Social norms and the prevention of alcohol misuse in collegiate contexts. *J Stud Alcohol.* 2002;(suppl 14):164–172.

5. Perkins HW, Haines M, Rice R. Misperceiving the college drinking norm and related problems: a nationwide study of exposure to prevention information, perceived norms and student alcohol misuse. *J Stud Alcohol.* 2005;66:470–478.

6. Borsari B, Carey KB. Peer influences on college drinking: a review of the research. *J Subst Abuse.* 2001;13:391–424.

7. Perkins HW, Meilman P, Leichliter JS, Cashin JR, Presley C. Misperceptions of the norms for the frequency of alcohol and other drug use on college campuses. *J Am Coll Health.* 1999;47:253–258.

8. House of Commons of Canada. Bill C-38: An act to amend the Contraventions Act and the Controlled Drugs and Substances Act. Ottawa, Ontario, Canada: House of Commons; 2003.

9. Adlaf EM, Demers A, Gliksman L. *Canadian Campus Survey 2004*. Toronto, Ontario, Canada: Centre for Addiction and Mental Health; 2004.

10. American College Health Association. The American College Health Association National College Health Assessment (ACHA-NCHA), Spring 2003 Reference Group data report (Abridged). *J Am Coll Health.* 2005;53:199–210.

11. Martens MP, Page JC, Mowry ES, Damann KM, Taylor KK, Cimini MD. Differences between actual and perceived student norms: an examination of alcohol use, drug use, and sexual behavior. *J Am Coll Health.* 2006;54:295–300.

12. Kilmer JR, Walker DD, Lee CM, et al. Misperceptions of college student marijuana use: implications for prevention. *J Stud Alcohol.* 2006;67:277–281.

13. Neighbors C, Geisner IM, Lee CM. Perceived marijuana norms and social expectancies among entering college student marijuana users. *Psychol Addict Behav.* 2008;22:433–438.

14. Perkins HW. Misperceptions of peer drinking norms in Canada: another look at the "reign of error" and its consequences among college students. *Addict Behav.* 2007;32:2645–2656.

15. American College Health Association. The American College Health Association National College Health Assessment (ACHA-NCHA), Spring 2005 Reference Group data report (Abridged). *J Am Coll Health.* 2006;55:5–16.

16. American College Health Association. The American College Health Association National College Health Assessment (ACHA-NCHA), Spring 2007 Reference

Group data report(Abridged). *J Am Coll Health.* 2008;56:469–479.

17. Tabachnick BG, Fidell LS. *Using Multivariate Statistics.* 4th ed. Boston, MA: Allyn & Bacon; 2001.

18. Adlaf EM, Gliksman L, Demers A, Newton-Taylor B. Cigarette use among Canadian undergraduates. *Can J Public Health.* 2003;94:22–24.

Key and challenging words

normative, protocol, dichotomize, synergistic effect, discrepancy

Questions

1. Summarize the purpose and justification for the study.
2. Analyze the essay's Introduction, paying particular attention to organization and other strategies leading to comprehension (for example, topic sentences, transitions, and use of rhetorical patterns).
3. In your own words, explain the significance of Figure 1, using the information in the text section "Results" as well as the bolded text below the graphs.
4. What are the main findings in the section "Do Substance Norms Predict Self-reported Substance Use?" Paraphrase one of these findings.

5. In the "Comment" section, usually titled "Discussion" in Type B essays, identify by paragraph number and briefly summarize the following: (a) a main result; (b) the way it compares to a prior study; (c) a suggestion for further research. Note that there is more than one example of (a), (b), and (c) in the "Comment" section.
6. (a) Explain the importance of the "Limitations" section to the study as a whole; (b) briefly analyze the authors' effectiveness in addressing *one* of the study's limitations.

Post-reading

1. Referring to one of the study's findings, such as the bias of Canadian students to overestimate substance use by other students on campus (see p. 185), come up with a hypothesis that could be the basis of an experiment to extend the findings of the current study. Then, give a two-sentence description of the design of such a study—i.e., give a brief description of its methodology. (See "Methods," p. 182 or Chapter 3, Type B essays.)
2. *Collaborative activity:* In the "Comment" and "Conclusions" sections, the authors suggest

interventions to help reduce substance use on Canadian campuses. Design an intervention campaign for use by your institution's Health Services in which you consider the "relationship between social norms and the targeted substance" (p. 185). Your intervention campaign could consider other strategies and interventions as well, but you must refer to the key finding in the study (see p. 185, "Comment" section, paragraph 1). Summarize the main features of your campaign.

Additional library reading

Perkins, H.W. (2007). Misperceptions of peer drinking norms in Canada: Another look at the "reign of error" and its consequences among college students. *Addictive Behaviors, 32*(11), 2645–2656. doi:10.1016/j.addbeh.2007.07.007.

Demers, A. Beauregard, N. & Gliksman, L. (2013).

College alcohol-control policies and students' alcohol consumption: A matter of exposure? *Contemporary Drug Problems, 40*(2), 191–214.

Higdon, L.I. (2011). How to make students uncomfortable with drinking. *The Chronicle of Higher Education, 57*(37), A36-A37.

CANADA IN THE WORLD

Tarmageddon: Dirty oil is turning Canada into a corrupt petro-state

Andrew Nikiforuk
(1,604 words)

Pre-reading

1. Who is Andrew Nikiforuk? Do an online or library search on the author to determine his qualifications for writing this essay, professional background, publications, etc.
2. Do a library search on "oil sands" or "tar sands" to get an idea of the controversy surrounding the Alberta Oil Sands project. Scan the titles (and, if possible, the abstracts/summaries) of the 5–10 most recent articles in journals, magazines, and newspapers. What kinds of periodicals do the articles appear in (e.g., business, environmental)? Are they primarily informative or argumentative articles? If the latter, what position is taken (i.e., pro/con)?

1 Europeans once regarded Canada as a decent "do-gooder" democracy, celebrated for its vast forests, pristine waters, and pleasant cities. But the rapid development of the tar sands, the world's largest energy project, has not only blackened the country's environmental reputation, but also dramatically undermined its political and economic character.

2 Oil, a politically corrosive resource, has unsettled the nation. Ever since Canada supplanted Mexico and Saudi Arabia nearly a decade ago as the No. 1 oil supplier to the United States, the federal government has become an increasingly aggressive defender of hydrocarbons and little else.

3 The nation's dismal record on climate change, and minimal investments in green energy, simply reflect a growing dependence on oil revenue, oil volatility, and petroleum lobbyists. As a consequence, Canada now shares the same sort of unaccountability and lack of transparency that marks fellow petrostates such as Saudi Arabia. Nowadays, Canada is, as one *Toronto Star* columnist pointedly put it, "a nation that doesn't say much, doesn't do much, and doesn't seem to stand for much."

4 Canada's dramatic transformation began with the rapid exploitation of the tar sands in the mid-1990s. This resource, a true symbol of peak oil, is neither cheap nor light. Bitumen, an inferior and ultra-heavy hydrocarbon that resembles asphalt, is so thick that it can't move through a pipeline unless diluted with a solvent.

5 Bitumen also contains so much carbon (and so little hydrogen) that it must be upgraded into "synthetic crude," a product with a higher sulphur, acid, and heavy metal content than West Texas crude or North Sea oil. As a consequence, bitumen remains the world's most capital-intensive oil at $60–80 a barrel; in contrast, US domestic crude can be produced at $10 a barrel.

6 Although industry studies claim that bitumen production is only 15 per cent dirtier than light oil, the facts speak otherwise. The U.S. National Energy Technology Laboratory, for instance, recently calculated that jet fuel made from bitumen has a carbon footprint 244 per cent greater than fuel made from US domestic crude. While Statoil, Norway's state-owned company, reports greenhouse gas emissions of 8 to 19 kilograms per barrel in the North Sea, production emissions in the tar sands range from 22 to 417 kilograms or higher. In addition, scientists report a disturbing lack of public transparency on tar sands emissions reporting.

7 Nevertheless, every major global oil company has joined the bitumen boom. To date, the $200 billion scramble has directly industrialized 1.4 million hectares of forest—the equivalent of 40 Denvers or 17 Berlins.

8 The spectacle has not been pretty. Open pit mines the size of cities excavate shallow bitumen deposits in the forest, while steam plants inject deeper formations with as many as 12 barrels of steam to melt

just one barrel of bitumen. Both recovery methods create enormous environmental messes.

9   The mines generate extraordinary volumes of toxic waste, which companies store in massive unlined dykes. These geologically unstable "tailing ponds" occupy 140 square kilometres of forest along the Athabasca River and contain a variety of fish-killers and cancer-makers, including arsenic, cyanide, naphthenic acids, and polycyclic aromatic hydrocarbons. Any breach of these impoundments would be catastrophic for the world's third-largest watershed, the Mackenzie River Basin.

10   Federal and provincial standards for reporting the volume of pollutants in these waste sites, and for reducing mining waste, didn't materialize until 2009. Even Boston-based Cambridge Energy Research Associates has decried the total lack of transparency on the reporting of tar ponds seepage into ground water or surface water.

11   The steam plants have equally impressive footprints. These heavily subsidized enterprises are fragmenting a forest the size of England with wells and pipelines. A fifth of Canada's natural gas demand goes into boiling the water to melt out the bitumen. This makes the energy intensity of steam plants so high that, at one joule of energy to make 1.4 joules of bitumen, there is little net gain in energy from the process.

12   The amount of groundwater pumped through these steam plants keeps growing, and threatens the hydrology of the entire region. Opti-Nexen, a large steam plant operator, initially calculated that it would take two barrels of steam to make one barrel of bitumen. Now the company boils up to six.

13   Due to its energy and water intensity, the tar sands has become its own carbon-making nation within Canada. It now accounts for 5 per cent of the nation's emissions and pollutes the global atmosphere with 40 megatonnes of greenhouse gases a year. That's nearly double the annual emissions of Estonia or Latvia. By 2020, the project will likely exceed the emissions of Belgium, a nation of 10 million people. (These industry calculations do not include the burning of the oil in cars or the destruction of peat-lands, forests, and grasslands by the mines and natural gas drillers.)

*

14   The most poisonous legacy of the tar sands project has been its impact on public policy. Canada, once a global leader on tackling ozone pollution and acid rain, now has no effective climate change policy. Canada is the only signatory to the Kyoto Protocol that has completely abandoned its targets. It now ranks 59th out of 60 countries on responsible climate action: only Saudi Arabia boasts a worse record.

15   At the failed Copenhagen talks last year, an almost invisible Canada, one of the world's top ten emitters, gave a mere three-and-a-half-minute presentation. Even Saudi Arabia managed a six-minute talk.

16   Canada's Prime Minister, Stephen Harper, the son of an Imperial Oil executive, hails from the tar sands-producing province of Alberta, where a third of the population conveniently does not believe in climate change. Like many of Saudi Arabia's elites, Harper remains a bona-fide climate change skeptic—if not an outright denier. He has also appointed climate change deniers to important scientific posts. One of his close associates, Ken Boessenkool, even works as an oil industry lobbyist. Many of his fishing buddies support the country's pro-oil, anti-climate-action lobby group, Friends of Science.

17   Given that corporate taxes on tar sands production yield the federal government nearly \$5 billion a year, steady oil revenue has trumped the public interest. The country has opposed low carbon fuel standards in the US, while Canada's Foreign Affairs branch says it "will resist efforts to label one form of energy as appropriate, such as renewables." Canada's Environment Minister, Jim Prentice, openly criticizes provinces such as Quebec for implementing green policies that reduce fossil fuel consumption.

18   Like Saudi Arabia, Canada has increasingly relied on foreign temporary workers, whose numbers (250,000) now exceed permanent immigrants, to develop its oil fields. In 2008, Alberta actually had 20 times as many temporary foreign workers (from places as diverse as China, South Africa, and the Philippines) as the US in proportion to its population.

19   Abuses by brokers and employers abound. A 2009 report by the University of Sussex concluded that Canadian authorities, much like Saudi politicians, view temporary workers as "stocks that can be bought in or out as required." The Canadian and Alberta

governments have also failed to consult local workers, unions, and the general public about their temporary foreign worker programs.

*

20   Although industry and government describe the tar sands as "Canada's new economic engine," the project has in reality given Canada a bad case of the Dutch Disease. This economic malaise, a form of deindustrialization, takes its name from a 1977 *Economist* article that detailed how a natural gas boom hollowed out the manufacturing base of the Netherlands. Gas exports inflated the value of the Dutch guilder, which in turn undermined the ability of its manufacturers to export their goods.

21   Thanks to rapidly growing tar sands exports (from 600,000 barrels a day in 2000 to 1.3 million barrels today), the loonie, as the Canadian dollar is known, has now reached parity with—and may soon surpass—the US dollar in value. But the high-priced loonie has made it particularly difficult for Canadian manufacturers to sell their goods. A 2009 study by Luxembourg's Centre for Research in Economic Analysis confirmed that Canada's oil-priced currency has indeed hammered industries as varied as textile mills, electronics, fabricated metal, and paper. It concluded that 54 per cent of the nation's manufacturing employment losses (nearly 5 per cent of the workforce) were due to the rapid tar sands development from 2002 to 2007.

22   Unlike Norway, the world's most transparent petro-state, Canada has also failed to exercise any fiscal accountability over its non-renewable oil wealth. The country has no sovereign fund and has saved no wealth to date, much to the consternation of the Organization for Economic Cooperation and Development (OECD), which concluded in a damning 2008 report that "other nations have shown much more restraint and foresight in managing their resource revenues to mitigate boom-and-bust cycles."

23   In addition, neither Canada nor Alberta charges much for the bitumen. Alberta has even described its royalty regime as a "give-it-away" scheme. Alberta's share from a $60 barrel of oil is a mere 30 cents, one of the lowest royalties in the world. The province also permits corporations to deduct royalties for federal corporate tax purposes.

24   Nevertheless, Alberta still garners nearly a third of its revenue from hydrocarbons. To date, much of it has been used to lower taxes, manipulate public sentiment, and recklessly build infrastructure to fuel more tar sands development. Ruled by one political party for an astounding 38 years, Alberta's government has been increasingly described as incompetent, authoritarian, and corrupt.

25   Canada has yet to have a national debate about the pace and scale of the tar sands development. Until it acknowledges the project's cancerous hold on national life, Canada will increasingly become an unstable petro-state marginalized by oil price volatility and global carbon politics.

CCPA Monitor. 2010. May 17 (1).

Key and challenging words

corrosive, volatility, breach (n.), decry, hydrology, malaise, consternation, mitigate, authoritarian

Questions

1.   Does Nikiforuk provide a successful introduction? Briefly analyze the first paragraph.

2.   Using a reliable source, such as an encyclopedia, research bitumen, determining whether the description of this substance, along with the facts about its effects and extraction methods discussed in paragraphs 4–10, seems accurate.

3.   Analyze Nikiforuk's use of compare and contrast in his essay: a) Identify two passages in which he uses a comparison, analyzing them for their effectiveness;

b) Why does Nikiforuk often compare Canada to Saudi Arabia, and what are the effects of such comparisons?

4. How many main points does Nikiforuk's essay contain? Which point do you believe is the most important one for his argument? Why?

5. From paragraph 9, a) Define "'tailing ponds'" in your own words; b) What is the significance of the word "Even" in the last sentence of paragraph 10?

6. Does Nikiforuk present all his points fairly? Identify any examples of slanted language and of logical or ethical fallacies. Explain why you think they undermine (or do not undermine) his claim.

7. Explain what is meant by the "Dutch Disease" (paragraph 20) and how this "disease" could affect Canada's economy.

Post-reading

1. Find two reviews of Nikiforuk's book *Tar Sands: Dirty Oil and the Future of a Continent* (these could be in a journal, magazine, or newspaper, but not a personal website or blog). Compare and contrast the two reviews in approximately 500 words. Or, compare and contrast Nikiforuk's essay on the oil sands with an essay that takes the opposing view (for example, McLellan, listed below. Remember that you are evaluating the effectiveness of each argument, not expressing your own viewpoint about the oil sands.

2. *Collaborative or individual activity:* Discuss or debate one of the following topics: a) How is the development of the Alberta Oil Sands project affecting Canada's reputation internationally or how do you think it will affect Canada's reputation? b) Do you believe Nikiforuk successfully defends the claim he makes in the title and introduction?

3. Do you believe the absence of cited sources reduces Nikiforuk's credibility? Do you believe it reduces his credibility for readers of the *CCPA Monitor*? (To answer the second question, you should access the home page of the publication in which this essay appeared in order to determine the kind of audience he is writing for.)

Related websites of interest

Friends of Science (mentioned in the essay, paragraph 15):
www.friendsofscience.org/

Alberta government "Oil Sands" website:
www.oilsands.alberta.ca/

The Tyee (an online magazine for which Andrew Nikiforuk has written many articles as its first "writer in residence"; browse by topic [energy] or search for Nikiforuk from the home page to access articles):
http://thetyee.ca/

Additional library reading

McLellan, D.A. (2013, January 4). The oil sands' benefits. *Financial Post.* Retrieved from http://opinion.financialpost.com/2013/01/14/the-oil-sands-benefits/

The ugly Canadian

Amir Attaran
(4,297 words)

Pre-reading

1. Scanning the essay, note differences between this essay and scholarly essays you have encountered before (in this book or in other books or journals). What could account for these differences? How is this essay similar to scholarly essays you have encountered?
2. Does the simple title suggest the content of the essay? What about the headings? In one sentence, summarize what you think the essay will be about.

1   On April 22 of this year, a mysterious four-month-long nightmare ended for Robert Fowler and Louis Guay, the Canadian diplomats abducted in Niger by a shadowy group calling itself al Qaeda in the Islamic Maghreb. Fowler and Guay were on a secret mission for the secretary general of the United Nations, although when they were abducted they were on a private trip to a Canadian-run goldmine, travelling without a protective escort. The kidnappers ripped them from their UN-marked vehicle with such intensity of purpose that the engine was left idling and nothing was stolen. The village where it happened was named Karma.

2   The story had a happy ending, at least in terms of Fowler and Guay's physical health. Yet all kinds of questions hang in the air, beginning with what exactly did al Qaeda receive—and from whom—in exchange for the hostages. Prime Minister Stephen Harper adamantly denied that Canada pays ransoms or releases prisoners to satisfy kidnappers, but it is clear from news reports that a complex negotiation took place involving several countries and that money, prisoners, or both probably changed hands. But there are other questions as well: Why was there such a silence in Canada over those four months? Didn't we care that two of our top diplomats had been seized in this way? Officially the silence was said to be for their security, but it is also true that many in Ottawa's establishment disliked the reminder that to be Canadian no longer implies beneficence and safety from harm. In the face of a national mythology that everyone loves Canadians—a mythology that has resulted in innumerable maple leaves being stitched like amulets onto countless backpacks—the Fowler and Guay episode was a cold wind of reality.

3   When ill fate strikes one's country, it is awkward or even taboo to pose the question of whether it is deserved, for lack of a better word. In the wake of 9/11, Americans reacted ferociously to anyone who dared to hint that they shared in the blame. Yet many foreigners knew America had it coming and, after a dignified period of mourning, they said so. On the first anniversary of the Twin Towers attack Prime Minister Jean Chrétien famously reminded Americans that "you cannot exercise your powers to the point of humiliation of the others." Canadians agreed with him, and in a 2002 poll by *The Globe and Mail*, 84 per cent believed that America bore partial or total responsibility for the attacks.

4   But the notion that there is karma for a country, which trips so easily off the tongue when tut-tutting about the United States, is surely not a notion from which Canada is exempt. Canada too makes the mistake of exercising powers to the point of humiliation of the others, and it would be fanciful to imagine that Canada lacks the biblical sin of pride. Indeed, if one takes an unflinching look at Canadian conduct in the world, the evidence permits no conclusion other than that the country has lately been engaged in a liquidation of its internationalism. Canada has lost the outward gaze that the British Empire imposed, and that Prime Minister Lester Pearson cultivated. Today's Canadians, just 0.5 per cent of the world's population, are more insular than even their modest numbers suggest.

5   I do not make this criticism in the spirit of an unpatriotic hatchet job. Unlike Canadians born in this

country, I came to it by choice, faults and all. As a born Californian with a Berkeley and Oxford education, probably I could live elsewhere, but I was attracted to this very Pearsonian country in the 1990s. I settled in Vancouver, studied law at the University of British Columbia and became a Canadian. While I love this place, learning it through its laws has also shown me a dark side.

6   In a democracy where legislation is freely chosen, laws are a country's DNA: they are the code the country lives by, and if the code is ugly, by merciless logic so too will be the country. On that level, Canada's laws give objective evidence that Pearson's Canada is comatose, if not dead. Today's Canada would not please Pearson, and he would find the country's outlook on foreign people and international obligations oddly picayune and ignorant. He might even say that we are hazardously far down the road of becoming a country of diverse but ugly Canadians—and if we do not check this tendency, karma could pay us back.

Belonging

7   Lester Pearson was a great many things, but complex was not one of them. By a certain age, he had a formula—be assiduous, be respectful, be canny, be humorous, be mindful of who is on the way up, be a dove and a hawk, be principled but not dogmatic—and it served him (and Canada) so well he rarely deviated from it. In Pearson's five years as a minority prime minister, he enacted laws and policies for universal health care, official bilingualism, colour-blind immigration, crop insurance, student loans and the national pension.

8   Yet nothing drove Pearson more than the will to find solutions short of war. He was hardly a pacifist: as a youth he enlisted in the Great War, and later in life he cut short a vacation to be at his diplomatic post in London during the Blitz. War taught him the value of its avoidance and the importance of countries honouring diplomatic commitments to live together harmoniously.

9   Pearson made it his business to slip velvet handcuffs on the exercise of state power. He did this as a diplomat long before being prime minister, by building international institutions and making Canada an early and eager joiner: the United Nations, the

North Atlantic Treaty Organization, and the Food and Agriculture Organization were all largely shaped by Pearson at their creation. When international crises emerged—Palestine, or Suez, for example—it was to the international organizations that Pearson turned. He knew Canada would lose some sovereignty through its chronic reliance on internationalism, but as Canada had only just gained sovereignty from Empire, giving or taking a little sovereignty bothered Pearson less than it might politicians today. This flexibility was shared by Pearson's contemporaries, such as Eleanor Roosevelt with her human rights treaties, or Robert Schuman with his European Coal and Steel Community, which later became the European Union, and it was their vision that unlikely sounding legal institutions could bind countries and cement the peace. Like so many Lilliputians, these great thinkers believed that bureaucrats, lawyers, and businesspeople could tie down generals, demagogues, and terrorists—and actually win.

10   Sixty years later, the internationalists' experiment must be judged a qualified success. The UN is warily regarded: it struggles against incoherent and wasteful complexity, but sometimes inspires by averting a war, epidemic, famine, or other nightmare. The EU is unimaginably successful: not only are Europeans richer and healthier than ever, but the decision to take dominion over the raw materials of war—coal and steel were chosen for a reason—has given Europe an antidote to the poisonous tribalism that for a millennium made it the world's bloodiest continent. NATO has a celebrated past and uncertain future: as a bureaucratic organization it kept the peace during the Cold War, but forced to become a war-making organization in Afghanistan, it is struggling.

11   The lesson of these three cases is subtle: the Lilliputians of the international institutions can preserve the commonweal, but only if governments perpetuate their Pearsonian enchantment with building institutions (as with the EU), while at the same time discouraging bloat (the UN) and avoiding infirmity of purpose (NATO). Left–right politics has little to do with it. Simply put, internationalism is a pragmatic lesson in how collectively to make the world, and Canada, a safer and more prosperous place.

12   Of course, none of this is really new. Pearson did not invent any guiding ideas, so much as raise

them to a functional place in statecraft. Centuries ago, Thomas Hobbes wrote of people's need for "a common power to keep them all in awe," else they revert to the "war of all against all." In the war-weary generation of Pearson, politicians had learned by blood that "if there be no power erected, or not great enough for our security, every man [or country] will and may lawfully rely on his own strength and art for caution against all other[s]," as Hobbes wrote. How remote those days seem now, as the Pearsonian belief in a larger common power has been throttled by Blairs and Bushes who believed foremost in the exceptionalism of their own countries and the dangerous conceit that they might become the common power. It has not ended well for Blair and Bush and their countries.

Backtracking

13   But just as exceptionalism is going back out of fashion, along comes Canada to dumbly clench it. Our recent history is embarrassingly rich in examples of joining institutions and then breaking the rules. Saddest of all, Canadian exceptionalism is frequently arbitrary, unexplained, or self-sabotaging, and the rest of the world is left baffled about the motivations for our country's behaviour. In this, Canadian exceptionalism often makes even less sense than American exceptionalism: at least when Washington thumbs its nose at the international order, it does so with undeterred conviction and a raft of intellectually veneered (if often wrong) arguments. A look at Canada's laws across the board—in matters of economics, health, or human rights—shows how pointless Canadian exceptionalism has become.

14   ***Global Trade Law.*** Before the current global recession, the most prominent globalization debate, which nearly killed the Doha round of World Trade Organization negotiations, was whether free trade advanced developed and developing country interests alike. The debate is not new, and three decades ago it dogged the international trade system, until countries agreed on a principle of "differential and more favourable treatment." The thought was that if richer countries such as Canada opened their markets, for instance by discounting tariff rates preferentially for poorer exporting countries, the latter could gain a toehold on the free trade bandwagon. This lopsided deal would eventually pay itself back, as the poor countries

grew, became rich and became new export markets; in the long run everyone would win. Nothing could be more internationally minded, and so as poorer countries fought their corner, Ottawa decided to be as accommodating as it could.

15   But since then, the way in which Canada applies differential and more favourable treatment is nothing short of bizarre.

16   In law, the Governor-in-Council decides which developing countries get the preference of exporting to Canada at a discounted tariff rate. While that is supposed to be a decision based on countries' poverty and need, politics plays a role too. Hence democratic Belize and Botswana get the preference, but despotic Belarus and Burma do not. Neither, obviously, do developed Belgium and Bulgaria.

17   But how does one explain the Governor-in-Council's decision to give Vladimir Putin's Russia or Robert Mugabe's Zimbabwe the preference? Neither seems a democratic government. Why do Hong Kong, Israel, South Korea, and Singapore get the preference? Certainly none is poor or developing. The height of absurdity is Qatar: it gets the preference too, although per capita it is the world's richest country.

18   When we twist global trade rules so arbitrarily, imagine how it represents Canadian values. Foreigners might wonder: Are Canadians cruel or are they fools? Cruel, because we give a preference intended for the poor to the rich, or fools, for handing rich countries unnaturally low tariffs to clobber our industries? Not only do Canada's random actions misrepresent Canadian values, whether among leftist bleeding hearts or rightist free traders, but they also damage our prosperity and economy.

19   ***Corporations Law.*** A more extreme example of exceptionalism departing from Canadian values is in the morally undisputed area of corruption. Corruption is bad. Countries that coddle corruption are bad. Yet Canada deliberately maintains the loosest corruption laws of any developed country.

20   A decade ago, the Organisation for Economic Co-operation and Development advanced a treaty, called the Anti-Bribery Convention, which aimed to criminalize the giving of bribes to foreign public officials. Canada signed on and passed a law to fulfil the Anti-Bribery Convention's purpose. A self-congratulatory press release at the time quotes justice minister

Anne McLellan touting Canada as "a constant supporter of international anti-corruption efforts."

21   That was, and remains, deeply untrue. Far from targeting international corruption, Canada's law criminalizes only corruption in Canada. Injecting accuracy where its own minister would not, the Department of Justice writes that "Canada has jurisdiction over the bribery of foreign public officials when the offence is committed in whole or in part in its territory." Thus if a Canadian corporation passes cash-stuffed envelopes in Caracas and Harare, rather than Calgary and Halifax, it is allowed. None of the other 29 OECD countries has this loophole and, despite mighty complaints from abroad, Canada cravenly refuses to close it.

22   In fact, Canada is now arguably the "leading" advanced country in which to base a corrupt international business. In 2007, the same year that the United States prosecuted 67 violations of the Anti-Bribery Convention, Canada prosecuted only one. By giving Canadian firms a loophole in international bribery rules, Ottawa gives them an incentive to perfect skills in giving *baksheesh* rather than skills for real competitiveness. Neither the right nor the left can possibly consider this a long-run strategy for Canada's prosperity.

23   ***Health Law.*** While it is bad enough that Canadian exceptionalism costs this country money, taken a bit further, it can kill. When the SARS epidemic hit Toronto and claimed 44 lives in 2003, residents were stunned that the World Health Organization recommended not travelling to their city. Although SARS affected dozens of countries, only two drew WHO's wrath: China, because the apparatchiks in Beijing would not provide information on the epidemic's spread, and Canada, because the bureaucrats in Ottawa could not provide that information. When WHO asked about Toronto's epidemic, an epic cat fight erupted between federal and provincial officials over the answer. Left hanging, WHO had no option but to do the prudent thing and isolate Toronto—a decision that embarrassed Canada and cost it more than a billion dollars.

24   You might think that this humbling experience would have taught Ottawa a lesson about playing well with international organizations, but you would be wrong. WHO learned during SARS that it needed a stronger commitment from governments to disclose information on epidemics, before they become globally threatening. More than 190 countries agreed and, in 2007, WHO's revised International Health Regulations came into force. These regulations oblige national governments—meaning Ottawa, not the provinces—to share epidemiological information during outbreaks.

25   Yet Canada has done nothing to write WHO's new rules into Canadian law. Although the Harper government passed a law to establish the new Public Health Agency of Canada, it deliberately kept the agency toothless. Canada's auditor general complains that without mandatory powers, PHAC "relies on the goodwill of the provinces"—not law—to obtain epidemic information in emergencies. Goodwill, of course, is what failed during SARS. The auditor general also warns that PHAC is "not assured of receiving timely, accurate and complete information" in a future epidemic. Of the ten provinces, PHAC has reached formal agreement with only one (Ontario) to share information during an emergency—and even that agreement is a failure because it is secret and not legally binding. Thus even as listeria-contaminated meat was killing Canadians last year, Ottawa still refused to tell Ontario which stores and restaurants were affected.

26   More than any other example, epidemic preparedness shows how Canadian exceptionalism is a knife pointed outward and inward simultaneously. Senior WHO officials privately admit that Canada is a country of concern, because without a national agency having powers over epidemiological information, Canada could seed deadly infections in other countries before officials become aware. WHO's fears are well founded, because if Canada's governments are too secretive to share information on a comparatively minor listeriosis outbreak, it is fanciful to think that openness will characterize a larger emergency such as an influenza pandemic, during which PHAC expects "between 15 and 35 per cent of Canadians could become ill . . . and between 11,000 and 58,000 deaths could occur." With the H1N1 virus certain to reappear in the 2009 autumn influenza season, perhaps in deadlier form, and our laws still not conforming to WHO's wise direction, Canadians could pay with their lives.

27   ***Human Rights Law.*** Up to this point, I have stuck to politically neutral examples of Canadian exceptionalism. Everyone loves money, and nobody wants to die of a deadly pandemic, so these issues raise few ideological hackles. But not everyone loves humans, or rather, not every human is easy to love—there is

Omar Khadr. Exceptionalism in this territory is harder to evaluate because it reflects ideological choices. Even so, there are clear examples that reveal the pointlessness of Canada's human rights exceptionalism.

28   Consider the violation known as the enforced disappearance of persons, which is basically state-orchestrated secret kidnapping. Security never demands it, as governments can engage in lawful preventive detention or deportation without shadowy disappearances. The only "advantage" in disappearing persons is to ward off pesky lawyers and to keep loved ones in confusion and terror—a handy trick if the government intends to torture or assassinate a person, as military dictatorships in Argentina, Brazil, and Chile did, and as the United States has done in undisclosed CIA "dark sites" in recent years.

29   You might think that Canada, which, under both left- and right-wing governments has nurtured a global reputation as a human rights defender, could not move quickly enough to sign a treaty against enforced disappearances. But again, you would be wrong. The UN's International Convention for the Protection of All Persons from Enforced Disappearance has been open for signatures since 2007, and so far 81 countries have signed. The Harper government refuses to sign, although it assured the UN General Assembly that Canada was "pleased to support" the treaty. In short, our government lied and reneged.

30   Currently, a disturbingly possible reason for Canada not signing the enforced disappearance treaty is that Canada is committing enforced disappearances. In Afghanistan, the Canadian Forces detain persons secretly, without criminal charges, without notice to their families, and without recourse to law. When lawyers asked General Rick Hillier for access to these detainees, he refused. A few hundred detainees—the exact number is classified—have been transferred by the Canadian Forces to the Afghan secret police this way, in full knowledge that those police torture. When a Canadian Foreign Affairs official visited some transferred detainees in the Afghan prison in November 2007, he found not only allegations of torture, but the torture implements themselves:

> When asked about his interrogation the detainee came forward with an allegation of abuse . . . . He alleged that during the [censored] interrogation, [censored] individuals held him to the ground [censored] while the other [censored] beating him with electrical wires and rubber hose. He indicated a spot on the ground in the room we were interviewing in as the place where he was held down. He then pointed to a chair and stated the implements he had been struck with were underneath it. Under the chair, we found a large piece of braided electrical wire as well as a rubber hose. He then showed us a bruise (approx. 4 inches long) on his back that could possibly be the result of a blow.

31   The federal court now notes several instances where detainees were apparently tortured or went "missing."

32   Seizing persons and disappearing them to the purveyors of torture is the sort of conduct one associates with the United States; no wonder Washington rejects the enforced disappearance treaty. But love or hate Washington's choices, America is more honest than Canada, because it never pretended to have a great commitment to human rights law. For the US, rejection works—the world has low expectations, and American power makes for distinction in other ways—but for a country otherwise as unadorned as Canada, faith toward certain national ideals is its identity and branding. Stripped of its human rights reputation, Canada is like Switzerland without neutrality, Italy without fashion, or Tanzania without safaris.

Belonging Again

33   I have outlined four completely different examples of pointless Canadian refusal to go along with the global rules—so pointless that the outcome is actually to diminish Canadians' wealth, health, and standing in the world. I could outline more negative examples—Canada's directionless foreign aid, its contempt for global climate change initiatives, and its densely layered disincentives to foreign investment—or acknowledge some positive examples—the landmines treaty, or certain aspects of Canada's mission in Afghanistan. There is no need, because they do not change this central point: Canada's foreign and trade policies are so irrational as to violate the global rules even when we are victims of the violation.

34   Fixing this situation—as is only wise—requires major improvements to the low quality of Canada's foreign and trade policy establishment.

35   Most importantly, Canada needs serious ministers in the foreign and trade portfolios. Pearson was secretary of state for external affairs for nine unbroken years—a tenure instrumental to his and Canada's success. Yet in the last decade, Canada has had five trade ministers and seven foreign ministers. You have to go back to 1989 in the United States to count a total of seven secretaries of state. Allies and enemies who see Canada swapping its top representatives even more often than Japan changes prime ministers can only conclude that Canadian diplomacy is not serious—and they will walk all over us.

36   Intellect and dedication also matter. Pearson was an Oxford-educated university professor with a hyperactive work ethic. If finding a comparable candidate requires the prime minister bypassing elected members of Parliament to appoint an outsider by way of the Senate, that is a lesser evil than entrusting a diffident poseur like Maxime Bernier with the job of picturing Canada to the world.

37   The Department of Foreign Affairs and International Trade also needs a near-complete makeover to make it less picayune and more insightful about the world. As the Maher Arar inquiry so pointedly illustrated, even the most senior and worldly seeming Canadian diplomats can be ignorant of obvious realities. Recall Franco Pillarella, formerly DFAIT's human rights chief and ambassador to Syria during Arar's ordeal, answering no when asked if he was aware of "serious human rights abuses . . . being committed" in that country. His consul, Leo Martel, testified to doing "*le maximum et plus*" for Acar, but also admitted ignorance of public reports concerning Syria's human rights record. Many DFAIT officials lacked the insight to perceive and act on the foreign realities ensnaring Arar, Abdullah Almalki, Ahmad El Maati, Muayyed Nureddin—and now Abousfian Abdelrazik. (How odd that the same DFAIT bureaucracy which was so incapable of helping these Muslim men swung into high action when the victims were Brahmins such as Robert Fowler or Louis Guay.)

38   One wants not to ascribe this pattern to intentional racism in DFAIT, so one requires an alternative hypothesis. Mine is that DFAIT failed on these and unrelated challenges (so, not simply racism) because it is actually quite naive, and lacks a culture with empathic imagination for foreign persons or foreign realities—a *sine qua non* of good diplomacy. Currently, DFAIT's senior ranks are a monoculture of the scions of *pure laine* Canadian families of European descent, so how surprising is it that Canadian diplomacy is complaisant and Eurocentric in outlook?[1] Even the Canadian Space Agency now hires more "aliens," of the visible minority kind, than xenophobic DFAIT. A large-scale effort to employ more minorities or recent immigrants and to make DFAIT's culture more heterogeneous, as other outward-facing agencies have done (e.g., the Immigration and Refugee Board, Passport Canada), would go a long way toward giving it the imagination and flexible *Weltanschauung* it now lacks. Obviously, a diplomatic corps that can better understand foreigners and better explain Canadian actions to them will better advance Canada's political and economic interests abroad.

39   While it is a subtle point, Canada also needs a civil society that is less captured by government. Some of my fellow academics, particularly in schools of government or international affairs, fear criticizing the emperor's wardrobe too vigorously because support from government agencies might dry up. Self-censorship also stymies those Canadian non-governmental organizations whose core budgets depend on government grants; they should really be called GOs, but calling them so is to hint they are unnecessary. The practice, firmly established in DFAIT, of hand-picking scholars and NGOs for patronage is highly dangerous, for just when Canada's diplomatic or trade interests may call for *les vérités qui dérangent*, the temptation is greatest to solicit *les mensonges qui arrangent* from a sycophantic gallery. A wise federal government would recognize this fact and dispense academic funding only through the arm's-length research councils, would cap Ottawa's largesse to NGOs and would reform the tax laws so that a larger charitable sector financed by private benefactors could fill the void. These changes would favour neither the right nor the left, and would create a more vibrant brain trust of truly non-governmental analysts to impose accountability and, especially, purpose on Canada's lackluster foreign and trade policy.

40   If Canada is a magnificent country, which it is, then it should look itself in the mirror and fearlessly examine the evidence of its conduct in the world. Currently, that evidence teaches that the high-functioning diplomacy of Pearson's era is a thing of

the past, to the shocking extent that Canada lets slip even those international obligations that economically and socially benefit Canadians. Self-neglect is our clearest warning that Canada's global outlook is misguided. We can take the warning and do what is best for ourselves and others, or we can wait for a meeting with karma to announce that Canada has chosen a wrong road.

Literary Review of Canada.2009. June 17 (5).

Note

1. A glance at DFAIT's organizational chart, available on its website at <www.international.gc.ca> (under "About the Department"), shows an apparent dearth of non-European surnames among DFAIT's senior officials. Knowing most of those officials, I can confirm this is the case.

Key and challenging words

amulet, unflinching, insular, picayune, assiduous, dogmatic, Lilliputian, commonweal, throttle (v.), conceit, undeterred, veneer, cravenly, renege, recourse, purveyor, diffident, scion, complaisant, stymie

Questions

1. Who are Robert Fowler and Louis Guay? Using reliable sources, like newspapers or magazines, answer this question. From your research, does it appear that the author's concerns about the government's actions and statements are valid? Why does Attaran begin with their story?
2. Why does the author refer to his own background in paragraph 5? Why does he declare he is not a Canadian by birth? Do his statements in this paragraph affect his credibility?
3. Who does Attaran believe is the key figure in creating Canada's positive international reputation? In a brief paragraph summarize this person's role.
4. Attaran characterizes the "internationalists' experiment" as "a qualified success" (paragraph 10). Does such a claim strengthen or weaken his argument? Explain.
5. What is the significance of the ideas of Thomas Hobbes to the essay (paragraph 12)? Using a reliable source, briefly explain Hobbes's ideas on statecraft and their importance to Attaran's argument.
6. What main rhetorical pattern does the author use to support his points? Choose one subsection under the heading "Backtracking" and discuss his strategies to increase reader comprehension. Could he have used other strategies to help? How does that subsection function within the larger section, contributing to its effectiveness?
7. Referring to paragraph 32 and at least one other paragraph in which the US is mentioned, explain the author's reasons for comparing the Canada to the US. How do the comparisons advance his argument?
8. Summarize paragraphs 35–37 in two or three sentences.
9. Analyze Attaran's argument as a whole. You could consider purpose and audience, order of points, use of appeals, and other argumentative strategies.

Post-reading

1. In about 500 words, analyze the role of a Canadian prime minister after Lester Pearson (for example, Pierre Elliott Trudeau) in promoting Pearson's ideals of internationalism, as described in Attaran's essay. Use at least two reliable sources.
2. *Collaborative or individual activity:* Do you agree with Attaran's assessment concerning Canada's international reputation? What evidence have you seen that convinces you that Canada's status is declining (or not declining)? Such evidence could be based on news reports, discussions with friends, observations, etc.

Related websites of interest

"The ugly Canadian" refers in passing to many Canadian and international organizations, whose pages can be searched for more specific information. For example, information on the Anti-Bribery Convention (see paragraph 20) can be found by performing a search at the Organisation for Economic Co-operation and Development (OECD) homepage.

Organisation for Economic Co-operation and Development:
www.oecd.org

World Health Organization:
www.who.int/en

World Trade Organization/Tariffs:
www.wto.org/english/tratop_e/tariffs_e/tariffs_e.htm

International Convention for the Protection of All Persons from Enforced Disappearance:
www2.ohchr.org/english/law/disappearance-convention.htm

Additional library reading

Thérien, Jean-Philippe, and Gordon Mace. "Identity and Foreign Policy: Canada as a Nation of the Americas." *Latin American Politics & Society* 55.2 (2013): 150–68. Print.

Shooting the messenger: Why Canadians don't often blow the whistle on wrongdoing

Suanne Kelman
(3,575 words)

Pre-reading

1. What is "WikiLeaks"? Using at least two reliable sources, write a one- or two-paragraph description of this incident. Include a brief summary of the opposing sides to the WikiLeaks controversy.
2. Reflect on your own attitude to whistleblowing in a response. Are most whistleblowers heroes, traitors, or something in between? Support your thesis through the use of critical thinking.
3. After reading paragraphs 1–9, come up with a reading hypothesis (see chapter 5, p. 51) that includes argumentative purpose, audience, and any relevant features that could help guide your reading of the essay—for example, tone and linguistic/stylistic techniques.

1   When WikiLeaks funnelled endless secret documents to the press last year, there was only one possible reaction for all true Canadians: an immediate, obsessive hunt for evidence that we exist. Fortunately, we could breathe a sigh of relief after the first comb-through: not only did we show up in a lot of diplomatic cables, but Julian Assange's outfit eventually released a list of our most important and sensitive infrastructure and resources in case anyone wanted to attack.

2   Still, it is lucky that our hunger for attention is modest, because our presence in the mountain of leaked documents was relatively meagre. Much of the commentary on us was uncomplimentary, but we are used to that; like some collective middle child, we just cannot stand to be ignored.

3   A few Canadians bestirred themselves to express outrage over the leaks themselves, especially that list of valuable terrorist targets: the historian J.L. Granatstein demanded that WikiLeaks be shut down immediately for criminal incitement. Tom Flanagan—a former advisor to Stephen Harper—told the CBC that the U.S. government should take out a contract on Assange, later explaining away the remark as a joke.

4   Somewhere in the Canadian psyche there seems rooted the belief that whistleblowing is not nice. But here is an interesting feature that no one seems to have noticed: there is no solid evidence that Canadian officials provided any of this mountain of secret information. WikiLeaks did publish almost 2,000 messages from the Canadian embassy in Washington, but those may simply have been intercepted—quite possibly by some of our American friends.

5   Why didn't any Canadians, as far as we know, funnel secrets to WikiLeaks? Where is our Bradley Manning?

6   It is not as if Canada has no homegrown whistleblowers. We boast our own honour roll; heroic Canadians have exposed corruption, protected veterans' benefits, revealed major safety concerns and saved taxpayers millions of dollars. They even have their own website—fairwhistleblower.ca—where anyone can follow their activities and revelations.

7   Moreover, Canada has an explicit policy of openness—of encouraging whistleblowers in the public sector. That is why the federal government created the Office of the Public Sector Integrity Commissioner of Canada in 2007, to embolden civil servants to report on waste, mismanagement and corruption. As things have turned out, however, our practice is largely divorced from that policy. Our governments are increasingly fond of secrecy and most Canadians do not seem to mind much.

8   So few Canadians applauded Julian Assange's release of thousands of government secrets. There was little discussion in this country of the central issues: whether complete transparency is desirable; whether some government activities, notably diplomacy, truly require secrecy; whether the public had a right to this sudden avalanche of information about their own elected governments. Most of the discussion centred either on that dratted list of targets or on more peripheral issues, such as Assange's character.

9   We were not alone in our ambivalence; commentators almost everywhere worried about the revelations ruining sensitive negotiations and making the world less safe. But many Canadians radiated an aura of prissy disapproval. A lot of the people I have spoken with seem to feel that Assange's exposés were not just dangerous; they were impolite and gauche. Somewhere in the Canadian psyche there seems rooted the belief that whistleblowing is not nice. But surely we have the right and the need to know if our money is being wasted, if our politicians are lying to us, if our allies despise us, if we are violating international law, if other nations are spying on us. Why don't we stick up for whistleblowers? We have never needed them more.

10   To be fair, there were Canadians who praised Assange's assault on secrecy, although not a great many of them. He led a list of last year's heroes compiled by *The Toronto Star*'s Olivia Ward, for his "crusade to make government more transparent and accountable." The left-wing magazine *Canadian Dimension* suggested that he receive the Nobel Peace Prize for similar reasons. He has proved popular with the people who phone in to chat on the CBC's *Cross Country Checkup*.

11   The praise, you will notice, came exclusively from the left. There does seem to be a pattern here: Assange was booed or dismissed by the *National Post*, *Maclean's*, Conrad Black and *The Globe and Mail*'s Margaret Wente, who compared him to Ted Kaczynski, the Unabomber, after calling him "an information

terrorist" in an earlier column. Interestingly, Wente's attack was based on the idea that Assange was masquerading as an advocate for the public's right to know, when his actual aim was more revolutionary. She quoted him directly: "It is not our goal to achieve a more transparent society; it's our goal to achieve a more just society." So her underlying assumption appears to be that transparency is a good in itself, that the public does have a right to know. I have found, in general conversation, that you can usually count on journalists, political activists and lawyers to share that belief, even in Canada.

12   But why is there so little street-level support in Canada for the idea that governments enjoy entirely too much secrecy and too much power? Have we ceased to recognize the crucial role that whistleblowers play in keeping our governments honest?

13   It is comparatively easy to explain such an attitude in the United States. The September 11 attacks were so deeply traumatizing—and so cleverly exploited by the George W. Bush government—that the traditional American reverence for privacy and individual liberty came to seem close to treasonous. That Washington would have to come down hard and heavy seemed obvious, even in some sense comforting. Canada was not attacked, but our government's passion for secrecy has burgeoned, as evidenced by closed trials with unnamed charges for suspected terrorists, the withdrawal of the compulsory census and, perhaps above all, the centralized control of contact with the media in institutions ranging from the federal government to your local hospital.

14   Exhibit A of this ominous Canadian trend comes, astonishingly, from the very office set up to protect government whistleblowers. Christiane Ouimet, Canada's first-ever public sector integrity commissioner, resigned last October after her own staff blew the whistle on her to the auditor general. Charged with handling complaints from civil servants about wrongdoing in their workplaces, Ouimet had considered only seven of the 228 complaints she had received worth investigating and none of them proved conclusive. The auditor general, in a report released in December, also found patterns of intimidation and retaliation in Ouimet's treatment of her own department's employees.

15   Ouimet's defence, by the way, was that she was in fact investigating 15 files, not seven, and that her staff were hostile and jealous. The Conservative government was apparently not wholly dissatisfied with her performance: she received a severance package worth $534,000 in addition to her pension. There are those who might say that she did exactly what she was expected to do—neglect the complaints until they withered away.

16   In such a climate, it is not surprising that it is hard to identify a Canadian whistleblower who would qualify as a hero/martyr on the scale of the American Karen Silkwood, Britain's Dr David Kelly or Israel's Mordechai Vanunu.

17   To refresh your memory: Silkwood was a chemical technician and union activist at an Oklahoma nuclear plant. She died under suspicious circumstances after investigating irregularities—and worse—at the plant. Kelly apparently killed himself—although rumours of murder persist—after being unmasked as a major source for the BBC on the issue of Saddam Hussein's non-existent weapons of mass destruction.

18   Vanunu leaked information about Israel's nuclear program to the British press in 1986. A Mossad Mata Hari then lured him to Italy, from whence, heavily drugged, he was repatriated to Israel. After a trial, he served 18 years there and was released in 2004 on parole conditions so restrictive that he has twice returned to jail for violating them. They include a ban on talking with anyone who is not an Israeli—a limitation even more draconian than the parole conditions for some of Canada's G20 protestors. Amnesty International has labelled Vanunu a prisoner of conscience.

19   But many Israelis regard Vanunu as a traitor rather than a whistleblower. And this is where things get tricky. There are traitors, there are whistleblowers, there are leakers, there are spies. To my mind Vanunu qualifies as a whistleblower because he took his information to the media for general distribution, not to another government for its own advantage as a spy would have done. And there is nothing heroic about a party functionary who leaks damaging revelations about the opposition to the press. Whistleblowers are not seeking personal gain. Their motives are altruistic. Although they may

prefer to hide in the shadows, they are taking genuine risks.

20   And Canada has such people, committed to transparency and prepared to suffer for their good deeds. It is not our way to hound them to death; our country prefers to harass and neglect them into silence.

21   The most recent major example is diplomat Richard Colvin, who in 2009 testified to a parliamentary committee that Afghan authorities had tortured detainees handed over to them by Canadian troops. His lawyer alleged that Canadian authorities had tried to silence him. Colvin is still employed in intelligence at the Canadian embassy in Washington, but he will no doubt pay a price, no matter who is in power in Ottawa. The intelligence community does not look kindly on squealers.

22   Colvin is not alone. Linda Keen, the former head of the Canadian Nuclear Safety Commission, lost her job after refusing to permit the Atomic Energy of Canada Limited to reopen its Chalk River facility until the plant insured higher safety standards, and publicly accusing the government of trying to interfere with the commission, an independent body. She now has her own firm, which advises companies on enterprise risk management. In last month's federal election, she endorsed the Green Party.

23   There are names familiar at least to readers who follow the news: Sean Bruyea, who revealed in 2005 that a proposed federal program for injured soldiers would actually greatly reduce their compensation. Dr Nancy Olivieri, who released research findings in 1998 suggesting that a drug she was testing had dangerous, possibly fatal side effects. Corporal Robert Read, fired for investigating corruption at the Canadian High Commission in Hong Kong—a firing upheld in 2005 by the Federal Court, which rebuked Read for "a lack of loyalty to the government." Brian McAdam, who also exposed corruption at the Canadian Consulate in Hong Kong and the infiltration of Chinese organized criminals and spies into this country. That good deed ended his 30-year career in the foreign service.

24   Allan Cutler has proved more resilient. He is the civil servant who was almost fired in 1996 for documenting and later filing a formal complaint about the financial transactions at the Department of Public Works that came to be known as the sponsorship scandal. Cutler managed to hold on to his job until 2004; an official inquiry into the scandal began the following year. He also ran for the Conservatives in the 2006 election (he was defeated by David McGuinty) and founded a website, Canadians for Accountability (canadians4accountability.org).

25   And then there is Joanna Gualtieri. She exposed a pattern of outrageously excessive purchases by the Department of Foreign Affairs and International Trade for embassies and diplomatic residences abroad, and felt victimized and harassed thereafter, even though the inspector general and auditor general upheld her accusations. When she left her job and tried to sue the government, the Department of Justice argued that she had no right to do so, that her proper avenue for recourse was to submit a grievance—to the same people she was accusing. The Ontario Court of Appeal agreed with her unanimously, so she won her suit twelve years after launching it. The government's response was to pass, in 2003, the *Public Service Modernization Act*, which bars civil servants from suing their employers.

26   But Gualtieri is a fighter. She founded the Federal Accountability Initiative for Reform—FAIR—and served as its director for ten years. FAIR's website remains the best resource on whistleblowing in Canada.

27   These are worthy people, even heroic. But none has come close to achieving the iconic status of Daniel Ellsberg—the man who gave the *New York Times* and other media the Pentagon Papers on the Vietnam War—or Jeffrey Wigand, the former executive who first told the world that tobacco companies were manipulating the ingredients of cigarettes to make them more addictive.

28   Why? In part because none of our media has the same impact as the *New York Times* or *60 Minutes*. More crucially, there are no blockbuster movies about our whistleblowers. Russell Crowe (who played Jeffrey Wigand in *The Insider*) is unlikely ever to be cast as Richard Colvin. Meryl Streep, who starred in *Silkwood*, was not tapped to impersonate Nancy Olivieri.

29   But which is the chicken and which is the egg? We do make movies—even if they do not achieve the

same profile as American star vehicles. But we do not make movies about Canadian officials or executives who tell tales out of school. Our whistleblowers do not become popular heroes. Why not?

30 One normal Canadian answer would be self-abasement: we are cowardly and mediocre and we cut down tall, outspoken poppies every chance we get. Another equally normal response in this country would be to quietly display our superiority: our discretion, our loyalty, our unwillingness to seek attention or betray a confidence.

31 There is, I think, some truth in both visions. But they leave out some important factors.

32 For one thing, information does filter out regularly in Canada through at least apparently unofficial channels. The alert citizen eventually acquires a great deal of information that governments and corporations would like to keep hidden. Damning reports from the auditor general hit the papers early. Discreet tips led opposition members and the press to Shawinigate or, in Ontario, to eHealth's untendered contracts and dubious expense claims.

33 These stories do not appear by magic; someone is quietly handing over confidential documents or pointing out likely places to look and reminding reporters and opposition members of Parliament, in the words of Deep Throat, to follow the money.

34 In recent years, the leakers of information and documents have been joined by an even more valuable resource: the amateur videographers. Their footage has had an incalculable impact on our understanding of police conduct during the G20 protests.

35 And they are not all anonymous. Without one of them, the public might never have learned what actually happened to Robert Dziekanski, the Pole who died after the RCMP tasered him at Vancouver International Airport. I wonder how many Canadians recall the name of the public-spirited soul who not only filmed the incident, but also went to court to force the police (who had confiscated the video) to return it and then released it to the media. It is Paul Pritchard, a man who deserves to be remembered, but probably will not be.

36 As a nation, we do not have much long-term memory for whistleblowers—never mind systems for protecting and rewarding them. To find the last time

our country really celebrated revelations of wrongdoing, you have to go all the way back to Igor Gouzenko. And he was not a Canadian or even a real whistleblower; he was a cipher clerk at the Soviet embassy in Ottawa who defected in 1945, bringing with him 109 documents on Soviet espionage. He was spilling someone else's secrets.

37 I mention him because Canada rewarded his courage—or treachery, if you choose to side with Joseph Stalin. He and his wife were fitted out with new identities and lived into the 1980s in a Toronto suburb. Canada expressed its gratitude in other ways: the government generously bestowed the Governor General's Award for fiction on Gouzenko's *The Fall of a Titan* in 1954.

38 Today's homegrown whistleblowers are not so lucky. Their moment in the spotlight will be fleeting. Federal legislation or no, they are likely to find their jobs intolerable, even if they manage to hold on to them. The best they can hope for is a favourable editorial or column or two—and then, good luck.

39 The issue does not engage our legal system deeply. The *Public Servants Disclosure Protection Act* (the legislation Ouimet was charged with carrying out) extends only to the civil service, not to private corporations. It does not link an investigation that finds wrongdoing to any sanctions for the guilty. It lacks effective mechanisms for shielding employees who come forward. FAIR, the organization devoted to promoting honesty in government and the protection of whistleblowers, italicizes this warning in its critique of the act:

> You need to understand that expressing truths that are inconvenient to those in power is inherently dangerous and can cause serious harm to your career, to you and your family's wellbeing, even to your physical and mental health.

40 And that is the message from the organization that works to encourage whistleblowing in Canada.

41 This is not a new problem. I am a reformed gossip columnist: Almost 20 years ago, I regularly received phone calls from terrified whistleblowers who had just grasped what was going to happen to their careers if I published their stories. But I think there is some evidence of a cultural shift that is making things worse.

42   Here is the emblematic quotation from FAIR's document on Canada's attitude to governance and the release of information:

> From 2004 to 2007 Canada Public Service Agency reported annual statistics on the implementation of the Treasury Board Policy on the *Prevention and Resolution of Harassment in the Workplace*. [Note: This is the kind of treatment faced by whistleblowers like Joanna Gualtieri, Brian McAdam and Robert Read, the petty tactics that make a workplace as unpleasant as possible and ensure that careers are stalled.] These reveal a gradually worsening situation, until in 2008 the agency simply stopped issuing these reports.

43   This is not a unique instance of closing off access to unwelcome news. Nor is the problem restricted to the federal government. At all levels, our governments seem to be running on the motto "Don't ask, don't tell."

44   Could it be that potential whistleblowers are genuinely afraid of physical repercussions? That seems unlikely in Canada. The RCMP has been accused of a great many things in recent years—thanks in part to a small host of leakers and whistleblowers—but I do not believe that anyone, even Randy Quaid, suspects them or CSIS of carrying out political assassinations. A whistleblower certainly faces dismissal here. Lawsuits are always possible. Life can become very unpleasant indeed. But it is unlikely that anyone will be waterboarded or executed for speaking up.

45   The larger question is: why do we, the public, allow this culture of silence and intimidation to thrive? Why has official Ottawa been able to keep the vast majority of its employees quiescent and obedient in the face of an ever-more-muffling fog of obfuscation and ignorance?

46   They could not get away with this if the public seemed to care. But it does not. Perhaps terminal cynicism has set in, a sense that dirty laundry aired is just business as usual. Whatever the reason or reasons, only a minority of voters appear to focus on the issues of transparency and honesty. Just a few months ago, Canada's minister of international cooperation admitted that she had fibbed to the House of Commons—that she was the one who changed a document to justify cutting funding for the charity KAIROS. That used to be called contempt of Parliament, a pretty serious charge. Last month, the voters of Durham returned Bev Oda to office with a whopping majority.

47   So for this issue, it may not matter all that much which party is in power in Ottawa. Once governments have acquired new powers, they are notoriously reluctant to relinquish them, which is why Homeland Security in the United States has not withered away during the presidency of Barack Obama.

48   Moreover, while Americans take umbrage over nasty revelations about their friends, Canadians seem to disapprove of blowing the whistle against anyone. South of the border, Republicans can be very protective of their allies' personal and financial history; some Democrats seemed to feel that Bill Clinton's shenanigans were nobody's business. But Canadians are more likely to feel discomfort with revelations about any party, any company, any person. Our recent political history suggests that a surprising number of us do not mind straightforward abuse—especially in a political ad or debate—but we instinctively cringe at hearing a secret.

49   Perhaps this should not be a surprise. The citizens of many other countries are rioting in the streets for the right to free elections; over the past few months, untold numbers of Canadians whined about having to vote yet again—after only three years of freedom from the burden of casting a ballot. Since marking an X does not really tax anyone's strength, presumably they resented the hard work of having to absorb information and think about how to cast that vote.

50   It is really no wonder, in such an environment, that most Canadians hesitate to come forward and sound the alarm about corruption, lying or waste. More information is likely to provoke not just indifference, but outright hostility. Where so much of the population despises the privilege of staying informed, there will always be the temptation to shoot the messenger.

Literary Review of Canada. June 2011.

Key and challenging words

peripheral, resilient, self-abasement, quiescent, obfuscation

Questions

1. Using reliable research sources, briefly identify Bradley Manning (paragraph 5). Why do you think Kelman does not explain who he is?
2. Paraphrase paragraph 35. Why, according to the author, will Pritchard not be remembered?
3. Comment on Kelman's use of questions throughout her essay. Consider their purpose as well as their effectiveness, ensuring that you refer to specific examples in your answer.
4. (a) Discuss the importance of examples to the essay's development and organization; (b) analyze Kelman's use of two specific examples.

5. Analyze Kelman's style in paragraphs 15–18, including in your answer at least three of the following: level of language, diction, tone, paragraphing, sentence structure, and use of dashes (you can also consider other significant features).
6. Analyze the effectiveness of Kelman's argument. Ensure that you include specific textual references in your analysis.

Post-reading

1. Using your critical thinking skills, respond to one of the following statements. You could focus on how Kelman uses the statement and how it supports her thesis (if it does) or express your own views on the statement. Ensure that you support your points:
   a. "Somewhere in the Canadian psyche there seems rooted the belief that whistleblowing is not nice" (paragraph 4)

   b. "Where so much of the population despises the privilege of staying informed, there will always be the temptation to shoot the messenger" (paragraph 50).

   This could also be used as collaborative or group activity.

Related website of interest

Federal Accountability Initiative for Reform:
fairwhistleblower.ca/

Discourse and dialogue between Americans and Canadians— Who is talking to whom?

Douglas C. Nord
(5,906 words)

Pre-reading

1. Are you familiar with the "traditional story" of Canada–US relationships in which the attention and concern are all on one side—Canada's? If you subscribe to this belief, where did it come from? Friends, classmates, family? Media reports? Reflect on your beliefs and observations on the nature of Americans' perception of Canada and Canadians in one or two paragraphs.
2. a) Summarize the two quotations below the essay's title; b) Why do you think the author begins his essay with these quotations?

For all of our pressing our noses up against the glass of American prosperity and achievement, we cherish our separateness—our unassuming civility, our gift of irony and understatement in a world of exaggerated claims and excess, the myriad "intangibles" we are certain that set us apart. . . . (Michael Adams in *Fire and Ice*, 2002)

The difference between America and Canada is that Americans don't care what the difference between America and Canada is. (American quotes by Mark Steyn in Maclean's, 2005)

1   US–Canadian relations are not a significant focus of attention in most of the areas of the world today. Outside of Canada, they tend not to be a major source of conversation. This is particularly true in the United States. Few Americans spend much time considering their interactions with Canadians. Very little in the way of official pronouncements on the state of relations between the United States and Canada are generated by government, business, or other societal leaders. While public opinion among Americans tends to reflect some degree of positive affect toward their "neighbor to the north," it is largely devoid of a particular center or focus of interest. Canada continues as a "good friend" and as a "cooperative neighbor," but the rationale for this positive assessment is rarely explored at any level of thoroughness.[1]

2   In Canada, the situation is far different. The United States occupies a major and continuing focus of attention for most Canadians. Events taking place in the United States are regularly covered by the Canadian press and media. American leaders and personalities are well known by Canadians. The topic of relations between the two countries is a regular part of Canadian conversations both at the elite and mass levels. While there exists a significant store of positive affect towards Americans on the part of many Canadians, there also can be found a major reservoir of skepticism and critical attitudes directed toward recent American political leaders and policies. The Canadian vision of the United States tends to be far more developed and differentiated than the American vision of Canada.[2]

3   This asymmetry in attention and attitude has been presented as a long-standing feature of the bilateral relationship. It has been accounted for by various theories which point to the relative difference in power and position of the two countries within the global community. The "elephant and the mouse" metaphor has been regularly presented to capture the observed difference in impact and attention that has tended to be part of the US–Canadian relationship. While Americans seem to be regularly oblivious to the ways in which their society has a continuing impact on their "northern neighbors," Canadians are well aware of nearly every "twitch and grunt" that emanates from south of the line.[3] This is the traditional story and Canadians are fond of telling it—perhaps too much so.

4   The question that this essay seeks to explore is whether this traditional depiction of the bilateral relationship is a completely accurate one today. Since much of the existing discourse on US–Canadian relations has originated from Canadian sources, might it not be useful to explore what Americans may be thinking about the present bilateral relationship and how they might conceive of it? What is the current US vision of Canada and what are its present sources? What may be some of the concerns, issues, and problems that they see as central to the relationship? In what fashion may US-based academics and policymakers find Canada to be a useful comparative case in their research, scholarship, and teaching? All of these questions seem worthy of some further consideration if we are to accurately gauge the full features of the US–Canadian relationship.

The American Vision of Canada

5   It is true that the American vision of Canada is not as extensive and discriminating as Canadians would like it to be. As noted above, it is not an image that occupies the mind of most residents of the United States on any regular basis. Canadians have traditionally taken a perverse delight in discussing this fact among themselves. Whether it be Walter Stewart relating "stupid American jokes" some 40 years ago or Rick Mercer "Talking with Americans" more recently, there exists a seemingly insatiable need among Canadians to point out how Americans know very little about them or their society.[4] The assumption tends to be that there is no vision of Canada held by Americans beyond a series of stereotypes and stale clichés. Yet is this really the case?

6   While the American vision of Canada can be limited at times, it is not entirely devoid of any significant content. There are some basic images of Canada and Canadians that are largely shared by Americans that if carefully considered should not make Canadians either despair or blush. The average American tends to see Canada and Canadians along four dimensions. The first of these relates to being a "neighbor" of the United States. This basic geographic and social reality is well-known by most Americans—especially those who reside along the northern border. Most Americans are usually familiar with the countless ways in which the two societies interact with one another economically,

politically and socially.[5] They tend to see Canadians as "the people who live next door" and who share much in common with them. Often there is the expectation that because of this closeness, Canadians will think and act like Americans. This can be off-putting at times to Canadian sensibilities, but it should not be confused as a rejection of Canadian distinctiveness. Most Americans know that Canadians often prefer to go along their own path and do not think this is unacceptable. Rather, they are intrigued by the idea of an alternative approach existing within a most similar society.

7   The second dimension along which most Americans see Canada relates very much to this latter point. Canada for many Americans represents an alternative model by which they can judge many aspects of their own society. Because the "neighbors to the north" are seen to be so similar in so many ways to Americans, the observed differences in everyday conduct or in more formal public policy choices are seen as particular points of interest—sometimes engendering praise, sometimes criticism. Most Americans are quite aware that Canadians enjoy a high standard of living and experience levels of social welfare similar to their own country. Many perceive there to be higher levels of environmental awareness and greater social equality north of the line. Especially for those who have traveled to Canada there is a sense that the country is a more peaceful and less conflict-oriented society than their own.[6] Often Canada is seen by Americans as a "societal laboratory" where significant public policy options are incubated and evaluated before they are proposed for introduction into the United States. Over the past two decades there has been regular reporting of Canadian actions regarding aboriginal rights, climate change, and bilingualism by the American press and media. Canadian examples regarding the provision of health care, the regulation of guns, and the recognition of same-sex marriage have been widely discussed south of the line. On occasion, these policy choices have been the focus both of praise and criticism from different political sectors of American society.[7] Regardless, however, there is a significant awareness in the United States that important ideas and policy options are being circulated north of the line and they are worthy of notice.

8   A third dimension of the American image of Canada relates to the country's status of being a strong economic partner to the United States. An increasing number of Americans have become very much aware of the size and importance of the trade and investment taking place between the two countries every day. They have become ever more attuned to the fact that Canada is the number one international supplier of energy resources to the United States. American business and political leaders are well aware of the growing economic interconnectedness of the two national economies spurred on by the advent of the Canada–US Free Trade Agreement (FTA) and the North American Free Trade Agreement (NAFTA). They are knowledgeable of the extent to which North American prosperity is supported and enhanced by common marketing, transportation, and distribution networks. They are cognizant of the opportunity to facilitate the greater movement of skilled labor across the bilateral border, as well as the need to commit to joint efforts at research and development and environmental protection.[8] Interestingly, the results of the recent economic recession have contributed to more Americans looking northward toward Canada for examples as to how successful macroeconomic policy may be fashioned, whether this be in the areas of budget allocation, deficit reduction, or banking regulation.

9   A fourth dimension along which Canada is viewed by many Americans relates to its international profile. While many Americans see their own country as being one the last of the great powers, they often look at Canada as operating within the international community in a far different fashion. They see Canada as choosing to involve itself not only for the sake of defending or extending its influence in the world, but in order to address major global concerns—be these environmental, human rights, or security based. Canada's reputation as an international peacekeeper and as an active global donor and participant within international organizations is well known in the United States.[9] Sometimes there is a belief among Americans that Canada is more attuned to the needs and priorities of the global community than their own country. There is a sense that Canada has a greater ability to build and maintain friendships in areas of the world that the United States is less capable of operating in because of the former's established linkages with the

Commonwealth and the Francophone communities. The recent hosting of the Winter Olympics in Vancouver conveyed to many Americans the impression that Canada and Canadians seemed far more welcoming to the world than the United States. From a different vantage point, Canada tends also to be regarded by many Americans as a dependable ally of the United States in conflict-oriented arenas of the world. This can be seen in American appreciation for Canada's military and economic contributions to the Afghanistan War effort and to that country's commitment to the global initiative against terrorism. Most Americans recall the fact that Canada was there when needed at the time of the attacks of September 11, 2001, and the country serves as a regular defense partner in NATO, NORAD, and in other mutual security pacts.[10]

10   Taken together, these four dimensions of the American image of Canada suggest that the US understanding of its northern neighbors and its relationships to them may not be as limited and simplistic as some Canadians might like to believe. Americans do have awareness and a degree of understanding of Canada and Canadians that exceeds much of the popular myth that circulates north of the border. It is an image that has its origins on both sides of the common frontier. Part of it is fashioned by distinctive American needs and objectives. Other parts of it are reflections of images that Canadians themselves project to the United States and seek to promote. In the following section an effort will be made to address both sources.

The Sources of the American Image of Canada

11   As noted above, the vision of Canada that many Americans hold has its origins on both sides of the international border. To a significant degree it is composed of a mixture of images that Canadians, themselves, have helped to craft—sometimes without forethought, sometimes with great calculation. A good portion of this vision is derived from people-to-people connections that come through multiple forms of contact—commercial, social, and cultural. A large percentage of what Americans think Canada is all about stems from their interaction with colleagues, customers, friends, and family who live on the other side of the line. This is particularly true for Americans

residing relatively close to the border.[11] While this vision of Canada and Canadians can be highly idiosyncratic, there are certain common features that regularly appear in it. These include images of friendliness, honesty, innovation, cleanliness, competitiveness, and being environmentally attuned. As can be seen, these perceptions are largely positive in nature and contribute to each of the four conceptual dimensions along which Americans tend to evaluate Canada and Canadians.

12 Beyond such informal influencing of American perceptions, however, the northern neighbors have devoted considerable time, attention, and resources to attempting to shape American perceptions of Canada and Canadians. Sometimes this is done through the specific actions of government and sometimes through the private sector. For more than a century now, Canadian diplomacy has been directed in no small degree toward fashioning both elite and mass American opinion of Canada and its people. This has been undertaken through a variety of means including the cultivation of important American political, business, media, and cultural leaders both at national, regional, and local levels by representatives of the Canadian embassy in Washington, DC, and through the country's 16 consular offices scattered across the United States.[12] Within this undertaking, there has been the normal effort to influence political action on a variety of bilateral concerns and agendas between Canada and the United States. Canadian government representatives have also sought to expand trade, investment, and commercial interaction between the two countries, as well as to promote innovative Canadian products and technology in American markets. It also has included a vigorous effort toward promoting and partially funding the study of Canada at American universities and think tanks. At a broader level of public diplomacy, Canadian government representatives have helped to draw American attention to the contributions of various Canadian artists and cultural figures and to the vibrancy of contemporary Canadian culture. Similar efforts across most of these same fields of endeavor have also been undertaken by Canadian provincial governments—with Quebec and Alberta leading the way.[13]

13 Canadian private business and financial leaders have also seen substantial merit in attempting to influence the American mindset. Historically, this has been done both as an effort to sell Canada as a dependable source of needed goods and services, and as a sound business partner and good place for American investment. The natural abundance of the land and the skilled workforce of the country have been regularly promoted among the American business community by Canadian commercial, financial, and investment firms. With the steady expansion and growing interconnectedness of American and Canadian business enterprises over the past half century, there have been similar efforts by Canadian business leaders to encourage a North American orientation to commercial undertakings that have manifested themselves in the FTA and the NAFTA. Similar efforts have been undertaken by the Canadian business community to expand markets for new Canadian products, technology, and services.[14]

14 One other source from the Canadian side of the border that has regularly influenced the American image of Canada is its tourism message. It should not be forgotten that the tourism industry across Canada usually occupies either the first or second largest component of the economies of most provinces—with the American market being a major focus of attention. Over many years—and into our own era—the tourism promotions, which the Canadian governmental and private sectors have directed toward the United States, have had a major impact on what Americans believe Canada to be all about. They contribute significant content to the four thematic dimensions that form the American vision of Canada. Sometimes the imagery that is conveyed is based on unfortunate clichés—such as the proverbial "moose, mountains, and Mounties"—that occupied the heart of Canadian tourism promotions in the decades of the 1960s through the 1980s.[15] In more recent periods, Canadian tourism messages have focused on the themes of world-class cities and cultures, a society in harmony with nature and its diverse peoples, and a country close to the United States. Regardless of their specific content, it is often forgotten that these are images created by Canadians themselves and are carefully directed toward American audiences for their consideration and consumption. Such tourism messages are among the most readily absorbed information about the Canadian country and peoples that is received by

the American mass public. It raises an interesting question: If a regular concern of Canadians is that Americans have such inaccurate information about them, should they not be more interested in the specific content of the tourism messages they are sending to Americans?

15   Some of the sources of the American vision of Canada can clearly be found on the US side of the border. It includes the personal experiences of Americans who have traveled, worked or studied in Canada. In general, these have been good experiences and contribute to the overall positive affect that can be found at the heart of the American image of Canada. It is augmented by the presence of a large number of Canadians in residence in the United States who provide many of their American neighbors with a significant amount of current information and insights into their northern homeland. Often this Canadian community blends rather easily into the American setting and reinforces themes of common values, needs, and goals. On the other hand, Canadian affinity groups like CanDiego in southern California help to maintain awareness among the broader American population that the two societies are not entirely the same. So too does the occasional rivalry that bursts forth at times, such as during the hockey finals of the recent Winter Olympics.[16]

16   To a large extent, however, the image of Canada that is derived from American sources tends to be forged in the same manner by which most Americans have traditionally assessed most other countries of the world. Put very bluntly, it relates to the extent to which the foreign state or society is seen to be in harmony with primary American values, objectives, and concerns. Americans tend to place great store in the extent to which the societal values of another country are seen to be in conformity with those of their own. In the case of Canada, Americans have generally seen a similarity here—though not always.[17] Both in earlier centuries and at points in more recent times, Americans have seen Canadians at odds with some of their most cherished beliefs and public policies. However, the memories of these events—be they anti-republicanism in the nineteenth century or opposition to the Vietnam War in the twentieth—are usually quickly forgotten by the vast majority of Americans. They are overwhelmed by a sense of common cause and purpose.

17   This leads to the second domestic source of the American image of Canada. It is based on the notion that the two countries, in addition to being North American neighbors, are allies in the broader field of international politics and security. Most Americans view Canada as a dependable political and military partner. They can recall the two countries fighting together in most of the major international conflicts of the last century. They are aware that the two countries have been partners within NATO and NORAD during years of the Cold War era and its aftermath. They know that Ottawa and Washington are jointly committed to opposing international terrorism in the post-9/11 world.[18] As such, they see Canada among the ranks of the most dependable of the United States' foreign allies and friends. On occasion they wonder when Canada appears to break ranks, as in the case of the Vietnam War and Iraq, but again the clear majority of Americans consider this to be a temporary aberration rather than a betrayal. Canada, from an American vantage point, is to be seen as a supportive, loyal, and trustworthy partner.

18   The third domestic source of American perceptions of Canada can be seen to arise from the perceived economic complementariness of the two countries. For many years, Americans have seen Canada as a reliable source of natural resources, a conveniently close market for their products and services, and a good place for their investments. Such perceptions gave rise to a view of Canada that sometimes bordered on seeing the country as simply an economic extension of corporate America—much to the annoyance of many Canadians. More recently, however, it has evolved into a more complex and differentiating perception. Large numbers of Americans now see Canada as part of a tripartite North American business partnership. Ever since the coming of the NAFTA, Canada has tended to be increasingly placed in the same conceptual box as the other neighbor, Mexico. Such a change in perception carries with it a variety of potential challenges and opportunities to the traditional Canadian–American economic relationship.[19] Canadians tend to emphasize the former while an increasing number of Americans perceive the latter.

19   Taken together these several sources of the American image of Canada provide a much more complex and differentiated content than is popularly

presented on either side of the border. It suggests that there are a series of directing themes within the four dimensions of the American vision of Canada that require closer attention and examination. It also begs the question of how this American perspective on the relationship can be better presented and articulated.

Current American Discourse on US–Canadian Relations

20   At the present moment, while there seems to be a multifaceted American vision of their relations with Canadians, it is not well voiced. Whether this is at an official governmental level or that of private sector discourse, the United States has some difficulty in articulating its thoughts. Partly this is due to the fact that Americans have rarely been called on to express themselves on such matters. Ironically, Canadians have seemingly been quite content to provide both sides of the conversation. A quick survey of recent writings on the theme of contemporary relations between the two societies reveals that Canadians are the overwhelming authors of most of this analysis—often at a ratio of 10 to 1 in publication.[20] This dominance of the discourse suggests that Canadians are not only much more preoccupied with the relationship than are Americans, but also that they are quite content to tell Americans what Americans should think about their own relations with Canada. Clearly there is a need to develop both the American voice and to expand its presence within the conversation.

21   As opposed to the representatives of the Canadian federal and provincial governments, American government officials consistently offer very little in the way of formal pronouncements on their dealings with Canada. It is usually very difficult to get the State Department in Washington, DC, or the US Embassy in Ottawa or the various American consulates across Canada to formally articulate what American interests and objectives are in their dealings with the northern neighbor.[21] This is sometimes excused by suggesting that the extent of the interaction between the two governments is so broad that it would be impossible to easily summarize American priorities and goals. Sometimes, it is also suggested that any effort in this direction might be judged by Canadians as Americans attempting to unduly control

or dominate the bilateral agenda. However, it seems clear that the paucity of American governmental statements on US interests in Canada may also be the direct result of a lack of concentrated and sustained effort to define them. Especially in recent years, many of the US government representatives who have been given the responsibility to articulate American perspectives on the bilateral relationship have lacked any formal education or background in this area. As a result, there has been an over-reliance on vague but comforting statements about continued partnership within the hemisphere—often with Canada being viewed through the primary lens of NAFTA.

22   As opposed to the extensive undertakings of the Canadian government to promote the study of Canada within the academic, cultural, and policy making circles of the United States, there have only been minimal efforts by the US government to promote American Studies north of the line. Again, this is partly excused by the pronouncement that Canadians "know all they need to know" about their southern neighbors due to regular flow of information and cultural images northward across the border. Similarly, there has also existed a belief that too much official promotion of the United States within Canada risks being interpreted by some Canadian nationalists as an attempt to dominate their community. While there are a growing number of American Studies programs and centers in Canada, interestingly, most are funded from Canadian sources.[22]

23   State and regional governments within the United States have sometimes done a better job in articulating American goals and objectives than has the Federal government. This is particularly the case for those which find themselves to be relatively close neighbors of Canadian provincial governments. In recent decades, we have witnessed the expansion of a number of originally US-based regional organizations in the Great Lakes, New England and the Pacific Northwest to incorporate various Canadian provincial members. In so doing, American state and local officials have had the opportunity to present their views and priorities directly to their Canadian counterparts not only on matters related to local border concerns but also broader issues of bilateral trade, resource development, transportation, and environmental protection. A series of bilateral state-to-province linkages have been established by a number of American governors in collaboration with various Canadian premiers in which major concerns such as climate change, the provision of health services, and technological innovation have been articulated. Interestingly, such discussions have tended to receive the attention and interest of the media and general public on both sides of the border.[23]

24   Within the private sector, there are some initiatives to articulate the American perspective on the relationship. Many of the large American corporations that have operated within Canada over the years have undertaken sustained efforts to explain to their Canadian customers, shareholders, and the general public the reasons for their presence in the country and the particular business objectives that they seek to achieve. In recent decades, this activity has grown as key areas of their participation in the Canadian economy—such as in auto manufacturing, oil and gas exploitation, and mineral and forest resource development—have become the focus of extensive coverage by the media in both Canada and the United States. More non-traditional American businesses operating within the Canadian marketplace, such as those in media, financial services, and the entertainment industries, have undertaken new efforts to introduce themselves and their brand to Canadian consumers. Both types of American business entities have sought to explain their roles within FTA and NAFTA frameworks to Canadian audiences.[24]

25   This quick overview of the character of the current American voice with respect to US–Canadian relations suggests that some additional progress needs to be made on the American side if there is to be a true and sustained dialogue between the two communities. Americans need to focus their attention on how they might better frame and articulate their goals and priorities in their dealings with their northern neighbor and how these can be more effectively communicated to Canadians. An effort is made in the following section to suggest some steps that might be undertaken to achieve these objectives.

Enhancing the American Voice in US–Canadian Relations

26   If the American contribution to the discourse on bilateral relations is to be improved, it seems that at least three steps must be undertaken now and continued over the foreseeable future. Each of these three steps seeks to address a specific limitation in the present manner in which the American discussion of relations with Canada takes place. Taken together, it is suggested that a more focused and clearly articulated vision of what Americans seek to achieve in their interaction with their northern neighbors can be presented. While the vast majority of the proposed initiatives demand specific effort on the part of Americans, some also require the helpful collaboration of Canadians.

27   Perhaps the first step that must be taken to improve the American contribution to this bilateral discourse is for US government and various private sectors actors to become more aware and informed regarding the wide array of issues and concerns that should be the focus of this conversation. Unfortunately, Americans have tended to lag behind their northern neighbors in educating themselves on these matters. They have been far too ready to direct their attention and interest either to "domestic" concerns or to regions of the globe that are seen as presenting more difficult challenges. With regard to Canada, there has been far too much reliance upon an attitude of benign neglect which suggests that problems and differences between the two countries can be best solved by either ignoring them, pretending that they don't exist, or by papering over them with the rhetoric of Canada being our "best friend and ally."[25]

28   During a period of significant economic, political, and security challenges to this country, Americans need to become more aware of the extent to which Canada is vital to United States in addressing each of these types of concerns. Investments must be made, of both a short-term and continuing nature, in bringing Canada to a more central position in the American domestic and foreign policy conversation. Some of this is already taking place, as was related above. However, much more could be profitably undertaken at this time regarding trade, health, energy, security, and environmental matters. There is an identifiable need for the US government and its diplomatic representatives to become more conversant regarding such bilateral matters, along with ways in which carefully cultivated relations with Canada can advance national goals and priorities. Within both the business and educational communities, additional resources need to be directed towards informing students, employees, and investors

regarding the neighbors to the north and the significant manner in which their lives and fortunes are linked to those on the other side of the border. Again, some headway has been made in this regard over the past few decades, but such efforts at education and information sharing need to be addressed more from an American perspective and funded more extensively by American sources.

29   The second step that needs to be undertaken at this time to enhance the American voice in discussing the bilateral relationship is for Americans to become much more specific regarding their needs and expectations of Canadians. As was noted above, for far too long Americans have tended to be less than precise in identifying their specific goals and objectives regarding their dealings with Canadians. Over the coming years, it would seem to be a marked improvement if Americans from government, business, and other communities could be much more specific regarding the economic, political, social, and environmental issues that they see as central to their interaction with Canadians.[26] This ability to speak in a more direct and focused fashion would enhance their specific contributions to the discourse and assure Canadians that the necessary study and care required for solving problems has been made. This might also help to retire the lingering image of the elephant and the mouse.

30   Becoming more focused and specific in their discussion of issues and problems does not mean that Americans should expect that Canadians will always agree with or accept the vantage point or proposal offered from south of the line. These more direct and frank discussions should allow for the specific opportunity to "agree to disagree" over particular issues or policy measures without lingering concern over future discord or retaliation. As several scholars from both sides of the border have argued, it is time for US–Canadian relations to become a more equal and mature partnership in which there is an expectation that different needs and priorities may exist among the two countries and different policy options can be freely chosen and respected.[27]

31   The third step required to enhance the American voice in this bilateral discourse is directed, in part, from this last observation. Interestingly, it is a step that requires the careful consideration of Canadians as much as Americans. As noted earlier, a good deal of the present discussion of US–Canadian relations is undertaken and dominated by Canadians. If we are to encourage more participation by American policymakers, academics, and the general public in this conversation we need to provide them with more opportunities for them to enter it. This means not only offering them space to speak but also allowing them to contribute to the framing of the discourse. Too often, at present, the agenda and issues "of concern" are almost exclusively identified by Canadians. If we are to have healthy US participation in future bilateral discussions, Americans need to be given a significant opportunity to address and discuss those topics that appear to be of most interest to them.[28]

32   It should not be assumed that Canadians always have an accurate read or understanding of American interests and priorities. Over the past decade, it has been apparent that on more than one occasion they have badly misread American interest and desire to discuss specific topics. Issues that may generate avid attention and wide discussion north of the border may have far less resonance south of the line. This can be seen in the case of both softwood lumber and the Northwest Passage. In the future there must be an equal partnership between Americans and Canadians in determining what they choose to address in their dialogue. In this manner it is far more likely that sustained interest from both sides can be achieved.

Some Final Thoughts

33   It is useful on occasion to look at a much studied problem from a somewhat different perspective. This is what this article has attempted to do. It has considered the bilateral relationship between the United States and Canada from the vantage point of the former rather than the latter. As noted above, this is not frequently done and it seems to rearrange some of the standard assumptions regarding how this relationship operates now and in the future. The article has suggested that there is an American voice to be heard in discussing the interaction between the two communities. It may not be as well developed as the Canadian voice, but it can be discerned if listened to with some care.

34   This article has sought to stress the importance of considering the sources, goals, and priorities of the

American vision of the relationship not because they are any more significant than those of the Canadian perspective, but because they have tended to get overlooked in most of the traditional presentations of Canadian–American relations. If we are to better understand the true dynamics of this important international relationship, we need to consider the American side of the equation as well as the Canadian component. Also, if we truly want to create a dialogue between Americans and Canadians we need to ensure that the American contribution is a regular element of the discourse.

35   Finally, if we are to engage the interest and attention of Americans with regard to Canada, we must give greater emphasis to exploring why Canada should be of interest to this country—in both broad and narrow terms. American policymakers and academics need to be provided more of an opportunity to discover for themselves those issues and topics of the relationship that they find the most interesting and compelling. We need to move away from Canadians regularly telling Americans what they should be thinking about Canada—and what the "important" problems are. As in any bilateral relationship, there has to be room for individual discovery and reflection as well as joint problem-solving.

American Review of Canadian Studies. 2011. 41 (4).

Notes

1. Norman Hillmer and J.L. Granatstein, *For Better or For Worse: Canada and the United States in the Twenty-First Century*. Toronto: Thomson/Nelson, 2007, pp. 14–15.

2. See for instance: John Holmes, *Life with Uncle: The Canadian–American Relationship*. Toronto: University of Toronto Press, 1981; Richard Gwyn, *The 49th Paradox: Canada In North America*. Toronto: Collins Publishers, 1986.

3. Norman Hillmer, "Reflections on the Unequal Border" *International Journal* (Spring 2005) 60: 331–340.

4. Walter Stewart, *As They See Us*. Toronto: McClelland and Stewart, 1977; "Canadian Jon Stewart Explains Thanksgiving," National Public Radio, Weekend Edition. October 9, 2010.

5. Brian Buckley, "The News and the Neighbors: The Media and Canadian–American Relations" in David Carment, et al., eds. *Coping with the American Colossus*. Don Mills: Oxford University Press, 2003, pp. 75–99.

6. Michael Adams, *Fire and Ice: The United States, Canada and the Myth of Converging Values*. Toronto: Penguin Canada, 2003, pp. 48–49.

7. Leslie A. Pal, "Between the Sights: Gun Control in Canada and the United States" in David M. Thomas, ed., *Canada and the United States: Differences that Count*, 2nd Edition, 2000, pp. 68–93.

8. Paul Cellucci, *Unquiet Diplomacy*. Toronto: Key Porter Books Ltd., 2007, pp. 122–24.

9. Cynthia Kite and Douglas C. Nord, "Canadian Foreign Policy" in Patrick James and Mark Kasoff, eds., *Canadian Studies in the New Millennium*. Toronto: University of Toronto Press, 2008.

10. Bernard J. Brister, "The Same Yet Different: The Evolution of the Post-9/11 Canada–US Security Relationship" in Monica Gattinger and Geoffrey Hale, eds., *Borders and Bridges: Canada's Policy Relations in North America*. Don Mills: Oxford University Press, pp. 83–85.

11. Donald K. Alper and James Loucky, *Canada–US Border Securitization: Implications for Binational Cooperation*. Orono, ME: Canadian–American Public Policy #72, 2007.

12. Evan Potter, *Branding Canada: Projecting Canada's Soft Power through Public Diplomacy*. Montreal and Kingston: McGill-Queen's University Press, 2009, pp. 97–127.

13. Richard Vengroff and Jason Rich, "Foreign Policy by Other Means: Paradiplomacy and the Canadian Provinces" in Patrick James, et al., eds. *Handbook of Canadian Foreign Policy*. Latham, MD: Lexington Books, 2006, pp. 105–130.

14. Christopher Waddell, "Erasing the Line: Rebuilding Economic and Trade Relations After 11 September" in Carment, op.cit, pp. 57–58.

15. Douglas C. Nord, "American Images of Canada—Courtesy of the Canadian Tourism Industry" *North Dakota Quarterly* 52 (Summer 1984) 257–288.

16. Barbara Yaffe, "Americans Must Understand that Border Barriers Will Hurt Them Too," *Vancouver Sun*, February 16, 2010.

17. Seymour Martin Lipset, *Continental Divide: The Values and Institutions of the United States and Canada*. New York: Routledge, 1990.

18. Louis W. Pauly, "Canada in a New North America" in Peter Andreas and Thomas J. Biersteker, eds., *The Rebordering of North America*. New York: Routledge, 2003, pp. 90–109.

19. Peter Kresl, "NAFTA and Its Discontents" *International Journal* 60 (Spring 2005) 417–428.

20. See for instance, David Thomas and Barbara Boyle Torrey, eds., *Canada and the United States: Differences That Count*, 3rd Edition, Peterborough: Broadway Press, 2008.

21. Norman Hillmer, *Partners Nevertheless: Canadian–American Relations in the Twentieth Century*. Toronto: Copp-Clark Pittman, Ltd. 1989 pp. 3–4.

22. Such as those at the University of Western Ontario and the University of Toronto.

23. Earl Fry, "Federalism and the Evolving Cross Border Role of Provincial, State and Municipal Governments" *International Journal* 60 (Spring 2005) 471–482.

24. Christopher Kukucha, "Sub-Federal Trade and the Politics of North America Integration: Evaluating the Cross-Border Exports of American States" in Gattinger and Hale, op.cit. pp. 270–288.

25. Charles Doran, "Canada–US Relations: Personality, Pattern and Domestic Politics" in Patrick James, et al., pp. 389–408.

26. Andrew Cohen, "Canadian–American Relations: Does Canada Matter in Washington? Does It Matter If Canada Doesn't Matter?" in Norman Hillmer and Maureen Appel Molot, eds. *A Fading Power*. Toronto: Oxford University Press, 2002, pp. 34–48.

27. Hillmer and Granatstein, op.cit, pp. 319–322.

28. Douglas C. Nord, "Canadian Foreign Policy Viewed from South of the Line—An American Perspective" *Canadian Foreign Policy* 14 (Winter 2007) 69–75.

Key and challenging words

asymmetry, incubate, aberration, insatiable, cognizant, idiosyncratic, conversant

Questions

1. Explain why the use of questions in paragraph 4 might be an appropriate way to expand on the author's thesis.

2. (a) Briefly summarize the "four dimensions" that help explain how Americans see Canadians; (b) show, using examples, the importance of these dimensions to the essay as a whole (to do this, you will need to refer to more than the section "The American Vision of Canada").

3. Referring to one section in the essay, identify *two* rhetorical patterns (chapter 6, pages 79–80) and explain how *each* pattern helps develop this section of the essay.

4. Taking one paragraph of substantial length, analyze it for its organization and readability. For example, you could consider topic sentence, rhetorical pattern, paragraph wrap, prompts, repetition, transitions, and the like.

5. How important is it that the author assumes an objective stance and a neutral tone in his essay? Does he succeed in doing so? Referring to at least two specific passages, analyze his stance and tone with these two questions in mind.

6. Of the recommendations that Nord makes near the end of his essay, which do you think is the most useful and/or realistic? Why?

Post-reading

1. Who does Nord blame for the failure of Americans to pay attention to Canada? Refer to specific passages in your answer.

2. *Collaborative activity:* As the founding members of a civic provincial or national organization (you can give it an appropriate name), your mission is to encourage greater American presence in US–Canada relations. Develop a set of policies and/or strategies that define your approach: (a) identify the purpose and scope of your organization; (b) identify and describe your objectives and your audience (for example, citizens, educational, government, or business leaders); and (c) how you would accomplish them. Besides providing broad-based goals, be specific in regards to strategies and initiatives. Refer to Nord's essay at least twice. (This could be a written or oral project.)

Related websites of interest

Rick Mercer Talking to Americans:
www.youtube.com/watch?v=seYUbVa7L7w

Matthew Santoro. 10 Differences between Canadians and Americans:
www.youtube.com/watch?v=3liA1GLKbW4

Additional library reading

Alm, Leslie R., and Ross E. Burkhart. Canada–US Border Communities: What the People Have to Say. *American Review of Canadian Studies*. 43.1 (2013): 86–106. Print.

Sands, Christopher. "America and the Canadian Presence: As the United States Faces Global Challenges, How Does Canada Fit In?" *American Review of Canadian Studies* 42.4 (2012): 482–88. Print.

Listen to the North

John Ralston Saul
(4,115 words)

Pre-reading

1. After scanning the article, list five ways that it differs from the academic/scholarly essay as it is discussed in Chapter 2.
2. Come up with a one-sentence definition of "colonialism" or "colonial," using freewriting or another pre-writing technique, if you wish, to generate ideas. When you read the essay, note the uses of the term, beginning with paragraph 1. Are Saul's uses consistent with your definition?

1   Sometimes we understand events in our lives immediately. Sometimes it takes decades. I have gradually realized over the last year that my view of Canada, indeed my view of how my own life could or should be lived, was radically transformed late in the winter of 1976 on my first trip to the Arctic. I was 29, fresh from seven years in France, first writing my PhD, then running a small investment firm in Paris. Those are experiences that produce a southern, urban, European-oriented self-confidence, which could also be described as the attitude of a classic colonial Canadian.

2   I travelled north with Maurice Strong, the founding chair and CEO of Petro-Canada. It had begun operations on the first of January that year. Maurice was its first employee. As his assistant, I was the second and so doubled the size of the national oil company. It was a Crown corporation and had inherited the shares the government held in some of the private companies exploring for oil and gas in the High Arctic islands. The government had financed some of these risky ventures or rescued them. And so we were going north to look over our property; that is, the people's property.

3   On our way to the High Arctic islands, we flew into Inuvik—then an oil and gas boom town—on the delta of the Mackenzie River where it flowed into the

Canada in the World **217**

Arctic Ocean. The first meeting Maurice had organized was with the local hunters and trappers associations. I believe they represented the Inuit, the Dene, and the Gwich'in. I went into the room filled with goodwill, thanks to my urban, southern, western views—in other words, I was out to lunch. An hour and a half later I walked out in a state of deep confusion. It seemed that there was another way of looking at society, another way of looking at the land, at human relationships, and the relationship between society and the land.

4   This other view was not necessarily to the left or the right, for or against oil exploration or other forms of development. This was a different philosophy, a Canadian philosophy, not derivative of the South or the West. It existed outside of those rational structures of thought that aim to separate humans from everything else in order to raise us to a privileged position in which our interests trump those of the place in which we exist. Whatever the advantages of this approach, we are now faced with unintended outcomes such as climate change. This other philosophy, when I first heard it applied in Inuvik, is just as interested in human well-being, but sees it in a context integrated with the place. And so these hunters were asking tough questions about the broader, longer-term impacts of each narrow southern-style proposal for what we thought of as progress.

5   In those days, you could get through school and university, get a PhD, and live an intellectually active life in Canada without anyone mentioning this more integrated, in many ways more modern, way of thinking. Today this would not be so easily possible. And yet what people in the South do know today will still have been delivered to them in southern, western forms. You could say that northern ideas are still so deformed by southern intellectual and political systems that the situation is almost worse. There is now an assertion of understanding and sympathy so constructed on the western model that we are protected against deep confusion; in other words, we are protected from the possibility of listening and understanding.

6   Ever since 1976, I have gone north as often as I can. This year those of us who organize the LaFontaine-Baldwin Lecture with the Institute for Canadian Citizenship held it in Iqaluit. The Inuit leader Siila Watt-Cloutier spoke about the North and about Canada as a whole as seen from a northerner's point of view (a transcript is available on the ICC's

website at www.icc-icc.ca). And that really is the point. The key to Canada as a northern or Arctic or circumpolar nation is the people of the North.

*

7   People like myself ought therefore to be happy with the place the North and the Arctic in particular are now playing in our news and sometimes in our daily conversations. I read. I listen. Yet what I hear is mainly the South talking to the South and sometimes to the outside world about the North. There are a few signs, but very few, of any attempt to see the North from the North's point of view.

8   Most of the sovereignty debate has been framed in old-fashioned western empire terms: *We have a distant frontier that must be defended. This frontier is ours, not theirs*, whoever they may be. It is only in this context that the people of the North are mentioned, as if the reason for their existence were to serve Canadian Sovereignty. There is little sense in all of this that the well-being and success of the people of the North is a purpose in and of itself. And they do not need to be the guarantors of our sovereignty—even though they are—in order to deserve well-being and success. They deserve these exactly as any other Canadian citizen deserves them.

9   Besides, the whole idea of sovereignty is meaningless if we cannot sustain a long-term, solid northern policy. Today there is southern-style enthusiasm. Very little of this seems attached to such northern realities as housing shortages, ill-adapted school curricula, and difficult communications of every sort. And this raises the old fear that something else will soon catch our fancy and the North will retreat once again from the general public consciousness and that of the government.

10   This failure to build and maintain a strong, integrated northern policy and northern foreign policy is clearly laid out in *Arctic Front: Defending Canada in the Far North*, a book written by Ken Coates, Whitney Lackenbauer, William Morrison, and Greg Poelzer, four sensible northern experts. They argue that this is just a continuation of Canada's incapacity as a state to sustain any serious level of attention on the North. Northern success is all about continuity and maintenance, internally and internationally. Periodic enthusiasms do not do the trick.

*

11   This essay focuses on the Arctic. But the larger context is that we are a northern nation. Two thirds of our country lies in what is normally categorized as North lands. One third of our gross domestic product comes out of the three territories and the equally isolated northern parts of our provinces. And that one third is what makes us a rich, not a poor, country. Our cities, our high-tech service-based lives are built upon the foundation provided by that one third of riches. And now the South believes that the percentage of the GDP coming from the Arctic section of the North will grow. We ought to be a central player in the northern world in general and in particular in the circumpolar world. But first we all need to see ourselves as part of it and, at the moment, we do not.

12   The current Arctic enthusiasm instead resembles an updated manifestation of George Brown's old rep by pop argument, in which the shape and direction of Canada are supposed to be controlled simply by those who have the most votes. We act as if the second largest country in the world is only real in a handful of southern cities. That is why our current approach to Arctic sovereignty has such a Toronto-Montreal-Ottawa-Calgary-Vancouver feel to it. And that is why there is little sign of the balance between people and place that has always been and remains central to Canada's success. In this atmosphere, the point of view of northerners is treated as if it weighed three House of Commons seats, which is what a strict geographical definition of the region allots them: three territories, one seat apiece. And so, throughout our history, when the moment comes to spend the money or talk about the issues, ministers tend to become distracted by a bridge in their riding or in a swing riding, and the northern monies evaporate.

13   Our contemporary northern history therefore looks like this. In the early 1970s, there was little southern interest in things northern. Then came the oil crisis and with it a southern passion for energy sources under the ice. The Berger Commission revealed, even to the half-asleep majority, that northerners had a point of view and enough power to impose themselves. Then the South slipped back into disinterest. Suddenly a US ship—the *Manhattan*—made its way through the Northwest Passage. This produced a sovereignty panic in the 1980s. A flood of ardent reactive policies followed. These quickly evaporated and the South fell back asleep.

But northerners and a small number of committed southerners worked hard through the 1990s to produce real action—not reaction, but something healthy, with roots. The result was a series of northern land settlements, the growth of Nunavik, the creation of Nunavut, the Arctic Council, a serious northern foreign policy in 2000 and so on. The twenty first century brought a brutal political reaction against these initiatives, as if our infatuation with economic integration with the United States meant that we were an urban people for whom the northern nature of our country was an embarrassment. In effect, the South once again forgot the North. There was, however, a strong enough northern and pro-North institutional base for quiet work to continue. The Makivik Corporation in Nunavik expanded. Leaders such as Paul Okalik, Nellie Cournoyea, Mary Simon, Siila Watt-Cloutier and others worked ceaselessly; northern studies expanded in the universities. All of this was happening below the political radar.

14   And then the most recent sovereignty panic began, largely spurred by the rapider-than-expected effects of climate change. With the northern icefields turning into navigable ocean passages, other countries began viewing "our" North as an international highway. Overnight, urgent reactive promises were again being made in Ottawa by the very people who five years before had denigrated northern policies. People have the right to change their minds. And the difference this time is that northerners are far better organized and are prepared to navigate the political waters. And yet the new promises and policies continue to resemble old-fashioned southern views of the North.

15   Northerners keep pointing this out. But in order to be heard, ideas and arguments must pass through the national communications systems. And these systems, whether political or journalistic are run through a reconceptualization process in three southern cities.

*

16   Take a very simple example. Among all the new military promises, only one directly involves northerners. The Rangers are a highly successful part-time force of 4,000 spread throughout the northern two thirds of Canada. They play both a military and a search and rescue role, as well as an important social function for youth with the Junior Rangers. For example, hunters are traditionally men. Through the Junior Rangers,

teenage girls are becoming good shots and then hunters, which can give them great self-confidence.

17   Throughout the North, the Rangers are the most important presence of the Canadian state. They have great experience on the land. And yet there are virtually no regular force officers involved. And there are virtually no northerners serving in command positions above their particular communities. The Ranger Patrols—as they are called—are trained by very good regular force warrant officers who, from what I have seen, love working outside the normal army system and being in the community.

18   The costs of all of this are minimal. On parade the Rangers wear a red sweatshirt and baseball cap, although this is now changing. Their rifles are basic, but good. Almost everything else is their own.

19   The new national policy is to expand the Rangers to 5,000, and that is a good thing. But there is no public debate about the existing model and whether it should change. For example, the Rangers could be structured into a formal regiment, to put them on the same level as the rest of the regular and militia forces. Their regions could be structured as battalions and integrated on an east-west northern basis. Under the current system each Ranger area is tributary to the southern commands immediately below them—a perfectly colonial structure.

20   One of the other new promises is for an Arctic training centre. Again a good idea, but for what purpose? It could be used to bring northerners into the full-time regular army at all rank levels so that the new regiment would be led increasingly by northerners, just as all our other regiments are led largely by people from the part of Canada in which they are based. This process could be sped up by the new Aboriginal Leadership Opportunity Year (ALOY) program, which is run out of the Royal Military College in Kingston and aims to draw aboriginal youth into the officer corps. In other words, the Rangers could become a regiment with a core of regular force, largely northern leaders and a majority remaining in the militia.

21   But let's go back to the conceptualization process. If this is a northern unit, why are the Rangers dressed in baseball caps and sweatshirts? You can't wear this outfit outside ten months of the year. Of course, this is more or less a dress uniform, but why a dress uniform that has to be worn inside? The whole idea and reality of the Rangers is that they are outside and on the land. Their outfit is symbolic of a southern view, symbolic of a generalized southern failure to support the development of northern equipment.

22   For example, we do not produce snowmobiles appropriate to the Arctic. Each time I am with Rangers, they point out the weaknesses of what is available. The best machines are made by Bombardier in Finland. The explanation no doubt is that our Arctic market is not big enough for such specific-use machines. Why, then, are those machines made in Finland (population five million)?

23   When you are out on the land in full winter most of the machines Canadians use freeze up so badly overnight that the common way to get them going is to turn the machine on its side (even the block is placed according to southern logic). Then all the men stand in a circle and pee on the block. This is just the beginning of a 30-minute start-up process—not very helpful in a crisis. I have thought, while standing in these circles, that basic details often reveal how Canada's practical imagination has not focused on the North; and how the practical imagination of northerners has been prevented form shaping what is done.

24   When you look at the heavy hand of the South on northern architecture or power systems or education methods or food supply systems, you begin to realize how difficult it has been and remains for the new Arctic leadership in particular to put a northern perspective in place. Not always, but very often, the insistent and unimaginative ideas coming from the South have solved immediate specific difficulties while creating systemic problems.

*

25   If southern Canadians are now seriously concerned about the status of the North, then this is an ideal moment to listen to what northerners are saying. They are continuing to suggest a myriad of approaches, practical and philosophical. The latter, among the Inuit, is often called IQ—Inuit Qaujimajatuqangit. This is often translated as traditional ways or culture. But as Peter Irniq and Frank Tester point out in the December 2008 issue of *Arctic*, that suggests something anthropological, something locked in the past. Or it is seen as "a 'holistic' concept that includes spiritual as well as factual knowledge." This western

interpretation suggests that "understanding the whole can be achieved by understanding the parts."

26   This is just the sort of interpretation that comforts southern-style science in the North. It involves endlessly collecting information that is meant one day to add up to something. That's fine. By all means keep collecting. The results are fascinating and no doubt useful. But it is this approach that has comforted two decades of inaction. For example, the science of glaciers is fascinating. There is more to learn. But precise pictures have been taken of them for a half-century. Anyone can hold those pictures in their hands and fly low over the glaciers and compare. The glaciers are melting. The next step is action. Or as Watt-Cloutier put it in her LaFontaine-Baldwin Lecture: "Slowing down climate change would be the best long-term solution to enforcing Canada's Arctic sovereignty." After all, that sovereignty is only in question because the ice is melting.

27   The point of IQ, or, more broadly, northern philosophies, is that they provide a completely different approach to the Arctic reality—a non-western, non-silo, non-sum-of-the-parts approach. Irniq and Tester call this a seamless approach. It is one in which the human is seen as an integrated part of the place. And so IQ relates to the Cree idea of Witaskewin—*living together in the land*—and the West Coast Nuu-chah-nulth worldview of Tsawalk—*everything is one*.[1]

28   These are philosophies of harmony and balance. They are indeed seamless and appropriate evocations of our physical reality. They remove the separation of the human from the place—that separation that has brought us many wonderful things, more recently along with global warming and an incapacity to act when what we think of as scientific progress seems to contradict the stability of our physical reality. The southern idea is that progress is an uncontroversial reality that solves problems. Anyone sitting on the outside of western philosophy simply responds: What do you mean by progress?

29   No one in the North is saying that southern science or its concepts of progress should simply go away. What northerners are perhaps saying is that the philosophical concepts that shape most southern ideas are undermining the advantages and promoting destructive side effects. And these side effects are now becoming their principal outcome. Northern architecture, for example, continues to evolve largely from southern assumptions. Technical problems, such as dealing with cold, are solved on a one-off basis. But there is no debate about what Arctic buildings should look like and what their relationship to each other should be. What should the underlying principles of those shapes be? Do southern assumptions and solutions about housing cause family and even broad social problems while concentrating on heating systems?

30   The stubbornness of the western intellectual approach and the relentless self-promotion of its silo structures make it very difficult for northern leaders to inject their own philosophical approaches into the heart of their own policy making. The southern, western system insinuates itself everywhere with religious fervor.

31   And yet there are breakthroughs. Nunavut is now building a cultural school, called Piqqusilirivvik, and is doing so with interesting architecture. It will be in Clyde River, up the east coast of Baffin Island. The school will promote the reality of a fundamentally northern and non-western philosophy. And Nunavut is working hard to get itself out from under the Alberta school curriculum, which shapes Arctic schools in a way that undermines Inuktituk and an integrated northern life. The recent *Nunavut Education Act* is making another stab at correcting this problem.

32   Perhaps most problematic is that there is still no university in the Canadian North. We remain the only circumpolar country without northern or Arctic universities.

33   We have hundreds, perhaps thousands, of northern experts. Almost all of them are based in southern universities. All our Arctic study centres are in southern universities. Millions of public dollars are invested every year in these southern universities to work on the North. And most of this money stays in the south. Doctorates on the North are organized and written in the South, with periodic trips up to check things out. MAs on the North are done in the South, perhaps with one or two research visits to the distant frontier. Lecturers are hired in the South. Tenure track is in the South.

34   Yes, there are worthwhile programs aimed at producing northern lawyers, nurses, and so on. These contractual arrangements with southern universities are delivered by excellent northern colleges, but the intellectual form, the conceptualization, the real control remain largely in the South.

35   What this means is that there are no intellectual centres based in the North at which students can

gather and then make their way. Why? Because they are all in the South. And public money—federal and provincial—keeps it this way.

36 This is a fundamental Canadian failure. It is a failure of our intellectual class. What we have is a colonial structure.

37 Four other circumpolar countries, each with populations a fraction of ours, have healthy northern universities, as does Alaska, as does Russia. Canada alone continues to treat northern higher education in a colonial manner.

38 Among the new policies coming out of Ottawa is the promise of an Arctic research centre. Another good idea. But without universities in the North, this will simply comfort our southern institutions in their "live south, work south, invest south, think south, visit north" structure. Norway—population four million—has leapt far ahead of Canada—population 33 million—with their Arctic research centre. Theirs is served by a very good northern university. Ours will serve universities in the South.

39 What is our excuse? Usually that we don't have the concentration of population or the infrastructure necessary to justify such universities. No other circumpolar country says this. Why? Because they believe that part of being a northern country is that you must create the intellectual and physical infrastructure in the North from which everything can grow. Imagine five federal research chairs in each of three northern universities. The reality of centres of excellence would rush north overnight.

40 In the meantime southern Canada, with the national government, the universities and businesses, continues to act as if northerners were not full Canadians and the North not an integrated part of who we are. Above all, the south still has not absorbed the reality that northerners have modern leadership views—both philosophical and practical—on how their part of the country could function.

41 Three universities in the North (or one with three different campuses) matter because they are the key to building fully rounded northern communities. These are institutions northerners could attach themselves to, places young southerners would be attracted to. They would immediately become a reason for young northerners to finish high school, as they are continually admonished to do in an old-fashioned southern way—*Get an education and get a job.* But what sort of education? Will it relate to the North? Will it help young people to build their north or cut them off from it, and make them insecure because it only makes sense in the South? And what kind of job? Where?

42 These simple questions could be partially answered in a positive way if there were northern-imagined centres of excellence in the North. Which raises the strategic point in conceptualizing these universities, one that relates to IQ and northern approaches to learning.

43 There are already good colleges in the three northern capitals. They need to be strengthened and expanded to fully cover the essential areas of utilitarian training. But there is no need for universities that are basically fancy training centres, or for imitation southern universities in the North.

44 This is what an increasing number of northerners who have made their way through the southern system are saying. One group of young lawyers and public administrators in Iqaluit—Sandra Inutiq, Elisapi Davidee-Aningmiuq, Kirt Ejesiak, Hugh Lloyd, and Aaju Peter—has created the Ilitturvik University Society to advance the idea of programs "politically, economically, culturally and socially relevant to the Arctic and Inuit."[2] Another group, in the Northwest Territories, has created a project called Dechinta, aimed at a field school approach toward post-secondary education.[3]

45 These young people have all more than proved themselves in the southern university system. They are a small part of a growing critical mass of young northern leaders.[4] What they are saying is that those southern systems are not appropriate to the North. So there is now a remarkable opportunity to break away from the disease of the silo education and utilitarian approaches, which have so damaged our southern universities. We have the opportunity to recognize that this approach is central to our incapacity to act when faced by crises such as climate change.

46 We have seen that model fail when faced with the reality of the North, the needs of the North. There is every reason to embrace the seamless model being put forward by an increasing number of northerners.

Literary Review of Canada. 2009.
October 17 (8).

Notes

1. See, for example, Harold Cardinal and Walter Hildebrandt's *Treaty Elders of Saskatchewan*(University of Calgary Press, 2000) or Umeek-E Richard Atleo's *Tsawalk, A Nuu-chah-nulth Worldview*(University of British Columbia Press, 2004).
2. See <www.ilitturvik.org>
3. See <www.dechintabushuniversity.ca>
4. For example, see those who have spoken out in *Northern Exposure: Peoples, Powers and Prospects in Canada's North*, edited by Frances Abele, Thomas Courchene, Leslie Seidle and France St.-Hilaire and produced by the Institute for Research on Public Policy in 2009.

Key and challenging words

derivative, guarantor, ardent, reactive, denigrate, utilitarian

Questions

1. a) Identify Saul's thesis; b) Provide descriptive headings for the different sections in the essay; c) In which section does Saul provide the most direct support for his thesis?
2. a) In paragraph 4, what does Saul suggest is to blame for climate change? b) Summarize the two different philosophies referred to in the opening paragraphs and their aims.
3. What two main rhetorical patterns does Saul use in the consecutive paragraphs 12 and 13? In paragraph 13, identify the sentence that announces this pattern.
4. Explain the problems Saul finds with the way the Canadian Rangers are being used.
5. Demonstrate the way Saul uses the example of snowmobiles (paragraphs 22–23) to support his point in paragraph 21; analyze his argument in these paragraphs for its logic and effectiveness.
6. What is IQ (paragraphs 25–27) and how does it differ from the traditional use of the concept by western/southern societies?
7. Discuss Saul's use of comparisons in the last section of his essay, showing how they contribute to this section as a whole.
8. Using a reliable reference source, define the term "centres of excellence" (first mentioned in paragraph 39) and explain how they are connected to other institutions or organizations mentioned in the essay.
9. Analyze Saul's use of personal experience in his essay, referring to specific passages. Does it affect his credibility and help support his argument?

Post-reading

1. Find a recent news item about Canada's north and analyze the author's point of view about the north or the views of those mentioned in the article. Would you consider the views that inform the article "southern" or "northern," according to Saul's distinction?
2. Write a one-paragraph mission statement for a prospective university in the Canadian north; to get an idea of what such statements look like, you could consult the one for your own university or check another university's statement, such as that of the University of Northern British Columbia: www.unbc.ca/about/
3. *Collaborative or individual activity:* What is "Arctic sovereignty"? Consider the following questions, among others of your choosing: How might the definition of "Arctic sovereignty" be different for Canada compared to that of other circumpolar countries? How might it be different for a non-Arctic country? Do you believe this is an issue that will affect future generations? Why or why not?

Related websites of interest

Canadian Rangers:
www.army.forces.gc.ca/land-terre/cr-rc/index-eng.asp

Canada's Northern Strategy:
http://northernstrategy.gc.ca

VOICES WITHIN CANADA

Of hockey, Medicare and Canadian dreams

Stephen J. Toope
(1,968 words)

Abstract

As Canada approaches its 150th anniversary, Canadians need to decide what we want to be when we grow up. Our national sport and Medicare alone will not define us. Understanding our strengths and facing our problems squarely, what visions could Canadians be dreaming of as we face a stormy future?

———

1   Hockey is a great, fast-paced sport, and it has served well as an emblem for Canadians' sense of self. Set in winter snows, demanding agility and fortitude in the face of harsh conditions, and requiring a robust competitive spirit, hockey speaks both to what Canadians have inherited from a frontier history and to what we hope to be.

2   It is too bad that the national game is dominated by an NHL that seems greedier, insensitive to the expectations of fans and dominated by the need to satisfy a US market. And the increasingly obvious risks associated with out-of-control violence may one day bring the current hockey regime to account.

3   Medicare is a great social policy achievement, and it has served well as an emblem for Canadians' sense of self. Emerging from the wide plains of Saskatchewan, and reflecting a desire to protect the vulnerable amongst us, Medicare speaks to an open spirit and an aspiration towards social equality.

4   Too bad the system underperforms less costly systems in Europe and fails to produce health outcomes that an advanced society should expect to see. The costs keep rising, crowding out other social expenditures of both federal and provincial governments. And access seems to depend too often on who you know.

5   Is this the best we can do as Canadians? Are hockey and Medicare our defining features? Do they best represent who we are and what we hope to become? As Canada approaches its 150th anniversary, we Canadians need to push ourselves a little to figure out what we want to be when we grow up.

6   It may seem strange to say that we aren't grown up yet, for we are among a handful of countries that has managed democratic rule for so long. Yet our democracy has, for much of its history, been a dependent one, first on the United Kingdom and then on the United States. It was only after the First World War that Canada began to develop an independent set of relationships with foreign states, and only in 1931, with the passing of the Statute of Westminster, that the Canadian Parliament was accorded status equal to the Parliament of the UK. Our economic policy was long constrained by our absolute dependence upon the United States in foreign trade. From the 1960s

through to the early 2000s, the share of Canadian trade with the US rose from roughly 60 per cent of total trade to over 80. With more attention to Asia in the last few years, the concentration of trade with the US has fallen, but remains over 70 per cent. For much of our history in the twentieth century, Canada hid behind the US on major matters of foreign policy as well. Although we liked to think of ourselves as "honest brokers," much of the world saw us merely as somewhat gentler versions of Americans.

7   These hard-sounding comments should not be mistaken for self-loathing. Canadians have much to be proud of, as our country has evolved through the last century. We have created a society marked by relative openness to immigration, especially in comparison with most of Europe. Our ability to attract large numbers of people from foreign shores, respecting and even borrowing from many of their traditions, while encouraging social integration, is enviable. It is practically unmatched in other liberal democracies. It is a truism, for example, that Vancouver is now the largest Asian city outside Asia, but what is truly remarkable is the ability of immigrants from China, Korea and elsewhere to build lives that are still connected to their histories and to have other Canadians acknowledge that history. UBC has the largest Mandarin language programme in North America, and many of its students are Anglo-Canadian, of Korean and Japanese origin, or foreign students from around the world.

8   Canadians should also be proud of our history of social mobility. Today, when many influential Americans, like Nobel Prize-winning economist Joseph Stiglitz, worry that the US is no longer a "land of opportunity," Canada is out-performing the US as a place where it is possible to rise from distinctly modest backgrounds to find economic security. A major reason for that continuing mobility is that education is publicly financed to a large extent, from day care right through to doctoral programmes. University and college education is still relatively affordable in Canada, opening up worlds of opportunity for new generations of students, from here and from around the globe.

9   On the cultural front, Canada has also seen an explosion of talent and global recognition over the last few years. Canadian authors like Atwood, Gallant, Hagi, Huston, Laferrière, Martel, Munro, and Ondaatje are international best-sellers and prize winners. Canadian actors star in major Hollywood films. Although English-Canadian cinema is not in its strongest period, Quebec cinema continues to produce inventive and influential films, including three nominated for best foreign-film Oscars in the last three years. In pop music, airwaves and iPods around the world are filled with the likes of Drake, Justin Bieber, Celine Dion, Carly Rae Jepsen, and Leonard Cohen. The Vancouver school of conceptual and post-conceptual photography is globally influential, with artists like Jeff Wall offered retrospectives at major galleries world-wide.

10   Canadians have lots to celebrate, aside from hockey and Medicare, though we tend not to celebrate very loudly. How many Canadians even know that Nancy Huston, a Calgarian by origin but writing in French, won France's prestigious Prix Fémina, or that Canadian composer Howard Shore has won three Oscars, three Golden Globes and four Grammies for his film scores? Just last year, Canadians could have celebrated the thirtieth anniversary of the *Canadian Charter of Rights and Freedoms*, a constitutional text that has influenced legal systems around the world, in part through direct borrowing and in part through the work of the Canadian Supreme Court which, since the advent of the *Charter*, has proven to be one of the most internationally cited courts in the world. Small-minded politics out of Ottawa precluded much attention to this anniversary.

11   But amidst the many reasons that we should celebrate, there are also reasons to worry. While we continue to target for roughly 250,000 new immigrants each year, their integration into our economy has faltered, even though they are better educated than ever before. Between 2000 and 2005, according to Statistics Canada, the income gap between Canadian-born workers and recent immigrants with university degrees widened significantly. Our productivity as a nation has also stagnated. Over the last thirty years, the productivity gap between Canadian and US workers has increased to almost $10,000 a person per year. This is not because Canadians don't work hard, but because our business performance in innovation is tepid at best. The Jenkins Panel on Canadian innovation reported to the federal government in 2010 that the expenditure of Canadian business on research and development had fallen since 2006, declining to the

level of 2000, when Canada was already merely at the average of Organization for Economic Cooperation and Development (OECD) countries.

12   Consider also what has happened to real wages over the last thirty years. Statistics Canada reports that average real wage rates increased by only 14 per cent in Canada from 1981 to 2011, failing to match the rising cost of living. Even though social mobility is better than in the United States, it is less robust than in many European countries, which have traditionally been seen as bastions of privilege. The Conference Board of Canada laments that from 1990 to 2013, the wealthiest Canadians have significantly increased their proportion of total national income, while the poorest, and even middle-income groups, have lost ground.

13   Like the inhabitants of many other advanced economies, Canadians may live through a slow-moving demographic train wreck over the next few years. Not only are there likely to be too few working people to support the social safety net for the Boomer generation, but even now a growing gulf is opening between generations, with younger Canadians worrying that they won't ever find meaningful jobs or be able to afford their own homes. UBC's Professor Paul Kershaw demonstrates that the average household income for young Canadian couples has stagnated since the mid-1970s, adjusting for inflation, while average housing prices in Canada have skyrocketed by 76%. Culturally, many of our once-treasured institutions and organizations are in perilous straits. In 2012 to 2013, funding cuts to arts organizations kicked in at the federal and provincial levels. The Playhouse Theatre in Vancouver closed, The Toronto Symphony operated in deficit, one of the last major Canadian independent publishers, Douglas & McIntyre, filed for bankruptcy protection, and the National Gallery of Canada cut staff to address a budget crunch.

14   Incanting the names of Sidney Crosby, Roberto Luongo and Carey Price just won't be good enough to protect Canadians from the storms to come, or to ground a rich sense of identity. Nor will Medicare alone be our sure port. Understanding our strengths and facing our problems squarely, Canadians need to figure out who we are, now that we really are quite close to grown up. What visions could Canadians be dreaming to as we face a stormy future? What might a robust sense of Canadianness, of pride in our society, look like 50 years or so from now, at the 200th anniversary of Confederation?

15   The social inclusion that we have offered to generations and generations of immigrants will continue, and be buttressed by better economic integration. That inclusive spirit will finally be matched by a respect for the traditions of the First Nations and other aboriginal Canadians, and society-wide efforts to help ensure their economic, social and cultural vitality. We will have recaptured our fundamental, if demanding, connections to the land and the landscape, defined so clearly in Margaret Atwood's *Survival* or Margaret Laurence's *The Stone Angel*. Those connections will imply a profound commitment to understanding and upholding the delicate balancing required in the exploitation of resources and treasuring the natural environment.

16   Canadians will have re-imagined our place in the world, recognizing that our social and economic links to Asia are an important trade strength, but that the greatest source of long-term opportunity might well be in Africa. We will admit that we cannot secure our future through military adventures because we will never have the staying power required to deal with internal conflicts and guerrilla-style war on foreign shores. Our focus, instead, will be on entrepreneurial social, cultural and economic engagement around the world, matched with military training missions and limited participation in collective security efforts designed to protect vulnerable populations. We will finally have cracked the code on Canadian-style social and economic innovation, innovation that draws on the diverse talents of an astonishingly intercultural and multilingual society with deep family, social, cultural and economic connections that span the globe. To spur that innovation in all fields of endeavour, Canadians will have found the will to risk for the great, rather than settling for the good.

17   And yes, hockey will still matter, but a hockey that has re-found its connection to people more than dollars, and a hockey that doesn't sacrifice the well-being of players in an attempt to mimic ultimate fighting. Canadians will have employed our new-found social innovation mojo to re-engineer Medicare to ensure its fiscal sustainability and improve health outcomes.

18   Canadians' dreams will be about hockey, healthy kids and pensioners, friends from all parts of the world, gorgeous natural vistas and culturally rich urban neighbourhoods, and work in far-away places where Canadians are welcomed as partners in creative social and economic initiatives. Adult dreams.

Canadian Issues.
2013. Summer.

Note

1. The views expressed are personal and should not be attributed to the University of British Columbia.

Key and challenging words

truism, preclude, retrospective (n), tepid, incant, buttress

Questions

1. Identify, then paraphrase, Toope's thesis (recall that not all theses take the form of a statement).
2. Analyze the author's brief introduction, commenting on any stylistic features, such as repetition, that contribute to its effect or that suggest the essay's purpose.
3. Summarize paragraph 6 in which Toope explains why he believes Canada is not "grown up yet."
4. Discuss Toope's use of (a) examples and (b) statistics in developing his argument. Refer specifically to the text.
5. Discuss the strategies that Toope uses to avoid coming across as too negative in his essay. You could discuss his language, tone, rhetorical/argumentative strategies or any other relevant features.
6. Explain the purpose of the following paragraphs and their function in the essay: (a) 15–16; (b) 17–18.

Post-reading

1. Do you think that Toope is essentially an optimist or a pessimist in his vision of Canada—present and past? Provide textual to support your claim.

Related website of interest

Social Science and Humanities Research Council:
www.sshrc-crsh.gc.ca/society-societe/community-communite/Imagining_Canadas_Future-Imaginer_l_avenir_du_Canada-eng.aspx

Which "Native" history? By whom? For whom?

J.R. (Jim) Miller
(2,267 words)

Pre-reading

1. Using a dictionary of usage or a reliable online source, define the terms "First Nations," "Inuit," and "Métis." Then, look up "aboriginal," "native," and "indigenous" to determine distinctions among them. Scan "Which 'Native' history?" for these words. Does their usage seem to conform to the definitions you have looked up?

Abstract

Although "Native" history is often discussed as though it were a single type of scholarship, in reality it takes many forms. Different rules apply to the different varieties, and some research methods are more applicable to one type than to others. In most cases, the approach known as Native-newcomer history, which focuses on the evolving relationship between indigenous and immigrant peoples, is the most useful.

*

1   During the last twenty years, controversies have occasionally erupted over "Native" history. Who should write it? For whom is it intended? Greater illumination and less heat would be achieved if authors were clear about what they mean when they say they are writing "Native" history. The indiscriminate use of the term to cover several distinct, though related, historical approaches has resulted in a great deal of confusion and not a little acrimony. The fact of the matter is that "Native" and "Native history" are not simple or unproblematic terms. Authors and speakers have used "Native" history when addressing one of several genres that exist under the term, with the result that gate-keepers have sometimes got up in arms when there was no necessity for them to do so. Particularly in the 1990s, and still sometimes in the twenty-first century, non-Aboriginal scholars writing on indigenous subjects have been accused of "appropriating the voice" of Native people. Usually, however, the charge is unjustified because what is being considered is not something that pertains specifically or exclusively to

Native peoples. It is helpful to be clear about what sort of history is under consideration before worrying about appropriation.

2   Certainly, there are topics involving Native people to which they alone have a proprietary right. In general, these are matters that involve personal or family property, or things that have great spiritual significance to Aboriginal people. So, for example, a Potlatch song or a dance might belong to a family; others have no right to sing or perform it without the family's permission. To ignore this property right is akin to violating copyright or a trademark. Other cases involve ceremonies of great spiritual significance, or rituals that are associated with certain seasons of the year among particular indigenous people. To perform the ceremonies indiscriminately is rude and disrespectful; to tell stories at the wrong season of the year is inappropriate, and might be considered threatening by the people to whom they matter a great deal. In these areas, simple courtesy requires scrupulous observation of the norms that prevail among the peoples whose ceremonies, stories, or dances are being considered. It is worth noting, though, that such indigenous practices rarely figure directly in what we usually think of as "Native" history.

3   The study of the distinctive role of the First Nations, Métis, or Inuit in historical events since contact with Europeans is a second genre of what is said to be "Native" history. A clear example can be found in the Northwest Rebellion of 1885, a topic that has attracted a great deal of attention. Until comparatively recently, most of the writing on this confrontation was the work of non-Native scholars and journalists. This writing tended to range widely over

the motives and actions of the non-Native settlers and government, Métis, and First Nations in the events in the Saskatchewan country and the consequences for them. In the 1990s, however, a pair of historians, one First Nations and the other non-Native, decided that it was time that the particular role of First Nations in the Rebellion be studied carefully and in detail. Blair Stonechild of the First Nations University of Canada and Bill Waiser of the University of Saskatchewan joined forces to study the actions of the First Nations in 1885 and their consequences. They first consulted a number of First Nations Elders and chiefs to ensure that their inquiries would not be considered offensive. Reassured that their project was welcome and would receive support, they plunged into the research.

4   Stonechild and Waiser conducted their research in a thoroughly bicultural manner. Both were intimately involved in the research, as they were later in the writing of the resulting book based on both documentary and interview evidence. With the cooperation and guidance of Elders and political leaders on individual reserves, they hired First Nations interviewers, who worked with Elders to identify and interview members of the communities with the necessary historical knowledge. First Nations protocol was observed at all meetings, including those attended by Stonechild and Waiser, by presenting tobacco and cloth before asking an individual to speak. The result of this bicultural project was *Loyal Till Death: Indians and the Northwest Rebellion* (Fifth House, 1997), which substantially revised understanding of the forces involved in the events of 1885. These scholars and their informants showed convincingly that First Nations involvement was minimal and usually the result of individual motives rather than community will. *Loyal Till Death* refuted the sixty year-old view, first promulgated by G.F.G. Stanley in *The Birth of Western Canada: A History of the Riel Rebellions* (Longmans, Green, and Co, 1936) that Louis Riel had been at the head of an alliance of Métis and First Nations. Stonechild and Waiser showed convincingly that the 1885 rising in Saskatchewan was not a Métis movement. As a result, they provided a fuller and more rounded version of the 1885 events than earlier works.

5   A bicultural approach can also be found in the work of a single scholar. The Anicinabe of what is now southern Ontario have been prominent practitioners of this style of history. In the first half of the nineteenth century, Ojibwa historians such as Peter Jones (Kahkewaquonaby) and George Copway (Kahgegagahbowh) produced histories of their own people. These writers were the beneficiaries of substantial Euro-Canadian education, which they combined with their understanding of their Aboriginal heritage to interpret and explain their people's history. Their twentieth-century intellectual descendant is John Borrows, a Chippewa of Newash, who has enjoyed a distinguished academic career. Educated first in history and then in law, Borrows became an academic lawyer and is now based at the University of Victoria. His legal analyses are grounded both in history and law, employing Anicinabe and Euro-Canadian ways of knowing. His many articles and his recent book, *Recovering Canada: The Resurgence of Indigenous Law* (University of Toronto Press, 2002), skillfully combine evidence from both intellectual traditions. For example, he frequently employs wampum and government documents, or Anicinabe stories and Euro-Canadians' letters to support his arguments. Borrows, Copway, and Jones are prime examples of a bicultural approach to history executed by a single, broadly educated, and especially well-informed person.

6   The work of these three has sometimes been exclusively about Native peoples and sometimes about Native-newcomer relations. The latter, which is increasingly being noticed as a distinct genre called Native-newcomer history, is in fact what most of the work on "Native" history is actually about. Native-newcomer history is the story of the change over time in the relationship between indigenous and immigrant peoples, usually in the western hemisphere, and most commonly in what is now Canada. For example, it examines the shift in relations that began with commercial interactions in the fur trade and imperial rivalries, and continued into the era of agricultural settlement, mining and other resource-extractive industries, and urban-industrial society. This style of inquiry always focuses in the first instance on the interaction between the immigrant and indigenous people.

7   Native-newcomer history also studies the impact that the successive changes in the relationship had on both parties. For example, in the fur trade, Aboriginal people were affected by positive influences, such as European technology, as well as negative forces, such

as epidemic disease and distilled alcohol. For their part, the newcomers found that local knowledge and indigenous technology, particularly in transportation, brought them great wealth. A similar pattern of beneficial and detrimental forces flowing from contact was also found in later eras.

8   Native-newcomer history requires a special set of skills that is not the exclusive preserve of either Aboriginal or non-Aboriginal researchers. Of course, the historian's standard tool kit of investigation, analysis, synthesis, and exposition are essential, but more is required. Researchers need some awareness of the techniques of other disciplines, including art, literature, law, political studies, and, above all, oral research and cultural anthropology. Why is such a diverse range of skills needed? Changes in the native-newcomer relationship were reflected in literature and art, or in political attitudes and behaviour. A great deal of Native-newcomer history was inspired by the need to prepare claims, especially land claims, and a good deal of that history is embodied in court rulings. The evolution of the courts' attitudes and treatment of indigenous people, as in the case of the complex issue of Aboriginal title, both reflects societal changes and stimulates further development of the native-newcomer relationship.

9   Why is some familiarity with anthropology a major asset to working in Native-newcomer history? The answer can be summarized in one word: ethnohistory. Ethnohistory, which was invented in the 1930s by Canadian historian Alfred G. Bailey (*The Conflict of European and Eastern Algonkian Cultures, 1504–1700: A Study in Canadian Civilization*, New Brunswick Museum, 1937), became prominent in North America in the 1950s, as American anthropologists became involved in claims research for cases going to the US Indian Claims Commission. To put it simply, anthropologists had to learn to work with historical documents to back their claims with longitudinal analysis. The blend of anthropology and history that resulted from their innovative research became known as ethnohistory. Ethnohistory involves the analysis of documents that historians have used for some time, though now European and Euro-American documents are interpreted in light of the additional cultural knowledge that anthropologists bring to their examination. With knowledge of kin-based indigenous societies,

researchers could read accounts of Natives' speeches in which they referred to themselves as "children" and the French or English governor as "father," and understand that the familial language conveyed not notions of dependence on the part of Natives, but mutuality and reciprocal obligation. For example, it is impossible to study the history of treaty-making between the Crown and Native peoples, without an appreciation of the significance of the kinship terminology that was used in negotiations. Historians and ethnohistorians have been learning about kinship from anthropology.

10   Similarly, anthropology was the main source of oral research that historians have begun to employ in their research concerning the Native-newcomer relationship. Aboriginal peoples were not initially literate in European languages, although they often had other ways to record important events, such as wampum in the northeast woodlands or winter counts on the plains. Sometimes oral accounts were written down and could be interpreted from the documents following the guidelines of ethnohistorical practice. In other cases, oral history had to be collected for research because memories of the question being investigated had not yet been gathered. Treaty-making is an example of the former situation, with residential schooling being an example of the latter. In both cases, oral history research permits a fuller understanding of the process and results.

11   It should be obvious that Native-newcomer history has the advantage of inclusiveness. When it comes to researching and writing this style of history, it is a field for both Aboriginal and non-Aboriginal students and scholars. Native-newcomer history is for all or it is for none, because it deals with past events and processes in which people from both societies were involved. If non-Native researchers should refrain from studying Native-newcomer history, then so should Native investigators. Who, then, will research the history of the Beothuk, the Newfoundland First Nation that became extinct in 1829? At the consumption end of Native-newcomer historical production, the benefits flow broadly as well. Because so much of Canadian history is the story of the interactions of indigenous peoples and immigrants, the study of changes in their relationship over time is relevant to Canadians today.

12   A Native-newcomer approach to history also produces more rounded informative accounts of events

from our past. It is possible to study treaty-making from a predominantly Euro-American point of view, but this does not take into account the rich contribution of First Nations to the process. It is possible as well to study the history of treaty-making by concentrating on the Native role, as American legal scholar Robert Williams did in *Linking Arms Together: American Indian Treaty Visions of Law and Peace, 1600–1800* (Oxford University Press, 1997). However, the author completely neglected the Royal Proclamation of 1763, the single most important document in the history of treaty-making, as well as the emergence of territorial treaties, the predominant form of treaty in North American history. While *Linking Arms Together* is a valuable work in many ways, it is not the comprehensive treatment that a question like treaties between indigenous and immigrant peoples in North America requires. A better model is found in the historiography of the Northwest Rebellion of 1885. Blair Stonechild and Bill Waiser's *Loyal Till Death* explains the insurrection more fully and accurately than G.F.G. Stanley's *Birth of Western Canada*.

13   The most useful answer to the question "Which "Native" history?" is "Native-newcomer history". Historical study of the relationship enriches our understanding of the past by focusing on intercultural processes and their results. It provides a fuller and more comprehensive understanding of the history of Canada over the past four hundred years than more parochial approaches. It is a historical genre that requires the application of methods and insights from many disciplines, but it is also a field of inquiry to which all are welcome as both producers and consumers of research.

14   Which "Native" history? Native-newcomer history. By whom? Any and all students who are qualified and willing to carry out its methods. For whom? All Canadians.

Canadian Issues. 2008.
Fall 33-35.

Key and challenging words

acrimony, proprietary, scrupulous, longitudinal, reciprocal, parochial

Questions

1. How could you describe the author's tone in paragraph 1? From the tone, what can you infer about the purpose of the essay? What does it suggest about Miller's audience?

2. What primary organizational method (rhetorical pattern) is used in the essay? Identify a different pattern that Miller uses to develop one of his paragraphs.

3. Explain why the Northwest Rebellion of 1885 provides a good example of a historical event to analyze for Miller's purposes. How does the approach of non-Native historians differ from that of Stonechild and Waiser?

4. Find two reviews of the book *Loyal Till Death: Indians and the Northwest Rebellion* from an academic journal, a historical society website, or another reliable source. Do the reviewers' conclusions about the book differ from those of Miller? Write a 500–750 word analysis of one of the reviews, comparing the reviewers' comments with those of Miller.

5. In one or two sentences, explain the distinction between the second and third genres of Native history discussed in the essay.

6. What term is used in paragraphs 6–7 to identify non-Aboriginal peoples? Do you believe it is an appropriate term?

7. a) What are the advantages that Native-newcomer history offers over other kinds of Native history? b) Why does Miller state, "If non-Native researchers should refrain from studying Native-newcomer history, then so should Native investigators" (paragraph 11)?

8. Analyze the rhetorical effectiveness of the concluding two paragraphs.

Post-reading

1. *Collaborative activity:* Discuss the significance of names, labels, and titles as they have been applied to cultural groups in the past; how could a label affect the identity of a group or individual in the group? You could consider, for example, stereotypes associated with the word "Indian."

Related websites of Interest

Aboriginal Expression in the Arts and Media:
mediasmarts.ca/diversity-media/aboriginal-people/
aboriginal-expression-arts-and-media

Media—Magazines:
www.ammsa.com/publications/windspeaker
www.theturtleislandnews.com/

Additional library reading

King, Thomas. "Godzilla vs. Post-colonial." *Journal of Postcolonial Writing* 30.2 (1990): 10–16. Print.
Miller, J.R. *Skyscrapers Hide the Heavens. A History of Indian-White Relations in Canada.* 3rd ed. Toronto: University of Toronto Press, 2000. Print.

Retzlaff, Steffi. "What's in a Name? The Politics of Labelling and Native Identity Constructions." *The Canadian Journal of Native Studies* 25.2 (2005): 609–26. Print.
Aboriginal Expression in the Arts and Media:
mediasmarts.ca/diversity-media/aboriginal-people/
aboriginal-expression-arts-and-media

A sorry state

Mitch Miyagawa
(5,043 words)

Pre-reading

1. Using reliable sources, such as media coverage, create a timeline of Canadian government apologies to minority groups in Canada, starting with the 1988 apology to Japanese Canadians for internment during World War II. Summarize in a couple of sentences each the nature of the apology and the response of the group to which the apology was directed.
2. How important do you think it is that governments issue apologies for past injustices? Have too many or too few apologies been made by the Canadian government? Reflect on this issue and its importance today in one or two paragraphs.

1   The government of Canada gave my family our first apology, for the internment of Japanese Canadians during World War II, in 1988. I was seventeen, and I don't remember any of it. I had other things to worry about. My mom had just left my dad, Bob Miyagawa. She'd cried and said sorry as my brother and I helped her

load her furniture into the back of a borrowed pickup. Her departure had been coming for a while. At my dad's retirement dinner the year before, his boss at the Alberta Forest Service had handed him a silver-plated pulaski, a stuffed Bertie the Fire Beaver, and a rocking chair. My mom, Carol—barely forty years old and chafing for new adventures—took one look at the rocking chair and knew the end was near.

2   Three months after she left, on September 22, Brian Mulroney rose to his feet in the House of Commons. The gallery was packed with Japanese Canadian seniors and community leaders, who stood as the prime minister began to speak. "The Government of Canada wrongfully incarcerated, seized the property, and disenfranchised thousands of citizens of Japanese ancestry," he intoned. "Apologies are the only way we can cleanse the past." When he finished, the gallery cheered, in a most un-Japanese Canadian defiance of parliamentary rules.

3   The clouds may have suddenly parted in Ottawa; the cherry blossoms in Vancouver may have spontaneously bloomed. I missed it all. It was graduation year. Every day after school, I worked at West Edmonton Mall, diving elbow deep in Quarterback Crunch ice cream so I could save up for a pool table. Weekends, I visited my mom at her new place, a small apartment within walking distance of the tracks by Stony Plain Road.

4   Up until then, and perhaps to this day, being half Japanese had just been something I used to make myself unique. A conversation starter. A line for picking up girls. The internment my dad and 22,000 others like him suffered was something to add to the story. It increased the inherited martyr value.

5   I didn't get many dates.

6   Four years earlier, when Brian Mulroney was leader of the Opposition, he'd asked Pierre Trudeau to apologize to Japanese Canadians. Exasperated, Trudeau shot back, "How many other historical wrongs would have to be righted?" It was Trudeau's last day in Parliament as prime minister. He finished his retort with righteous indignation: "I do not think it is the purpose of a government to right the past. I cannot rewrite history."

7   Trudeau must have known that the apology door, once opened, would never be closed. Mulroney might have known, too. Redress for Japanese Canadians was the beginning of our national experiment with institutional remorse—an experiment that has grown greatly over the past twenty years, intertwining itself with my family's story.

8   I like to look at the glass as half full: my parents' divorce was not so much a split as an expansion. They both remarried, so my kids now have more grandparents than they can count. And I've gained the most apologized-to family in the country—maybe the world.

9   I watched Stephen Harper's apology for Indian residential schools with my dad's wife, Etheline, on a hot night in the summer of 2008. Etheline was the third generation of her Cree family to attend an Indian mission school. She went to Gordon Residential School in Punnichy, Saskatchewan, for four years. Gordon was the last federally run residential school to be closed, shutting down in 1996 after over a century in operation.

10   When I talked to my mom in Calgary afterward, she casually mentioned that her second husband Harvey's father had paid the Chinese head tax as a child. Harper apologized to head tax payers and their families in 2006.

11   I was aware that my family had become a multiculti case study, but when I realized the government had apologized to us three times it went from being a strange coincidence to a kind of joke. (*Q: How does a Canadian say hello? A: "I'm sorry."*) Soon, though, I started wondering what these apologies really meant, and whether they actually did any good. In seeking answers, I've mostly found more questions. I've become both a cynic and a believer. In other words, I'm more confused than ever before. I'm no apology expert or prophet. I'm so sorry. All I can offer is this: my apology story.

12   In the fall of 2008, I travelled from my home in Whitehorse to Vancouver. The National Association of Japanese Canadians had organized a celebration and conference on the twentieth anniversary of Redress. It rained as I walked toward the Japanese Hall on Alexander Street in East Vancouver, in what was once the heart of the Japanese community. In the distance, giant red quay cranes poked above the buildings along Hastings, plucking containers from cargo ships anchored in Burrard Inlet. The downpour soaked the broken folks lined up outside the Union

Gospel Mission at Princess and Cordova, a few blocks from the hall. Some huddled under the old cherry trees in Oppenheimer Park, beside the ball field where the Asahi baseball team, the darlings of "Japantown," played before the war.

13 Inside the hall, a few hundred people milled about, drinking green tea and coffee served from big silver urns by bluevested volunteers. The participants on the first panel of the day, titled Never Too Late, took seats on the wide stage at the front. They represented the hyphenated and dual named of our country: a Japanese-, Chinese-, Indo-, Black, Aboriginal, and Ukrainian-Canadian rainbow behind two long fold-out tables. Their communities had all been interned, or excluded, or systematically mistreated. Apology receivers and apology seekers. A kick line of indignation, a gallery of the once wronged. (*A Japanese-, Chinese-, Indo-, Black, Aboriginal, and Ukrainian- Canadian all go into a bar. The bartender looks at them and says, "Is this some kind of joke?"*)

14 In the fictional world of *Eating Crow*, a "novel of apology" by Jay Rayner, the hottest trend in international relations is something called "penitential engagement." To deal with the baggage from the wars, genocides, and persecutions of the past, the United Nations sets up an Office of Apology. The protagonist of the novel, Marc Basset, is hired as Chief Apologist, partly because of his tremendous ability to deliver heartfelt apologies, but also because of his "plausible apologibility." His ancestors captained slave ships, ran colonies, slaughtered natives, and waged dirty wars. Backed by a team of researchers and handlers, Basset circles the globe, delivering statements of remorse.

15 Penitential engagement is closer to reality than you'd think. The Japanese government has made at least forty "war apology statements" since 1950. All of Western Europe remembers German chancellor Willy Brandt's famous *Kniefall* in 1970, when he fell to his knees on the steps of the Warsaw Memorial, in silent anguish for the victims of the Warsaw Ghetto uprising. During the past twenty years, Italian prime minister Silvio Berlusconi has apologized for the colonial occupation of Libya, South African president Frederik W. de Klerk has apologized for apartheid, and the Queen has issued a Royal Proclamation of regret to the Acadians in the Maritimes and Louisiana. In 1998, the Australian government began its annual National Sorry Day for the "stolen generations" of aboriginal children. In 2005, the US Senate apologized for its failure to enact federal anti-lynching legislation. And both houses of Congress have now passed apologies for slavery.

16 At the 2001 UN World Conference against Racism, Racial Discrimination, Xenophobia and Related Intolerance, held in Durban, more than 100 countries called "on all those who have not yet contributed to restoring the dignity of the victims to find appropriate ways to do so and, to this end, appreciate those countries that have done so." Working toward this goal is the International Center for Transitional Justice in New York, which "assists countries pursuing accountability for past mass atrocity or human rights abuse." As if in response, jurisdictions across Australia, the United States, and Canada are passing apology acts designed to allow public officials to apologize without incurring legal liability.

17 Concerned about our precious self-image as a peacemaking, multicultural country, Canada has been making every effort to lead the sorry parade. In addition to the residential school and Chinese head tax apologies, the federal government has also now said sorry for the *Komagata Maru* incident, when a ship full of immigrants from India was turned away from Vancouver Harbour, and established a historical recognition program "to recognize and commemorate the historical experiences and contributions of ethno-cultural communities affected by wartime measures and immigration restrictions applied in Canada." And we became the first Western democracy to follow South Africa in establishing a truth and reconciliation commission, for the residential schools.

18 Not surprisingly, other groups have come knocking on Ottawa's door. Among them are Ukrainian Canadians, on behalf of those interned during World War I, and the residents of the bulldozed Africville community in Halifax, now a dog park. Some who have already received an apology clamour for more, or better. Harper's *Komagata Maru* apology was issued to the Indo-Canadian community outside Parliament. Now they want the same as every other group: an official, on-the-record statement.

19 I sat down on a plastic-backed chair in the deserted second row. Seconds later, an old *Nisei*, a second-generation Japanese Canadian named Jack

Nagai, plunked down beside me. He sighed and lifted the glasses hanging around his neck to his face. "Gotta sit close for my hearing aid," he said, then looked at me and grinned. I pulled out a notebook, and he watched me out of the corner of his eye, fingering the pen in his breast pocket.

20   *Black scuffs*, I wrote. The pearly walls and floor of the Japanese Hall auditorium were marked and streaked. A fluorescent light fifteen metres above my head flickered and buzzed. The hall had a school gym wear and tear to it. Jack noticed my scribbling and jotted down something on the back of his program.

21   ·   The brown spots on his bald head reminded me of my Uncle Jiro, who passed away suddenly in 2005 at the age of seventy-seven. As it turned out, Jack was from Lethbridge as well, and had known my uncle from the city's Buddhist Church. My Uncle Jiro, "Jerry" to his non-Japanese friends, had helped the blind to read, bowled every Sunday, and kept a meticulous journal of the prices he'd paid for groceries and the sorry state of his golf game. He'd been a bachelor, mateless and childless, like several others on my dad's side.

22   Those few of us in my family who now have kids have Caucasian spouses, so our strain is becoming less and less Asian. The Miyagawa name may disappear here with my two sons, and with the name would go a story seeded a hundred years ago.

23   My grandmother and grandfather farmed berries on three hectares of rocky slope in Mission, BC, starting in the 1920s. They were their own slave-drivers, labouring non-stop to clear the land and get the farm going. Grandmother produced the workforce, delivering a baby a year for a decade. My dad was near the end, the ninth child of ten. By 1941, the Japanese controlled the berry industry in BC. My grandparents' farm expanded and flourished.

24   Then came Pearl Harbor, war with Japan, and the dislocation of more than 20,000 Japanese Canadians from the West Coast. On a spring day in 1942, my dad and his family carried two bags each to the station and boarded a train bound for the sugar beet fields of southern Alberta. They never made it back to Mission. The Japanese Canadians weren't allowed to return to BC until four years after the war was over, so the family instead settled in Lethbridge. Dad moved away soon after he came of age, and ended up in Edmonton, where I was born.

25   For my dad, the apology was pointless. Like many others in the Japanese Canadian community, he had already turned the other cheek. *Shikata ga nai*, the saying goes—what's done is done.

26   I admire and marvel at his ability to let go of the past. He even calls his family's forced move across the Rockies a "great adventure." For a ten-year-old, it was a thrill to see the black smoke pouring from the train engine's stack as it approached the Mission station.

27   Mist softens a train platform in the Fraser Valley. Last night's rain drips from the eaves of the station, clinging to the long tips of cedar needles. All over the platform, families are huddled together by ramshackle pyramids of suitcases. Children squat around a puddle on the tracks, poking at a struggling beetle with a stick. A distant whistle; their mother yells at them in Japanese; they run back to stand beside her. Their father stands apart, lost in thought. He's trying to commit to memory the place where he'd buried his family's dishes the night before, in one of his berry fields a few kilometres away.

28   Clickety-clack. Clickety-clack. A screech of brakes, a sizzle of steam. The train pulls in, the doors open, each one sentinelled by a Mountie with arms crossed.

29   The families become mist, along with their suitcases and the Mounties. Everything disappears except the train. It's quiet. An old conductor in a blue cap sticks his head out the window. No need for tickets on this train, he says. Step right up. Welcome aboard the Apology Express.

30   The conference began, and Jack and I leaned forward to hear. The panellists took their turns bending into low mikes, paying homage to the hallowed ground zero of apologies. Chief Robert Joseph, a great bear of a man in a red fleece vest, hugged the podium and said, "The Japanese Canadian apology was a beacon." Everyone at the tables looked tiny, posed between the high black skirting framing the stage and the minuscule disco ball that hung above them.

31   The people telling the stories of their communities were the same ones who had put on their best shoes to walk the marbled floors of Parliament, who had filed briefs for lawsuits. They spoke in the abstract— reconciliation, compensation, acknowledgement— and kept up official outrage as they demanded recognition for their causes. "We have to remember,

so it will never happen again" was the panel's common refrain. After an hour, Jack's eyes were closed, and he'd started to lean my way. I could hear soft snoring from the other side of the room, where a group of seniors slumped and tilted in their chairs.

32   This wasn't what I'd come to hear either. After studying and listening to official expressions of remorse to my family and others, after reading the best books on the subject (*The Age of Apology*; *I Was Wrong*; *On Apology*; *Mea Culpa*), I'd come to believe that government apologies were more about forgetting than remembering.

33   I righted Jack as best I could, and snuck out the back of the hall for some fresh air.

34   I've always imagined that my mom met Harvey Kwan in a room full of light bulbs. They both worked for the Energy Efficiency Branch of the provincial government. She wrote copy for newsletters; he did tech support. In my mind, Mom would watch the way Harvey methodically screwed the bulbs into the bare testing socket. She appreciated his size. Not quite five feet tall, my mom likes her husbands compact (though she did dally for a time with a rather tall embezzler from Texas). She was further attracted to Harvey's quiet voice, his shy smile as he explained wattages and life cycles. Perhaps they reached for the same compact fluorescent and felt a jolt as their fingers touched.

35   Mom and "Uncle Harv" were both laid off soon after they started dating, so they moved from Edmonton to Calgary, closer to their beloved Rockies, and became true weekend warriors, driving past the indifferent elk on Highway 1 to Canmore and Banff to hike and camp and ski. Mom was afraid of heights; Harv took her hand and led her to the mountaintops.

36   Harvey's father had sailed to Canada aboard the *Empress of Russia* in 1919, at the age of fourteen. He paid the $500 head tax, then rode the CPR with his father to the railroad town of Medicine Hat, on the hot, dry Alberta prairie. Around the time he became an adult, in 1923, the Canadian government passed a *Chinese Immigration Act*, which remained in force for twenty-five years. Under the act, no new Chinese immigrants could come to Canada, so a young bachelor like him could only have a long-distance family. He managed to sire three sons with his first wife in China during that time, but she never made it to Canada, dying overseas. He eventually took a second wife, Harvey's mom, who had to wait several years

before she could enter the country. In the meantime, she lived unhappily with Harvey's father's mother, probably waiting on her like a servant.

37   And that's all Harvey knows. He doesn't know about his father's life, those twenty-five years away from his first wife and their children, then his second. He doesn't know his grandfather's name. He doesn't know what his grandfather did. He doesn't know where the man is buried. They never spoke of that time.

> Mr. Speaker, on behalf of all Canadians and the Government of Canada, we offer a full apology to Chinese Canadians for the head tax and express our deepest sorrow for the subsequent exclusion of Chinese immigrants . . . No country is perfect. Like all countries, Canada has made mistakes in its past, and we realize that. Canadians, however, are a good and just people, acting when we've committed wrong. And even though the head tax—a product of a profoundly different time—lies far in our past, we feel compelled to right this historic wrong for the simple reason that it is the decent thing to do, a characteristic to be found at the core of the Canadian soul.

> —*Stephen Harper, June 22, 2006*

38   Apology comes from the Greek *apo* and *logos* ("from speech"), and as every first-year philosophy student who reads Plato's *Apology* knows, it originally meant a defence of one's position. But somewhere along the line, it became a Janus word, adopting its opposite meaning as well. Rather than a justification of one's position or actions, it became an admission of harm done, an acceptance of responsibility. When Harper spoke on the head tax, you could see both faces of the word at work: *Those were different times. We're not like that now. We should, in fact, be proud of ourselves. Pat ourselves on the back. Reaffirm our goodness today by sacrificing the dead and gone.*

39   Rather than bringing the past to life, statements like these seem to break our link with history, separating us from who we were and promoting the notion of our moral advancement. They also whitewash the ways in which Canadians still benefit from that past, stripping the apologies of remorse. Rendering them meaningless. Forgettable.

40   I wasn't the only one taking a break from the conference. I followed a Japanese Canadian woman

with short grey hair down the street to Oppenheimer Park, watching from a distance as she placed her hand, gently, on the trunk of one of the old cherry trees. I later learned that these were memorial trees, planted by Japanese Canadians thirty years ago. The City of Vancouver had been planning to chop them down as part of a recent redevelopment scheme, but the Japanese Canadian community rallied and saved them (though the old baseball diamond will still be plowed under).

41   I arrived back at the hall in time for lunch. Ahead of me in line was the author and scholar Roy Miki, one of the leading figures in the movement for Japanese Canadian redress and a member of the negotiating committee for the National Association of Japanese Canadians. Miki was an "internment baby," born in Manitoba in 1942, six months after his family was uprooted from their home in Haney, BC. He laughed when I told him about my family and, intrigued, pulled up a chair beside me for lunch. He had neat white hair, parted to one side, and wore blue-tinted glasses. We balanced bento boxes on our knees, and he told me something that astounded me: the negotiators hadn't wanted an apology very badly.

42   "We wanted to shine a light on the system—to show its inherent flaws," he said. "Our main concern wasn't the apology or the compensation. The real victim was democracy itself, not the people." What those pushing for redress wanted was an acknowledgement that democracy had broken down, and that people had benefited from the internment of Japanese Canadians. They wanted to change the system in order to protect people in the future.

43   Miki remained wary of government expressions of remorse, concerned that the emotional content of apologies—the focus on "healing"—distracted from the more important issue of justice. "Now the apology has become the central thing," he said. "It allows the government to be seen as the good guy. But there's a power relationship in apologies that has to be questioned; the apologizer has more power than the apologized-to."

44   Mulroney, in his apology to Japanese Canadians, said the aim was "to put things right with the surviving members—with their children and ours, so that they can walk together in this country, burdened neither by the wrongs nor the grievances of previous generations." Both the victimizer and the victim are freed from their bonds. Japanese Canadian internment "went against the very nature of our country." With the apology, so the redemption narrative went, Mulroney was returning Canada to its natural, perfect state. Cue music. Roll credits. The lights come up, and all is right with the world again. I find the storyline hard to resist, especially when the main characters are long gone. But of course not all of these dramas took place once upon a time.

45   My dad met his second wife, Etheline Victoria Blind, at a south Edmonton bingo. Yes, he found a native bride at a bingo, in front of a glass concession case where deep-fried pieces of bannock known as "kill-me-quicks" glistened under neon light.

46   I was working for an environmental organization at the time. Like most Alberta non-profits, we depended on bingos and casinos as fundraisers. Dad was one of our A-list volunteers. He was retired, reliable, and always cheerful, if a bit hard of hearing. Etheline, on the other hand, was on the long-shot volunteer list. She was the mother of the high school friend of a colleague. I didn't know her, but I called her one night in desperation.

47   I don't remember seeing any sparks fly between Dad and Etheline. He was sixty-five at the time, and not seeking to kick at the embers of his love life. But Etheline invited him to play Scrabble with her, and so it began.

48   Dad and Etheline had a cantankerous sort of affair, from my point of view. They lived separately for many years—Dad in a condo on Rainbow Valley Road, Etheline in an aging split-level five minutes away—but moved gradually toward each other, in location and spirit, finally marrying a few days after Valentine's Day, eight years after they met. I flew down from Whitehorse with my son, just a year old then. He was the only person at the wedding wearing a suit, a one-piece suede tuxedo.

49   And so Etheline became my Indian stepmother.

50   Stephen Harper's apology to residential school survivors was a powerful political moment. You had to be moved by the sight of the oldest and youngest survivors, side by side on the floor of Parliament—one a 104-year-old woman, the other barely in her twenties. The speeches were superb, the optics perfect. Yet personally, I felt tricked. Tricked because the apology

distilled the entire complicated history of assimilation into a single policy, collapsing it like a black hole into a two-word "problem": residential schools. Here was the forgetful apology at its best. By saying sorry for the schools, we could forget about all the other ways the system had deprived—and continued to deprive—aboriginal people of their lives and land. The government had created the problem, sure, but had owned up to it, too, and was on its way to getting it under control, starting with the survivors' prescription for recovery. If they were abused, they merely had to itemize their pain in a thirty-page document, tally their compensation points, stand before an adjudicator to speak of their rape and loneliness, and receive their official payment. All taken care of.

51   And yet. And yet.

52   Etheline, I apologize. I knew you for ten years and never really knew where you came from. I'm educated, post-colonial, postmodern, mixed race, well travelled, curious, vaguely liberal, politically correct. "You're the most Canadian person I know," I've been told. And yet I never once asked you about your time in residential school. I never really related until that night, after we'd watched Harper's shining moment, that powerful ceremony—and I'd watched how it moved you, felt the hair on my arms rise and a shiver in my back when we talked late and you told me how your grandfather was taken from his family when he was four, the same age my oldest son is now; told me how he'd never known his parents, but relearned Cree ways from his adopted family and became a strong Cree man even after his own children were taken away; how he'd raised you when your mother couldn't; how you were in the mission school, too, for four years, and your grandfather wouldn't let them cut your braids, and you'd feel the cold brick walls with your hands, and the laundry ladies would only call you by your number, and you would stare out the window toward the dirt road that led away from the school and cry for your *Kokum* and *Meshom*. I never knew. Or if you told me, I only listened with half an ear. And I apologize again, for bringing it all up, for writing down your private pain. But I know we need to tell it again and again. It has to be there; it has to get into people's hearts.

53   And here I make an apology for the government apology. For whatever I feel about them, about how

they can bury wrongs in the past instead of making sure the past is never forgotten, about how they can use emotion to evade responsibility, they have indeed changed my life. They've made me rethink what it means to be a citizen of this country. They've brought me closer to my family.

54   Near the end of the conference, the woman with short grey hair stood up and told a story. After World War II, when she was a schoolgirl, she'd one day refused to read out loud from a textbook with the word "Jap" in it. She was sent home, where she proudly told her father what she'd done. He slapped her across the face. The apology, she told everyone at the hall, had restored her dignity. The conference ended the next day, and I returned home with something to think about.

55   It's summer as I write, almost a year since the conference, and the apologies have kept coming. The state of California apologized for the persecution of Chinese immigrants last week. Thousands of former students of Indian day schools, feeling left out of the residential school apology, filed a statement of claim at the Manitoba legislature yesterday.

56   I'm sitting on the beach of Long Lake, just outside Whitehorse. Though it's hot outside, the water here always stays cold, because the summer's not long enough to heat it. Still, my two boys are hardy Yukoners, and they're running in and out of the water, up to their necks. I watch their little bodies twist and turn, then look at my own thirty-eight-year-old paunch and search the sky. What will we be apologizing for when my children are adults? Temporary foreign workers? The child welfare system?

57   Tomio bumps into Sam, knocking him to the ground. Sam cries. "Tomio," I tell my oldest, "say sorry to your brother." "Why?" he asks. "I didn't mean to do it."

58   "Say sorry anyway," I reply.

59   We say sorry when we are responsible and when we are not. We say sorry when we were present or when we were far away. We are ambiguous about what apologies mean in the smallest personal interactions. How can we expect our political apologies to be any less complicated?

60   A long time ago—or not so long ago, really, but within our nation's lifetime—another train hustled along these tracks: the Colonial Experiment. She was a beaut, shiny and tall. Ran all the way from Upper Canada; ended here in this lush Pacific rainforest. The Colonial Experiment was strictly one way, so it's up to the Apology Express to make the return trip.

61   Watch as we go by: a Doukhobor girl peeks out from under her house, her head scarf muddy. The police officers who took her sister and her friends away to the school in New Denver are gone and won't be back for another week. A Cree boy, hair freshly shorn into a brush cut, stares out the window of a residential school in the middle of the Saskatchewan grasslands, watching his parents' backs as they walk away. A Japanese fisherman hands over the keys to his new boat. A Ukrainian woman swats the mosquitoes away,

bends to pick potatoes at Spirit Lake, and feels her baby dying inside her. A Chinese man living under a bridge thinks about his wife at home and wonders if he'll see her again.

62   But take heart: at every stop on the way back, someone important will say sorry for their lot. Just like the man in the top hat on my son's train engine TV show, he'll make it all better, no matter how much of a mess there's been.

63   All aboard. If you feel a little sick, it's just the motion of the cars. Close your eyes. Try not to forget.

Speaking My Truth, Vol. 3, *Cultivating Canada.*
2012.

Key and challenging words

redress, Janus word, grievance, cantankerous

Questions

1. How much of the essay would you consider the introduction? Explain.
2. Comment on Miyagawa's use of personal experience in his essay, referring specifically to at least one example from the introduction and at least one from another part of the essay.
3. Why does Miyagawa use an example from fiction (paragraph 14)? How does it help support his point?
4. Find one example each of a passage that uses narration, description, and analysis. Briefly explain how the use of each contributes to the essay as a whole.

5. Why does the author consider himself an authority on apologies? How does he show his expertise? Find an example of another authority and discuss how he or she is used to develop a point.
6. Identify two passages in which Miyagawa uses a specific or distinct tone (the tone should not be the same in both). How do the different tones affect the reader? How do they help develop the part of the essay in which they occur?
7. After reading the essay, analyze Miyagawa's attitude toward apologies. Use specific textual references in your analysis.

Post-reading

1. Find two individual reactions from members of the same racial/cultural group to whom the Canadian government has apologized. Using summary and analysis, compare and contrast their reactions.
2. The federal and provincial governments have made several apologies for racist behaviours in the past.

Choose one example of a government apology other than that made by the government to Aboriginal peoples in 2008. In one paragraph, summarize the issue(s) that occasioned the apology; in another paragraph, summarize the responses of those to whom the apology was made.

Related websites of interest

Miyagawa, Mitch. "A Sorry State." Online Video Clip. YouTube. YouTube, 2013. 15 Oct. 2014:
<http://tvo.org/video/184814/sorry-state>.

Rogers, Shelagh. Foreword. Speaking My Truth. Aboriginal Healing Foundation Research Publications. 2012. Web. 15 Oct. 2014:
<http://speakingmytruth.ca/v2a/?page_id=177>.

Truth and Reconciliation Commission of Canada:
www.trc.ca/websites/trcinstitution/index.php?p=3

Additional library reading

Bombay, Amy, Kimberly Matheson, and Hymie Anisman. "Expectations among Aboriginal Peoples in Canada Regarding the Potential Impacts of a Government Apology." *Political Psychology* 34.3 (2013): 443–60.

Jacobs, Beverley. "Response to Canada's Apology to Residential School Survivors." *Canadian Woman Studies* 26.3/4 (2008): 223–25.

The Senate and the fight against the 1885 Chinese Immigration Act

Christopher G. Anderson
(4,254 words)

Pre-reading

1. Anderson's essay is occasioned by the apology of Prime Minister Stephen Harper to Chinese Canadians for the Head Tax of 1885 and other discriminatory policies of the late nineteenth- and early twentieth centuries in Canada. a) Using a reliable source, such as an encyclopedia or recent government document, research the history of Chinese immigration to Canada from 1885 to 1923, including the laws enacted to limit or exclude Chinese immigration; b) Using a reliable dictionary, find a definition for "racism" or "racial discrimination."

1   On June 22, 2006, the Prime Minister rose in the House of Commons to "offer a full apology to Chinese Canadians for the head tax and express our deepest sorrow for the subsequent exclusion of Chinese immigrants." After recalling the fundamental role that Chinese Canadians had played in the nation-building construction of the Canadian Pacific Railway (CPR), the Prime Minister observed how—once the line was completed—"Canada turned its back on these men" as it imposed a $50 Head Tax on Chinese migrants in 1885, increased this to $100 in 1900 and then to $500 in 1905, and finally expanded the scope of its exclusionary measures in 1923 to make it all but impossible for Chinese immigrants to resettle legally in Canada through into the post–Second World War period. Although

the various race-based measures instituted to exclude Chinese migrants were deemed to be legal at the time, they were, according to the Prime Minister, "inconsistent with the values that Canadians hold today." This article argues that at the time of the 1885 legislation, and for some time after, there were voices that spoke out against these discriminatory policies. Most specifically, this sentiment dominated debates on the question in the Canadian Senate between 1885 and 1887, and it did so to such an extent that government supporters had to resort to some clever procedural maneuvers to see the law passed and amended against the will of the majority of Senators. In an important sense, then, these restrictive measures are not only "inconsistent with the values that Canadians hold today," but also conflict with values held by Canadians in the late nineteenth century, values that can be traced to a set of liberal beliefs on the rights of non-citizens inherited from Britain. The debates that took place in the Senate are, therefore, both interesting and important because they provide greater depth to our understanding of the historical record of race relations in Canada. They also speak to the more general issue of the role of the Senate in Canadian politics.

2   Although Chinese migrants had lived in Canada since as early as 1858, it was not really until the 1880s that their numbers began to rise appreciably. Thus, while 4,383 were identified in the 1881 Canadian census, the population is then thought to have grown to around 10,550 by September 1884 as the construction of the Canadian Pacific Railway picked up steam. More generally, some 16,000 to 17,000 Chinese migrants probably came to Canada during the early 1880s to work on the rail line.[1] For economic and geographic reasons, Chinese migrants generally arrived and lived in British Columbia, and it is from there that the most persistent and vocal cries were heard for greater control from the late nineteenth century onward.

3   At first, the reception of the Chinese was relatively cordial: "Colonial British Columbians were initially remarkably tolerant of the thousands of Chinese who came. British officials refused to countenance any discrimination, and whites, rather than pressing for hostile action, boasted of the British justice enjoyed by the Chinese."[2] Although there were certainly incidents of racism, including violence, against the Chinese, British liberalism formed the basis of the government's response to their presence in the colony. While Britain itself had had very limited experience with receiving Chinese migrants, the country's official position on the presence of non-citizens was primarily defined at this time by a recognition of the right of foreigners to enter and remain, which precluded any wholesale restriction.[3] However, after British Columbia joined Confederation in 1871, local politicians (first at the provincial level and then at the federal level) began to pressure Ottawa to pass legislation to restrict the ability of the Chinese to immigrate to or—for those who had already arrived—find work in Canada.[4]

4   The first major effort in the House of Commons was undertaken by Arthur Bunster (Vancouver Island), who sought and failed to convince his fellow MPs in 1878 to make it illegal to hire people to work on the construction of the CPR if their hair was greater than 5.5 inches in length—an obvious attack on the Chinese, whose hair was generally worn in long queues.[5] In words that recalled those famously used by Lord Palmerston some 20 years earlier in the defence of the rights of foreigners in Britain,[6] Prime Minister Alexander Mackenzie stated that the motion "was one unprecedented in its character and altogether unprecedented in its spirit, and at variance with those tolerant laws which afforded employment and an asylum to all who came within our country, irrespective of colour, hair, or anything else."[7] Mackenzie did not "think it would become us, as a British community, to legislate against any class of people who might be imported into, or might emigrate to, this country."[8]

5   Although calls for "repressive measures" against the Chinese—including their forced removal from the country—were made time and again in Parliament through into the 1880s, Prime Minister John A. Macdonald, while he personally opposed such immigration, appointed two separate commissions of inquiry to investigate the situation in 1879 and 1884. Once the CPR was completed, however, the government introduced changes in May 1885 to the proposed *Electoral Franchise Act* before Parliament to deny any person of Chinese origin the right to vote in federal elections.

6   John A. Macdonald justified this action on the grounds that the Chinese migrant "is a stranger, a sojourner in a strange land . . . [H]e has no common interest with us . . . [H]e has no British instincts or British feelings or aspirations, and therefore ought not to have a vote."[9] Moreover, if given the vote, he warned,

the Chinese would likely elect a sufficient number of Chinese-origin MPs in British Columbia to force the rest of the country to adhere to their "eccentricities" and "immorality."[10] The Prime Minister's move received strong support from a number of MPs (especially those from British Columbia), but it also sparked some vocal opposition. For example, L.H. Davies (Queen's) argued that "If a Chinaman becomes a British subject it is not right that a brand should be placed on his forehead, so that other men may avoid him."[11] For his part, Arthur H. Gillmor (Charlotte), while he did "not think they are a desirable class of persons," argued all the same that "as British subjects, we ought to show them fair play."[12] Despite such protests, however, the motion was carried. For reasons that are not clear, such voices became mute when the House turned to consider the government's legislation to restrict Chinese immigration two months later.

7   It was left to Secretary of State Joseph A. Chapleau to explain Bill 125 (later renumbered Bill 156) "to restrict and regulate Chinese Immigration into the Dominion of Canada" to the House, and he did so with such an expression of regret as to lead one MP to comment that "one would almost imagine [that he] were in opposition to the Bill rather than in favour of it."[13] Chapleau began by declaring that he had been surprised when

> a demand was made for legislation to provide that one of the first principles which have always guided the English people in the enactment of their laws and regulations for the maintenance of the peace and prosperity of the country, should be violated in excluding from the shores of this great country, which is a part of the British Empire, members of the human family.[14]

8   Although he agreed that it was a good thing to ensure the continuance of a "white" British Columbia, he took issue with the way in which the Chinese had been demonized. As co-chair of the 1884 commission, he had found little evidence to support the uniformly negative image put forward by those who wanted to prevent their arrival; moreover, he had concluded that such migration had had a generally positive impact on the regional economy. Chapleau had come to see, however, that when it came to the Chinese people Canadians were "naturally disposed, through inconscient prejudices, to turn into defects even their virtues."[15]

9   The law would not only impose a $50 "Head Tax" (or "Capitation Tax") on Chinese migrants before they could be landed, but would also put in place several other restrictions. For example, only one Chinese passenger was to be allowed per each 50 tons weight of the arriving vessel (s.5), and a system of certificates was to be put in place to control those who desired to leave and return without paying the Head Tax again (s.14). Those most in favour of restriction were not wholly satisfied by these proposals but saw in them "the thin end of the edge" in the creation of a more extensive system of control.[16] Indeed, amidst concerns over the administration of the legislation, the only opposition came from those who wanted to make it more restrictive, although these critics supported Bill 156 all the same as it passed easily through the House.

10   Subsequently, amendments were introduced to the *1885 Chinese Immigration Act* during the next two years. In 1886, the government sought to enforce compulsory registration of those already in Canada (with penalties for non-compliance), expand the scope of the law to cover trains as well as ships, and remove merchants from the list of those exempt from paying the Head Tax. Although the bill was passed in the Lower Chamber with little dissent, it was ultimately held up in the Senate by the opponents of restriction. In 1887, the government introduced new amendments that were notable for the absence of any further restrictions, save a change to allow the Chinese only three months leave from the country before having to repay the Head Tax.[17] Even these proposals, however, barely made it through the Upper Chamber, and that lone restrictive feature was ultimately removed.

11   There was an intimation of the level of support that the Chinese might receive in the Senate during its debate on the 1885 *Electoral Franchise Act*. "I cannot myself see the propriety," Alexander Vidal commented, "of excluding the Mongolians, who have shown themselves to be patient, industrious and law-abiding, from privileges which are given to every other member of the human family in this country."[18] For his part, Lawrence G. Power did not think "the Parliament of Canada should make any distinction of race at all; that the Chinese, Negroes, Indians and Whites should be on the same footing; that no exceptions should

be made in favour of one or against another race."[19] Striking a position that would be repeated by a number of his colleagues when Bill 156 arrived not long thereafter, Richard W. Scott observed that having sought to open up China to the world, Canada should not "set up a Chinese wall on our side," for to do so would be "entirely contrary to the principles of the Empire."[20] Despite such objections, however, the franchise legislation was passed. The protests that were made over denying the Chinese the right to vote paled, however, in comparison to the outrage expressed by the many Senators who spoke against the restriction of Chinese migration.

The Senate in Defence of the Chinese (1885–87)

12   Early on in the debate, Alexander Vidal set the tone for the majority in the Senate when he declared: "I think it is entirely inconsistent with the very fundamental principle of the British constitution that legislation of this kind should find a place on the statute book."[21] To pursue such a course as that proposed in Bill 156, observed James Dever, would tarnish the reputation of the country:

> We, who pride ourselves on the freedom of our institutions, and the abolition of slavery in the United States, and who fancy we are going over the world with our lamp in our hand shedding light and lustre wherever we go—that we should become slave-drivers, and prohibit strangers from coming to our hospitable shore because they are of a different colour and have a different language and habits from ourselves, in deference to the feelings of a few people from British Columbia, is a thing I cannot understand.[22]

13   To the extent to which the law would discriminate against a particular group, concluded William Almon, it remained "contrary to the genius of the nineteenth century."[23] Moreover, it was suggested that if the Chinese did not seem to adapt well to Canadian society, then this was in part the fault of Canadians themselves when they instituted such barriers as disenfranchisement and the prevention of family reunification. Indeed, it was observed that the Chinese became further excluded from European Canadian society by the stereotypes that the latter employed.

14   Although the opponents of restriction were unable to prevent the passage of the bill, the way in which it was returned to the House is worth noting, for it was only on account of some fancy procedural footwork on the part of the government side that it happened with so little disturbance. William Almon had "given notice that [he] would oppose it at the third reading, and that [he] would move that it be read the third time three months hence"—thereby making it impossible for the legislation to pass that session.[24] The Senator, however, apparently committed a procedural error that allowed the legislation to emerge from the committee stage unscathed and pass through Third Reading without any discussion. Not only did Almon not give notice in writing, but he also wrongly assumed that debate could not pass through two stages on the same day. As a result, his efforts to scuttle the bill were sidestepped and it was returned to the House of Commons without a word altered, despite the considerable opposition to the very principles on which it was based that had been expressed. Almon's frustration comes through quite clearly, as does his firm conviction that it was a fundamentally illiberal piece of legislation:

> I think such legislation is a disgrace to humanity. I think it is rolling back civilization from the end to the beginning of the nineteenth century. The early part of this century did away with the Slave trade, with the *Test Act,* and gave Catholic emancipation and abolished slavery in the West Indies. We now enact a law which is as vile as any of those to the repeal of which I have just alluded, and I think it will impress an indelible disgrace on this House and on the Dominion.[25]

15   The chances that Almon's effort might otherwise have succeeded would seem to be slim—after all, it was fairly rare for a government bill to be turned back in the Senate, especially when the same party controlled both chambers—but the fate of the government's attempt to amend the 1885 *Chinese Immigration Act* by passing Bill 106 the following year makes it difficult to claim that there were none. As noted above, the proposed amendments in 1886 were mostly restrictionist in nature, but rather than simply

debate these measures, opponents attacked the law itself. While much of the criticism trod upon familiar ground (e.g., "It is so repugnant to all that is English, and honourable or right that one can hardly discuss it in a proper frame of mind"),[26] there were important developments as well.

16　For example, Alexander Vidal raised the question of Canadian sovereignty and the country's right to restrict entry at its borders, and he suggested that this should not be held to be absolute but rather ought to conform to the principles on which the land had come to be settled. He began by inquiring as to the foundations of Britain's occupation of North America:

> By what royal right have we and our fathers crossed the ocean and taken possession of this western continent? What right had we to come here and dispossess the Indians, native proprietors of this country, and take possession of their lands? . . . [Do we] not only consider that we have a better right to it than they have, but to consider it so exclusively our own as to shut out from sharing in the advantages of this country others of God's people who have as much right to it as we have?[27]

17　The land was taken not by right, he claimed, but "because we believed that where our civilization and enlightenment have been introduced we have carried with us the blessings of Christianity to the people amongst whom we have settled."[28] To restrict other people now from coming to live in the country on the basis of race, he concluded, was so "utterly inconsistent with our professions as Christians and with the vaunted freedom we profess to cherish as a British people" that it undermined the basis on which the land had been occupied—the superiority of "the Anglo-Saxon race."[29] Thus, while Senators often still viewed the issue from a race-based and even missionary perspective, they also operated within a rights-based framework, with potentially quite important policy implications for Chinese Canadians.

18　Even George W. Allan, who introduced the amendments in the Senate for the government, said that he had "no special leaning towards this Chinese legislation."[30] Given the level of agreement against the proposals, it would be, Richard W. Scott averred, "a service to the empire if we allow this question to stand over another year."[31] By that time, he hoped, passions

in British Columbia might have calmed somewhat and a more reasonable examination of the question might be assayed. Thus, the same Senate that had seemed to sanction the 1885 *Chinese Immigration Act* now let the debate on its amendment stand for six months, thereby signaling an unwillingness to allow the law to be changed in a more restrictive manner.

19　The government's second attempt to amend the law, Bill 54, responded to some of the criticisms that had been expressed in the Senate by removing the restrictive elements included in the previous bill. Moreover, the one aspect of the new bill that would have made it more difficult for Chinese migrants—the three-month return clause—was first extended to six months and then dropped altogether. Nonetheless, the legislation received extended criticism ("a diabolical Bill . . . [that] has not a shadow of justice or right on its side"),[32] out of which emerged—amidst the old complaints—other lines of argumentation. For example, Almon asked: "How will it be now if we pass [this] Act to say that there is a dividing line between Canada and the United States? . . . Can we any longer point with pride to our flag and say that under that emblem all men, be they Mongolian, Circassian or Caucasian, are equally free?"[33]

20　The Senator who sponsored the bill on the government's behalf, future Prime Minister John J.C. Abbott, agreed that the principle that lay behind the 1885 *Chinese Immigration Act* was offensive to the chamber, but he argued all the same that the amendments on the floor might help to temper the harshness of the law. If too many alterations to the proposed bill were presented to the House, he cautioned, then it would reject them, with the result that the modest positive alterations that could be made would not come into effect, leaving the Chinese worse off than they might otherwise have been. This line of reasoning found some sympathy but little support, as "the sentiment of the Senate seemed to be that the Act should be wiped off the Statute Book."[34] Indeed, Vidal introduced Bill P to do just that, and he had such backing that Abbott himself admitted that it would likely pass on a vote. The justification for repeal was succinctly expressed by Robert Haythorne, who declared that "it is a difficult thing to amend a Bill based upon a wrong principle, and the principle upon which [the 1885 *Chinese Immigration Act* is] based is a bad and cruel one."[35] Even if the House would not accept it, Vidal argued, passage of Bill P would "show that we have proper views of British freedom and the responsibilities that are attached to our professions as Christians."[36]

21   The government side, however, was once again able—through procedural means—to steer its legislation through the chamber. It argued successfully before the Speaker that since the law involved the collection of revenue—the Head Tax—the Senate could not seek to repeal it. The Speaker based his ruling on s.53 of the 1867 *BNA Act* ("Bills for appropriating any Part of the Public Revenue, or for imposing any Tax or Impost, shall originate in the House of Commons") and on the 47th Rule of the Senate according to *Bourinot* ("The Senate will not proceed upon a Bill appropriating public money that shall not within the knowledge of the Senate have been recommended by the Queen's representative"). The question of the Senate's authority to amend money bills would long trouble Parliament and was eventually the subject of a Special Committee of the Senate in 1917. In response to this decision, Vidal argued: "I can easily understand that if we found the word 'Chinese' between cheese and cigars in the tariff bill that we could not touch it, but it is an extraordinary thing that we cannot amend a public Bill simply because there is a penalty attached for which the Government derives a revenue."[37] Although the purpose behind the Head Tax was clearly one of policy (that is, to restrict the entry of Chinese migrants) rather than one of generating revenue, the Speaker supported the government's line of reasoning. Thus, not only was Vidal's initiative ruled out of order but any chance of pursuing meaningful change to the bill seemed to have been thwarted. With the wind so completely and effectively taken out of the opposition's sails, Third Reading was speedily accomplished. It would be some years before the Senate would again exhibit such a rights-based outlook on the issue of migration control, even as the government expanded the scope of its restrictions towards Chinese migration as well as all other non-white, non-Christian, and non-British groups.

22   After coming into effect in January 1886, the 1885 *Chinese Immigration Act* doubtless contributed to the low levels of Chinese migration to Canada that occurred during the remainder of the 1880s. It is difficult, however, to assess the effect of the new law as there was an anticipated reduction in arrivals due to the completion of the CPR, which led many to leave the country, either to return to China or to try their fortunes in the United States. However, throughout the 1890s the number of entries recorded each year grew, if somewhat erratically, sparking a new wave of restrictive measures towards Chinese migration that culminated in the extremely effective 1923 *Chinese Immigration Act*. Indeed, according to official tallies, only eight Chinese immigrants were landed in Canada between 1924–25 and 1938–39—less than one every two years.

Conclusions

23   This examination of the response in the Senate to the government's first attempts to control Chinese immigration between 1885 and 1887 is instructive in at least two major respects. First, it uncovers an important feature of the history of Canadian state relations with Chinese migrants that has too long been overlooked. While it is certainly true that the Chinese had few friends willing to support them in Canada, they could count a large number of Senators amongst them. Thus, Senator William J. Macdonald, himself a representative of British Columbia, took note of the role that many of his colleagues were playing:

> I wish to express my satisfaction at the fact that a people who have been treated so rigorously and ungenerously, who are unrepresented, and who have been hunted to the death, should have found representatives to stand up on the floor of this House and speak on their behalf.[38]

24   Of course, rights-based British liberalism was not the sole motivation for opposition to the 1885 *Chinese Immigration Act*. Indeed, there were traces of distrust of organized labour, alongside a desire that business should have access to such—as one Senator would put it a few years later—"good labour-saving machines."[39] Moreover, an opposition to discrimination did not necessitate admiration for the Chinese either as individuals or as a group (although it often was joined to such sentiments).[40] It also was at times connected to an opinion that "whites" were superior to the Chinese,[41] and for some Senators accepting such migrants in Canada was an important means by which

the Chinese might be converted to Christianity.[42] Nonetheless, there is a clearly expressed respect for the individual rights of the Chinese that comes through in these debates, one that found widespread support amongst the opponents of restriction. Their racism, in short, did not fully displace their belief in equality, and they were able to support, as a result, radically different policy options from those that were being pursued by the government, and that would ultimately be transformed into a source of national shame.

25   As well as recalling an important piece of Canadian history, one that has been completely ignored or overlooked in the literature, the relevance of these Senate debates today can also be seen in the extent to which members of that institution sought to institute a policy position that is much more in keeping with what we understand to be modern values held by Canadians. This not only suggests that Canadians possess a much richer and more complex political history than is often recognized, but it also underlines the potential role for the Senate in broadening our political ideas and language, of providing the sort of sober second thought that was supposed to be one of its central functions in the Canadian political system.

Canadian Parliamentary Review.
2007. Summer 30 (2).

Notes

1. Patricia E. Roy, *A White Man's Province: British Columbia Politicians and Chinese and Japanese Immigrants, 1858–1914* (Vancouver: University of British Columbia Press, 1989), x–xi.

2. *Ibid.*, 4. See also W. Peter Ward, *White Canada Forever: Popular Attitudes and Public Policy Toward Orientals in British Columbia*[Second Edition] (Montreal and Kingston: McGill-Queen's University Press, 1990), 24–29.

3. See Colin Holmes, *John Bull's Island: Immigration and British Society,*1871–1971 (London: Macmillan Education Ltd., 1988).

4. See Bruce Ryder, "Racism and the Constitution: The Constitutional Fate of British Columbia Anti-Asian Immigration Legislation, 1884–1909," *Osgoode Hall Law Journal*, Volume 29, Number 3 (1991), 619–76.

5. 1207. See also James Morton, *In the Sea of Sterile Mountains: The Chinese in British Columbia* (Vancouver: J.J. Douglas Ltd., 1973), 43–44.

6. "Any foreigner, whatever his nation, whatever his political creed, whatever his political offences against his own Government may, under this Bill, as he does today, find in these realms a safe and secure asylum so long as he obeys the law of the land." Quoted in T.W.E. Roche, *The Key In The Lock: A History of Immigration Control in England from 1066 to the Present Day* (London: John Murray, 1969), 58.

7. Canada, House of Commons, *Debates*, March 18, 1878, p. 1209.

8. *Ibid.*

9. *Ibid.*, May 4, 1885, p. 1582.

10. *Ibid.*, p. 1588.

11. *Ibid.*, p. 1583.

12. *Ibid.*, p. 1585.

13. *Ibid.*, Edgar C. Baker (Victoria), July 2, 1885, p. 3013.

14. *Ibid.*, p. 3003.

15. *Ibid.*, p. 3006.

16. *Ibid.*, Noah Shakespeare (Victoria), July 2,1885, p. 3011.

17. The new bill kept a provision to allow Chinese travelers in transit to pass through Canada without paying the Head Tax, while it added a clause to allow the Chinese wife of a white man to enter without paying the Head Tax, and another that would ensure that a portion of the Head Tax was sent to provincial coffers in Victoria.

18. Canada, Senate *Debates*, July 13, 1885, p. 1276.

19. *Ibid.*, p. 1280.

20. *Ibid.*

21. *Ibid.*, p. 1297.

22. *Ibid.*, p. 1298.

23. *Ibid.*, p. 1295.

24. *Ibid.*, July 18, 1885, p. 1411.

25. *Ibid.*

26. *Ibid.*, Richard W. Scott, January 30,1886, p. 692.

27. *Ibid.*, May 21, 1886, p. 687.

28. *Ibid.*

29. *Ibid.*

30. *Ibid.*

31. *Ibid.*, May 26, 1886, p. 747.

32. *Ibid.*, William J. Macdonald, June 10, 1887, pp. 311–12.

33. *Ibid.*, p. 299.

34. *Ibid.*, Richard W. Scott, June 13, 1887, p. 349.

35. *Ibid.*, June 10, 1887, p. 313.

36. *Ibid.*, p. 307.

37. *Ibid.*, June 14, 1887, p. 396.

38. *Ibid.*, June 10, 1887, p. 311.

39. *Ibid.*, Henry A.N. Kaulbach, July 8, 1892, p. 497.
40. See W. Peter Ward, *White Canada Forever: Popular Attitudes and Public Policy Toward Orientals in British Columbia* [Second Edition] (Montreal and Kingston: McGill-Queen's University Press, 1990), Chapter 1.
41. According to Vidal, for example, the "superior civilization" of the "Anglo-Saxon race" meant that whites should have no fear of being overpowered by the Chinese; see Canada, Senate, *Debates*, July 13, 1885, p. 1297.
42. See *ibid.*, William Almon, p. 1296.

Key and challenging words

exclusionary, cordial, demonize, intimation, propriety, disenfranchisement, illiberal, indelible, restrictionist, aver, succinctly, appropriate, culminate

Questions

1. Identify in Anderson's introduction the justification for his essay and his thesis; paraphrase the thesis.
2. Construct a timeline for the most significant events referred to in the essay from 1878 to 1887.
3. a) Identify a primary source used in the first three paragraphs of the essay; b) Select a primary source that is set up in the block format and show its importance to the passage in which it occurs and the essay as a whole.
4. Briefly discuss the function of paragraph 11, which focuses on a time before Bill 125 (156) was introduced.

5. Explain in your own words the basis of the government manoeuvre that prevented Bill 54 from being repealed. How was faulty reasoning involved?
6. Explain how the views expressed by the senators who opposed the Head Tax exemplified a "rights-based" outlook (paragraphs 17 and 21) that characterized British thought in the nineteenth century.
7. According to the author in his conclusion, what can be learned from the debate in the Senate from 1885–7?

Post-reading

1. *Collaborative or individual activity:* After coming up with a working definition of "racism" or "racial discrimination," consider whether the views expressed by the senators who opposed the Chinese Head Tax were, in fact, racist or discriminatory. Defend your point of view, making specific references to the senators' speeches.

2. Essays in the humanities often put forward a new interpretation of primary source material, arguing that the new interpretation is more valid than older interpretations or represents a significant perspective that is worthy of consideration. In 500 words, analyze the effectiveness of Anderson's argument; what made it convincing or not?

Related websites of interest

Address by the Prime Minister on the Chinese Head Tax Redress, 22 June 2006:
http://pm.gc.ca/eng/media.asp?id=1220

CBC Archives:
http://archives.cbc.ca/society/immigration/topics/1433/

Citizenship and Immigration Canada: Chinese Head Tax Redress:
www.cic.gc.ca/english/multiculturalism/programs/redress.asp

Developing better political leaders: The case for a school of government

Paul G. Thomas
(2,013 words)

Pre-reading

1.   What are your expectations of politicians today? Do you believe that the nature of the political process or the qualities of politicians need to change? How could this be done? Reflect on these and other relevant questions in one or two paragraphs.

1   Opinion surveys tell us that among occupations, politicians are ranked last in terms of trustworthiness. The same surveys also reveal low levels of public confidence in the capacity of governments to deal effectively with such major policy challenges as climate change, healthcare reform, poverty, aboriginal issues and law and order.

2   Mistrust of politicians and pessimism about the capabilities of governments are related. Politicians have become both the creators and the captives of an increasingly cynical public. Over the years political parties and their leaders have made election promises which they never intended to adopt or which were too good for the voters to resist and impossible to implement. Along with over promising and under delivering, politicians have shown little regard for the intelligence of voters and their potential to learn about complicated policy issues. Instead of seeking to play an informing and educational role, politicians use polling, focus groups, psycho-demographic analysis of the electorate and sophisticated communications strategies to arouse an apathetic public and to manipulate public opinion to gain voter support.

3   It has been said that politicians campaign in poetry and govern in prose. During elections, simple, emotive stories are used to establish a dominant narrative and to make an emotional connection with voters. Between elections the proceedings of legislatures, especially as covered by the media, resemble a permanent election campaign in which the competing political parties engage in highly adversarial, negative, personal and theatrical attacks. Governments attempt to "spin" stories and to manage the news, while opposition parties interpret every revelation of a problem in a highly suspicious, accusatory light.

Very little informed, balanced discussion of their real issues of governing complex societies takes place and very little learning for the parties or the public (if it is watching) takes place. Slogans, sound bites and feigned indignation certainly ignore the ambiguities, uncertainties and risks of governing in the 21st century.

4   Partisanship, competition and some degree of negativity are appropriate in a pluralistic society where there are legitimate disagreements over both the ends and means of public policy. Competition among parties provides the energy which drives elections and the legislative process. Parties help to shape voter choices at election time, they serve as recruitment agencies to fill public offices, they perform the roles of government and oppositions in our cabinet-parliamentary system of government, and in these ways they provide a basis for achieving responsiveness and accountability to citizens.

5   If politics is essentially about the representation and accommodation of divergent values and interests, the channeling of social conflicts in a constructive manner and the mobilization of public consent and support for new directions within society, then we need better informed and more skillful political leaders. We also need a higher quality and more constructive partisanship from all the political parties which compete for office in this country. Yearning for charismatic, transformational political leaders who by the power of their ideas and their eloquence transcend social divisions and unify large majorities behind a shared vision is an unrealistic basis for the achievement of good government.

6   The novelist Robert Louis Stevenson once observed that "politics is the only occupation for

which no preparation is thought to be necessary." This is wrong. Even in previous centuries when the scope and complexity of government was far less challenging, "amateur" politicians and their parties still found it difficult to diagnose social problems, gain public support for their policy ideas, set agendas within government and translate their ideas into effective programs.

7   Over time politics has become more professionalized, but the emphasis within political parties has been on campaigning and communication to build support, not on the tough tasks of developing sound policy ideas and building skills to lead public organizations. Despite generous public subsidies, political parties have invested little time and effort into policy development. Campaign schools for candidates and short orientation programs for newly elected legislators do not prepare people for the real challenges of public life. Working in legislatures is something like attending a school of politics, but the mindless partisanship and the lack of meaningful opportunities to gain in-depth knowledge, and even more importantly to apply that knowledge in a constructive manner, means that the talents of most elected representatives are not developed or fully utilized.

8   In order to obtain sound policy advice and the managerial skills to implement public programs effectively, governments have created public service schools, executive development programs and exchanges with the private sector. Few such opportunities exist for politicians. When ministers are not well prepared in terms of background knowledge and leadership skills there is the risk that senior public servants will dominate the partnership of shared leadership which we depend upon for creative, quality government.

A School of Government for Politicians

9   The most basic question is whether politics can be taught. I believe that it can. The National School of Government in the United Kingdom and the Graduate School of Political Management in Washington, D.C. have produced graduates who practice politics effectively and with greater ethical awareness because of the opportunity to broaden their perspectives and to gain new skills. Some individuals will have more innate skills as leaders, but everyone can learn how to be a better leader. These schools are not involved in training more spin doctors, pollsters and media manipulators; their goal is to provide elected representatives with a broad education that enables them to cope with rapid change, uncertainty and issues which are divisive and seem to be intractable.

10   The proposed school of government would have a number of broad educational goals. One would be to develop a sense of history, but also to cultivate an awareness of the dangers of simple lesson drawing from the past. Helping politicians to think in systems terms and developing greater capacity to understand complex causal relationships between proposed policy interventions and potential outcomes in society would be another goal. In addition to strategic and integrative thinking skills, graduates would possess greater tolerance for ambiguity and uncertainty. They would become longer term in their thinking, something which election cycles and the problem-specific nature of the parliamentary and media processes discourage. They would accept the need to plan, but also the necessity for improvisation. Awareness of the potential and the limits of various policy instruments available to governments would reduce the frequency of policy failures or disappointments. A great deal of policy-making represents a form of hypotheses testing: through trial and error governments seek to learn what works. As part of this experimental approach, politicians would develop greater skills in risk analysis and the identification of valid evidence and usable knowledge for feasible policy making.

11   Numerous operational issues are involved with creation of the school, only a few of which can be considered in the space available here. The first is who will be admitted to the school. I would propose that the school be open to all "freshmen" legislators from across the country who would take a set of core introductory courses. Another set of courses would be designed for cabinet ministers and "shadow" cabinet ministers in opposition with the goal of easing the transition into leading departments and managing portfolios of non-departmental bodies. Courses should also be developed for political staff who represent a growing and influential group of actors within government.

12 A second issue is what should be taught. The school should develop courses in such areas as Canadian society and the economy, the constitution, including federalism, the *Charter of Rights and Freedoms*, the principles of collective and individual ministerial responsibility, the machinery of government, including the role of the public service, public finances and the budgetary process, the numerous accountability requirements which now apply to public office holders and the increased importance of values and ethics in public life. Along with these broad core subjects, there should be customized, more applied courses for ministers on such topics as agenda setting and leading a department, policy and risk analysis, decision-making for busy people, working with public servants, dealing with lobbyists, preparing for parliamentary business (Question period and committee appearances), communications and political messaging.

13 Most politicians enter public life from other occupations, which means that the school will involve adult education. It is also the case that few politicians are lacking in terms of ego, confidence and ambition. These facts mean that the "faculty" in the school must have credibility (not just credentials), excellent presentation skills and the confidence to deal with controversy in a way that will promote learning rather than talking past others. To bridge theory and practice, there must be a carefully selected mix of faculty—including former respected politicians and public servants, consultants, think tank representatives, communications specialists and academics who are leading-edge researchers but also excellent communicators. The pedagogical approach must involve active learning with a minimum of formal presentations, lots of group discussion, the use of role playing, including taped sessions, the analysis of cases, group projects and so on. The content of the courses will have to reflect the shifting context of Canada's public sector.

14 Good schools seek to measure and to improve their performance. Success for the proposed school of national government will have many dimensions:

- The reputation of the school and the demands for its courses;
- The careers and reputations of its graduates in terms of their sense of responsibility to serve the public interest;

- The achievement of a better balance in political life between the current heavy emphasis on the skills and techniques of "retail politics" and the knowledge and skills required to govern productively and ethically;
- The gradual emergence of more systematic, evidence-based approaches to policy formulation;
- Greater respect and support for the role of an impartial, professional public service as a partner in the production of quality government;
- Less highly charged partisanship in legislatures and more constructive exchanges across party lines, especially in relation to matters where partisan philosophical differences are not relevant.

15 One of the benefits of the school will be to allow individuals from more diverse social and occupational backgrounds to enter and be successful in elected public office.

16 Even if a persuasive case can be made for a school of government, there is still the practical problem of how it will be created and financed. There is the existing Canada School of the Public Service (CSPS) (previously the Canadian Centre for Management Development) in Ottawa which, after several shifts in focus over the years now concentrates on leadership development in the senior public service. Sporadically it has involved politicians and political staff in its programs, but mainly it has sought to create a "safe" place where public managers can discuss issues, including the constraints arising from the political process, in a candid manner.

17 The proposed school could operate as a virtual, networked institution, using venues and faculty from across the country. The existing Canada School of the Public Service in Ottawa might provide the physical home for the school which would have a small staff, mainly a director and administrative support personnel. Courses could be open to interested federal, provincial, territorial and city politicians. Fees could be charged, but on the assumption that improved governing benefits society at large, private donations could also be sought. Scheduling courses and finding time for politicians from across the country to participate would be difficult, but on-line sessions and

material distributed electronically would provide some flexibility.

18   Foresight, intelligence, judgment, prudence, civility and integrity are far more important in public life than the skills of selling illusions and attacking political opponents. Now is the time to invest in the development of better political leaders.

Canadian Parliamentary Review.
2009. Autumn.

Key and challenging words

pluralistic, mobilization, charismatic, intractable

Questions

1. Explain in your own words what the author means by "It has been said that politicians campaign in poetry and govern in prose" (paragraph 3).
2. What is Thomas referring to when he follows the quotation by Robert Louis Stevenson by the statement "This is wrong"? Summarize paragraph 6, where this statement occurs.
3. Unlike many non-academic essays, Thomas's essay does not include a clear thesis in the first few paragraphs. Do you think this absence detracts from the essay or the writer's credibility, or is it clear what the writer will be arguing—even without a thesis? Do you think it is a better essay *without* a thesis statement? Explain your answer by specific textual references.

4. In paragraph 10, Thomas discusses the goals of a school for politicians: (a) summarize these goals in 50–60 words; (b) identify which goal you believe is the most important one. Use critical thinking to support your points.
5. Analyze the writer's organization in the section "A School of Government for Politicians." You could consider the order of points, paragraph development and coherence, and use of other organizational strategies.
6. Find at least one example of each of the following argumentative strategies (see chapter 9, p. 114) and explain its use in the selected passage: a) concession; b) precedent; c) emotional *or* ethical appeal.

Post-reading

1. Respond to one of the following statements, using critical thinking to analyze its validity: (a) "Along with over promising and underdelivering, politicians have shown little regard for the intelligence of voters and their potential to learn about complicated policy issues" (par. 2); (b) "...[F]ew politicians are lacking in terms of ego, confidence and ambition" (par. 13).

2. To be considered seriously by a reader, proposal arguments need to be seen as both necessary (e.g., the proposal will address an important issue) and feasible (i.e., practical and realistic). Write an analysis of Thomas's argument in which you consider both these requirements.

Related website of interest

Taxpayer.com: Official site of the Canadian Tax-payers Federation, a citizens advocacy group *dedicated to lower taxes, less waste and accountable government:*
www.taxpayer.com/

Additional library reading

Arterton, Chris. A School for Politicians and Political Staffers. *Canadian Parliamentary Review* 30.3 (2007): 17–21. Print.

Missing in action: Gender in Canada's digital economy agenda

Leslie Regan Shade

(2,355 words)

Pre-reading

1. After reading the title and first paragraph and noting the name of the journal in which the essay appeared, (a) write a one-paragraph reading hypothesis that includes purpose, audience, and rhetorical mode; or (b) paraphrase paragraph 1.
2. *Collaborative or individual activity:* Were you aware that online gender equity was an issue for some Canadians? Reflect on/discuss the importance of this issue and possible ways to increase women's digital inclusion.

1   Global public interest advocates have hailed Canada, which has been developing federal policy and programs to increase citizens' Internet access since the 1990s, as an early promoter of online gender equity. But twenty years later, market fundamentalism and a retreat from the public interest by the Conservative-led federal government have diminished this progressive agenda, and concern with gender—especially the notion of gender equity—has palpably dissipated. Yet digital inclusion is still a persistent issue in Canada. As Internet governance becomes more globally implicated, feminist interventions in activism and scholarship are key to creating and sustaining innovative strategies of inclusion.

2   Perhaps the biggest policy sellout in the past decade in Canada has been the hollowing out of the principle of universality and a concomitant withering of public interest in social welfare. This includes digital policy, as evidenced by the gradual yet crucial disinvestment in funding for programs for Internet access. Consider how the rhetoric surrounding digital technologies has evolved: In the mid-1990s, hyperbole about information highways had politicians boasting that Canada would be the most wired nation in the world. The "roaring nineties" were characterized by the mantra of the marketplace (Stiglitz 2003) but also by the recognition that government funding for community Internet projects could ameliorate digital divides, notably through Industry Canada's Community Access Program (CAP). The dot-com euphoria of the late 1990s, critical policy research on the knowledge-based economy, and

dreams of media convergence were quickly eclipsed by more sobering analyses of the tech crash amid the widely hyped new economy. Information highways transformed to broadband and fiber-to-the-home applications, while public concerns over privacy and security after September 11, 2001, created new policy and legislative regimes that often trumped human rights.

3   Modernizing the telecommunications landscape was the objective of the 2005 Telecommunications Policy Review Panel, which was tasked with formulating recommendations for a globally competitive regulatory environment; its final report called for market forces to prevail, bringing into question whether Canadians would be entitled to an affordable, universally accessible, and democratically accountable telecommunications system (Longford, Moll, and Shade 2012). In his 2010 Throne Speech before Parliament, the prime minister launched a strategy to "drive the adoption of new technology across the economy," to reintroduce copyright reform legislation, and to discuss increasing foreign ownership in the telecommunications sector, thus "giving Canadian firms access to the funds and expertise they need" (Government of Canada 2010).

4   Despite the documented boon it provided for community economic and cultural development, the CAP program was terminated in 2012 (*CBC News* 2012). Until recently, Canada could bask in its reputation as an international innovator in broadband access, but Canada now has the embarrassing distinction as a broadband laggard, sparking contentious debates

between industry, government, the Canadian Radio-television and Telecommunications Commission, and public interest groups over whether regulatory intervention can increase competition in the broadband sector.

5   Concern with women's equality has also diminished in the past decade. Status of Women Canada became a federal departmental agency in 1976, with a mandate to coordinate policy and programs with respect to the status of women. Over the years the agency provided core funding for women's groups working in areas such as health care, education, anti-poverty initiatives, and antiracism. In 2006, however, the Conservative federal government announced that Status of Women Canada would no longer fund groups engaged in advocacy, lobbying, or research. Following the government's directive, Status of Women closed regional offices; canceled the Policy Research Fund, which had supported independent policy research; changed funding eligibility criteria to allow for-profit organizations to apply alongside nonprofit groups; and, most notoriously, dropped the word "equality" from its mandate (Standing Committee on the Status of Women Canada 2007).

6   The rise and fall of CAP, the persistence of the market mantra, and a palpable contempt for equality issues are salient examples of discursive and material shifts in social and digital policy in the past decade, from promoting Internet access so as to foster and nurture participatory citizenship toward a discourse that merely advantages consumers' access to goods and services.

In the Good Old Days . . .

7   Early Internet policy recommendations regarded gender as an essential component for universal access, with Status of Women Canada funding research on Internet usage by women's groups and the potential of the Internet to foster women's citizenship (Shade 1996). Several declarations were issued in 1995 alone: the Federal Plan for Gender Equality stated that "the absence of equity and access-related research [regarding the information infrastructure] is of growing concern" (Status of Women Canada 1995, par. 270); the Coalition for Public Information (CPI), a nongovernmental organization aligned with the Ontario Library

Association, integrated gender issues into its public policy framework (Skrzeszewski and Cubberley 1995); and the final report from the federally mandated Information Highway Advisory Council recognized that an attention to gender disparities was necessary to ensure equitable and universal Internet access (Industry Canada 1995).

8   In the 2000s, Canada played an international role in promoting gender equity in access to the Internet. The Canadian International Development Agency worked with the International Telecommunications Union's Task Force on Gender Issues to include gender mainstreaming in telecom programs and policies (ITU 2008). During the drafting of the World Summit on the Information Society (WSIS)'s "Declaration of Principles" (2012), the Canadian government collaborated with the summit's Gender Caucus to include a paragraph on gender equality (see also Gallagher 2011). And as part of Canada's participation in the second phase of WSIS, the Canadian Commission for UNESCO organized a conference that produced the "Canadian Civil Society Communiqué," affirming human rights, equality, cultural diversity, freedom of expression, privacy, and gender equality as Canadian values (CPSR 2005).

Digital Skills for Whom and for What?

9   The issue of social inclusion has been almost absent from recent digital policy, although the government's consultation paper on the digital economy did consider "digital skills": "the ability to locate, organize, understand, evaluate, create and share information using digital technology" (Industry Canada 2010a; see also Industry Canada 2010b). Emphasized was the need for a "sufficient quantity of qualified ICT [information and communication technology] workers" to form the "backbone" of a "strong, globally competitive information and communications technology sector," and one barrier to this goal was identified as the emergent "digital skills divide," which affected not just labor participation but "all . . . Canadians, be they homemakers, students or seniors" (Industry Canada 2010a).

10   In analyzing how digital skills are framed in the consultation paper, and in public submissions strategizing about best practices for addressing the

digital divide, it becomes clear that digital skills were primarily couched in economic terms.[1] Infused with the technological imperative, submissions argue that digital skills are needed to function, participate, be productive, compete globally, spark innovation, prosper, prepare Canadians for the jobs of tomorrow, and meet the demands of market forces. Digital skills make for better workers. Better workers equate with better consumers, who create prosperity. More prosperity equates with global competitiveness—a veritable virtuous circle. Missing, however, is a more holistic vision that sees building digital skills as an element of citizenship and social justice. A blind spot in the submissions is a nuanced consideration of race, class, and gender inequalities.

11   More than two hundred organizations submitted briefs on digital skills, including an array of universities, colleges, and their associations; libraries and library associations; cultural groups; and a sprinkling of independent media companies, public interest groups, literacy organizations, and small Internet service providers. Themes that emerge from an analysis of submissions include identification of the educational sector as the conduit for training, strategies for increasing access to technology through libraries and community sites, increasing digital literacy, and ensuring broadband access for rural and remote communities, especially for First Nations communities.

12   Two organizations concerned with integrating women into the technological workforce submitted comments. Women in Film and Television—Toronto is a nonprofit professional organization that promotes, mentors, and trains women in the screen-based media industry and has a mandate to promote digital literacy skills. Its brief urges the government to conduct large-scale surveys on employment trends and skills gaps in the digital sector in order to ascertain gender disparities (WFTT 2010). The Canadian Advanced Technology Alliance (CATA; the largest high-tech professional association in Canada) and its Women in Technology Forum recommended redressing the gender imbalance in science and technology through education for young girls, promoting the participation and advancement of women in the tech sector, and improving work-life balance (CATA WIT Forum 2010). While these are laudable goals, the

diverse echelons and practices within digital work—from paid higher-level programming, managerial skills, and lower-level data entry to the more contingent and affective labor practices of "prosumers" (online brand consumers and influencers) need to be differentiated, as many feminists argue (Scott-Dixon 2008; Gill 2010; Fortunati 2011).

13   Two other submissions also considered gender. OCAD University commented on gender representation in screen-based programming, including video games, and on the dearth of women serving as owners and workers in small technology companies, the mobile phone industry, and the social media industry (OCAD University 2010). A consensus document on the digital economy—the result of a roundtable organized at the University of Toronto and signed by over eighty academics, public interest stakeholders, and citizens—is notable because it highlights a citizen-based strategy emphasizing affordable, universal access, including a legal right to broadband Internet access, participatory citizenship and social inclusion, and promotion of privacy and other civil liberties ("Consensus Submission" 2010).

14   As is clear from the submissions and government paper on the digital economy, digital policy frames skill as the ability to participate in the labor force and to purchase and consume products and services. It emphasizes consumer rights rather than the rights of citizens to access ICTs in order to create content and participate meaningfully in democratic public life. Contemporary communications-policy discourse makes the terms "citizen" and "consumer" interchangeable, such that the "ubiquitous discourse of choice and empowerment" relegates the citizen solely to the market (Livingstone and Lunt 2007, 53). Indeed, Canadian digital policy has shifted from a semblance of citizen-based universality to a regime of market-generated rules for consumers. Programs and policies fixate on the technical, rather than social, infrastructure. Missing is a consideration of the nexus of technology, citizenship, and social justice. Despite the Canadian government's siren call for market forces to meet accessibility needs, numerous digital divides and differentials in digital skills persist, demarcated by socioeconomic status, demographics (including gender and generation), and geographic

location (rural vs. urban). It is thus crucial to address these digital fissures and examine the relationships among four key variables in the adoption of digital skills: accessibility, affordability, usability, and value. Needed is a move from digital divides to digital capabilities, an approach that interrogates the texture of communication rights and entitlements. Digital skills can strengthen citizens' rights—the ability to create and participate meaningfully in democratic, social, and public life and thus contribute to social inclusion.

15   In her incisive feminist intersectional critique and analysis of the deployment of digital technologies in US society through federal programs, Virginia Eubanks (2011, xv) argues that optimistic "magical thinking" about technology disguises and heightens digital inequalities and that investments in technology, without simultaneous investment in social justice, merely increase inequalities at the structural, political, and sociocultural levels. As she argues, digital policy too often assumes middle-class values and experiences, neglecting or obscuring the insights and struggles of poor and working-class people. The shuttering of the CAP program in Canada is also a gender equity issue. Community networks serve the economically disadvantaged, with women in the lower socioeconomic strata using the facilities to improve their situation and overcome technological disadvantages (Moll and Fritz 2012).

16   During the 2011 federal election, social media was widely deployed to raise awareness about the erosion of social welfare programs and policies. A popular website, ShitHarperDid.com, featured short informational videos delivered by low-key comedic hipsters. One video asked, "Do you know the pickup line that goes over the best for Canadian women?" The answer: "I am not Stephen Harper." Featuring a montage of young women addressing the camera, the script reads as follows:

> Harper has closed twelve out of sixteen Status of Women offices in Canada. He eliminated funding for Legal Voices for Women, including the National Association for Women in Law. He eliminated funding for Sisters in Spirit, an internationally praised organization, leading an investigation into six hundred murdered Aboriginal women and

girls. Since 2006 Stephen Harper has cut funding for women's advocacy by 43 per cent. That's why, as a proud Canadian woman, I will be voting. And I will *not* be voting for Stephen Harper's Conservatives.[2]

17   The 2011 election did usher in an antiequality majority government, and as political scientist Sylvia Bashevkin ruefully comments, "Harper's track record of implementing regressive changes will probably continue now that his party controls both houses of parliament" (2012, 5). This does not bode well for digital inclusion. The ability to track key indicators of household and workplace Internet access that have been collected since the mid-1990s by Statistics Canada, the primary source of Canadian socioeconomic data, is imperiled now that the government has made cuts that affect thirty-four surveys (Bednar and Stabile 2012).

18   What is now needed more than ever is funding for collaborative research on digital inclusion that brings together academics and advocacy groups. Evidence-based policy making does not have to be merely quantitative, and qualitative work that engages community members and intermediaries who serve as gateways to the Internet and broadband for many low-income Canadians can add much richness and depth to policy evidence. Aligning with Eubanks's research, a focus on social inclusion can enable us to learn from the media justice movement's awareness of wider social justice issues and attention to systemic issues of race, class, and gender. Feminist gender justice advocacy around policy issues within the media reform movement is crucial (Dougherty 2010; Shade 2011).

19   Ensuring a broadband-enabled digital society will take, as Catherine Middleton argues, "engaged, informed and digitally literate citizens" (2011, 11) and will involve the participatory development of applications and services that are valuable, affordable, and accessible. This, I argue, is a priority for feminist activism and scholarship, which can be at the vanguard of critiques and constructions of the digital economy.

Signs. 2014.
Summer 39 (4).

Notes

1. For public submissions regarding the digital skills divide, see the "Building Digital Skills" page of Industry Canada's website for the Digital Economy in Canada at www.digitaleconomy.gc.ca/eic/site/028.nsf/eng/h_00492.html.

2. ShitHarperDid, "Canadian Women's Favourite Pick-Up Line," YouTube video. 1:09, posted by "ShitHarperDid," April 20, 2011, www.youtube.com/watch?v5KmthTK SWFWw&feature5bf_prev&list5UUz6NBjskef0fNb8w XqLlD5A.

References

1. Bashevkin, Sylvia. 2012. "Regress Trumps Progress: Canadian Women, Feminism and the Harper Government." Perspective paper, Friedrich Ebert Stiftung, Washington, DC, July. http://library.fes.de/pdf-files/id/09205.pdf.

2. Bednar, Vass, and Mark Stabile. 2012. "Statistics Canada Cuts Compromise the Tools Used to Understand the State." *Toronto Star*, July 10. www.thestar.com/opinion/editorialopinion/article/1224561-statistics-canada-cuts-compromise-the-tools-used-to-understand-the-state.

3. CATA WIT Forum (Canadian Advanced Technology Alliance Women in Technology Forum). 2010. "Addressing the Shortage of Women in ICT." Report submitted to the Government of Canada, The Digital Economy in Canada, Industry Canada, Ottawa, July 12. www.digitaleconomy.gc.ca/eic/site/028.nsf/eng/00362.html.

4. CBC News. 2012. "Ottawa Cuts CAP Public Web Access Funding." April 6. www.cbc.ca/news/canada/calgary/story/2012/04/06/ns-cap-funding-cut.html.

5. "Consensus Submission to the Federal Government Consultation on a Digital Economy Strategy for Canada." 2010. Report convened by Andrew Clement and Karen Louise Smith with support from the University of Toronto Faculty of Information, Identity, Privacy and Security Institute, and the Knowledge Media Design Institute, submitted to the Government of Canada, The Digital Economy in Canada, Industry Canada, Ottawa, July 13. www.ic.gc.ca/eic/site/028.nsf/eng/00284.html.

6. CPSR (Computer Professionals for Social Responsibility). 2005. "Canadian Civil Society Communiqué." Document WSIS-II/PC-3/CONTR/13-E, prepared on behalf of Canadian Civil Society, World Summit on the Information Society, Winnipeg. www.itu.int/wsis/docs2/pc3/contributions/Co13.pdf.

7. Dougherty, Ariel. 2010. "Snapshot of Foundation Support for Feminist Gender Justice Media." Media Equity Collaborative, Truth or Consequences, NM. http://old.gfem.org/sites/gfem.org/files/FNJn2010_SNAPSHOT_FdnFGJM_MEC.pdf.

8. Eubanks, Virginia. 2011. *Digital Dead End: Fighting for Social Justice in the Information Age.* Cambridge, MA: MIT Press.

9. Fortunati, Leopoldina. 2011. "ICTs and Immaterial Labor from a Feminist Perspective." *Journal of Communication Inquiry* 35(4):426–32.

10. Gallagher, Margaret. 2011. "Gender and Communication Policy: Struggling for Space." In *The Handbook of Global Media and Communication Policy*, ed. Robin Mansell and Marc Raboy, 451–66. Malden, MA: Wiley-Blackwell.

11. Gill, Rosalind. 2010. "'Life Is a Pitch': Managing the Self in New Media Work." *In Managing Media Work*, ed. Mark Deuze, 249–62. London: Sage.

12. Government of Canada. 2010. "Addressing the Shortage of Women in ICT." Speech from the Throne, March 3. www.ic.gc.ca/eic/site/028.nsf/eng/00362.html.

13. Industry Canada. 1995. "Connection, Community, Content: The Challenge of the Information Highway." Final report, Information Highway Advisory Council, Industry Canada, Ottawa.

14. ———. 2010a. "Building Digital Skills for Tomorrow." Consultation paper, Industry Canada, Ottawa. www.ic.gc.ca/eic/site/028.nsf/eng/00041.html.

15. ———. 2010b. "Shaping Canada's Strategy for the Digital Economy." Report, Industry Canada, Ottawa. www.ic.gc.ca/eic/site/ich-epi.nsf/eng/02090.html.

16. ITU (International Telecommunications Union). 2008. "Gender Mainstreaming Activities." Working document, International Telecommunications Union, Geneva. www.itu.int/ITU-D/gender/gender_mainstreaming_activities.html.

17. Livingstone, Sonia, and Peter Lunt. 2007. "Representing Citizens and Consumers in Media and Communications Regulation." *Annals of the American Academy of Political and Social Science*, no. 611, 51–65.

18. Longford, Graham, Marita Moll, and Leslie Regan Shade. 2012. "There and Back to the Future Again: Community Networks and Telecom Policy Reform in Canada, 1995–2010." In *Connecting Canadians: Investigations in Community Informatics*, ed. Andrew Clement, Michael Gurstein, Graham Longford, Marita

Moll, and Leslie Regan Shade, 439–69. Edmonton: Athabasca University Press.

19. Middleton, Catherine. 2011. "From Canada 2.0 to a Digital Nation: The Challenges of Creating a Digital Society in Canada." In *The Internet Tree: The State of Telecom Policy in Canada 3.0*, ed. Marita Moll and Leslie Regan Shade, 3–13. Ottawa: Canadian Centre for Policy Alternatives.

20. Moll, Marita, and Melissa Fritz. 2012. "Keeping in Touch: A Snapshot of Canadian Community Networks and Their Users—Report on the CRACIN Survey of Community Network Users." In *Connecting Canadians: Investigations in Community Informatics*, ed. Andrew Clement, Michael Gurstein, Graham Longford, Marita Moll, and Leslie Regan Shade, 61–89. Edmonton: Athabasca University Press.

21. OCAD University. 2010. "Digital Economy/Digital Society." Report submitted to the Government of Canada, The Digital Economy in Canada, Industry Canada, Ottawa, July 13. http://digitaleconomy.gc.ca/eic/site/028.nsf/eng/00330.html.

22. Scott-Dixon, Krista. 2008. "Long (Standing) Digital Divisions: Women's IT Work in Canada." *Atlantis* 32(2):18–32.

23. Shade, Leslie Regan. 1996. "Report on the Use of the Internet in Canadian Women's Organizations." Report, Status of Women Canada, Ottawa.

24. ———. 2011. "Wanted, Alive and Kicking: Curious Feminist Digital Policy Geeks." *Feminist Media Studies* 11(1):123–29.

25. Skrzeszewski, Stan, and Maureen Cubberly. 1995. "Future-Knowledge: A Public Policy Framework for the Information Highway." Report prepared for Canada's Coalition for Public Information, Coalition for Public Information/Ontario Library Association, Toronto.

26. Standing Committee on the Status of Women Canada. 2007. "The Impacts of Funding and Program Changes at Status of Women Canada." Report, House of Commons Canada, Ottawa, May. www.parl.gc.ca/HousePublications/Publication.aspx?Language5E&Mode51&Parl539&Ses51&DocId52876038&File55.

27. Status of Women Canada. 1995. "Setting the Stage for the Next Century: The Federal Plan for Gender Equality." Report, Status of Women Canada, Ottawa.

28. Stiglitz, Joseph E. 2003. *The Roaring Nineties: A New History of the World's Most Prosperous Decade*. New York: Norton.

29. WFTT (Women in Film and Television—Toronto). 2010. "Women in Digital Media." Report submitted to the Government of Canada, The Digital Economy in Canada, Industry Canada, Ottawa, July 6. www.digitaleconomy.gc.ca/eic/site/028.nsf/eng/00465.html.

30. WSIS (World Summit on the Information Society). 2012. "Declaration of Principles. Building the Information Society: A Global Challenge to the New Millennium." Report, December 12. www.itu.int/wsis/docs/geneva/official/dop.html.

Key and challenging words

concomitant, hyperbole, ameliorate, laggard, contentious, palpable, salient, veritable, echelon, contingent, dearth, relegate, nexus, demarcate, fissure, incisive, rueful

Questions

1. a. Identify the main rhetorical patterns in (i) paragraphs 2–3 and (ii) in paragraphs 8–9. b. for either (i) or (ii), discuss strategies that the author uses to increase comprehension, referring to the text.

2. Scan the essay for references to Industry Canada's Community Access program (CAP). Explain the importance of this organization to feminist goals of digital inclusion.

3. Analyze the rhetorical and stylistic effectiveness of paragraph 14. You could consider some of the features discussed in question 1 as well as those discussed in chapter 6, p. 76, such as the use of repetition, parallel structures, and transitions.

4. Comment on the use of direct quotations in the essay. In your answer, refer to at least two direct quotations and analyze their function within the selected passages.

5. Using critical thinking and your knowledge concerning the differences between quantitative and qualitative sources (see chapter 3), explain Shade's

statement in paragraph 18 that more quantitative research is needed today.

6. Is Shade's essay about only gender inclusiveness? What groups lack an internet presence? Do her references to these other underrepresented groups help or hinder her credibility, do you think?

7. Analyze Shade's introduction (par. 1) and conclusion (paragraphs 18–19). In addition to analyzing the effectiveness of her argument there, explain whether you think they are too brief in an essay of this length, supporting your explanation by critical thinking and your knowledge of argument.

Post-reading

1. *Collaborative activity:* Design an information campaign that draws attention to the need and suggests practical means for increasing online gender equity in Canada or another specific place, such as your campus. Along with outlining the problem and proposing solutions, decide on a specific audience for the campaign (for example, a branch of government/administration, a citizens' action group, or other feasible target). Refer to Shade's essay at least twice in your presentation/report.

Related websites of interest

Digital Canada 150: Addressing the Shortage of Women in ICT:
www.ic.gc.ca/eic/site/028.nsf/eng/00362.html

UN Women—United Nations Entity for Gender Equality and the Empowerment of Women:
www.unwomen.org/ru/digital-library/publications/2012/10/un-women-sourcebook-on-women-peace-and-security

National Council of Women of Canada:
www.ncwc.ca/aboutUs.html

Media Smarts: Canada's Centre for Digital and Media Literacy:
mediasmarts.ca/gender-representation

Sexuality and sexual health of Canadian adolescents: Yesterday, today, and tomorrow

Eleanor Maticka-Tyndale
(4,973 words)

Pre-reading

1. Scan the title, abstract, headings, and subheadings to help determine the essay's content and organization. Why is organization so important in a review essay?

2. Review essays usually synthesize many sources. What can you tell from the "References" pages about the kinds of sources used in the essay? Are there a large number? A wide variety of kinds of sources (e.g., not all scholarly articles)? Does the name of the essay's author appear among the references? Why might this be important?

Abstract

A profile of the sexual health and behaviours of contemporary Canadian adolescents is developed based on current research and compared to adolescents in the latter half of the twentieth century. While notable changes occurred in the sexual lives of youth between the late 1950s and the early 1990s, the patterns of behaviour established in the latter part of the twentieth century have continued into recent years. There is strong evidence that today's youth are experiencing better sexual health and taking more measures to protect their sexual health than prior generations of youth did. However, problems remain. Canadian teens and young adults continue to be challenged by STIs; many GLBTQ youth continue to face homonegativity and discrimination in their schools and communities; youth living in poverty, in rural areas, and aboriginal youth carry the greatest burdens of poor sexual health and are the most poorly served by sexuality education and sexual health care. Recommendations are made to strengthen both sexuality education and sexual health services to meet the needs of all Canadian youth.

Introduction

1　Those who rely on media reports to keep them up to date about the sexual health of Canadian adolescents may well have come to the conclusion that we live in particularly troubling times. Over the past few years we have been told that pregnancies are sought after with little thought of the long-term needs of a child (Gulli, 2008; Lunau, 2008); there is a widening repertoire of sexual acts such as masturbatory displays for others via webcams and oral sex "games" that are believed to have become part of what teenagers regularly do in their sexual lives (Stepp, 1999; Wilson, 2004); teens are easy victims for adult predators who have ready access to them, especially via the Internet (CBC News, 2008b); and dramatic increases in sexually transmitted infections are a growing threat to the sexual and reproductive health of our youth (Pearce, 2008). There is also a persistent interest in age of first intercourse among teens and the sense that this is happening much earlier than in the recent past. In these and other such cases, we, the professionals and organizations who are the sources for the stories, are at times insufficiently careful in the way we present and explain our findings. When we turn to the actual research, we find that the impressions created by most of these claims arise from misunderstanding or misinformation reinforced by an underlying expectation that the news about adolescent sexuality and sexual health has to be bad. What the research evidence suggests is that although there remains room for improvement, the picture of the sexual health and well-being of today's Canadian teens is, in many ways, more positive than in previous generations. The picture is also far more complex and context laden than is often portrayed. This article reviews the evidence, considers the context, and suggests possible future directions for supporting the sexual health of youth in Canada.

Adolescent Sexuality and Sexual Health: Yesterday and Today

2　Comparing adolescents in the most recent 10 years to earlier generations we find that the major changes in what adolescents 'do' sexually occurred between the 1950s and late 1960s. There have been few changes in the patterns of teenage sexuality since the time when many of today's adults were teens (1970s), and many aspects of adolescent sexual health have improved since then. Using data for recent adolescents from the *National Longitudinal Survey of Children and Youth* (NLSCY) and for adolescents in earlier generations from the *National Population Health Survey* (NPHS) (Statistics Canada, 1998)—two national surveys using comparable research methodologies—and comparing these data to findings from various other large-scale studies conducted nationally or regionally (Boyce, 2004; Boyce, Doherty, Fortin, & MacKinnon, 2003; McCreary Centre Society, 2004; Rotermann, 2008; Saewyc, Taylor, Homma, & Ogilvie, 2008; Tonkin, Murphy, Lee, Saewyc, and the McCreary Centre Society, 2005), we find that since the 1970s the age of first sexual intercourse has remained relatively stable. For the large majority, first sexual intercourse occurs at 16 to 18 years of age. Also relatively consistent throughout this period has been that around 15–22 per cent have first intercourse before 16 years of age, with this percentage being lower for the most recent cohort than for earlier ones. Clearly, teens are not initiating sexual intercourse earlier, but rather slightly later than their parents' generation did.

3 What about claims of a more "casual" approach to sex, of oral sex becoming a common and early activity, and of teens engaging in virtual (or display) sex over the Internet? The best we can do in assessing the "casualness" of adolescent sexual encounters is to consider the number of partners they have. Comparing results from the *Canada Youth and AIDS Study* conducted in the late 1980s (King et al., 1988) to its sequel, the *Canadian Youth Sexual Health and HIV/ AIDS Study* conducted after 2000 (Boyce et al., 2003) we find youth currently in-school reporting slightly fewer lifetime sexual intercourse partners in the more recent than in the earlier study. If we assume that more partners suggests more "casualness" about sex, these results suggest that we are seeing somewhat less "casualness" among current adolescents than we were 10–15 years ago.

4 With respect to oral sex, it is important to remember that over the last 30 to 40 years oral sex has become a normative aspect of the adult sexual script and this trend has been followed by youth. Studies conducted on adolescent populations in the United States and Canada during and since the 1970s consistently show that oral sex is about as common as sexual intercourse, is most typically initiated at about the same time as intercourse, but precedes first coital activity for 15–25 per cent of adolescents (for US see: DeLamater & MacCorquadale, 1979; Lindberg, Jones & Santelli, 2007; Newcomer & Udry, 1985; for Canada see: Boyce et al., 2003; Gillis, 2005; Herold & Way, 1985; Warren & King, 1994).

5 Something that is new with the most recent generations of teens is the role played by communications technologies such as cell phones and the Internet. Here we have very little research other than basic counts that confirm what we already know, i.e., that adolescents and young adults are using cell phones and the Internet to an increasing extent and more than those who are older. An entirely new language and culture of communication has developed for text messaging and chat rooms. In her doctoral research, Smylie (2008) found that younger teens, who had more limited access to transportation or lived in peri-urban or rural areas, relied heavily on cell phones to connect with each other and maintain relationships while older, more urban adolescents relied more on face-to-face contact. Levine (2002), in interviewing adolescents in the United States about their sexual experiences quoted one 13-year-old girl as saying that she prefers experimenting sexually on-line because face-to-face is too "gropey" whereas on-line there is more talk. With every new technology—the printing press, movie theatres, telephones, automobiles, drive-in-theatres—youth have found ways to incorporate the technology into their rituals of "connecting" and adults have expressed dismay over what the implications are for morality and safety. What we can conclude about the sexual behaviours of contemporary Canadian teens is that they are maintaining patterns established in the late 1960s and early 1970s.

Sexual Health Trends

Pregnancy and Parenting

6 The majority of Canadian adolescents are taking responsibility for their own sexual health by accessing contraception, using condoms, and seeking out abortion when necessary far more than any previous Canadian generation (compare, for example, trend data reported in Maticka-Tyndale, McKay and Barrett, 2000, to that in more recent reports on youth, e.g., Boyce, 2004; Boyce et al., 2003; McKay, 2006; Saewyc et al., 2008). In preventing pregnancies and postponing parenthood, teens today benefit from changes that were just beginning to be realized in the 1970s and '80s such as legal access to contraception and abortion as well as more recent changes such as the availability of emergency contraception (Pancham & Dunn, 2007). Legal access does not, however, guarantee access to all. Rural and very young teens remain poorly served by sexual and reproductive health services (e.g., Langille, Flowerdew & Andreou, 2004; Shoveller et al., 2007) and access to abortion remains limited or non-existent in some provinces and all territories. The continuing declines in pregnancy and birth rates (see McKay, 2006) speak not only to the greater availability of contraception and abortion today, but also to the ability of the vast majority of today's teens to take the necessary actions to prevent pregnancy and postpone parenthood.

Sexually Transmitted Infections

7   In comparison to pregnancy prevention, the picture for sexually transmitted infections (STI) is not as positive. Following a steady decline in reported rates for chlamydia among youth into the mid-1990s, rates rose steadily among 15- to 19- and 20- to 24-year olds from 1997–2004. Paradoxically this increase in teen chlamydia rates occurred concurrently with a decline in teenage pregnancy rates and an increase in teen condom use over the same time period (compare teen condom use data from repeated surveys conducted among British Columbia youth in 1992, 1998, and 2003 as reported in Saewyc et al., 2008). These trends seem inconsistent with the increase in reported rates of chlamydia among teens and raise the question of whether increasing rates necessarily reflect an increase in prevalence of infection. Rising rates would also occur with introduction of more sensitive testing methods and more frequent testing, both of which would detect more cases but would not necessarily indicate a rise in the percentage infected (McKay & Barrett, 2008). However, regardless of whether the prevalence of chlamydia among youth has or has not increased, the present levels of infection are still grounds for concern. Many STI carry long-term consequences for health and reproductive potential (MacDonald & Brunham, 1997; PHAC, 2007) and efforts to raise the low levels of chlamydia screening of all sexually active 15- to 24-year-old youth by physicians (Hardwick, McKay & Ashem, 2007; Moses & Elliott, 2002) are thus an important health promotion priority. Indeed, a range of STI (in particular, human papilloma virus, HPV, and herpes simplex virus, HSV, as well as chlamydia) are common in the teen population and require a sustained prevention effort from the education and health care systems.

Sexual Abuse

8   While data on pregnancies and STI, and policies and programs designed to address them are within the domain of public health, sexual abuse, which is also a component of sexual health, is within the domain of the criminal justice system. Data on the actual prevalence of sexual abuse are not readily available, since only cases that are reported to the police are recorded and research suggests that this is a minority of cases. Several small-scale and regional studies conducted in Canada provide some insight into the extent of this threat to sexual health. Sexual harassment and unwanted sexual comments are experienced by the majority of female and gay adolescents of varying ages and this is the most prevalent form of sexual abuse (Berman, McKenna, Arnold, Taylor, & MacQuarrie, 2000; BC Ministry of Children and Family Development, 2002; Egale, 2008). As the severity of the sexual abuse increases, fewer adolescents are affected. However, various forms of unwanted sexual contact (being verbally, physically, or forcefully coerced into sex play or sexual intercourse) are reported by up to 35 per cent of adolescent women and approximately 15 per cent of adolescent men (Bagley, Bolitho, & Bertrand, 1997; Bagley, Wood & Young, 1994; Murray & Henjem, 1993; Newton-Taylor, DeWit, & Giiksman, 1998; Rhynard & Krebs, 1997; Saewyc et al., 2008). Women are consistently more likely to be victims of all forms of sexual abuse (from unwanted comments and harassment to forced sex) than are men, and reports of sexual abuse increase as teens get older. Multivariate analyses conducted on data collected from youth across British Columbia show that experiencing sexual abuse is a precursor for other threats to sexual health such as very early sexual intercourse (before age 14), experiencing or causing a pregnancy, and lower likelihood of using condoms (Saewyc, Magee & Pettingell, 2004; Saewyc et al., 2008). A persistent finding across all studies is that sexual harassment, coercion, and violence are perpetrated most often by someone known to the victim. This extends from classmates, co-workers, and neighbours, to friends and family members. Despite the "truism" that the danger most often originates within our circle of acquaintances, media attention and public fear focus on the danger posed by strangers, often identifying them as sexual predators.

Internet Concerns

9   As Internet chat rooms and social networking sites have become more popular among teens, fears have mounted about sexual predators who make contact with teens via the Internet and lure them into sexual liaisons. Parents are advised to monitor Internet use and teens are cautioned against providing personal information or arranging face-to-face meetings with those met on-line. Police and service providers tell us that, as with all forms of sexual violence or abuse, the

majority of cases are not reported, but that the dangers abound. Researchers from the Crimes Against Children Research Center and Family Research Laboratory at the University of New Hampshire recently published the first study of online predators and victims (Wolak, Finkelhor, Mitchell, & Ybarra, 2008). Based on their research, they conclude that social networking, posting personal information, and engaging in conversations with 'strangers' over the Internet are not associated with any elevated danger for teenagers. While there are adults who solicit sex from adolescents via the Internet, this is rarely done surreptitiously such as by feigning friendship or pretending to be a teenager. Rather, adults and adolescents searching for partners (of any age) for sexual conversation or sex in virtual or real time tend to be open about their interest and age. Most adolescents do not report distress over these encounters and "click off" when they encounter such communications, especially from adults. Wolak and her colleagues found that teenagers who engaged in Internet communication with adults about sex or met these adults did not display naivety about the Internet or about these encounters. They were fully aware and willingly engaged in sexual liaisons in the virtual and/or the real world. Wolak et al.'s study suggests that with encounters initiated via the Internet, there is considerably less danger than we have assumed and adolescents are generally able to, and do, effectively protect themselves. These findings are less inflammatory than some police and media reports but are unlikely to dispel fears about safety surrounding Internet use by adolescents.

10   Concern over the safety of younger adolescents from older sexual predators, especially those encountered over the Internet, was voiced as a primary motivator for recent changes in age-of-consent laws in Canada (CBC News, 2008a). Bill C-22, which received Royal assent on May 1, 2008, raised the age of consent from 14 to 16 years with a "close in age" (five or less years) exemption. Critics of the change have questioned its necessity and raised concerns about its consequences including the concern that it may discourage youth under 16 from seeking preventive or therapeutic health care (for discussion see Wong, 2007). What is criminalized in age-of-consent laws is consensual sex based on age categories. Under the law's premise of providing new protection for 14- and 15-year-olds, the age of their chosen partner is regulated. While

12- to 15-year-olds are considered capable of consenting to sexual intercourse, they are not considered capable of consenting to sexual intercourse with partners who are more than five years older than they are. Under the new law, adolescents and youth of 18 (or even 17), 19, 20, and 21 years (as well as older youth and adults) are charged as felons if they engage in consensual sex with partners who are 12, 13, 14, or 15 years respectively. Such a charge carries a lifelong designation as a sex offender, exclusion from various occupations, prohibition on travel to some countries (e.g., the United States), and community ostracization. The way the new law will be implemented and its implications for Canadian youth remain to be determined.

Sexual Health Inequities

11   The picture of adolescent sexual health, as indicated by pregnancies, STI, and sexual aggression or violence is not the same for all Canadian adolescents. The burden of poor sexual health is unevenly distributed across the adolescent population. Within Canada, teens who experience the poorest sexual health live in regions where families with particularly low incomes and tenuous connections to the labour force are concentrated (Hardwick & Patychuk, 1999; Langille et al., 2004), in more isolated and rural areas (Shoveller et al., 2007), and in provinces and territories with greater concentrations of rural and aboriginal populations (Canadian Federation for Sexual Health, 2007). In these regions, geographical, social, and economic forces interact to create environments that increase the likelihood that youth will become sexually active early in their teens, will experience early pregnancies, will be victims of sexual abuse, and will be more susceptible to STI. Social and health policies, programs, and services are critical to improving the sexual health and well-being of youth living in these circumstances.

12   Another group of adolescents whose sexual health is particularly threatened is teens who are gay, lesbian, bisexual, transgender, or questioning (GLBTQ). Because of the heterosexist bias and homonegativity that permeate our social institutions and even the personal thinking of many Canadians, GLBTQ teens often struggle in isolation to make sense of their feelings and experiences and to develop a sexual identity in relation to their other identities (e.g., ethnic, familial,

religious). Research in the United States has consistently shown that when youth are identified as GLBTQ they run the risk of psychological and physical assault and rejection by fellow students, co-workers, and even teachers, "friends" and family (Savin-Williams, 1999). Although Canadians are considered more accepting of diversity in sexual orientation and more supportive of equal rights than are Americans (Alderson, 2002), research has consistently demonstrated that GLBTQ students face psychological and physical harassment and violence in their schools precisely because they are GLBTQ (Bortolin, Adam, Brooke, & McCauley, unpublished; Bortolin, 2008; Egale, 2008; Saewyc et al., 2006; Sims, 2000; Youthquest, 2002). Preliminary findings from 1,200 respondents drawn from all provinces, territories, and sexual orientations to an on-line survey about school climate launched in December 2007 by Egale together with University of Winnipeg faculty (www.climatesurvey.ca) show that sexual minority youth are far less likely to feel safe in their schools and are far more likely to have been verbally and physically harassed, or to have skipped school for safety reasons than majority youth (www.egale.ca/extra/1393-HomophobiaBackgrounder.pdf). The consequences of the sexual violence perpetrated on GLBTQ youth include higher school drop-out rates (Saewyc et al., 2006) as well as higher rates of depression and other forms of psychological distress, substance use, and suicide than experienced by "straight" youth (Savin-Williams 1999). Homonegativity and heterosexism also pose barriers to access to social and health services. In both American and Canadian studies, GLBTQ youth report high levels of distrust of health and social service providers and feel they need to hide their identities to ensure better quality care (Barbara, Quandt, & Anderson, 2001; Travers & Schneider, 1996). Clearly, despite legal advances for gay and lesbian adults, GLBTQ adolescents continue to face serious impediments to their sexual health primarily as a result of the homonegativity and homophobia that continue to permeate many Canadian institutions.

Changing Contexts

13   The changed biological and social contexts within which today's adolescents experience their sexuality present new challenges for their sexual and reproductive health. Teens today are looking towards more years as sexually mature singles than did previous generations. The age of sexual maturation has continued to dip below the teenage years while the median age of first marriage and childbearing remains at 29–34 years (Statistics Canada, 2006), leaving the majority of Canadian youth with many years from sexual maturation to first marriage. If the trend toward delayed childbearing continues, many of today's adolescents will be trying to become pregnant during years when the fertility of women is naturally declining. Given the negative impact of STI on sexual and reproductive health of both men and women, couples are more likely to face difficulties in becoming pregnant or maintaining a pregnancy (MacDonald & Brunham, 1997; PHAC, 2007). Increasing numbers are likely to seek fertility assistance or adoption, while others will not have children.

14   Relationship and family forms are also undergoing profound changes. With each succeeding census (Statistics Canada, 2006), there are increasing numbers of Canadians living in relationships and family forms other than the traditional form of two parents with biological children. Increasing numbers of today's adolescents are likely to find themselves living in such situations as common-law couples, gay and lesbian marriages and families, singles, childless couples, divorced parents, blended families, and long-distance or geographically separated families. What do we know about the implications of these diverse forms of family and relationship for sexual health and well-being? Research, public health programs, sexual health education, and popular discourse have focused considerable attention on sexuality and sexual health during the adolescent years, most often with a focus on the burden of STI and their sequelae and the issues of unintended pregnancy and early parenthood faced by some teens. Less attention has been paid to the pervasive discrimination and threats faced by adolescents who are gay, lesbian, questioning, or transgender (Egale, 2008), to the effects of legislation on the sexual wellbeing of adolescents, or to the challenges accompanying the changing social fabric of Canada. Yet, it is long-term changes in the social fabric that are likely to have the most profound effects on adolescent sexual health and well-being in the future.

Facing the Challenges

15   A central challenge for policy makers and programmers is deciding how to promote and develop educational and health services and environments that enhance sexual health and well-being for all Canadian adolescents not only today, but throughout their lives. We are strongly influenced when setting policy and programs by the discourse of risky, irresponsible youth and sexual danger that permeates both media and public policy, much of it imported from our close neighbour, the United States (US). Our media report events, evidence, and the ideological discourse from the US as if they were our own. This is so despite the distinct differences between Canada and the US in terms of demography, attitudes toward adolescent sexuality, adolescent sexual health outcomes (e.g., teen pregnancy and STI rates), and provision of sexuality education and health care. Perhaps more importantly, if we wish to set a course to improve adolescent sexual health and well-being we should look to countries with strong records of sexual health among their adolescents. For such examples, we are best to turn to western Europe (Singh & Darroch, 2001).

16   International cross-country comparative studies of developed countries conducted under the direction of the Alan Guttmacher Institute (Darroch, Frost, Singh & The Study Team, 2001) and by Advocates for Youth (2000) identified some of the environmental contributors to better sexual health among adolescents. Sex education and sexual health services for adolescents in North America are influenced by a pervasive concern about when, and in what type of relationship, it is desirable for youth to become sexually active. In the United States this is evidenced in a focus on promoting abstinence-until-marriage in sex education programs, as well as on the reduction of sexual health services available to adolescents, and increased requirements of parental notification and approval to receive services or participate in education programs. Even the more "comprehensive" sexuality education programs have been increasingly labelled as "abstinence-plus" programs. This contrasts with sex education programs in western European countries which are more often based on the assumption, and acceptance, that adolescents and young adults will engage in sexual activity prior to marriage or without it. Programs are founded on and teach values of responsibility, integrity, respect for self and others, together with techniques that contribute to safety and pleasure (Advocates for Youth, 2000; Darroch et al., 2001; Levine, 2002; Schalet, 2004). Freely available health care, accessible to adolescents without requiring parental approval, accompanies quality sex education in most western European countries. Contrary to concerns voiced by some in Canada (and more generally in the United States) that such permissiveness and openness to adolescent sexual activity will lead to earlier sexual activity and elevate the dangers to sexual health, the timing and forms of sexual activity among western European adolescents and young adults closely parallel those in Canada and indicators of sexual health point to better sexual health for western European youth (Darroch et al., 2001; Singh & Darroch, 2001). The example of western Europe, together with evaluations of sex education programs delivered in diverse countries, is clear. The focus on abstinence that permeates sex education and the shift toward greater external regulation and control of the sexual lives and activities of adolescents evidenced in the United States do not contribute to an environment conducive to sexual health (Bruckner & Bearman, 2005; Darroch et al., 2001). Instead, the approach that Canada has already begun to take in the development of the *Canadian Guidelines for Sexual Health Education* (Health Canada, 1994, 2003) and in setting a framework for improving sexual and reproductive health (Health Canada, 2002) offers a far more promising direction.

17   There are, however, gaps to be filled and improvements to be made. With respect to professional education, a national study of sexual health-related residency training of physicians (Barrett & McKay, 1998) found considerable variability between programs with a sizeable degree of under-coverage of key field-specific topics. McKay and Barrett (1999) found decided limitations in the extent and content of sexual health pre-service training of teachers which they described as a missed opportunity to prepare educators to deliver sexuality education early in their training (thus placing greater pressure on in-service training thereafter). Canadian physicians do the sexual health assessments and routine chlamydia screening of all sexually active 15- to 24-year-old female patients.

18   (Hardwick et al., 2007; Moses & Elliott, 2002) at a frequency considerably below that recommended by the *Canadian Guidelines on Sexually Transmitted Infections* (Public Health Agency of Canada, 2006). Although the reasons for the low screening rates are complex, Hardwick et al. (2007) suggest a number of interventions to increase testing frequency given the time pressures of busy practices. A first essential step to filling the gaps in these and other areas of sexual health training and service is to prioritize the kind of training that will best prepare teachers to deliver broadly-based sexual health education and physicians to counsel and provide sexual health preventive, diagnostic, and treatment services to all Canadians. Broadly-based sexual health education as conceptualized in the *Canadian Guidelines for Sexual Health Education* (2003) that is accessible to all students in all schools is a must.

19   While we may well look to western Europe for examples of approaches that produce an environment conducive to sexual health and well-being among adolescents, Canadians must also consider several unique circumstances in Canada which are unlike those found in western European countries. Distinct subgroups of Canadian adolescents carry the very highest burden of poor sexual health. These include, first and foremost, aboriginal youth (Canadian Federation for Sexual Health, 2007; Devries, Free, Morison, & Saewyc, 2007) and also poor and rural youth (Hardwick & Patychuk, 1999; Langille et al., 2004; Shoveller et al., 2007). Broadly-based sexual health education and provision of better sexual health services suited to the environments in which these youth live are essential. But they are only a first step in relieving this burden. Policy and program initiatives that address the poverty, isolation, and lack of future opportunity are also necessary to improve sexual health and prepare these adolescents for the challenges of the future.

20   Canada also has a unique multicultural profile. We are second only to Australia in receiving immigrants, with increasing numbers of new Canadians coming from regions of the globe where sexuality is grounded in different social and cultural roots than those that dominate in Canada. These new immigrants and their children face unique challenges in adapting to the "sexual scene" they experience in Canada (e.g., Shirpak, Maticka-Tyndale & Chinichian, 2007) and to accessing sexual health care (e.g., Maticka-Tyndale, Shirpak, & Chinichian; 2007). Our official policy of multiculturalism provides an ideological guide for development of policies and programs that respect the integrity and address the needs of diverse cultural groups. Unfortunately, our ability and commitment to working out ideological disagreements about the delivery of sexuality education and sexual health services has considerable room for improvement. All too often we respond to disagreements by allowing parents to restrict their children's access to education and services. This reinforces divisions between groups and detracts from the weaving of a cohesive social fabric by creating two classes of adolescents (and future adults): those who have had education and access to care and those who did not. Canada needs to lead the way in developing models of sexuality education and health care that respect and weave together diversities and differences whether they are differences in ethnicity, attitudes toward sexual orientation, or religion.

21   The sexual health and well-being of Canadian adolescents has fared relatively well compared to earlier generations. Challenges remain, including unwanted pregnancies; the sequelae of STI; psychological and physical violence perpetrated against primarily women and GLBTQ teens; changing social, sexual and relationship structures; inequities in health and well-being based on geographical region, economic status, and sexual orientation; and ideological differences that restrict the access of some adolescents to the education and services they deserve. These are the realities that should stir news commentators and motivate public policy, educational programming, and improvements in health care services. Much can be learned by looking to the examples set by countries in Western Europe where the sexual health of adolescents is better than in Canada (see Maticka-Tyndale, 2001). However, there are also situations unique to Canada where we need to find our own solutions.

The Canadian Journal of Human Sexuality. 2008. 17 (3).

References

Advocates for Youth. (2000). *Adolescent Sexual Health in Europe and the US - Why the difference?* 2nd ed. Washington, DC: Advocates for Youth.

Alderson, K. (2002). Reflecting on shattered glass: Some thoughts about gay youth in schools. *The Alberta Counsellor, 27,* 3–11.

Bagley, C, Bolitho, F., & Bertrand, I. (1997). Sexual assault in school, mental health and suicidal behaviors in adolescent women in Canada. *Adolescence, 32,* 341–366.

Bagley, C, Wood, M., & Young, I. (1994). Victim to abuser: Mental health and behavioral sequels of child sexual abuse in a community survey of young adult males. *Child Abuse and Neglect, 18,* 683–97.

Barbara, A.M., Quandt, S.A., & Anderson, R.T. (2001). Experiences of lesbians in the health care environment. *Women and Health, 14,* 45–61.

Barrett, M., & McKay, A. (1998). Training in sexual health and STD prevention in Canadian medical schools. *The Canadian Journal of Human Sexuality, 7,* 305–320.

Berman, H., McKenna, K., Arnold, C, Taylor, G., & MacQuarrie, B. (2000) Sexual harassment: Everyday violence in the lives of girls and women. *Advances in Nursing Science, 22,* 32–46.

British Columbia Ministry of Children and Family Development. (2002). *The health and well-being of Aboriginal children and youth in British Columbia.* Vancouver, BC: BC Ministry of Children and Family Development.

Bortolin, S., Adam, B.D., Brooke, C, & McCauley, J. (unpublished ms) Gay, lesbian and bisexual youth's experiences of school climate. University of Windsor.

Bortolin, S. (2008). Exploring the interplay of masculinities and homophobia in the high school climate. MA thesis. University of Windsor.

Boyce, W. (2004). *Young People in Canada, Their Health and Well-Being.* Ottawa, ON: Health Canada.

Boyce, W, Doherty, M., Fortin, C, & MacKinnon, D. (2003). *Canadian Youth, Sexual Health and HIV/AIDS Study: Factors influencing knowledge, attitudes and behaviours.* Toronto, ON: Council of Ministers of Education, Canada.

Bruckner, H., & Bearman, P. (2005). After the promise: The STD consequences of adolescent virginity pledges. *Journal of Adolescent Health, 36,* 271–278.

Canadian Federation for Sexual Health. (2007). *Sexual Health in Canada: Baseline 2007.* Ottawa, ON: Canadian Federation for Sexual Health.

CBC News. (April 29, 2008b). Internet predator stalking Surrey teens: RCMP. Retrieved June 20, 2008, from www.

cbc.ca/canada/british-columbia/story/2008/04/29/bc-sun-ey-predator.html.

CBC News. (May 1, 2008a). Canada's age of consent raised by 2 years. Retrieved May 15, 2008, from www.cbc.ca/canada/story/2008/05/01/crime-bill.html.

Darroch, J.R., Frost, J.J., Singh, S., & The Study Team. (2001). *Teenage Sexual and Reproductive Behavior in Developed Countries: Can more progress be made.* Occasional Report No. 3. New York, NY: Alan Guttmacher Institute.

DeLamater, J., & MacCorquodale, P. (1979). *Premarital Sexuality.* Madison, WI.: University of Wisconsin Press.

Devries, K.M., Free, C.J., Morison, L. & Saewyc, E. (2007) Factors associated with the sexual behavior of Canadian aboriginal young people and their implications for health promotion. *AJPH,*

Dryburgh, H. (2000). Teenage pregnancy. *Health Reports,* 72(1), Statistics Canada, Catalogue 82-003.

Equality for Gays and Lesbians Everywhere Canada (EGALE). (2007). *The First National School Climate Survey on Homophobia in Canadian Schools* in conjunction with the University of Winnipeg. Retrieved January 12, 2008, from www.climatesurvey.ca.

Equality for Gays and Lesbians Everywhere Canada (EGALE). (2008). *Preliminary Results of the First National School Climate Survey.* Retrieved June 15, 2008, from www.egale.ca/extra/1393-Homophobia-Backgrounder.pdf.

Gay, Lesbian and Straight Education Network (GLSEN). (2005). *The 2005 National School Climate Survey: The experiences of lesbian, gay, bisexual and transgender youth in our nation's school* (2005). New York, NY: GLSEN National.

Gillis, R. (2005) Examining the *National Longitudinal Survey of Children and Youth:* A profile of Canadian adolescent sexuality. MA thesis. Windsor, ON: University of Windsor.

Gulli, C. (2008). Suddenly teen pregnancy is cool? For the first time in years, more kids are having kids—and not just in the movies. *Maclean's,* 17 January 2008.

Hardwick, D., McKay, A., & Ashem, M. (2007) Chlamydia screening of adolescent and young adult women by general practice physicians in Toronto, Canada: Baseline survey data from a physician education campaign. *The Canadian Journal of Human Sexuality, 16,* 63–76.

Hardwick, D., & Patychuk, D. (1999). Geographic mapping demonstrates the association between social inequality, teen births and STDs among youth. *The Canadian Journal of Human Sexuality. 8,* 77–90.

Health Canada. (1994). *Canadian Guidelines for Sexual Health Education.* First edition. Ottawa, ON: Minister of National Health and Welfare. Division of STD Control,

Health Protection Branch and Health Services Systems Division, Health Programs and Services Branch, Health Canada.

Health Canada. (2003). *Canadian Guidelines for Sexual Health Education.* (Second edition). Ottawa, ON: Minister of Health. Community Acquired Infections Division, Population and Public Health Branch, Health Canada.

Health Canada. (1999). *A Report from Consultations on a Framework for Sexual and Reproductive Health.* Ottawa, Government of Canada. Health Canada. (2002). Reported *genital chlamydia/gonnorhea cases and rates in Canada by age group and sex.* Division of Sexual Health Promotion and STD Prevention and Control, Bureau of HIV/AIDS, STD and TB. Ottawa, Government of Canada, www.hc-sc.gc.ca/pphb-dgspsp.

Herold, E., & Way, L. (1985). Oral–genital sexual behavior in a sample of university females. *The Journal of Sex Research. 19,* 327–338.

King, A.J.C., Beazley, R.P, Warren, W.K., Hankins, CA., Robertson, A.S., & Radford, J.L. (1988). *Canada Youth and AIDS Study.* Ottawa, ON: Health and Welfare Canada.

Langille, D., Flowerdew, G, & Andreou, P (2004). Teenage pregnancy in Nova Scotia communities: Association with contextual factors. *The Canadian Journal of Human Sexuality, 13,* 83–94.

Lindberg, L.D., Jones, R., & Santelli, J.S. (2007). Noncoital sexual activities among adolescents. *Journal of Adolescent Health, 42,* S44–S45.

Levine, J. (2002). *Harmful to Minors.* Madison, WI: University of Wisconsin Press.

Lunau, K. (2008). Babies are the new handbag. *Maclean's.* January 17, 2008.

MacDonald, N.E., & Brunham, R. (1997). The effects of undetected and untreated sexually transmitted diseases: Pelvic inflammatory disease and ectopic pregnancy in Canada. *The Canadian Journal of Human Sexuality, 6,* 161–170.

Maticka-Tyndale, E. (2001). Sexual health and Canadian youth: How do we measure up? *The Canadian Journal of Human Sexuality, 10,* 1–17.

Maticka-Tyndale, E., Barrett, M., & McKay, A. (2000). Adolescent sexual and reproductive health in Canada: A review of national data sources and their limitations. *The Canadian Journal of Human Sexuality, 9,* 41–65.

Maticka-Tyndale, E., McKay, A., & Barrett, M. (2001). *Teenage Sexual and Reproductive Behavior in Developed Countries: Country Report for Canada.* Occasional Report No. 4. New York, NY: Alan Guttmacher Institute.

Maticka-Tyndale, E., Shirpak, K.R., & Chinichian, M. (2007). Providing for the sexual health needs of Canadian immigrants: The experience of immigrants from Iran. *Canadian Journal of Public Health. 98,* 183–186.

McCreary Centre Society. (2004). *Healthy Youth Development: Highlights from the 2003 Adolescent Health Survey III.* Vancouver, BC: McCreary Centre Society.

McKay, A. (2006). Trends in teen pregnancy in Canada with comparisons to USA. and England/Wales. *The Canadian Journal of Human Sexuality, 15,* 157–161.

McKay, A., & Barrett, M. (2008). Rising reported rates of chlamydia among young women in Canada: What do they tell us about trends in the actual prevalence of the infection? *The Canadian Journal of Human Sexuality, 17,* 61–69.

McKay, A., & Barrett, M. (1999). Pre-service sexual health education training of elementary, secondary, and physical education teachers in Canadian faculties of education. *The Canadian Journal of Human Sexuality, 8,* 91–101.

Moses, S., & Elliott, L. (2002). Sexually transmitted diseases in Manitoba: Evaluation of physician treatment practices, STD drug utilization, and compliance with screening and treatment guidelines. *Sexually Transmitted Diseases, 29,* 840–846.

Murray, J., & Henjum, R. (1993). Analysis of sexual abuse in dating. *Guidance & Counseling, 8,* 181–202.

National Longitudinal Survey of Children and Youth (NLSCY); Human Resources Development Canada and Statistics Canada, www.statcan.ca/english/sdds/4450.htm.

Newcomer, S.Q, & Udry, R.J. (1985). Oral sex in an adolescent population. *Archives of Sexual Behavior, 14,* 41–46.

Newton-Taylor, B., DeWit, D., & Giiksman, I. (1998). Prevalence and factors associated with physical and sexual assault of female university students in Ontario. *Health Care for Women International, 19,* 155–165.

Pancham, A., & Dunn, S. (2007). Emergency contraception in Canada: An overview and recent developments. *The Canadian Journal of Human Sexuality, 16,* 129–133.

Pearce, T. (2008). Chlamydia in teens jumps 50%. *Globe and Mail.* February 13, 2008.

Public Health Agency of Canada. (2007). *Supplement: 2004 Canadian Sexually Transmitted Infections Surveillance Report. ccdr* 2007, 33S1, 1–69.

Public Health Agency of Canada (PHAC). (2006) *Canadian Guidelines on Sexually Transmitted Infections.* Ottawa, ON: Public Health Agency of Canada.

Rhynard, J., & Krebs, M. (1997). Sexual assault in dating relationships. *Journal of School Health, 67,* 89–93.

Rotermann, M. (2008) Trends in teen sexual behaviour and condom use. *Health Reports, 19(3).* Statistics Canada, Catalogue no. 82-003-XPE.

Saewyc, E.M., Magee, L.L., & Pettingell, S.E. (2004). Teenage pregnancy and associated risk behaviors among sexually abused adolescents. *Perspectives on Sexual and Reproductive Health, 36,* 98–105.

Saewyc, E.M., Skay, C.L., Pettingell, S.L., Reis, E.A., Bearinger, L., Resnick, M., Murphy, A., & Combs, L. (2006). Hazards of stigma: The sexual and physical abuse of gay, lesbian, and bisexual adolescents in the United States and Canada. *Child Welfare, 85*, 195–213.

Saewyc, E., Taylor, D., Homma, Y, & Ogilvie, G (2008). Trends in sexual health and risk behaviours among adolescent students in British Columbia. *The Canadian Journal of Human Sexuality, 17*, 1–13.

Savin-Williams, R.C. (1999). Matthew Shepard's death: A professional awakening. *Applied Developmental Science, 3*, 150–154.

Schalet, A. (2004). Must we fear adolescent sexuality? *Medscape General Medicine, 6*. 22 pages. Retrieved March 3, 2006, from www.medscape.com/viewarticle/494933_print.

Shirpak, K.R., Maticka-Tyndale, E., & Chinichian, M. (2007). Iranian immigrants' perceptions of sexuality in Canada: A symbolic interactionist approach. *The Canadian Journal of Human Sexuality, 16*, 113–128.

Shoveller, J., Johnson, J., Prkachin, M., & Patrick, D. (2007). "Around here, they roll up the sidewalks at Night": A qualitative study of youth living in a rural Canadian community. *Health and Place, 13*, 826–838.

Shoveller, J., Johnson, J., Langille, D.B., & Mitchell, T. (2004). Socio-cultural influences on young people's sexual development. *Social Science and Medicine, 59*, 473–487.

Warren, W.K., & King, A.S. (1994). Development and evaluation of an AIDS/STD/sexuality program for grade 9 students. Kingston, Ontario. Social Programs Evaluation Unit, Queen's University.

Wilson, S. (2004). Good girls do. *Globe and Mail*. 1 February 2004.

Wolak, J., Finkelhor, D., Mitchell, K.J., & Ybarra, M. (2008). Online "predators" and their victims. *American Psychologist, 63*, 111–128.

Youthquest. (2002). Youthquest! Low-cost, high impact: Programs for lesbian, gay, bisexual and transgender youth. *Youthquest! 2002 Strategic Services Plan*. Retrieved from www.youthquest.bc.ca/servplan2002/needassessment.htm#ftnref2.

Sims, M.W. (2000). Gay/straight alliance clubs—understanding our differences. Retrieved from sss.bchrs.gov.bc.ca/PressRelease2000.asp.

Singh, S., & Darroch, J. (2001). Adolescent pregnancy and childbearing: Levels and trends in the developed countries. *Family Planning Perspectives, 32*, 14–23.

Smylie, L. (2008). The influence of social capital on the timing of first sexual intercourse among Canadian youth. Doctoral dissertation. University of Windsor.

Statistics Canada. (1998). *National Population Health Survey (NPHS)*, 1996–1997. Ottawa, Canada.

Statistics Canada. (2006). Family portrait: Continuity and change in Canadian families and households in 2006: Highlights. Retrieved June 20, 2008, from www12.statcan.ca/english/census06/analysis/famhouse/highlights.cfm.

Stepp, L.S. (July 8, 1999). Unsettling new fad alarms parents: Middle school oral sex. *Washington Post*. July 8, 1999.

Tonkin, R.S., Murphy, A., Lee, Z., Saewyc, E., and The McCreary Centre Society. (2005). *British Columbia Youth Health Trends: A Retrospective, 1992–2003*. Vancouver, BC; McCreary Centre Society.

Travers, R., & Schneider, M. (1996). Barriers to accessibility for lesbian and gay youth needing addictions services. *Youth & Society, 27*, 356–378.

Key and challenging words

coercion, precursor, surreptitious, feign, inflammatory, consensual, homonegativity, permeate, sequela, pervasive

Questions

1. Consult the "References" list for the works referenced in paragraph 1. Which titles seem to most clearly support the author's point about media "misunderstanding or misinformation" (paragraph 1)? Does she solely blame the media for misleading stories?

2. What specific bases of comparison does Maticka-Tyndale use for comparing this generation's sexuality and sexual health to that of previous generations?

3. Does the author seem to feel that the role played by new technologies in sexuality represents a threat to adolescent safety or morality? Why or why not?

4. Using one of the first three subheadings in the section "Sexual health trends," analyze in one paragraph the subsection, showing how Maticka-Tyndale's presentation of the information assists with clarity and coherence; if appropriate, you could

consider what she could have done to improve ease of reading.

5. Why does the author devote so much space to Wolak et al. in the subsection "Internet concerns"? Why might these findings be significant?

6. Does the author appear to have concerns about Bill C-22? What can be inferred about her opinion of the bill? In your answer, refer to specific features (such as language) of the paragraph.

7. In the subsection "Sexual health inequities," a) summarize paragraph 11; b) in paragraph 12, explain why the author has put "friends" and "straight" in quotation marks; c) paraphrase the last sentence of paragraph 12.

8. How do the sex education and sexual health education objectives and services differ in the US as compared to many Western European nations? According to the author, how has the media affected policy making in Canada in the past and how is it likely to affect policies in the future?

9. What specific challenges to adolescent sexual health confront Canadian policy makers as distinct from those of other nations? How can these challenges be overcome?

Post-reading

1. "Abstinence-plus" programs, prominent in the US, are mentioned in paragraph 16. Using a reliable source, such as a scholarly review article, newspaper/magazine article, or health-related website, define "abstinence-plus" education and summarize the effectiveness of such programs, according to researchers or other experts.

2. *Collaborative activity:* Discuss or debate approaches to health/sex education received in high school (of course, this could differ considerably among high schools). Consider such factors as resources available, access to resources, health/sex education classes or classes that include a health-sex education component, teaching methods, and attitude toward health/ sex education. What is the need or value of such classes? How could they be improved?

3. Identify central issues or problems in sexual health education today in Canadian high schools and suggest ways they could be addressed. This could take the form of an informal report in which you begin with an introduction that states the problem; follow with paragraphs that summarize the most relevant information, such as the findings of studies and/or current statistics; and conclude with a list of recommendations. Include references to "Sexuality and sexual health of Canadian adolescents: Yesterday, today and tomorrow" in your report; if your instructor permits, you may use additional sources.

Related website of interest

Canadian Guidelines for Sexual Health Education (2012):
www.cfsh.ca/resources/educational_and_training_
tools/healthcanadaguidelines.aspx

MEDIA AND IMAGE

Advice to teens

Nicola Phillips
(2,246 words)

Pre-reading

1. Are you aware of the concern with the mounting national student debt? Does or will the issue of debt affect you and/or any of your friends? Reflect on this issue in one to two paragraphs.
2. Scan the article. Does it seem different from other news stories on the subject of youth debt? Come up with a reading hypothesis that includes essay purpose and audience.

1   As we grapple with economic crises and easy credit, government overspending and a generation of parents whose expenditure threatens to saddle their children with crippling debts, concerns about profligacy and indebtedness have grown. The Citizens' Advice Bureau lists debt as a major issue facing young people under 25, most of which relates to personal loans, overuse of store cards and bank overdrafts. Buying goods on credit rather than with cash is commonplace and students face unprecedented levels of debt from the moment they start university. In the early 19th century, when the use of credit was equally ubiquitous, questions about the acquisition and responsibility for debt were remarkably similar to those faced by families today. Who is most at fault? The youth who cannot control his desire to buy fashionable goods, the shopkeepers who encourage purchases on credit, or the parent who has failed to instil a sense of financial responsibility? And who is legally or morally liable for the repayment of such debts?

2   The family of William Collins Jackson, an East India Company merchant, struggled to deal with just such questions, with ultimately tragic consequences. At just 19 years old, their son William was a handsome, charming, educated and fashionably dressed young man, for whom a bright future was predicted. In 1810, however, angry creditors had him arrested and locked within the Fleet Debtors' prison. Most creditors hoped debtors' sufferings in gaol would prompt their friends and family to raise the necessary funds before a case came to court. Indeed, debtors from wealthier families often spent time in a private debtors' lock up, or "sponging house" (so called because they were designed to wring every last penny from the debtor), while they attempted to raise enough bail to prevent imprisonment. William had written numerous frantic letters from a sponging house in Palsgrave Place but, despite the fact that his father was a wealthy man, his family ignored his pleas. Why? Because Mr Jackson believed his son was a profligate, who had failed to control his financial (and immoral) impulses. He needed to be taught a lesson before his actions led to his own and his family's ruin.

3   In the 18th and early-19th century fears were expressed about parents who dissipated their offspring's inheritance in the interests of preserving landed estates. Contemporary advice, such as that offered by William Fleetwood in *The Relative Duties of Parents and Children* (1811), urged children to pay off their parents' debts unless they had been "so extravagant that there would be no end of paying for them." Signs of profligacy in young men provided equal cause for concern. In art and literature a profligate son was a stereotypical character, accounts of whose fall from grace were intended to improve the morals and conduct of youths. Sarah More's novel *The Cheapside Apprentice* (1796) aimed to show "how a gay life may prove a short one" by recounting the story of a young man who inherited £3,000 and indulged in such profligacy that his fortune disappeared and he turned to forgery to cover his debts, a path that inevitably led to the gallows.

4   Youthful indebtedness, then as now, did not necessarily lead to a life of crime, but two commonly cited causes were peer pressure and the dangers of the desire to be seen as "fashionable." William Jackson was brought up in the expectation of inheriting in excess of £50,000 (worth well over £1 million today). He had been sent to the best schools and his friends included the sons of landed gentry, whose elegant dress, expensive leisure pursuits and sexual exploits he sought to emulate. But, as Isaac Taylor warned in his *Advice to the Teens* (1818), young gentlemen fresh from school should avoid trying to "keep on a par" with those "more richly supplied or more fashionably connected." Impatience "for gratification that could not wait until your finances were in better shape," he added, could only lead to increasing debts that would blight their adult life and the humiliation of borrowing from friends to pay them off. Among the vast amounts of stylish accoutrements William bought were a pair of exquisite, expensive duelling pistols that instantly confirmed the 17-year-old as both a man of fashion and of sufficient status to duel with other gentlemen. But he had insufficient funds to pay the gunmaker, or to repay the friends who had lent him money. All too soon he had to use the pistols in a duel with his creditors and former friends, and his family were forced to purchase a commission in the army so that he could temporarily leave the country to escape his debts.

5   The prevailing culture of purchasing goods on credit, a shortage of circulating coin caused by the wars with France and the legal confusion over liability for debts contracted by a minor made it easy for William to acquire modish merchandise, which he expected his father to pay for. William's gentlemanly attire, polite manners and the knowledge that his father was a wealthy man encouraged shopkeepers to offer the long-term credit expected by elite customers and to accept from him various forms of paper "promises to pay." Under civil law fathers were obliged to maintain their children in a manner suited to their social status until the age of 21. Sons who purchased goods were assumed to be acting with the permission of their fathers, who could then be held liable for payment of "necessary" goods. However, the courts struggled to define what items could be deemed necessary to preserve a young man's honour and social status. In one case the Lord Chief Justice decreed that it was

necessary for a young officer's honour and position to buy livery for his manservant (but not cockades for his soldiers). William Jackson insisted that his military officer's uniform was a necessary expense that he should not be expected to pay for from his monthly allowance, which he considered "insufficient to dress like a gentleman."

6   Court records show that William was just one of many male adolescents, including undergraduates, who exploited these legal uncertainties when obtaining credit from shopkeepers. However, they were also vulnerable to exploitation by men with a vested interest in helping youths get even further into debt under the guise of helping them escape from it. Moneylenders, like today's loan sharks, received a particularly bad press. John "Jew" King was a very wealthy money broker who specialised in lending funds to impoverished young heirs and improvident aristocrats. He was frequently attacked for his immoral earnings and fraudulent schemes, but continued to attract clients from the highest echelons of society. King complained about the number of public school boys who quickly learned "all the mysteries of borrowing at high interest" and even more quickly "how to cancel the obligation afterwards," but William swiftly became trapped in a spiral of dangerous borrowing. He was introduced to King by an unscrupulous attorney, who specialised in debt avoidance and the hiring of men to stand bail (at extortionate rates) to secure a debtors' release from gaol. But once in thrall to a bail man many debtors found they could not escape, even after paying what they believed they owed, because if they defaulted on any sum set by the bail man he could return them to prison.

7   Despite the recent acquisition of great wealth and aspirations of social improvement for his son, Mr Jackson remained wedded to his middle-class merchant roots, moral conservatism and strictly prudent economic principles. He did not share his son's view of what goods could be considered necessary purchases, particularly when the sums spent exceeded many hundreds of pounds. Mr Jackson was equally concerned about the morality of the means by which William acquired credit, declaring that he himself could not be held liable for any debts that had been contracted "dishonourably." This reflected in part his belief that his son had deliberately altered the way he

signed his name on credit notes to make it more similar to his father's signature—an act that could be considered forgery—and his fear that he could not afford to pay the mounting debts without ruining himself. Yet there was broader public concern about the difference between what was considered a lawful or fraudulent means of contracting debts.

8   Many creditors believed it fraudulent to promise repayment without a "reasonable" expectation of being able to do so or a prudent anticipation of "avoidable" difficulties. Living "extravagantly" after borrowing money could also be construed as fraudulent behaviour. Creditors made calculated choices about whether to prosecute under civil or criminal law when they sought to get their money back. On more than one occasion creditors threatened to arrest William for debt but, when his father refused to pay them off, sought redress under criminal law in the hope that the more severe consequences might force Mr Jackson to settle out of court. These moral judgements rarely corresponded with the beliefs of debtors such as William, whose consciences provided a range of justifications for their risky financial transactions; nor did they reflect the credit expectations of wealthy men. When he was eventually found guilty of fraud, William wrote to the Prince Regent in 1813 claiming that: "The misdemeanour I have been guilty of in drawing upon a banking house, having no effects [i.e. funds] there, is a crime half the nobility are daily guilty of."

9   The prince did not reply, but public concern about youthful immorality and indebtedness had been greatly increased by his own behaviour as a young man. During the 1790s Parliament had debated how best to deal with the prince's massive debts (of over £500,000) and to what extent his father, the thrifty George III, should be held liable for them. During one such debate in 1795 an MP asked "how many Members of that House were wild in their youth? Had they not been forgiven and had their debts paid?" In another, it was suggested that the king could combat his reputation for parsimony by paying off his son's debts and thus earning the "most valuable species of compound interest . . . ample return of love, affection and veneration" from both his son and his subjects. Then, as now, the giving or refusing of money to family members also had emotional implications. In his *Enquiry into The Duties of Men* (1811) Thomas Gisborne explained

that it was important for a father to set the amount of his son's allowance at the right level to reflect his rank in society, but also because "to fix [it] lower is to teach him to think himself treated with unkindness, and authorised to endeavour to maintain the station which he conceives to belong to him" by less scrupulous means.

10   In 18th-century families the relationship between parents and children was commonly conceptualised as "friendship," which implied an obligation to offer assistance. William often asked his father to behave as his "friend" and provide practical or financial help. But family relationships were also reciprocal; if William misbehaved or disobeyed him, Jackson considered the obligation broken and increasingly refused to help. He also believed that he had a duty to society to prevent William defaulting or defrauding more tradesmen. He argued that, if he settled one creditor's claims, he would have to settle them all and William would continue to sink further into debt. Jackson's actions echo the guidance given on websites today, which offer legal advice on the extent to which parents are responsible for their children's debts. Modern parents are warned not to bail out their children because doing so will not teach them how to solve the problem. William bitterly resented his father's refusal to settle. Only once did he concede it might prove a useful strategy; some creditors gave up pursuing him when he was imprisoned because they realised neither he nor his father would pay.

11   For these reasons Mr Jackson resisted pleas from all William's creditors, but he also railed against the system of consumer credit, which he believed was equally responsible for his son's ruin, and blamed tradesmen for their lack of care when granting it. "It is solely owing to the facility with which boys of the present age can obtain goods from men in business by fallacious statements that so many of them are brought to ruin," Jackson berated one shopkeeper. Unable to change the culture of credit, or control William by exercising parental authority, Jackson sought to teach his son a lesson by locking him in debtors' prisons. In May 1810 Jackson had written to the Attorney General in Guernsey (where William was serving with his regiment) and asked for him to be imprisoned until he mended his ways. In December that year when William was committed to the Fleet, Jackson refused to

help gain his release for seven months, at which point William reached a temporary agreement with his creditors. And he was not, as Pierce Egan's witty verse in *Life in London* (1821) suggests, the only "youth, whose father, for reform,/Has shut him up where countless vices swarm."

12   Mr Jackson's strategy was unsuccessful. William's inability to escape his creditors made him adopt ever more desperate and illegal means of obtaining money and resulted in his eventual transportation to Australia in 1814.

13   Today, draconian debt laws do not drive young people to desperation, but the temptation to borrow remains, so too does the facility to gain easy credit. Parents thus face similar challenges about how best to help their offspring with the problem of debt.

History Today. 2013. December.

Key and challenging words

profligacy, ubiquitous, dissipated, accoutrement, liability, modish, livery, improvident, echelon, unscrupulous, extortionate, thrall, redress, parsimony, rail (v), fallacious, draconian

Questions

1. Summarize paragraph 5; paraphrase sentences 3–5 of this paragraph.
2. What kinds of sources are used in the essay? Analyze the effectiveness of two sources from different disciplines, referring specifically to the text.
3. (a) How does Phillips use the case of William Jackson to represent upper-class youth during his time period? (b) Choosing one specific passage, show how she uses synthesis to link the general (youth debt) and the specific (Jackson).
4. How do you think the questions in paragraph 1 are answered in the essay? Using critical thinking and referring to specific passages in the text, explain the author's answer to the question, "Who is most at fault?"
5. Analyze Phillips's use of comparisons in the essay. Using at least two examples, explain whether you think she successfully compares youth in the past to youth in the present.

Post-reading

1. Compose a letter from a son or daughter to a parent that argues for an increase in spending allowance due to peer pressure and the need to succeed (see paragraph 4). Compose a suitable reply from the parent. In both letters, refer to some of the arguments (justifications) mentioned in the essay (obviously, all the arguments referred to won't be applicable). (You can set the letters in the nineteenth, twentieth, or twenty-first century.)

Related websites of interest

Managing Your Finances:
www.youth.gc.ca/eng/topics/money/manage_finances.shtml

Youth on Credit and Debt:
www.youtube.com/watch?v=oJgz3rDo6tE

Additional library reading

Wright, L. Walters, D., & Zarifa, D. (2013). Government student loan default: Differences between graduates of the liberal arts and applied fields in Canadian colleges and universities. *Canadian Review of Sociology, 50*(1), 89–115. doi:10.1111/cars.12004

Sotiropoulos, V., & D'Astous, A. (2012). Social networks and credit card overspending among young adult consumers. *Journal of Consumer Affairs, 46*(3), 457–484. doi:10.1111/j.1745–6606.2012.01239.x

In defence of the iGeneration

Renée Wilson
(3,158 words)

> ### *Pre-reading*
>
> 1. *Collaborative or individual activity:* (a) Do you think that the "iGeneration" is misunderstood or unfairly judged by earlier generations? Reflect on this question in one to two paragraphs or discuss in groups; OR (b) Brainstorm a list that includes both strengths and weaknesses of the "iGeneration." Pick at least two strengths and two weaknesses in order to come up with a representative "profile" of a member of this generation. Write up this profile in a paragraph.
> 2. After reading the essay's title and scanning the first three paragraphs, come up with a reading hypothesis (see p. 51); it should include the essay's purpose and intended audience.

A scientific and anecdotal rumination on why today's kids are more than alright—they're the best generation yet

-----

1   I had only been a College professor for three years when Gregory Levey's controversial and much-discussed magazine piece "Lament for the iGeneration" was published in 2009. I interpreted it as a cautionary tale: if we're in the hands of the next generation, we're really screwed. Levey, a Ryerson communications professor, basically argued he's pretty sure education has tanked; the iGeneration (those born in the 1990s) can't handle post-secondary learning; and that the gap between the schools and the kids is too huge to mend. Dismal stuff, but I understood where Levey was coming from—kind of.

2   I was terrified when I first started teaching. I didn't have any teacher training. I got hired via email. There was no mentoring, no lesson plans, no prep. One day I was writing a magazine column in my crap clothes from home, and the next I was dressed like a grown up stammering through a lesson at the helm of a full class. I just wanted them to like me. I guess that's why I took it personally when they paid more attention to Facebook than they did to me during a lecture. It was an out-of-body experience to have to tell them to turn their computers off and listen to me. I felt the same frustration Levey described in his article: "Radical advances in technology over the past decade have made today's young minds incompatible with traditional learning. It isn't just what they know or don't know. It's also how they know things at all."

3   Seven years later, I still die inside a little bit when, inevitably, I have to give the speech about shutting down screens when I'm directly addressing them.

I hate that I have to say it, but now I don't take it personally. I still worry that they won't get the crux of the lesson if they don't give me their full attention, but I know they're not mentally flitting around out of disrespect. Instead of finger wagging, I immersed myself in learning what makes them tick. Asking them to drop their tech would be like asking you to wear your shoes on the wrong feet. It's do-able, of course, but does it ever feel wrong. What I found is that this generation multi-task very well, and that the cynicism surrounding the iGeneration is dead wrong. Not only are the kids alright, they could be the best generation yet.

4   My cynical generation is great at slapping critical labels on the iGeneration. We do it all the time. "Everyone dumps on the youngest generation," says Giselle Kovary, co-founder and Managing Partner of Toronto-based Ngen People Performance Inc., which specializes in managing generational differences in the workplace. "But this generation is scary smart."

————

5   The generation born in the 1990s has pretty much always known things we haven't: Facebook (est. 2004), YouTube (est. 2005), Twitter (est. 2006), Google (est. 1996) and Wiki (est. 2001). Social networking to them is what colour TV was to GenX: It's hard to remember life before it—and just like TV used to be the big scare, we are obsessed over what the internet does to children of the iGeneration, especially now that they're growing up. All of this freaky attachment to tech is seriously messing with the "social" part of their brains, some experts say. Everyone—including iGeneration itself—is extremely sensitized to the way young people interact with technology. The list of scientific studies on the topic is as expansive as the more amateur commentary making its way through social media circuits.

6   The conclusions that such technology-attached-brain studies and commentaries reach are overwhelmingly scary. They ring not of advancement and exciting future possibilities, but of one word: beware. Take, for instance, the conclusions of one cautionary book. "Besides influencing how we think, digital technology is altering how we feel, how we behave, and the way in which our brains function," says Gary Small in his book, *iBrain: Surviving the technological alteration of the modern mind*, which he co-wrote with his wife, Gigi Vorgan, in 2008. "As the brain evolves and shifts its focus toward new technological skills, it drifts away from fundamental social skills, such as reading facial expressions during conversation or grasping the emotional context of a subtle gesture."

7   In other words, the iGeneration's techno brains are morphing them into socially inept robots. It's easy—perhaps too easy—to agree with this assessment, but I don't buy it. In my seven years in the classroom, I've witnessed how much more mature this generation is than I ever was as a student. On the upside, this techno brain phenom has resulted in a cohort that can think on its feet, make snap decisions and, on the flip-side of all the negative studies about them turning into social morons, there's just as much research to show that students who use tech to communicate are actually fantastic collaborators. It's like they're wired for it. They are fearless about pushing buttons—literally and figuratively—and, as one article put it, it's "as if they've been programed how to know what to do."

8   I'm in constant contact with my students, partly because they demand it and partly because it's just easier that way. Why wait a week to get an answer from me, when they can fire off a quick message, get the direction they need and then press on with an assignment? Isn't that just working smarter? I've talked a student through a class project at 8 p.m., while she was still at school and I was grocery shopping. I've conducted a class from my hotel room at Disney World during March Break without a single hiccup. The students didn't think twice about passing me around on an iPad to answer questions. What's more, they all showed up to class, even though they knew I wouldn't be there in body.

9   "This generation is known for its innovation and creativity," laughs Kovary over the phone. "Think outside of the box? Um, they don't even know there is a box." This generation only knows a world where the next-best version is released quarterly. What they've internalized is that there's no need to wait until every detail is perfect. Instead, you make adjustments as needed, in real time. This freedom of approach is what, perhaps, makes them the gutsiest of all generations. As Kovary adds, the iGeneration doesn't get stuck in the older generation's static world, or even in the status quo. Change is okay. In fact, it's great.

————

10   If the box no longer exists, neither does any sort of social or geographical barrier. Enter the now ubiquitous crowd-sourcing movement. What once was a small world has become a teeny, tiny world and no generation is more adept at taking advantage of that than the iGeneration. When I was a kid (Ugh. Did I just say that?), I wanted to be a travel agent. (Don't laugh. Who saw Expedia coming in the '80s?). But I didn't know anyone in the field, I couldn't find a college or university program, and that dream died. Today, those obstacles don't exist. The iGeneration doesn't blink at the thought of finding valuable life, job, or education connections through technology or social media. Just as those from other generations might ask their spouse, mentor or close friend, the iGeneration will source hundreds of "friends" and "followers" for love advice, career advice, and even thoughts on what to eat for lunch.

11   It can seem gutsy to put out a public SOS on Facebook or Twitter, but that's the way the iGeneration rolls. "They will crowd source, no matter what the challenge," says Kovary. "Their 'pack' is 700 people." While critics lambast the generation for its me-me-me focus, the truth is that collaboration comes naturally to this extended pack. Their willingness to source what other people have to say almost makes relying on others second nature.

12   In one class, for instance, I blindfolded my students and told them to make their way around the classroom, being sure to touch each of the four walls before returning to their chairs, in an unconventional attempt to teach them about deadlines (newsflash: I set them because I can see what's coming). Almost the entire group instinctively worked as a team, made a human chain and executed the task in a pack. In the end, I made my point about deadlines (my due date is preventing you from ramming into the proverbial desk you didn't see) and they reinforced the notion that there is power, and trust, in a pack.

13   Perhaps surprisingly, rather than creating a generation of followers and drifters—as is so often suggested—this ask-everybody-and-anybody-everything-and-anything attitude has created a cohort of peers. This extends to all areas, including business, and pretty much anything where top-down leadership was once instinctive. Now, says Kovary, everyone within a corporation is a peer. "If a senior manager says 'email me,' [this

generation] will," she adds. "If you're going to tout open communication, get ready!"

14   Whereas other generations were meant to maintain respectful distance, connecting with people—all people—is the iGeneration's natural expectation. Or as 23-year-old Katie Fewster-Yan puts it, because her generation is able to make so many easy connections with people, the top-down model of leadership seems unappealing, even obsolete. Instead, she suggests the term micro-leaders. She is co-founder of Ruckus Readings. Ruckus is a Toronto-based reading series that promotes spoken word literature, one of many, she admits, that exists in Toronto—an exercise in diversifying options, instead of competing for an audience. "Since it's so easy to connect with people," she adds, "You can really choose to follow the ones you're drawn to."

15   For Fewster-Yan, this has nothing to do with a sense of entitlement (another common, and tired, criticism of today's twentysomethings.) In fact, she mostly feels like she has the inverse of entitlement: that her resume is one small sheet in a massive stack of overqualified resumes, not even entitled to minimum wage despite her university education. She guesses that, more than anything, is why many of the iGeneration start things on their own, like she did with Ruckus Readings. It's not that they feel entitled to be happy or immediately successful or even that they should jumpfrog over others with more experience. Rather, there is a general sense that the old model of "shimmying in at the bottom, hanging tight and working your way up" is broken. And why, in this new world of change and crowd-sourcing wouldn't it seem that way? "I think of plenty of people as role models," says Fewster-Yan, "but I see them more as exemplary peers than superiors."

16   Or, as 22-year-old Chanelle Seguin says: "The best part is that the older generations are learning from the iGen." Seguin is the sole staff reporter at the *Pincher Creek Echo* in Alberta, where she is responsible for writing and designing the weekly community newspaper. In addition to putting in a solid eight hours at the paper, she also works part-time at Walmart to pay off the line of credit she needed to move from Ontario to Alberta for the reporting gig. Plus, she is a volunteer Girl Guide leader, is planning to coach hockey and is working on her own sports magazine start-up, *Tough Competition*.

17   She says her generation was forced to become leaders. They had to teach themselves how to use Facebook, Twitter, smartphones, Bluetooth—and the list goes on. Her generation doesn't, she adds, follow the same way other generations did. In that way, she admits, they kind of deserve the selfish moniker everyone slaps on them. "We are almost selfish," says Seguin, "because we lead ourselves and don't consider following anyone."

———

Traditionalists: 1922–1945

IN A WORD: STABLE

CATCH PHRASE: "If it ain't broke, don't fix it."

CHARACTERISTICS: stayed in the same company, doing the same job, forever; stayed married forever; change only happens for a good reason; maintaining the status quo is just fine

Baby Boomers: 1946–1964

IN A WORD: CAUTIOUS

CATCH PHRASE: "Change fatigue."

CHARACTERISTICS: many lost their jobs during the recessions of the '80s and '90s; had to endure "flavour of the month" leadership changes resulting in lack of enthusiasm for new changes; very politically savvy; must poke holes in a project before committing to it

Generation X: 1965–1980

IN A WORD: CYNICAL

CATCH PHRASE: "What's in it for me?"

CHARACTERISTICS: skeptical of leader's motivations and intentions; if they see what's in it for them, they will act as great champions for change; witnessed corporate downsizing, the dot-com bubble burst, and the scandals on Wall Street; expect change to happen

Generation Y: 1981–2000

IN A WORD: FLEXIBLE

CATCH PHRASE: "Do it now. Fix it later."

CHARACTERISTICS: have grown up in a world where technology changes every three-to-six months; don't long for the past; constantly seeking the newest, latest improvement; can become frustrated when faced with a reluctance to change; can't stand lip-service; no need to wait until every detail is perfect; make adjustments as needed, in real time

Summarized from Upgrade Now, *a guidebook for how to work harmoniously in a multi-generational workforce, by Adwoa Buahene and Giselle Kovary of Ngen People Performance Inc.*

18 Even so, don't ask for an iGeneration's undivided attention because you're not going to get it. It would be like asking a GenX to go back to changing channels without a clicker, or trying to convince a Traditionalist that debt is good. It just feels wrong. The iGeneration is of the "do it now, fix it later" mentality. But why wouldn't they be? They've come of age at a time when technology changes quarterly. Change is good. Rapid change means things are getting cooler.

19 Some have labelled this trait as the desire for immediate gratification, or a lack of stick-with-it-ness, but I think they're wrong. I think it's a matter of momentum. They can't stay static because everything around them, the social life-sustaining technology that triggers their all-consuming dopamine, is in perpetual change. Science tells us that brain function from age 15 to 25 is dopamine induced, which is why this is life's most emotionally powerful span. It isn't until later, sometime from age 25 onward, that the ability to control impulses kicks in. Dopamine is the feel-good chemical, it's that little Russell Brand voice in your head that whispers, "Go ahead, luv, have another piece of cake."

20 The iGeneration is swimming in it. Science also tells us that hits of dopamine, for the iGeneration, come from things like Facebook status likes and ReTweets. It's easy to confuse this with narcissism. While nearly all researchers peg key human development on ages birth to three years, prominent figures in adolescent research beg to elaborate. They say people ultimately become who they are during adolescence. The prefrontal cortex—the steady-eddie part of our brain—starts developing just before adolescence and doesn't stop until we're in our mid-twenties, which means from puberty until then everything feels really intense. We can blame this intensity on dopamine, a neurotransmitter that helps control the brain's reward and pleasure centres and gushes when we do something that feels good. This entire process is about preparing young people to shape their own notion of who they are as people, as they strive for self-actualization.

21 In Jennifer Senior's article, "Why You Truly Never Leave High School," published in January in *New York* magazine, the power of dopamine is explored. She quotes studies on the "reminiscence bump"—the term used for the fact that, "when given a series of random prompts and cues, grown adults will recall a disproportionate number of memories from adolescence."

This explains BOOM radio, mullets in 2013, why NKOTB can still sell out, and why otherwise placid grandparents can still bust a mean jive at a wedding reception. Societal circumstances change with the generations, but basic brain development doesn't. The drastic variable with the iGeneration, though, is the breakneck speed of technology. According to *iBrain*, we haven't seen this kind of leap since humankind first learned how to use a tool.

22 Every human being experiences the same stages of brain development, in that we're all in prefrontal cortex development from puberty to our mid-twenties. The difference today is that dopamine hits are coming from tech, and tech is everywhere, and tech equals perpetual change. According to Joel Stein's article, "The Me Me Me Generation," published in May in *Time* magazine, in order to retain this generation in the workforce, companies must provide more than just money; they must also provide self-actualization. "During work hours at DreamWorks (for example)," Stein writes, "you can take classes in photography, sculpting, painting, cinematography and karate."

23 This whole self-actualization thing is a bit *much* for GenXers and Boomers to stomach, especially in the workplace. I get it. And it took me a few runs at it, but I now see that self-actualization is the only way to truly reach the iGeneration in the classroom. I don't fancy myself Michelle Pfeiffer's character in *Dangerous Minds*, and I certainly have nothing on *Dead Poets Society's* captain-my-captain, but when I handed out marshmallows to students in a magazine writing class I knew I grabbed them tighter than Facebook in that lesson. I had found a way to tap into their value system. It was all about them (ahem, self-actualization), yes, but I knew every student also had a story to tell.

24 Still, I had completely underestimated the power of my marshmallow lesson. I was humbled when one student's composition described how it made him feel when he and his sister roasted marshmallows by candle flame because, as "apartment kids", they never had the privilege of a backyard campfire. In "Marshmallow", I expected a literal description of the taste of a marshmallow. Perhaps I underestimated the trust they had in me, and in their classmates, to share such personal stories. Educators need to find out what iGeneration's values are by sneaking up on them with unconventional lessons.

25   I remember another lesson, where I had students write a hate letter to anyone or anything. Dear Money. Dear Coffee. Dear Dad. Anything. One girl, a Harley-Davidson employee, addressed her letter as: Dear Chrome-Loving Douche Bag. Of course, when I read it aloud to the class, there was an extended laughter pause, but the content of the letter revealed a real revulsion, and fear of, a middle-aged man who flirted with her during a sale. It's bizarre. I've had some of the best Canadian journalists come speak in my classes, and I still catch students sneaking Facebook during the session. Yet, the Douche-Bag letter warranted undivided attention.

26   In a world so saturated with noise, it's like the iGeneration is thirsty for honesty and direct, transparent communication. If you spin an inauthentic response, they will quickly abandon ship. I have to admit, there's something endearing about a generation who wants to cut through the bullshit—much of it knee-jerk criticism of themselves.

This. 2013. November/December.

Key and challenging words

rumination, ubiquitous, saturated

Questions

1. Summarize paragraph 19 in which the author discusses studies on the effects of dopamine on the adolescent brain.
2. Discuss Wilson's use of anecdotal and/or first-person evidence in her essay. In your answer, include the following, along with any other relevant issues: examples of this kind of evidence; an analysis of its contribution to the essay; an analysis of how this kind of evidence is used to enhance credibility and whether it succeeds in this purpose.
3. In addition to anecdotal evidence (see question 2), identify at least one example each of the following kinds of evidence and analyze their contribution to the essay: (a) expert/authority; (b) analogy.
4. Comment on the effectiveness of Wilson's writing style, including tone, level of language, and diction. Consider her target audience in your answer and the suitability of her tone for this audience.

5. (a) Analyze the author's argument, including her use of inductive and deductive reasoning. To help analyze inductive reasoning, ask if she has provided adequate support for her claims; to help analyze deductive reasoning, ask if her generalizations are valid and supportable; (b) has she made any logical fallacies—for example, oversimplifications?
6. What is the function of the sidebar (p. 276)? Do you think it adds to or detracts from the article? Explain your reasoning.
7. Respond to one of the following statements, using critical thinking to analyze its validity: (a) "[T]he iGeneration's techno brains are morphing them into socially-inept robots" (paragraph 7); (b) "What [this generation has] internalized is that there's no need to wait until every detail is perfect. Instead, you make adjustments as needed, in real time" (paragraph 9).

Post-reading

1. *Collaborative or individual activity:* How applicable are Wilson's points to your own university experience? Be specific by referring to passages in the essay as well as in analyzing your own experiences at university (or high school/college).
2. Access "Lament for the iGeneration," by Gregory Levey (see paragraph 1), published in 2009 in *Toronto Life Magazine.* Scan the essay, looking for its main ideas. (a) Write a summary of Levey's essay in 200–250 words (about 10 percent of the original); or (b) write a compare–contrast critical analysis of both essays with at least two bases of comparison.

Related website of interest

Erin Millar, and Ben Coli. "Lament for the Lament for the iGeneration: Are Today's Students so Tapped into Twitter and Facebook That They're Unteachable?" Macleans.ca. *Macleans, 5 Oct. 2009. Web. 15 Oct. 2013.*

www.macleans.ca/education/uniandcollege/lament-for-the-lament-for-the-igeneration/

A ban on marketing of foods/beverages to children: The who, why, what and how of a population health intervention

Daniel J. Dutton, Norman R.C. Campbell, Charlene Elliott, and Lindsay McLaren
(1,766 words)

Pre-reading

1. Read the title and abstract, and scan the essay, noting headings and topic sentences. Write a one- to two-paragraph reading hypothesis (see p. 51) that considers the essay's purpose, audience, and main points.

Abstract

There is increasing recognition in Canada and elsewhere of the need for population-level interventions related to diet. One example of such an intervention is a ban on the marketing of foods/beverages to children, for which several health organizations have [developed] or are in the process of developing position statements. Considering the federal government's inaction to impose restrictions that would yield meaningful impact, there is opportunity for the health community to unite in support of a stronger set of policies. However, several issues and challenges exist, some of which we outline in this commentary. We emphasize that, despite challenges, the present and predicted future of diet-related illness in Canadian children is such that population-level intervention is necessary and becoming increasingly urgent, and there is an important role for the health community in facilitating action.

-----

1   To achieve significant and sustained reduction in various health risk factors, the need for population-level intervention (i.e., intervention [policy or program] operating within or outside the health sector, that targets a whole population[1,2]) is increasingly recognized. One current example is diet. Approximately 40% of deaths from non-communicable diseases worldwide are attributed to excess consumption of saturated fats, trans fats, sugar and salt.[3] This applies to children as well: Canadian children, on average, do not eat enough fibre[4] or fruits and vegetables[5] and consume too much sodium.[6] Accordingly, it has been predicted that the current generation of children could live a shorter life span than their parents; this would be unprecedented.[7]

2   Several population-level interventions have been suggested, one of which is banning marketing to children (e.g., ref. 8). Marketing to children includes traditional forms of marketing, such as television or print advertisements, as well as internet or cellular

phone-based promotion, games and contests, and in-store promotions targeting children.[9] A reasonable evidence base exists to support a ban on marketing to children, although much of the evidence to date pertains to television advertising. Advertisements appear to have a strong influence on children's preference, according to a review commissioned by the World Health Organization (WHO), which included both observational and controlled experimental trials. This review concluded that children exposed to advertising exhibit preferences towards food they see advertised, a tendency towards purchasing and requesting the foods they see advertised, and a greater consumption of those foods.[10] Cecchini et al.[11] estimated that, among various interventions used to tackle unhealthy diet and physical inactivity, the largest overall gains in disability-adjusted life years (DALYS) in a developed country would come from regulation of food advertisements to children, the benefits of which would accrue over the lifetime of the children.

3   One clear lesson from the history of public health is that even a robust evidence base often is not sufficient to ensure the adoption and implementation of specific policies—particularly those that are upstream in nature.[12] To achieve the desired population-level impact, interventions will need to have a significant structural or regulatory component,[13] due to inherent weaknesses of a voluntary, company-initiated approach. However, the current political environment in Canada is not supportive of this: in a regime characterized by active and passive encouragement of market forces,[14] government action to regulate private industry and potentially restrict profits by corporations is unpalatable to some. This is illustrated by the federal government's preference for voluntary rather than regulatory approaches in dietary policy.[8] That government has identified diet-related health issues as a priority (www.phacaspc.gc.ca/media/nr-rp/2011/2011_0307-eng.php) yet fails to implement policy that would have the desired impact, makes the government potentially vulnerable to a health lobby. There is opportunity for the health community to unite around a call for population-level interventions that require regulation and enforcement, such as banning marketing to children. However, for such a call to have credibility, the health community needs to be cognizant of the issues and challenges, some of which we outline here.

The Who: Creating a Health Lobby

4   There is opportunity for health organizations (including professional organizations in public health and health care, and non-profit groups) to unite in favour of banning marketing to children. While some in the public health community may readily support this, other health organizations may encounter challenges. For example, the disease-specific focus of some federal or provincial non-governmental organizations lends itself to a "downstream" orientation whereby the organization's funding is predominantly for biomedical and/or clinical research activities. For these organizations, supporting a call for banning marketing to children may be viewed as "too upstream" to be consistent with the organization's mandate. Ultimately, these organizations are accountable to their donor base, so support for a ban may be achieved through increased support for upstream policies from the general public, which includes the donor base, as well as organizational leadership. To secure the buy-in of these organizations, it may be necessary to actively promote the value (i.e., evidence base, potential impact) of such population health interventions. Such promotion, or education, could occur via communication (e.g., newsletters) to membership, as well as through conventional channels such as increased media attention to the determinants of health through newspapers and other mainstream media.

The Why: "Health" May not be the Most Effective Rationale

5   Although an evidence base exists to support banning marketing to children for health reasons, health communications scholars have argued that "health" may not be the most effective rationale. In particular, the "health pitch" has been shown to be vulnerable to manipulation by industry.[15] For example, towards ostensibly aligning with health goals, some companies have been keen to brand their foods as "healthier" than alternatives by emphasizing particular characteristics of their product, though in a misleading manner. For example, a company may emphasize elevated levels of desirable content (such as fibre), while other characteristics of the product may be questionable from a nutrition point of view; alternatively, they

may advertise decreased levels of less desirable content (such as sodium) "per serving," which is achieved by reducing serving size rather than through product reformulation. That health branding is vulnerable to manipulation reflects attributes of the regulatory system (i.e., manipulation would not occur if the system was designed to disallow it), and regulatory systems in turn are often developed in conjunction with industry, thus raising the broader issue of potential conflict of interest when industry is involved in the development of government-set regulations. While the expertise and advocacy of the health sector is integral to the proposed ban, an important complement is the ethical case for a ban: children are a vulnerable group. Health professionals, who are understandably accustomed to viewing health as sufficient rationale to implement an activity such as a ban, may need prompting to look beyond "health" as the only or most important rationale, and endorse the critical role of the ethical case. Further, privileging the ethical case may appeal to sectors of the general population who are not as convinced by a health rationale. There is a precedent for the value of privileging the ethical case: under sections 248 and 249 of the Consumer Protection Act, Quebec has banned advertising to children since 1980.[16] The ban was challenged by industry, but the Supreme Court of Canada upheld the ban on the basis that children are unable to critically assess advertising (which may be coercive or misleading), and thus advertising to children is not ethically defensible.[17] For a health lobby to be effective, health and health care professionals need to recognize and emphasize the ethical rationale of a ban, in addition to the health rationale. Privileging the ethical justification for a ban would also solve some of the problems with the vulnerability of existing initiatives, as noted above, to manipulation of what constitutes "healthier."

The What and How: The Nuts and Bolts of the Intervention, and Jurisdictional Issues

6   Banning "marketing" to children is, in fact, complex. Other well-known public health bans have focused more on single products (e.g., cigarettes) or mediums (e.g., television) than on target audiences. While we can avoid the complexity posed by the large diversity of products (foods/beverages) by calling for a complete ban on all products, questions remain about how to operationalize marketing to a target audience. For example, how do we determine the audience targeted by marketing, including their age? How do we ensure that all important media (i.e., television, internet, cell phones, video games, etc.) are included?

7   The Quebec case is instructional. Although there are guidelines on what constitutes advertising to children,[17] the guidelines are open to interpretation. Monitoring of the Quebec ban comes mostly in the form of complaints by advocacy groups that direct attention to potential violations of the ban, and the onus is on the complainants to emphasize that the delivery and/or content of the advertisement is directed at children (such as the Coalition Poids www.cqpp.qc.ca/en). While it is operationally easy to extend the Quebec model to every other province in Canada, it is not clear that a grassroots monitoring approach would be appropriate or effective at the national level. Without comprehensive national rules, regional discrepancies could give rise to both unequal enforcement of such a ban as well as differential interpretations across regions of what counts under the ban, which would lead to future national enforcement difficulties. The need for a national policy and enforcement is consistent with discussion of jurisdictional issues in public health generally: while public health delivery is largely a provincial responsibility, a coordinated central response federally is necessary for successful intervention, especially when the costs of the intervention are likely to be unequal across provinces.[18]

Conclusion

8   The Canadian government has identified certain diet-related health issues as priorities, yet their actions are insufficient to achieve meaningful change to the food environment. There is an opportunity for the health community to unite around population-level interventions such as a ban on marketing to children, and such a lobby could potentially be very powerful in the face of government hypocrisy. For a health lobby to be effective, there is need for cognizance of key issues and challenges, some of which we outline here. However these challenges should not be seen as

reasons not to proceed, considering what is at stake. The present and predicted future of diet-related illness in Canadian children is such that population-level intervention is necessary and becoming increasingly urgent. Although the action suggested, and issues raised, in this commentary may be known to experts with regard to the relationship between health and marketing in children, we propose that this relatively small number of experts will be limited in their ability to enact change unless they have the active support of the general health community.

Conflict of Interest: Dr. Norman R.C. Campbell received financial travel support from Boehringer Ingelheim to attend hypertension meetings in 2010. Otherwise, the authors have no conflicts of interest to declare.

Canadian Journal of Public Health. 2012. 103 (2).

References

1. Rose G. *The Strategy of Preventive Medicine*. Oxford, UK: Oxford University Press, 1992. [Reprinted. *Rose's Strategy of Preventive Medicine*. Oxford: Oxford University Press, 2008.]

2. Hawe P, Potvin L. What is population health intervention research? *Can J Public Health* 2009;100(Suppl 1):S8–S14.

3. Beaglehole R, Bonita R, Horton R, Adams C, Alleyne G, Asaria P, et al. Priority actions for the non-communicable disease crisis. *Lancet* 2011;377(9775):1438–47.

4. Health Canada. Do Canadian Children Meet their Nutrient Requirements through Food Intake Alone? 2009. Cat. No. H164–112/1–2009E-PDF. Available at: www.hc-sc.gc.ca/fn-an/alt_formats/pdf/surveill/nutrition/commun/art-nutr-child-enf-eng.pdf (Accessed February 8, 2012).

5. Garriguet D. Canadians' eating habits. *Health Rep* 2007;18(2):17–32.

6. Garriguet D. Sodium consumption at all ages. *Health Rep* 2007;18(2):47–52.

7. Olshansky SJ, Passaro DJ, Hershow RC, Layden J, Cames BA, Brody J, et al. A potential decline in life expectancy in the United States in the 21st Century. *N Engl J Med* 2005;352:1138–45.

8. Sodium Working Group. Sodium Reduction Strategy for Canada: Recommendations of the Sodium Working Group. Health Canada, 2010. Available at: www.hc-sc.gc.ca/fn-an/nutrition/sodium/strateg/index-eng.php (Accessed February 8, 2012).

9. Harris J, Pomeranz J, Lobstein T, Brownell KD. A crisis in the marketplace: How food marketing contributes to childhood obesity and what can be done. *Annu Rev Public Health* 2009;30:211–25.

10. Hastings G, McDermott L, Angus K, Stead M, Thomson S. The Extent, Nature and Effects of Food Promotion to Children: A Review of the Evidence. World Health Organization, 2007. Available at: www.who.int/dietphysicalactivity/publications/Hastings_paper_marketing.pdf (Accessed February 8, 2012).

11. Cecchini M, Sassi F, Lauer JA, Lee YY, Guajardo-Barron V, Chisholm D. Tackling of unhealthy diets, physical inactivity, and obesity: Health effects and cost-effectiveness. *Lancet* 2010;376(9754):1775–84.

12. Siegel M, Doner Lotenberg L. *Marketing Public Health: Strategies to Promote Social Change*, 2nd ed. Sudbury, MA: Jones and Bartlett Publishers, 2007.

13. McLaren L, McIntyre L, Kirkpatrick S. Rose's population strategy of prevention need not increase social inequalities in health. *Int J Epidemiol* 2010;39: 372–77.

14. Eikimo TA, Bambra C. The welfare state: A glossary for public health. *J Epidemiol Community Health* 2008;62:3–6.

15. Elliott C. Marketing fun foods: A profile and analysis of supermarket food messages targeted at children. *Can Public Policy* 2008;34(2):259–73.

16. Éditeur officiel du Québec. *Consumer Protection Act*. 1978;248–49.

17. Jeffery B. The Supreme Court of Canada's appraisal of the 1980 ban on advertising to children in Québec: Implications for "misleading" advertising elsewhere. *Loyola of Los Angeles Law Review* 2006;39:237–76.

18. Wilson K. The complexities of multi-level governance in public health. *Can J Public Health* 2004;95(6): 409–12.

Key and challenging words

unpalatable, cognizant, coercive, onus, differential, jurisdictional

Questions

1. Briefly discuss the importance of the studies mentioned in paragraph 2 to the authors' purpose.
2. Explain why the authors state that "even a robust evidence base often is not sufficient to ensure the adoption and implementation of specific policies" (paragraph 3).
3. Identify the authors' thesis, and comment on its rhetorical effectiveness; for example, you could consider language, tone, or appeals designed for the essay's audience.
4. Define *upstream* (paragraph 3) and *downstream* (paragraph 4) approaches and explain the difference between them. Try to use context to answer the question before referring to a business dictionary.

5. (a) Discuss the strategies the authors use to aid comprehension in the section "The why: 'Health' may not be the most effective rationale." You could consider organization, rhetorical patterns, transitions, and the like; (b) if you were to divide this long paragraph into three shorter paragraphs, where would you make the separations? Justify your choices and provide headings for each subsection.
6. Analyze the authors' use of precedent and one other argumentative strategy in their essay (see p. 109).
7. Analyze the authors' conclusion, keeping in mind the audience they are addressing.

Post-reading

1. As a group lobbying for health interventions for children, use the information and approaches discussed in this essay (along with other sources if appropriate) to create a brief report/presentation. Your audience will not be health professionals but government representatives in a position to recommend or implement the kinds of interventions discussed in the essay.

Related website of interest

Childhood Obesity Foundation:
www.childhoodobesityfoundation.ca/

Additional library reading

Campbell, N., Pipe, A., & Duhaney, T. (2014). Calls for restricting the marketing of unhealthy food to children: Canadian cardiovascular health care and scientific community get ignored by policy makers. What can they do? *Canadian Journal of Cardiology, 30*(5), 479–481. doi:10.1016/j.cjca.2013.11.025

Elliott, C., & Brierley, M. (2012). Healthy choice?: Exploring how children evaluate the healthfulness of packaged foods. *Canadian Journal of Public Health, 103*(6), e453–e458.

Elliott, C. (2012). Packaging health: Examining 'better-for-you' foods targeted at Children. *Canadian Public Policy, 38*(2), 265–281. doi:10.1353/cpp.2012.0010

Reality TV gives back: On the civic functions of reality entertainment

Laurie Ouellette
(3,029 words)

Pre-reading

1. Consider the documentaries you have watched. What were their names? What was their purpose? Their main features? Do they fit the description of the "documentary tradition" outlined in paragraph 1?
2. This essay has no descriptive (content) headings. Determine where the introduction ends and the body paragraphs begin. Read the first sentences of the first few paragraphs. Does it appear that they are topic sentences that can help you determine the essay's content?

Abstract

Reality TV is more than a trivial diversion. Civic aims historically associated with documentaries (particularly citizenship training) have been radically reinterpreted and integrated into current popular reality formats.

Keywords: citizenship, civic experiment, documentary, public service, reality TV.

*

1   In his influential 2002 essay "Performing the Real: Documentary Diversions," John Corner identified a *lack of civic purpose* as reality TV's defining attribute. His point of reference was the documentary tradition, from which the surge of "unscripted" entertainment since the late-1990s has selectively borrowed. Reflecting on the early stages of this development, Corner worried that if television programs like *Big Brother* drew from the look and style of serious documentary, they eclipsed its historical "civic functions," defined as official citizenship training, journalistic inquiry and exposition, and (from the margins) radical interrogation (48–50). Designed "entirely in relation to its capacity to deliver entertainment" and achieve "competitive strength" in a changing marketplace, reality TV repurposed "documentary as diversion," Corner argued (52). Serious techniques of observation, documentation, investigation, and analytic assessment were fused to the pleasure principles of soap opera and gaming—and focused inward. Cameras and microphones captured the performance of selfhood and everyday life within artificial settings and contrived formulas. For Corner, this interior play with the discourse of the real was symptomatic of a larger trend with troubling implications. Changing the whole point of documentary since the late-1800s, the new reality programming addressed TV viewers as consumers of entertainment instead of citizens. Would purposeful factual forms of television—and democracy itself—survive?

2   The broader institutional context for such concerns was—and is—the waning public service tradition. Public broadcasters such as the British Broadcasting Corporation (BBC) in the United Kingdom and to a lesser extent the Public Broadcasting Service (PBS) in the United States have played a major role in defining and developing television's civic potentialities (Scannell; Ouellette). Envisioning the medium as an instrument of education, not a mover of merchandise, public broadcasters embraced documentary and other nonfiction formats as a dimension of their broader mission to serve and reform citizens so they might better fulfill their national "duties and obligations" (Ang 29). Factual programming high in civic legitimacy but low in "exchange value" (Corner 52) was faithfully circulated as a "cultural resource for citizenship" as well as an instrument for enlightening and guiding national populations (Murdock 186). Since the 1990s, however, this commitment has been subject to reinterpretation and flux. As BBC scholar Georgina Born points out, the "concept and practice" of public broadcasting has been "radically transformed" across Western capitalist democracies by market liberalization, deregulation, digital technologies, and the post-welfare impetus

to reform and downsize the public sector in general (Born, "Digitalising" 102; see also *Uncertain Vision*). Faced with budget cuts, entrepreneurial mandates, and heightened competition from commercial channels and new media platforms, many public broadcasters have backed away from traditional public service–inflected programming with limited audience appeal. At a juncture when citizens are increasingly hailed as enterprising subjects and consumers of do-it-yourself lifestyle resources, major European public broadcasters have embraced many of the popular reality conventions critiqued by Corner. The BBC, for example, helped pioneer the hybridization of documentary and entertainment, and is now a major player in the global circulation of unscripted formats. With fewer resources, PBS has also experimented with the popular reality show in an attempt to bolster ratings. With the market logic responsible for "documentary as diversion" operating across public and private channels, the conditions for fostering documentary as a civic project would appear to be closing down.

3   Although the further decline of journalistic and investigative documentary material on television is difficult to dispute, I want to suggest that the medium has not entirely withdrawn from civic engagement since Corner's essay was published—far from it. Many of the functions ascribed to the documentary and the public service tradition in general—particularly citizenship training—have been radically reinterpreted and integrated into popular reality formats. While the specific aims and techniques have changed, reality TV continues to be mobilized as a resource for educating and guiding individuals and populations. If the civic functions of reality entertainment are more difficult to recognize, it is partly because they now operate *within* market imperatives and entertainment formats, but also because prescriptions for what counts as "good citizenship" have changed. Unlike the cultural resources for citizenship provided by the (partly) tax-funded public service tradition, reality TV's civic aims are also diffuse, dispersed, commercial (especially in the United States), and far removed from any direct association with official government policies or agendas.

4   In *Better Living through Reality TV: Television and Post-Welfare Citizenship*, James Hay and I argue that, particularly in the United States, reality TV does not

"divert" passive audiences from the serious operations of democracy and public life, as much as it translates broader sociopolitical currents and circulates instructions, resources, and scripts for navigating the changing expectations and demands of citizenship. Many reality programs explicitly address TV viewers as subjects of capacity who exercise freedom and civic agency within (not against) entertainment and consumer culture. This is not particularly surprising, to the extent that reality TV took shape alongside the neoliberal policies and reforms of the 1990s, including the downsizing of the public sector, welfare reform, the outsourcing of state powers and services, the emphasis on consumer choice, and heightened expectations of personal responsibility. Within this context, we suggest, the application of documentary techniques to the demonstration, performance, and testing of self and everyday life makes reality entertainment potentially useful to new strategies of "governing at a distance" that deemphasize public oversight and require enterprising individuals to manage their own health, prosperity, and well being (Rose). From *The Apprentice* to *The Biggest Loser*, reality games command an indirect and unofficial role in constituting, normalizing, educating, and training the self-empowering the citizens beckoned by political authorities. However artificial and staged these programs appear on the surface, they help to constitute powerful truths concerning appropriate forms of civic conduct and problem-solving. To the extent that reality TV's civic functions are also marketable, affective, entertaining, and executed through dispersed partnerships among the television industry, sponsors, nonprofit agencies, celebrities, and TV viewers, they parallel with (and have helped to constitute) the "reinvention of government" in the United States (under Clinton and Bush) as a series of decentralized public-private partnerships on one hand, and self-enterprising citizens on the other (Ouellette and Hay 18–24).

5   Cultural studies scholar Toby Miller once theorized citizenship as an ongoing pull between the "selfish demands" of the consumer economy and the "selfless requirements" of the political order (136). This tension takes on an even greater degree of intensity as the line between consumerism and public politics further collapses, and the requirements of citizenship come to include the actualization of the self through consumer culture and the execution of compassion and ethical responsibility to others. We are expected

to actualize and maximize ourselves in a world of goods and perform as virtuous subjects whose voluntary activities in the public world are, as George W. Bush explained during his inaugural address, "just as important as anything government does." In addition to calling on nonprofits, charities, and faith-based organizations to temper gaps left by the downsized welfare state, both the Bush and Clinton administrations promoted volunteerism as a preferred mode of privatized civic empowerment. Reality TV's contributions to what might be called post-welfare civic responsibility manifested within this milieu and are particularly evident in the "do-good" experiments that have flooded the airwaves since the millennium.

6   From *American Idol Gives Back* to *Oprah's Big Give*, a stream of high-profile helping ventures has appeared to redeem reality TV's scandalous associations with bug eating, navel gazing, and bed swapping. These programs (and the marketing discourses that surround them) make explicit claims about reality TV's civic importance. Do-good programs can take on a variety of formats—from the audience participation show to the competition to the makeover—but all reject the earlier notion of public service as education and preparation for participation in the official political processes. Reality entertainment instead intervenes directly in social life, enacting "can do" solutions to largely personalized problems within emotional and often suspenseful formats. The template was established by *Extreme Makeover Home Edition* (2002–present), a successful ABC program that mobilizes private resources (sponsors, experts, nonprofits, volunteers) in a "race against time" to revamp the run-down houses of needy families (see Ouellette and Hay 42–56). The participants are selected by casting agents who find the most "deserving" and marketable stories of hardship from tens of thousands of applications weekly. Products and brand names are woven into the melodramatic interventions, and as many critics have noted, complex issues and socioeconomic inequalities are simplified and downplayed. Still, to dismiss these ventures as trivial or somehow less than "real" would be to overlook their constitutive role as technologies of citizenship, private aid, and volunteerism.

7   On *Home Edition*, for example, TV viewers are "activated" to practice compassionate citizenship by volunteering for nonprofit partners such as Habitat for Humanity and Home Aid. The ABC website provides direct links, publicity on sponsors and partners, advice on getting involved, and tips from volunteer agencies, thus further stitching the production and active consumption of reality TV into privatized networks of assistance and self-care. While often endorsed by public officials, do-good programs circulate as alternatives to the various ills (inefficiency bureaucracy, dependency, centralized control) ascribed to the welfare state. Needy subjects and their problems provide the raw material for the manufacture of entertainment commodities and circulation of advertising that cannot be zapped. The best and only solution to unmet needs and human hardships (private charity) is offloaded onto the private sector and TV viewers. More explicitly than other reality subgenres, the helping trend acknowledges the limitations of self-maximization and pure market logic—and capitalizes on the result.[1]

8   Do-good television is especially common on commercial channels in the United States. Although European public broadcasters offer reality-based lessons on living, most lack the resources to intervene directly in reality on a philanthropic scale. Why would the television industry take on such projects, given its historical avoidance of public service obligations? For one thing, do-good experiments are fully expected to be profitable. More importantly, they also allow media outlets to cash in on marketing trends such as "citizen branding" and corporate social responsibility (CSR). Because networks are offered as branded interfaces to suggested civic practices, good citizenship—and the ethical surplus it is assumed to generate—can be harnessed to build consumer loyalty. This makes it possible to differentiate brands of television in a cluttered environment and exploit what business historian David Vogel calls the burgeoning "market for virtue." For example, ABC (home to many do-good ventures) brands itself as a Better Community, while the reality-based cable channel Planet Green provides a branded interface to green citizenship and environmental problem-solving. Recently, MTV (owned by Viacom) announced its intention to replace trivial reality entertainment with issue-oriented and civic-minded material. Last year, the wealthy debutantes of *My Sweet Sixteen* were sent to impoverished global locations to improve their character and ethics

in a program called *Exiled*. The contestants on the third season of sister channel VH1's *Charm School* are currently being instructed on the importance and procedures of volunteering and performing community service. The change is part of MTV and VH1's efforts to re-brand their programming—and their images—in the wake of young people's overwhelming support of Barack Obama. Tellingly, *Charm School's* off-screen male narrator not only sounds a lot like Obama, he also punctuates the ongoing question of whether the show can transform party girls into "model citizens" with the slogan, "Yes, we can." As this example attests, the spirit of accountability public sector renewal ushered in by the election can easily be evoked as a new justification for the enactment of philanthropy and self-help—in part because of television's commercial investments in these solutions as branding devices and marketing strategies.

9   If CSR is becoming the new public service, we need critical frameworks for assessing its cultural output. My aim here is not to fault Corner's early evaluation of mainly British reality TV but to begin to unravel the complexities of reality entertainment in its current forms. I have been arguing that any attempt to theorize the civic functions and consequences of popular reality will need to also address its constitutive relationship to changing and colluding dynamics of commerce and governance. It also seems crucial to recognize the residual, emergent, and sometimes contradictory logics operating within the genre. For example, however market-driven and stitched into the circuitry of privatization, do-good reality programming does provide all-too-rare visibility on US television for the poor, the sick, the unemployed, the homeless, and the uninsured. As Anna McCarthy convincingly argues, it bears witness to the "trauma" of everyday life under neoliberal conditions, even as it deflects the causes and commodifies the consequences. Reality TV's helping interventions disrupt the calculated rationality of today's enterprise culture, encouraging visceral and affective reactions to poverty not unlike the industrial slum photographs of Jacob Riis or the gas company–funded social problem documentaries of John Grierson (see Winston). In the wake of the current financial crisis and recession, these dimensions of reality TV may be intensifying—as suggested by the recent Fox program *Secret Millionaire* (2008–09).

10   Developed by the UK company RDF Media, *Secret Millionaire* originated in 2006 on Channel 4, a publicly owned but commercially funded British channel. RDF developed the format for Fox Television last year, using US participants and locations but keeping the generic template and the series name intact. Conceived and marketed as reality entertainment, *Secret Millionaire* combines the techniques of the documentary, the social experiment, and the melodrama. Each week, a designated millionaire goes "undercover" into impoverished communities to observe hardship firsthand and give away one hundred thousand dollars of his money (tellingly, the millionaire is almost always white and male) while the cameras roll. The benefactors are required to give up their mansions, fancy cars, expensive restaurants, electronic gadgets, and other taken-for-granted consumer privileges and subsist on "welfare wages" like the struggling individuals and families they encounter. They perform hard labour, eat cheap food, live in substandard housing, and interact socially with have-nots, often for the first time in their lives. Along the way, they scout around for people and projects to donate a chunk of their fortune to. Eventually, the expected "reveal" occurs: The millionaire unmasks his true identity and surprises the deserving recipients with a spectacular cash donation.

11   In the debut episode of the US version, a wealthy California lawyer who is also a successful business owner goes to live among the poor with his teenaged son. They perform temporary construction work, reside in a cheap motel, and quickly discover how much they have to learn about the "real world." What is innovative and potentially disruptive about the program is not its authenticity per se (the artificial conditions and staged aspects of other reality shows are readily apparent) but the alternative manner through which the intervention unfolds. In many respects, the formula draws from and exploits dominant representations of socioeconomic inequality: wealth is individualized, and only those "others" who are judged deserving on the basis of uncontrollable circumstances and/or exemplary character are candidates for assistance. Yet, unlike other do-good television programs, the *Secret Millionaire's* purpose is ultimately *not* to evaluate or make over the poor. Nor is it to shower them with branded consumer goods

(courtesy of sponsors) or to enact enterprising solutions to their complex social problems. Its point is to evaluate, educate, guide, enlighten, and transform the richest people in North America. Throughout the debut episode, father and son learn about routine dimensions of socioeconomic difficulties not from experts, but from the experiences and commiserations of people who mistakenly believe they share something in common with the main characters. A middle-aged, uninsured woman who became homeless for a time when she suffered a major back injury provides them breakfast and encouragement. She had subsequently found work at the same construction site and—unaware of their true identity (the cameras are ascribed to a documentary filming)—tries to help the best she can. Another family with a chronically ill child and no health coverage explains the everyday stresses and difficulties of making ends meet and their eventual slide into bankruptcy. While this constitution of the worthy poor is characteristic of other do-good reality experiments, *Secret Millionaire* also identifies the undernourished and collapsing public sector as a structural factor in their situations. TV viewers are allowed to identify with shared problems and difficulties that no television program can fix.

12   The millionaires perform extreme empathy and shock on hearing the hardship stories. As with all reality entertainment, their reactions are shaped and accentuated by casting, editing, camera work, and music. Yet, this artifice does not prevent the series from contributing in potentially useful ways to the "truth" about class and wealth in the current era. In the premiere, father and son undergo a process of self-recognition in which they become increasingly aware of their privilege. They come to see themselves as thoughtless and selfish and are unable to rationalize their "luxury spending" in the midst of unmet human needs and chronic suffering. While this recurring lesson can be easily dismissed as a cultural tempering of growing resentment against the business elites responsible for the current economic crisis, it also reworks the civic logic orienting of much of reality TV by reversing the process and subjects of transformation. Within this context, the millionaire's cash donation can be interpreted as a technology of private aid, but it can also be seen as enacting a reevaluation (if not quite a redistribution) of the allotment of resources and wealth in the United States. The lack of product placements in *Secret Millionaire* reinforces this possibility—not only because a consumer address is contained in the commercial breaks, but because the problem of uneven wealth cannot be resolved by a trip to Disney World or the installation of a free washing machine. Alas, this lack of marketability will undoubtedly keep the civic possibilities opened up by programs such as *Secret Millionaire* in check. Such are the limits of reality TV in its current form.

Journal of Popular Film and Television. 2010.
April–June 38 (2).

Note

1.   For a more detailed analysis of the governmental dimensions of do-good TV (from which this article draws), see Ouellette and Hay ch. 1, "Charity TV: Privatizing Care, Mobilizing Compassion."

Works Cited

Ang, Ien. *Desperately Seeking the Audience*. London: Routledge, 2001. Print.

Born, Georgina. "Digitalising Democracy." *What Can Be Done? Making the Media and Politics Better*. Ed. J. Lloyd and J. Seaton. Oxford: Blackwell, 2006. 102–23. Print.

———. *Uncertain Vision: Birt, Dyke and the Reinvention of the BBC*. London: Secker and Warburg, 2004. Print.

Bush, George W. "Inaugural Address." *American Rhetoric Online Speech Bank* 20 Jan. 2001. Web. 11 May 2009. <www.americanrhetoric.com/speeches/gwbfirstinaugural.htm.>

Corner, John. "Performing the Real: Documentary Diversions." *Television and New Media* 3 (2002): 255–69. Rpt. in *Reality TV: Remaking Television Culture*. Ed. Susan Murray and Laurie Ouellette. New York: NYU Press, 2009. 44–64. Print.

McCarthy, Anna. "Reality Television: A Neoliberal Theater of Suffering." *Social Text* 25.4 (2007): 17–41. Print.

Miller, Toby. *The Well-Tempered Self: Citizenship, Culture and the Postmodern Subject*. Baltimore: Johns Hopkins UP, 1993. Print.

Murdock, Graham. "Public Broadcasting and Democratic Culture: Consumers, Citizens and Communards." *A Companion to Television.* Ed. Janet Wasco. Malden: Blackwell, 2005. 174–98. Print.

Ouellette, Laurie. *Viewers Like You? How Public Television Failed the People.* New York: Columbia UP, 2002. Print.

Ouellette, Laurie, and James Hay. *Better Living through Reality TV: Television and Post-Welfare Citizenship.* Malden: Black-well, 2008. Print.

Rose, Nikolas. "Governing 'Advanced' Liberal Democracies." *Foucault and Political Reason: Liberalism, Neoliberalism and Rationalities of Government.* Ed. Andrew Barry, Thomas Osbourne, and Nikolas Rose. Chicago and London: University of Chicago Press, 1996. 37–64.

Scannell, Paddy. "Public Service Broadcasting and Modern Public Life." *Media Culture Society* 11 (1989): 135–66. Print.

Vogel, David. *The Market for Virtue: The Potential and Limits of Corporate Social Responsibility.* Washington, DC: Brookings Institute Press, 2005. Print.

Winston, Brian. *Claiming the Real: Documentary, Grierson and Beyond.* New York: Palgrave Macmillian, 2008. Print.

Key and challenging words

contrived, symptomatic, entrepreneurial, juncture, bolster, milieu, mobilize, constitutive, philanthropic, burgeoning, attest, collude, residual, visceral, benefactor, commiseration

Questions

1. a) In two sentences, summarize the views of John Corner as expressed in paragraph 1; *OR* b) In two sentences, summarize the abstract of John Corner's article "Performing the Real: Documentary Diversions" (*Television and New Media* 3.3 [2002]: 255–69).

2. Explain the different uses for quotation marks around the following words in paragraph 1: "unscripted," "civic functions," and "entirely in relation to its capacity to deliver entertainment."

3. Explain how the view of public broadcasting today differs from the traditional view. What accounts for these differences?

4. Type A essays often make connections between forms of art or entertainment and the "real" world, claiming universal relevance for such art. Show how Ouellette connects reality TV in the 1990s to political, social, or economic forces at play during that time (see paragraph 4).

5. a) Analyze Ouellette's use of synonyms, rephrasing, repetition, and sentence transitions to contribute to coherence in paragraph 5; b) Analyze the effectiveness of paragraph transitions by looking at two of the following, considering how the last sentence of the earlier paragraph is connected to the first sentence of the following one: paragraphs 5–6, 6–7, 7–8, 8–9, or 9–10.

6. What is *branding* (paragraph 8)? Explain how branding can be applied to "do-good television" and why it is important, according to the author.

7. a) In one paragraph, explain why *Secret Millionaire* (paragraphs 10–12) is a good illustration of what Ouellette discusses in the previous paragraphs; b) Compare *Secret Millionaire* with other "do-good" reality shows discussed in the article, noting at least one similarity and difference.

8. Analyze the conclusion of the essay for its effectiveness.

Post-reading

1. *Collaborative activity:* a) Discuss or debate the validity of Ouellette's main points about reality TV today. Refer to specific reality shows you have watched or are familiar with; *OR* b) Discuss or debate the concept of "reality" TV. How real is reality TV?

2. Access the home page of one of the TV shows mentioned in the article, such as *Charm School* or *Secret Millionaire*, or another "do-good" reality TV show. Is there a summary of the show itself (rather than episode summaries)? Does the description of the show

stress what Ouellette considers its citizenship function? Summarize the website's description of the show and its function or purpose.

3. Find an argumentative essay on some aspect of reality TV in a popular (non-academic) source, like a magazine or a blog. Analyze the argument, first summarizing its thesis and main points, and then evaluating the effectiveness of the argument.

Additional library reading

Many studies on reality programming have been published in the last ten years and can be accessed through your library's databases. The first and third articles below are empirical studies of reality TV; the second focuses on the reality TV show *Charm School*, which is discussed in Laurie Ouellette's essay.

Barton, Kristin M. "Reality Television Programming and Diverging Gratifications: The Influence of Content on Gratifications Obtained." *Journal of Broadcasting & Electronic Media* 53.3 (2009): 460–76. Print.

Papacharissi, Zizi, and Andrew L. Mendelson. "An Exploratory Study of Reality Appeal: Uses and Gratifications of Reality TV Shows." *Journal of Broadcasting & Electronic Media* 51.2 (2007): 355–70. Print.

Holbrook, Alice, and Amy E. Singer. "When Bad Girls Go Good." *Journal of Popular Film & Television* 37.1 (2009): 34–43. Print.

Post-princess models of gender: The new man in Disney/Pixar

Ken Gillam and Shannon R. Wooden
(4,993 words)

Pre-reading

1. Are you aware that Disney animated films have long been criticized for their stereotypical and sexist portrayals of their main characters? Consider one Disney animated film you have seen or for which you know the plot, focusing on its male and/or female stereotypes.

2. Scan the abstract and first paragraph of the essay: a) Identify two examples of *jargon* in the abstract (i.e., words/phrases used within the discipline that a knowledgeable reader would be expected to understand but that a non-specialist might not understand); b) Why do you think the authors chose to begin their essay with a brief personal narrative?

Abstract

Unlike most Disney animated films, which have been criticized for decades for their stereotypical female leads and traditional representations of gender, all the major features released by Disney's Pixar studios since 1990 have featured masculine protagonists. These male plots are remarkably alike, and together, we argue, they indicate a rather progressive postfeminist model of gender. Beginning with alpha-male traits in common, from emotional inaccessibility to keen competitiveness, the stars of these stories follow similar *Bildungsroman* plots. In this article, we chart the pattern of masculine development in three of these films—*Cars*, *Toy Story*, and *The Incredibles*—noting that Pixar consistently promotes a new model of masculinity. From the revelation of the alpha male's flaws, including acute loneliness and vulnerability, to figurative emasculation through even the slightest disempowerment, each character travels through a significant homosocial relationship and ultimately matures into an acceptance of his more traditionally "feminine" aspects.

Keywords: animated film, *Bildungsroman*, Disney, gender studies, homosociality, masculinity, Pixar, Eve Sedgwick

*

1   Lisping over the Steve McQueen allusion in Pixar's *Cars* (2006), our two-year-old son, Oscar, inadvertently directed us to the definition(s) of masculinity that might be embedded in a children's animated film about NASCAR. The film overtly praises the "good woman" proverbially behind every successful man: the champion car, voiced by Richard Petty, tells his wife, "I wouldn't be nothin' without you, honey." But gender in this twenty-first-century *Bildungsroman* is rather more complex, and Oscar's mispronunciation held the first clue. To him, a member of the film's target audience, the character closing in on the title long held by "The King" is not "Lightning McQueen" but "Lightning the queen"; his chief rival, the always-a-bridesmaid runner-up "Chick" Hicks.

2   Does this nominal feminizing of male also-rans (and the simultaneous gendering of success) constitute a meaningful pattern? Piqued, we began examining the construction of masculinity in major feature films released by Disney's Pixar studios over the past thirteen years. Indeed, as we argue here, Pixar consistently promotes a new model of masculinity, one that matures into acceptance of its more traditionally "feminine" aspects. Cultural critics have long been interested in Disney's cinematic products, but the gender critics examining the texts most enthusiastically gobbled up by the under-six set have so far generally focused on their retrograde representations of women. As Elizabeth Bell argues, the animated Disney features through *Beauty and the Beast* feature

a "teenaged heroine at the idealized height of puberty's graceful promenade. . ., [f]emale wickedness. . . rendered as middle-aged beauty at its peak of sexuality and authority [. . ., and] [f]eminine sacrifice and nurturing. . . drawn in pear-shaped, old women past menopause" (108). Some have noted the models of masculinity in the classic animated films, primarily the contrast between the ubermacho Gaston and the sensitive, misunderstood Beast in *Beauty and the Beast*,[1] but the male protagonist of the animated classics, at least through *The Little Mermaid*, remains largely uninterrogated.[2] For most of the early films, this critical omission seems generally appropriate, the various versions of Prince Charming being often too two-dimensional to do more than inadvertently shape the definition of the protagonists' femininity. But if the feminist thought that has shaped our cultural texts for three decades now has been somewhat disappointing in its ability to actually rewrite the princess trope (the spunkiest of the "princesses," Ariel, Belle, Jasmine, and, arguably, even Mulan, remain thin, beautiful, kind, obedient or punished for disobedience, and headed for the altar), it has been surprisingly effective in rewriting the type of masculine power promoted by Disney's products.[3]

3   Disney's new face, Pixar studios, has released nine films—*Toy Story* (1995) and *Toy Story 2* (1999); *A Bug's Life* (1998); *Finding Nemo* (2003); *Monsters, Inc.* (2001); *The Incredibles* (2004); *Cars* (2006); *Ratatouille* (2007); and now *WALL•E* (2008)—all of which feature interesting male figures in leading positions. Unlike many of the princesses, who remain relatively static even through their own adventures, these male leads are actual protagonists; their characters develop and change over the course of the film, rendering the plot. Ultimately these various developing characters—particularly Buzz and Woody from *Toy Story*, Mr. Incredible from *The Incredibles*, and Lightning McQueen from *Cars*—experience a common narrative trajectory, culminating in a common "New Man" model[4]: they all strive for an alpha-male identity; they face emasculating failures; they find themselves, in large part, through what Eve Sedgwick refers to as "homosocial desire" and a triangulation of this desire with a feminized object (and/or a set of "feminine" values); and, finally, they

achieve (and teach) a kinder, gentler understanding of what it means to be a man.

Emasculation of the Alpha Male

4   A working definition of *alpha male* may be unnecessary; although more traditionally associated with the animal kingdom than the Magic Kingdom, it familiarly evokes ideas of dominance, leadership, and power in human social organizations as well. The phrase "alpha male" may stand for all things stereotypically patriarchal: unquestioned authority, physical power and social dominance, competitiveness for positions of status and leadership, lack of visible or shared emotion, social isolation. An alpha male, like Vann in *Cars*, does not ask for directions; like Doc Hudson in the same film, he does not talk about his feelings. The alpha male's stresses, like Buzz Lightyear's, come from his need to save the galaxy; his strength comes from faith in his ability to do so. These models have worked in Disney for decades. The worst storm at sea is no match for *The Little Mermaid's* uncomplicated Prince Eric—indeed, any charming prince need only ride in on his steed to save his respective princess. But the post-feminist world is a different place for men, and the post-princess Pixar is a different place for male protagonists.

5   *Newsweek* recently described the alpha male's new cinematic and television rival, the "beta male": "The testosterone-pumped, muscle-bound Hollywood hero is rapidly deflating . . . . Taking his place is a new kind of leading man, the kind who's just as happy following as leading, or never getting off the sofa" (Yabroff 64). Indeed, as Susan Jeffords points out, at least since *Beauty and the Beast*, Disney has resisted (even ridiculed) the machismo once de rigueur for leading men (170). Disney cinema, one of the most effective teaching tools America offers its children, is not yet converting its model male protagonist all the way into a slacker, but the New Man model is quite clearly emerging.

6   *Cars*, *Toy Story*, and *The Incredibles* present their protagonists as unambiguously alpha in the opening moments of the films. Although Lightning McQueen may be an as-yet incompletely realized alpha when *Cars* begins, not having yet achieved the "King" status of his most successful rival, his ambition and fierce competitiveness still clearly valorize the alpha-male model: "Speed. I am speed . . . . I eat losers for breakfast," he chants as a prerace mantra. He heroically comes from behind to tie the championship race, distinguishing himself by his physical power and ability, characteristics that catapult him toward the exclusively male culture of sports superstars. The fantasies of his life he indulges after winning the coveted Piston Cup even include flocks of female cars forming a worshipful harem around him. But the film soon diminishes the appeal of this alpha model. Within a few moments of the race's conclusion, we see some of Lightning's less positive macho traits; his inability to name any friends, for example, reveals both his isolation and attempts at emotional stoicism. Lightning McQueen is hardly an unemotional character, as can be seen when he prematurely jumps onto the stage to accept what he assumes to be his victory. For this happy emotional outburst, however, he is immediately disciplined by a snide comment from Chick. From this point until much later in the film, the only emotions he displays are those of frustration and anger.

7   *Toy Story's* Buzz Lightyear and Sheriff Woody similarly base their worth on a masculine model of competition and power, desiring not only to be the "favourite toy" of their owner, Andy, but to possess the admiration of and authority over the other toys in the playroom. Woody is a natural leader, and his position represents both paternalistic care and patriarchal dominance. In an opening scene, he calls and conducts a "staff meeting" that highlights his unambiguously dominant position in the toy community. Encouraging the toys to pair up so that no one will be lost in the family's impending move, he commands: "A moving buddy. If you don't have one, GET ONE." Buzz's alpha identity comes from a more exalted source than social governance—namely, his belief that he is the one "space ranger" with the power and knowledge needed to save the galaxy; it seems merely natural, then, that the other toys would look up to him, admire his strength, and follow his orders. But as with Lightning McQueen, these depictions of masculine power are soon undercut. Buzz's mere presence exposes Woody's strength as fragile, artificial, even arbitrary, and his "friends," apparently having been drawn to his authority rather than his character, are

fair-weather at best. Buzz's authority rings hollow from the very beginning, and his refusal to believe in his own "toyness" is at best silly and at worst dangerous. Like Lightning, Buzz's and Woody's most commonly expressed emotions are anger and frustration, not sadness (Woody's, at having been "replaced") or fear (Buzz's, at having "crash-landed on a strange planet") or even wistful fondness (Woody's, at the loss of Slink's, Bo Peep's, and Rex's loyalty). Once again, the alpha-male position is depicted as fraudulent, precarious, lonely, and devoid of emotional depth.

8   An old-school superhero, Mr. Incredible opens *The Incredibles* by displaying the tremendous physical strength that enables him to stop speeding trains, crash through buildings, and keep the city safe from criminals. But he too suffers from the emotional isolation of the alpha male. Stopping on the way to his own wedding to interrupt a crime in progress, he is very nearly late to the service, showing up only to say the "I dos." Like his car and toy counterparts, he communicates primarily through verbal assertions of power—angrily dismissing Buddy, his meddlesome aspiring sidekick; bantering with Elastigirl over who gets the pickpocket—and limits to anger and frustration the emotions apparently available to men.

9   Fraught as it may seem, the alpha position is even more fleeting: in none of these Pixar films does the male protagonist's dominance last long. After Lightning ties, rather than wins, the race and ignores the King's friendly advice to find and trust a good team with which to work, he browbeats his faithful semi, Mack, and ends up lost in "hillbilly hell," a small town off the beaten path of the interstate. His uncontrolled physical might destroys the road, and the resultant legal responsibility—community service—keeps him far from his Piston Cup goals. When Buzz appears as a gift for Andy's birthday, he easily unseats Woody both as Andy's favourite and as the toy community's leader. When Buzz becomes broken, failing to save himself from the clutches of the evil neighbour, Sid, he too must learn a hard lesson about his limited power, his diminished status, and his own relative insignificance in the universe. Mr. Incredible is perhaps most obviously disempowered: despite his superheroic feats, Mr. Incredible has been unable to keep the city safe from his own clumsy brute force. After a series of lawsuits

against "the Supers," who accidentally leave various types of small-time mayhem in their wake, they are all driven underground, into a sort of witness protection program. To add insult to injury, Mr. Incredible's diminutive boss fires him from his job handling insurance claims, and his wife, the former Elastigirl, assumes the "pants" of the family.

10   Most of these events occur within the first few minutes of the characters' respective films. Only Buzz's downfall happens in the second half. The alpha-male model is thus not only present and challenged in the films but also is, in fact, the very structure on which the plots unfold. Each of these films is about being a man, and they begin with an outdated, two-dimensional alpha prototype to expose its failings and to ridicule its logical extensions: the devastation and humiliation of being defeated in competition, the wrath generated by power unchecked, the paralyzing alienation and fear inherent in being lonely at the top. As these characters begin the film in (or seeking) the tenuous alpha position among fellow characters, each of them is also stripped of this identity—dramatically emasculated—so that he may learn, reform, and emerge again with a different, and arguably more feminine, self-concept.

11   "Emasculated" is not too strong a term for what happens to these male protagonists; the decline of the alpha-male model is gender coded in all the films. For his community service punishment, Lightning is chained to the giant, snorting, tar-spitting "Bessie" and ordered to repair the damage he has wrought. His own "horsepower" (as Sally cheerfully points out) is used against him when literally put in the service of a nominally feminized figure valued for the more "feminine" orientation of service to the community. If being under the thumb of this humongous "woman" is not emasculating enough, Mater, who sees such subordination to Bessie as a potentially pleasurable thing, names the price, saying, "I'd give my left two lug nuts for something like that!"

12   Mr. Incredible's downfall is most clearly marked as gendered by his responses to it. As his wife's domestic power and enthusiasm grow increasingly unbearable, and his children's behaviour more and more out of his control, he surreptitiously turns to the mysterious, gorgeous "Mirage," who gives him what he needs

to feel like a man: superhero work. Overtly depicting her as the "other woman," the film requires Elastigirl to intercept a suggestive-sounding phone call, and to trap her husband in a lie, to be able to work toward healing his decimated masculinity.

13   In *Toy Story*, the emasculation of the alpha male is the most overt, and arguably the most comic. From the beginning, power is constructed in terms conspicuously gender coded, at least for adult viewers: as they watch the incoming birthday presents, the toys agonize at their sheer size, the longest and most phallic-shaped one striking true fear (and admiration?) into the hearts of the spectators. When Buzz threatens Woody, one toy explains to another that he has "laser envy." Buzz's moment of truth, after seeing himself on Sid's father's television, is the most clearly gendered of all. Realizing for the first time that Woody is right, he is a "toy," he defiantly attempts to fly anyway, landing sprawled on the floor with a broken arm. Sid's little sister promptly finds him, dresses him in a pink apron and hat, and installs him as "Mrs. Nesbit" at her tea party. When Woody tries to wrest him from his despair, Buzz wails, "Don't you get it? I AM MRS. NESBIT. But does the hat look good? Oh, tell me the hat looks good!" Woody's "rock bottom" moment finds him trapped under an overturned milk crate, forcing him to ask Buzz for help and to admit that he "doesn't stand a chance" against Buzz in the contest for Andy's affection, which constitutes "everything that is important to me." He is not figured into a woman, like Buzz is, or subordinated to a woman, like Lightning is, or forced to seek a woman's affirmation of his macho self, like Mr. Incredible is, but he does have to acknowledge his own feminine values, from his need for communal support to his deep, abiding (and, later, maternal) love of a boy. This "feminine" stamp is characteristic of the New Man model toward which these characters narratively journey.

Homosociality, Intimacy, and Emotion

14   Regarding the "love of a boy," the "mistress" tempting Mr. Incredible away from his wife and family is not Mirage at all but Buddy, the boy he jilted in the opening scenes of the film (whose last name, Pine, further conveys the unrequited nature of their relationship). Privileging his alpha-male emotional

isolation, but adored by his wannabe sidekick, Mr. Incredible vehemently protects his desire to "work alone." After spending the next years nursing his rejection and refining his arsenal, Buddy eventually retaliates against Mr. Incredible for rebuffing his advances. Such a model of homosocial tutelage as Buddy proposes at the beginning of the film certainly evokes an ancient (and homosexual) model of masculine identity; Mr. Incredible's rejection quickly and decisively replaces it with a heteronormative one, further supported by Elastigirl's marrying and Mirage's attracting the macho superhero.[5] But it is equally true that the recovery of Mr. Incredible's masculine identity happens primarily through his (albeit antagonistic) relationship with Buddy, suggesting that Eve Sedgwick's notion of a homosocial continuum is more appropriate to an analysis of the film's gender attitudes than speculations about its reactionary heteronormativity, even homophobia.

15   Same-sex (male) bonds—to temporarily avoid the more loaded term *desire*—are obviously important to each of these films. In fact, in all three, male/male relationships emerge that move the fallen alphas forward in their journeys toward a new masculinity. In each case, the male lead's first and/or primary intimacy—his most immediate transformative relationship—is with one or more male characters. Even before discovering Buddy as his nemesis, Mr. Incredible secretly pairs up with his old pal Frozone, and the two step out on their wives to continue superheroing on the sly; Buddy and Frozone are each, in their ways, more influential on Mr. Incredible's sense of self than his wife or children are. Although Lightning falls in love with Sally and her future vision of Radiator Springs, his almost accidentally having befriended the hapless, warm Mater catalyzes more foundational lessons about the responsibilities of friendship—demanding honesty, sensitivity, and care—than the smell-the-roses lesson Sally represents. He also ends up being mentored and taught a comparable lesson about caring for others by Doc Hudson, who even more explicitly encourages him to resist the alpha path of the Piston Cup world by relating his experiences of being used and then rejected. Woody and Buzz, as rivals-cum-allies, discover the necessary truths about their masculine strength only as they discover how much they need one another. Sedgwick further describes the ways in

which the homosocial bond is negotiated through a triangulation of desire; that is, the intimacy emerging "between men" is constructed through an overt and shared desire for a feminized object. Unlike homosocial relationships between women—that is, "the continuum between 'women loving women' and 'women promoting the interests of women'"—male homosocial identity is necessarily homophobic in patriarchal systems, which are structurally homophobic (3). This means the same-sex relationship demands social opportunities for a man to insist on, or prove, his heterosexuality. Citing Rene Girard's *Deceit, Desire, and the Novel*, Sedgwick argues that "in any erotic rivalry, the bond that links the two rivals is as intense and potent as the bond that links either of the rivals to the beloved" (21); women are ultimately symbolically exchangeable "for the primary purpose of cementing the bonds of men with men" (26).

16   This triangulation of male desire can be seen in *Cars* and *Toy Story* particularly, where the homosocial relationship rather obviously shares a desire for a feminized third. Buzz and Woody compete first, momentarily, for the affection of Bo Peep, who is surprisingly sexualized for a children's movie (purring to Woody an offer to "get someone else to watch the sheep tonight," then rapidly choosing Buzz as her "moving buddy" after his "flying" display). More importantly, they battle for the affection of Andy—a male child alternately depicted as maternal (it is his responsibility to get his baby sister out of her crib) and in need of male protection (Woody exhorts Buzz to "take care of Andy for me!").[6] *Cars* also features a sexualized romantic heroine; less coquettish than Bo Peep, Sally still fumbles over an invitation to spend the night "not with me, but . . ." in the motel she owns. One of Lightning and Mater's moments of "bonding" happens when Mater confronts Lightning, stating his affection for Sally and sharing a parallel story of heterosexual desire. The more principal objects of desire in *Cars*, however, are the (arguably) feminized "Piston Cup" and the Dinoco sponsorship. The sponsor itself is established in romantic terms: with Lightning stuck in Radiator Springs, his agent says Dinoco has had to "woo" Chick instead. Tia and Mia, Lightning's "biggest fans," who transfer their affection to Chick during his absence, offer viewers an even less subtly gendered goal, and Chick uses this to taunt Lightning. It is in

the pursuit of these objects, and in competition with Chick and the King, that Lightning first defines himself as a man; the Piston Cup also becomes the object around which he and Doc discover their relationship to one another.

The New Man

17   With the strength afforded by these homosocial intimacies, the male characters triumph over their respective plots, demonstrating the desirable modifications that Pixar makes to the alpha-male model. To emerge victorious (and in one piece) over the tyrannical neighbour boy, Sid, Buzz and Woody have to cooperate not only with each other but also with the cannibalized toys lurking in the dark places of Sid's bedroom. Incidentally learning a valuable lesson about discrimination based on physical difference (the toys are not monsters at all, despite their frightening appearance), they begin to show sympathy, rather than violence born of their fear, to the victims of Sid's experimentation. They learn how to humble themselves to ask for help from the community. Until Woody's grand plan to escape Sid unfolds, Sid could be an object lesson in the unredeemed alpha-male type: cruelly almighty over the toy community, he wins at arcade games, bullies his sister, and, with strategically placed fireworks, exerts militaristic might over any toys he can find. Woody's newfound ability to give and receive care empowers him to teach Sid a lesson of caring and sharing that might be microcosmic to the movie as a whole. Sid, of course, screams (like a girl) when confronted with the evidence of his past cruelties, and when viewers last see him, his younger sister is chasing him up the stairs with her doll.

18   Even with the unceremonious exit of Sid, the adventure is not quite over for Buzz and Woody. Unable to catch up to the moving van as Sid's dog chases him, Woody achieves the pinnacle of the New Man narrative: armed with a new masculine identity, one that expresses feelings and acknowledges community as a site of power, Woody is able to sacrifice the competition with Buzz for his object of desire. Letting go of the van strap, sacrificing himself (he thinks) to Sid's dog, he plainly expresses a caretaking, nurturing love, and a surrender to the good of the beloved: "Take care of Andy for me," he pleads. Buzz's own moment of truth comes from seizing his power as a toy: holding Woody, he glides into the family's car and back into Andy's care, correcting Woody by proudly repeating his earlier, critical words back to him: "This isn't flying; it's falling with style." Buzz has found the value of being a "toy," the self-fulfillment that comes from being owned and loved. "Being a toy is a lot better than being a space ranger," Woody explains. "You're *his toy*" (emphasis in original).

19   Mr. Incredible likewise must embrace his own dependence, both physical and emotional. Trapped on the island of Chronos, at the mercy of Syndrome (Buddy's new super-persona), Mr. Incredible needs women—his wife's superpowers and Mirage's guilty intervention—to escape. To overpower the monster Syndrome has unleashed on the city, and to achieve the pinnacle of the New Man model, he must also admit to his emotional dependence on his wife and children. Initially confining them to the safety of a bus, he confesses to Elastigirl that his need to fight the monster alone is not a typically alpha ("I work alone") sort of need but a loving one: "I can't lose you again," he tells her. The robot/monster is defeated, along with any vestiges of the alpha model, as the combined forces of the Incredible family locate a new model of post-feminist strength in the family as a whole. This communal strength is not simply physical but marked by cooperation, selflessness, and intelligence. The children learn that their best contributions protect the others; Mr. Incredible figures out the robot/monster's vulnerability and cleverly uses this against it.

20   In a parallel motif to Mr. Incredible's inability to control his strength, Buddy/Syndrome finally cannot control his robot/monster; in the defeat, he becomes the newly emasculated alpha male. But like his robot, he learns quickly. His last attempt to injure Mr. Incredible, kidnapping his baby Jack-Jack, strikes at Mr. Incredible's new source of strength and value, his family. The strength of the cooperative family unit is even more clearly displayed in this final rescue: for the shared, parental goal of saving Jack-Jack, Mr. Incredible uses his physical strength and, with her consent, the shape-shifting body of his super-wife. He throws Elastigirl into the air, where she catches their baby and, flattening her body into a parachute, sails gently back to her husband and older children.

21   Through Lightning McQueen's many relationships with men, as well as his burgeoning romance with Sally, he also learns how to care about others, to focus on the well-being of the community, and to privilege nurture and kindness. It is Doc, not Sally, who explicitly challenges the race car with his selfishness ("When was the last time you cared about something except yourself, hot rod?"). His reformed behaviour begins with his generous contributions to the Radiator Springs community. Not only does he provide much-needed cash for the local economy, but he also listens to, praises, and values the residents for their unique offerings to Radiator Springs. He is the chosen auditor for Lizzy's reminiscing about her late husband, contrasting the comic relief typically offered by the senile and deaf Model T with poignancy, if not quite sadness. Repairing the town's neon, he creates a romantic dreamscape from the past, a setting for both courting Sally ("cruising") and, more importantly, winning her respect with his ability to share in her value system. For this role, he is even physically transformed: he hires the body shop proprietor, Ramone, to paint over his sponsors' stickers and his large race number, as if to remove himself almost completely from the Piston Cup world, even as he anticipates being released from his community service and thus being able to return to racing.

22   Perhaps even more than Buzz, Woody, and Mr. Incredible do, the New Man McQueen shuns the remaining trappings of the alpha role, actually refusing the Piston Cup. If the first three protagonists are ultimately qualified heroes—that is, they still retain their authority and accomplish their various tasks, but with new values and perspectives acquired along the way—Lightning completely and publicly refuses his former object of desire. Early in the final race, he seems to somewhat devalue racing; his daydreams of Sally distract him, tempting him to give up rather than to compete. The plot, however, needs him to dominate the race so his decision at the end will be entirely his own. His friends show up and encourage him to succeed. This is where the other films end: the values of caring, sharing, nurturing, and community being clearly

present, the hero is at last able to achieve, improved by having embraced those values. But Lightning, seeing the wrecked King and remembering the words of Doc Hudson, screeches to a stop inches before the finish line. Reversing, he approaches the King, pushes him back on the track, and acknowledges the relative insignificance of the Piston Cup in comparison to his new and improved self. He then declines the Dinoco corporate offer in favor of remaining faithful to his loyal Rust-eze sponsors. Chick Hicks, the only unredeemed alpha male at the end, celebrates his ill-gotten victory and is publicly rejected at the end by both his fans, "the twins," and, in a sense, by the Piston Cup itself, which slides onto the stage and hits him rudely in the side.

Conclusion

23   The trend of the New Man seems neither insidious nor nefarious, nor is it out of step with the larger cultural movement. It is good, we believe, for our son to be aware of the many sides of human existence, regardless of traditional gender stereotypes. However, maintaining a critical consciousness of the many lessons taught by the cultural monolith of Disney remains imperative. These lessons—their pedagogical aims or results—become most immediately obvious to us as parents when we watch our son ingest and express them, when he misunderstands and makes his own sense of them, and when we can see ways in which his perception of reality is shaped by them, before our eyes. Without assuming that the values of the films are inherently evil or representative of an evil "conspiracy to undermine American youth" (Giroux 4), we are still compelled to critically examine the texts on which our son bases many of his attitudes, behaviours, and preferences.

24   Moreover, the impact of Disney, as Henry Giroux has effectively argued, is tremendously more widespread than our household. Citing Michael Eisner's 1995 "Planetized Entertainment," Giroux claims that 200 million people a year watch Disney videos or films, and in a week, 395 million watch a Disney TV show, 3.8 million subscribe to the Disney Channel, and 810,000 make a purchase at a Disney store (19). As Benjamin Barber argued in 1995, "[T]he true tutors of our children are not schoolteachers or university professors but filmmakers, advertising executives and pop culture purveyors" (qtd. in Giroux 63). Thus we perform our "pedagogical intervention[s]" of examining Disney's power to "shap[e] national identity, gender roles, and childhood values" (Giroux 10). It remains a necessary and ongoing task, not just for concerned parents, but for all conscientious cultural critics.

Journal of Popular Film and Television. 2008. 36 (1).

Notes

1.   See Susan Jeffords, "The Curse of Masculinity: Disney's *Beauty and the Beast*," for an excellent analysis of that plot's developing the cruel Beast into a man who can love and be loved in return: "Will he be able to overcome his beastly temper and terrorizing attitude in order to learn to love?" (168). But even in this film, she argues, the Beast's development is dependent on "other people, especially women," whose job it is to tutor him into the new model of masculinity, the "New Man" (169, 170).

2.   Two articles demand that we qualify this claim. Indirectly, they support the point of this essay by demonstrating a midcentury Disney model of what we call "alpha" masculinity. David Payne's "Bambi" parallels that film's coming-of-age plot, ostensibly representing a "natural" world, with the military mindset of the 1940s against which the film was drawn. Similarly, Claudia Card, in "Pinocchio," claims that the Disneyfied version of the nineteenth-century Carlo Collodi tale replaces the original's model of bravery and honesty with "a macho exercise in heroism [. . . and] avoid[ing] humiliation" (66–67).

3.   Outside the animated classics, critics have noted a trend toward a post-feminist masculinity—one characterized by emotional wellness, sensitivity to family, and a conscious rejection of the most alpha male values—in Disney-produced films of the 1980s and 1990s. Jeffords gives a sensible account of the changing male lead in films ranging from *Kindergarten Cop* to *Terminator 2*.

4.   In Disney criticism, the phrase "New Man" seems to belong to Susan Jeffords's 1995 essay on *Beauty and the Beast,* but it is slowly coming into vogue for describing other post-feminist trends in masculine identity. In popular culture, see Richard Collier's "The New Man: Fact or Fad?" online in *Achilles Heel: The Radical Men's Magazine* 14 (Winter 1992/1993). www.achillesheel.freeuk.com/article14_9.html. For a literary-historical account, see *Writing Men: Literary Masculinities from*

Frankenstein to the New Man by Berthold Schoene-Harwood (Columbia UP, 2000).

5. Critics have described the superhero within some framework of queer theory since the 1950s, when Dr. Fredric Wertham's *Seduction of the Innocent* claimed that Batman and Robin were gay (Ameron Ltd, 1954). See Rob Lendrum's "Queering Super-Manhood: Superhero Masculinity, Camp, and Public Relations as a Textual Framework" (*International Journal of Comic Art* 7.1 [2005]: 287–303) and Valerie Palmer-Mehtan and Kellie Hay's "A Superhero for Gays? Gay Masculinity and Green Lantern" (*Journal of American Culture* 28.4 [2005]:

390–404), among myriad nonscholarly pop-cultural sources.

6. Interestingly, Andy and *Toy Story* in general are apparently without (human) male role models. The only father present in the film at all is Sid's, sleeping in front of the television in the middle of the day. Andy's is absent at a dinner out, during a move, and on the following Christmas morning. Andy himself, at play, imagines splintering a nuclear family: when he makes Sheriff Woody catch One-Eyed Black Bart in a criminal act, he says, "Say goodbye to the wife and tater tots . . . you're going to jail."

Works Cited

Bell, Elizabeth. "Somatexts at the Disney Shop: Constructing the Pentimentos of Women's Animated Bodies." Bell, *From Mouse to Mermaid* 107–24.

Bell, Elizabeth, Lynda Haas, and Laura Sells, eds. *From Mouse to Mermaid: the Politics of Film, Gender, and Culture.* Bloomington: Indiana UP, 1995.

Card, Claudia. "Pinocchio." Bell, *From Mouse to Mermaid* 62–71.

Cars. Dir. John Lasseter. Walt Disney Pictures/Pixar Animation Studios, 2006.

Collier, Richard. "The New Man: Fact or Fad?" *Achilles Heel: The Radical Men's Magazine* 14 (1992–93). <www.achillesheel.freeuk.com/article14_9.html>.

Eisner, Michael. "Planetized Entertainment." *New Perspectives Quarterly* 12.4 (1995): 8.

Giroux, Henry. *The Mouse that Roared: Disney and the End of Innocence.* Oxford, Eng.: Rowman, 1999.

The Incredibles. Dir. Brad Bird. Walt Disney Pictures/Pixar Animation Studios, 2004.

Jeffords, Susan. "The Curse of Masculinity: Disney's *Beauty and the Beast.*" Bell, *From Mouse to Mermaid* 161–72.

Lendrum, Rob. "Queering Super-Manhood: Superhero Masculinity, Camp, and Public Relations as a Textual Framework." *International Journal of Comic Art* 7.1 (2005): 287–303.

Palmer-Mehtan, Valerie, and Kellie Hay. "A Superhero for Gays? Gay Masculinity and Green Lantern." *Journal of American Culture* 28.4 (2005): 390–404.

Payne, David. "Bambi." Bell, *From Mouse to Mermaid* 137–47.

Schoene-Harwood, Berthold. *Writing Men: Literary Masculinities from Frankenstein to the New Man.* Columbia: Columbia UP, 2000.

Sedgwick, Eve Kosofsky. *Between Men: English Literature and Male Homosocial Desire.* New York: Columbia UP, 1985.

Toy Story. Dir. John Lasseter. Walt Disney Pictures/Pixar Animation Studios, 1995.

Wertham, Fredric. *Seduction of the Innocent.* New York: Reinhart, 1954.

Yabroff, Jennie. "Betas Rule." *Newsweek* 4 June 2007: 64–65.

Key and challenging words

nominal, retrograde, trope, trajectory, valorize, stoicism, paternalistic, precarious, diminutive, emasculate, gendered (adj.), decimate, arsenal, tutelage, coquettish, insidious, nefarious, pedagogical, purveyor

Questions

1. In the Introduction, identify a) the justification for the study; b) the thesis statement and the type of thesis (i.e., simple or expanded).

2. Scholarly studies in the humanities often utilize a theoretical perspective, interpreting primary sources in light of that perspective. Is it clear from the introduction that the authors will be using

theory? What theorist will they be using and what is her discipline/field of study? (You may have to do some research to answer the second part of the last question.)

3. In paragraph 5, the authors use a direct quotation from the magazine *Newsweek*. What purpose does it serve? Why might it be appropriate for the authors to

use a variety of non-academic sources in this essay (see "Works Cited")?

4. In analyzing literature, students are often told to avoid simple plot summary. Why is plot summary necessary in this essay, and what are its main functions? Refer to specific passages in your answer.

5. From their contexts, define in one or two sentences "homosocial continuum" (paragraph 14) and "triangulation of desire" (paragraphs 15 and 16).

6. Name the three primary sources analyzed in the essay. Which one do the authors believe provides the best or strongest support for their claim about the new man? Why?

7. As is typical in humanities essays, the authors synthesize primary sources to support their points. Analyze the use of synthesis in paragraph 9, 15, or 16 (these paragraphs use at least two primary sources).

8. Analyze the rhetorical effectiveness of the Conclusion; in what way(s) does it broaden, expand on, or universalize the thesis?

Post-reading

1. *Collaborative activity:* a) Discuss the concept of the "alpha male," finding examples from literature and history, or from your observation or knowledge of Western society; *OR* b) Discuss the concept of the "new man" as analyzed in the essay, finding other examples.

2. *Collaborative or individual activity:* Consider the validity or truth of the following direct quotation, exploring its significance to our society: "'[T]he true tutors of our children are not school teachers or university professors but filmmakers, advertising executives and pop culture purveyors'" (paragraph 24).

Additional library reading

Brydon, Suzan G. "Men at the Heart of Mothering: Finding Mother in *Finding Nemo.*" *Journal of Gender Studies* 18.2 (2009): 131–46. Print.

Wohlwend, Karen E. "Damsels in Discourse: Girls Consuming and Producing Identity Texts through Disney Princess Play. *Reading Research Quarterly* 44. 1 (2009): 57–83. Print.

Zarranz, Libe Garcia. "Diswomen Strike Back? The Evolution of Disney's Femmes in the 1990s." *Atenea* 27.2 (2007): 55–67. Print.

AGGRESSION AND SOCIETY

Imagining a Canadian identity through sport: A historical interpretation of lacrosse and hockey

Michael A. Robidoux

(6,772 words)

Pre-reading

1. How important is hockey to the concept of a Canadian identity? Using a pre-writing technique, explore your beliefs and opinions on the connections between hockey and national identity.

Sport in Canada during the late nineteenth century was intended to promote physical excellence, emotional restraint, fair play, and discipline; yet these ideological principles were consistently undermined by the manner in which Canadians played the game of hockey. This article explores the genesis of violence in hockey by focusing on its vernacular origins and discusses the relevance of violence as an expression of Canadian national identity in terms of First Nations and French-Canadian expressions of sport.

*

1   In *Imagined communities*, Benedict Anderson convincingly reduces the concept of nationalism to an imagining—imagined "because members of even the smallest nation will never know most of their fellow-members, meet them, or even hear of them, yet in the minds of each lives the image of their communion" (1991:6). It is this notion of communion that motivates nations to define and articulate their amorphous existence. If Anderson is correct—which I believe to be the case—the task of defining a national identity is a creative process that requires constructing a shared history and mythology(ies) that best suit the identity *imagined* by those few responsible for responding to this task. For a nation as young as Canada (confederated in 1867), this constructive process is somewhat recent and largely incomplete, which is disconcerting for Canadians who have twice witnessed the threat of national separation.[1] As a result, what it means to be Canadian is often scrutinized, lamented, and at times even celebrated (most recently through a Molson Canadian beer advertisement).[2] Yet through all of this there has been one expression of nationalism

that has remained constant since Confederation, that being the game of ice hockey.[3]

2   Since World War II, Canadians have been internationally perceived more as peacekeepers and, perhaps, even as being unreasonably polite—both political constructions in themselves—which makes it difficult to comprehend why a game such as hockey, known for its ferocity, speed, and violence, would come to serve as Canada's primary national symbol. The mystery intensifies if we consider that the game of hockey was born out of a period of social reform in Canada, where popular pastimes that involved violence, gambling, and rowdiness were being replaced by more "civilized" leisure pursuits imported from Europe. For instance, cricket, as Richard Gruneau states, was

> especially palatable to Canada's colonial merchants and aristocrats because it combined an excellent and enjoyable forum for learning discipline, civility, and the principles of fair play with a body of traditions and rules offering a ritual dramatization of the traditional power of the colonial metropolis and the class interests associated with it. [1983:104]

3   The question becomes, then, how did a game such as hockey not only take shape in Canada but become "frequently cited as evidence that a Canadian culture exists" (Laba 1992:333)? Furthermore, to what extent does the game of hockey embody a Canadian collective sensibility, or is this *imagining* of Canadian identity without justification even at a symbolic level? In order to respond to these questions, it is necessary to

explore early vernacular forms of sport in this nation and consider how these sensibilities have maintained themselves in a contemporary sporting context.

The Process of Modernization

4   Sport historians and sociologists have documented extensively the development of physical activity from a traditional folk (vernacular) pastime to a modern organized event.[4] Much of this discourse, however, concerns itself with the impact of modernization on traditional physical activities without taking into account the influences of traditional sporting behaviour and its role in shaping (at least from a Canadian perspective) a national sport identity. Colin Howell is critical of these prejudicial tendencies and writes:

> Modernization theory views history as a linear continuum in which any given circumstance or idea can be labeled "pre-modern" or traditional, and thus, can safely be ignored as something that the seemingly neutral process of "modernization" has rendered anachronistic. [1995:184][5]

5   What needs to be understood is that the process of modernization is not, in fact, a linear progression but rather a series of contested stages that maintain certain aspects of the past, while housing them in an entirely different framework. Before further discussing the relationship between traditional and modern sport, a brief explanation of these terms is necessary.

6   In sport theory, loosely organized, periodic, and self-governed sporting contests fit under the rubric of *traditional* sport (Metcalfe 1987:11). This form of physical activity is devoid of field or participant specifications and "was closely interwoven with established conventions of ritual . . . as well as the daily and seasonal rhythms of domestic and agrarian production, entertainment and religious festivals" (Gruneau 1988:12–13). There is a tendency to refer to traditional sport as rural, tribal, and in the past tense; in truth, however, this manner of participation continues to exist in a variety of forms. An example would be road/ball/ pond hockey in which people engage in variations of the game of hockey in unspecified locales, with unspecified participants in terms of age, number, gender, and skill; these spontaneous games are performed around daily routines, whether these routines be dictated by

work, school, personal, or familial responsibilities. For this reason, I have substituted the term *traditional* with *vernacular*, as it connotes similar meanings but remains viable in a contemporary context and is, in fact, clearer.

7   The significance of the term *modern* sport is twofold in that it relates not only to the changes that have taken place in the way people engage in play, but *modern* also implies the political motivations that dictated these changes. To begin, modern sport is not a random pursuit but rather a highly organized event played within specific boundaries and performed with uniform rules maintained by leagues and organizations. In time, equipment becomes standardized, and play becomes recorded and measured. The result is greater uniformity over time and space, reducing the "localized forms of individual and community-based expressions of pleasure, entertainment, physical prowess, and ritual display" (Gruneau 1988:13). Importantly, the consequence of this reductive process was not simply the limiting of specific expressions of sport, but behaviour itself has been reduced to satisfy a limited and highly specific social order. Pierre Bourdieu explains that "it would be a mistake to forget that the modern definition of sport is an integral part of a 'moral ideal,' that is, an ethos which is that of the dominant fractions of the dominant class" (1993:344), notions that were instilled and maintained by religious and education institutions (Wheeler 1978:192). It is through the standardization of sport that undesirable qualities of vernacular play could be eliminated—behaviours such as violence, public disorder, and mass rowdiness—thus controlling behaviour to ensure a compliant and nonvolatile populace. However, it must be stressed that while levels of control were successfully manufactured through sport, and play was indeed standardized, "undesirable" vernacular elements were not, in fact, entirely reduced but actually remain critical features of specific sports such as lacrosse and hockey.

8   The political motivations behind the modernization of sport cannot be separated from the actual changes that occurred in expressions of physical activity. In Canada, these motivations stemmed from a British Victorian sensibility. By the turn of the eighteenth century, sport in Britain was being realized as an excellent means of social control and conditioning (Jarvie and Maguire 1994:109). The successes that church and school officials had enjoyed by providing

the ever-increasing urban working class with productive non-threatening activities, such as cricket and (a "refined" version of) football, were soon being implemented in the colonies as a means of "correcting" the rougher, more vulgar vernacular pastimes. Perhaps even more importantly, there was symbolic value in having newly colonized peoples engaging in these uniquely British activities; thus, regulated sport quickly became a vehicle for cultural imperialism. Metcalfe speaks to the imperialistic role of cricket by stating that it "illustrated the powerful forces of tradition and the way in which dominant social groups perpetuated their way of life in the face of massive social change" (1987:17).

9   In early nineteenth-century Canada, attempts were well underway to introduce imported European games such as cricket and curling to a nation only beginning to take shape. However, in its earliest stages, organized sport was something suitable only for "gentlemen" and not worthy of the working class or ethnic minorities. Howell points out that while "middle-class reformers advocated a more disciplined and rational approach to leisure, seeking to replace irrational and often turbulent popular or working-class recreations with more genteel and improving leisure activities," these "bourgeois sportsmen" primarily "concentrated their attention on the improvement of middle-class youth" (1995:14). It was not until later in the century that schools and churches began to take a more active role in introducing structured forms of physical activity to Canadians of various class and ethnic backgrounds. The intent of making sport and physical activity more socially democratic was threefold: to acquire levels of control over increased amounts of leisure time made possible by industrialization and a shorter workweek; to reduce class conflict by enabling male participants of various backgrounds to compete on an equal playing field; and to build a physically fit yet subordinate workforce, ensuring maximum levels of industrial production. In short, advocating for institutionalized sport served as an important means of reproducing a Victorian social order in Canada, where young men learned to be honourable and genteel gentlemen. As with any hegemonic process,[6] however, control was never absolute, and almost immediately emergent and residual cultures affected the desired outcome in unexpected ways.

Resisting an Imported Canadian Identity

10   The development of "controlled" sport took an important turn by the middle of the nineteenth century with a new emergent class—led by Montreal-born dentist, George Beers—responding to impositions of British nationalism in Canada. Beers's role in Canadian sport history was that of a romantic nationalist, as his politics were comparable to Herder's romantic nationalism of eighteenth-century Germany. Like Herder, Beers understood that to construct a national identity, two things needed to occur. First, foreign influence needed to be eliminated—Herder contended with French influence; Beers contended with English imperialism. And second, a national history/mythology needed to be consciously constructed. Instead of turning to indigenous poetry and language as Herder did, Beers turned to indigenous sport as a means of portraying the soul of a nation. What better place to look, he surmised, than Canada's First Peoples whose game of *baggataway*—filled with speed, violence, and skill—appeared to best embody the harsh and gruelling existence of Canadian natives as well as the trials of early Canadian settlers in this new and untamed land.

11   The game *baggataway*, renamed lacrosse by French settlers,[7] was played by many First Nations (Native Canadians) across North America prior to European contact, and it proved to be a game that both fascinated and repulsed early settlers (Eisen 1994:2). Some English Europeans were least sympathetic to First Nations' leisurely activities largely because of puritanical sensibilities that tended to perceive all forms of play as wasteful and unproductive. It is not surprising that English observations of lacrosse disparaged the violence; yet negative comments were often countered with admiration for First Nations players who exuded remarkable sportsmanship and respect for their opponents. One late eighteenth-century account reads:

> The Chippewas play with so much vehemence that they frequently wound each other, and sometimes a bone is broken; but notwithstanding these accidents there never appears to be any spite or wanton exertions of strength to affect them, nor

do any disputes ever happen between the parties. [Carver 1956:237]

12   More detailed accounts of lacrosse come from French missionaries and settlers, who, unlike the English, lived with First Nations peoples and made efforts to learn their language, customs, and social practices. One of the earliest accounts comes from Nicolas Perrot, who encountered the game while living as a *coureur de bois*[8] between 1665 and 1684:

> Il y a parmy eux un certain jeu de crosse qui a beaucoup de raport avec celuy de nostre longue paume. Leur coustume en joüant est de se mettre nation contre nation, et, s'il y en a une plus nombreuse que l'autre, ils en tirent des hommes pour rendre égale celle qui ne l'est pas. Vous les voyez tous armez d'une crosse, c'est à dire d'un baston qui a un gros bout au bas, lacé comme une raquette; la boule qui leur sert à joüer est de bois et à peu près de la figure d'un oeuf de dinde. [1973:43–44][9]
>
> [Among them there is a certain game of crosse that compares to our tennis. Their custom is to play nation (tribe) against nation (tribe), and if one side has more players than the other, more players are brought forth to ensure a fair game. Each has a stick, called a crosse, that has a big curve at the end that is laced like a racket; the ball that they play with is made of wood and looks a little bit like a turkey's egg.]

13   He continues by describing the violent nature of the sport:

> Vous entendez le bruit qu'ils font en se frapant les uns contre les autres, dans le temps qu'ils veulent parer les coups pour envoyer cette boule du costé favorable. Quand quelqu'un la garde entre les pieds sans la vouloir lascher, c'est à luy d'eviter les coups que ses adversaires luy portent sans discontinuer sur les pieds; et s'il arrive dans cette conjuncture qu'il soit blessé, c'est pour son compte. Il s'en est veü, qui ont eü les jambs cassées, d'autres les bras, et quelques uns ont estez mesme tüez. Il est fort ordinaire d'en voir d'estropiez pour le reste de leurs jours, et qui ne l'ont esté qu'à ces sortes de jeu par un effect de leur opiniâtreté. [1973:45]
>
> [One can hear the noise they make when they hit one another, while they attempt to avoid receiving blows in order to throw the ball to a favourable location. If one secures the ball in his feet without letting it go, he must fend off blows from his opponents who continually strike his feet; and if in this situation he is injured, it is his own concern. Some are seen with broken legs or arms, or are even killed as a result. It is common to see players maimed permanently, yet this does not change the way they play the game on account of their obstinacy.]

14   For many young French males, the rough nature of the sport was appealing, and as a result, these men became enamoured with not only the game of lacrosse but with its participants as well.

15   The radical impositions of European colonization on North American indigenous peoples has been taken to task in recent academic and popular discourse; clearly, arguments that perceive this relationship to be unidirectional are often overstated. In *The skyscrapers hide the heavens*, Miller offers some balance to this historical analysis by revisiting early Euro-Indian relations and discussing them in terms of cultural change, both "non-directed" and "directed" (2000:95). In other words, Miller understands these relations as being far more equitable than is often portrayed. Not only did First Nations peoples often *willingly* take advantage of such things as European technology to benefit their own situations, but Miller documents, as well, the gross reliance of European settlers on First Nations knowledge and technologies. In fact, he states that European survival in Canada would not have been possible without First Nations assistance and charity. Furthermore, and more importantly for our purposes, is the knowledge concerning the extensive cultural borrowings of European settlers (in this case French) from First Nations peoples.

16   For a certain sector of French Canadian males—later known as *les Canadiens*—the First Nations male provided an alternative model of masculinity to what they had known in France, one where physicality, stoicism, and bravado were valued and celebrated, not repressed, as was the typical Christian model of masculinity:

> The young voyageurs struggled to copy the Indians' stoicism in the face of adversity and their endurance when confronted with hardship, deprivation, and pain. They also copied, to the extent that their

employers and governors could not prevent, the autonomy that Indian society inculcated in its young. French males found the liberated sexual attitudes of young Indian women before matrimony as attractive as the missionaries found them repugnant. [Miller 2000:54]

17   Early French settlers began emulating First Nations males and, in doing so, began sharing in their cultural practices. Occupational and survival-related pursuits such as canoeing, snowshoeing, and hunting were some of the obvious activities that were learned and performed. Native team sports such as lacrosse also proved to be of tremendous interest to *les Canadiens*, as these games gave both First Nations and French males the opportunity to prove their worth to one another as men. According to Joseph Oxendine, these white settlers did not fare very well, however, "because of the Indian's clear superiority of the game. Indians were frequently reported to have used fewer players in an effort to equalize the competition" (1988:48). First Nations proficiency at lacrosse was highly regarded by early sport enthusiasts, but these skills were also perceived by others to be violent and dangerous, a perception that began generating its own folklore among the early North American settlers.

18   Perhaps the most popularly known lacrosse event was a legendary contest between two First Nations tribes at Fort Michilimackinac in 1763—an ambush disguised as a sporting contest. According to Alexander Henry's account of the "contest," the tribes used lacrosse as a means of staging an attack on the British fort during the Pontiac Rebellion (Henry 1901). Francis Parkman supports this in his account, which states:

> Suddenly, from the midst of the multitude, the ball soared into the air and . . . fell near the pickets of the fort. This was no chance stroke. It was part of a preconcerted stratagem to insure the surprise and destruction of the garrison. . . . The shrill cries of the ballplayers were changed to the ferocious warwhoop. The warriors snatched from the squaws the hatchets, which the latter . . . had concealed beneath their blankets. Some of the Indians assailed the spectators without, while others rushed into the fort, and all was carnage and confusion. [1962:254]

19   It was the legendary status the sport commanded that made it the perfect vehicle for George Beers's nationalist agenda. The game ran counter to British bourgeois sensibilities that understood sport to be refined and gentlemanly, one that could ultimately serve as a breeding ground for proper British mores and values. Instead, lacrosse was a display of rugged, brutal, and aggressive behaviours that were said to embody what it meant to be a Canadian settler in this unforgiving northern territory. Thus, Beers called on Canadians to refrain from engaging in the imperial pursuit of cricket and take up lacrosse as the new national game, in effect ridding Canada of foreign influences and acquainting the new populations with the soul of the nation.

20   In order to make this fictious proposal possible, the native game needed to be claimed by the male settlers and then incorporated into a modern sporting climate. *Baggataway*, as First Nations peoples played it, was not merely a sport but a spiritual and religious occasion, often having healing or prophetic significance.[10] The game also had regional and tribal idiosyncrasies, which meant that there was no standard form of play, making Euro-Canadian adoption difficult. Thus, *baggataway* as a native vernacular entity needed to be transformed into lacrosse, which meant claiming the game and eliminating traits that were linked to First Nations culture. To achieve this transformation, it was necessary to standardize the rules to create a sense of uniformity. An important step was made, in fact, by George Beers, who published the first rules of lacrosse under the name "Goal-keeper" in a series of advertisements in the *Montreal Gazette* in 1860 (Cosentino 1998:15). These rules were later adopted by the Montreal Lacrosse Club and became the "official" rules of lacrosse, later republished in the *Montreal Gazette* in July of 1867 (Morrow 1989:47). Efforts to standardize the game not only eliminated regional variation but also seemed to dictate how the game of lacrosse was to be played. All that was left, then, was to attract people to the game, and, again, in this Beers was instrumental.

21   Through various print forms (magazines and newspapers), Beers began to promote lacrosse as Canada's national game and in the process deride cricket as foreign and irrelevant to Canadians. In an article that appeared in the *Montreal Gazette* in August of 1867, suitably entitled, "The national game," Beers writes:

> As cricket, wherever played by Britons, is a link of loyalty to bind them to their home so may lacrosse be to Canadians. We may yet find it will do as much for our young Dominion as the Olympian games did for Greece or cricket for our Motherland. [1867]

22   Of course, Beers makes no apologies for appropriating an Aboriginal game and promoting it as the national pastime. Instead, he sees appropriation as an accurate depiction of European presence in Canada and argues, "just as we claim as Canadian the rivers and lakes and land once owned exclusively by Indians, so we now claim their field game as the national field game of our dominion" (1867). Beer's proselytizing was enormously effective, to the extent that a National Lacrosse Association was formed— the first national sporting body in Canada—and lacrosse was being touted by many as Canada's official national game.[11]

23   These developments, which documented how a vernacular sporting pastime was transformed into a modern sport, were not as complete as scholars have suggested. Sports historian Don Morrow claims: "At first heralded in adoption, then transformed in nature, the Indian origins of the game were finally shunned by nineteenth-century white promoters and players" (1989:46). While ritual/sacred components and regional variations were erased from modern lacrosse competitions, there were native/vernacular elements of the game that remained, largely to the chagrin of elite sporting officials who were governing these developments. To begin, the popularization of lacrosse did not arise merely because of Beers's ideological ravings. It is incorrect to claim, as Morrow does, that the new national affinity of lacrosse was achieved through the word of George Beers. Crediting only one person simply does not allow for human agency, and while public consciousness can be influenced, it is not something that can be dictated. In other words, there needed to be some pre-existing value in lacrosse that allowed it to be so willingly adopted by Canadian sport enthusiasts. It is here, then, that we can begin examining the cultural value of lacrosse (and later hockey) and its relationship to Canadian identity.

Sport Sensibilities in Conflict

24   One of the primary reasons lacrosse served as a viable alternative to imported British sports such as cricket was its emphasis on physical aggression, volatility, and danger. The game appealed to males who identified with a more physically aggressive notion of masculinity rather than the reserved and civil expressions of masculinity exemplified in cricket. In essence, the attraction to lacrosse was an extension of early French Canadians' infatuation with First Nations masculinity, where the emphasis was on physical superiority, bodily awareness, and perseverance. Lacrosse provided males the opportunity to display these heralded qualities and challenge themselves through formal competitions. However, in the attempt to modernize lacrosse and market it to a broader audience, the game needed to become less violent and needed to be played in a manner more suitable for "gentlemen"; otherwise the game would not enter dominant sport culture. Efforts were in place to sanitize the game, but they were not entirely successful. In fact, those who were most successful at the sport were First Nations and working-class players who played the game as it was originally designed—aggressively and intensely. Attempts to turn the game into something else merely put those who engaged in it as "gentlemen" at a clear disadvantage to those who maintained its aggressive style of play. One team renowned for its aggressive play was the Montreal Shamrocks, who "were, without question, the most successful team prior to 1885. . . . The Shamrocks were out of place both socially and athletically. Social misfits on the middle-class playing fields, the Shamrocks were Irish, Roman Catholic, and working-class" (Metcalfe 1987:196).

25   What is critical here is that the ideological and political value of lacrosse as advocated by those in power paled in relation to the actual meanings early participants experienced through playing it. Colin Howell, also a sports historian, correctly observes that lacrosse was "a relatively minor sport" that "was suddenly elevated to prominence because of the symbolic role that was associated with it at the time of Confederation" (Howell 1995:103). However, those elite officials who helped elevate the status of lacrosse understood the sport symbolically, not according to its literal value as a meaningful expression of Canadian consciousness. I do not wish to imply that this is a singular phenomenon, but there is evidence that lacrosse did have value for certain Canadian males as an identifiable articulation of who they were as men. In essence, lacrosse did signify class, gender, and ethnic values, but these values were generally unacknowledged by elite sporting officials who were suddenly threatened by their own ideological manoeuvrings. The official recourse was to prohibit the "people" from playing the game and to attempt to make it instead the game of an exclusive minority:

> The logical conclusion for lacrossists was that the incidence of disputes, violence, and undesirable conduct on the field of play could mean only one thing—some players were not gentlemen. The truth of this observation was given substance by the presence of Indians, who always played for money and, by race alone, could not be gentlemen, and of the working-class Shamrock team. [Metcalfe 1987:195]

26   This prohibition of undesirable participants eventually led to the introduction of amateurism.

27   Amateur athletics in Canada did not merely function as a means of ensuring that athletes engage in sport in a gentlemanly manner[12] but served as a discriminatory system that prevented "undesirable" players from playing. Prior to 1909, the year when a national amateur athletic union was formed in Canada, national sporting bodies used the concept of amateurism to best suit their sport's needs. In the case of the National Lacrosse Association, league officials decided to make it an "amateur" association restricted to those players who fit under the definition of amateur. An amateur was conveniently defined by the Amateur Athletic Union of Canada as someone who had "never competed for a money prize, or staked bet with or against any professional for any prize" or one who had "never taught, pursued, or assisted in the practice of athletic exercises as a means of obtaining a livelihood" (Metcalfe 1987:105–106). The stipulations were highly restrictive and deliberate in design.

28   First, the new requirements made working-class participation virtually impossible in that wage earners were no longer able to receive financial compensation for taking time off from work to play. Keeping in mind that it was illegal to play sports on Sunday and that the workweek ran from Monday to Saturday, working-class participation in sport was restricted generally to Saturday afternoons. As a result, players were not only prevented from receiving payment for time lost at work, but those players who at one time received compensation for their services were no longer eligible to play. The second aspect of the restrictions was equally effective because it denied access to individuals who at one time gambled on sport. During this period in Canadian history, gambling and sport were virtually inextricable: gambling made up part of the fabric of vernacular sporting pastimes. For First Nations cultures in particular, gambling in sport (by spectators and participants) was deeply ingrained in their traditions and at times even played a role in their overall economies (Oxendine 1988:31). Therefore, by these first two stipulations alone, most ethnic minorities and working-class players were considered ineligible and could no longer play amateur athletics. The final stipulation reinforced economic divisiveness further by making it clear that sport was not the property of the people but, rather, of men who "had the leisure, economic resources and social approval to explore intensive athletic training in a financially disinterested manner" (Burstyn 1999:224).

29   The restrictive measures imposed by the National Lacrosse Association did not go unchallenged, however. Teams tried to circumvent the rules by covertly using "professional" players to become more competitive and in certain cases even paid players for their services. In response, the National Lacrosse Association was compelled to enforce disciplinary measures to contend with these dissident organizations. Teams caught cheating were brought before the Canadian Amateur Athletic Union to face arbitration and potential censuring.[13] As these arbitration cases grew in number, tremendous pressures were being placed on the National Lacrosse Association to retract its strictly amateur policy and permit both professionals and amateurs into the league. Despite this, the National Lacrosse Association remained steadfast in its position to prohibit professional players and was ultimately successful in maintaining itself as an amateur association; this success, however, proved to be its inevitable downfall.

30   By maintaining its exclusive membership, the National Lacrosse Association forced

potential lacrosse players to pursue alternative sporting options. Other team-sport leagues (i.e., baseball, football, and hockey) were not as resistive to the influences of professionalism, and thus, they provided working-class and ethnic minority players alternatives to play in these sports and be financially compensated at the same time. While baseball and football did attract many of the players, these sports did not possess the symbolic and literal value found in lacrosse. Instead, it was hockey that early Canadian sport enthusiasts embraced by the turn of century, for the same reasons they were attracted to lacrosse 20 years earlier. Unlike baseball or football, hockey was seen as uniquely Canadian in origin and character. An amalgam of modern and vernacular sporting pastimes, hockey resembled lacrosse in design and in the manner it was played. Play was aggressive and often violent, providing men the opportunity to display this emergent notion of masculinity. At a symbolic level, it was played on a frozen landscape, perfectly embodying what life as a Canadian colonialist was supposed to be like. Thus, hockey provided all that lacrosse entailed but without the restrictions of amateurism. By the 1920s, hockey had succeeded in becoming Canada's national sport pastime.

Violence, Masculinity, and Canadian Identity

31   It is here, then, that we return to the politics of identity and the manner in which hockey, a game notoriously aggressive and violent, serves as a potential symbol for national expression. Along with other social scientists,[14] I have been critical of popular discourse that tends to mythologize hockey and locate it as a unifying force in this nation. Gruneau and Whitson astutely observe:

> The myth of hockey as a "natural" adaptation to ice, snow, and open space is a particularly graphic example of what Barthes is alerting us to—about how history can be confused with nature. . . . This discourse of nature creates a kind of cultural amnesia about the social *struggles* and vested interests— between men and women, social classes, regions, races, and ethnic groups—that have always been part of hockey's history. [1993:132]

32   While these sentiments are certainly valid, it would be incorrect to say that hockey is without cultural or historical relevance in Canada. In fact, it is my contention that hockey is more than a mythological construct; it is a legitimate expression of Canadian national history and identity. Hockey *does* speak to issues of gender, race, ethnicity, and region in this nation, albeit not in an entirely positive manner. For this reason, hockey moves beyond symbol and becomes more of a metaphoric representation of Canadian identity.

33   First, hockey was born out of post-Confederation Canada,[15] in a period of political uncertainty and unrest. Canada was a disparate nation, divided in terms of language, region, and ethnicity—lacking in identity and national unity. Thus, while hockey was used ideologically to express national sentiment, its value as a vernacular entity was equal to, if not greater than, its symbolic value. From the outset, hockey's violent and aggressive style separated itself from other bourgeois (European) pastimes, including the increasingly popular game of baseball that was entering Canada from the United States. Early games often appalled certain sport writers and sport officials who saw the violence on the ice and in the stands as unfit for gentlemen. J.W. Fitsell provides two accounts of the first recorded game of hockey, which took place in 1875. The first, from *The Daily British Whig*, states that "Shins and heads were battered, benches smashed and the lady spectators fled in confusion" (Fitsell 1987:36). The other report from *The Montreal Witness* claimed that:

> Owing to some boys skating about during play an unfortunate disagreement arose: one little boy was struck across the head, and the man who did so was afterwards called to account, a regular fight taking place in which a bench was broken and other damages caused. [Fitsell 1987:36]

34   These accounts of violence are undoubtedly extreme, yet what is significant is that even in its earliest stages hockey was a sport perceived as excessively aggressive and violent within a modern European context.

35   It was largely because of this excessive violence that hockey became a sport Canadians could call their own, and they quickly began to showcase it in international contexts. By the mid-1890s, competitions were

FIGURE 1 Odds and ends at the hockey struggle.

FIGURE 2 American cartoonists took to the slash and crash of Canadian players in Pittsburgh.

being staged between Canadian hockey teams and American ice-polo teams. The Canadian teams dominated these early competitions and revelled in the press they received. Newspapers did applaud their skill, but at the same time reports were critical of their rough play. *The Daily Mining Gazette* of Houghton, Michigan, described one game as "rush, slash and check continually. . . . Calumet were knocked off the puck by Portage Lakes 'any old way.' Many a man had to be carried to the dressing room" (Fitsell 1987:120). In a game in Sault Ste. Marie, Michigan, an incident occurred where "Stuart [an American player] was laid out by a board check from Jack Laviolette. He recovered and tangled with the same player, fans rushed on the ice and as Stuart bled from the facial cuts, police were called in" (Fitsell 1987:120). These accounts illustrate that within 20 years of organized existence, hockey was internationally known as being first, Canadian, and second, notoriously violent. Further evidence of this is found in two American cartoons depicting Canadians playing hockey in Pittsburgh in 1904.[16]

36   The distinction hockey received as being a rough sport also served as a means for Canadians to display their proficiency in the clearly demarcated context of a sporting event, making hockey a valuable vehicle for expressing national identity. But it was not simply proficiency on the ice, it was physical proficiency within the masculinist tradition that was earlier identified in relation to lacrosse. Hockey displayed men who were perceived to be stoic, courageous, and physically dominant: precisely the same images of masculinity valued in First Nations culture and later by early Canadian settlers. These historically pertinent attitudes attracted Canadians to hockey, as the game provided Canadian males with an identifiable image outside of a British Victorian framework. Moreover, through hockey competitions, Canadians could exude superiority over Americans, illustrating for many a "victory for the industrious Canadian beaver over the mighty U.S. eagle" (Fitsell 1987:106). In essence, hockey became a vehicle of resistance against British and American hegemony, something that Canadians continue to call on in periods of political or national uncertainty.

37   The political implications went beyond resistance to British and American rivalries. One such occasion was the 1972 Summit Series in which Canadian professional hockey players engaged in an eight-game series against the Soviet Union national hockey team. The event was a debacle, yet it is considered by many to be the greatest Canadian story ever told. The series was described as East meets West—communism versus capitalism. So as the players rightfully admitted, it was no longer just about hockey. Reflecting on the series, Team Canada member Phil Esposito stated: "It wasn't a game anymore; it was society against society . . . it wasn't fun. It was not fun" (*September 1972–1997*). The series was filled with incidents of extreme violence: one Canadian player (Bobby Clarke), following instructions from a coach, broke a Soviet player's ankle with his stick. Other incidents involved a Soviet referee nearly being attacked by a Canadian player; throat-slitting gestures; kicking (with skates); fighting; and a *melee* with NHL Players Association executive director Alan Eagleson, the Soviet Guard, and the Canadian hockey team. The event, which was advertised as an expression of goodwill between nations, turned sour when the favoured Canadians were defeated in the initial games and obviously outclassed in terms of skill and sportsmanship. Canadian players were simply unaware of the tremendous abilities of the Soviets and were, hence, humiliated both on the ice by the Soviets and off the ice by an unforgiving Canadian public who lambasted them with jeers.

38   In response to their dire predicament, Canadian players resorted to bullying and intimidation tactics and literally fought their way back into contention. In a miraculous comeback, overcoming real and imagined barriers, the Canadian team proved victorious, winning the final game and the series. Their "heroism" became permanently etched into the memory of Canadians, despite actions that have recently been described by two American journalists as "hacking and clubbing the Soviet players like seal pups and bullying their way to a thrilling, remarkable comeback" (Klein and Reif 1998:31). While there have been critics of the series, the games in the Canadian collective consciousness remain as "an orgy of self-congratulation about the triumph of 'Canadian virtues'—individualism, flair, and most of all, character" (Gruneau and Whitson 1993:263). Historically speaking, these seemingly appalling behaviours are compatible with Canadian hockey in general and for this reason are embraced, not denounced. The players performed in a manner consistent with Canadian play, illustrating a Canadian

character that has yet to be defined in more concrete fashion. Therefore, despite Canadian behaviour that was an assault on international hockey, and on international competition in general, this assault was distinctly Canadian, something that is invaluable for the construction of a national identity.

Conclusion

39 The connection I have made between hockey and Canadian nationalism is very real.

40 I do not make the claim that Canadians are predisposed to violence or that they condone violent behaviour. Rather, I argue that hockey enabled Canadians to display qualities that have been valued in patriarchal relations: stoicism, courage, perseverance, and proficiency. The singularity of the game and the manner in which it was played were critical for a young and disparate nation to have as its own as it faced encroaching social, political, and cultural interests from Europe and the United States. At a more pedestrian level, hockey was accessible to men of various ethnic and class backgrounds, and thus, to a greater degree than lacrosse, it became a game of the people. The fact that "people" here is specific only to males established hockey as a male preserve, making it a popular site for males to define their worth as men, drawing on notions of masculinity that date back to seventeenth-century Canada. In this sense, understanding hockey beyond its mythological rhetoric acknowledges the "social *struggles* and vested interests—between men and women, social classes, regions, races, and ethnic groups" and confirms that hockey was, as Gruneau and Whitson state, "all of these" (1993:132).

41 Finally, by linking hockey to Canadian nationalism I am not situating either as being positive. In fact, the Canadian penchant to understand itself through hockey repeats masculinist formulas of identification that reflect poorly the lives of Canadians. The physically dominant, heterosexist, and capitalist associations of this specific identity are certainly exclusionary, but for that matter, all nationalist expressions cannot suitably speak for the polyphony of a nation. Despite the obvious fallibility of nationalistic representation, the legitimacy of nationalistic expression remains. Canada's history is located firmly in patriarchy, heterosexism, and capitalism; thus, the use of hockey to promote national pride and unity was not random then, nor is it today. Playing hockey is a means of constructing an image of a nation in the manner in which dominant forces within it wish to be seen. With this, hockey does not merely symbolize the need to define a national identity, it offers insight into the actual imaginings of what this identity entails. Hockey provides Canada a means by which to be distinguished. As Benedict Anderson astutely observes, such distinction ought not to be characterized by the dichotomy of "falsity/genuineness", but by the style in which it is 'imagined'" (1991:6).

Journal of American Folklore. 2002. 115 (45).

Notes

1. The province of Quebec has twice voted to separate from Canada (1980 and 1995). The most recent referendum saw only 51 per cent of Quebecers voting "no" to separation.
2. The television commercial gained national notoriety because of its pro-Canadian stance. It depicts an ordinary "Joe" pronouncing his Canadian identity in contrast to perceived stereotypes of Canadians.
3. From this point forward ice hockey will be referred to as hockey.
4. See Gruneau 1983, 1988; Gruneau and Whitson 1993; Dunning 1975; Hargreaves 1986; Burstyn 1999; Metcalfe 1987; Morrow et al. 1989; Guttmann 1994; and Guay 1981.
5. Richard Gruneau in "Modernization and hegemony" similarly recognizes the shortcomings of "overlooking, or misconstruing, the importance of social and cultural continuities in sport" (1988:19).
6. Guttmann expresses his dissatisfaction with the term *cultural imperialism* to describe sport diffusion. Instead, he prefers the term *cultural hegemony*, which better communicates the lively "contestation that has accompanied ludic diffusion" (1994:178).
7. It has been argued that the term *la crosse* was applied to the game because the sticks used by the participants resembled a bishop's crozier (Thwaites 1959:326). Maurice Jetté argues, however, that the name comes from "an old French game called 'la soule' which was

played with a 'crosse' very similar to the Indian implement" that was also cross-like in shape (1975:14).

8. Literally means, "runner of the woods." More specifically, *coureurs de bois* were French male fur traders and trappers who lived as the indigenous population did during the seventeenth century. J. R. Miller writes that these young males were "neither French peasants nor Indian braves, they were a bit of both" (2000:56).

9. All translations provided by Robidoux unless otherwise stated.

10. Jean de Brébeuf, a Jesuit priest, writes in 1636: "There is a poor sick man, fevered of body and almost dying, and a miserable Sorcerer [Shaman] will order for him, as a cooling remedy, a game of crosse. Or the sick man himself, sometimes, will have dreamed that he must die unless the whole country shall play crosse for his health" (Thwaites 1959:185).

11. Despite claims made in *The story of nineteenth-century Canadian sport*(1966) and the 1894 edition of the *Dictionnaire canadien-français* that lacrosse was the national game of Canada, there are no official records that substantiate this claim (Morrow 1989:52–53).

12. Varda Burstyn writes, "For many of the founding sport associations of the late-nineteenth century, 'amateur' athletics meant 'gentlemen' athletics" (1999:49).

13. The Amateur Athletic Association of Canada changed its name in 1898 to the Canadian Amateur Athletic Union in an attempt to strengthen its position as a national sport governing body (Metcalfe 1987:110).

14. See Robidoux (2001); Gruneau and Whitson (1993); and Laba (1992).

15. Canada became a confederation in 1867, and the first recorded game of hockey took place in 1875.

16. The figures and caption are taken from J.W. Fitsell's *Hockey's captains, colonels and kings* (1987:119). The cartoons depict games that took place in Pittsburgh in 1904. No information is provided to indicate where they were originally published.

References

1. Anderson, Benedict. 1991 [1983]. Imagined Communities: Reflections on the Origin and Spread of Nationalism. New York: Verso.

2. Beers, W.G. 1867. National Game. Montreal Gazette, August 8.

3. Bourdieu, Pierre. 1993. "How Can One Be a Sports Fan?" *In* The Cultural Studies Reader. Simon During, ed. pp. 339–358. London: Routledge.

4. Burstyn, Varda. 1999. The Rites of Men: Manhood, Politics, and the Culture of Sport. Toronto: University of Toronto Press.

5. Carver, J. 1956 [1796]. Travels through the Interior Parts of North America. Minneapolis: Ross and Haines, Inc.

6. Cosentino, Frank. 1998. Afros, Aboriginals and Amateur Sport in Pre-World War One Canada. Ottawa: Canadian Historical Association.

7. Dunning, Eric. 1975. Industrialization and the Incipient Modernization of Football. Stadion 1(1):103–139.

8. Eisen, George. 1994. Early European Attitudes toward Native American Sports and Pastimes. *In* Ethnicity and Sport in North American History and Culture. George Eisen and David K. Wiggins, eds. pp. 1–18. Westport, CT: Greenwood Press.

9. Fitsell, J. Williams. 1987. Hockey's Captains, Colonels, and Kings. Erin, Ontario: The Boston Mills Press.

10. Gruneau, Richard. 1983. Class, Sports, and Social Development. Amherst: University of Massachusetts Press.

11. ———. 1988. Modernization or Hegemony: Two Views on Sport and Social Development. *In* Not Just a Game: Essays in Canadian Sport Sociology. Jean Harvey and Hart Cantelion, eds. pp. 9–32. Ottawa: University of Ottawa Press.

12. ———, and David Whitson. 1993. Hockey Night in Canada: Sport, Identities and Cultural Politics. Culture and Communication Series. Toronto: Garamond Press.

13. Guay, D. 1981. L'Histoire de l'Éducation Physique au Québec: Conceptions et Évènements (1830–1980). Chicoutimi: Gaetan Morin.

14. Guttman, Allen. 1994. Games and Empires: Modern Sports and Cultural Imperialism. New York: Columbia University Press.

15. Hargreaves, John. 1986. Sport, Power and Culture: A Social and Historical Analysis of Popular Sports in Britain. New York: St. Martin's Press.

16. Henry, Alexander. 1901 [1809]. Travels and Adventures in Canada and the Indian Territories between the Years 1760 and 1776. James Bain, ed. Toronto: G.N. Morang.

17. Howell, Colin D. 1995. Northern Sandlots: A Social History of Maritime Baseball. Toronto: University of Toronto Press.

18. Jarvie, Grant, and Joseph Maguire. 1994. Sport and Leisure in Social Thought. London: Routledge.

19. Jetté, Maurice. 1975. Primitive Indian Lacrosse: Skill or Slaughter? Anthropological Journal of Canada. 13(1):14–19.

20. Klein, Jeff Z., and Karl-Eric Reif. 1998. Our Tarnished Past. Saturday Night Magazine 113(10):30–33.

21. Laba, Martin. 1992. Myths and Markets: Hockey as Popular Culture in Canada. *In* Seeing Ourselves: Media Power and Policy in Canada. Helen Holmes and David Taras, eds. pp. 333–444. Toronto: Harcourt Brace Jovanovich Canada.

22. Metcalfe, Alan. 1987. Canada Learns to Play: The Emergence of Organized Sport, 1807–1914. Toronto: McClelland and Stewart.

23. Miller, J.R. 2000 [1989]. Skyscrapers Hide the Heavens: A History of Indian-White Relations in Canada. 3rd edition. Toronto: University of Toronto Press.

24. Morrow, Don. 1989. Lacrosse as the National Game. *In* A Concise History of Sport in Canada. Don Morrow, Mary Keyes, Wayne Simpson, Frank Cosentino, R. Lappage, eds. pp. 45–68. Toronto: Oxford University Press.

25. ———, M. Keyes, W. Simpson, F. Cosentino, and R. Lappage, eds. 1989. A Concise History of Sport in Canada. 3rd edition. Toronto: Oxford University Press.

26. Oxendine, Joseph B. 1988. American Indian Sports Heritage. Champaign, IL: Human Kinetic Books.

27. Parkman, Francis. 1962. The Conspiracy of Pontiac. 10th edition. New York: Collier Books.

28. Perrot, Nicolas. 1973 [1864]. Mémoire sur les Moeurs, Coustumes, et Relligion des Sauvages de l'Amérique Septentrionale. Publié pour la première fois par J. Tailhan. Montréal: Éditions Élysée.

29. Robidoux, Michael A. 2001. Men at Play: A Working Understanding of Professional Hockey. Montreal: McGill-Queen's University Press.

30. September 1972. 1997. By Ian Davey. August Schellenberg, narrator. Robert MacAskill, dir. Ian Davey and Robert MacAskill, producers. CTV.

31. Thwaites, Reuben G., ed. 1959. The Jesuit Relations and Allied Documents: Travels and Explorations of the Jesuit Missionaries in New France, 1610–1791, vol. 10. New York: Pageant Book Company.

32. Wheeler, Robert F. 1978. Organized Sport and Organized Labour: The Workers' Sports Movement. Journal of Contemporary History 13:191–210.

Key and challenging words

amorphous, disconcerting, connote, hegemonic, enamour, proselytize, resistive, amalgam, disparate, debacle, pedestrian (adj.), masculinist, dichotomy, polyphony

Questions

1. Identify Robidoux's thesis statement and comment on the form it takes. The author does not include a literature review early in the body of his essay, but he does refer to the work of sports historians in note 4. Why do you think he does not include a full literature review?

2. Briefly consider why it is beneficial for the author to define the following concepts before proceeding to the body, or main part, of his essay: a) nationalism (paragraph 1); b) modernization (paragraph 4).

3. What is the function of the first main section, "The process of modernization," in terms of the overall essay?

4. The author uses several primary sources in his essay. Referring to one example of a primary source, briefly explain its purpose and effectiveness. Note: You can consider any original source in this essay as a primary source even if Robidoux cites it from a secondary source.

5. Why is it important for Robidoux's purposes that he draws attention to the "often overstated" perception that European colonization imposed only negative effects on the indigenous population (paragraph 15)?

6. Does Robidoux consider the role of George Beers an important one in the rise of the popularity of lacrosse as a national game (paragraphs 10, 19–23)? Explain his reliance (or lack of reliance) on Beers in his essay.

7. Summarize Robidoux's point concerning the regulations imposed by the National Lacrosse Association and the way they worked to exclude participation in the sport by the working-class and First Nations peoples.

8. Identify the paragraph in which the author makes the transition from discussing lacrosse to discussing hockey. Why is this an important paragraph?

9. In the final two paragraphs preceding his conclusion, Robidoux uses a relatively familiar (1972) example of hockey operating within a political/nationalistic framework. What does this detailed example contribute to the author's thesis and to the effectiveness of the essay as a whole? What is the author's tone in this passage, and how is it conveyed?

10. What do the two cartoons (figures 1 and 2) contribute to the essay?

Post-reading

1. *Collaborative activity:* Do you think that Robidoux would subscribe to the common perception that sports builds character? Why or why not? *OR* Do you believe that participation in sports builds character? Discuss or debate one of these questions.

2. Write a critical analysis of the final two paragraphs. Support your analysis by specific references to the text. *OR* Write a critical response to the author's critique of the 1972 "Summit Series" (the final two paragraphs before the conclusion).

Additional library reading

Allain, K.A. (2011). Kid Crosby or golden boy: Sidney Crosby, Canadian national identity, and the policing of hockey masculinity. *International Review for the Sociology of Sport, 46*, 3–22. doi:10.1177/1012690210376294

The more you play, the more aggressive you become: A long-term experimental study of cumulative violent video game effects on hostile expectations and aggressive behavior

Youssef Hasan, Laurent Bègue, Michael Scharkow, and Brad J. Bushman
(2,814 words)

Pre-reading

1. *Collaborative or individual activity:* Using your observations and other kinds of anecdotal evidence, discuss/reflect on the link between violent video games and aggressive behaviour. Is it a causal relationship; that is, do you believe that playing video games causes violent behaviour? If so, do you believe the link is weak or strong, short-term or long-term?

Abstract

It is well established that violent video games increase aggression. There is a stronger evidence of short-term violent video game effects than of long-term effects. The present experiment tests the cumulative long-term effects of violent video games on hostile expectations and aggressive behavior over three consecutive days. Participants ($N = 70$) played violent or nonviolent video games 20 min a day for three consecutive days. After gameplay, participants could blast a confederate with loud unpleasant noise through headphones (the aggression measure). As a potential causal mechanism, we measured hostile expectations. Participants read ambiguous story stems about potential interpersonal conflicts, and listed what they thought the main characters would do or say, think, and feel as the story continued. As expected, aggressive behavior and hostile expectations increased over days for violent game players, but not for nonviolent video game players, and the increase in aggressive behavior was partially due to hostile expectations.

Introduction

1   In a classic Calvin and Hobbes cartoon, Calvin is shown watching a violent television program. He has the following internal dialog: "Violence in the media. Does it glamorize violence? Sure. Does it desensitize us to violence? Of course. Does it help us tolerate violence? You bet. Does it stunt our empathy for our fellow beings? Heck yes. Does it *CAUSE* violence? . . . Well, that's hard to prove. The trick is to ask the right question."

2   Contrary to what Calvin thinks, experimental studies do allow for causal inferences. Although it is not ethical for researchers to allow assaults, rapes, and murders to occur in laboratory settings, numerous experimental studies have shown a causal relationship between violent media exposure and less serious forms of aggression (Anderson & Bushman 2002a). One problem with experimental studies, however, is that they typically last less than 1 h, although there are some exceptions (e.g., Bushman & Gibson 2011).

3   It is not so much the immediate short-term causal effects of media violence that are of concern, but rather the cumulative long-term causal effects. Long-term effects are generally assessed in longitudinal studies. However, because longitudinal studies employ correlational methods, it is difficult to make strong causal inferences based on longitudinal data. Although single-session experiments allow one to make causal inferences about violent video game effects, they do not allow one to test whether violent video games have a cumulative effect on aggressive thoughts and behaviors. The present research is the first experiment to test the cumulative causal effects of violent video games on aggression over a relatively long period of time—three days.

4   Smoking provides a useful analogy for the importance of this work. Smoking one cigarette will probably not cause lung cancer, but repeatedly smoking cigarettes for days, weeks, months, and years, greatly increases the risk. Similarly, playing a violent video game once will probably not cause a person to become more aggressive, but repeatedly playing violent games for days, weeks, months, and years may increase the risk. In the ideal experiment, participants would be randomly assigned to play violent or nonviolent video games for weeks, months, or years. However, it is not feasible (or ethical) to do such an experiment. Thus, we limited our experiment to three days. If the effects accumulate over three days, they may accumulate even more over weeks, months, and years.

Theoretical Foundation

5   There are theoretical reasons to predict that repeated exposure to violent video games has cumulative effects over time. According to cognitive neoassociative-theory (Berkowitz 1990), human memory can be thought of as a network represented by nodes and links. The nodes represent concepts and the links represent relations among concepts. Once a concept is processed or stimulated, activation spreads out along the network links and primes (activates) associated or related concepts as well. In addition, thoughts are linked, along the same sort of associative lines, not only to other thoughts but also to emotional reactions and behavioral tendencies. Thus, exposure to violent media can prime a complex of associations consisting of aggressive ideas, angry feelings, and the impetus for aggressive actions. According to this theory, repeated exposure to media violence over longer periods of time can create a rich, intricate network of aggressive associations that can be more easily primed by violent media.

6   Cognitive information-processing models also posit that exposure to violent media should have a cumulative effect over time. One model emphasizes scripts, beliefs, and observational learning (Huesmann 1988, 1998; Huesmann & Eron 1984). In a play or movie, scripts tell actors what to say and do. In human memory, scripts define situations and guide behavior: The person first selects a script for the situation and then assumes a role in the script. Scripts that produce good outcomes become more likely to be used again. Scripts that produce bad outcomes become less likely to be used again. Scripts can be learned by direct experience or by observing others, including mass media characters. According to this theory, repeated exposure to media violence results in the practice and rehearsal of aggressive scripts, and the creation and reinforcement of a hostile worldview over time.

7   Another model emphasizes attributions (e.g., Dodge 1980; Dodge & Frame 1982; Fite, Goodnight, Bates, Dodge, & Pettit 2008). Attributions are the explanations people make about why others behave the way they do. For example, if a person bumps into you, a hostile attribution would be that the person did it on purpose to hurt you. Repeated exposure to violent media can lead people to develop hostile attribution biases. People who consume a heavy dose of violent media eventually come to view the world as a hostile place.

8   The General Aggression Model (e.g., Anderson & Bushman 2002b; DeWall, Anderson & Bushman 2011) encompasses all of these models.

Mediating Role of Hostile Expectations

9   As a possible causal mechanism of the link between exposure to violent video games and aggression, we focus on the hostile expectation bias, defined as the tendency to expect others to react to potential conflicts with aggression (Dill, Anderson, Anderson, & Deuser 1997). When people expect others to behave aggressively, they should be more likely to behave aggressively themselves. In the General Aggression Model (Anderson & Bushman 2002b), hostile expectations are conceptualized as mediators of violent video game-related aggression. Our previous research has supported these theoretical predictions. Playing violent video games increases hostile expectations (Bushman & Anderson 2002), and hostile expectations, in turn, are positively related to aggressive behavior (Hasan, Bègue, & Bushman 2012).

Overview

10   Participants in the present experiment were exposed to violent or nonviolent video games for three consecutive days. We predict that violent games (but not nonviolent games) will increase hostile expectations and aggressive behaviors, and the effects will become stronger each day. That is, we expect a cumulative effect of violent video games on both hostile expectations and aggressive behaviors over time. We also predict that hostile expectations will mediate the effect of violent games on aggressive behaviors.

Method

Participants

11   Participants were 70 French university students (50% female; M_{age} = 24.4, SD = 13.4). They were paid 10€ ($13) each day for three consecutive days.

Procedure

12   Participants were told that the researchers were conducting a 3-day study on the effects of brightness of video games on visual perception. After informed consent was obtained, participants were randomly assigned to play a violent or nonviolent game for 20 min. To increase the generalizability of findings (Wells & Windschitl 1999), we used three violent games (*Condemned 2*, *Call of Duty 4*, and *The Club*; all rated 18+) and three nonviolent games (*S3K Superbike*, *Dirt 2*, and *Pure*; all rated 10+). By the flip of a coin, participants played either a violent game or a nonviolent game for 20 min each day for three consecutive days. They played a different game each day. The order of games was randomized.

13   After playing the game, participants completed one of three ambiguous story stems each day (Dill et al. 1997). For example, in one story a driver crashes into the back of the main character's car, causing a lot of damage to both vehicles. After surveying the damage, the main character approaches the other driver. Participants are asked: "What happens next? List 20 things that the (main character) will do or say, think, and feel as the story continues." They completed a different story stem each day. The order of the story stems was randomized.

14   Next, participants were told that they would compete with a same-sex opponent (actually a confederate) on a 25-trial computer game in which they had to respond to a visual cue faster than their partner, with the loser receiving a noise blast through a pair of headphones. Participants thought they were playing against a different same-sex opponent each day. The intensity and duration of the noise were determined by each individual at the beginning of each trial, from 60 dB (Level 1) to 105 dB (Level 10; about the same level as a smoke or fire alarm). A nonaggressive no-noise level was also offered (Level 0). Participants could also determine how long their opponent suffered by setting the noise duration from 0 to 5 s, in 0.5-second increments. The noise was a mixture of sounds that many people find very unpleasant, such as fingernails scratching a chalkboard, dentist drills, and ambulance sirens. The intensity and duration of the noise participants gave the confederate were used to measure aggression. The opponent set random intensity and duration levels across the 25 trials. Participants lost half the trials (randomly determined). Basically, within the ethical limits of the laboratory, participants controlled a weapon that could be used to blast their opponent with unpleasant noise. The construct validity of this task is well established (Anderson & Bushman 1997; Bernstein, Richardson, & Hammock 1987; Giancola & Zeichner 1995). It has been used for decades as a reliable and valid measure of laboratory aggression (Taylor 1967).

15   Next, participants rated how absorbing, action-packed, arousing, boring, difficult, enjoyable, entertaining, exciting, frustrating, fun, involving, stimulating, and violent the video game was (1 = *not at all* to 7 = *extremely*). They also rated how bright the display was, which was the ostensible purpose of the study. The violent rating was used as a manipulation check. The other ratings were used as possible covariates to control for the differences between video games besides violent content. To control for habitual exposure to violent video games, participants also listed their three favorite games, and we counted the number of violent games rated 18+ (for players 18 years and older). Because the same pattern of results was obtained with and without the covariates, we used the simpler analyses that excluded the covariates. A debriefing followed, which included a probe for suspicion. No participant expressed suspicion about the study.

Results

Preliminary Results

Exemplars of violent and nonviolent video games

16   There were no significant differences among the three violent video games, or among the three nonviolent video games, on hostile expectations or aggressive behaviors. Thus, the data were collapsed across exemplars of video game types for subsequent analyses.

Manipulation check of violent content of video games

17   As expected, violent video games were rated as more violent than nonviolent video games on all three days (p's < .0001, d's > 1.75). Thus, the violent game manipulation was successful.

Reliability of story stem completions

18   Independent coders, blind to experimental conditions, counted the number of aggressive behaviors, thoughts, and feelings the participants listed when completing the story stems. The intraclass correlations were .81, .86, and .74, for aggressive behaviors, thoughts, and feelings, respectively (Shrout & Fleiss 1979). Because the intraclass correlation coefficients were relatively high, the scores from the two raters were averaged.

Sex differences

19   There were no significant main or interactive effects involving sex of participant on either hostile expectations or aggressive behaviors, so the data from men and women were combined.

Primary results

20   Noise intensity and duration levels across the 25 trials were significantly correlated on all three days (r's > .90), so noise intensity and duration were standardized and averaged to form a more reliable measure of aggression.

21   As can be seen in Fig. 1, hostile expectations and aggressive behaviors both increased over time for violent video game players but not for nonviolent video game players. Latent growth curve analysis (Muthen & Curran 1997) shows that playing a violent game had a significant positive effect on both the intercept (b = 0.46, β = .38) and the slope (b = 0.49, β = .94) for hostile expectations. Violent game players start off with more hostile expectations than nonviolent game players on day 1, and hostile expectations increase on subsequent days. There is no increase in hostile expectations for nonviolent game players. Turning to aggressive behavior, the intercept is significantly higher than in the nonviolent video game group (b = 1.11, β = .38), and there is also a significant effect on the slope factor (b = 1.05, β = .33). Thus, violent game players start off more aggressive than nonviolent game players on day

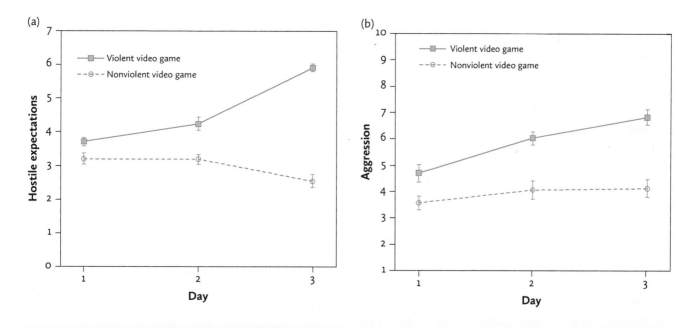

FIGURE 1.a   Effect of video game content on hostile expectations over time. Capped vertical bars denote 1 standard error. b. Effect of video game content on aggressive behavior over time. Capped vertical bars denote 1 standard error.

1, and become even more aggressive on subsequent days. There is no increase in aggression for nonviolent game players. Finally, a cross-sectional model showed that hostile expectations mediated the effect of violent video game exposure on aggressive behavior ($b = 0.17$, 95% bootstrap CI: .01 to .62, which excludes the value zero; Hayes 2009).

Discussion

22   In the cartoon cited at the beginning of this article, Calvin asked a question that many others have asked: "Do violent media cause violence?" Although one cannot determine whether violent media cause criminal acts of violence (e.g., rape, assault, murder), because it is unethical to study such behaviors in laboratory settings, one can determine whether violent media cause an increase in less serious forms of aggressive behavior (e.g., blasting a person with loud, unpleasant noise through headphones) and on aggression-related thoughts and feelings (e.g., hostile expectations). Importantly, one can also test whether these causal effects are cumulative. The present research clearly showed a cumulative effect of violent video

games on hostile expectations and aggressive behaviors. Because we used the experimental method, we can infer that playing violent video games caused both hostile expectations and aggressive behaviors to increase over the three-day study period. These findings are consistent with cognitive neoassociative-theory (e.g., Berkowitz 1990) script theory (e.g., Huesmann 1988), attribution theory (e.g., Dodge 1980), and the General Aggression Model (e.g., Anderson & Bushman 2002b). All of these models propose that exposure to violent media can have a cumulative effect of aggressive thoughts and behaviors over time.

23   In addition, replicating our previous work (Hasan et al. 2012), hostile expectations mediated the link between exposure to violent video games and aggression. Violent video games increased hostile expectations. Hostile expectations, in turn, were positive related to aggression.

Limitations and Future Research

24   The present experiment is not without limitations. One limitation is that we only considered one possible underlying mechanism in the link between

exposure to violent video games and aggression—hostile expectations. We chose to focus on hostile expectations because we expected hostile expectations to cumulate over time. We also wanted to replicate our previous findings showing that hostile expectations mediate the effect of violent video games on aggression (Hasan et al. 2012). However, there are surely other important mediators of violent video game-related aggression that we did not consider, such as angry feelings, physiological arousal, and brain processes. Future research can examine whether other mediators also accumulate over time in response to violent game play in the way that hostile expectations do.

25   Another limitation is that our experiment lasted only three days. We wish we could have conducted a longer experimental study, but that was not possible for practical and ethical reasons. Although we predict violent video game effects to cumulate beyond three days, we cannot be sure, nor can we be sure of the shape of the curve. During our three-day study, the increase was linear for both hostile expectations and aggressive behaviors, but over a longer period of time the curves might asymptote or possibly even decrease (although we can think of no theoretical reason why it would decrease). Future research should examine the cumulative effects of violent video games on aggressive behaviors and aggression-related thoughts and feelings over a more extended period of time.

Conclusion

26   Although previous experiments have shown that violent video games can cause a short-term, immediate increase in aggression, until now no experimental study has tested the long-term cumulative causal effects of violent video games on aggression. Although longitudinal correlational studies can investigate cumulative effects of violent video exposure, they cannot be used to make strong causal statements. The present 3-day experiment showed that violent video games increased both hostile expectations and aggression, and the effects increased each day. As predicted, hostile expectations mediated the effect of violent video game exposure on aggression. When people expect others to behave aggressively, they are more likely to behave aggressively themselves. In sum, violent video games do cause an increase in aggression, and the effects are cumulative and can be relatively long-lasting.

Journal of Experimental Social Psychology. 2013. 49.

References

Anderson, C.A., & Bushman, B.J. (1997). External validity of "trivial" experiments: The case of laboratory aggression. *Review of General Psychology 1*, 19–41.

Anderson, C.A., & Bushman, B.J. (2002a). Media violence and societal violence. *Science 295*, 2377–2378.

Anderson, C.A., & Bushman, B.J. (2002b). Human aggression. *Annual Review of Psychology 53*, 27–51.

Berkowitz, L. (1990). On the formation and regulation of anger and aggression: A cognitive-neoassociationistic analysis. *American Psychologist 45*, 494–503.

Bernstein, S., Richardson, D., & Hammock, G. (1987). Convergent and discriminant validity of the Taylor and Buss measures of physical aggression. *Aggressive Behavior 13*(1), 15–24.

Bushman, B.J., & Anderson, C.A. (2002). Violent video games and hostile expectations: A test of the General Aggression Model. *Personality and Social Psychology Bulletin 28*, 1679–1689.

Bushman, B.J., & Gibson, B. (2011). Violent video games cause an increase in aggression long after the game has been turned off. *Social Psychological and Personality Science 2*, 29–32.

DeWall, C.N., Anderson, C.A., & Bushman, B.J. (2011). The general aggression model: Theoretical extensions to violence. *Psychology of Violence 1*(3), 245–258.

Dill, K.E., Anderson, C.A., Anderson, K.B., & Deuser, W.E. (1997). Effects of aggressive personality on social expectations and social perceptions. *Journal of Research in Personality 31*, 272–292.

Dodge, K.A. (1980). Social cognition and children's aggressive behavior. *Child Development 51*, 620–635.

Dodge, K.A., & Frame, C.L. (1982). Social cognitive biases and deficits in aggressive boys. *Child Development 53*, 620–635.

Fite, J.E., Goodnight, J.A., Bates, J.E., Dodge, K.A., & Pettit, G.S. (2008). Adolescent aggression and social cognition in the context of personality: Impulsivity as a moderator of predictions from social information processing. *Aggressive Behavior 34*(5), 511–520.

Giancola, P.R., & Zeichner, A. (1995). Construct validity of a competitive reaction-time aggression paradigm. *Aggressive Behavior 21*, 199–204.

Hasan, Y., Bègue, L., & Bushman, B.J. (2012). Viewing the world through "blood-red tinted glasses": The hostile expectation bias mediates the link between violent video game exposure and aggression. *Journal of Experimental Social Psychology 48*, 953–956.

Hayes, A.F. (2009). Beyond Baron and Kenny: Statistical mediation analysis in the new millennium. *Communication Monographs 76*, 408–420.

Huesmann, L.R. (1988). An information processing model for the development of aggression. *Aggressive Behavior 14*, 13–24.

Huesmann, L.R. (1998). The role of social information processing and cognitive schema in the acquisition and maintenance of habitual aggressive behavior. In R.G. Geen, & E. Donnerstein (Eds.), *Human aggression: Theories, research, and implications for policy.* (pp. 73–109). New York: Academic Press.

Huesmann, L.R., & Eron, L.D. (1984). Cognitive processes and the persistence of aggressive behavior. *Aggressive Behavior 10*, 243–251.

Muthen, B.O., & Curran, P.J. (1997). General longitudinal modeling of individual differences in experimental designs: A latent variable framework for analysis and power estimation. *Psychological Methods 2*, 371–402.

Shrout, P.E., & Fleiss, J.L. (1979). Intraclass correlations: Uses in assessing rater reliability. *Psychological Bulletin 86*, 420–428.

Taylor, S.P. (1967). Aggressive behavior and physiological arousal as a function of provocation and the tendency to inhibit aggression. *Journal of Personality 35*, 297–310.

Wells, G.L., & Windschitl, P.D. (1999). Stimulus sampling and social psychological experimentation. *Personality and Social Psychology Bulletin 25*, 1115–1125.

Key and challenging words

cumulative, longitudinal, attribution, confederate (n), replicate, asymptote

Questions

1. After reading the first four paragraphs, explain why the authors might have chosen to begin the way they do with a joke from a Calvin and Hobbes cartoon.

2. Identify the two main problems facing researchers exploring a link between video game playing and aggression.

3. (a) Briefly explain the function of the section "Theoretical foundation" to the essay as a whole; (b) Summarize paragraph 5 or 6 in one or two sentences.

4. (a) Explain why so much detail is needed in the "Method" section; (b) explain the purpose of the "manipulation check" (you may need to read the "Results" section to answer this).

5. Using figures 1a and 1b, along with textual information, explain the results of the subjects' hostile expectations and aggression measures.

6. Show how the "Discussion" section fulfils the requirements of an experimental study (Type B essay), identifying at least three of the features mentioned on p. 23.

Post-reading

1. Referring to the sub-section "Limitations and future research" in "Discussion," come up with a hypothesis that could be the basis of an experiment to remedy a limitation or extend the finding of the current study.

Then, give a two-sentence description of the design of such a study—i.e., give a brief description of its methodology. (See "Method," p. 315 and Chapter 3, Type B essays.)

Related website of interest

Media Smarts, Canada's Centre for Digital and Media Literacy:

mediasmarts.ca/video-games

Additional library reading

Thomas, K.D., & Levant, R.F. (2012). Does the endorsement of traditional masculinity ideology moderate the relationship between exposure to violent video games and aggression? *The Journal of Men's Studies, 20*(1), 47–56. doi:10.3149/jms.2001.47

Saleem, M., Anderson, C.A., & Gentile, D.A. (2012). Effects of prosocial, neutral, and violent video games on college students' affect. *Aggressive Behavior, 38,* 263–271. doi:10.1002/ab.21427

Trends in North American newspaper reporting of brain injury in ice hockey

Michael D. Cusimano, Bhanu Sharma, David W. Lawrence, Gabriela Ilie, Sarah Silverberg, and Rochelle Jones
(4,596 words)

Pre-reading

1. *Collaborative or individual activity:* Are you aware of the increasing attention paid to brain injuries in sports, particularly hockey? To what extent is the media responsible for bringing this to the attention of the public? Should they or other bodies, such as hockey administrators, player representatives, or team owners, play a larger role?
2. *Collaborative or individual activity:* To what extent do you believe that brain injuries like concussions are "part of the game" and are thus unavoidable?

Abstract

The frequency and potential long-term effects of sport-related traumatic brain injuries (TBI) make it a major public health concern. The culture within contact sports, such as ice hockey, encourages aggression that puts youth at risk of TBI such as concussion. Newspaper reports play an important role in conveying and shaping the culture around health-related behaviors. We qualitatively studied reports about sport-related TBI in four major North American newspapers over the last quarter-century. We used the grounded-theory approach to identify major themes and then did a content analysis to compare the frequency of key themes between 1998–2000 and 2009–2011.

The major themes were: perceptions of brain injury, aggression, equipment, rules and regulations, and youth hockey. Across the full study period, newspaper articles from Canada and America portrayed violence and aggression that leads to TBI both as integral to hockey and as an unavoidable risk associated with playing the game. They also condemned violence in ice hockey, criticized the administrative response to TBI, and recognized the significance of TBI. In Canada, aggression was reported more often recently and there was a distinctive shift in portraying protective equipment as a solution to TBI in earlier years to a potential contributing factor to TBI later in the study period. American newspapers gave a greater attention to 'perception of risks' and the role of protective equipment, and discussed TBI in a broader context in the recent time period. Newspapers from both countries showed similar recent trends in regards to a need for rule changes to curb youth sport-related TBI. This study provides a rich description of the reporting around TBI in contact sport. Understanding this reporting is important for evaluating whether the dangers of sport-related TBI are being appropriately communicated by the media.

Introduction

1   Concussions and other forms of mild traumatic brain injuries occur at least 1.7 million times a year in North America and account for about 75% of all traumatic brain injuries (TBI) [1,2,3]. Sport-related head trauma is a common cause of TBI in youth, and every year in North America, nearly half million youth aged 14 years or less need hospital-based care for this injury [3,4]. The Centers for Disease Control and Prevention (CDC) recently declared that sport concussions are a "silent epidemic" and that they deserve further research [3].

2   Repeated concussions and TBI are of particular concern as they may cause life-lasting cognitive and psychosocial deficits [5,6]. These injuries are common in all contact sports, but those who play ice hockey are at particular injury risk [7,8,9,10]. The potential long-lasting effects of TBI suggest that these injuries are an important threat to public health [11]. Prevention of sport-related TBIs requires multifaceted approaches that consider issues related to the nature of play and the culture existent within ice hockey [12,13].

3   At elite levels, such as the National Hockey League (NHL), aggression (i.e., a purposeful physical act driven by intent to cause physiological or psychological harm) is valued and has been considered to be an effective success strategy [14,15]. Aggressive players are quickly recognized for their style of play by coaches, management, other players, and fans [16]. Moreover there still exists, among the sports community, a widespread attitude that concussions are "a part of the game" and resiliency to medical counsel is considered a sign of "toughness" [17]. These issues hinder prevention and treatment efforts and call for research to address these concerns.

4   An attitude that stresses "toughness" and "ruggedness" of players who can "heroically brush off" injuries often pressures players to neglect their own safety and health for the game [16]. Social learning theory proposes that such aggressive play is encouraged and fostered in ice hockey culture, and by learning of the positive rewards of aggression in ice hockey, aggressive behaviour continues within the sport [18]. Since aggressive play in ice hockey can increase injury incidence by making high-speed collisions more likely and by fostering an "intent-to-harm" attitude among players [19], understanding the media portrayal of TBI in ice hockey is important for evaluating whether the clinical severity of these injuries is being appropriately communicated.

5   To better understand how the mass media and popular culture report TBI in sports like ice hockey, we studied a sample of newspaper articles. The manner by which newspapers portray ice hockey–related TBIs and how this has changed over time has not yet been examined. The purpose of our paper was to inductively identify themes in Canadian and American newspaper reports of ice hockey–related TBIs, and to determine if, over time, there has been any change in the content and nature of these reports. Our goal was to understand the reporting of these injuries and the implications of this reporting.

Methods

Sample

6   We performed a qualitative analysis of newspaper articles published, between 1985 and 2011, in the Chicago Tribune (CT), New York Times (NYT), Toronto Star (TS), and Vancouver Sun (VS). We selected these newspapers based on the size of their readership. Furthermore, we sought to represent (1) Canada and the United States; (2) east and west coast ice hockey media reports; and (3) both original-six and expansion-era ice hockey teams. We chose newspapers with a local nature rather than a national coverage because they would likely report in more detail about local hockey market issues. Furthermore, by analyzing local instead of national newspapers, it was possible to evaluate whether the

ice hockey culture in different localities was consistent within and across localities. The four newspapers had a cumulative average weekly circulation of over 13 million copies in 2011 [20,21].

Data collection

7   We retrieved all newspaper articles electronically from the ProQuest™ database, an online periodical index part of the Cambridge Information Group. To locate and retrieve newspaper articles that discussed ice hockey brain injuries we used the following search terms: *Hockey (in citation and document text) AND "concuss*" OR "head injur*" OR "head trauma" OR "brain injur*" OR "brain trauma" OR "banged head" OR "bell rung" OR "conscious*" (in citation and abstract).* Key scientific and colloquial terms were included in the search algorithm as newspapers were likely to use both sets of terms. We included newspaper articles in our study if they referred to one or more of the key terms a minimum of three times within the body and/or headline of that article.

8   Newspaper articles published before January 1st, 1985 were not available from ProQuest™; we collected data after this point until the end of the 2011 NHL season (June 15th, 2011). We reviewed and analyzed articles from each of 4 time intervals, that is, 1985–1989, 1990–1999, 2000–2009, and 2010–2011. The number of analyzed articles published in each time interval varied. A total of 541 newspaper articles were analyzed; 49, 185, 187, 120 were published in 1985–1989, 1990–1999, 2000–2009, and 2010–2011, respectively. Furthermore, the number of newspaper articles published by each print media source varied, as 120, 126, 140, 155 articles were analyzed from the CT, NYT, TS, and VS, respectively.

Data analysis

9   We used the grounded-theory approach as a framework for a thematic analysis to provide rich descriptions of the nature and character of newspaper articles on the topic of interest over time [22]; categories and themes were allowed to emerge from the data inductively and were not pre-identified by a *priori* hypotheses [23,24]. We recorded data into meaningful pieces of information known as meaning units (MU) [25]. After we coded MUs, they were used to create broad categories, which were later classified into specific themes and sub-themes. We used the constant comparison method throughout the coding process in that as each MU emerged, it was compared to other MUs that were similarly categorized to determine appropriate classification. In addition, we did a content analysis by counting the frequency with which MUs occurred within the sample text [23].

10   All retrieved newspaper articles were imported as text files into HyperRESEARCH™ qualitative research software, formerly used in qualitative healthcare investigations [26,27,28]. The MUs from each article were coded using HyperRESEARCH™. Three members of the research team, who met on a weekly basis to discuss the coding process, independently completed all coding. We continued to review newspaper articles until we reached saturation of information in each time interval. In all cases, analyzing 50 articles per newspaper per time interval exceeded data saturation [29].

11   To investigate specific trends over time, we focused on the time periods 1998–2000 and 2009–2011. Since the time period of 2009–2011 is four years after the 2004–2005 NHL lockout, we chose a comparison time period that was four years before this lockout (i.e. 1998–2000). We compared these time periods by means of a thematic and content analysis to explore the nature of and frequency distribution of MUs between time periods and geographical regions (i.e., Canada and America). Three members of the team reviewed the articles, and collaboratively discussed any discrepancies in the classifications of MUs. We assessed coder agreement by means of inter-rater reliability (Cronbach's alpha for coding of MUs was 0.91).

Results

Thematic Analyses

12   Five main themes, each comprised of several subthemes, emerged and they are described in Table 1. These five themes were highly recurrent across all media sources in all time intervals and were prominent in both countries.

13   **Canadian newspapers.** Canadian newspapers disapproved of and condemned needless aggression

Table 1   The five major themes—and associated sub-themes—identified while conducting the analysis.

Theme	Subtheme	Discussion points
Aggression	Aggression as cause of injury	• How aggressive play contributes to head injuries
		• How many head-injuries could be avoided if aggressive play was minimized
	Contributors to aggression	• What fuels aggressive behaviour in players
		• Demand for aggressive play
	Attitudes on aggression	• The need to curb aggression
		• The importance of aggressive play to the culture of hockey
Perceptions of brain injury	Risk perceptions	• Perceived clinical severity of injury
		• Perceived dangers of repeat injury
		• Long-term consequences of brain-injury
	Impact of injury	• Impact of injury on team standings and success
		• Impact of injury on player short-and long-term health
Equipment	Attitudes on the role of equipment	• Equipment as a means to prevent brain injuries
		• Equipment as a contributor to brain injuries
	Effectiveness of equipment	• The need for better equipment to prevent more brain injuries
		• The inability of helmets to prevent brain injuries
Rules & regulations	Attitudes on rules and regulations	• The need for more stringent rules and regulations in ice hockey
		• The need for more liberal rules and regulations in ice hockey to 'let the players play'
		• The (in)ability of rules and regulations to prevent brain injuries in ice hockey
Youth hockey	Attitudes on youth hockey	• The importance of keeping young ice hockey players safe
		• The dangers of a brain injury to the development of youth
		• The pressure youth face from parents and coaches to return to play as soon as possible

Examples of the discussion points that comprise a given sub-theme are provided above. All Meaning Unit codes (N = 1535) were sorted under one of the above themes. doi:10.1371/journal.pone.0061865.t00

and violence in ice hockey as expressed in these excerpts:

> I know of no other way of expressing our shame and dissatisfaction with the violence and unnecessary fighting that seems to be the present image for hockey—VS, 1999
>
> Canadians were just treated to some amazing hockey at the Olympics and nowhere was fighting or head-hunting seen. The game can survive and thrive without it—TS, 2010

14   Canadian newspapers consistently reported that TBIs in ice hockey were serious injuries. However, these newspapers also reported that these injuries are just a part of the game, and that they are essentially an unavoidable occupational hazard.

15   In the earlier time period, protective equipment was often described as a solution to ice hockey's brain injury problem; wearing more protective equipment was thought to improve player safety. In contrast, during the recent time period, the emphasis shifted distinctly and it was reported that protective equipment makes players feel invulnerable to injury, and this causes them to take more potentially harmful physical liberties.

16   Canadian newspapers consistently reported how poor the NHL was at enforcing rules on player safety. Although the need for a culture change in ice hockey was consistently discussed, recent reports

placed responsibility on the NHL to make the game safer:

> It would be nice to say the NHL is attacking this [concussion] problem with zest, but, as is generally the case with Bettman's aimless administration, the words aren't being backed up with action—TS, 2000
>
> To their great discredit, the league and its general managers have dragged their feet on the [brain injury] issue. . . . the league took some half-hearted steps to protect players against the worst effects of head-injuries—TS, 2011

17   Recently, reports began to state there is enough inherent excitement in ice hockey given the finesse of the sport that the need for aggressive and violent play is *unnecessary*. Table 2 provides quotes that illustrate the themes seen in Canadian newspapers.

18   **American newspapers.** Similar themes and trends emerged in the American newspaper articles. In both time periods, American newspapers reported that aggression was an integral ingredient to ice hockey and that brain injuries should be accepted as a part of ice hockey. However, both American and Canadian newspapers expressed much more concern recently about the potential long-term clinical impacts of brain injuries. The focus during the earlier time period was to report TBIs only when they occurred to star players, with little mention to the overall extent of the issue:

> The league is concerned about the growing number of concussions that sidelined such headliners as Paul Kariya, Eric Lindros and Pat LaFontaine last season—CT, 1998

19   In contrast, the more recent trend has been to describe the broader impact of TBIs to the cross section of the league and to set star players' injuries into the bigger context of the overall problem:

> Repeated concussions can have long-lasting effects and head injuries have caused several hockey players in recent years to end their careers prematurely, including Eric Lindros, Pat Lafontaine and Keith Primeau—CT, 2009

20   The serious nature of these injuries was noted in both time periods but the more recent reports stressed the need for a serious culture change within the sport *because* of TBIs:

> Only in the past few years has the NHL dropped its historically cavalier attitude toward concussions—NYT, 1998
>
> Calls are proliferating for changes to the culture of a sport that many see as too accepting of reckless body contact and serious injury—NYT, 2010

21   Reference to better equipment as a hazard as opposed to a protective factor was also noted in more recent American reports, as well as the need for the league to strengthen rules in an attempt to make the game safer by preventing brain injury. Although the risks of TBI to youth hockey players were consistently reported over time, more recently, calls for the elimination of such injuries to youth became more prominent. Table 3 provides illustrative quotes from American newspapers.

Content Analyses

22   A summary of the number of MUs associated with each theme and newspaper in both time periods is provided in Table 4. The findings from newspapers in each country were similar; there were only international, not intra-national, differences in media reporting of ice hockey head-injuries.

23   Canadian print media discussed aggression in ice hockey equally during both time periods. The content of discussions of TBI in the more recent time period more often dealt with the severity and impact of the injury. Discussion of rules and regulations recently increased in Canada.

24   In comparison to Canadian newspapers, American newspapers less frequently discussed aggression as a contributor to TBI in ice hockey but more often discussed perception of risks of brain injury. In contrast to Canadian newspapers, American ones more often report on equipment and rules during both time periods. Both American and Canadian media showed similar recent trends to increasingly report on the need for rule changes and the need to protect youth ice hockey players from TBI.

Theme	1998–2000	2009–2011
Aggression	**Gratuitous violence should be removed from the NHL**	
	*Without question, the gratuitous violence, hacking, slashing, cross checking and fisticuffs that so dominates the NHL game today is the main factor in my own loss of interest in the NHL—*VS, 1999	*Hockey is such a fast moving and exciting sport. There should be no time for fights, which are increasing arranged in advance by goons who get little ice time otherwise—*VS, 2009
Perceptions of brain injury	**Brain injuries are viewed as occupational hazards**	
	It's a physical game, so we all have to accept that there are going to be injuries— VS, 1999	*As long as people are playing collision sports and are moving at a high rate of speed, there will be some concussions—* VS, 2010
	The need for a culture change with respect to brain injuries	
	Hockey players from all levels who have suffered concussions and several prominent doctors, neurosurgeons, trainers and officials all agreed that a major shift has to take place in the culture of hockey to deal with the growing problem of brain injuries— TS, 1998	*What's unacceptable is the willful inability to grasp this issue of serious brain injury in hockey—and every "concussion" is serious, the effects are cumulative, some of the guys now on injury lists are going to suffer early dementias and cognitive loss later in life—* VS, 2011
Equipment	**Equipment and brain injuries**	
	Maybe I [player] won't have to recover from (a concussion) again. The precautions I've taken with a new helmet, mouthguard and visor should, hopefully, prevent that— TS, 1999	*There is talk of upgrading the quality of NHL helmets to reduce head injuries, but New Jersey Devils GM Lou Lamoriello says improved equipment only makes players take more liberties—* VS, 2009
Rules & regulations	***Poor governance in the NHL***	
	There is more of an emphasis on supplementary discipline for players guilty of delivering wanton blows to an opponent's head, but those penalties aren't particularly onerous given the damage sometimes done to the victim— TS, 1999	*First and most obvious, the performance of the league's referees in punishing headshots has been worse than abysmal. Again and again, the refs have failed to step up and administer the most immediate and effective punishment—* VS, 2010
Youth hockey	***Severity of youth brain injuries***	
	Concussions—long the most overlooked of serious sports injuries—are especially dangerous for young people because they affect the brain's ability to absorb new information— TS, 1999	*Various research has shown bodychecking is the leading cause of serious injuries—including concussions and fractures—in kids' hockey—* VS, 2011

Table 2 Quotes from Canadian newspapers that represent trends in reporting of brain injury in ice hockey.

doi:10.1371/journal.pone.0061865.t002

Discussion

25   We found several important trends about the reporting of TBIs in ice hockey. There has been a shift in not only reporting brain injuries when they occur to star players but also in reporting them more broadly across a variety of levels of skill. There is also a trend to recognizing the long-term severity and impact of TBI to the player and the need to take action against aggression, particularly at the youth levels. However, at the same time, there is a persistence of the theme that head injuries are *just a part of the game,* and that anyone who plays ought to just accept this occupational risk or not

play. Exposure to these conflicting views may make it difficult for the reader to adopt a stance on the issue of sport-related TBIs. This can be concerning as it has been shown that media messages that create confusion in the population can lead to unhealthy behaviours [30]. Furthermore, a shift in focus on equipment as a protective device to a potential cause of more aggressive behavior was seen in both countries. A shift in concern towards making youth play safer through rule changes was manifest recently in both countries and a call on the professional league to take responsibility and action towards effective solutions was also seen in the recent newspaper articles. The articles that we analyzed echo

Table 3   Quotes from American newspapers that represent trends in reporting of brain injury in ice hockey.

Theme	1998–2000	2009–2011
Aggression	**Aggression as an integral component to ice hockey**	
	It's also my [NHL VP and director of hockey operations] responsibility to keep hockey a physical game. After all, hits happen— CT, 1999	*Hitting is a big part of the game, and we have to be careful we don't go too far and make the game just a finesse game, just a skating game—* NYT, 2010
	When it's your turn to take the field, the court or the ice rink, you're ready to hand out a little punishment of your own . . . you're determined to do so, because that is how, according to today's broadcast sports discourse, you demonstrate athletic superiority— CT, 1999	*The NHL remains bound by an ethos of toughness, an arena where fighting is tolerated and even encouraged as rough justice, and where playing through concussions and gruesome lacerations are marks of courage—* NYT, 2011
Perceptions of brain injury	**Brain injuries are viewed as occupational hazards**	
	By the nature of its violent game, the NHL also can't prevent concussions. They're going to occur every so often— NYT, 1999	*Hockey is probably the fastest team sport out there, and it can get pretty violent . . . Getting hurt happens a lot. Nobody is really 100 percent healthy out there—* CT, 2010
Equipment	**Equipment and brain injuries**	
	LaFontaine tirelessly advocated ways to prevent serious concussions, stressing the importance of wearing mouth guards and more protective helmets— NYT, 1998	*Other sports have spent the last several years realizing that safety equipment can bring dangers of its own. Checking in professional hockey became considerably more vicious with the adoption of helmets in the 1970s and '80s—* NYT, 2011
Rules & regulations	**The need for stricter rules**	
	The league intends to apply a much stricter standard of supplementary discipline for any deliberate action by a player that is either directed to the head of an opponent or results in an injury to the head— NYT, 1998	*Under pressure from medical researchers, owners and even players, the general managers are expected to strengthen Rule 48, the league's bylaw governing checks to the head, which was instituted this season—* NYT, 2010
Youth hockey	**Severity of youth brain injuries**	
	Two or more significant blows to the head while playing sports can harm teenagers' thinking abilities for years to come— CT, 1999	*This approach toward eliminating head contact, both incidental and intentional, is critically important for our youth players—* NYT, 2011

doi:10.1371/journal.pone.0061865.t003

Table 4   The number of MUs (N = 1535) pertaining to the identified themes, as per time period and geographic region.

Country	Time period	Aggression	Perceptions of brain injury	Equipment	Rules & regulations	Youth hockey
Canada	1998–2000	76	182	11	12	6
	2009–2011	157	122	7	46	33
America	1998–2000	83	247	34	27	18
	2009–2011	97	214	26	88	49

Kruskal-Wallis tests revealed ns effects of country, or time period, on each of the identified categories.

doi:10.1371/journal.pone.0061865.t004

the recent shift in scientific literature that documents the detrimental effects of TBI in sport [31,32,33]. The effect of TBI on the cognitive and psychosocial development of *youth* also seems to be accurately portrayed in the analyzed newspaper articles [5,6]. Reports of brain injury as an unchanging "occupational hazard" reflect a stark contrast to the calls for rule changes and action by the most elite professionals in these newspaper articles.

26 Several useful models help us to understand how the media shapes individuals' knowledge, attitudes, and practices of injury-related risk-taking. Iyengar's (1991) model focuses on the intended and real effects of media including information-provision, setting agendas, framing, and persuasion [34]. By contrast, McGuire's (2001) approach considers the following factors important to media impact: source (credibility), message and content, channel, and audience variables [35]. Together, these models describe two dimensions of communication relevant to understanding the impact of the media on individuals' knowledge, attitudes, and practices of risk-taking: the intended and real effects (at an intermediate or macro-social level) of communication, as well as the qualities of presentation, content, and context that have been shown to produce changes in individuals' opinions and behaviours.

27 We are sensitive to Herman and Chomsky's classic argument that media discourse can be biased and reflect the interests of power elites including government officials and corporate or industry groups [36]. We like others, found that media reports often emphasized the aggressive and violent nature of games often in what seemed to be means to incite interest in the event by as many people as possible.

28 The role that such media reports have on youth attitudes and the culture of hockey cannot be ignored. While we recognize that family and close personal friends can influence individuals' formation of opinions and judgments, we also share Katz and Lazarfield's (1955) argument that individuals' interpretation of media messages can be directly shaped by opinion leaders in their communities as reported in the media [37]. Since young media consumers are particularly impressionable [38], it is not surprising that research has shown that youth exposed to themes of aggression and violence in the media are more likely to develop tendencies of physical aggressiveness, violent and delinquent

behaviour, and conduct issues [39]. Furthermore, studies show that youth who are repeatedly exposed to violence and aggression in the media view violence and aggression as the appropriate means for solving conflict in all aspects of life [40]. So, it is likely that the reporting on TBI that we have documented is also a likely factor that contributes to a culture that normalizes aggressive and violent behaviour [41,42].

29 Media reporting on health issues can also help shape positive health-related attitudes and behaviours [43]. During the SARS crisis, media reports on this disease outbreak were largely responsible for altered consumer behaviours, causing many to change their travel plans to avoid areas that the media decreed highly infectious [44]. Chapman et al. (2005) found that in four Australian states, in the two weeks after the media announced singer and pop-icon Kylie Minogue was diagnosed with breast cancer, bookings for mammographies increased by 40% [45]. This sort of reporting may also have unhealthy effects [46]. Jordan et al. (2008) propose that the media has contributed to the childhood obesity pandemic by advertising the unhealthy foods and beverages that children now demand and regularly consume [47]. This suggests that media reports of an issue such as TBI in sport can contribute to an altered culture. Those charged with promoting healthy behaviors would benefit from understanding these trends in the media reports.

30 The results and implications of this study need to be considered in light of the investigation's limitations. Although the newspapers analyzed in this investigation are highly circulated, they represent only a small proportion of all daily, paid North American newspapers. Additionally, we only reviewed the articles of 4 largely circulated newspapers—it is not clear whether similar trends were reported in other newspapers, on radio, television and through other online sources. To assess the impact on such media reports on the public would require prospective studies with large numbers of people, a study beyond the scope of the present investigation.

Conclusion

31 We have shown that reporting of TBI and its context has changed substantially over time. That our findings were consistent within and across countries, with scientific reporting around TBI and over time provides evidence for the robustness of our findings. Future work that builds upon our findings should focus on how reporting of TBI in ice hockey can affect public discourse and the shaping of programs and policies that have positive effects on public health.

Plos One. 2013. 8 (4).

Author Contributions

Author Contributions Conceived and designed the experiments: MDC BS DWL GI SS RJ. Performed the experiments: MDC BS DWL GI SS RJ. Analyzed the data: MDC BS DWL GI SS RJ. Wrote the paper: MDC BS DWL GI SS RJ.

References

1. Bazarian JJ, Veazie P, Mookerjee S, Lerner EB (2006) Accuracy of mild traumatic brain injury case ascertainment using ICD-9 codes. Acad Emerg Med 13: 31–38.
2. Faul M, Xu L, Coronado VG (2010) Traumatic brain injury in the United States: emergency department visits, hospitalizations, and deaths. CDC National Center for Injury Prevention and Control, United States.
3. National Center for Injury Prevention & Control (2003) Report to Congress on mild traumatic brain injury in the United States: Steps to prevent a serious public health problem. Atlanta, GA: Centers for Disease Control and Prevention.
4. Halstead ME, Walter KD (2010) Sport-related concussion in children and adolescents. Pediatrics 126: 597–615.
5. Wetjen NM, Pichelmann MA, Atkinson JL (2010) Second impact syndrome: concussion and second injury brain complications. J Am Coll Surg 4: 553–557.
6. Lord-Maes J, Obrzut JE (1996) Neuropsychological consequences of traumatic brain injury in children and adolescents. J Learn Disabil 29: 609–617.
7. Stevens ST, Lassonde M, de Beaumont L, Keenan JP (2006) The effect of visors on head and facial injury in National Hockey League players. J Sci Med Sport 9: 238–242.
8. Wennberg RA, Tator CH (2003) National Hockey League reported concussions, 1986–1987 to 2001–2002. Can J Neurol Sci 30: 206–209.
9. Wennberg RA, Tator CH (2008) Concussion incidence and time lost from play in the NHL during the past ten years. Can J Neurol Sci 35: 647–651.
10. Benson BW, Meeuwisse WH, Rizos J, Kang J, Burke CJ (2011) A prospective study of concussions among National Hockey League players during regular season games: the NHL-NHLPA Concussion Program. CMAJ 183: 905–911.
11. Marchie A, Cusimano MD (2003) Bodychecking and concussions in ice hockey: Should our youth pay the price? CMAJ 169: 124–128.
12. Cusimano MD, Taback NA, McFaull SR, Hodgins R, Bekele TM, et al. (2011) Effect of bodychecking on rate of injuries among minor hockey players. Open Med 5: 57–64.
13. Widmeyer WN, Birch JS (1984) Aggression in professional ice hockey: a strategy for success of a reaction to failure? J Psychol 177: 77–84.
14. Gee CJ (2010) Aggression in competitive sports: Using direct observation to evaluate incidence and prevention focused intervention. In: Luiselli JK, Reed DD, editors. Behavioural sport psychology: Evidence-based approaches to performance enhancement. New York: Springer. pp. 199–210.
15. Sheldon JP, Aimar CM (2001) The role aggression plays in successful and unsuccessful ice hockey behaviours. Res Q Exerc Sport 72: 304–309.
16. Cusimano MD, Chipman ML, Volpe R, Donnelly P (2009) Canadian minor hockey participants' knowledge about concussion. Can J Neurol Sci 36: 315–320.
17. Kepner T (2012) Line drive strikes Tigers starter, and prompts concerns. New York Times: New York.
18. Bandura A (1978) Social learning theory of aggression. J Commun 28: 12–29.
19. Stuart MJ, Colbenson CM, Kronebusch SP (2000) A psychosocial perspective of aggression in ice hockey. In: Ashare, editor. Safety in ice hockey. West Conshohocken: American Society for Testing and Materials. pp. 199–200.
20. Audit Bureau of Circulations (2011) Average circulation at the top 25 U.S. daily newspapers. ABCInteractive, United States.
21. Newspapers Canada (2011) Daily Newspaper Circulation by Province. Newspapers Canada, Canada.
22. Patton MQ (2002) Qualitative research and evaluation methods (3rd ed.). California: Sage Publications. 688 p.
23. Bauer MW, Gaskell G (2000) Qualitative researching with text, image and sound: A practical handbook. London: Sage Publications. 374 p.
24. Strauss A, Corbin JM (1998) Basics of Qualitative Research: Techniques and Procedures for Developing Grounded Theory. California: Sage Publications. 336 p.
25. Tesch R (1991) Computer programs that assist in the analysis of qualitative data: An overview. Qual Health Res 1: 309–325.
26. Bergeron RL (2002) Family preservation: An unidentified approach in elder abuse protection. Fam Soc 83: 547–556.

27. Putnam JM (2007) Combining telehealth and e-learning: A case study in smoking cessation programming. Am J Health Stud 3: 130–138.

28. Ward-Smith P, Forred D (2005) Participation in a dementia evaluation program: perceptions of family members. J Neurosci Nurs 37: 92–96.

29. Morse JM (1995) The significance of saturation. Qual Health Res 5: 147–149.

30. Youl PH, Janda M, Kimlin M (2009) Vitamin D and sun protection: The impact of mixed public health messages in Australia. Int J Cancer 124: 1963–1970.

31. Macciocchi SN, Barth JT, Alves W, Rimel RW, Jane J (1996) Neuropsychological functioning and recovery after mild head injury in collegiate athletes. Neurosurgery 39: 510–514.

32. Rabadi MH, Jordan BD (2001) The cumulative effect of repetitive concussion in sports. Clin J Sport Med 3: 194–198.

33. Bowen AP (2003) Second impact syndrome: a rare, catastrophic, preventable complication of concussion in young athletes. J Emerg Nurs 29: 287–289.

34. Iyengar S (1991) Is anyone responsible?: How television frames political issues. Chicago: University of Chicago Press. 206 p.

35. McGuire WJ, Rice RE, Atkin CK (2001) Input and output variables currently promising for constructing persuasive communications. In: Rice RE, Atkin CK, editors. Public communication campaigns. Thousand Oaks: Sage. pp. 22–48.

36. Herman ES, Chomsky N (2002) Manufacturing consent: The political economy of the mass media. New York: Pantheon Books. 412 p.

37. Katz E, Lazarsfeld PF (1955) Personal influence: The part played by people in the flow of mass communication. New York: The Free Press. 434 p.

38. Kirsh SJ (2010) Media and youth: A developmental perspective. United Kingdom: Wiley-Blackwell. 328 p.

39. Boxer PL, Huesmann R, Bushman BJ, O'Brien M, Moceri D (2009) The role of violent media preference in cumulative developmental risk for violence and general aggression. J Youth Adolesc 38: 417–428.

40. Anderson CA, Huesmann LR (2007) Human aggression: A social-cognitive view. In: Hogg MA, Cooper J, editors. The SAGE Handbook of Social Psychology. Thousand Oaks: Sage. pp. 296–323.

41. Cantor J (2000) Media violence. J Adolesc Health 27: 30–34.

42. Anderson CA, Bushman BJ (2002) Human Aggression. Annu Review Psychol 53: 27–51.

43. Lupton D, McLean J (1998) Representing doctors: discourses and images in the Australian press. Soc Sci Med 46: 947–958.

44. Ali SH, Keil R (2006) Global cities and the spread of infectious disease: The case of severe acute respiratory syndrome (SARS) in Toronto, Canada. Urban Stud 43: 491–509.

45. Chapman S, McLeod K, Wakefield M, Holding S (2005) Impact of news of celebrity illness on breast cancer screening: Kylie Minogue's breast cancer diagnosis. Med J Aust 5: 247–250.

46. Strasburger VC (2011) Children, adolescents, obesity, and the media. Pediatrics 128: 201–208.

47. Jordan AB, Kramer-Golinkoff EF, Strasburger VC (2008) Does adolescent media use cause obesity and eating disorders? Adolesc Med State Art Review 19: 431–449.

Key and challenging words

a priori, invulnerable, inherent, integral, cavalier, proliferate, detrimental, incite

Questions

1. (a) Discuss how the authors show the importance of their topic in their introduction; (b) how do they justify their study?

2. Summarize paragraph 6; paraphrase the same paragraph, making sure you include the authors' reasons for choosing the four newspapers for analysis.

3. In your own words, explain what the authors mean when they state, "[C]ategories and themes were allowed to emerge from the data inductively and were not pre-identified by *a priori* hypotheses" (paragraph 9).

4. Analyze the use of tables to aid in comprehension and organization in the "Methods" section.

5. In the "Thematic analyses" part of the "Results" section, identify two differences between the early versus recent time periods (they could apply to Canadian newspapers, American newspapers, or both), and infer the reason(s) why these differences might have occurred.

6. Analyze the authors' organizational/rhetorical strategies in paragraph 25 that enable them to convey information clearly. For example, you could consider

the use of a topic sentence, rhetorical patterns, transitions, repetition, emphasis, and the like.

7. Show how the authors use one source about media reporting unrelated to hockey to develop a point about media reporting of head injuries in hockey.

8. Why is it important in the Discussion section that the authors acknowledge previous models relating to the media? Summarize one of these models.

Post-reading

1. Find one similarity and one difference in the "Methods" and/or "Results" sections of "Trends in North American Newspaper Reporting" and the corresponding section(s) in "Community Perspectives on the Impact of Climate Change," p. 388, another essay that uses the qualitative research method.

2. Locate two in-depth articles written on head injuries in hockey, one of which was published within the last

five years and one of which was published before 2004. (a) Identify common "themes" (see Table 1 of "Trends in North American Newspaper Reporting" for examples, but other themes might be applicable); (b) write a compare–contrast analysis of the articles, using at least two bases of comparison.

Related website of interest

Brain Injury Association of Canada: Concussion Information/Management:
biac-aclc.ca/category/concussion-management-and-information/

Additional library reading

Warsh, J.M., Constantin, S.A., Howard, A., & Macpherson, A. (2009). A systematic review of the association between body checking and injury in youth ice hockey. *Clinical Journal of Sport Medicine, 19*(2), 133–144. doi:10.1136/ip.2009.022764

Emery, C.A., Hagel, B., Decloe, M., & McKay, C. (2010). Risk factors for injury and severe injury in youth ice hockey: A systematic review of the literature. *Injury Prevention, 16*(2), 113–118. doi:10.1136/ip.2009. 022764

Addressing driver aggression: Contributions from psychological science

Christine M. Wickens, Robert E. Mann, and David L. Wiesenthal
(2,572 words)

Pre-reading

1. *Collaborative or individual activity:* Has aggressive driving affected you or someone you know—either as a perpetrator or a victim? What were the circumstances, causes, and/or consequences of the incident(s)? Could anything have been done to minimize the likelihood of the incident(s) (for example, reducing driving speed, clearer signalling, etc.)?

2. Read the abstract and first paragraph to determine how this essay conforms to the conventions of a Type C (critical review) essay. Write a one-paragraph reading hypothesis (see p. 51) that establishes a plan or strategy for reading the essay.

Abstract

Aggressive roadway behavior contributes to motor-vehicle collisions, resulting in significant injuries, fatalities, and related financial costs. Psychological models have identified person- and situation-related variables that are predictive of driver aggression, and these have been used to develop strategies to alleviate aggressive roadway behavior. Future psychological research directions are discussed.

-----

1   Aggressive roadway behavior increases the risk of motor vehicle collisions and is associated with greater injury severity resulting from such collisions (Galovski, Malta, & Blanchard, 2006; Paleti, Eluru, & Bhat, 2010). Although estimates of the prevalence of aggressive driving vary considerably (see Galovski et al., 2006), the AAA Foundation for Traffic Safety (2009) reported that 56% of fatal crashes in the United States from 2003 through 2007 involved at least one driver action that is typically associated with driver aggression, such as excessive speeding or reckless/careless driving. Although 78% of Americans recognize the danger and resulting health and financial impact of aggressive driving, a significant number of American drivers admit to speeding to beat a yellow light (58%), pressuring other motorists to speed up (26%), and tailgating (22%; AAA Foundation for Traffic Safety, 2009). Given this paradox of attitude versus behavior, psychological science clearly has a role to play in furthering our understanding of what factors contribute to aggressive driver behavior and identifying potential solutions to the problem.

Defining Aggressive Driver Behavior

2   In addressing the issue of driver aggression, the first step must be to define the term. Most available statistics, including those cited in the prior paragraph, are based on a broad interpretation of aggressive driving; however, there has been controversy concerning which aggressive acts meet the inclusion criteria. Many researchers have argued that the aggressive action must be deliberate. If one motorist has an accidental lapse in judgment and does not leave enough space when pulling in front of another driver, is this an example of aggressive driving? Another definitional issue involves the nature of the intention. Must the driver be motivated by hostility toward another motorist to be considered aggressive, or can the driver be motivated by impatience or an attempt to save time? Some researchers have argued that there is a distinction between aggressive and risky driving. The former involves harmful intent directed toward another motorist, whereas the latter involves exclusively selfish motives such as time urgency or thrill-seeking (for a thorough review of this debate, see Galovski et al., 2006; Wiesenthal, Lustman, & Roseborough, in press). For the purposes of streamlining the current review of a vast literature, *driver aggression* will be used to refer to violations of highway traffic laws (e.g., speeding, tailgating, reckless driving) and less serious anger expressions (e.g., swearing, obscene gestures) that are assumed to result from hostility directed toward another motorist; *driver violence* will be used to refer to violations of criminal laws (e.g., threatening harm, assault). These acts are not errors or lapses in judgment; they are aberrant driving behaviors (see Reason, Manstead, Stradling, Baxter, & Campbell, 1990) motivated specifically by hostility. Psychologists have postulated many theoretical models explaining driver aggression that hypothesize a combination of person-related and situational variables (e.g., Shinar, 1998).

Person-Related Contributors

Demographics

3   Person-related variables are those factors that are specific to the driver; arguably, they constitute the largest and most diverse class of contributory factors. Demographic characteristics are the most basic of these variables. Driver aggression is more common among the young and the unmarried, which may be explained by more frequent risk-taking behavior by these demographic groups. Driver aggression has also been seen more commonly among the well-educated and higher socioeconomic status groups, perhaps because they have more social engagements and may be more rushed for time, or they may be less deterred by the risk of fines should they be observed by the authorities (Wickens et al., 2012). Driver aggression has been shown to be greater among men than women, but the most significant gender difference is found with driver violence: men are much more likely to engage in this extreme behavior (Hennessy, Wiesenthal, Wickens, & Lustman, 2004).

Personality

4   Personality may affect our cognitive perception of a situation, our preferences regarding levels of arousal or stimulation, or our sensitivity to stress or threat, all of which play a role when we are driving (Matthews, Dorn, & Glendon, 1991). Drivers who frequently demonstrate high levels of verbal and physical aggression or anger in other aspects of their lives are generally more likely to do so in the driving environment (Deffenbacher, Deffenbacher, Lynch, & Richards, 2003). Narcissistic people are recognized as arrogant, selfish, and having a sense of entitlement. Narcissists have been found to engage in more retaliatory and vengeful behavior, perhaps because they are more likely to perceive ambiguous driving altercations as intentional or unjust (Lustman, Wiesenthal, & Flett, 2010). Sensation seeking, associated with a need for novel and intense stimuli, has generally been associated with risky driving behavior. This trait has also been identified as a significant predictor of driver aggression, perhaps because sensation seekers perceive less risk in, or accept the risk associated with, roadway aggression (Dahlen, Martin, Ragan, & Kuhlman, 2005). Impulsive people demonstrate poor control over thoughts and behaviors, often initiating behavior without significant forethought, and are more likely to use the vehicle as a weapon for retaliation (Dahlen et al., 2005). Type-A personality consists of a cluster of traits relevant to driver behavior including competitiveness, hostility, achievement motivation, and a sense of time urgency (Bone & Mowen, 2006; Wickens & Wiesenthal, 2005). Not surprisingly, Type-A personality is more common among aggressive than nonaggressive drivers (Miles & Johnson, 2003). Neuroticism is associated with feelings of anxiety, anger, envy, depressed mood, and poor emotional response to stress. Drivers high in neuroticism engage in more horn honking, tailgating, and using obscene hand gestures (Bone & Mowen, 2006). Other variables that have been found to contribute to driver aggression include machismo, extraversion, ego defensiveness, and emotional instability (Bone & Mowen, 2006; Krahé & Fenske, 2002; Neighbors, Vietor, & Knee, 2002; Sümer, Lajunen, & Özkan, 2005). There are also personality variables that have been found to reduce the likelihood that a driver will engage in roadway aggression, including high levels of conscientiousness and agreeableness (Bone & Mowen, 2006; Sümer et al., 2005).

Cognition

5   How we cognitively perceive a driving event will have a major impact on how we feel and eventually respond to the event. Stress researchers conceptualize cognition in driver aggression as involving appraisal of the demands of a stressful situation and ability to cope with them. A driver caught in a stressful driving situation characterized by crowded but quickly moving traffic, time urgency, and an unexpected near-collision may assess the situation as being greater than his/her personal resources can tolerate. The motorist may experience feelings of anger and may lash out aggressively (Matthews et al., 1991; Wickens & Wiesenthal, 2005). Attribution theorists have conceptualized the role of cognition as a series of judgments regarding why an event occurred and the level of responsibility assigned to an offending driver. If we are cut off on the highway and assume that the offending driver's actions were intentional, we feel angry and may respond in kind. However, if we attribute the driver's actions to an unintentional cause such as a sudden tire blowout causing the vehicle to swerve in front of us, then we may feel sympathy for the other motorist (Wickens, Wiesenthal, Flora, & Flett, 2011).

6   Cognitive biases can also influence the development of driver aggression. When interpreting the potentially offensive actions of other motorists, drivers tend to overestimate internal (e.g., personality) and underestimate external (e.g., situation) causes; however, drivers tend to do the opposite when making attributions for their own actions (i.e., the actor-observer bias; e.g., Herzog, 1994). Novice motorists tend to be overconfident of their driving skills (Mynttinen et al., 2009), thus lowering their tolerance for the perceived misdeeds of other motorists.

Alcohol, Drugs, and Mental Health

7   Alcohol-related problems, use of cannabis, and use of these substances immediately before driving increase one's risk of engaging in driver aggression

(Butters, Mann, & Smart, 2006; Wickens et al., 2012). Drivers reporting the use of cocaine, ecstasy (MDMA), or both are more likely to commit violent roadway behavior (Butters et al., 2006). The pharmacological effect of these substances on mood and inhibition, along with personality characteristics (e.g., trait anger or aggression, sensation seeking) common to drinkers, drug users, and aggressive drivers, may also explain the overlap in these behaviors.

8   Various psychiatric disorders have also been implicated as contributors to driver aggression. Intermittent explosive disorder is an impulse control disorder characterized by extreme expressions of anger out of proportion to the provoking stimulus. In a study of treatment-seeking aggressive drivers in Albany, New York, approximately one third of these drivers met criteria for intermittent explosive disorder, significantly more than a control sample of non-aggressive drivers (Galovski et al., 2006). Attention deficit hyperactivity disorder is characterized by inattention, impulsivity, and hyperactivity and is associated with increased self-reports of driving violations, anger, and aggression (Barkley & Cox, 2007). Attention deficit hyperactivity disorder often co-occurs with other disruptive behavior disorders, such as conduct disorder and oppositional defiant disorder. Relative to a sample of nonaggressive control subjects, these disorders have been found to be more prevalent among aggressive drivers (Malta, Blanchard, & Freidenberg, 2005). Personality disorders, such as antisocial personality disorder and paranoid personality disorder, are also more likely to be found among aggressive than nonaggressive drivers (Galovski et al., 2006). Psychiatric distress, which includes symptoms of both depression and anxiety, has been found to significantly increase the odds of perpetrated driver violence (Butters et al., 2006). Nonetheless, studies examining the impact of anxiety and mood disorders on driver aggression have generated mixed findings, providing some support for this relationship but necessitating additional research (Wickens, Mann, Butters, Smart, & Stoduto, in press). Finally, it is also important to note that medications used to ameliorate psychiatric problems may influence, and perhaps increase, driver aggression (Wickens, Mann, Butters, et al., in press).

Situation-Related Contributors

Environmental Factors

9   Sights, sounds, and smells can all play a role. The visual content of the roadside environment can influence the level of stress and negative affect experienced by drivers; urban roadways lined with commercial buildings and billboards generate more stress than rural roadways lined with natural vegetation (Parsons, Tassinary, Ulrich, Hebl, & Grossman-Alexander, 1998). Likewise, hostile cues such as aggressive billboard advertising or a gun rack in the window of a pickup truck increase driver anger and aggression (Ellison-Potter, Bell, & Deffenbacher, 2001). Sounds within the vehicle can also influence stress levels; self-selected music reduces stress experienced in heavy traffic congestion (Wiesenthal, Hennessy, & Totten, 2000). Likewise, the smell of peppermint decreases drivers' frustration, anxiety, and fatigue (Raudenbush, Grayhem, Sears, & Wilson, 2009), and rising ambient temperature increases drivers' horn honking (Kenrick & MacFarlane, 1986).

Situational Factors

10   Within the driving environment, aspects of the situation can also elicit or augment anger behind the wheel that would not otherwise have emerged. Offensive driving by another motorist can provoke roadway anger and aggression (Wickens et al., 2011), but situational factors can further increase the likelihood of an aggressive response. Traffic congestion is a major source of roadway stress, and the resulting frustration may be directed aggressively at other motorists (Shinar, 1998). Daily hassles and job-related stresses can make traffic congestion or an offensive driver action seem much more upsetting (Matthews et al., 1991; Wickens & Wiesenthal, 2005). Likewise, time urgency can make traffic congestion or an otherwise benign traffic situation seem much more stressful (Wickens & Wiesenthal, 2005), which can lead to driver aggression.

11   Attributions of other drivers' roadway actions are influenced by the visible characteristics of that driver and the features of their vehicle. Female drivers are judged to be more careless and less aggressive

than male drivers, and drivers of BMWs are judged to be more aggressive than drivers of Smart cars (Lawrence & Richardson, 2005). The relative status of vehicles also makes a difference in the likelihood of aggression; when blocked by a "middleclass" vehicle stopped at a green light, drivers of upperclass vehicles honk their horns more quickly than drivers of middle-class vehicles, who honk more quickly than drivers of lower-class vehicles (Diekmann, Jungbauer-Gans, Krassnig, & Lorenz, 1996).

Alleviating Aggressive Driver Behavior

12   Beyond bettering our understanding of the factors that contribute to driver violence and aggression, psychological science is also developing strategies to alleviate the behavior. Programs to treat aggressive drivers are now being developed using cognitive-behavioral therapy, attributional retraining, and relaxation training (Galovski et al., 2006). These programs teach drivers to identify the triggers of their roadway anger and aggression, to recognize cognitive distortions that contribute to their anger, and to control their breathing and relax their muscles when an anger-provoking event is encountered. Additional evidence-based curricula could be added, such as recognizing the tendency to overestimate our own driving skills and emphasizing the importance of roadway communication (e.g., signaling lane changes, flashing headlights as a sign of gratitude; Wickens et al., 2011). Although development of these programs is in the early stages, the success of similarly-intended programs for persons convicted of driving while intoxicated (e.g., Wickens, Mann, Stoduto, Flam Zalcman, & Butters, 2013) suggests that these programs could substantially improve traffic safety if implemented on a large scale. These programs could also be beneficial if presented early in a novice driver's training.

13   Other attempts at behavior modification have included incentives for good driving: Instrumented vehicles or monitored traffic zones identify and reward law-abiding drivers with entries in a lottery or direct monetary compensation (Battista, Burns, & Taylor, 2010; Haggarty, 2010). Directed passenger feedback has also been used to encourage drivers to better monitor their speed and mirrors (Hutton, Sibley, Harper, & Hunt, 2002), although it is unclear how long this effect might persist, whether it could be used to reduce retaliatory aggression, and whether it is affected by the type of relationship between the driver and the passenger (e.g., teen driver and parent; see Wiesenthal et al., in press).

14   Psychological science can also advise police by identifying specific driving behaviors for enforcement campaigns and when these efforts should occur (Wickens, Wiesenthal, Hall, & Roseborough, 2013). It can inform public service and education campaigns through identification of the audience to target and the most effective focus of the public appeal (e.g., emotional versus informational; Lewis, Watson, White, & Tay, 2007). Psychological science also allows for the evaluation of various technological solutions to the driver aggression problem, including photo radar, red-light cameras, and electronic message boards over the highway for safety appeals or in the rear window of a passenger vehicle to facilitate inter-vehicle communication (e.g., Chen, Meckle, & Wilson, 2002; Retting, Williams, Farmer, & Feldman, 1999; Smart, Cannon, Howard, & Mann, 2005).

Future Directions

15   Psychology is advancing our knowledge of factors contributing to driver aggression, adding to the list of relevant variables and expanding our understanding of existing factors. Person-related and situational variables operate together; thus, it is imperative that we continue to investigate how the contributions of multiple factors combine and interact to influence aggressive roadway behavior. We also need to understand the mechanisms underlying the influence of contributory factors. Personality, cognition, and affect all influence each other, and an improved assessment of the temporal order and strength of these influences is needed. Efforts to apply this information to modify driver aggression through policy, incentive-based approaches, psychotherapeutic programs (e.g., attributional retraining), and technological innovations to the vehicle and the roadway environment (e.g., electronic message boards) are in their infancy but possess great potential for impact.

Current Directions in Psychological Science. 2013. 22 (5).

Declaration of Conflicting Interests

The authors declared that they had no conflicts of interest with respect to their authorship or the publication of this article.

Funding

This work was supported by a grant from AUTO21, a member of the Networks of Centres of Excellence program that is administered and funded by the Natural Sciences and Engineering Research Council, the Canadian Institutes of Health Research, and the Social Sciences and Humanities Research Council (SSHRC), in partnership with Industry Canada. C.M. Wickens was supported by Postdoctoral Fellowships from the SSHRC and the Centre for Addiction and Mental Health, and R.E. Mann acknowledges ongoing funding support from the Ontario Ministry of Health and Long-Term Care.

References

AAA Foundation for Traffic Safety. (2009, April). *Aggressive driving: Research update.* Washington, DC: Author.

Barkley, R.A., & Cox, D. (2007). A review of driving risks and impairments associated with attention-deficit/hyperactivity disorder and the effects of stimulant medication on driving performance. *Journal of Safety Research 38,* 113–128.

Battista, V., Burns, P., & Taylor, G. (2010). *Using rewards to influence driving behaviour: A field operational trial.* Proceedings of the 20th Canadian Multidisciplinary Road Safety Conference, Niagara Fall, Ontario, Canada.

Bone, S.A., & Mowen, J.C. (2006). Identifying the traits of aggressive and distracted drivers: A hierarchical trait model approach. *Journal of Consumer Behaviour 5,* 454–464.

Butters, J.E., Mann, R.E., & Smart, R.G. (2006). Assessing road rage victimization and perpetration in the Ontario adult population. *Canadian Journal of Public Health 97,* 96–99.

Chen, G., Meckle, W., & Wilson, J. (2002). Speed and safety effect of photo radar enforcement on a highway corridor in British Columbia. *Accident Analysis & Prevention 34,* 129–138.

Dahlen, E.R., Martin, R.C., Ragan, K., & Kuhlman, M.M. (2005). Driving anger, sensation seeking, impulsiveness, and boredom proneness in the prediction of unsafe driving. *Accident Analysis & Prevention 37,* 341–348.

Deffenbacher, J.L., Deffenbacher, D.M., Lynch, R.S., & Richards, T.L. (2003). Anger, aggression, and risky behavior: A comparison of high and low anger drivers. *Behaviour Research and Therapy 41,* 701–718.

Diekmann, A., Jungbauer-Gans, M., Krassnig, H., & Lorenz, S. (1996). Social status and aggression: A field study analyzed by survival analysis. *The Journal of Social Psychology 136,* 761–768.

Ellison-Potter, P., Bell, P., & Deffenbacher, J. (2001). The effects of trait driving anger, anonymity, and aggressive stimuli on aggressive driving behavior. *Journal of Applied Social Psychology 31,* 431–443.

Galovski, T.E., Malta, L.S., & Blanchard, E.B. (2006). *Road rage: Assessment and treatment of the angry, aggressive driver.* Washington, DC: American Psychological Association.

Haggarty, E. (2010, December 9). Speed camera lottery pays drivers for slowing down. *The Toronto Star.* Retrieved from www.thestar.com/news/world/2010/12/09/speed_camera_lottery_pays_drivers_for_slowing_down.html.

Hennessy, D.A., Wiesenthal, D.L., Wickens, C.M., & Lustman, M. (2004). The impact of gender and stress on traffic aggression: Are we really that different? In J.P. Morgan (Ed.), *Focus on aggression research* (pp. 157–174). Hauppauge, NY: Nova Science Publishers.

Herzog, T.A. (1994). Automobile driving as seen by the actor, the active observer, and the passive observer. *Journal of Applied Social Psychology 24,* 2057–2074.

Hutton, K.A., Sibley, C.G., Harper, D.N., & Hunt, M. (2002). Modifying driver behavior with passenger feedback. *Transportation Research Part F 4,* 257–269.

Kenrick, D.T., & MacFarlane, S.W. (1986). Ambient temperature and horn honking: A field study of the heat/aggression relationship. *Environment & Behavior 18,* 179–191.

Krahé, B., & Fenske, I. (2002). Predicting aggressive driving behavior: The role of macho personality, age, and power of car. *Aggressive Behavior 28,* 21–29.

Lawrence, C., & Richardson, J. (2005). Gender-based judgments of traffic violations: The moderating influence of car type. *Journal of Applied Social Psychology 35,* 1755–1774.

Lewis, I.M., Watson, B., White, K.M., & Tay, R. (2007). Promoting public health messages: Should we move beyond fear-evoking appeals in road safety? *Qualitative Health Research 17,* 61–74.

Lustman, M., Wiesenthal, D.L., & Flett, G.L. (2010). Narcissism and aggressive driving: Is an inflated view of the self a road hazard? *Journal of Applied Social Psychology 40,* 1423–1449.

Malta, L.S., Blanchard, E.B., & Freidenberg, B.M. (2005). Psychiatric and behavioral problems in aggressive drivers. *Behaviour Research and Therapy 43,* 1467–1484.

Matthews, G., Dorn, L., & Glendon, A.I. (1991). Personality correlates of driver stress. *Personality and Individual Differences 12,* 535–549.

Miles, D.E., & Johnson, G.L. (2003). Aggressive driving behaviors: Are there psychological and attitudinal predictors? *Transportation Research Part F 6*, 147–161.

Mynttinen, S., Sundström, A., Koivukoski, M., Hakuli, K., Keskinen, E., & Henriksson, W. (2009). Are novice drivers overconfident? A comparison of self-assessed and examiner-assessed driver competences in a Finnish and Swedish sample. *Transportation Research Part F 12*, 120–130.

Neighbors, C., Vietor, N.A., & Knee, C.R. (2002). A motivational model of driving anger and aggression. *Personality and Social Psychology Bulletin 28*, 324–335.

Paleti, R., Eluru, E., & Bhat, C.R. (2010). Examining the influence of aggressive driving behavior on driver injury severity in traffic crashes. *Accident Analysis & Prevention 42*, 1839–1854.

Parsons, R., Tassinary, L.G., Ulrich, R.S., Hebl, M.R., & Grossman-Alexander, M. (1998). The view from the road: Implications for stress recovery and immunization. *Journal of Environmental Psychology 18*, 113–139.

Raudenbush, B., Grayhem, R., Sears, T., & Wilson, I. (2009). Effects of peppermint and cinnamon odor administration on simulated driving alertness, mood and workload. *North American Journal of Psychology 11*, 245–256.

Reason, J., Manstead, A., Stradling, S., Baxter, J., & Campbell, K. (1990). Errors and violations on the roads: A real distinction? *Ergonomics 33*, 1315–1332.

Retting, R.A., Williams, A.F., Farmer, C.M., & Feldman, A.F. (1999). Evaluation of red light camera enforcement in Oxnard, California. *Accident Analysis & Prevention 31*, 169–174.

Shinar, D. (1998). Aggressive driving: The contribution of the drivers and the situation. *Transportation Research Part F 1*, 137–160.

Smart, R.G., Cannon, E., Howard, A., & Mann, R.E. (2005). Can we design cars to prevent road rage? *International Journal of Vehicle Information and Communication Systems 1*, 44–55.

Sümer, N., Lajunen, T., & Özkan, T. (2005). Big five personality traits as the distal predictors of road accident involvement. In G. Underwood (Ed.), *Traffic and transport psychology: Theory and application—Proceedings of the ICTTP 2004* (pp. 215–227). New York, NY: Elsevier.

Wickens, C.M., Mann, R.E., Butters, J., Smart, R.G., & Stoduto, G. (in press). Road rage. In I. Treasaden & B. Puri (Eds.), *Forensic psychiatry: Fundamentals and clinical practice*. Boca Raton, FL: CRC Press.

Wickens, C.M., Mann, R.E., Stoduto, G., Butters, J.E., Ialomiteanu, A., & Smart, R.G. (2012). Does gender moderate the relationship between driver aggression and its risk factors? *Accident Analysis & Prevention 45*, 10–18.

Wickens, C.M., Mann, R.E., Stoduto, G., Flam Zalcman, R., & Butters, J. (2013). Alcohol control measures in traffic. In P. Boyle, P. Boffetta, W. Zatonski, A. Lowenfels, O. Brawley, H. Burns, & J. Rehm (Eds.), *Alcohol: Science, policy and public health*(pp. 378–388). New York, NY: Oxford University Press.

Wickens, C.M., & Wiesenthal, D.L. (2005). State driver stress as a function of occupational stress, traffic congestion, and trait stress susceptibility. *Journal of Applied Biobehavioral Research 10*, 83–97.

Wickens, C.M., Wiesenthal, D.L., Flora, D.B., & Flett, G.L. (2011). Understanding driver anger and aggression: Attributional theory in the driving environment. *Journal of Experimental Psychology: Applied 17*, 354–370.

Wickens, C.M., Wiesenthal, D.L., Hall, A., & Roseborough, J.E.W. (2013). Driver anger on the information superhighway: A content analysis of online complaints of offensive driver behaviour. *Accident Analysis & Prevention 51*, 84–92.

Wiesenthal, D.L., Hennessy, D.A., & Totten, B. (2000). The influence of music on driver stress. *Journal of Applied Social Psychology 30*, 1709–1719.

Wiesenthal, D.L., Lustman, M., & Roseborough, J. (in press). Aggressive driving: Current perspectives in theory and research. In A. Smiley (Ed.), *Human factors in traffic safety* (3rd ed.). Tucson, AZ: Lawyers & Judges Publishing Company.

Key and challenging words

postulate, deter, retaliatory, attribution, intermittent, ameliorate, alleviate

Questions

1. Summarize the nature of the paradox referred to in paragraph 1.

2. Why is it important that the authors define the term *driver aggression* (paragraph 2)? Paraphrase the definition given in paragraph 2.

3. Explain the importance of headings as an aid to essay organization.

4. Analyze the organization and development of paragraph 8, referring to strategies that make detailed content accessible. For example, you could consider

the topic sentence, paragraph development, rhetorical patterns, logical sentence order, sentence structure, transitions, and the like.

5. The authors not only report on studies but also sometimes speculate on (infer) the reason for the findings (for example, see the first half of paragraph 4 where they infer the reason why narcissistic and sensation-seeking drivers may drive more aggressively). Choose two findings that are not speculated on in this paragraph—for example, "machismo, extraversion, ego defensiveness, and emotional instability" are not discussed—and in one or two sentences infer why they might increase driver aggressiveness.

6. Explain which you think is the main factor in aggressive driving, choosing one of the subsections under person-related contributors or situation-related contributors. Use critical thinking and specific textual references to support your answer.

Post-reading

1. Create an educational and/or enforcement campaign to address aggressive driving. As part of your general strategy, choose the person- and situation-related contributors to aggressive driving you believe are most likely to reduce the incidence of aggressive driving. You can aim your strategy to a particular demographic if you think it will be effective to do so. (A substantial budget allows you to take a multi-pronged approach to the problem.)

Related website of interest

Traffic Injury Research Foundation:
www.tirf.ca/index.php

Additional library reading

Vanlaar, W., Simpson, H., Mayhew, D., & Robertson, R. (2008). Aggressive driving: A survey of attitudes, opinions and behaviors. *Journal of Safety Research, 39*(4), 375–381. doi: 10.1016/j.jsr.2008.05.005

Cyberbullying myths and realities

Russell A. Sabella, Justin W. Patchin, and Sameer Hinduja
(6,935 words)

Pre-reading

1. *Collaborative or individual question:* Identify/reflect on some of your beliefs about cyberbullying. For example, you could start with the five questions, *Who?, What?, When?, Where?,* and *How?* (e.g., Who is a typical cyberbully or victim?; What are the causes of cyberbullying?). Then, consider where these beliefs come from (e.g., family, peers, the media, teachers).

Abstract

Bullying has long been a concern of youth advocates (e.g., educators, counselors, researchers, policy makers). Recently, cyberbullying (bullying perpetrated through online technology) has dominated the headlines as a major current-day adolescent challenge. This article reviews available empirical research to examine the accuracy of commonly perpetuated claims about cyberbullying. The analysis revealed several myths about the nature and extent of cyberbullying that are being fueled by media headlines and unsubstantiated public declarations. These myths include that (a) everyone knows what cyberbullying is; (b) cyberbullying is occurring at epidemic levels; (c) cyberbullying causes suicide; (d) cyberbullying occurs more often now than traditional bullying; (e) like traditional bullying, cyberbullying is a rite of passage; (f) cyberbullies are outcasts or just mean kids; and (g) to stop cyberbullying, just turn off your computer or cell phone. These assertions are clarified using data that are currently available so that adults who work with youth will have an accurate understanding of cyberbullying to better assist them in effective prevention and response. Implications for prevention efforts in education in light of these revelations are also discussed and include effective school policies, educating students and stakeholders, the role of peer helper programs, and responsive services (e.g., counseling).

1. Introduction

1   Teens now have in their hands the same amount of computing ability that, just a decade ago, only large businesses could afford. How does a young person manage ever-increasing access to technology and, by extension, the power it imbues? Most students use technology responsibly, but some have chosen to use it in careless and inappropriate ways by hurting, humiliating, embarrassing, and personally attacking others (Hinduja & Patchin, 2012b; Kowalski, Limber, & Agatston, 2008; Patchin & Hinduja, 2010). This phenomenon has been termed cyberbullying, which has been defined as *"willful and repeated harm inflicted through the use of computers, cell phones, and other electronic devices"* (Hinduja & Patchin, 2009, p. 5, 2012a).

2   In several ways, cyberbullying may be perceived as more sinister than "off-line" (i.e., traditional or schoolyard) bullying because the attacks can be more intense, frequent, unsuspecting, and seemingly difficult to stop (Hinduja & Patchin, 2009). Compared to traditional bullies, cyberbullies are not restrained by space or time. Some cyberbullies may hide under a cloak of anonymity, in essence allowing them to easily attack others at any time and from any place they want (Kowalski et al., 2008). With modern technology, cyberbullying can occur at the "speed of thought" and in front of much larger audiences than those behaviors confined to the schoolyard. Online bullies also can potentially be even more cruel than off-line bullies because, in addition to words, they can incorporate as part of their attacks a rich array of media including sounds, altered photos, text, video, slide shows, and polls (Li, 2007; Sabella, 2008).

3   Though it occurs in cyberspace, this problem should not be trivialized since it has been linked to real-world consequences. For example, research has found that cyberbullying is associated with negative emotions such as sadness, anger, frustration, embarrassment, or fear (Hinduja & Patchin, 2007; Patchin & Hinduja, 2011; Ybarra & Mitchell, 2007), and these emotions have been correlated with delinquency and interpersonal violence among youth and young adults (Aseltine, Gore, & Gordon, 2000; Broidy & Agnew, 1997; Mazerolle, Burton, Cullen, Evans, & Payne, 2000; Mazerolle & Piquero, 1998). Furthermore, cyberbullying has been linked to low self-esteem and suicidal ideation, recent school difficulties, assaultive conduct, substance use, carrying a weapon to school, and traditional bullying offending and victimization (Hinduja & Patchin, 2007, 2008, 2009; Schneider, O'Donnell, Stueve, & Coulter, 2012; Ybarra, Diener-West, & Leaf, 2007; Ybarra & Mitchell, 2004a). It is for these reasons that youth-serving professionals should seek to gain and share knowledge related to the identification, prevention, and response of this problem.

4   One of the dangers, however, of doing cyberbullying risk-reduction work is that, in the course of educating students, staff, parents, and others, we can unwittingly contribute to the "hype" generated by a mass media that focuses on the dramatic and erratic. Recent headlines can serve to fuel what may be a distorted and artificially inflated view of cyberbullying—one not based on reality (Magid, 2011). Without a careful review of the professional literature, counseling or

educating students about cyberbullying may unintentionally stem from rumor or extreme and rare cases. Without carefully differentiating fact from fallacy, our good intentions can lead to erroneous decisions, harmful attitudes, and ineffective programmatic strategies (Kowalski et al., 2008; Willard, 2007a, 2010).

5   When working with students or others within the school community, youth educators (which may include, and from hereafter, refers to school counselors, researchers, policymakers, and, in general, youth advocates) must take care to provide accurate information and guidance supported by existing research. In this article, we seek to identify and clarify common myths surrounding cyberbullying by presenting research-supported realities that call into question some of the conventional wisdom concerning this problem. The myths included in this article were identified through various sources. First, we conducted an extensive review of the available professional literature and mass media publications. Second, we have heard these myths frequently professed through our work with thousands of educators and students while providing consultation, training, and policy development in the area of cyber-safety. Finally, we informally surveyed the online community called the Embrace Civility Network (formerly the *Youth Risk Online Professional Network*)—a consortium of over 250 recognized experts in the field, as well as educators, counselors, attorneys, CEOs/CSOs of online safety organizations, scholars, and legislators. This list is not intended to be exhaustive as there are unquestionably other statements that frequently appear in popular media and professional literature that lack adequate substantiation. The current work, however, is intended to clarify some of the more commonly referenced "facts" about cyberbullying. It should also be acknowledged that even the empirical research in this area is still evolving and therefore needs to be considered with a critical eye on operationalization and methodology. We begin with myth #1 which discusses this issue and its implications for our understanding of cyberbullying even further.

2. Myth 1: Everyone Knows What Cyberbullying Is

6   Many individuals may believe that they already fully understand and can recognize what cyberbullying is. The reality, however, is that there exists much variability in the way cyberbullying is defined and considered—even among cyberbullying researchers (Menesini & Nocentini, 2009; Oblad, 2012; Ybarra, Boyd, Korchmaros, & Oppenheim, 2012). As discussed by Patchin and Hinduja (2012), some researchers use very broad definitions of the problem that include every possible experience with any form of online aggression. Others focus only on specific types of harm, such as humiliation or threats to one's physical safety, without also including other forms like name-calling, insults, or social exclusion. Some cover any and all media and venues through which cyberbullying can occur, while others may leave out a few technologies (such as webcams) or environments (such as in online gaming networks). To confuse matters even further, in many languages other than English, there is no equivalent word for the term "bullying," which can affect the reported prevalence rates, especially when considering data collected internationally (Craig, Henderson, & Murphy, 2000; Smorti, Menesini, & Smith, 2003).

7   The varied conceptualizations are not surprising because, in reality, a continuum of behaviors exists, ranging from annoying or disappointing to severe, persistent, and pervasive attacks on others. At what point on the continuum does an incident make the leap from being one of poor judgment to one that we would call cyberbullying—or even one that may be criminal? The answers to these questions are still unclear and in need of further formal inquiry and examination.

8   One problem with not having a reliable and widely accepted definition of cyberbullying is that the inconsistencies lead to different measurements of the nature and extent of harassment in cyberspace, which at best provides an incomplete picture and at worst leads to misinformation and confusion (Mishna, Pepler, & Wiener, 2006; Patchin & Hinduja, 2012). Another problem with inconsistent definitions is that the terms *"bullying"* and *"cyberbullying"* are arguably now being overused among both adults and children alike. For example, some students are claiming that they are being bullied because they were not invited to a popular party, because they were accidentally pushed in the hallways, or perhaps teased, lied about, or made fun of *one time* (Williams & Guerra, 2007; Wolak, Mitchell, & Finkelhor, 2007). It is important for all

members of the school community to understand that peer conflict does not equate to bullying. To reiterate, arguing, bantering back-and-forth, ignoring, rough-housing and fighting are not necessarily instances of bullying, whether they occur online or via traditional venues (Willard, 2007c). Instead, cyberbullying, like traditional bullying, is characterized by intention, repetition, harm, and power imbalance (Patchin & Hinduja, 2006; Wolak et al., 2007). Not every conflict meets these criteria (Baas, de Jong, & Drossaert, 2013). Educators should help students understand and differentiate between situations that would and would not be considered bullying, perhaps through the presentation of examples, scenarios, and even role-playing exercises (see e.g., Sabella, 2012b).

3. Myth 2: Cyberbullying Is Occurring at Epidemic Levels

9   Consider these actual news headlines and stories:

- "Cyber bullying is a growing epidemic in communities, including ours" (Chin, 2011).
- "Cyberbullying: A National Epidemic" (Education Insider, 2010).
- "Cyber bullying spiralling out of control in schools" (McDougall, 2011).
- "Curing Utah's 'silent epidemic': Finding a solution to teen suicide" (Wood, 2013).
- "Child advocates say a growing epidemic of 'cyberbullying'—the use of computers, cell phones, social-networking sites and other technology to threaten or humiliate others" (Billitteri, 2008).

10   These are just a few examples of the many headlines that are seen through mass media that reinforce the notion that both bullying and cyberbullying have reached sweeping proportions. To be sure, one incident of any form of bullying is too many. However, making a serious issue such as cyberbullying seem more problematic than it really is, is in itself problematic. First, some students are apt to believe that if the majority of their peers are being bullied and bullying others, then it can be considered normative

behavior and consequently "not a big deal" (Hinduja & Patchin, 2012b). Second, the purported cyberbullying epidemic seems to be giving our youth a bad reputation, contributing to what some have referred to as "*juvenoia*" (Finkelhor, 2011). Conventional wisdom suggests that "kids these days" are more violent and less respectful than a generation ago. It is doubtful that this is true, especially since every generation seems to think that the youth of today are worse than when they were growing up. In fact, strong evidence exists to suggest that violence among youth, especially in schools, has actually decreased in the last decade (Finkelhor, 2013; National Center for Education Statistics, 2013). Finally, labeling cyberbullying an epidemic leads to some level of hysteria which may contribute to overzealous adults making uninformed and unwise decisions in an attempt to control youth behavior (e.g., zero-tolerance policies; taking away cell phones or other access to technology) (Hinduja & Patchin, 2009).

11   A precise measure of the prevalence of cyberbullying among teens is impossible to determine, partly related to Myth #1 (inconsistent definitions) but also due to varied methodological approaches. Some studies ask their teen participants about *any* experience with cyberbullying, while others focus on "online youth" who experience specific types of high-tech harm within the previous 30 days. One published study found that 72% of youth have experienced cyberbullying (Juvonen & Gross, 2008) whereas other published research has put this number at less than 7% (Ybarra, 2004; Ybarra & Mitchell, 2004a). The majority of studies estimate that anywhere from 6% to 30% of teens have experienced some form of cyberbullying, while the number of youth who admit to cyberbullying others at some point in their lives ranges from about 4% to 20% (Patchin & Hinduja, 2012). Of course this means that 70–80% of youth have not been cyberbullied, and have not cyberbullied others.

4. Myth 3: Cyberbullying Causes Suicide

12   Over the last few years, there have been several high-profile incidents where teenagers and young adults have taken their own lives in part because of experiences with bullying and cyberbullying (Bazelon, 2010;

Boyette, 2013; Halligan, 2006; High, 2007; Jones, 2008; Marr & Field, 2001). The viral nature of these stories in the media is especially troubling because exposure to news items on suicide has been cited as one of the numerous risk factors contributing to suicidal behavior (Beautrais, Collings, & Ehrhardt, 2005; Hawton & Williams, 2001). Also, the impact of news media reporting on suicidal behavior appears to be strongest among young people (WHO, 2000). Despite these tragedies, the vast majority of cyberbullying victims do not kill themselves, and those who do typically have experienced a constellation of stressors and other issues operating in their lives, making it difficult to isolate the influence of one specific personal or social problem as compared to others (Hinduja & Patchin, 2010a).

13   That said, research has shown that being involved in bullying (both as a victim and a bully) as a young person increases the risk for experiencing factors which are associated with suicidal thoughts, suicidal attempts, and completed suicides (Bauman, Toomey, & Walker, 2013; Campbell, Spears, Slee, Butler, & Kift, 2012; Klomek, Sourander, & Gould, 2010; Klomek et al., 2009; Rigby & Slee, 1999; Skapinakis et al., 2011). Kim and Leventhal (2008), for example, conducted a meta-analytical review of 37 different studies that examined the association between bullying and suicide, with an emphasis on the strengths and limitations of each of the study's research designs. Their review concluded that any participation in bullying increases risk factors such as depression and anxiety, which can be associated with suicidal ideation and/or behaviors in a broad spectrum of youth.

14   Recently, Hinduja and Patchin (2010a) conducted a study on teen technology use and misuse involving approximately 2000 randomly selected middle school students from one of the largest school districts in the United States. Results showed that youth who experienced traditional bullying or cyberbullying, as either an offender or a target, were more likely to report suicidal thoughts and to have previously attempted suicide than those who had not experienced such forms of peer aggression. The authors found that traditional bullying victims were 1.7 times more likely and traditional bullying offenders were 2.1 times more likely to have attempted suicide than those who were not traditional victims or offenders (Hinduja & Patchin, 2010a). Similarly, cyberbullying victims were 1.9 times more likely and cyberbullying offenders were 1.5 times more likely to have attempted suicide than those who were not cyberbullying victims or offenders. Winsper, Lereya, Zanarini, and Wolke (2012) conducted a study that focused on the prospective link between involvement in bullying (bully, victim, bully/victim) and subsequent suicide ideation in preadolescent children in the United Kingdom. These authors concluded that being a target of bullying, especially as a bully/victim, significantly increases the risk of suicide ideation in preadolescent children.

15   Given all of this research, one might ask: Why is it a myth that "cyberbullying causes suicide?" The answer to this question lies in the important difference between the nature of *correlation* and *causation*. While it is true that there exists a *relationship* between bullying and suicide (a connection or correlation), no conclusive statistical evidence has shown that a cyberbullying experience directly "leads to" or *causes* suicide. As previously stated, most youth who are cyberbullied do not take their own lives. So, the best that we can confidently say is that, among some young people, cyberbullying and suicide may be co-occurring (or are "co-related") with at least one of many other factors such as depression, social withdrawal, disability, social hopelessness, or other psychiatric morbidity (Skapinakis et al., 2011). That is, cyberbullying may aggravate the victim's already existing vulnerabilities. As Hinduja and Patchin (2010a) concluded, ". . . it is unlikely that experience with cyberbullying *by itself* leads to youth suicide. Rather, it tends to exacerbate instability and hopelessness in the minds of adolescents already struggling with stressful life circumstances" (p. 217). Unfortunately, some research findings have shown that the primary focus of news items in this context is on the technology involved in the cyberbullying and not the suicide events themselves or other important factors that may have contributed to the suicides, such as victims' mental well-being (Thom et al., 2011).

5. Myth 4: Cyberbullying Occurs More Often Now than Traditional Bullying

16   Conventional wisdom would have us believe that since technology has proliferated over the last

decade and stories of cyberbullying are frequently mentioned in the news, it is likely more prevalent than traditional, schoolyard bullying. However, research demonstrates that this is not the case (at least not yet). For example, according to the National Center for Educational Statistics (2013) report, *Indicators of School Crime and Safety*, (which reported data from 2011), 27.8% of students reported being the victim of bullying during the school year while only 9% of students had been cyberbullied. Ybarra et al. (2012) recently found that 25% of students had been bullied in person while 10% had been bullied online. Overall, most research demonstrates that cyberbullying still occurs less frequently than bullying, though that could change in the future. Jones, Mitchell, and Finkelhor (2013) collected data from students across the US in 2000, 2005, and 2010 and saw a modest but steady increase in cyberbullying between 2000 and 2010 (from 6% to 11%).

17   Beran and Li (2007) reviewed several published studies, all of which suggest that cyberbullying and traditional bullying occur at a comparable rate. One possible explanation for the similar rates of traditional bullying and cyberbullying is that there seems to be a significant overlap among students who are involved in both forms (Beran & Li, 2007; Cross et al., 2009; Hinduja & Patchin, 2008; Raskauskas & Stoltz, 2007; Smith et al., 2008; Vandebosch & Van Cleemput, 2009; Ybarra & Mitchell, 2004a). For example, Beran and Li (2007) surveyed 432 students from grades 7–9 in Canadian schools about their victimization experiences, and found that one third of children bullied in cyberspace were also bullied at school. In addition, Ybarra and Mitchell (2004a) found that many cyberbullies were also cybervictims, and that almost half of the cyberbullies reported having been victims of traditional bullying. Recognizing this overlap in behaviors is important, since it affects decision-making that determines a school's goals/focus and commitment of resources. Focusing on cyberbullying as a priority at the expense of addressing traditional bullying is a mistake. Both should be addressed as different manifestations of the same underlying issues.

6. Myth 5: Like Traditional Bullying, Cyberbullying Is a Rite of Passage All Teens Experience

18   "Boys will be boys." "It'll toughen him up." "It will help her grow a backbone so she can handle life." "That which does not kill you only makes you stronger." These statements are sometimes used by both children and adults to normalize or minimize hurtful behavior among children and teens, sometimes even as a way of coping with cyberbullying after it occurs (Parris, Varjas, Meyers, & Cutts, 2012). The message that these perspectives send to our youth is that social cruelty has been common to one degree or another among past generations and, because they survived, experiencing bullying is some sort of ritual that we all must go through during the course of normal maturation. This is simply not true. In fact, U.S. President Barack Obama cogently emphasized this point during a conference on preventing bullying at the White House on March 10th, 2011 when he said:

> If there's one goal of this conference, it's to dispel the myth that bullying is just a harmless rite of passage or an inevitable part of growing up. It's not. Bullying can have destructive consequences for our young people. And it's not something we have to accept. As parents and students, as teachers and members of the community, we can take steps—all of us—to help prevent bullying and create a climate in our schools in which all of our children can feel safe; a climate in which they all can feel like they belong. As adults, we all remember what it was like to see kids picked on in the hallways or in the schoolyard. And I have to say, with big ears and the name that I have, I wasn't immune. I didn't emerge unscathed. But because it's something that happens a lot, and it's something that's always been around, sometimes we've turned a blind eye to the problem. We've said, "Kids will be kids." And so sometimes we overlook the real damage that bullying can do, especially when young people face harassment day after day, week after week (2011).

19   In reality, no matter how prevalent or pervasive bullying has been in our history, it was not acceptable then and it is not acceptable now. In her book, *Cyberbullying: What Counselors Need to Know*, Bauman (2011) presented a significant body of evidence supporting the idea that there are negative consequences of bullying for all involved youth. She presented various relevant research studies that demonstrate that victims *and* bullies have more social, emotional, behavioral, and academic problems than others who are not involved. As described above, victims are more likely to suffer from depression, anxiety, low self-esteem, and loneliness, and these consequences are still detected when the victims are adults. Various studies that have found that peer rejection, delinquency, criminality, violence, and suicidal ideation were additional outcomes of involvement in bullying (Bauman, 2008; Farrington, 2012; Fekkes, Pijpers, & Verloove-VanHorick, 2004; Hinduja & Patchin, 2007; Mynard, Joseph, & Alexander, 2000; Sharp, 1995; Smokowski & Kopasz, 2005). Having a "thick skin" or even notable coping skills may not be enough for some youth to navigate the pain, embarrassment, humiliation, and horror of victimization. Although many students are resilient and may even summon inner strength they did not know they had in order to deal with bullying or cyberbullying, some simply are unable to do so. Besides, there is no valuable life lesson that one can learn from enduring bullying that cannot be taught in a more humane way.

7. Myth 6: Cyberbullies Are Outcasts or Just Mean Kids

20   Some seem to believe that the majority of youth who cyberbully others simply do it for the sake of inflicting harm, as some sort of antisocial or even sadistic behavior inspired by their online activity (Finkelhor, 2011). As is often the case, there is a measure of truth to this, as some adolescent developmental experts and philosophers view bullying as driven by a need for control and domination by a child who perceives that his/her actions will lead to greater peer acceptance and recognition (Adler & Adler, 1995, 1996; Faris & Felmlee, 2011; Vaillancourt & Hymel, 2006). However, the weight of the research has shown, instead, that most youth participate in cyberbullying to get revenge or because they are "just playin'" (König, Gollwitzer, & Steffgen, 2010; Sanders, 2009; Varjas, Talley, Meyers, Parris & Cutts, 2010). As Elizabeth Englander (2008) concluded after surveying youth who admitted to cyberbullying others: "Cyberbullies themselves identify their own anger and desire for revenge as the major immediate motive for engaging in cyberbullying. A second motive is identified by students who report that they engage in cyberbullying 'as a joke.'" (p. 8)

21   It seems that many cyberbullies who retaliate are often angry, frustrated, or otherwise emotionally distraught and are simply acting out using the technology that is readily at their fingertips. Others participate in cyberbullying because they want retribution by returning a hurt or injury or to seek justice and teach a lesson. Still others casually dismiss the gravity of their cyberbullying behaviors because they do not make the connection between their online behavior and the offline consequences. These aggressors have also been referred to as "inadvertent" cyberbullies (Willard, 2007c) because, although their postings were intentional, they intended no harm. At the time, inadvertent cyberbullies believed that what they were doing was benign, and they were just "having fun" or "messing around." Although those who are mean to others in real life often behave similarly online, this is not always the case. Instead, some cyberbullies may be perceived among teachers and peers as kind and responsible students while in school, even when they could be actively involved in bullying others outside the purview of adults. For example, Hinduja and Patchin (2012b) found that those students who reported earning grades of mostly A's were just as likely to be involved in cyberbullying (both as a target and a bully) as those students who reported that they typically earned C's or D's. Just because certain students do well academically does not mean they are less likely to mistreat others. Those who subscribe to this myth may also mistakenly conclude that cyberbullies are easily identified and generally known among students and teachers. In fact, some parents and teachers would be shocked to know that some "good" students are also involved in the problem behavior.

8. Myth 7: To Stop Cyberbullying, Just Turn Off Your Computer or Cell Phone

22   It may seem logical at first to consider turning away from technology as a means to stopping cyberbullying from occurring (Englander & Muldowney, 2007). Encouraging youth to turn off or avoid technology, however, is an unrealistic and overall ineffective long-term strategy (Hinduja & Patchin, 2009). Technology is ubiquitous and now integrated in virtually all aspects of their lives (Madden, Lenhart, Duggan, Cortesi, & Gasser, 2013). Moreover, technology is an important social and educational tool for teens, and someone who is being cyberbullied should not have to miss out on all of the benefits technology has to offer (Hinduja & Patchin, 2012b). Finally, if the target of the cyberbullying didn't do anything wrong, why should he or she be punished by not being able to use their favorite electronic devices? Since when has it been appropriate to blame the victim? Advising a student to avoid technology in response to cyberbullying is like advising someone being bullied at school to quit going to school. Also consider that turning off the computer or cell phone does not stop many forms of cyberbullying (Hinduja & Patchin, 2009). A student does not need to be online for someone to create a mean or hurtful Web page about him or her. Rumors can be circulated via cell phone or online text messages without the victim being involved. A harassing online profile can be created without a target even knowing about it.

23   We need to acknowledge how essential connected technology is to teens. In particular, text messaging has become the primary way that teens reach their friends, surpassing face-to-face contact, email, instant messaging and voice calling as the go-to daily communication tool for the 14–17 year old age group (Madden et al., 2013). Being forced to disconnect for an extended period of time is not a realistic long-term solution. Second, telling a child to ignore noxious messages and postings can be difficult. Once images and negative content is witnessed, they cannot be "unwitnessed." Asking a child to simply delete unpleasant content does not solve the problem either. To the contrary, deleting posts, texts, emails, or other aggressive content destroys

the evidence often needed to eventually identify and respond to the cyberbully (Kowalski et al., 2008; Willard, 2007b).

24   In short, it is clear that avoiding technology will do little to solve the problem of cyberbullying. Instead, counselors need to educate students with information and skills they can use to effectively respond when it does happen. These might include blocking harassing messages, removing hurtful content (after it is archived), or talking with a trusted adult to get additional assistance.

9. Armed with Accurate Information About Cyberbullying, Educators Can Help

25   This article has identified and clarified several myths that are associated with adolescent cyberbullying. Existing research has helped to shed empirical light on the conventional wisdom surrounding the experiences of teens online. For instance, we know that cyberbullying is not an epidemic inducing large numbers of teens to commit suicide. However, that certainly does not exempt us from addressing it before and when it happens. Cyberbullying is a significant problem for many teens, and efforts should be taken to prevent and respond to it, and to equip youth with ways that empower them to reduce their own victimization risk (Chibarro, 2007). No one person, professional, or even organization will be able to effectively accomplish the systematic changes that need to occur and pervade our society. Cyberbullying risk reduction will require comprehensive and collaborative efforts among various youth advocates. School counselors in particular can play a critical role and can help in significant ways. For instance, Sabella (2012b) suggests that school counselors take the lead with a comprehensive approach that includes five areas, all of which have a basis in empirical support (see e.g., Pearce, Cross, Monks, Waters, & Falconer, 2011; Ttofi & Farrington, 2011). These include: (1) facilitating the development of effective school policies; (2) educating parents; (3) educating students; (4) developing peer helper programs; and (5) providing responsive services such as reporting and counseling opportunities. These efforts must include all stake holders such as teachers, school support services,

educational leaders, community leaders, legislators, parents, and, of course, students.

9.1. Effective School Policies

26 According to the American School Counselor Association's position statement about bullying (ASCA, 2005), leadership in the form of policy development is an appropriate role and responsibility of the school counselor:

> Professional school counselors collaborate with others to promote safe schools and confront issues threatening school safety. Professional school counselors encourage the development of policies supporting a safe school environment, and they provide leadership to the school by assisting in the design and implementation of school wide violence prevention activities and programs.

27 Hinduja and Patchin (2009) also argue that "one of the most important steps a district can take to help protect its students and protect itself from legal liability is to have a clear and comprehensive policy regarding bullying and harassment, technology, and their intersection: cyberbullying" (p. 188). Forty-nine states have bullying laws that require schools to have policies about bullying and most of these now include requirements to address electronic forms of harassment (Hinduja & Patchin, 2012a). School counselors can suggest the development of policies as described by Franek (2006), who stated that all forms of cyberspace harassment either during school hours or after school hours should not be tolerated. An anti-cyberbullying policy should also include establishing a prevention program and an annual assessment of such a program to determine its effectiveness (Diamanduros, Downs, & Jenkins, 2008; Hamburger, Basile, & Vivolo, 2011). In addition to legislation, most state departments of education have provided model anti-bullying policies (Hinduja & Patchin, 2012a) and the United States Department of Education released a report, *Analysis of State Bullying Laws and Policies* (Temple et al., 2012), which can serve as helpful references for school counselors towards this end. It is essential that counselors review and understand their school policy concerning cyberbullying so that they are able to respond to behaviors within the appropriate framework established by the policy.

9.2. Educating School Staff and Parents

28 School counselors also can serve as key players in providing parents, guardians, and school staff with the professional development or training they need to work to reduce the risk of cyberbullying among students (Bauman, 2011; Beale & Hall, 2007; Bhat, 2008; Maher, 2008; Winburn, Niemeyer, & Reysen, 2012). At a fundamental level, adults, including teachers and parents, need to keep pace with new technology to understand how students communicate online and how cyberbullying happens. The results of one study indicated that school adults provide limited help, which might be caused by their lack of understanding and training in how to deal with the issue (Li, 2010).

29 In collaboration with community groups and parent/teacher associations, school counselors also can enhance the way caretakers protect and inform their children by providing them with solutions from both human/relational and technological perspectives (Bradshaw, Sawyer, & O'Brennan, 2007). This is especially important given that there exists some evidence of a familial pattern to bullying whereby sometimes multiple children from the same family (and sometimes within the same school) are identified bullying perpetrators (Chan, 2006). Human/relational solutions to reducing cyberbullying include encouraging the development of relationships that facilitate trust and open lines of communication (Sabella, 2008, 2012b). School counselors also should encourage parents to learn about what their children are doing online and work to better understand the technology they are using. Understanding Facebook's privacy settings, for example, will enable parents and teachers to educate children about how to protect their personal information to the maximum extent possible (ASCA & iKeepSafe, 2011). Parents can also monitor the online activities of their children by being involved in these environments along with them such as watching a few funny YouTube videos together, "Skyping" with distant family members, using Pinterest to collect their favorite pieces of online content, or checking out Tumblr blogs from around the world.

30 School counselors can also coordinate efforts among educators and youth advocates to pass along information to parents about specific technological solutions (such as filtering, blocking, or tracking software) that may be helpful in deterring inappropriate behaviors or in collecting evidence of cyberbullying. To be sure, these products are never a replacement for active human engagement and intervention. Counselors, parents, and other adults have an obligation to help children become knowledgeable about the use (and misuse) of technology, to teach them how to make good decisions about how they use technology, and to help them to police themselves (and perhaps each other). Technological solutions can be an effective complement or backup to how youth are educated and supervised (Ybarra & Mitchell, 2004b). These include, but are not limited to, password protecting home wireless networks, using Internet safety services/software, subscribing to a digital reputation monitoring service, and/or exploring cell phone parental controls (Kowalski et al., 2008).

9.3. Educating Students

31   In collaboration with other educators, student training (also known as classroom guidance) should be provided to confront cyberbullying by including student competencies which help youth recognize legal and personal consequences of cyberbullying, improve social problem-solving and anger management skills, encourage prosocial behavior, and increase the ability to empathize with victims (Bradshaw, Waasdorp, O'Brennan, & Gulemetova, 2011; Hazler, 2006; Limber, Kowalski, & Agatston, 2009; Lund, Blake, Ewing, & Banks, 2012; Macklem, 2003). Students who witness or learn about cyberbullying happening to others should also learn about their responsibilities and how best to support each other (Li, 2010).

32   Although an abundance of cyberbullying and Internet safety related resources are available online, few sequenced and comprehensive lesson plans exist. Moreover, none of these has been formally evaluated. That said, some promising approaches do exist (see e.g., Sabella, 2012a for a compilation of recommended cyberbullying lesson plans) which include many of the components of cyberbullying prevention education recommended by other researchers (e.g., Diamanduros et al., 2008; Hinduja & Patchin, 2009).

9.4. Peer Helper Programs

33   Together with teachers, parents, and other youth advocates, school counselors should also take advantage of the expertise that already exists in their buildings. That is, they can use students to help educate their classmates about using technology responsibly. Led by the school counselor, educators can train students to work with and educate younger peers so that they make wise decisions online starting at an early age. Students can also work with others who are "at risk" as well as with those who are experiencing typical childhood problems and concerns, and thereby play important roles in both intervention and prevention (ASCA, 2008). Myrick, Highland, and Sabella (1995) indicated that the advantages of using peer helpers in general may include: better communication and relationships among students; the generation of positive sentiments and a healthier climate across campus; wider message delivery, higher visibility, and the promotion of positive public relations to the school; evaluation of lesson plans, content, or learning activities by those who likely have the most insight into what works and what does not; and the provision of platforms on which peer helpers can model appropriate behavior for others to emulate. Along similar lines, Mustacchi (2009) has eloquently described how her students assisted her in developing lesson plans, materials, and ultimately teaching other students about cyberbullying and other technology related issues:

> When I began implementing this curriculum the next fall, I noticed how much the 8th graders knew and were eager to impart to one another—with almost desperate urgency. As if riding a rollercoaster, students relayed stories and advice to one another, hitting highs and lows at breakneck speed. They were experts in some aspects of online interaction and risks but complete novices in others. I realized that their knowledge and thirst to exchange information provided a rare opportunity. So I charged my 8th grade students with the job of teaching my 6th graders. . . . Their talks, materials, and activities kept the younger students fully engaged. They asked questions and got their peers to think and reflect, sometimes with creative tactics (p. 80).

9.5. Responsive Services

34   Finally, school counselors, social workers, psychologists and community mental health workers (those who can provide personal/social counseling services) should provide help to both cyberbullies and their targets in the form of responsive services. This refers to specific activities designed to meet students' immediate needs and concerns such as individual or small-group counseling and crisis response (ASCA, 2012). Through these mechanisms, appropriate student support service personnel can help perpetrators to better understand the consequences of their actions, find better ways to resolve anger and conflict, and make more thoughtful and responsible choices about social interactions (Beaty & Alexeyev, 2008; Borg, 1998; Camodeca & Goossens, 2004; Haynie et al., 2001; Pellegrini, Bartini, & Brooks, 1999). Counselors also can help cyberbullying victims who may need help with issues of post-traumatic stress. Many counseling approaches exist that can be helpful in working with students involved in cyberbullying situations. Sabella (2012b) recommended three models in particular that are effective for both victims and perpetrators: Solution Focused Brief Counseling (SFBC), Reality Therapy (RT), and Rational Emotive Behavioral Therapy (REBT). All three models can help aggressors to take responsibility for their actions and correct their behaviors while also empowering targets to successfully cope and respond.

35   It should be noted that small group counseling has been specially recognized as an effective way to help students who experience bullying. For example, Young (1998) described a procedure and process for how school counselors can conduct support groups among the victim's identified supporters, the perpetrator, and those perceived to be supporters of the perpetrator. Reber (2012) provides some evidence about the positive impact of an eight (8) session group counseling experience on the self-esteem levels of students who have been identified as the targets of bullying aggressors. In another example, Hall (2006) proposed a "Solving Problems Together" (SPT) group in which the school counselor can help students develop the knowledge, attitude, and skills that will enable them to deal more effectively with bullying. Relatedly, Perkins and Williamson (2010) described how they incorporated cyberbullying prevention groups in schools as part of a service learning project designed and implemented by counseling graduate students. These suggested efforts hold much promise if counselors can take the lead and perform the required steps to educate and enlist youth (and other educators on campus) towards the common goal.

10. Conclusion and Future Directions

36   The current work is certainly not exhaustive in its attempt to illuminate the facts and debunk the myths about cyberbullying, as other misconceptions about the behaviors of teens online exist and warrant empirical scrutiny. An even more systematic review of popular media accounts of these problems would no doubt reveal additional unsubstantiated, questionable, or patently false claims about the nature, extent, causes, and consequences of cyberbullying behaviors. It is essential to compare these assertions to the body of scientific evidence that is available to separate fact from fiction. To be sure, there is still much that is not known about cyberbullying, especially about the efficacy of efforts to intervene. For instance, as of this writing, there have been no formal process or outcome evaluations of programs designed to prevent or respond specifically to cyberbullying.

37   Anecdotally, there is much talk about "what works" and "what doesn't," but data need to be collected about the short- and long-term outcomes associated with these initiatives. And, because cyberbullying includes so many different people and organizations (e.g., students, school personnel, parents, cell phone service providers, social networking companies, gaming companies, legislators, and police), future research must be comprehensive in scope. Many important questions still remain unanswered such as: (a) What types of parental actions/responses are most effective in preventing and responding to cyberbullying? (b) How effective are peer helpers as compared to adults when delivering cyberbullying risk-reduction strategies? (c) How effective are self-led online tutorials (e.g., videos or interactive games) in reducing the prevalence and incidence of cyberbullying? (d) What reporting procedures and processes

are best for preventing and responding to cyberbullying? and, (e) What specific supervising and monitoring techniques, both human and technological, work best?

38 According to Pearce, Cross, Monks, Waters, and Falconer (2011), the special characteristics of cyberbullying pose new challenges to future anti-bullying research. As mentioned earlier, these include the anonymous nature of the problem, greater breadth of audience, the lack of authority in cyberspace, and 24-h access to technology, as well rapid technological changes continually providing new means by which harm can be inflicted.

These challenges, together with the rapidly changing landscape of technology, will continue to make future research in this area as difficult as it is necessary. In the meantime, educators and other youth advocates should be careful to use information, curricula, and other resources that are informed by the most current and valid research available. Otherwise, by default, they risk falling into the trap of relying on conventional wisdom and media hyperbole in their well-intentioned efforts to address cyberbullying.

Computers in Human Behavior. 2013. 29.

References

Adler, P.A., & Adler, P. (1995). Dynamics of inclusion and exclusion in preadolescent cliques. *Social Psychology Quarterly, 58*(3), 145–162. http://dx.doi.org/10.2307/2787039.

Adler, P.A., & Adler, P. (1996). Preadolescent clique stratification and the hierarchy of identity. *Sociological Inquiry, 66,* 111–142. http://dx.doi.org/10.1111/j.1475-682X.1996.tb00213.x.

ASCA (2005). *The professional school counselor and bullying, harassment and violence prevention programs: Supporting safe and respectful schools (Position Statement).* American School Counselor Association. <www.schoolcounselor.org/content.asp?pl=325&sl=127&contentid=178>.

ASCA (2008). *The professional school counselor and peer helping (Position Statement).* American School Counselor Association. <http://asca2.timberlakepublishing.com//files/PS_PeerHelping.pdf>.

ASCA & iKeepSafe (2011). *Facebook for School Counselors.* <https://www.facebook.com/safety/groups/teachers/>.

ASCA (2012). *The ASCA national model: A framework for school counseling programs* (3rd ed.). Alexandria, VA: American School Counselor Association.

Aseltine, R.H., Gore, S., & Gordon, J. (2000). Life stress, anger and anxiety, and delinquency: An empirical test of general strain theory. *Journal of Health and Social Behavior, 41*(3), 256–275.

Baas, N., de Jong, M., & Drossaert, C. (2013). Children's perspectives on cyberbullying: Insights based on participatory research. *Cyberpsychology, Behavior, and Social Networking, 16*(4), 248–253.

Bauman, S. (2008). Effects of gender, grade, and acculturation on overt and relational victimization and depression in Mexican American elementary school students. *Journal of Early Adolescence, 28,* 528–554.

Bauman, S. (2011). *Cyberbullying: What counselors need to know.* Alexandria, VA: American Counseling Association.

Bauman, S., Toomey, R.B., & Walker, J.L. (2013). Associations among bullying, cyberbullying, and suicide in high school students. *Journal of Adolescence, 36*(2), 341–350.

Bazelon, E. (2010). *What really happened to Phoebe Prince?* (Retrieved 12.06.13). <www.slate.com/articles/life/bulle/features/2011/what_really_happened_to_phoebe_prince/the_untold_story_of_her_suicide_and_the_role_of_the_kids_who_have_been_criminally_charged_for_it.html>.

Beale, A.V., & Hall, K.R. (2007). Cyberbullying: What schools administrators (and parents) can do. *The Clearing House, 81*(1), 8–12. http://dx.doi.org/10.3200/TCHS.81.1.8–12.

Beaty, L.A., & Alexeyev, E.B. (2008). The problem of school bullies: What the research tells us. *Adolescence, 43*(169), 1–11.

Beautrais, A.L., Collings, S.C., & Ehrhardt, P. (2005). *Suicide prevention: A review of evidence of risk and protective factors, and points of effective intervention.* Wellington, New Zealand: Ministry of Health.

Beran, T., & Li, Q. (2007). The relationship between cyberbullying and school bullying. *Journal of Student Wellbeing, 1*(2), 15–33.

Bhat, C.S. (2008). Cyber bullying: Overview and strategies for school counselors, guidance officers, and all school personnel. *Australian Journal of Guidance and Counseling, 18*(1), 53–66. http://dx.doi.org/10.1375/ajgc.18.1.53.

Billitteri, T.J. (2008, May 2). *Cyberbullying* (Retrieved 28.02.13). <http://library.cqpress.com/cqresearcher/document.php?id=cqresrre2008050200&PHPSESSID=o6qklm45di95pqru6uiftj3ba0>.

Borg, M.G. (1998). The emotional reaction of school bullies and their victims. *Educational Psychology, 18*(4), 433–444.

Boyette, C. (2013). *N.Y. police probe possible cyberbullying after girl found hanged* (Retrieved 12.06.13). <www.cnn.com/2013/05/23/us/new-york-girldeath>.

Bradshaw, C.P., Sawyer, A., & O'Brennan, L. (2007). Bullying and peer victimization at school: Perceptual differences between students and school staff. *School Psychology Review, 36*(3), 361–383.

Bradshaw, C.P., Waasdorp, T.E., O'Brennan, L.M., & Gulemetova, M. (2011). *Findings from the National Education Association's nationwide study of bullying: Teachers' and education support professionals' perspectives.* Washington, DC: National Education Association.

Broidy, L.M., & Agnew, R. (1997). Gender and crime: A general strain theory perspective. *Journal of Research in Crime and Delinquency, 34*(3), 275–306.

Camodeca, M., & Goossens, F.A. (2004). Aggression, social cognitions, anger and sadness in bullies and their victims. *Journal of Child Psychology and Psychiatry, 46,* 186–197.

Campbell, M., Spears, B., Slee, P., Butler, D., & Kift, S. (2012). Victims' perceptions of traditional and cyberbullying, and the psychosocial correlates of their victimisation. *Emotional & Behavioural Difficulties, 17*(3/4), 389–401. http://dx.doi.org/10.1080/13632752.2012.704316.

Chan, J.H.F. (2006). Systemic patterns in bullying and victimization. *School Psychology International, 27*(3), 352–369. http://dx.doi.org/10.1177/0143034306067289.

Chibarro, J.S. (2007). School counselors and the cyberbully: Interventions and implications. *Professional School Counseling, 11*(1), 65–68.

Chin, A. (2011). *Police try to prevent cyber bullying.* <www.kktv.com/news/headlines/Police_Try_To_Prevent_Cyber_Bullying_121227869.html>.

Craig, W.M., Henderson, K., & Murphy, J.G. (2000). Prospective teachers' attitudes toward bullying and victimization. *School Psychology International, 21*(1), 5–21. http://dx.doi.org/10.1177/0143034300211001.

Cross, D., Shaw, T., Hearn, L., Epstein, M., Monks, H., Lester, L., et al. (2009). *Australian covert bullying prevalence study.* Safe Schools Research. <www.deewr.gov.au/Schooling/NationalSafeSchools/Pages/research.aspx>.

Diamanduros, T., Downs, E., & Jenkins, S.J. (2008). The role of school psychologists in the assessment, prevention, and intervention of cyberbullying. *Psychology in the Schools, 45*(8), 693–704.

Education Insider (2010). *Cyberbullying: A national epidemic.* <http://educationportal.com/articles/Cyberbullying_A_National_Epidemic.html>.

Englander, E.K. (2008). *Research brief: Cyberbullying & bullying in Massachusetts: Frequency & motivations.* <http://webhost.bridgew.edu/marc/MARC%20findings%20summary%202008.pdf>.

Englander, E.K., & Muldowney, A. (2007). Just turn the darn thing off: Understanding cyberbullying. In D.L. White, B.C. Glenn, & A. Wimes (Eds.), *Proceedings of persistently safe schools: The 2007 national conference on safe schools* (pp. 83–92). Washington, DC: Hamilton Fish Institute, The George Washington University.

Faris, R., & Felmlee, D. (2011). Status struggles: Network centrality and gender segregation in same- and cross-gender aggression. *American Sociological Review, 76*(1), 48–73. http://dx.doi.org/10.1177/0003122410396196.

Farrington, D.P. (2012). Childhood risk factors for young adult offending: Onset and persistence. In F. Losel, A. Bottoms, & D.P. Farrington (Eds.), *Young adult offenders: Lost in transition?* (pp 48–64). London: Routledge.

Fekkes, M., Pijpers, F.I.M., & Verloove-VanHorick, S.P. (2004). Bullying behavior and associations with psychosomatic complaints and depression in victims. *Journal of Pediatrics, 144*(1), 17–22.

Finkelhor, D. (2011). *The Internet, youth deviance and the problem of Juvenoia.* <www.unh.edu/ccrc/pdf/Juvenoia%20paper.pdf>.

Finkelhor, D. (2013). Trends in bullying and peer Victimization. <www.unh.edu/ccrc/pdf/CV280_Bullying%20&%20Peer%20Victimization%20Bulletin_1-23-13_with%20toby%20edits.pdf>.

Franek, M. (2006). Foiling cyberbullies in the new wild west. *Educational Leadership, 63*(4), 39–43.

Hall, K.R. (2006). Solving problems together: A psychoeducational group model for victims of bullies. *The Journal for Specialists in Group Work, 31*(3), 201–217. http://dx.doi.org/10.1080/01933920600777790.

Halligan, J. (2006). *Ryan Patrick Halligan* (Retrieved 23.01.08). <www.ryanpatrickhalligan.org/>.

Hamburger, M.E., Basile, K.C., & Vivolo, A.M. (2011). *Measuring bullying victimization, perpetration, and bystander experiences: A compendium of assessment tools.* Atlanta, GA: Centers for Disease Control and Prevention, National Center for Injury Prevention and Control. <www.cdc.gov/ViolencePrevention/pub/measuring_bullying.html> (Retrieved 02.03.13).

Hawton, K., & Williams, K. (2001). *The connection between media and suicidal behavior warrants serious attention 22*(22), 137–140. http://dx.doi.org/10.1027//0227-5910.22.4.137.

Haynie, D., Nansel, T., Eitel, P., Crump, A., Saylor, K., & Yu, K. (2001). Bullies, victims and bully/victims: Distinct groups of at-risk youth. *Journal of Early Adolescence, 21*(1), 29–49.

Hazler, R.J. (2006, March 18, 2006). *Essential techniques for successful intervention and prevention of bullying,* Carrollton, GA.

High, B. (2007). *Bullycide in America–Moms speak out about the bullying/suicide connection.*

Hinduja, S., & Patchin, J.W. (2009). *Bullying beyond the schoolyard: Preventing and responding to cyberbullying.* Thousand Oaks, CA: Sage Publications (Corwin Press).

Hinduja, S., & Patchin, J.W. (2012a). *School climate 2.0: Preventing cyberbullying and sexting one classroom at a time.*

Hinduja, S., & Patchin, J.W. (2012b). *Bullying and cyberbullying laws.* <www.cyberbullying.us/Bullying_and_Cyberbullying_Laws.pdf>.

Hinduja, S., & Patchin, J.W. (2007). Offline consequences of online victimization: School violence and delinquency. *Journal of School Violence, 6*(3), 89–112.

Hinduja, S., & Patchin, J.W. (2008). Cyberbullying: An exploratory analysis of factors related to offending and victimization. *Deviant Behavior, 29*(2), 1–29.

Hinduja, S., & Patchin, J.W. (2010a). Bullying, cyberbullying, and suicide. *Archives of Suicide Research, 14*(3).

Jones, T. (2008). *A deadly Web of deceit: A teen's online 'friend' proved false, and cybervigilantes are avenging her.* <www.washingtonpost.com/wp-dyn/content/article/2008/01/09/AR2008010903367_pf.html> (Retrieved 10.01.08).

Juvonen, J., & Gross, E.F. (2008). Extending the school grounds?—Bullying experiences in cyberspace. *Journal of School Health, 78,* 496–505.

Kim, Y.S., & Leventhal, B. (2008). Bullying and suicide. A review. *International Journal of Adolescent Medical Health, 20*(2), 133–154.

Klomek, A.B., Sourander, A., & Gould, M. (2010). The association of suicide and bullying in childhood to young adulthood: Review of cross-sectional and longitudinal research findings. *Canadian Journal of Psychology, 55*(5), 282–288.

Klomek, A.B., Sourander, A., Niemela, S., Kumpulainen, K., Piha, J., Tamminen, T., et al. (2009). Childhood bullying behaviors as a risk for suicide attempts and completed suicides: A population-Based birth cohort study. *Child & Adolescent Psychiatry, 48*(3), 254–261.

König, A., Gollwitzer, M., & Steffgen, G. (2010). Cyberbullying as an act of revenge? *Australian Journal of Guidance and Counselling, 20*(2), 210–224.

Kowalski, R.M., Limber, S.P., & Agatston, P.W. (2008). *Cyber bullying: Bullying in the digital age.* Malden, MA: Blackwell Publishing.

Li, Q. (2007). Bullying in the new playground: Research into cyberbullying and cyber victimisation. *Australasian Journal of Educational Technology, 23*(4), 435–454.

Li, Q. (2010). Cyberbullying in high schools: A study of students' behaviors and beliefs about this new phenomenon. *Journal of Aggression, Maltreatment & Trauma, 19*(4), 372–392. http://dx.doi.org/10.1080/10926771003788979.

Limber, S.P., Kowalski, R.M., & Agatston, P.W. (2009). *Cyberbullying: A prevention curriculum for grades 6–12.* Center City, MN: Hazelden.

Lund, E.M., Blake, J.J., Ewing, H.K., & Banks, C.S. (2012). School counselors' and school psychologists' bullying prevention and intervention strategies: A look into real-world practices. *Journal of School Violence, 11*(3), 246–265. http://dx.doi.org/10.1080/15388220.2012.682005. <www.tandfonline.com/doi/pdf/10.1080/15388220.2012.682005> (Retrieved 02.03.13).

Macklem, G.L. (2003). *Bullying and teasing: Social power in children's groups.* New York: Kluwer Academic/Plenum.

Madden, M., Lenhart, A., Duggan, M., Cortesi, S., & Gasser, U. (2013). *Teens and technology 2013.* <www.pewinternet.org/Reports/2013/Teens-and-Tech.aspx> (Retrieved 12.06.13).

Magid, L. (September 17, 2011). *Cyberbullying is a serious problem, but is it an epidemic? Huff Post.* <www.huffingtonpost.com/larry-magid/cyberbullying-is-a-seriou_b_967310.html>.

Maher, D. (2008). Cyberbullying: An ethnographic case of one Australian upper primary school class. *Youth Studies Australia, 27*(4), 50–57.

Marr, N., & Field, T. (2001). *Bullycide: Death at playtime—An expose of child suicide caused by bullying.* London: Success Unlimited.

Mazerolle, P., Burton, V., Cullen, F.T., Evans, D., & Payne, G.L. (2000). Strain, anger, and delinquent adaptations: Specifying general strain theory. *Journal of Criminal Justice, 28,* 89–101.

Mazerolle, P., & Piquero, A. (1998). Linking exposure to strain with anger: An investigation of deviant adaptations. *Journal of Criminal Justice, 26*(3), 195–211.

McDougall, B. (2011). *Cyber bullying spiralling out of control in schools.* The Daily Telegraph. <www.news.com.au/technology/cyber-bullying-spirallingout-of-control-in-nsw-schools/story-e6frfro0-1226233680802>.

Menesini, E., & Nocentini, A. (2009). Cyberbullying definition and measurement: Some critical considerations. *Zeitschrift für Psychologie/Journal of Psychology, 217*(4), 230–232.

Mishna, F., Pepler, D., & Wiener, J. (2006). Factors associated with perceptions and responses to bullying situations by children, parents, teachers, and principals. *Victims & Offenders, 1*(3), 255–288. http://dx.doi.org/10.1080/15564880600626163.

Mustacchi, J. (2009). R U safe? *Educational Leadership, 66*(6), 78–82.

Mynard, H., Joseph, S., & Alexander, J. (2000). Peer victimization and posttraumatic stress in adolescents. *Personality and Individual Differences, 29*(5), 815–821.

Myrick, R.D., Highland, W.H., & Sabella, R.A. (1995). Peer helpers and perceived effectiveness. *Elementary School Guidance and Counseling, 29*(4), 278–288.

National Center for Educational Statistics (2013). *Indicators of school crime and safety: 2012.* <http://nces.ed.gov/programs/crimeindicators/crimeindicators2012/>.

Obama, B. (2011). *Remarks by the president and first lady at the White House conference on bullying prevention.* <www.whitehouse.gov/the-pressoffice/2011/03/10/remarks-president-and-first-lady-white-house-conferencebullying-prevent>.

Oblad, T. (2012). *Understanding cyberbullying in the net generation: A meta-analytic review.* Masters thesis. <http://repositories.tdl.org/ttu-ir/handle/2346/47526>.

Parris, L., Varjas, K., Meyers, J., & Cutts, H. (2012). High school students' perceptions of coping with cyberbullying. *Youth & Society, 44*(2), 284–306. http://dx.doi.org/10.1177/0044118X11398881.

Patchin, J.W., & Hinduja, S. (2006). Bullies move beyond the schoolyard: A preliminary look at cyberbullying. *Youth Violence and Juvenile Justice, 4*(2), 148–169.

Patchin, J.W., & Hinduja, S. (2010). Changes in adolescent online social networking behaviors from 2006 to 2009. *Computers and Human Behavior, 26*, 1818–1821.

Patchin, J.W., & Hinduja, S. (2011). *Traditional and nontraditional bullying among youth: A test of general strain theory.* Youth and Society.

Patchin, J.W., & Hinduja, S. (2012). *Preventing and responding to cyberbullying: Expert perspectives.* Thousand Oaks, CA: Routledge.

Pearce, N., Cross, D., Monks, H., Waters, S., & Falconer, S. (2011). Current evidence of best practice in whole-school bullying intervention and its potential to inform cyberbullying interventions. *Australian Journal of Guidance & Counselling, 21*(1), 1–21. http://dx.doi.org/10.1375/ajgc.21.1.1.

Pellégrini, A.D., Bartini, M., & Brooks, F. (1999). School bullies, victims, and aggressive victims. Factors relating to group affiliation and victimization in early adolescence. *Journal of Educational Psychology, 91*(2), 216–224.

Perkins, G.W., & Williamson, M.L. (2010). *A service learning approach to cyberbullying prevention.* Ideas and research you can use: VISTAS 2010. <http://counselingoutfitters.com/vistas/vistas10/Article_63.pdf>.

Raskauskas, J., & Stoltz, A.D. (2007). Involvement in traditional and electronic bullying among adolescents. *Developmental Psychology, 43*(3), 465–475.

Reber, C. (2012). *The impact of group counseling on the self-esteem levels of students who have been identified as the targets of bullying aggressors.* <http://digitalcommons.brockport.edu/edc_theses/130> (Retrieved 02.03.13).

Rigby, K., & Slee, P.T. (1999). Suicidal ideation among adolescent school children, involvement in bully-victim problems, and perceived social support. *Suicide and Life Threatening Behavior, 29*(2), 119–130.

Sabella, R.A. (2008). *GuardingKids.com: A practical guide to keeping kids out of high-tech trouble.* Minneapolis, MN: Educational Media.

Sabella, R.A. (2012a). *Cyberbullying/technology safety lesson plans.* <http://bit.ly/cyberbullying-curr-table>.

Sabella, R.A. (2012b). Cyberbullying: How school counselors can help. In J.W. Patchin & S. Hinduja (Eds.), *Cyberbullying prevention and response: Expert perspectives.* New York: Routledge.

Sanders, J. (2009). Cyberbullies: Their motives, characteristics, and types of bullying. In *Paper presented at the XIV European conference of developmental psychology*, Vilnius, Lithuania.

Schneider, S.K., O'Donnell, L., Stueve, A., & Coulter, R.S. (2012). Cyberbullying, school bullying, and psychological distress: A regional census of high school students. *American Journal of Public Health, 102*(1), 171–177. http://dx.doi.org/10.2105/AJPH.2011.300308.

Sharp, S. (1995). How much does bullying hurt? The effects of bullying on the personal well-being and educational progress of secondary aged students. *Educational and Child Psychology, 12*, 81–88.

Skapinakis, P., Bellos, S., Gkatsa, T., Magklara, K., Lewis, G., Araya, R., et al. (2011). The association between bullying and early stages of suicidal ideation in late adolescents in Greece. *Psychiatry, 11*(1), 22.

Smith, P.K., Mahdavi, J., Carvalho, M., Fisher, S., Russell, S., & Tippett, N. (2008). Cyberbullying: Its nature and impact in secondary school pupils. *Journal of Child Psychology and Psychiatry, 49*(4), 376–385.

Smokowski, P.R., & Kopasz, K.H. (2005). Bullying in schools: An overview of types, effects, family characteristics and intervention strategies. *Children & Schools, 27*(2), 101–110.

Smorti, A., Menesini, E., & Smith, P.K. (2003). Parents' definitions of children's bullying in a five-country comparison. *Journal of Cross-Cultural Psychology, 34*(4), 417–432. http://dx.doi.org/10.1177/0022022103034004003.

Temple, J.R., Paul, J.A., van den Berg, P., Le, V.D., McElhany, A., & Temple, B.W. (2012). Teen sexting and its association with sexual behaviors. *Archives of Pediatrics and Adolescent Medicine*, 1–6.

Thom, K., Edwards, G., Nakarada-Kordic, I., McKenna, B., O'Brien, A., & Nairn, R. (2011). Suicide online: Portrayal of website-related suicide by the New Zealand media. *New Media & Society, 13*(8), 1355–1372. http://dx.doi.org/10.1177/1461444811406521.

Ttofi, M.M., & Farrington, D.P. (2011). Effectiveness of school-based programs to reduce bullying: A systematic and meta-analytic review. *Journal of Experimental Criminology, 2011*(7), 1. http://dx.doi.org/10.1007/s11292-010-9109-1.

Vaillancourt, T., & Hymel, S. (2006). Aggression and social status: The moderating roles of sex and peer-valued characteristics. *Aggressive Behavior, 32*, 408–596. http://dx.doi.org/10.1002/ab.20138.

Vandebosch, H., & Van Cleemput, K. (2009). Cyberbullying among youngsters: Profiles of bullies and victims. *New Media and Society, 11*(8), 1349–1371.

Varjas, K., Talley, J., Meyers, J., Parris, L., & Cutts, H. (2010). High school students' perceptions of motivations for cyberbullying: An exploratory study. *Western Journal of Emergency Medicine, 11*(3), 269–273.

WHO (2000). *Preventing suicide. A resource for media professionals. Geneva: Mental and behavioural disorders.* Department of Mental Health, World Health Organisation.

Willard, N.E. (2007a). The authority and responsibility of school officials in responding to cyberbullying. *Journal of Adolescent Health, 41*, S64–S65.

Willard, N.E. (2007b). *Cyber-safe kids, cyber-savvy teens, helping young people use the internet safely and responsibly.* San Francisco, CA: Jossey-Bass.

Willard, N.E. (2007c). *Cyberbullying and cyberthreats: Responding to the challenge of online social aggression, threats, and distress.* Champaign, IL: Research Press.

Willard, N.E. (2010). *School response to cyberbullying and sexting: The legal challenges.* Center for Safe and Responsible Internet Use. <http://csriu.org/documents/documents/cyberbullyingsextinglegal_000.pdf>.

Williams, K., & Guerra, N.G. (2007). Prevalence and predictors of Internet bullying. *Journal of Adolescent Health, 41,* S14–S21.

Winburn, A., Niemeyer, R., & Reysen, R. (2012). Mississippi principals' perceptions of cyberbullying. *Delta Journal of Education, 2*(2), 1–15. <www.deltastate.edu/PDFFiles/DJE/Niemeyer%20Final%20for%20Publication.pdf>.

Winsper, C.C., Lereya, T.T., Zanarini, M.M., & Wolke, D.D. (2012). O-61—Involvement in bullying in childhood and suicide ideation at 11 years: A prospective birth cohort study. *European Psychiatry, 271* http://dx.doi.org/10.1016/S0924–9338(12)74161–5.

Wolak, J., Mitchell, K., & Finkelhor, D. (2007). Does online harassment constitute bullying? An exploration of online harassment by known peers and online-only contacts. *Journal of Adolescent Health, 41,* S51–S58.

Wood, B. (2013, Feburary 24). *Curing Utah's "silent epidemic": Finding a solution to teen suicide.* Desert News. <www.deseretnews.com/article/865574056/Curing-Utahs-silent-epidemic.html> (Retrieved 28.02.13).

Ybarra, M.L. (2004). Linkages between depressive symptomatology and Internet harassment among young regular Internet users. *CyberPsychology and Behavior, 7*(2), 247–257.

Ybarra, M.L., Boyd, D., Korchmaros, J.D., & Oppenheim, J. (2012). Defining and measuring cyberbullying within the larger context of bullying victimization. *Journal of Adolescent Health, 51*(1), 53–58.

Ybarra, M.L., Diener-West, M., & Leaf, P.J. (2007). Examining the overlap in internet harassment and school bullying: implications for school intervention. *Journal of Adolescent Health, 41,* S42–S50.

Ybarra, M.L., & Mitchell, J.K. (2004a). Online aggressor/targets, aggressors and targets: A comparison of associated youth characteristics. *Journal of Child Psychology and Psychiatry, 45,* 1308–1316.

Ybarra, M.L., & Mitchell, J.K. (2004b). Youth engaging in online harassment: Associations with caregiver–child relationships, Internet use, and personal characteristics. *Journal of Adolescence, 27*(3), 319–336.

Ybarra, M.L., & Mitchell, K.J. (2007). Prevalence and frequency of internet harassment instigation: Implications for adolescent health. *Journal of Adolescent Health, 41,* 189–195.

Young, S. (1998). The support group approach to bullying in schools. *Educational Psychology in Practice, 14*(1), 32–39. http://dx.doi.org/10.1080–0266736980140106.

Key and challenging words

ideation, erroneous, pervasive, purport, overzealous, exacerbate, proliferate, cogently, resilient, emulate, debunk, efficacy

Questions

1. (a) Identify the essay's justification and its thesis; (b) paraphrase the passage in the introduction that discusses the essay's limitations.

2. What do the authors mean by *conventional wisdom* (see, for example, paragraphs 5 and 16)? Explain the term in your own words.

3. Although the authors primarily summarize the results of studies, they often use lengthy direct quotations (see, for example, pars 9, 18, 26, and 33). Explain the importance of direct quotations in the essay, using at least two examples from the text.

4. In the abstract, the authors identify their audience as "adults who work with youth." Find two examples in the essay itself where members of this target audience are addressed, and explain the contribution of each to the section in which it occurs.

5. Clear organization is an important feature of Type C (review) essays. Show how a) the essay's organization facilitates comprehension (e.g., use of markers, such as headings and section summaries; order of points; repetition; and prompts); b) choosing either section 3 or section 8, discuss organization and/or rhetorical strategies that make the section easy to follow (some of the above features could apply, along with topic sentences, diction, transitions, and the like).

6. The authors do not usually just dismiss the "myths" they discuss; rather, they use critical thinking to analyze their validity. Show how the authors achieve their balanced and objective approach to the myth discussed in the section "Myth 6: Cyberbullies Are Outcasts or Just Mean Kids."

Post-reading

1. Explain which of the five approaches mentioned in section 9 of the article you think will best help combat cyberbullying. Justify your answer by using critical thinking and information in the article, along with your own observations, if applicable.

2. In paragraph 37, the authors pose some unanswered questions about cyberbullying. Design an experiment in order to attempt to answer one of these questions. Include a hypothesis (see p. 31) and a one-paragraph summary of the method you would use to test the hypothesis.

3. *Collaborative or individual activity:* You are a member of the Canadian citizens' group, "Anti-bull Canada," whose mission is to dispel myths about bullying, especially cyberbullying, while promoting anti-bullying strategies and actions. Using information from section 9 and/or other parts of "Cyberbullying Myths and Realities," along with other sources, if appropriate, design a campaign for a specific group—for example, parents, school counsellors, government, etc.

Related websites of interest

PREVNet: Canada's Authority on Bullying:
www.prevnet.ca/bullying/cyber-bullying

Define the Line: Clarifying the Blurred Lines between Cyberbullying and Digital Citizenship:
definetheline.ca/dtl/category/cyberbullying/

Additional library reading

Walker, Carol M., Beth Rajan Sockman, and Steven Koehn. "An Exploratory Study of Cyberbullying with Undergraduate University Students." *TechTrends* 55.2 (2011): 31–38.

Cassidy, Wanda, Karen Brown, and Margaret Jackson. "'Under the Radar': Educators and Cyberbullying in Schools." *School Psychology International* 33.5 (2012): 520–32.

INTERSECTIONS WITH SCIENCE

Pharmaceutical innovation: Can we live forever? A commentary on Schnittker and Karandinos

Joel Lexchin
(1,954 words)

Pre-reading

1. Access your library's database and read the abstract for "Methuselah's medicine: Pharmaceutical innovation and mortality in the United States, 1960–2000," the basis for Lexchin's commentary. Who was Methuselah? Summarize the article's abstract in two sentences.
2. Does the title suggest Lexchin's thesis or approach? Scan the first two paragraphs in order to determine this information and come up with a reading hypothesis.

1   If we discover enough new drugs can we live forever, or at least for a lot longer than we currently do? This is the thesis that Schnittker and Karandinos set out to explore in "Methuselah's Medicine: Pharmaceutical Innovation and Mortality in the United States, 1960–2000" in this issue of Social Science & Medicine (Schnittker & Karandinos, 2010). More specifically, they look at the relationship between pharmaceutical innovation and life expectancy between 1960 and 2000 in the United States (US). The amount of pharmaceutical innovation is measured by the number of new molecular entities (NME) approved by the Food and Drug Administration and mortality—life expectancy at birth and age-specific mortality—is examined as a function of NME approvals within a given year. In addition to drug approvals they also consider the role that per-capita gross domestic product (GDP) and health-specific spending play in increasing longevity. Although they find that GDP has a larger association with life expectancy than NME, they also conclude that their "study demonstrates a significant relationship between pharmaceutical innovation and life expectancy at birth" (Schnittker & Karandinos, 2010).

2   This paper joins a growing list of publications, chiefly from Frank Lichtenberg (2007), that argue that the more new drugs there are the better off we are. However, just as Lichtenberg has his critics (Baker & Fugh-Berman, 2009) so too there are issues with this present paper that need to be debated and clarified before its conclusions can be accepted. Before doing that, though, let us give some new drugs their due—the antiretroviral drugs for HIV/AIDS certainly have extended the lives of people with that disease; the antithrombolitics are extremely valuable for treating patients with acute myocardial infarctions. Clearly, some new drugs are valuable but can that conclusion be generalized in the way that Schnittker and Karandinos have done?

3   All NMEs are not the same; the first angiotensin converting enzyme (ACE) inhibitor or the first proton pump inhibitor yielded significantly more benefits than the second or third or fourth in the class and many of the NMEs that have appeared in the 40 years being considered by the authors are "add-ons" to existing drug classes. Furthermore, many NMEs have nothing to do with increasing life expectancy. Terbinafine is a good drug for treating toenail fungal infections, but no one dies from infected toenails. Minoxidil has some benefit in male pattern alopecia, but baldness is not a fatal disease. What percent of NME introductions since 1960 have the potential for altering mortality patterns? That question is not explored in this present study.

4   The French drug bulletin, *La revue Prescrire*, analyzes the therapeutic value of new drugs (and new indications for older drugs) introduced into the French

market. Out of 983 new drugs or new indications for existing drugs marketed between 1996 and 2006, only 4.1 per cent offered major therapeutic gains and an additional 10.8 per cent had some value but did not fundamentally change present therapeutic practice ("A look back at pharmaceuticals in 2006: aggressive advertising cannot hide the absence of therapeutic advances," 2007). Garattini and Bertele (2002) examined 12 new anticancer drugs approved in Europe between 1995 and 2000 which contained new molecular entities or known active principles with new indications and concluded that none of the 12 offered any significant improvement in action. Of the 61 new biotechnology products introduced in Europe between 1995 and 2003 for therapeutic purposes, only 2 were approved on the basis that they were superior to existing therapies using hard clinical endpoints (Joppi, Bertele, & Garattini, 2005). According to Schnittker and Karandinos (2010), the major benefit has come from the introduction of new drugs that treat cardiovascular disease and, as I acknowledged above, certain new drugs are extremely valuable in these conditions. But, on-the-other hand, the thiazide diuretics, some of which were introduced before 1960, are at least as good and possibly superior to the much newer ACE inhibitors and calcium channel blockers in preventing the complications of hypertension (The ALLHAT officers and coordinators for the ALLHAT collaborative research group, 2002). Aspirin, which was available long before 1960, is a major factor in decreasing mortality from cardio and cerebrovascular disease.

5   The data presented by Schnittker and Karandinos show that mortality reduction is greatest in the 15–19 year age group (Schnittker & Karandinos, 2010). What are the major causes of mortality in that group? According to the US National Center for Injury Prevention and Control the three leading causes of death in the 15–19 age group are unintentional injury, homicide, and suicide (National Center for Injury Prevention and Control, 2009). Neither unintentional injury nor homicide is preventable by pharmacotherapy and the value of antidepressants in reducing deaths by suicide is far from clear (Jureidini & McHenry, 2009). The other 7 leading causes of death in this age group, which may be modifiable by drug treatment, account for little more than 12 per cent of mortality. Even if pharmaceuticals eliminated every

death in each of these 7 causes, the overall impact on deaths would be minimal.

6   Schnittker and Karandinos note that their findings are for the US and that results in other countries may differ for a variety of reasons including how extensive health insurance is (eliminating financial barriers to prescription drugs) and the degree of innovation in the country. With these caveats in mind how do changes in life expectancy in the US compare to what has happened in other developed countries? Life expectancy in the United States in 1960 was 73.1 years for women and 66.6 years for men. In that year, the US ranked 14th among the Organisation for Economic Co-operation and Development countries for women and 20th for men. By 2000 US life expectancy for women and men was 79.5 and 74.1, respectively and the US ranked 22nd and 21st (Directorate for Employment, 2009). At the same time as the US is losing ground in life expectancy compared to European countries, the European Federation of Pharmaceutical Industries and Associations is complaining that innovation in Europe is lagging behind the US (European Federation of Pharmaceutical Industries and Associations, 2009) and other work shows that new drugs become available much faster in the US than in other developed countries (Office of Fair Trading, 2007). Clearly there are other factors involved in changes in national mortality figures, but if new drugs are helping the US then they are significantly outweighed by these other considerations.

7   Schnittker and Karandinos state that "new drugs tend to be used promptly" and "this implies a relatively quick impact on mortality" (Schnittker & Karandinos, 2010). The first statement is certainly true, and this uptake is significantly fuelled by an annual $57.5 billion promotional budget (Gagnon & Lexchin, 2008). But there is good reason to question the latter claim. Knowledge about the safety of new drugs is minimal at best because they have only been tested in highly selective populations and in patient numbers that preclude identification of less common side effects. One indication of the unrecognized dangers from new drugs is that half of the drugs withdrawn from the US market for safety reasons occur within two years of marketing (Lasser et al., 2002). The example of what happened with rofecoxib should make us sceptical of claims that new drugs lead to rapid declines in

mortality. Graham and colleagues estimate that in the five years that rofecoxib was on the US market there were between 88,000 and 140,000 excess cases of serious coronary heart disease with a case-fatality rate of 44 per cent (Graham et al., 2005).

8   Finally, and more generally, the paper by Schnittker and Karandinos (2010) buys into the notion that we will be saved by innovation. On a micro level, innovation is important and many people are better off due to technological advances, but on a population level, it is harder to prove that more innovation and technology is the most important reason for better health outcomes. The US has significantly more neonatologists and neonatal intensive care beds than Australia, Canada, or the United Kingdom but does not have better birth weight-specific mortality rates than these three other countries (Thompson, Goodman, & Little, 2002). A recent systematic review that I participated in compared health outcomes in the US and Canada for patients treated for similar underlying medical conditions; in effect we were comparing higher overall expenditures and more technology (US) with a universal public insurance plan where inpatient care is almost completely delivered by private not-for-profit institutions (Canada): "Studies addressed diverse problems, including cancer, coronary artery disease, chronic medical illnesses, and surgical procedures. Of 10 studies that included extensive statistical adjustment and enrolled broad populations, five favoured Canada, two favoured the United States, and three showed equivalent or mixed results. Overall, results for mortality favoured Canada" (Guyatt et al., 2007, p. e27).

9   Drugs that are important advances in medical care are few and far between. We definitely need more of them and their development should be encouraged but, despite new drugs, I'm not counting on living to 150.

Social Science & Medicine. 2010. (70).

References

A look back at pharmaceuticals in 2006: aggressive advertising cannot hide the absence of therapeutic advances. (2007). *Prescrire International, 16,* 80–86.

Baker, D., & Fugh-Berman, A. (2009). Do new drugs increase life expectancy? A critique of a Manhattan institute paper. *Journal of General Internal Medicine, 24,* 678–682.

Directorate for Employment, Labout, and Social Affairs. (2009). *OECD health data 2008-frequently requested data.* Organisation for Economic Co-operation and Development.

European Federation of Pharmaceutical Industries and Associations. (2009). *The pharmaceutical industry in figures: Key data – 2009 update.* Brussels: EFPIA.

Gagnon, M.-A., & Lexchin, J. (2008). The cost of pushing pills: a new estimate of pharmaceutical promotion expenditures in the United States. *PLoS Medicine, 5,*e1.

Garattini, S., & Bertele, V. (2002). Efficacy, safety, and cost of new anticancer drugs. British Medical Journal, 325, 269–271.

Graham, D. J., Campen, D., Hui, R., Spence, M., Cheetham, C., Levy, G., et al. (2005). Risk of acute myocardial infarction and sudden cardiac death in patients treated with cyclo-oxygenase 2 selective and non-selective non-steroidal anti-inflammatory drugs: nested case-control study. *Lancet, 365,* 475–481.

Guyatt, G. H., Devereaux, P. J., Lexchin, J., Stone, S. B., Yalnizyan, A., Himmelstein, D., et al. (2007). A systematic review of studies comparing health outcomes in Canada and the United States. *Open Medicine, 1,* E27–E36.

Joppi, R., Bertele, V., & Garattini, S. (2005). Disappointing biotech. *British Medical Journal, 331,* 895–897.

Jureidini, J. N., & McHenry, L. B. (2009). Key opinion leaders and paediatric antidepressant overprescribing. *Psychotherapy and Psychosomatics, 78,* 197–201.

Lasser, K. E., Allen, P. D., Woolhandler, S. J., Himmelstein, D. U., Wolfe, S. M., & Bor, D. H. (2002). Timing of new black box warnings and withdrawals for prescription medications. *JAMA, 287,* 2215–2220.

Lichtenberg, F. (2007). *Why has longevity increased more in some states than in others? The role of medical innovation and other factors.* New York: Manhattan Institute.

National Center for Injury Prevention and Control. (2009). *10 leading causes of death, United States 2006, all races, both sexes.* Atlanta: Centers for Disease Control and Prevention.

Office of Fair Trading. (2007). Annexe D: global overview of the pharmaceutical industry.

Schnittker, J., & Karandinos, G. (2010). Methuselah's Medicine: Pharmaceutical innovation and mortality in the United States, 1960–2000. *Social Science & Medicine, 70,* 961–968.

The ALLHAT officers and coordinators for the ALLHAT collaborative research group. (2002). Major outcomes in high-risk hypertensive patients randomized to angiotensin-converting enzyme inhibitor or calcium channel blocker vs diuretic: the antihypertensive and lipid-lowering treatment to prevent heart attack trial (ALLHAT). *JAMA, 288,* 2981–2997.

Thompson, L. A., Goodman, D. C., & Little, G. A. (2002). Is more neonatal intensive care always better? Insights from a cross-national comparison of reproductive care. *Pediatrics, 109,* 1036–1043.

Key and challenging words

pharmaceutical, therapeutic, modifiable, caveat

Questions

1. What is the function of paragraph 1? How does it differ from introductions in the kinds of essays you might be asked to write?

2. a) What specific argumentative strategy does Lexchin use in paragraph 2? b) Paraphrase the last sentence in this paragraph.

3. Explain in your own words the problems with Schnittker and Karandinos's methodology and/or the assumptions on which part of the study is based (see paragraph 3), according to Lexchin.

4. Analyze the development of paragraph 6 (e.g., you could consider the rhetorical pattern, the placement of the topic sentence, use of deductive versus inductive development, etc.).

5. What kind of evidence does Lexchin use throughout the body paragraphs to support his claims? Pointing to at least one body paragraph show how his use of evidence provides support for his claim.

6. How does the claim in paragraph 8 differ from that of the other paragraphs? Why do you think he addresses this issue in his second-last paragraph rather than in an earlier paragraph?

7. Explain the extensive use of the Guyatt et al. study in paragraph 8.

Post-reading

1. *Collaborative activity:* a) Discuss or debate central issues related to health care in Canada versus in the US. b) Could the fact that the Schnittker and Karandinos study is based on US statistics affect its applicability to Canada? If so, how?

2. Access the Guyatt et al. study mentioned in paragraph 8. Note that it is found in the open access journal *Open Medicine* (www.openmedicine.ca/). a) What are open access sources? According to the website, why is open access publishing particularly important in the field of medicine? b) Summarize the "Discussion" section of the Guyatt et al. study in approximately 150 words (the section is 1,500 words).

3. In the same issue of *Social Science & Medicine* (volume 70, issue 7, 2010), Schnittker and Karandinos respond to Lexchin's commentary as well as to another commentary. Summarize Schnittker and Karandinos's response to Lexchin; then briefly explain whether you think it was an adequate response (make your summary and analysis 300–400 words).

Doping is a threat to sporting excellence

John William Devine
(2,695 words)

Abstract

Savulescu *et al* have argued that the risk to athletes' welfare provides the only legitimate ground for restricting the use of performance enhancing drugs in sport. In this paper, it is argued that the idea of "sport," properly understood, provides further reason to impose such restrictions. A "balance of excellences" argument is proposed whereby doping is considered objectionable on account of its disrupting the relation between the excellences around which sporting competition is organised. We have reason to restrict the use of performance enhancing drugs in sport not only because of the threat they pose to athletes' health but also because of the threat they pose to athletes' displaying the relevant types of sporting excellence.

-----

1   "If a drug does not expose an athlete to excessive risk, we should allow it even if it enhances performance."[1]

2   Savulescu *et al* have argued in this journal that the only legitimate ground for restricting the use of performance enhancing drugs in sport (doping) is the risk that those drugs pose to an athlete's welfare. On this view, once it has been established that a drug is safe or tolerably unsafe, we have no reason to limit its use in sporting competition, however much it enhances an athlete's performance. I argue that a proper understanding of the purposes of sport provides us with reason to object to the use of performance enhancing drugs, quite apart from any harm that athletes might risk by doping (while this argument applies to the justifiability in sport of any type of enhancement, its application is restricted here to the case of doping).

3   In the first section, I argue that sporting competition should be understood as an excellence-based activity, that is, as an activity organised at least in part around the purpose of encouraging competitors to display certain kinds of excellence. In the second section, I contend that doping threatens to obscure the display of at least some relevant sporting excellences. As such, doping threatens to undermine a central purpose of sport. We have reason to prohibit in sport any practice that undermines a central purpose of sport. Hence, a careful examination of sport reveals that, in addition to harm, consistency with the purposes of sport provides us with a reason to restrict the use of performance-enhancing drugs in sport.

Sport as an Excellence-Based Activity

4   Rules in sport present competitors with obstacles which preclude the pursuit of the ends of the sport (e.g., crossing the finish line, winning points, scoring tries) by the most causally efficacious means possible (in this respect, the author follows Bernard Suits' analysis of games[2]). Runners must remain within the confines of their lane, even when running outside their lane would enable them to reach the line more quickly; tennis players must use rackets to

return the ball even though a gun that fired the ball back would be more effective in winning points; and rugby players must never pass the ball forwards even when so doing would prove a more efficient means of scoring a try.

5   A variety of explanations are consistent with this feature of sport. Rules in sport may arise from, for instance, mere convention, a desire to create an interesting spectacle or to ensure that competitors have fun playing the sport. In the era of professionalism, it seems likely too that rules would be designed with one eye on commercial interests. The author does not attempt to settle which, if any, of these ends should feature in a comprehensive account of the purposes of sport. Instead, he argues for the more modest claim that a component of *any* plausible conception of sport is the idea that the rules of sport are at least partly organised so that competitors can reliably succeed only if their performances display an appropriate combination of physical, psychological and strategic excellences (for other virtue-based accounts of sport, see Sandel[3] and McNamee[4]).

6   This explanation is borne out in public debate about the rules of sport. Such discussions typically proceed at least in part on the basis of whether the proposed changes would affect the level of difficulty or the skills necessary for success in the sport (See the discussions of proposed changes to the laws of rugby union at URL: www.rugby-heaven.co.nz/4405748a22442.html and to more recent changes at URL: www.guardian.co.uk/sport/blog/2009/dec/02/elvs-laws-irbinternational-rugby-board [both accessed on 13 December 2009]. Both discussions are conducted in terms of whether the proposed changes are consistent with the central skills and excellences of the sport.). Of course, many rules in sport are not directly formulated to encourage the display of excellence. The rules of sport are a complex mixture of rules of different standing. Some are central to the purpose of the sport ("players shall use only rackets to strike the ball"), and some have little to commend them beyond tradition ("players shall wear predominantly white attire"). (This is not to say that every rule will not influence the excellences necessary to succeed at the sport. For instance, even if the scoring in tennis arose from such arbitrary considerations as the markings on the clock-face, the

requirement of winning at least four points to win a game and at least six games to win a set and at least two sets to win a match poses different physical, psychological and strategic challenges than if matches were decided, for instance, according to who had won the most points after a given period of time had elapsed.) However, the authors' claim is only that at least *some* rules in every sport are excellence-based. Central to every sport are rules that are designed to challenge competitors to display distinct kinds of excellence. The author remains agnostic about *why* the display of excellence is valued in sport.

7   According to this understanding, we do not, for example, allow high jumpers to use ladders in competition because this would make it possible for competitors to win races without displaying the relevant excellence around which the high jump is organised—the ability to *jump* high to clear the bar. Similarly, we do not allow rowers to attach motors to their boats because the use of a motor is not consistent with the purpose of the sport—cross the finishing line using only oars to propel the boat forward.

Doping as a Threat to Sporting Excellence

8   Not only are the rules organised around the display of different types of excellence; they are organised so that different excellences contribute to the outcome of sporting competition to different degrees. There is an internal relationship between the excellences that a sport is organised around. Different excellences should make only a certain contribution to performance relative to the other relevant excellences which are valued in that sport. That is, different excellences should play only so important a role in determining the outcome of competition relative to the other relevant excellences. For example, in the late 1990s, the men's singles tennis championships at Wimbledon was criticised as being dominated by powerful serving. While this may partly have been a complaint about the spectacle of tennis losing some its appeal for fans, it can also be understood as a complaint that one type of excellence—powerful serving—assumed too much prominence in the style of tennis that prevailed at the time. That is, while the rules of tennis still allowed for the display of all the excellences valued in tennis, developments in the biomechanics of serving and advances in racket

technology meant that the contribution of different excellences to the outcome of competition shifted in such a way that one excellence came to dominate, and others, such as deftness of touch and patient strategic play, no longer made a significant contribution to the performance of those who were successful in the sport. In response to these criticisms, tennis authorities changed the court surface and pressure of the balls to encourage the longer, more strategic rallies that were seen to be missing from competition. These measures might be best explained as an attempt to redress the internal relationship between the excellences around which the sport is organised.

9   The author's central contention is that doping may similarly alter to an objectionable degree the relationship between the various excellences that a sport is designed to call forth, that is, doping may upset the "balance of excellences" that inheres in a sport. Consider the following thought experiment:

> *Amazon Plant Case*: On an expedition deep in the Amazon rain forest, an athlete stumbles upon a previously unknown plant. When she returns to the lab to conduct tests on the plant, she discovers that consumption of this plant by humans leads to muscle growth greater than any previously known food or drug. Ingesting the plant before competition allows her to jump 50% further than she was previously capable of jumping.

10   In order to shield the use of the plant from unfairness concerns, let us assume that the plant can be mass produced very cheaply and made available across the world to whomever wants it. The plant occurs naturally in the Amazon rainforest, so concerns about it being an "unnatural" aid do not arise. Lastly, assume that consumption of the plant carries no risks to health. On what grounds, if any, might we object to an athlete using the Amazon Plant?

11   The enhancement derived from consumption of the plant might be considered problematic on account of the relatively significant contribution of the ability to metabolise the Amazon Plant to the outcome of performance as compared with other excellences relevant to the sport. While there is nothing intrinsically wrong with metabolisation being a determinant of performance—it seems impossible to imagine how it could not be for human beings—there may be

a limit to the benefit we are willing to allow athletes to derive from excellence in metabolision. In *Amazon Plant*, the ability to metabolise might be seen to determine performance to too great an extent relative to other excellences whose display should contribute to sporting performance. Even if some excellence is not an inappropriate determinant of sporting competition per se, its contribution to performance proportionate to the contribution of other excellences we wish to see displayed in a sport may be so great as to intolerably disturb the balance of excellences in that sport. Thus, the importance of other excellences in performance is diminished in a way that is inconsistent with the purposes around which the sport is organised.

12   Even if some types of enhancement can violate the balance of excellences in a sport, it is a further claim to suggest that enhancement achieved by any of the existing performance enhancing drugs can violate the balance of excellences of any existing sport. This judgement requires further empirical and theoretical study. More information is required concerning the contribution that modern doping techniques can make to the athletic performance of elite athletes. Further deliberation is needed about the level of enhancement we believe to be compatible with the display of sporting excellence. This requires reflection on the nature of sport and the purposes of individual sports so that we can determine a threshold beyond which doping becomes objectionable in different sports. This threshold will almost certainly be imprecise, but that should not deter us from positing such a threshold and using our judgement in its implementation.

13   If sport is organised around the pursuit of specific purposes, then we have reason against allowing any practice which runs counter to the effective pursuit of any one of those purposes. This is not to say that we have, all things considered, reason to prohibit a practice—assuming that effective prohibition procedures can be instituted—that impedes the pursuit of any purpose of a sport, however. As argued above, it seems plausible to suggest that sport is organised around a variety of purposes. A practice that presses against one purpose of sport may facilitate others. For instance, even though athletes who dope beyond a certain level may be thought incapable of displaying an appropriate balance of excellences, the effect of doping on their performance may be thought

justifiable for perceived improvements to the spectacle of that sport. My claim, then, is that the possibility of doping being disruptive to the balance of excellences in a sport, if true, would provide us with a reason that counts in favour of imposing a ban on doping. Unless a stronger reason against the ban could be identified, we would be justified in imposing a ban on doping beyond the level at which doping is thought to intolerably disrupt the balance of excellences in that sport.

Conclusion

14 While Savulescu *et al*[1] may be correct that harm to athletes' health provides us with a reason to restrict the use of performance enhancing drugs in sport, the author has argued against their contention that harm provides the *sole* criterion on which the ban can be justified. Any adequate justification of the ban must take account of the inherent tension between doping and the purposes of sporting competition. A proper understanding of the purposes of sport reveals the basis for restrictions on the permissibility of doping irrespective of whether those substances are harmful to the athlete or not.

15 Sporting bodies must reflect on what excellences their respective sports should be organised around and what internal relation those excellences should have to each other. The sport-specific nature of this justification for the ban implies that, contrary to the approach of the World Anti-Doping Agency (WADA) code,[5] doping policy should be tailored to individual sports rather than being universal to all sports (The author accepts that this sports-specific approach to the ban on doping may prove more difficult to implement than the blanket WADA code. However, his concern here is with what follows in principle from the balance of excellences argument.) Moreover, reflection on the balance of excellences within sports must be viewed as an ongoing process. Our understanding of different sports evolves over time as players, technology and our understanding of the game develops. The necessity of this ongoing debate militates against the possibility of reaching a precise, final answer with regard to the shape that the ban should take. We must be prepared to revise and challenge prevailing understandings of the purposes of our sports and be willing to adjust our doping policies according to revisions in this understanding.

16 The balance of excellences argument does not necessarily provide a reason to ban performance-enhancing drugs per se. Rather, it provides a reason to ban performance-enhancing drugs beyond the level at which they are believed to intolerably alter the balance of excellences in a particular sport. The mere presence in an athlete's system of certain performance-enhancing drugs may be sufficient to objectionably alter the balance of excellences in their performance in some sports. Alternatively, athletes may be able to use some considerable quantity of some drugs before their performance is considered incompatible with the prevailing balance of excellences in their sport. Consequently, it is difficult to specify exactly what practical applications follow from the balance of excellences argument for sport as currently constituted. Sporting bodies must determine how they understand the appropriate balance of excellences in their respective sports. Only then will it become apparent what level of which different performance-enhancing drugs are contrary to the balance of excellences in different sports.

17 While the contours of the ban must be debated within individual sports, the author has suggested, contra Savulescu *et al*,[1] that harm-based reasons are not the only considerations that count in favour of imposing limitations on doping. Doping may objectionably reorder the balance of excellences within a sport so that the ability to metabolise comes to influence to an objectionable degree the outcome of sporting competition. Consequently, doping, beyond a certain level at least, may be incompatible with a central organising principle of sport.

18 Performance-enhancing drugs—harmful or not—may impede the display of the excellences around which a sport is organised, thereby rendering athletes in that sport who dope unable to meaningfully participate in that sport by displaying the relevant excellences in appropriate balance. We have reason to restrict the use of performance-enhancing drugs in sport, then, not only because of the threat they pose to athletes' physical health but also because of the threat they pose to athletes' sporting excellence.

British Journal of Sports Medicine. 2011. 45.

Acknowledgements

Drafts of this paper were presented at the Applied Ethics Discussion Group in the Faculty of Philosophy, University of Oxford and at the Middle Common Room Graduate Colloquium in New College, Oxford. Many thanks to WB Devine, T Douglas, G Elford, T Hope, M Philp, J Savulescu and MA Shapiro for written comments at different stages of the paper's development.

References

1. Savulescu J, Foddy B, Clayton M. Why we should allow performance enhancing drugs in sport. *Br J Sports Med* 2004;38:666–70.
2. Suits B. *The grasshopper: games, life, and Utopia*. Toronto: University of Toronto, 1978 (Reprinted Peterborough: Broadview Press, 2005):54–5.
3. Sandel M. *The case against perfection*. Chapter 2. Cambridge, MA: Harvard, 2007.
4. McNamee M. *Sports, virtues and vices* Chapters 1–3. London: Routledge, 2007.
5. World Anti-Doping Agency. 'World Anti-Doping Code 2009.' www.nada-bonn.de/fileadmin/user_upload/nada/Downloads/Regelwerke/080305_WADA-Code_v2009_En.pdf (Accessed 13 December 2009).

Key and challenging words

preclude, efficacious, agnostic, redress, inhere, deter, posit, militated

Questions

1. Identify Devine's thesis and explain why the author might have chosen to make it as long as he did.
2. Summarize what Devine means by sport as an "excellence-based activity." Explain the importance of using examples to support his argument, referring specifically to the text.
3. Show how the author uses a "thought experiment" to support his claim that doping could disrupt the "balances of excellences" in a sport.
4. Discuss the author's use of specific strategies in paragraph 8 to increase reader comprehension.
5. Which of the three appeals discussed in "The Active Voice: The Rhetorical Analysis: The How, What, and Why" (pp. 95-97) does Devine rely on? Why might the other two kinds of appeals be less important for his argument?
6. Using critical thinking, explain why Devine might have asked J. Savulescu, whose argument he is challenging, to comment on his paper? (See "Acknowledgements" at the end of the essay).
7. Devine presents a formal argument in which his points are carefully laid out and, in some cases, qualified: (a) provide two examples of diction that demonstrate his careful approach to his topic; (b) Do you believe that such an approach makes his argument stronger or weaker overall? Explain your reasoning.

Post-reading

1. *Collaborative or individual activity:* What are some possible limitations of Devine's argument? Analyze the effectiveness of his argument and, if appropriate, consider ways in which his argument could be challenged.

Related website of interest

Canadian Centre for Ethics in Sport:
www.cces.ca/en/wada

Additional library reading

Schneider, Angela, and Jim Rupert. "Constructing Winners: The Science and Ethics of Genetically Manipulating Athletes." *Journal of the Philosophy of Sport* 36.2 (2009): 182–206. Print.

"Can the Scientists Keep Up?" *The Economist Technology Quarterly* 3 Mar. 2012: 13–15. Print.

The microscopic world

Bernard Lightman
(1,458 words)

Pre-reading

1. Scan the first three paragraphs of "The Microscopic World" to determine its target audience. How does the introduction appeal to this audience?

1   In *Drops of Water* (1851), the popularizer of science Agnes Catlow invited her readers to follow her into the invisible world of the minuscule. "My readers must fancy themselves spirits," she advised, "capable of living in a medium different from our atmosphere, and so pass with me through a wonderful brazen tunnel, with crystal doors at the entrance" (x). Catlow expected that her readers would react with astonishment to their first glimpse of the microscopic world. "Your minds are bewildered with the variety of new beings and forms you behold," she wrote, "all gliding and moving about without noise and at perfect ease" (xi). The popularizer of natural history Philip Henry Gosse also depicted the microscope as providing access to a hidden, wondrous world. "Like the work of some mighty genie of Oriental fable," he declared, "the brazen tube is the key that unlocks a world of wonder and beauty before invisible, which one who has once gazed upon it can never forget, and never cease to admire" (v).

2   The Victorians were excited by the new world revealed by the microscope. Beginning in the 1850s, the microscope became one of the most important instruments of the life sciences in the Victorian domestic parlour. Cheap instruments had become more widely available; specialist organizations, such as the Microscopical Society and the Quekett Club, held frequent soirees and public exhibitions; and popular scientific periodicals began to promote microscopy. At the same time, the practitioners of the life sciences were endorsing the microscope as the definitive laboratory instrument. In *The Microscope: and its Revelations* (1856), the biologist William Carpenter pointed to the "rapid increase which has recently taken place in the use of the Microscope,—both as an instrument of scientific research, and as a means of gratifying a laudable curiosity and of obtaining a healthful recreation" (v). Even novelists were caught up in the excitement. George Eliot, for example, was drawn into the culture of amateur microscopy through her relationship with George Lewes, and, as a result, her novel *Middlemarch* participates in the discourse.

3   We have scholarly studies on technical improvements to the microscope during the nineteenth century, on social interest in the microscope, and on its use by literary figures. But we have little on how

the microscopic world itself was perceived. When treated as an amusing optical gadget, the microscope was often seen as providing entertainment for the Victorian reading audience. The work of scholars on the visual culture of Victorian science might profitably be applied to an understanding of how reading audiences were introduced to the microscopic world. The microscope was, after all, an optical device like the stereoscope, kaleidoscope, and zootrope, all newly invented as part of the reorganization of vision that, Jonathan Crary has argued, created a new kind of observer. Optical illusions, panoramas, and spectacle were the popular amusements corresponding to this shift in visual culture.

4   Authors of books on the microscope often tapped into the discourse surrounding the new visual culture. In *Microscope Teachings* (1864), Mary Ward proposed to exhibit the wonders of the microscope "in the manner of a panorama" (vii). More common was the comparison between a spectacle and various scenes in the microscopic world. As the public lecturer Dionysius Lardner declared, "No person can witness without the highest degree of admiration the spectacle presented by certain parts of the structure of the more minute members of the animal kingdom, when viewed with a powerful microscope" (50). Indeed, science writers used the term "spectacle" to describe a large number of diverse animal structures viewed under the microscope, from a frog's foot to barnacles, sea-urchins, and gnats. Some authors drew attention to even smaller beings, referring, for example, to the wheel-like motion of the cilia of infusoria as a wondrous "spectacle" (Catlow 28). Many of these books on the microscopic world are richly illustrated, and the strategies for representing spectacle in pictorial form would be worth investigating.

5   The use of the term "spectacle" in relation to the microscopic world seems somewhat surprising, though not in light of Iwan Morus's recent work on the use of the oxyhydrogen microscope in magic lantern extravaganzas at the Adelaide Gallery and the Royal Polytechnic Institution. With its ability to entertain audiences with hugely magnified natural objects, the oxyhydrogen microscope was one of the technologies of spectacle (346–47). But for biologists

such as Carpenter, the size of the image produced by an optical device was irrelevant. The "extreme of minuteness" was "no less wonderful" and "no less majestic" than the "extreme of vastness" (37). Implying that the regular microscope was as powerful as the telescope, Carpenter asserted that one could be lost in "wonder and admiration" in looking at "countless multitudes of living beings which a single drop of water may contain" just as much as when one looked at the innumerable stars in the heavens. The images produced by the microscope were considered to be just as spectacular as those created by the oxyhydrogen microscope.

6   But, as Louisa Lane Clarke emphasized in *Objects for the Microscope* (1858), the microscope was to be used to edify, not just to entertain: "If we are wholly ignorant of the structure of plants, . . . we are apt to look at these slides for mere amusement, for the lust of the eye, pleased as a child or as a savage with strange forms or brilliant colours" (11). However, the lessons to be learned from the microscopic world varied according to the religious commitments of the writer. If we wish to understand how the Victorians regarded the microscope as a didactic tool, we must apply what we have learned from the scholarship on the development of scientific naturalism in the second half of the century. Thomas Henry Huxley, like other scientific naturalists, insisted that the microscope revealed a natural world composed purely of matter. During the 1860s and 1870s, Huxley was involved in a controversy over the unresolved structure of cell "protoplasm." Whereas vitalists maintained that the failure of microscopists to resolve any operative physical structure in protoplasm meant that the cell's life-sustaining activity could be explained only with reference to "vital" forces, Huxley maintained that the identification of a physiochemical basis for life would be discovered in the future when technical progress was sufficiently advanced (Gooday 421–22).

7   But when popularizers of science looked through the microscope, many of them saw a world completely unlike Huxley's—they were overwhelmed by the wondrous design and beauty of microscopic objects. They saw a world fraught with religious

significance. Thomas Dick, for example, declared that "ten thousand objects in the minute parts of creation" displayed "beauties, contrivances, and instances of divine mechanism, of which no one who has not looked at them through the microscope can form any adequate conception." Dick compared the finest works of human art to the works of nature, in particular the craftsmanship involved in the construction of microscopic objects. The closer you examined microscopic objects, "the more apparent is their supreme excellence," far beyond what humans could accomplish. Whatever Dick observed—whether plant leaves, a flea, or even the hair of a mouse—he was impressed and humbled by its beauty (Dick 120, 146, 160, 168, 170). Like Dick, Catlow, Gosse, Lane Clarke, Ward, and many others presented a picture of the microscopic world as filled with intricately designed, elegant beings and objects.

8 Popularizers were still offering this discourse of microscopic design to the reading audience at the end of the century, despite the efforts of Huxley and his allies to secularize nature. At century's end, Lewis Wright took Huxley, Ernst Haeckel, and Herbert Spencer to task for misusing the microscope to verify their materialism, arguing that if the microscope "could not reveal the Divine mystery of living existence, [it] at least manifested it to us as a greater Mystery than ever" (5). Despite what the "anti-teleologic and therefore unphilosophic biologist" maintained, Wright declared, the microscope unveiled organization: "The Microscope, then, has deserved well of the Christian believer" (6, 242).

9 Morus has argued that making nature visible in a spectacular fashion was a key aim of natural philosophy for much of the nineteenth century. The same can be said about the role of the microscope in natural history. It was used to make the Victorians aware of the spectacle that took place constantly in a world that eluded the unassisted human senses. Wondrous sights could be found in a drop of water, the wings of an insect, or the structure of inorganic matter. But microscopic ecosystems had also become the site of battle between scientific naturalists and those who wished to perpetuate the tradition of natural theology. Though miniscule physically, the microscopic world contained tremendous significance for those Victorians seeking to determine the ultimate meaning of nature.

Victorian Review. 2010. Fall 36 (2).

Works Cited

Carpenter, William B. *The Microscope: and Its Revelations*. London: John Churchill, 1856. Print.

Catlow, Agnes. *Drops of Water: Their Marvellous and Beautiful Inhabitants Displayed by the Microscope*. London: Reeve and Benham, 1851. Print.

Crary, Jonathan. *Techniques of the Observer: On Vision and Modernity in the Nineteenth Century*. London: MIT Press, 1990. Print.

Dick, Thomas. *The Telescope and Microscope*. New York: Lane and Scott, 1852. Print.

Gooday, Graeme. "Instrumentation and Interpretation: Managing and Representing the Working Environments of Victorian Experimental Science." *Victorian Science in Context*. Ed. Bernard Lightman. Chicago: U of Chicago P, 1997. 409–37. Print.

Gosse, Philip Henry. *Evenings at the Microscope; or Researches Among the Minuter Organs and Forms of Animal Life*. New York: D. Appleton, 1860. Print.

Lane Clarke, Louise. *Objects for the Microscope: Being a Popular Description of the Most Instructive and Beautiful Subjects for Examination*. 2nd ed. London: Groombridge and Sons, 1863. Print.

Lardner, Dionysius. *The Microscope*. London: Walton and Maberley, 1856. Print.

Morus, Iwan Rhys. "'More the Aspect of Magic than Anything Natural': The Philosophy of Demonstration." *Science in the Marketplace: Nineteenth-Century Sites and Experiences*. Ed. Aileen Fyfe and Bernard Lightman. Chicago: U of Chicago P, 2007. 336–70. Print.

Ward, Mary. *Microscope Teachings*. London: Groombridge and Sons, 1864. Print.

Wright, Lewis. *A Popular Handbook to the Microscope*. London: The Religious Tract Society, 1895. Print.

Key and challenging words

depict, gratify, laudable, extravaganza, innumerable, didactic, secularize, teleological

Questions

1. Identify, then summarize the essay's justification (see paragraph 3).
2. What does the author mean by the word *spectacle* (see paragraphs 4–5)? Give two examples of synonyms, or near-synonyms, of *spectacle* in the essay.
3. The title of this academic essay is uncharacteristically brief: (a) Suggest an informative subtitle that would expand on the subject of "The Microscopic World"; (b) Provide two or three descriptive section headings to follow the introduction and further inform the reader about content.
4. As an inter-disciplinary essay, "The Microscopic World" touches on several disciplines: (a) Identify three disciplines, in addition to science, relevant to the essay; (b) taking one of these, explain why the essay might be of interest or how it might be used by readers in that discipline.
5. Identify paragraphs that use the following rhetorical patterns and explain the contribution of two of them to the essay: (a) compare–contrast; (b) description; (c) examples.
6. (a) Consider the importance of primary sources in the essay (see p. 14). Choosing two examples from different paragraphs, discuss their role in developing the paragraph; (b) discuss the function of primary sources to help support the author's thesis and develop his essay; (c) explain the importance of Iwan Rhys Morus, a secondary source, to the essay.

Post-reading

1. Using at least two reliable sources, summarize Thomas Huxley's contribution to the development of Victorian science. Why might he be an apt representative of "scientific naturalism" (see paragraphs 6 and 9)?
2. Reflect on the nature of "spectacle" as described in "The Microscopic World." Is science or technology today capable of evoking this same sense of wonder? Explore the implications of this question in one or two paragraphs.

Related website of interest

The Victorian Web:
www.victorianweb.org/victorian/science/science&religion.html

Where are we going with preimplantation genetic diagnosis?

Timothy Krahn
(1,591 words)

Pre-reading

1. Using a reliable source, such as a medical encyclopedia or dictionary or an online source like IVF Canada (www.ivfcanada.com/services/index.cfm), find background information on preimplantation genetic diagnosis (PGD) and related areas (e.g., in-vitro fertilization, assisted reproduction). Come up with a one-sentence definition (paraphrase) of PGD and include a citation.

1 In Canada, preimplantation genetic diagnosis is governed by the Assisted Human Reproduction Act,[1] which received royal assent on 29 March 2004. Regulations for preimplantation genetic diagnosis in accordance with the act are currently being developed after a series of ongoing public consultations. To regulate uncertain and controversial public policy issues, such as assisted human reproduction, the Canadian government has an established history of taking its bearings from the best practises, policy precedents, and relevant regulatory structures in the United Kingdom.[2,3] In light of this history, it is fitting for us to pay attention to recent developments in the United Kingdom.

2 On 10 May 2006, the United Kingdom's Human Fertilisation and Embryology Authority published its decision to license preimplantation genetic diagnosis for hereditary breast and ovarian cancer (BRCA1 and BRCA2 mutations) and hereditary non-polyposis colorectal cancer.[4] These conditions are distinct from those previously licensed to be tested for in the United Kingdom because of a combination of 3 factors: they have a later age of onset, they are lower penetrance conditions (up to 80 per cent,[5] compared to the previous threshold of more than 90 per cent penetrance[6]) and they are potentially treatable. Before this decision, the Human Fertilisation and Embryology Authority had licensed preimplantation genetic diagnosis for conditions for which 1, or at most 2, of these 3 factors applied. By permitting preimplantation genetic diagnosis for these hereditary adult-onset cancers, the Human Fertilisation and Embryology Authority has effectively downgraded its criteria for "significant risk of being affected by a serious inherited genetic condition."[7] The purpose of this commentary is to consider the moral dangers associated with this ruling in terms of its potential resonating effects on the normative fabric of our culture.

3 In much of the Western world, where parents are having fewer children, where some parents are having children after the experience of infertility and where prenatal diagnosis and preimplantation genetic diagnosis are promoted as part of good prenatal care, we are developing a culture that is overly directed by the interests of some well-intentioned, but perhaps misguided, prospective parents (and possibly more exacting clinicians) committed to having healthy children. The underlying beliefs are as follows: Because parents are having fewer children, it is both common sense and in the best interests of the children that they be given the "best" genetic prospects. Moreover, from a societal perspective, if the health care system and social services are unable to assume the full burden of treating serious genetic conditions, then it seems only just that the present generation uses all reasonable means of preventing these conditions. Indeed, such reasoning probably explains a certain societal sympathy for people who want to test their embryos for potentially heritable conditions. The moral danger does not lie with the people who seek the testing; rather, the danger lies in how this testing could promote further stigmatization of and discrimination against people with "genetic impairments"[8-10] or their parents.[11] Indeed, testing could entrench a culture of prevention and perfectionism and promote a culture of intolerance.

4 As the number of genetic tests for conditions with lower penetrance increases and these tests become more widely available, parents may have increased expectations of having "normal and healthy" (i.e., unaffected) offspring. This desire could subtly shift parents' attitudes toward their embryos (and eventually their children) if their embryos are treated more and more like consumer products subject to a process of quality control.

5 One serious limitation of preimplantation genetic diagnosis is that it focuses narrowly on evidence of genetic anomalies (deviations from the norm that may not even be expressed). The risk is that evidence of genetic conditions or predispositions may become the overriding or sole factor in the process of embryo selection and that decision-makers may value only that which they can test for as dictated by the current state of available technology. In the end, this practice of selecting against certain genetic characteristics could further upgrade the standards of "normality" and compress the spectrum of "healthy," with the result that many human imperfections might become "less tolerated and less likely to be accepted as normal human variation."[12]

6 Widespread efforts at prevention and perfectionism could seed a culture of intolerance. Of particular concern is the risk of exacerbating social problems for people with conditions for which genetic testing is available. Increases could be seen in resources that are directed at finding ways to diagnose and screen embryos for genetic conditions by preimplantation genetic diagnosis. Correspondingly, reductions could be seen in resources to provide health care support and treatment for people living with these same conditions.[13],[14] Even the practice of labelling and singling out certain genetic conditions as "serious" and therefore test-worthy holds the danger of giving medical validation to some of our deepest fears and prejudices about what it is to live with, or to support people with, cognitive or physical impairments. Some have even suggested that we cannot brake on this slippery slope by applying more stringent criteria of what counts as a significant risk for a "serious" genetic condition (i.e., a condition valued negatively by the medical profession and society that is deemed worthy of screening against for reasons that extend beyond parental preference). From this perspective, to better avoid the prejudice and stigmatization of "impairment" associated with screening for serious conditions, it may be preferable to have parental choice alone as the sole justification required for screening. Otherwise, by marking off a special class of genetic conditions as serious we risk making it seem like the decision against having a child with a "serious" condition is prima facie more legitimate than the decision to resist this entrenched prejudice in our society.[14]

7   The recent decision by the Human Fertilisation and Embryology Authority has put us on an undetermined path where we could lose sight of, or even come to have contempt for, people who are "genetically disadvantaged." Given what we as Canadians can learn from British policy and practice in these matters, we need to ask ourselves: Where are we going with these new genetic technologies? Should we be so sanguine about having preimplantation genetic diagnosis take us there? What are we sacrificing to gain control over genetic conditions? Doesn't authentic control include knowing not only where to start, but also where to stop?

8   As archeologists know, future generations can learn about the values and norms of previous generations as much by examining their garbage as by examining their achievements. Given this analogy, what might our descendants learn about our culture by observing not only which policy choices are taken up, but also by which ones are discarded? Abby Lippman reminds us that "There are choices to be made and the choices will reflect our values and ideology. How we choose our culture (by the routes we take) is no less problematic than how we choose our children, and consequences from both will be among our legacies."[15] We would do well to heed her admonition.

CMAJ. 2007. May 176 (10).

*

Acknowledgements

I would like to thank Françoise Baylis, Olga Kits, and Lynette Reid for their comments on earlier drafts of this commentary.

This work was supported by a grant from the Canadian Institutes of Health Research (CIHR).

References

1. Assisted Human Reproduction Act, *SC* 2004, c 2, S10(2), 40(1).

2. Jones M, Salter B, Pigeon N. RES-000-22-0987 – Policy transfer in risk governance: lessons from the UK biotechnology framework. London (UK): Economic and Social Research Council; 2006. Available: www.esrc-societytoday.ac.uk/ESRCInfoCentre/Plain_English_Summaries/work_organisation/innovation_change/index27.aspx?ComponentId=15624&SourceP-ageId=1707 (accessed 2007 Mar 30).

3. Jones M. What can one nation learn from another? Exploring policy choice in the new Canadian framework for assisted human reproduction. London (UK): BioNews.org.uk; 2005 Oct 3. Available: www.bionews.org.uk/commentary.lasso?storyid=2765 (accessed 2007 Mar 16).

4. Human Fertilisation and Embryology Authority. Authority decision on the use of PGD for lower penetrance, later onset inherited conditions. London (UK):The Authority; 2006. Available: www.hfea.gov.uk/docs/The_Authority_decision__Choices_and_bound-aries.pdf (accessed 2007 April 2).

5. Human Fertilisation and Embryology Authority. Choices & boundaries report 2006: a summary of responses to the

HFEA public discussion. London (UK): The Authority; 2006. Available: www.hfea.gov.uk/cps/rde/xbcr/SID-3F57D79B-8FC36EC9/hfea/Choices_and_boundaries_Report_2006.pdf (accessed 2007 Mar 9).

6. Human Fertilisation and Embryology Authority. Choices and boundaries: Should people be able to select embryos free from an inherited susceptibility to cancer? London (UK): The Authority; 2005. Available: www.hfea.gov.uk/cps/rde/xbcr/SID-3F57D79B-5A0CC17F/hfea/Choices_and_Boundaries.pdf (accessed 2007 Mar 30).

7. Human Fertilisation and Embryology Authority. Code of practice. 6th ed. London (UK): The Authority; 2003. Available: www.hfea.gov.uk/cps/rde/xbcr/SID-3F57D79B-FAAAF985/hfea/Code_of_Practice_Sixth_Edition_-_final.pdf (accessed 2007 Mar 9).

8. Harris M, Winship I, Spriggs M. Controversies and ethical issues in cancer-genetics clinics. *Lancet Oncol* 2005;6: 301-10.

9. Asch A. Disability equality and prenatal testing: Contradictory or compatible? *Fla State Univ Law Rev* 2003;30: 315-42.

10. Matloff ET, Shappell H, Brierley K, et al. What would you do? Specialists' perspectives on cancer genetic testing, prophylactic surgery and insurance discrimination. *J Clin Oncol* 2000;18:2484-92.

11. Marteau TM, Drake H. Attributions for disability: the influence of genetic screening. *Soc Sci Med* 1995;40: 1127–32.

12. Beeson D. Social and ethical challenges of prenatal diagnosis. Med Ethics (Burlington, Mass) 2000 Winter;1–2,8. Available: www.lahey.org/Pdf/Ethics/Winter_2000.pdf (accessed 2007 Mar 30).

13. Holtzman NA, Shapiro D. Genetic testing and public policy. *BMJ* 1998;316:852–6.

14. Wasserman D, Asch A. American Medical Association. The uncertain rationale for prenatal disability screening. Virtual Mentor. 2006; 8: 53–56. Available: www.ama-assn.org/ama/pub/category/print/15809.html (accessed 2007 Mar 9).

15. Lippman A. Prenatal genetic testing and screening: constructing needs and reinforcing inequities. *Am J Law Med* 1991;17:15–50.

Key and challenging words

normative, stigmatization, entrench, anomaly, exacerbate, stringent, sanguine, admonition

Questions

1. What is Krahn's purpose in mentioning the date of the Assisted Human Reproduction Act and the current (2007) public consultations? How could the decision of the UK's Human Fertilisation and Embryology Authority affect Canadians?

2. Identify the author's thesis and account for its placement in the essay.

3. In paragraph 3, Krahn addresses the opposing viewpoint. Do you think he discusses these views reasonably and impartially? Do you believe this discussion helps his argument or weakens it? Why?

4. Several hypothetical outcomes of focusing too much on genetic anomalies are mentioned in paragraph 6.

Taking one of these possible outcomes, in a minimum of one paragraph evaluate its plausibility or validity.

5. Why does the author state "it may be preferable to have parental choice alone as the sole justification required for screening" (paragraph 6)?

6. Who is Abby Lippman, quoted in the essay's final paragraph? Do you think the ending is effective? Why or why not?

7. Analyze the effectiveness of Krahn's argument overall by considering such factors as the essay's organization, points, and support, the use of emotional or ethical appeals, or logical or emotional fallacies.

Post-reading

1. *Collaborative activity:* What are other controversial issues related to in-vitro fertilization that you have heard of? The discussion could focus on several of these issues, or one of the related issues could be debated (e.g., BeautifulPeople.com website).

2. *Collaborative or individual activity:* In a 2009 article (referenced below) in the same journal where Krahn's essay was published, the authors provide an overview of issues related to the genetic diagnosis of embryos, arguing that exaggerated rhetoric or unfounded fears could impact

research and public policy. Do you believe that this article undermines or calls into doubt Krahn's argument?

3. Using the criteria for determining source credibility discussed on pp. 145–147, evaluate one of the following secondary sources mentioned in Krahn's essay: Beeson, D. Social and ethical challenges of prenatal diagnosis; available:www.lahey.org/Pdf/Ethics/Winter_2000.pdf; or Wasserman, D., & Asch, A. The uncertain rationale for prenatal disability screening; available: www.ama-assn.org/ama/pub/category/print/15809.html.

Related websites of interest

Assisted Human Reproduction Canada:
www.ahrc-pac.gc.ca/index.php?lang=eng

Novel Tech Ethics, Dalhousie University:
www.noveltechethics.ca/

Additional library reading

Bouffard, C., Viville, S., & Knoppers, B.M. (2009). Genetic diagnosis of embryos: Clear explanation, not rhetoric, is needed. *CMAJ, 181,* 6–7. doi:10.1503/cmaj.080658. It may also be available online at www.cmaj.ca/cgi/content/full/181/6-7/387

Brezina, P.R. (2013). Preimplantation genetic testing in the 21st century: Uncharted territory. *Clinical Medicine Insights: Reproductive Health, 7,* 17–21. doi:10.4137/CMRH.S10914

Handyside, A. (2010). Let parents decide. *Nature, 464,* 978–979.

Järvholm, S., Broberg, M., & Thurin-Kjellberg, A. (2014). The choice of pre-implantation genetic diagnosis (PGD), a qualitative study among men and women. *Journal of Reproductive & Infant Psychology, 32*(1), 57–69. doi:10.1080/02646838.2013.851372

Speed that kills: The role of technology in Kate Chopin's "The story of an hour"

Jeremy Foote
(1,564 words)

Pre-reading

1. Read the short story that is analyzed by the author of the essay below (see pp. 372–373), noting themes, characters, setting, tone, language, and relevant techniques common to literary analyses. Summarize the story's theme(s) in one or two sentences.

2. *Collaborative or individual activity:* Reflect on the role of technology in our society today. Generate a list of the pros and cons; choosing one or two items from the list on each, explore their significance to you and your peers either orally or in writing.

1   Kate Chopin's "The Story of an Hour" has been taught and analyzed almost exclusively from a feminist perspective. As Lawrence Berkove writes, "There has been . . . virtual critical agreement on what the story says: its heroine dies, ironically and tragically, just as she has been freed from a constricting marriage and has realized self-assertion as the deepest element of her being" (1). Louise Mallard's sense of joy at her husband's apparent death, and her own death at his return, have become an archetype of feminine self-realization and the patriarchy that is always there to extinguish it (e.g., Harlow 501). Indeed, the feminist images of the story are so powerful that I believe critics have overlooked another theme. "The Story of an Hour" can be read as a protomodernist text. As also seen with later modernist writers, technology and the societal changes caused by technology play important roles in Chopin's story.

2   "The Story of an Hour" was first published in *Vogue* in 1894. More than a century later, now in the midst of our own technological revolution, it is difficult to grasp how fundamentally nineteenth-century technologies were altering the world in Chopin's time. Before the railroad, traveling was extremely difficult and dangerous. In the 1850s, it took an average of 128 days to traverse the Oregon Trail (Unruh 403), with a mortality rate of 4 per cent to 6 per cent (Unruh 408). The transcontinental railroad, completed in 1869, allowed the same journey to be made, safely and much more comfortably, in less than a week (Cooper). Perhaps more importantly, during the 1890s trains started to become part of daily life. In 1889 the first interurban electric rail lines were laid, and by 1894 hundreds of miles of track were being added every year (Hilton and Due 186–87).

3   Communications underwent an even more dramatic acceleration. The completion of the first successful transatlantic cable in 1866 meant news that had previously taken a week or more to travel between Europe and the Americas could now be sent nearly instantaneously. Like the railroad, while the initial invention had occurred years earlier, in the 1890s telegrams went from novel to quotidian. In 1870, Western Union relayed 9 million telegrams. By 1893, they were sending more than 66 million telegrams annually (United States Bureau of the Census 788).

4   Later writers would explore the effects of these and other technologies. In his 1909 "Futurist Manifesto," Filippo Marinetti gushes, "Time and Space died yesterday. We already live in the absolute, because we have created eternal, omnipresent speed." Not all writers would be as optimistic as Marinetti. A few decades after "Hour" was published, World War I would provide striking evidence of the destructive power of new technologies, and writers like Ezra Pound and T.S. Eliot would lament the new world that man had created. In "Hugh Selwyn Mauberly," for example, Pound claims that the world experienced "Fortitude as never before / Frankness as never before, / Disillusions as never told in the old days" (81–83). Pound felt that technology led to a world "as never before" but that these changes led to a "botched civilization" instead of a technological utopia (89).

5   "The Story of an Hour" can be read as a precursor to these more technophobic works. The story begins with news of Mr Mallard's death in a railroad disaster—received by telegram. This may be a commentary on the literal danger of riding trains in the 1890s, but we can also see the railroad's role in the story as a more subtle warning. While we don't know for certain why Mr Mallard would have been riding a train that day, Chopin describes him later as "a little travel-stained, composedly carrying his grip-sack and umbrella," bringing to mind the image of a commuter returning home from a day at the office (Chopin). The railroads, and the urbanization and industrialization that they symbolized and enabled, were changing how and where people worked. In Chopin's St. Louis, for example, the population had quintupled in her lifetime, as people moved away from their farms and into the cities (Gibson). Railroads meant that where people lived and where they worked could be far apart, giving rise to the commuter lifestyle (and the word *commuter*) (Paumgarten). Time that in previous generations had been spent with family was now spent apart, as family members sped away from one another. These changes certainly affected marital relationships and the experience of womanhood. Women were spending more and more time by themselves, with time to pursue their own interests. Perhaps it is these hours alone each day that leave Louise wanting more autonomy, dreaming of "no one to live for during those coming years" (Chopin).

6   In fact, the story gives evidence that Louise's emotions are affected by the physical absence of her husband. After recognizing the joy she feels upon learning of her husband's supposed death, Louise reflects on her feelings: "She did not stop to ask if it were or were not a monstrous joy that held her. . . . She knew that she would weep again when she saw the kind, tender hands folded in death; the face that had never looked save with love upon her, fixed and gray and dead" (Chopin). Confronted with her husband's body, she knows that she will feel differently. Her joyous reaction is to a distant, faceless death, unimpeded by the reality of an actual corpse—unattached to an actual person. The railroad provides this catalyst for Louise's self-realization, because it "killed" Mr Mallard both quickly and distantly. Indeed, the speed and remoteness of Mr Mallard's death seem to be primary causes of the speed and intensity of Louise's emotions. Instead of taking care of an ailing husband and preparing for his death, death is thrust upon her, forcing her to confront her entire reaction to his passing all at once.

7   While Brently's death and Louise's joyful reaction are enabled by the railroad, the story would be equally impossible without the technology of the telegraph. At the beginning of the story, Mr Mallard's friend hears of a telegram listing Brently Mallard as deceased. He decides to break the news to Louise, after having "taken the time to assure himself of its truth by a second telegram" (Chopin). Before telegrams, information could not travel faster than people. Mr Mallard would have arrived home, safe and sound, long before the news of his death could have reached his wife. "Slow" communications (i.e., everything before the telegraph) also had to be relayed person to person. Having people as part of the medium helped maintain the veracity and the context of messages. To send a telegram, on the other hand, words are converted into electrical impulses and then reinterpreted at their destination. They travel at the speed of light, without any substance, as disembodied information. "Hour" seems to be warning us that there are dangers in this separation of message from medium: the more information is isolated, the more meaning comes from the recipient's interpretation. The telegram that Louise receives is an example of this danger. There may very well have been a Brently Mallard killed in the railroad disaster, so the disembodied information was true,

---

The Story of an Hour

by Kate Chopin

Knowing that Mrs Mallard was afflicted with a heart trouble, great care was taken to break to her as gently as possible the news of her husband's death.

It was her sister Josephine who told her, in broken sentences; veiled hints that revealed in half concealing. Her husband's friend Richards was there, too, near her. It was he who had been in the newspaper office when intelligence of the railroad disaster was received, with Brently Mallard's name leading the list of 'killed'. He had only taken the time to assure himself of its truth by a second telegram, and had hastened to forestall any less careful, less tender friend in bearing the sad message.

She did not hear the story as many have heard the same, with a paralyzed inability to accept its significance. She wept at once, with sudden, wild abandonment, in her sister's arms. When the storm of grief had spent itself she went away to her room alone. She would have no one follow her.

There stood, facing the open window, a comfortable, roomy armchair. Into this she sank, pressed down by a physical exhaustion that haunted her body and seemed to reach into her soul.

She could see in the open square before her house the tops of trees that were all aquiver with the new spring life. The delicious breath of rain in the air. In the street below a peddler was crying his wares. The notes of a distant song which someone was singing reached her faintly, and countless sparrows were twittering in the eaves.

There were patches of blue sky showing here and there through the clouds that had met and piled one above the other in the west facing her window.

She sat with her head thrown back upon the cushion of the chair, quite motionless, except when a sob came up into her throat and shook her, as a child who has cried itself to sleep continues to sob in its dreams.

She was young, with a fair, calm face, whose lines bespoke repression and even a certain strength. But now there was a dull stare in her eyes, whose gaze was fixed away off yonder on one of those patches of blue sky. It was not a glance of reflection, but rather indicated a suspension of intelligent thought.

There was something coming to her and she was waiting for it, fearfully. What was it? She did not know; it was too subtle and elusive to name. But she felt it, creeping out of the sky, reaching toward her through the sounds, the scents, the colour that filled the air.

Now her bosom rose and fell tumultuously. She was beginning to recognize this thing that was approaching to possess her, and she was striving to beat it back with her will—as powerless as her two white slender hands would have been.

When she abandoned herself a little whispered word escaped her slightly parted lips. She said it over and over under her breath: "free, free, free!" The vacant stare and the look of terror that had followed it went from her eyes. They stayed keen and bright. Her pulses beat fast, and the coursing blood warmed and relaxed every inch of her body.

She did not stop to ask if it were or were not a monstrous joy that held her. A clear and exalted perception enabled her to dismiss the suggestion as trivial.

She knew that she would weep again when she saw the kind, tender hands folded in death; the face that had never looked save with love upon her, fixed and grey and dead. But she saw beyond that bitter moment a long procession of years to come that would belong to her absolutely. And she opened and spread her arms out to them in welcome.

There would be no one to live for her during those coming years; she would live for herself. There would be no powerful will bending hers in that blind persistence with which men and women believe they have a right to impose a private will upon a fellow creature. A kind intention or a cruel intention made the act seem no less a crime as she looked upon it in that brief moment of illumination.

And yet she had loved him—sometimes. Often she had not. What did it matter! What could love, the unsolved mystery, count for in face of this possession of self-assertion which she suddenly recognized as the strongest impulse of her being!

"Free! Body and soul free!" she kept whispering.

Josephine was kneeling before the closed door with her lips to the keyhole, imploring for admission. "Louise, open the door! I beg; open the door—you will make yourself ill. What are you doing, Louise? For heaven's sake open the door."

"Go away. I am not making myself ill." No; she was drinking in a very elixir of life through that open window.

Her fancy was running riot along those days ahead of her. Spring days, and summer days, and all sorts of days that would be her own. She breathed a quick prayer that life might be long. It was only yesterday she had thought with a shudder that life might be long.

She arose at length and opened the door to her sister's importunities. There was a feverish triumph in her eyes, and she carried herself unwittingly like a goddess of Victory. She clasped her sister's waist, and together they descended the stairs. Richards stood waiting for them at the bottom.

Someone was opening the front door with a latchkey. It was Brently Mallard who entered, a little travel-stained, composedly carrying his grip-sack and umbrella. He had been far from the scene of accident, and did not even know there had been one. He stood amazed at Josephine's piercing cry; at Richards' quick motion to screen him from the view of his wife.

But Richards was too late.

When the doctors came they said she had died of heart disease—of joy that kills.

but the substance of the information—that it was her husband who had been killed—was false. Even a second telegram was not enough to verify the truth, because the needed truth was found in the context, not in the information, and telegrams can only relay information.

8   "Hour" is not only about the danger of communications moving too quickly but also a warning about the overall increase in the speed of life. These technologies that were speeding up how people moved and communicated naturally sped up their lives, including their emotional lives. As the title tells us, this is a story about time; the rate at which things happen is important. Louise Mallard goes from devastation to euphoria to shock, all within an hour. Arguably, her death is more a result of how quickly her emotions occur, rather than the emotions themselves. Living in a time with twenty-four-hour news and ever-scrolling Twitter feeds, we know something of the dangers of not having enough time to process what is happening. The time needed to experience and analyze emotions has been eliminated, and the body (and soul) cannot keep up with that kind of schedule. Louise is forced to confront the great questions of life—death and love and self-actualization—in the space of an afternoon. It is no wonder that there are repercussions.

9   "The Story of an Hour" has long been heralded as a wonderful feminist text, which it is. The issues of male hegemony and feminine independence are dealt with in an important and powerful way. Chopin helps us realize, however, that other subtle factors are at play. This is a cautionary tale about a world that is speeding up; it is a warning about lives that move too quickly. The tragedy of Louise Mallard's death occurs not only because she is a woman but because she is a modern woman. This story would have unfolded very differently without the technologies of the railroad and telegraph; by exploring the effects of these technologies within a purposely feminine text, Chopin shows us that even such "timeless" issues as male and female relations can only be fully understood within the time and place in which they occur.

The Explicator. 2013. 71 (2).

Works Cited

Berkove, Lawrence I. "Fatal Self-Assertion in Kate Chopin's 'The Story of an Hour'." *American Literary Realism* 32.2 (2000): 152–58. Print.

Chopin, Kate. "The Story of an Hour." *Wikisource*. Web. 19 Jul. 2011. <http://en.wikisource.org/wiki/The Story of an Hour>.

Cooper, Bruce C. "Riding the Transcontinental Rails: Overland Travel on the Pacific Railroad—Introduction." *Central Pacific Railroad Photographic History Museum*. 2004. Web. 2 May 2011. <http://cprr.org/Museum/Riding the Rails Intro.html>.

Gibson, Campbell. "Population of the 100 Largest Cities and Other Urban Places in the United States: 1790 to 1990." Population Division Working Paper No. 27. U.S. Census Bureau. 1998. Web. 19 Jul. 2011. <www.census.gov/population/www/documentation/twps0027/twps0027.html>.

Harlow, Barbara. "From the Women's Prison: Third World Women's Narratives of Prison." *Feminist Studies* 12.3 (1986): 501–24. Print.

Hilton, George W., and John F. Due. *The Electric Interurban Railways in America*. Stanford, CA: Stanford UP, 2000. *Google Books*. Web. 21 Jul. 2011.

Marinetti, F.T. "The Futurist Manifesto." 1909. Web. 8 May 2012. <http://cscs.umich.edu/~crshalizi/T4PM/futurist-manifesto.html>.

Paumgarten, Nick. "[Annals of Transport:] There and Back Again." *The New Yorker*, 16 Apr. 2007. Web. 2 May 2012. <www.newyorker.com/reporting/2007/04/16/070416fa factpaumgarten>.

Pound, Ezra. "Hugh Selwyn Mauberley." 2007. *Project Gutenberg*. Web. 25 Apr. 2013.

United States Bureau of the Census. *Historical Statistics of the United States: Colonial Times to 1970*. Vol. 2. Washington, DC: U.S. Department of Commerce, Census Bureau, 1975. *Google Books*. Web. 21 Jul. 2011.

Unruh, John D. *The Plains Across: The Overland Emigrants and the Trans-Mississippi West, 1840–60*. Urbana: University of Illinois, 1993. *Google Books*. Web. 18 Jul. 2011.

Key and challenging words

patriarchy, quotidian, utopia, technophobic, precursor, autonomy, veracity, disembodied, euphoria, repercussion, hegemony

Questions

1. (a) Summarize the essay's justification; (b) paraphrase its thesis.
2. Discuss the importance of primary sources in Foote's essay, using at least two specific examples as support (one of the examples should be from a text other than "The Story of an Hour").
3. At what point does the author explicitly connect the story's themes to propose a unified reading of the text? Comment on its placement and effectiveness.
4. Does Foote's essay stress primarily the pros or the cons of technology during the 1890s? Explain your answer by referring specifically to the text.

5. Analyze paragraph 6, focusing on the rhetorical and/or organizational strategies used by the author. These could include language, parallel structures, repetition, sentence length/variety, paragraph structure, use of transitions, and the like.
6. Today's literary essays often look beyond the text being analyzed to embrace other disciplines and perspectives. Show how Foote uses non-literary sources to enrich his reading of "The Story of an Hour."

Post-reading

1. Foote makes many comparisons between Chopin's age and our own. Identifying one or two of these comparisons, discuss his success (or lack of it) in making the story relevant to today's reader.

2. Write a comparative analysis of "Speed That Kills" and "Advice to Teens" (p. 269), two humanities essays. As one of your bases of comparison, analyze the authors' attempts to make their essays relevant to today's readers.

Related website of interest

The Kate Chopin International Society:
www.katechopin.org/

Psychology's essential role in alleviating the impacts of climate change

Robert Gifford
(5,347 words)

Pre-reading

1. Scan the abstract, introduction, and headings in order to determine the essay's purpose (expository or argumentative?) and intended audience. From this information, formulate a reading hypothesis.
2. How might the IPCC Report, mentioned in the first sentence, have affected the timing of Gifford's essay?

Climate change is occurring: where is psychology? The conventional wisdom is that amelioration of the impacts of climate change is a matter for earth and ocean science, economics, technology, and policy-making. This article presents the basis for psychological science as a key part of the solution to the problem and describes the challenges to this both from within psychology and from other points of view. Minimizing the personal and environmental damage caused by climate change necessarily is a multidisciplinary task, but one to which psychology not only should, but must contribute more than it has so far.

Keywords: climate change, role of psychology, Canada

*

1   By now, the issue of whether or not climate change is occurring has been resolved for quite some time, and the fourth report of the Intergovernmental Panel on Climate Change (IPCC), in November 2007 has reiterated its conclusion. It is happening. Some may wish to debate the relative extent of natural and human causes of the change, but little doubt exists that human activities have been, and continue to be, one important force driving climate change. One can imagine that climate change might have some positive consequences for some people in some places, but according to many experts, climate change already is having, and will have many more, negative consequences for many people in many places.

2   The present thesis is that psychology, in concert with other disciplines, has an important role to play in easing the pain caused by climate change. Were this thesis widely recognized, the present article would be unnecessary. Unfortunately, the thesis is not broadly acknowledged. Anecdotally, I can report that I sat through a recent meeting of scientists from a variety of disciplines concerned with climate change and heard a leading natural scientist state that the large interdisciplinary grant proposal being discussed should not include any input from "fluff," by which he apparently meant the social sciences. More formally, the emerging discipline of sustainability science, clearly a first cousin to climate-change studies, has been advocated and defined by some authors (e.g., Clark & Dickson, 2003) without the slightest reference to possible contributions by psychologists. Are these assertions and omissions justified?

A Bit of Background

3   Each person on the planet, whether as an individual or as part of an organization, curates a stream of natural resources that are converted into products; the conversion process often creates greenhouse gases. Thus, as psychologists have long recognized, the fundamental unit of analysis for the human-caused portion of climate change is the person (Ehrlich & Kennedy, 2005; Gifford, 1987). Thus, ultimately, amelioration of that part of environmental problems such as climate change over which we have some potential control occurs at the individual level (Clayton & Brook, 2005).

4   Psychologists have long been concerned with individuals' behaviour that contributes to climate change.[1] In particular, environmental psychology,

---

[1] Ironically, this probably precedes the concern for climate change on the part of most of the 2000 or so natural scientists whose work was used by the Intergovernmental Panel on Climate Change, and thus basked in the shared glory of the 2007 Nobel Prize, with the notable exception of Al Gore himself.

a child of 1960s idealism, was conceived to solve environment-related problems through scientific evidence-based research. Research on energy conservation and other environmental problems has been going on for 35 years (e.g., Buckhout, 1972; Pallak & Cummings, 1976; Seligman & Darley, 1977). Derived in part from Kurt Lewin's mantra that nothing is so practical as a good theory, it has always been an approach that seeks to combine quality research with applications aimed at personal and organizational change. In doing so, it has developed a wide range of theories, models, and principles that can be used to design action research techniques for changing behaviour (e.g., Bechtel & Churchman, 2002; Gifford, 2007). A stream of special issues in journals on environmental problems has appeared since the 1980s (see Vlek & Steg, 2007, for a list), and they are the tip of an iceberg that includes hundreds of individual journal articles. In 40 years of existence, environmental psychologists have developed an extensive toolbox of ideas and techniques (e.g., Bechtel, Marans, & Michelson, 1987). They are based on hundreds of articles published in its two primary journals, the *Journal of Environmental Psychology* and *Environment and Behaviour*, and numerous allied journals, which form a very extensive information base for designing programmes and solutions to a variety of problems (Gifford, 2002b), including sustainability problems.

So Why Then Has Psychology Not Been a Climate-Change Player?

5   Discourse on climate change in the media and amongst policy-makers is virtually silent on the role of psychology. The conventional wisdom in the wider world of climate-change thought is that psychology has no important role to play. Why?

6   First, we must lay the blame in part on ourselves. Psychology, in general, has been accused of ignoring the environment by treating people as if they existed in a vacuum (nicely embodied in the blank four walls of the laboratory). As noted by Kidner (1994), the psychological scientist too often "perpetuates and legitimizes a world view in which the individual is seen as separate from the environment" (p. 362). Even environmental psychologists have largely kept their focus on individual-level influences on environment-related

behaviour: values, attitudes, motives, intentions, goals, social comparison, habits, and similar constructs. We have left the making of connections between these constructs—which *are* important, and policy—which is essential—to others. We write in our discussion sections that "someone" should take into account these important findings of ours. However, unfortunately, for the most part policymakers and natural scientists do not read our discussion sections. This is one reason sustainability science can be defined without reference to psychology.

7   Second, the kinds of effort needed to combat the consequences of climate change do not suit the academic context in which most established psychologists work. In this forum I need not elaborate on the ways and means needed to find an academic position, earn tenure, and win grants: usually it is to conduct many parametric experiments in laboratories with those handy introductory psychology students. This is not to blame graduate students and young PhDs who find themselves in this situation: the levers to success were not created by them.

8   Third, most policymakers in ministries and departments concerned with environmental problems were not trained in the behavioural sciences. Reser and Bentrupperbaumer (2001) estimate that functionaries in resource-related government agencies and departments trained in the natural sciences outnumber those trained in the social sciences by at least 50 to 1. With less or no social-science experience, these policymakers are unlikely to understand what the social sciences have to offer, and even if they were sympathetic to the idea, they would have difficulty understanding many of the concepts and results. This leads to fundamental misunderstandings of such concepts as values, valuation, and social impacts (Reser & Bentrupperbaumer, 2001). Some excellent but isolated progress has been made toward finding ways for natural and social scientists to communicate (e.g., Miller, 1985), but uneven numbers and inadequate communication and understanding remain serious problems.

9   Fourth, the role of psychology in climate change has so far been particularly neglected in Canada. Although discourse on the role of psychological science and climate change has been less than robust anywhere, it has at least existed in the United States and Germany (Oskamp, 2000; Schmuck & Schultz, 2002;

Stern, 1993), Australia (Reser, 2007), the Netherlands (Vlek, 2000), Sweden (Lundqvist & Biel, 2007), and the United Kingdom (Uzzell, 2007). I am unaware of any substantive previous discussion of psychology's role by a Canadian psychologist concerning the Canadian context. The leading proponent of environmental action in Canada was trained as a geneticist in a fruit-fly lab. How can psychologists expect to be players when we are silent?

The Basis for Psychology's Role

10   Each person, whether an average citizen or a CEO, has some level of choice and control over sustainability-related behaviours and actions. As Paul Stern (2005) has pointed out, these choices often are heavily constrained by contextual factors and one's own habits. Stern posits a hierarchical set of forces in which structural factors above or external to the individual usually are much more powerful influences on behaviour than individual-level influences.

11   Although one must acknowledge the power of context, and that Stern's hierarchy often accurately describes environmental behaviour choices, I maintain that individuals truly are the ultimate key to climate-change amelioration: policies, programmes, and regulations themselves do not change anything. For one thing, to be acceptable and efficacious to individuals; policies must be "bought into" by individuals. In short, policy beckons or even commands, but persons accept or refuse its demands. Behavioural change does not occur until this happens.

12   Many people do resist the temptation to engage in self-serving behaviours that contribute to climate change. Yet, admittedly, many do yield to the temptation. What will it take to change these people's behaviour? As a start—but only a start—understanding environment-related motivations, attitudes, social and organizational perceptions, rationales, biases, habits, barriers to change, life-context, and trust in government will help. Certainly, psychologists are already engaged in the effort on their own. For example, some have investigated the psychological dimensions of global warming (e.g., Dresner, 1989–90; Heath & Gifford, 2006; Nilsson, von Borgstede, & Biel, 2004). However, the major thesis of the present article is that we psychologists must do more.

13   I do not wish to argue that environmental psychology is, or even could be, a stand-alone panacea. For example, Schmuck and Vlek (2003) advocate that we work more closely with environmental scientists. However, I believe that we must work with at least four other groups to be effective: natural scientists, technical experts, policy experts, and local citizens' committees.

14   Fortunately, environmental psychologists have a history of interdisciplinary collaboration, beginning with geography and architecture, embodied in the collaborations between Robert Sommer, Humphry Osmond, and Kiyo Izumi in 1950s Saskatchewan (Sommer, 1983), or between Raymond Studer and David Stea in the United States (1966). More recently, and more pertinent to current concerns, fruitful collaborative work is being done in sustainability research (e.g., Schoot Uiterkamp & Vlek, 2007), including some collaborations that represent new bridges. Schoot Uiterkamp and Vlek (2007) describe five instances of collaborations, and their account is particularly valuable for its advice about the practicalities of engaging in multidisciplinary studies. This collaboration trend has been influenced, one suspects, by policies at national and international grant agencies that, for better or worse, virtually require interdisciplinary collaboration. In terms of influencing policy, collaborative efforts not only have "face credibility" based on the very breadth of their approach, but also success that is legitimately based on the increased validity of policy suggestions that emerge from studying a given problem with multiple valuable perspectives.

15   Gattig and Hendrickx (2007) bring perspectives from economics and behavioural decision theory into the mix. Discounting, the tendency to reduce the importance of an outcome with greater "distance" (temporally, socially, geographically, and probabilistically), is seen to be an important component of thinking about sustainability-related thinking. Fortunately, environmental problems appear to be less subject to discounting than some other matters. Although they incorporate some concepts from economics, Gattig and Hendrickx demonstrate why using those concepts in the same way that traditional economists do could lead to ineffective policies (cf. Stern, 1986). "Rational" discount rates are not the same as those of the public which, to its credit, seems to discount environmental

impacts less than in other domains. This helps to illustrate why other disciplines need psychology as much as psychology needs them.

16 Turning the policy issue upside down, some psychologists are examining the effects of policy strategies, as opposed to conducting studies that they hope will inform policy. Jager and Mosler (2007) are amongst those who use modeling to understand the outcomes of different policy choices. This form of active modeling offers the attractive advantage of trying out various policies before they are implemented and understanding why they might or might not work, thereby potentially avoiding expensive mistakes in policy-making. As Jager and Mosler point out, modeling can also be used to train policymakers. The very act of modeling encourages the idea that many policy alternatives exist, when often only a few may occur to a policymaker.

Technosalvation?

17 Technology is often promoted as the solution to many problems, including those related to climate change. Amongst these are biofuels, wind power, and solar power. Suspicion about the value of technology (e.g., Frank, 1966; Osborn, 1948) is longstanding and is justifiable in part. For example, growing biofuels requires the use of pesticides, reduces biodiversity, creates atmospheric pollution when burned, and has already caused large increases in food prices. Wind power creates noise, kills many birds, is unsightly, and negatively affects the rural lifestyle. Solar power requires the manufacture of photovoltaic cells, which creates a waste stream of cadmium, lead, and other heavy metal by-products. The downside of technology (pollution, health impacts, landfill contributions, accidents, energy consumed in production, and impacts on flora and fauna) is often overlooked in the touting of its benefits. As just one example that is not widely recognized, air pollution kills about 800,000 people each year (Kenworthy & Laube, 2002), and most air pollution is caused by technology in one form or another.

18 Of course, technology has another side to it, and as Midden, Kaiser, and McCalley (2007) clearly show, psychological scientists must deal with it because it is very unlikely to go away. It will not disappear because, despite its negative effects on people

and the environment, it undoubtedly has improved the quality of life for millions of other people, particularly when one thinks in terms of decades and centuries past (Simon, 1981). Assuming individuals have the motivation and appropriate skills, technology can assist in the goal of reducing greenhouse gas emissions. However, Midden et al.'s (2007) quite valid point is that the mere introduction of some new technology does not guarantee that it will be accepted and used by citizens, or that further investigation will not reveal that the cure is worse than the disease. Thus, policies aimed at facilitating the use by citizens of salutary technology must be encouraged, and the basis for such policies lies with research by environmental psychologists, who have the tools to understand why, whether, and when technology is accepted or not by citizens.

Three Models and Some Other Contributions of Psychology to Policy

19 Environmental psychologists share an interest in modeling with scientists in some other disciplines. The value of models is that they postulate relations amongst key influences and help to represent complex systems in understandable ways. They can stimulate investigation of the properties of the system and suggest predictions of future outcomes.

20 One such approach, Stern's (2000) values-beliefs-norms model (see Figure 1), postulates that behaviour is determined in part by a causal sequence that begins with deep-seated and quite-stable values, which strongly influence the more-mutable beliefs that one has, which set up the person's behavioural norms.

21 A second general approach is the social dilemma paradigm, which originated with Robyn Dawes' (1980) seminal article and has been expanded by Charles Vlek (1996). In essence, this paradigm asserts that individuals may act in self-interest or in the community interest; if they are amongst a few who act in self-interest they will prosper, but if many or most people act in self-interest, the environment (and they themselves) will suffer.

22 For the last several years, I have set myself the goal of integrating the many influences on, and outcomes

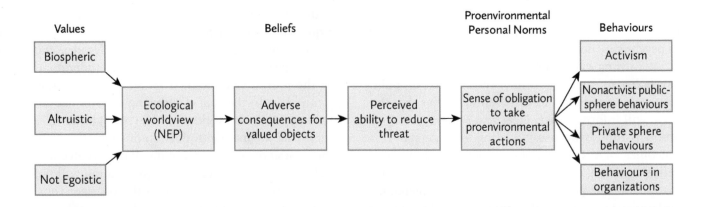

FIGURE 1 Stern's (2000) values-beliefs-norms model.

of, social dilemmas into a coherent and comprehensive model (Gifford, 2002a, 2008). Initially, I considered that influences on proenvironmental behaviour could be grouped into those associated with (a) the natural resource itself, such as its abundance or regeneration rate, (b) the decision-makers, such as their values and experience, (c) relations amongst decision-makers, such as trust and communication, and (d) the structure of the dilemma, such as the rules that govern environment-related actions (Gifford, 1987). Since then, the model has been expanding and relations amongst these categories of influence have been described and investigated (see Figure 2). In a meta-analysis Donald Hine and I (1991) conducted, about 30 different influences could be identified. This gradually led to the attempt to create a more comprehensive and organized model.

23   The model includes five categories of antecedent influences on a person's decisions, as shown in Figure 2: geophysical, governance (policies), interpersonal, decision-maker characteristics, and problem awareness. These influences are presumed to determine the different strategies or heuristics that individuals as decision-makers actually employ. Finally, two kinds of outcomes may be distinguished: those for decision-makers and their intimates, and those for the environment (the resource itself, the environment in general, and for other people in the community). Each element in the model includes numerous specific influences, which may be seen in Figure 2. A complete description of these influences may be found elsewhere (Gifford, 2007).

24   A mere listing of influences and outcomes is fairly straightforward; postulating and testing links amongst them is both more interesting and more challenging. For example, some decision-makers' strategy is geared toward sending a message to other decision-makers; the explicit message of some participants in our resource dilemma studies has been, for example: "Look, I am making sustainable choices, and I want you to do the same." Hence, a causal link exists between decision-maker strategies and interpersonal influences. At the larger social scale, consequences for climate change (environmental outcomes) often are reflected in changes in policies or regulations (governance influences). These hypothesized links between categories, and the conditions under which influence occurs or does not occur, represent the heuristic value of the model. Other direct and feedback links amongst the model's elements could be hypothesized and tested by psychologists, who alone amongst the climate-change players possess the necessary methodological tools to do so.

25   One recent example of this is provided by the work of Eek and Garling (2008). Social values (decision-maker influences) generally are thought to be associated with cooperative choices in resource dilemmas. One school of thought is that cooperation is actualized by a person's goals or aspirations (another decision-maker influence) that results in maximized outcomes for self and other (decision-maker outcomes). However, Eek and Garling convincingly make the case that a different goal, namely equal outcomes for all decision-makers, often is more influential than

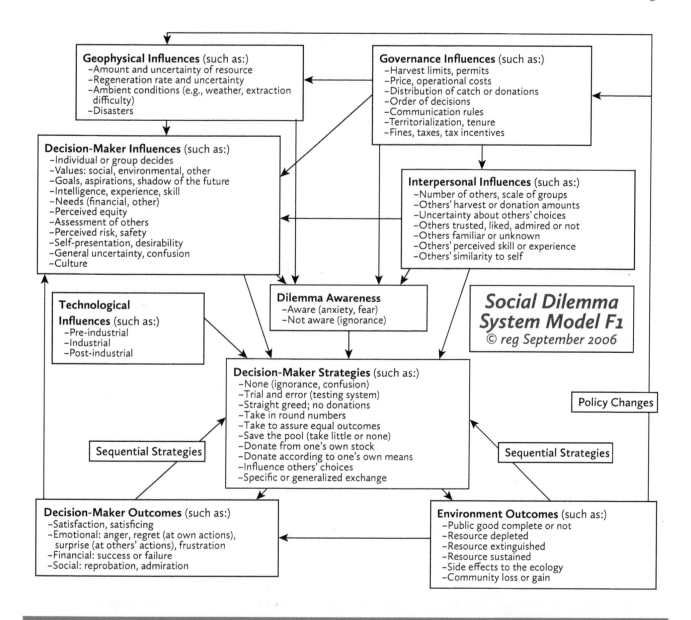

FIGURE 2 A model of the social dilemma approach to environmental problems that focuses on the decision-making of individuals (Gifford, 2008).

the joint maximization goal. Thus, choices presumably are a function of social values and goals, reflecting the model's implicit assertion that climate-change actions are multi-determined.

26 Another possibility is that over the course of time, different influences are regnant at different times (Gifford & Hine, 1997). This is reflected in the "sequential strategy" note in the model. Nevertheless, however helpful a comprehensive model might be for

visualizing the big picture in the model, the challenge for psychologists is to find ways to encourage those influences that promote behaviours that result in less greenhouse gas emissions.

27 Decision-makers usually are investigated as individuals by environmental psychologists, but in the everyday world decisions are sometimes, perhaps usually, made by groups such as boards of directors or government committees. Groups may be largely

unified in their goals and decisions, or not, which opens the door to group dynamics researchers, who often are psychologists. For example, Kazemi and Eek (2008) demonstrate the importance of considering the group as a decision-maker. Group goals (as well as individual goals) can affect the decisions made in the face of environmental problems. Clearly, given the ecological validity of the group as a decision-maker, this is an important direction for research to take. The model's decision-maker influences category obviously must include groups as well as individuals as the decision-makers. Its decision-maker strategies category includes several popular strategies used by decision-makers, and a link is necessary from that category to the interpersonal influences category, thereby postulating that strategies used by decision-makers will influence such within-group factors as trust, admiration, and perceived similarity to self.

The Challenges

28   Even a sustainability science that does include psychology must deal with several important human-nature challenges. The first is what has been called in other contexts mindlessness (Langer, Blank, & Chanowitz, 1978) or proximal cognition (Björkman, 1984), or what Dawes (1980) described in a more relevant context as limited-processing theory. Each of these constructs broadly asserts that humans often act without much reflection or rational planning. A few years earlier, I reported a little study in which university students were forced to navigate a path through some classroom desks that had been deliberately arranged to be difficult to navigate as they entered and left a classroom. Virtually all the students struggled through the desks, squeezing and turning, but when interviewed afterward, were almost completely unaware of their struggles. Their attention was largely allocated to thinking about the laboratory assignment they were conducting and probably other matters. I called this phenomenon "environmental numbness" (Gifford, 1976).

29   The notion of environmental numbness probably can be extended to the current climate-change crisis, in that most people, most of the time, simply are not thinking at all about climate change. Instead, they are (understandably) thinking about their work,

their friends and family, or the big game. The crucial challenges are to get as many people around the world as possible actively thinking about climate change, and to stimulate informed, evidence-based policy that creates accepted structural solutions, so that greenhouse gas emissions can be reduced whilst the rest of the people march, numb to the environment, through their days.

30   A second challenging element of the social dilemma is trust, or the lack of it (e.g., Brann & Foddy, 1987; Foddy & Dawes, 2008). When decision-makers remove less of the resource than they could have, or donors make a sizable contribution, many of them are trusting in a norm of fairness and reciprocity that, unfortunately, is not always shared by other decision-makers. Defectors or free-riders sometimes then see an opportunity for personal gain, and by acting in self-interest they harm the climate-change cause. For example, laboratory studies show that stealing from others in the commons is frequent (Edney & Bell, 1984). Lack of trust leads easily to reactance and denial. Read any online newspapers story about climate change, and below it will be comments deriding the scientific consensus that climate change is happening.

31   Third, a sense of community or group identity is important (Dawes & Messick, 2000). Where it is lacking, and around the globe it is tragically lacking, cooperation in our planetary commons is imperilled. For example, in one lab study, when harvesters thought of themselves more as individuals than as group members, they were more likely to overharvest the resource (Tindall & O'Connor, 1987). Another lab study did suggest that not much is required to create enough group identity to improve cooperation. In it, the only difference between "high-identity" and "low-identity" participants was that the high-identity participants came to the lab and received their instructions as a group (as opposed to singly), yet the high-identity harvesters cooperated more (Samuelson & Hannula, 2001). Unfortunately, given human history and current events, one is forced to wonder about the ecological validity of this encouraging finding. In December, 2007, China was rejecting mandatory emissions cuts because it said that the wealthy nations created the problem (Casey, 2007); this shows that people can have a strong identity (e.g., with their nation), but

lack sufficient identity with the environment to avoid destructive attitudes and behaviour.

32   A fourth challenge is that of human aspiration. Before we condemn the defectors and free-riders in our commons, we must confess that self-improvement is an essential part of human nature. This is the motive that Julian Simon (1981) celebrated as the solution to human problems. The "ultimate resource" that he believed in essentially was human ingenuity. When combined with the improvement motive, it has led to all the wonderful inventions that we enjoy today. However, in others, it also leads to venal self-aggrandizement (aided and abetted, of course, by the vast apparatus of persuasion that has been constructed in the modern consumption-oriented society). What to do? Use psychological science to reframe aspiration toward climate-amelioration ends. The other disciplines in sustainability science do not have the tools for this task, so it is up to us.

33   The fifth serious challenge problem is uncertainty, which can take several forms, such as in the absolute or relative amount of one's greenhouse gas emissions, the intentions of other decision-makers, the number of other decision-makers, the correct cost of a carbon credit, and so forth (e.g., Hine & Gifford, 1997). In fact, uncertainty can be a factor in every part of the model, from uncertainty about geophysical influences to uncertainty about quantitative and qualitative outcomes. For example, if someone drives 100 km in a particular car, it would not be difficult to measure the amount of greenhouse gases emitted. However, uncertainty about the effect of this emission on the atmosphere or whether the driver was wrong to drive at all is not easily decided. In sum, certainty may exist only under highly specific or highly aggregated conditions. For that reason, ecological validity in this area demands more studies of uncertainty in all the categories of the model.

34   A sixth challenge is that of perceived equity and justice, and the procedures designed to achieve these goals. Probably every researcher in the area, and certainly myself, has heard at least figurative and sometimes literal cries of revenge or anguish from participants who found the actions of others reprehensible. Therefore, justice-related issues cannot be ignored in social dilemma contexts. Four justice systems may be discerned: distributive, procedural, restorative, and retributive (Schroeder, Bembenek, Kinsey, Steel, & Woodell, 2008). Each system may be imposed from above (governance influences), or agreed-upon by decision-makers (interpersonal influences) but then are implemented as rules and regulations, thus creating a link between those two categories. Schroeder et al. (2008) believe that procedural justice systems will be more stable and cooperation-inducing than distributive justice systems, and explicitly argue that although such systems are best created through communication and agreements amongst those most affected (the decision-makers), they should become instituted as structural (i.e., rules and regulations) solutions to the eternal problem of transgressions in the commons. Clayton and Opotow (2003) discuss how justice is related to group and individual identity, and suggest that group identity promotes intergroup conflict, whereas its absence may allow individuals to experience their relation to nature as direct, which should lead to more pro-environmental behaviour.

35   The seventh challenge is the heavy weight of momentum. Although many people speak of changing their lives, the reality is that many people fail to achieve their goal of altering their behaviour patterns. Habit is not an exciting concept, but it is one important reason for the well-known gap between attitude and behaviour.

36   The eighth challenge is a widespread lack of a sense of efficacy, or perceived behavioural control. Many are hampered by the belief that they alone cannot change the global situation by anything that they do. Some acknowledge the truth that "every vote counts" without being able to muster the motivation (and often, the increased cost or inconvenience) of changing their behaviour in ways that would help to slow the forces that drive climate change.

37   The ninth challenge, and a potentially fatal one, is that of population size; this was central to Hardin's (1968) perspective, and current social scientists (e.g., McGinnis & Ostrom, 2008) quite naturally ask whether the often optimistic results obtained by those who work at the small-group level on common-resource problems would apply at larger scales. Of course, this question has been haunting psychologists for many years (e.g., Edney, 1981), particularly when many studies show a decline in cooperation as the size of the harvesting group grows, even in fairly

small groups (by societal standards) of 3 versus 7 (e.g., Sato, 1989). Nearly every study of group size has found that behaviour in resource management tends increasingly toward self interest as group size increases. Cooperation declines both as the number of decision-makers rises and as the number of groups within a commons with a constant total membership rises (Komorita & Lapworth, 1982). Good reasons for this are easy to list. As group size increases, the harm from any one participant's greed is spread thinner amongst the other participants: no single other decision-maker is badly hurt. Also, violations of sustainability or failures to donate are often less visible to others in larger groups. In addition, in large groups, the effect of the harm done to other decision-makers often is less visible to the violator (Edney, 1981); it is easier to inflict pain if one does not have to watch the victim experience pain. Finally, negative feedback or sanctions to violators or free-riders are increasingly difficult to manage in larger groups.

The Opportunities and Imperatives

38   If psychological science is to become recognized as an essential part of sustainability science and as an important player in the struggle to ameliorate the impacts of climate change, it must move toward a more serious engagement with the problem. If we do not, we run the danger of being viewed from the perspective of future citizens as the science that fiddled whilst the planet burned. One can either adopt the pessimistic view expressed by Garrett Hardin (1968) in his famous *Science* article, which most environmental psychologists have implicitly rejected by continuing to try to solve environmental problems, or one can adopt the view expressed in a more recent *Science* piece by Paul Ehrlich and Donald Kennedy (2005) that we "can organize fair and sustainable rules" (p. 563) to solve the problem.

39   Here is what we should do. First, obviously, we should conduct more research that bears directly on the many problems described above. Probably the central area of psychology for this task is environmental psychology, but we are a small group (about 650 worldwide who self-identify at least in part as environmental psychologists, according to a census I have undertaken this year, with only about two dozen in Canada). Other psychologists can help: how do people make climate-change-related decisions (cognitive and decision-science psychologists)? How can aspirations be reframed from owning more and more material goods to defining "improvement" as adopting climate-change amelioration behaviours (consumer psychologists)? How can helpful attitudes and lifestyles be more effectively taught (health psychologists)? How is acceptance of change related to the life cycle (life span psychologists)?

40   Second, we must engage policymakers (Clayton & Brook, 2005). A number of psychologists (e.g., Paul Stern) already are fully occupied in this crucial enterprise, and others have strongly advocated it (e.g., Vlek, 2000), but not enough of us are stepping off campus to do it. Green and green-leaning politicians now exist in much larger numbers in many countries, and these legislators both want and need quantified, substantiated information that they can use to enact more enlightened legislation. "Brown" politicians too should be our targets, perhaps more than green ones. Fritz Steele's (1980) notion of environmental competence includes knowing which political buttons to push, and psychologists have not done much button-pushing on climate change so far. The admirable fad in governments today is "evidence-based" policy (e.g., Davies, Nutley, & Smith, 2000). This new hunger for evidence-based policy is a huge opportunity for psychology, because of our methodological and research experience.

41   Because much in the way of needed change will occur (or not) at the level of individual citizens, environmental psychology is essential. Psychologists can serve as the key link between individuals—our traditional level of analysis—and policymakers. We can, and should, do the fundamental research on individuals and climate change, assess the acceptability of proposed policy and structural changes, and assess the impact of these changes on the behaviour, well-being, stress, and quality of life of individuals.

42   Third, we must seek out and interact with the other sustainability science players. We must tell the economists, technologists, and climate modellers what psychology can do. The climate scientists are merely the messengers, the technologists merely make machines, and the economists still think largely in

terms of pricing. Without the help of psychological science, these disciplines, although valuable in their own ways, will not be able to ameliorate the impacts of climate change.

Canadian Psychology. 2008. 49 (4).

*

I wish to acknowledge the contributions of Paul Stern, Joseph Reser, and Charles Vlek to my thinking on this issue. Naturally, however, I take responsibility for any views or fallacies expressed in this article that would not flatter them. I thank Donald Hine for his unintended challenge, and Brenda McMechan, Reuven Sussman, Leila Scannell, and Mary Gick for their comments and suggestions.

References

Bechtel, R. B., & Churchman, A. (2002). *Handbook of environmental psychology.* New York: Wiley.

Bechtel, R. B., Marans, R. W., & Michelson, W. (1987). (Eds.), *Methods in environmental and behavioral research.* New York: Van Nostrand Reinhold.

Björkman, M. (1984). Decision making, risk taking and psychological time: Review of empirical findings and psychological theory. *Scandinavian Journal of Psychology, 25,* 31–49.

Brann, P., & Foddy, M. (1987). Trust and the consumption of a deteriorating common resource. *Journal of Conflict Resolution, 31,* 615–630.

Buckhout, R. (1972). Pollution and the psychologist: A call to action. In J. F. Wohlwill & D. H. Carson (Eds.), *Environment and the social sciences* (pp. 75–81). Washington, DC: American Psychological Association.

Casey, M. (2007). China rejects mandatory emissions cuts. *The Globe and Mail,* December 8, p. A21.

Clark, W. C., & Dickson, N. M. (2003). Sustainability science. *Proceedings of the National Academy of Sciences, USA, 100,* 8059–8061.

Clayton, S., & Brook, A. (2005). Can psychology help save the world? A model for conservation psychology. *Analyses of Social Issues and Public Policy, 5,* 87–102.

Clayton, S., & Opotow, S. (2003). Justice and identity: Changing perspectives on what is fair. *Personality and Social Psychology Review, 7,* 298–310.

Davies, H. T. O., Nutley, S. M., & Smith, P. C. (2000). *What works? Evidence-based policy and practice in public services.* Bristol, United Kingdom: Policy Press.

Dawes, R. M. (1980). Social dilemmas. *Annual Review of Psychology, 31,* 169–193.

Dawes, R. M., & Messick, D. M. (2000). Social dilemmas. *International Journal of Psychology, 35,* 111–116.

Dresner, M. (1989–1990). Changing energy end-use patterns as a means of reducing global-warming trends. *Journal of Environmental Education, 21,* 41–46.

Edney, J. J. (1981). Paradoxes on the commons: Scarcity and the problem of equality. *Journal of Community Psychology, 9,* 3–34.

Edney, J. J., & Bell, P. A. (1984). Sharing scarce resources: Group-outcome orientation, external disaster, and stealing in a simulated commons. *Small Group Behavior, 15,* 87–108.

Eek, D., & Garling, T. (2008). A new look at the theory of social value orientations: Prosocials neither maximize joint outcomes nor minimize outcome differences but prefer equal outcomes. In A. Biel, D. Eek, T. Garling, & M. Gustaffson (Eds.). *New issues and paradigms in research on social dilemma* (pp. 10–26). New York: Springer.

Ehrlich, P. R., & Kennedy, D. (2005). Millennium assessment of human behavior. *Science, 309,* 562–563.

Foddy, M., & Dawes, R. M. (2008). Group-based trust in social dilemmas. In A. Biel, D. Eek, T. Garling, & M. Gustaffson (Eds.), *New issues and paradigms in research on social dilemma* (pp. 57–71). New York: Springer.

Frank, J. D. (1966). Galloping technology, a new social disease. *Journal of Social Issues, 12,* 1–14.

Gattig, A., & Hendrickx, L. (2007). Judgmental discounting and environmental risk perception: Dimensional similarities, domain differences, and implications for sustainability. *Journal of Social Issues, 63,* 21–39.

Gifford, R. (1976). Environmental numbness in the classroom. *Journal of Experimental Education, 44,* 4–7.

Gifford, R. (1987). *Environmental psychology: Principles and practice* (1st ed.). Newton, MA: Allyn & Bacon.

Gifford, R. (2002a). *Managing natural resources: A matter of life and death.* Keynote address to the International Congress of Applied Psychology, Singapore, July.

Gifford, R. (2002b). Making a difference: Some ways environmental psychology has improved the world. In R. Bechtel & A. Churchman (Eds.), Handbook of environmental psychology (2nd ed.). New York: Wiley.

Gifford, R. (2007). *Environmental psychology: Principles and practice* (4th ed.). Colville, WA: Optimal Books.

Gifford, R. (2008). Toward a comprehensive model of social dilemmas. In A. Biel, D. Eek, T. Gärling, & M. Gustaffson (Eds.), *New issues and paradigms in research on social dilemmas* (265–280). New York: Springer.

Gifford, R., & Hine, D. W. (1997). Toward cooperation in commons dilemmas. *Canadian Journal of Behavioural Sciences, 29,* 167–179.

Hardin, G. (1968). The tragedy of the commons. *Science, 162,* 1234–1248.

Heath, Y., & Gifford, R. (2006). Free-market ideology and environmental degradation: The case of beliefs in global climate change. *Environment & Behavior, 38,* 48–71.

Hine, D. W., & Gifford, R. (1991). *The commons dilemma: A quantitative review.* Canadian Psychological Association annual meetings, Calgary, June.

Hine, D. W., & Gifford, R. (1997). Individual restraint and group efficiency in commons dilemmas: The effects of two types of environmental uncertainty. *Journal of Applied Social Psychology, 26,*993–1009.

Jager, W., & Mosler, H.-J. (2007). Simulating human behavior for understanding and managing environmental resource use. *Journal of Social Issues, 63,*97–116.

Kazeemi, A., & Eek, D. (2008). Promoting cooperation in social dilemmas via fairness norms and group goals. In A. Biel, D. Eek, T. Garling, & M. Gustaffson (Eds.), *New issues and paradigms in research on social dilemmas*(pp. 72–92). New York: Springer.

Kenworthy, J., & Laube, F. (2002). Urban transport patterns in a global sample of cities and their linkages to transport infrastructures, land use, economics and environment. *World Transport Policy and Practice, 8,*5–20.

Kidner, D. W. (1994). Why psychology is mute about the environmental crisis. *Environmental Ethics, 16,*359–376.

Komorita, S. S., & Lapworth, C. W. (1982). Cooperative choice among individuals versus groups in an N-person dilemma situation. *Journal of Personality and Social Psychology, 42,*487–496.

Langer, E., Blank, A., & Chanowitz, B. (1978). The mindlessness of ostensibly thoughtful action: The role of "placebic" information in interpersonal interaction. *Journal of Personality and Social Psychology, 36,*635–642.

Lundqvist, L. J., & Biel, A. (2007). From Kyoto to the town hall: Making international and national climate policy work at the local level. Sterling, VA: Stylus.

McGinnis, M., & Ostrom, E. (2008). Will lessons from small-scale scale up?. In A. Biel, D. Eek, T. Garling, & M. Gustaffson (Eds.), *New issues and paradigms in research on social dilemmas*(pp. 189–211). New York: Springer.

Midden, C., Kaiser, F., & McCalley, T. (2007). Technology's four roles in understanding individuals' conservation of natural resources. *Journal of Social Issues, 63,*155–174.

Miller, A. (1985). Cognitive styles and environmental problem-solving. *Journal of Environmental Studies, 26,*535–541.

Nilsson, A., von Borgstede, C., & Biel, A. (2004). Willingness to accept climate change strategies: The effect of values and norms. *Journal of Environmental Psychology, 24,*267–277.

Osborn, F. (1948). *Our plundered planet.* Boston: Little, Brown.

Oskamp, S. (2000). The psychology of promoting environmentalism: Psychological contributions to achieving an ecologically sustainable future for humanity. *Journal of Social Issues, 56,*378–390.

Pallak, M. S., & Cummings, W. (1976). Commitment and voluntary energy conservation. *Personality and Social Psychology Bulletin, 2,*27–30.

Reser, J. (2007). Psychology and the natural environment: *A position paper for the Australian Psychological Society.* Melbourne, Australia: Australian Psychological Society.

Reser, J. P., & Bentrupperbaumer, J. M. (2001). "Social science" in the environmental studies and natural science arena: Misconceptions, misrepresentations, and missed opportunities. In G. Lawrence, V. Higgins, & S. Lockie (Eds.), *Environment, society, and natural resource management: Theoretical perspectives from Australasia and the Americas.* Northampton, MA: Edward Elgar.

Samuelson, C. D., & Hannula, K. A. (2001). *Group identity and environmental uncertainty in a sequential resource dilemma.* Unpublished manuscript, Department of Psychology, Texas A&M University.

Sato, K. (1989). Trust and feedback in a social dilemma. *Japanese Journal of Experimental Social Psychology, 29,*123–128.

Schmuck, P., & Schultz, W. P. (Eds.) (2002). *Psychology of sustainable development,* London: Kluwer Academic.

Schmuck, P., & Vlek, C. (2003). Psychologists can do much to support sustainable development. *European Psychologist, 8,*66–76.

Schoot Uiterkamp, A. J. M., & Vlek, C. (2007). Practice and outcomes of multidisciplinary research for environmental sustainability. *Journal of Social Issues, 63,*175–197.

Schroeder, D. A., Bembenek, A. F., Kinsey, K. M., Steel, J. E., & Woodell, A. J. (2008). A recursive model for changing justice concerns in social dilemmas. In A. Biel, D. Eek, T. Gärling, & M. Gustaffson (Eds.), *New issues and paradigms in research on social dilemmas*(pp. 142–158). New York: Springer.

Seligman, C., & Darley, J. M. (1977). Feedback as a means of decreasing residential energy conservation. *Journal of Applied Social Psychology, 62,*363–368.

Simon, J. (1981). *The ultimate resource.* Princeton, NJ: Princeton University Press. Sommer, R. (1983). *Social design: Creating buildings with people in mind.* Englewood Cliffs, NJ: Prentice Hall. Steele, F. (1980). Defining and developing environmental competence. In C. P. Alderfer & C. L. Cooper (Eds.), *Advances in experiential social processes*(Vol. 2), 225–244.

Stern, P. C. (1986). Blind spots in policy analysis: What economics doesn't say about energy use. *Journal of Policy Analysis and Management, 5,* 220–227.

Stern, P. C. (1993). A second environmental science: Human-environment interactions. *Science, 260,*1897–1899.

Stern, P. C. (2000). Towards a coherent theory of environmentally significant behavior. *Journal of Social Issues, 56,*407–424.

Stern, P. C. (2005, September 21). *Psychological research and sustain-ability science.* Keynote address to the 6th Biennial Conference on Environmental Psychology, Bochum, Germany.

Studer, R., & Stea, D. (1966). Architectural programming and human behavior. *Journal of Social Issues, 12,*1–14.

Tindall, D. B., & O'Connor, B. (1987, June). *Attitudes, social identity, social values, and behavior in a commons dilemma.* Presentation at the Canadian Psychological Association Conference, Vancouver, BC.

Uzzell, D. (2007). How the science of psychology can make a contribution to sustainable development. Working paper, British Psychological Society.

Vlek, C. (1996). Collective risk generation and risk management: The unexploited potential of the social dilemmas paradigm. In W. B. G. Liebrand & D. M. Messick (Eds.), *Frontiers in social dilemmas research* (pp. 11–38). New York: Springer-Verlag.

Vlek, C. (2000). Essential psychology for environmental policy making. *International Journal of Psychology, 35,* 153–167.

Vlek, C., & Steg, L. (2007). Human behavior and environmental sustain-ability: Problems, driving forces, and research topics. *Journal of Social Issues, 63,* 1–19.

Key and challenging words

amelioration, parametric, functionary, substantive, salutary, postulate (v.), antecedent, heuristics, regnant, reciprocity, deride, venal, aggrandizement, retributive

Questions

1. What is the function of the section "A Bit of Background"?

2. Why is it important to study the behaviour of individuals in a global phenomenon like climate change?

3. What is environmental psychology? How could it be a "player" in climate change policies? Why has it not been?

4. "We write in our discussion sections that 'someone' should take into account these important findings of ours. However, unfortunately, for the most part policymakers and natural scientists do not read our discussion sections" (paragraph 6): a) Why do you think Gifford included this criticism of psychologists? b) What are stereotypes that are applied to psychologists? To what extent do you believe these stereotypes are responsible for the lack of credibility Gifford addresses in this paragraph?

5. Summarize paragraphs 10–11 in which the author explains his disagreement with Stern.

6. In no more than two sentences provide a more complete caption for Figure 2, using the explanation in paragraph 23. Then, in about two additional sentences explain the nature of the relationship between any two parts of the diagram, using one of the examples that refer to Figure 2 in paragraphs 24–27.

7. Analyze one of the paragraphs in the section "The Challenges," showing how the writer creates a coherent, unified, and well-developed paragraph (do not analyze paragraphs 29, 35, or 36, as they are too short.

8. Which do you consider are the two most crucial challenges for psychologists among the nine discussed in this section? Write one paragraph each explaining why you believe it is so important in alleviating the effects of climate change.

9. In one or two paragraphs, analyze the rhetorical effectiveness of the concluding section, "The Opportunities and Imperatives," referring to specific passages.

Post-reading

1. *Collaborative or individual activity:* "The Tragedy of the Commons" (see paragraph 38) refers to an analogy used by Garrett Hardin of an open pasture in which herdsmen overuse a resource by applying a process of "rational" (though selfish) thinking. According to Hardin, each herdsman attempts to maximize his own profit by asking, "What is the utility *to me* of adding one more animal to my herd?" His reasoning is that if he adds one animal to the pasturage, he will be able to sell an additional animal at the market, whereas the group cost will be shared among all the herdsmen. Hardin concludes that "Each man is locked into a system that compels him to increase his herd without limit—in a world that is limited," which creates the tragedy. Hardin believed that humans are doomed by the tragedy of the commons, which makes it impossible to solve all such problems of the commons, like that of world overpopulation.

Discuss the apparent strengths and flaws in this concept, using, if possible, realistic examples from your own experience or observation about shared resources (for example, car-pooling lanes). Before discussing or debating this issue, you could read Hardin's essay, accessing it through a library database or at the address given below.

2. Do you believe the gap mentioned between academic studies and policymakers first mentioned in paragraphs 7 and 8 applies to social science research in general? Write a response to one of the following prompts: a) Social science research done at universities is remote from the concerns of everyday life; *OR*

b) Research in the social sciences done at universities could be made more relevant to everyday life and/or could affect policy decisions if. . . .

3. *Collaborative activity:* Do you believe that individuals are, in fact, the key to addressing climate change or that the key lies with politicians and other policymakers, rather than with individuals? What can individuals do to help alleviate climate change?

Related websites of interest

Intergovernmental Panel on Climate Change Fifth Assessment Report (AR5):
www.ipcc.ch/

Canada's Action on Climate Change (federal government site):
www.climatechange.gc.ca/default.asp?lang=En&n=E18C8F2D-1

The Pembina Institute (non-profit Canadian institute focused on sustainable energy policies):
http://climate.pembina.org/

Garrett Hardin, "The Tragedy of the Commons":
www.sciencemag.org/cgi/content/full/162/3859/1243

Additional library reading

Mark Van Vugt, M. (2009). Averting the tragedy of the commons: Using social psychological science to protect the environment. *Current Directions in Psychological Science, 18*(3), 169–173

Community perspectives on the impact of climate change on health in Nunavut, Canada

G.K. Healey et al.
(4,359 words)

Pre-reading

1. *Collaborative or individual activity:* What specific concerns or issues are you aware of concerning the effects of climate change on northern communities in Canada? Using a pre-writing technique (individual) or through discussion, come up with a list of at least five concerns or issues.

Abstract

The purpose of this study was to explore community perspectives on the most important ways that climate change is affecting the health of northern peoples. The study was conducted in Iqaluit, Nunavut, using a participatory action approach and the photovoice research method. Participants identified themes and patterns in the data and developed a visual model of the relationships between the themes identified. Five themes emerged from the data: the direct impacts of climate change on the health of individuals and communities, the transition from past climates to future climates, necessary adaptation to the changing climate in the North, the call to action (individual, regional, and national), and reflection on the past and changing knowledge systems. A climate change and health model was developed to illustrate the relationships between the themes. Participants in this study conceptualized health and climate change broadly. Participants believed that by engaging in a process of ongoing reflection, and by continually incorporating new knowledge and experiences into traditional knowledge systems, communities may be better able to adapt and cope with the challenges to health posed by climate change.

Introduction

1   The evidence that the climate is changing and that these changes can be attributed to human activities has become stronger in recent years (Hegerl et al., 2007). A recent report published by the Lancet Commission on Climate Change found that climate endangers health in six key ways: through changing patterns of disease and mortality, extreme weather events, food insecurity, water scarcity, heat waves, and threats to built structures, including housing and public infrastructure (Costello et al., 2009). The Arctic Climate Impact Assessment (ACIA) suggests that future climate change will be experienced earlier and more acutely in polar regions (ACIA, 2004). Indigenous peoples of the North are being affected by climate change, and future changes in climate are likely to pose serious challenges (World Health Organization, 2003; ACIA, 2004). However, the health-related impact on communities in northern Canada is not yet fully understood. Northern communities hold a close relationship with the land. Seals, whales, walrus, caribou, and other species provide highly nutritious food (Kuhnlein and Soueida, 1992) and provide a deep connection to the natural environment (Watt-Cloutier, 2004). The environment and the country foods that come from the land, lakes, rivers, and sea remain central to the way of life, cultural identity, and health of northern people (Egan, 1998; Duhaime et al., 2004; Watt-Cloutier, 2004; Van Oostdam et al., 2005). Hunting lies at the core of Inuit culture, teaching such key values as courage, patience, tenacity, and boldness under pressure, qualities that are required for both worlds—the modern and the traditional—in which Inuit live (Watt-Cloutier, 2004). For Inuit communities, sea-ice travel is critical to accessing wildlife resources and travelling between communities during winter months. Uncharacteristic weather patterns, storm events, and ice conditions are undermining the safety of travel and hunting or fishing activities (Furgal and Seguin, 2006). The increased risks to safety, as well as the longer traveling distances, are challenging the harvesting of country foods (Furgal and Seguin, 2006). The increasingly unpredictable weather patterns affect access to health services by threatening medical evacuation procedures that rural and remote areas rely upon for emergency and high-risk patient care. In addition to posing threats to livelihood and food security in the North, warming temperatures may be contributing to an increase in reports of never-before-seen species of biting flies and insects. Climate change is also proposed to pose the threat of increased vector-borne disease; however, this increase has not yet been clearly demonstrated (Kovats and Haines, 2005). Furthermore, permafrost melting attributable to a warmer climate will have serious implications for the structural integrity of northern houses and buildings (Furgal and Seguin, 2006). Northern community members have shared the concern that climate change, and the resulting changes in the environment and communities, may further compound existing health issues, including mental health and wellness, nutritional deficiencies, rates of respiratory illness, livelihood and economic stability, safety, and the spread of disease (Furgal and Seguin, 2006).

2   Research on the health impacts of climate change in northern Canada is a newer field. To date, the literature has largely focused on the collection of local indigenous

knowledge and observations about weather patterns, land and sea-ice conditions, animal behaviour, and species sightings (Furgal et al., 2002; Furgal and Seguin, 2006; Laidler, 2006; Laidler et al., 2008; Weatherhead et al., 2010); risk and community vulnerability to climate change (Ford and Smit, 2004; Ford et al., 2006; Ford, 2009; Laidler et al., 2009); and adaptation and adaptive capacity (Berkes and Jolly, 2001; Natural Resources Canada, 2004). Current approaches include a focus on indigenous knowledge and local observations of environmental change, as well as scientific assessments of the impacts associated with these and other forms of change (Furgal and Seguin, 2006).

Community-Led Research

3   Research that strives to understand how climate change affects the health of northern communities must elicit meaningful community involvement in the research process. Moreover, community participation and social mobilization are essential for identifying the factors that enhance or inhibit local adaptive capabilities in the face of climate change. The data presented here resulted from an initiative by Qaujigiartiit Health Research Centre, an independent community organization located in Iqaluit, Nunavut, in response to community requests for a forum in which to gain technical knowledge and hands-on experience of research. The Centre's mandate is to enable health research to be conducted locally, by Northerners and with communities, in a supportive, safe, culturally sensitive, and ethical environment, as well as to promote the inclusion of both Inuit *Qaujimajatuqangit* and Western science in addressing health concerns, creating healthy environments, and improving the health of Nunavummiut. The Centre is governed by a board of directors, whose members represent Nunavut-based research bodies, Inuit organizations, territorial and municipal governments, community members, and youth. This project was part of a research skills workshop held in Iqaluit on 12–14 May 2009, which included training in interviewing, survey administration, Inuit and community perspectives on ethics in research, and photovoice methodology. The photovoice research study presented in this paper took place over the course of that workshop.

4   This study explored community perspectives on the impact that climate change can and will have on the health of northern peoples. We combined a research project with an educational opportunity in order to build confidence and capacity so that Northerners may participate meaningfully in projects that come to their communities and eventually lead their own research projects on health, climate change, or both, in the future.

Methods

5   This exploratory, qualitative study used the photovoice research method. Six community participants from Nunavut communities (Gjoa Haven, Chesterfield Inlet, and Iqaluit), and two visiting graduate students took part in the training, data collection, and analysis of the study in Iqaluit, Nunavut. The participants were recruited through an open invitation sent by fax and e-mail to health centres, community organizations, and government and non-government agencies in Nunavut. The six participants volunteered to take part, and travel was provided to Iqaluit for the volunteers from other communities. The role of the graduate students was to learn about the research method and process and to record the discussion. The Participatory Action Research (PAR) approach (Macaulay et al., 1999) affords individuals the opportunity to participate directly in a study by sharing their knowledge and providing their perspectives on the research question. Participatory research attempts to negotiate a balance between developing valid, generalizable knowledge and benefiting the community that is being researched and to improve research protocols by incorporating the knowledge and expertise of community members. Collaboration, education, and action are the three key elements of participatory research. An advantage of a PAR approach in the North is that it stresses the relationship between researcher, participants, and community; capacity building in the community through research involvement; and the direct benefit to the community of the potential research outcomes (Macaulay et al., 1999). A goal is that research participants and collaborators should "own" the research process and use its results to improve the quality of life in the community. Photovoice (originally termed "photo novella") is referred to as an educational tool, an advocacy tool, and a participatory action research method (Wang and Burris, 1994, 1997; Wang et al., 1998). Rooted in the tenets of participation, empowerment, accessibility, and self-documentation, photovoice is a

technique for eliciting community perspectives and capturing everyday life experiences through photography (Moffitt and Vollman, 2004).

6   The photovoice technique was used to explore the impacts of climate change on health in Nunavut from the perspective of community members. The participants were the researchers and photographers: they own the data, and they were full participants in the analysis. Community participants were each provided with a camera and asked to photograph what they understood to be the most important effects of climate change on the health of the people in their communities. The photographs served to elicit individual perspectives and experiences in a group discussion about the effects of climate change on health. Participatory analysis emphasizes process, and participants are made central to this process (Moffitt and Vollman, 2004). Participants were asked to describe the rationale behind their photographs and to share the stories, perspectives, and experiences represented in these images. The printed photos were discussed one at a time, and the group members collaborated to select a "message" or "title" that they felt represented the photo. The photos were then grouped (and re-grouped) according to patterns the participants began to identify in the images. Photographs that they considered similar were placed together, and the messages attached to each photo at the beginning of the process formed the basis for the themes identified. This process led them to develop a visual model of relationships between these themes. With the group's permission, a written record of the discussion was kept.

7   As the participants in the project are the researchers and this project was initiated in Nunavut by Nunavummiut, this project was not eligible for review by a governing or legislative body. Therefore, a detailed discussion about community and Inuit perspectives on ethics was part of the process, and a locally developed "ethics checklist" was used as a guiding framework (Qaujigiartiit Health Research Centre, 2010). Additionally, the project adhered to the ethical principles developed by the Association of Canadian Universities for Northern Studies (ACUNS) and the Canadian Institutes of Health Research (CIHR) Guidelines for the Ethical Conduct of Health Research with Aboriginal Peoples (ACUNS, 2003; CIHR, 2008). Most importantly, the participants agreed to adhere to the Inuit principle of *Inuuqatigiittiarniq*, working in

an environment of respect and appreciation for one another. The participants collectively decided how to share the results of the study with their communities, the research community, and the public in general. They have used local newspaper and radio interviews, a research report, and an exhibit at the Nunatta Sunakkutaangit Museum in Iqaluit (all in both English and Inuktitut), as well as a poster presentation at an academic conference and the present paper.

Results

8   Five themes emerged from analysis and discussion of the photographic data: reflection on past and changing knowledge systems, direct impacts of climate change on health, transition from past climates to future climates, necessary adaptation to the changing climate in the North, and a call to action. The participants created a model of the themes identified during the analysis to illustrate visually the relationships they felt were crucial to understanding their perspective on climate change and health in their communities.

Reflection and Changing Knowledge Systems

9   Participants identified the theme of reflection and changing knowledge systems as central to the relationship between climate change and health. In the words of one participant, "We need to think about the past, reflect on our experiences, and look forward to the future." Participants saw the capacity to reflect on the past and preserve Inuit *Qaujimajatuqangit* (Inuit knowledge) as essential to coping with the effects of climate change on health (Fig. 1). They also recognized the importance of new knowledge about the changing environment and its implications for the land and for community health: in their view, incorporating new information into traditional knowledge systems is essential to managing the health effects of climate change.

The Impacts of Climate Change on Health

10   Direct effects of climate change on health were a prominent theme in group discussions. Participants thought that climate affects health in six key ways: through contamination of food, contamination of water, changes in weather patterns, melting permafrost, isolation due to restricted mobility, and loss of their way of life and their livelihood. One participant

Courtesy Arctic Institute of North America

FIGURE 1   A participant reading information about the historical context of the area displayed on a signpost outside of Iqaluit. This photo generated discussion about changes over time in the way knowledge is transmitted, as oral history was traditionally the primary means of sharing knowledge among Inuit, and now information comes in many forms, including written form.

Courtesy Arctic Institute of North America

FIGURE 2   This photo of a ski-doo with a "For Sale" sign was meant to convey the very real and immediate impact of climate change on community members if it results in a warming Arctic. Snowmobiles will become useless, and hunting practices and patterns may change. The group expressed grief at the idea that this photo may represent future events.

reflected that access to country food will be altered profoundly by climate change. Participants felt that community members will have to travel farther, in more dangerous conditions, and using different modes of transportation, in order to ensure country food security and maintain a traditional diet. The participant who photographed the ski-doo (Fig. 2) said, "We'll being seeing more of this . . . more machines for sale. We won't be able to use them any more when it warms up," highlighting her concern not only that ways of hunting will change, but also that people may not be able to hunt at all in the future.

The Transition from Past Climates to Future Climates

11   Participants reported that the transition from cold to hot was a particularly salient theme for the North, where history, health, and well-being are so intimately associated with colder environments. Figure 3, an image of ice and sand, is meant to represent the participants' perspective on the melting environment and the change from cold to warmer climates. Notions of change and transformation were discussed, and with these ideas emerged expressions of vulnerability. One participant said, "I feel vulnerable to the changes that may come. The snow is melting, the ice is melting. It will be different." Participants described feelings both of personal vulnerability (highlighted by the need to travel in dangerous conditions, for example) and of collective vulnerability (highlighted by the sense of collective cultural demise). Participants associated the sense of loss they feel with climate change in the North. For many, the transition from colder to warmer environments means a loss of livelihood, a loss of tradition, and a loss of preferred activities, such as snowmobiling, hunting, and camping.

Necessary Adaptation

12   Building upon the conclusion that transition is nearly inevitable, the participants highlighted the importance of adaptation for health and well-being in light of climate change. Participants proposed a variety of strategies for coping with climate change and reversing its ill effects. For example, referring to the image of the stop sign (Fig. 4), the photographer said, "I took this picture because it shows we can recycle things. The old oil drum is being re-used to help hold up signs. There are many more ways we can recycle if we think about it." These ways included improving personal choices, promoting sustainability, discouraging waste, cleaning up our own communities, and advocating for hope and survival in the face of adversity. The participants felt that collectively, Northerners can make changes to adapt to the changing climate and make lifestyle choices that may help reduce the effects of human-induced climate change.

Courtesy Arctic Institute of North America

FIGURE 3 This photo shows the meeting place of land and sea ice along a ski-doo trail on the beach in Iqaluit. The participants felt it was a metaphor for the receding ice in the Arctic.

The Call to Action

13   One participant, showing a picture of a sewage truck (Fig. 5), told the story of a recent event in her community. The local river eroded during the spring melt, washed out the bridge, and obstructed the route of the sewage-removal truck to the community. As a

result, the community was forced to dump its sewage into the sea. The contamination of sea waters with sewage was a serious concern to community members. The participant told this story to illustrate her feelings of being "stuck between a rock and a hard place," since communities in the North often have few alternatives, and thus little capacity to live more sustainably. Participants further indicated that geographic and environmental conditions in the North necessitate resource- and energy-intensive practices (such as sealift shipment, air cargo and air travel) and hinder environmentally friendly practices (such as recycling). The paucity of environmentally favourable alternatives for communities in the North was deemed, by participants, to be a call to action. One participant spoke of the need for action to protect our children from any harm or hazard that comes from human-induced climate change. In the context of the photo of a tricycle stuck in the snow (Fig. 6), this participant said: "This bike is stuck in the snow. Our children will be stuck in the future, too. They are stuck with what we leave for them. If we do nothing, they will be stuck with our mess."

14   Participants highlighted that action on an individual level can be two-pronged, involving education and responsible living. First, they suggested that information and education are essential to ensuring that individuals are knowledgeable about the effects of climate change in the North and can participate in meaningful, informed decision making on these issues. Secondly, they thought that individuals ought to be responsible for reducing consumption and living sustainably.

15   At the community level, it was believed that planning and consultation were essential to ensure successful management of climate-change effects on health. Engaging communities in political action was deemed imperative, and mechanisms of redistribution, or community sharing, ought to be strengthened to ensure more equitable access to country foods for communities whose access has been limited.

16   Participants associated a reduction in consumption with sustainable practices that would help mitigate the effects of climate change, and they stressed the need for investment in waste management services on a regional level, to ensure that recycling and compost

Courtesy Arctic Institute of North America

FIGURE 4 This photo of a stop sign anchored into place with an old oil drum demonstrates the recycling of old products. Many of the street signs in the Arctic can't be placed into the ground because of the permafrost. Anchoring the signs with old oil drums filled with rocks has been an innovative way to meet needs and re-use old materials.

programs have the capacity to operate throughout the territory. They felt it was also important to invest in territorial search-and-rescue programs, given the increasingly unpredictable weather patterns and sea-ice traveling conditions. Correspondingly, engaging policy makers was seen as essential to the promotion of environmentally friendly practices in Nunavut.

17   Finally, participants believed that the call to action on a national level involves a strengthening of knowledge sharing, consciousness-raising, and communication about the effects of climate change in the North. They believe that national policy makers can enforce corporate accountability and ban the dangerous chemicals that contaminate the environment and country foods in the North. Finally it was thought that investment should be made, at a national level, into alternative energy sources and innovative environmental practices.

The Climate Change and Health Model

18   The climate change and health model is a visual representation of the themes that emerged through the photovoice analysis process (Fig. 7). The model was created by the participants in the project. The placement of the themes around and within a circle, signifies interaction and overlap between ideas and messages. The theme of reflection and changing knowledge systems was identified as central to the relationship between climate change and health. The participants felt that knowledge, both past, present, and future, is one of the most important factors in mitigating the effects of climate change on health. From this central concept emerged four extensions: the themes of impacts, transition, adaptation, and action. Participants felt that the direct impacts of climate change both result from and contribute to the transition of the land, environment, and way of life of northern peoples. This transition has and will continue to

Courtesy Arctic Institute of North America

FIGURE 5 This photo shows a sewage truck removing waste from a home. Most homes in Nunavut are equipped with a water tank and a waste tank. Water is delivered to the home by truck and stored in the water tank. Used water and waste water are collected in the waste tank and removed by these trucks throughout the week. This photo prompted the telling of the story about river erosion in a community that blocked sewage trucks from accessing the treatment plant in 2008.

promote action at the individual, community, regional, and national levels. Action may take the form of an individual lifestyle change (i.e., using more energy-efficient light bulbs) or advocacy on a national political level. The actions are part of our collective adaptation to the changing climate. The adaptive capacity of communities will be affected by the level and extent of the actions undertaken. These adaptations could then potentially change or mitigate the continuing and future impacts of climate change on health in this cyclic model.

Courtesy Arctic Institute of North America

FIGURE 6 This photo of a child's tricycle stuck in the snow near a play area in Iqaluit was viewed by participants as representing how our children are "stuck" with what we leave them. They will inherit a planet, a land, and an environment that we are responsible for keeping in the best possible condition for them.

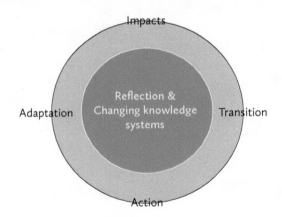

FIGURE 7 The Climate Change and Health Model developed by the study participants to visually represent how the themes identified in the data analysis process relate to each other. The model illustrates how the impacts of climate change can lead us to take action (or lead to inaction), which in turn changes the influence or impact. They interpreted these processes as cyclical, with the quality and accuracy of the knowledge available being one of the central influences in the entire process.

Discussion

19   Northern communities have figured prominently in recent research on climate change. However, little is known about the health effects of climate change in the North. What is more, community perspectives regarding these effects are largely absent from the literature. Our findings document the experience of a small group of community participants in Nunavut. Participants in this study conceptualized health and climate change broadly and identified the theme of reflection and changing knowledge systems as central to the relationship between the two concepts. They believe that by engaging in a process of ongoing reflection, and by continually incorporating new knowledge and experiences into traditional knowledge systems, communities may be better able to adapt and to cope with health-related challenges posed by climate change. It was in light of these ideas that the four additional themes emerged, and that the action plan was formulated. The five thematic areas identified by the participants in this study confirm, for the most part, the current, limited body of evidence on climate change and health.

20   Participants discussed personal and collective vulnerability in the context of the present climate transition. The concept of vulnerability to climate change has been discussed somewhat in the literature. Ford and Smit (2004) conceptualize vulnerability as a function of exposure to climatic stresses and the adaptive capacity to cope with these stresses. They argue that in order to identify needs and improve adaptive capacity, the process must begin with an assessment of the vulnerability of the group of interest, in terms of who and what are vulnerable, to what stresses, and in what way, and what capacity exists to adapt to changing risks. The results of the present study add to this body of work by highlighting the need to explore individual vulnerability to climate change and the mental, emotional, and spiritual impact of climate change on the health of Northerners, as well as the collective vulnerability of all northern indigenous peoples, communities, and cultures.

21   Models of climate change and its impact on the health of northern peoples are fairly new in the literature. Existing models explore vulnerability to climate change, exposure-sensitivity of a community to climate change effects, adaptive capacity to deal with exposures, and risks (including but not limited to those associated with climate change). They include buffering factors such as the nature of the community in question and its economy, location, and population (Ford et al., 2006). The model developed by participants in this study highlights the importance of community perspective, knowledge, and the cyclic nature of the relationships between events and reactions to climate change. This model also reflects well-known Inuit perspectives of the integral connection between personal and community health and the environment.

22   The theme of reflection and changing knowledge systems is important in the context of the literature reporting indigenous knowledge and perspectives on climate change. The participants in this study placed importance on the roles of both traditional and new Inuit knowledge about the land, changing environment and climate, and adaptations to these changes. How knowledge is gained, transmitted, and shared within and between northern communities has changed over time with globalization and increasingly accessible telecommunications technology and media. Reflection upon these changes and critical analysis of the information available were viewed as important responsibilities for community members in exploring adaptation to climate change.

23   The perspectives shared in this study are not meant to represent all northern communities. Our purpose was to shed light on the impact of climate change and health through the eyes of Nunavut community members with an interest in climate change research. The particular photographs, stories, and messages that emerged through this research process reflect a unique community perspective, rendering these findings particularly relevant to the North and significant for compelling community action around the issue of climate change. The findings show that perceived effects of climate change on health are varied and multifaceted. Accordingly, responsive action to these effects must transpire at multiple socio-ecological levels, ranging from individual choices to community, municipal, provincial or territorial, and federal strategies. The multilateral approach assumed in the participants' call to action reflects the multidimensional nature of the issue, as well as the varied opportunities for adaptation in the North.

Conclusion

24   Livelihood changes are predicted to continue and further alter Inuit communities and well-being (ACIA, 2004; Ford, 2009; Laidler et al., 2009). There will always be uncertainty about the magnitude of the adverse effects of climate change, and the burden of those effects will most probably fall predominantly on populations that have contributed little to the problem (Kovats and Haines, 2005). While the health impacts of climate change are not yet fully understood, this study contributes to the literature on perceived health effects of climate change in Inuit communities by identifying some community priorities surrounding this issue.

25   The culture, economy, and way of life of Inuit are under threat from human-induced climate change (Watt-Cloutier, 2004). The destruction of the age-old hunting economy presages destruction of the very culture of Inuit. The seriousness of the issue means that Inuit have to use every available avenue to bring their perspectives to the attention of decision makers who have the power to affect change (Watt-Cloutier, 2004; Kovats and Haines, 2005). This study further highlights the importance of participatory research and the merits of the photovoice technique in eliciting community perspectives and promoting social action from the individual to national level. Building

social capacity, thereby empowering communities to gain a sense of control, is essential to managing the health effects of climate change (Costello et al., 2009). Our findings support this notion and suggest that an investment in community is an essential strategy for mitigating the ill effects of climate change on health.

26   This study provides the foundation for continuing community-led research projects exploring the land-health environment relationship. Further community-led research using creative and participatory methods is needed to improve our understanding of the health implications of climate change in the North and to reduce health disparities between northern communities and the rest of Canada. This project provided community members with the opportunity to learn and apply new research skills and contribute to a growing body of knowledge about the effects on climate change on the health of Northerners. Given the health threats posed by climate change, further work should be done to bolster community involvement in these issues and to actualize change at multiple socio-ecological levels. It is by strengthening capacity that northern communities will be able to cope with, and potentially reverse, the effects of climate change on health in the North.

Arctic 64. 2011. 1.

Acknowledgements

The community participants/researchers in this project shared incredible stories and experiences that cannot be articulated in the limited scope of this paper.

For the opportunity to share and learn from each other, we are grateful. The funding for this research came from the Health Canada First Nations and Inuit Health Branch program entitled Climate Change and Health Adaptation in the North.

References

ACIA (Arctic Climate Impact Assessment). 2004. Impacts of a warming Arctic. Cambridge: Cambridge University Press.

Association of Canadian Universities for Northern Studies. 2003. Ethical principles for conduct of research in the North. http://acuns.ca/website/ethical-principles/.

Berkes, F., and Jolly, D. 2001. Adapting to climate change: Social-ecological resilience in a Canadian western Arctic community. Conservation Ecology 5(2): 18. [online] URL: www.consecol.org/vol5/iss2/art18/.

CIHR (Canadian Institutes of Health Research). 2008. CIHR guidelines for health research involving Aboriginal people. www.cihr-irsc.gc.ca/e/29134.html.

Costello, A., Abbas, M., Allen, A., Ball, S., Bell, S., Bellamy, R., Friel, S., et al. 2009. Managing the health effects of climate change. The Lancet 373:1693–1733.

Duhaime, G., Chabot, M., Fréchette, P., Robichaud, V., and Proulx, S. 2004. The impact of dietary changes among the Inuit of Nunavik (Canada): A socioeconomic assessment of possible public health recommendations dealing with food contamination. Risk Analysis 24:1007–1018, doi:10.1111/j.0272–4332.2004.00503.x.

Egan, C. 1998. Points of view: Inuit women's perceptions of pollution. International Journal of Circumpolar Health 57 (Suppl. 1):550–554.

Ford, J.D. 2009. Vulnerability of Inuit food systems to food insecurity as a consequence of climate change: A case study from Igloolik, Nunavut. Regional Environmental Change 9:83–100, doi:10.1007/s10113–008–0060-x.

Ford, J.D., and Smit, B. 2004. A framework for assessing the vulnerability of communities in the Canadian Arctic to risks associated with climate change. Arctic 57:389–400.

Ford, J.D., Smit, B., and Wandel, J. 2006. Vulnerability to climate change in the Arctic: A case study from Arctic Bay, Canada. Global Environmental Change 16:145–160, doi:10.1016/j.gloenvcha.2005.11.007.

Furgal, C., and Seguin, J. 2006. Climate change, health and vulnerability in Canadian northern Aboriginal communities. Environmental Health Perspectives 114:1964–1970.

Furgal, C., Martin, D., and Gosselin, P. 2002. Climate change and health in Nunavik and Labrador: Lessons from Inuit knowledge. In: Krupnik, I., and Jolly, D., eds. The earth is faster now: Indigenous observations of Arctic environmental change. Washington, D.C.: Arctic Research Consortium of the United States and Arctic Studies Centre, Smithsonian Institution. 266–300.

Hegerl, G.C., Zwiers, F.W., Braconnot, P., Gillett, N.P., Luo, Y., Marengo Orsini, J.A., Nicholls, N., Penner, J.E., and Stott, P.A. 2007. Understanding and attributing climate change. Chapter 9. In: Solomon, S., Qin, D., Manning, M., Chen, Z., Marquis, M., Avery, K.B., Tignor, M., and Miller, H.L., eds. Climate change 2007: The physical science basis. Contribution of Working Group I to the Fourth Assessment Report of the Intergovernmental Panel on Climate Change. Cambridge: Cambridge University Press.

Kovats, R.S., and Haines, A. 2005. Global climate change and health: Recent findings and future steps. Canadian Medical Association Journal 172:501–502, doi:10.1503/cmaj.050020.

Kuhnlein, H.V., and Soueida, R. 1992. Use and nutrient composition of traditional Baffin Inuit foods. Journal of Food Composition and Analysis 5:112–126, doi:10.1016/0889–1575(92)90026-G.

Laidler, G.J. 2006. Inuit and scientific perspectives on the relationship between sea ice and climate change: The ideal complement? Climatic Change 78:407–444.

Laidler, G.J., Dialla, A., and Joamie, E. 2008. Human geographies of sea ice: Freeze/thaw processes around Pangnirtung, Nunavut, Canada. Polar Record 44:335–361, doi:10.1017/S003224740800750X.

Laidler, G.J., Ford, J.D., Gough, W.A., Ikummaq, T., Gagnon, A.S., Kowal, S., Qrunnut, K., and Irngaut, C. 2009. Travelling and hunting in a changing Arctic: Assessing Inuit vulnerability to sea ice change in Igloolik, Nunavut. Climatic Change 94: 363–397, doi:10.1007/s10584–008–9512-z.

Macaulay, A.C., Commanda, L.E., Freeman, W.L., Gibson, N., McCabe, M.L., Robbins, C.M., and Twohig, P.L. 1999. Participatory research maximizes community and lay involvement. British Medical Journal 319:774–778.

Moffitt, P., and Vollman, A.R. 2004. Photovoice: Picturing the health of Aboriginal women in a remote northern community. Canadian Journal of Nursing Research 36:189–201.

Natural Resources Canada. 2004. Climate change impacts and adaptation: A Canadian perspective. Edited by D.S. Lemmen and F.J. Warren. Ottawa: Climate Change Impacts and Adaptation Division, Natural Resources Canada. http://adaptation.nrcan.gc.ca/perspective/profile_e.php.

Qaujigiartiit Health Research Centre. 2010. Reviewer health research ethics checklist (draft). Iqaluit, Nunavut: Qaujigiartiit Health Research Centre. www.nunavut.arctichealth.ca/apps/Docs/displayDocs.aspx.

Van Oostdam, J., Donaldson, S.G., Feeley, M., Arnold, D., Ayotte, P., Bondy, G., Chan, L., et al. 2005. Human health implications of environmental contaminants in Arctic Canada: A review. Science of the Total Environment 352:165–246.

Wang, C., and Burris, M.A. 1994. Empowerment through photo novella: Portraits of participation. Health Education Quarterly 21:171–186.

———. 1997. Photovoice: Concept, methodology, and use for participatory needs assessment. Health Education and Behavior 24:369–387.

Wang, C.C., Yi, W.K., Tao, Z.W., and Carovano, K. 1998. Photovoice as a participatory health promotion strategy. Health Promotion International 13:75–86.

Watt-Cloutier, S. 2004. Climate change and human rights. Human Rights Dialogue: "Environmental Rights." Series 2(11). New York: Carnegie Council.

Weatherhead, E., Gearheard, S., and Barry, R.G. 2010. Changes in weather persistence: Insight from Inuit knowledge. Global Environmental Change 20:523–528, doi:10.1016/j.gloenvcha.2010.02.002.

World Health Organization. 2003. Climate change and human health—Risks and responses: Summary. Edited by A.J., McMichael, D.H. Campbell-Lendrum, C.F. Corvalán, K.L. Ebi, A.K. Githeko, J.D. Scheraga, and A. Woodward. Geneva, Switzerland: World Health Organization. www.who.int/globalchange/publications/cchhsummary/en/.

Key and challenging words

tenacity, mandate, protocol, adhere, salient, paucity, equitable, mitigate, advocacy, presage, disparity

Questions

1. Explain why the introduction is divided into two sub-sections and analyze the functions of each.

2. (a) Which study of those mentioned in the Introduction appears closest to the authors' study? Explain. (b) Identify, then paraphrase, Healey et al.'s thesis.

3. In your own words, (a) define participatory research; (b) explain its importance as a research method; (c) explain its value to the community.

4. For the "Results" section, (a) discuss the importance of organization, identifying strategies that aid the reader's understanding; (b) focusing on any two of the first four sub-sections within "Results," identify specific strategies that aid the reader's comprehension of those sections.

5. Compare and contrast the "Results" section in this essay with the corresponding section in Youseff, "The more you play, the more aggressive you become," p. 316. For the general characteristics of Type B essays and the differences between those with quantitative and qualitative methodologies, see Chapter 3, p. 23, and Appendix B.

6. Explain the way in which the health model emerged from the photovoice analysis process and its importance to the study as a whole.

7. Referring to at least one paragraph in the "Discussion" section, show how the Healey et al. study contributes to the literature on climate change and health in northern communities.

8. Do you think the authors are essentially positive or negative about the ability of northern communities to meet the challenges posed by climate change? In your answer, refer to specific passages in the text.

Post-reading

1. *Collaborative activity:* After re-reading paragraphs 5–6 of the study, break into groups of 6 members each. Plan a qualitative study in which you address a problem at your university using the participatory research method and the photovoice technique. After identifying the problem and key research question(s), discuss what an "Introduction" and a "Methods" section would include. Group members should take photographs that reflect their concerns with the problem. Meet during a later class to choose representative photographs and discuss their significance in terms of the problem/research questions. Finally, identify "themes" emerging from the discussion (see paragraphs 6 and 8).

2. Write a brief (500- to 750-word) evaluative report (stressing assessment) or informational report (stressing content) on a website dedicated to the study of climate change in the Canadian Arctic. One such site mentioned in the article is ArcticNet; this site also contains links to similar sites that you could consider. Organize your report by appropriate formal or descriptive categories. Formal categories could include introduction, methods (basis of your evaluation), results, and conclusion. You could consider the website's purpose, credibility, main menu, links, navigation aids, accessibility, organization, visual appeal, quality and depth of information, use of charts to enhance understanding, and so on.

Related websites of interest

Nasivvik Centre for Inuit Health and Changing Environments:
www.nasivvik.ca

Network Environments for Aboriginal Health Research (NEAHR):
www.cihr-irsc.gc.ca/e/27071.html

Additional library reading

Furgal, C., & Seguin, J. (2006). Climate change, health, and vulnerability in Canadian northern Aboriginal communities. *Environmental Health Perspectives, 114*(12), 1964–1970. doi: 10.1289/ehp.8433

Lougheed, T. (2010). The changing landscape of Arctic traditional food. *Environmental Health Perspectives, 118*(9), 386–393. doi:10.1289/eph.118-a386

APPENDIX A
A Note on Statistics

What Do Students Need to Know about Statistics?

1   There are two main types of research: qualitative and quantitative. Both types help us to describe or explain a phenomenon (e.g., the experience of war veterans); however, each method goes about describing the situation in very different ways. Qualitative research uses non-numerical data, such as words or pictures, in order to describe a phenomenon. In-depth interviews and/or extensive observations are typically used in order to collect this type of data. An interview with a war veteran about his experience during the war is an example of a qualitative research approach. Quantitative research, on the other hand, uses numbers in order to describe or explain a phenomenon and typically investigates the relationship between variables (e.g., the relationship between war veterans and depression). Quantitative research typically includes questionnaires with large samples of participants and uses a strict methodology in order to control all factors that are related to the data and therefore may affect the interpretation of that data. A questionnaire mailed out to a random sample of 500 male war veterans across Canada between the ages of 65 and 85 who have no family history of depression is an example of a quantitative research approach.

2   The decision to use qualitative versus quantitative methods depends on the research question that you ask and the type of information you want to obtain. Qualitative research provides rich and detailed words to describe a phenomenon, but the data is situation- and context-specific. By contrast, quantitative research provides numerical data to describe the relationship between variables, and these relationships may be generalized to the population as a whole. In this essay, we will describe why and how quantitative research methods may be used to answer a research question.

3   In the social sciences, we conduct research because we are interested in better understanding human behaviour (e.g., frequency of drinking, reaction time, level of intelligence). Most of the time, however, we do not limit ourselves to describing just that behaviour, but we also want to know whether (and how) it is related to some other feature of the person or the situation. For example, suppose you are interested in studying the level of intelligence (IQ) of undergraduate students in linguistics. You might be wondering whether female and male students will have, on average, the same IQ or whether it varies depending on gender. That is, do female students have higher or lower IQ than males? In this case, IQ is what we call the dependent variable, and the feature in your study that you think has an influence on it—gender—is the independent variable.

Mean and Variance

4   Now suppose you recruit 10 male and 10 female students from one of your classes to answer this question. After administering an intelligence test to your 20 participants (N=20), you realize that each has a different IQ level. For some participants, their IQ value is 100, for others 130, and for still others 110. Because you want to compare the IQ of two groups (females vs males), you need a unique value, representative of each group, that would allow you to make this comparison. The best way to create that value is by averaging the individual IQ values within each group, creating the mean IQ for each group.

5   Because the mean is only an average of individual IQ values, it will not tell us much about each value from which it was calculated. For example, suppose the mean IQ of both the male and female groups is the same (e.g., 115). The single values used to compute those means could nonetheless be very different. Some males, for example, may have values of 90 and others 130, averaging out to 100, whereas the IQ values of females may be in general closer to the mean (e.g., some 115 and others 120) but also averaging out to 100. In other words, the group of males may have more variation in their IQ values than the group of females.

6   As you can probably infer by now, the mean becomes less trustworthy as an estimate of the group's IQ when the variation is greater. Therefore, it is useful to have information about how much the single values used to calculate the mean differ from this mean (i.e., a general measure of how spread these values are from the mean). You can obtain this information by calculating the variance.

7   Once you have the information about the mean IQ and the variance for each of your groups, you can use a statistical test of inference to determine whether the means of the two groups are actually different from each other. Recall that you were interested in determining whether, on average, females in your class have higher or lower IQ than males. If the mean IQ for males and females is exactly the same, you would intuitively conclude that females and males are equally smart (as measured by IQ). If they differ by one or two points, your conclusion would probably be the same, because you would consider those one or two points to be random and unimportant. However, what would you conclude if the two means differed by 10 points? How would you determine whether the two means are meaningfully different and that their difference is not just due to chance?

8   Researchers consider two means to be significantly different when there is a very small probability (less than .05 or less than 5 in 100 times) that these two means are different only by chance. In order to determine this probability there are a number of statistical tests you can use (see below, "Correlation and Prediction"). Returning to our example, if the mean IQ for female students was 130 and the mean IQ for male students was 120, and if the test you used indicated that there was a less than 5 in 100 probability that these two values differed by chance, then you could (sadly or happily) say that the girls in your class have a significantly higher IQ value than the boys. The standard of 5 in 100 for "statistical significance" is an arbitrary but useful convention in research. It does not refer to the social or practical significance of the result, because that is not a statistical issue.

9   If you had obtained the 20 participants from your class (i.e., your sample) using a random procedure, you could generalize the results of your study to your entire class (in this case, your population). However, notice that very rarely do researchers randomly select subjects to participate in their studies and, instead, the selection depends on other factors (e.g., those people who agree to participate in the study).

Correlation and Prediction

10   Say we want to know the relationship between high school GPA and university GPA. Our research question could be, What is the relationship between GPA in high school and GPA in university? A simple bivariate correlation can be used to answer this question. Correlations describe the extent to which two variables co-vary (e.g., as high school GPA goes up, so does university GPA).

11   However, say we determine that mothers' university GPA, fathers' university GPA, age, gender, and parents' income are also related (correlated) to GPA, and we want to know which factors influence university GPA the most. We can use multiple regression to answer this question. In multiple regression, all of the variables are entered into a regression (mathematical) equation, which then determines which factors most strongly influence university GPA when controlling for all other factors that were entered into the equation. Let's say fathers' university GPA and mothers' university GPA are revealed as the strongest factors influencing a university GPA. We can then use this information to screen and/or predict who will do the best in university based on their scores on the predictor variables. For example, if a student's mother and father had a high university GPA, we would predict that the student would have a high university GPA.

12   Another common statistical procedure is called an ANOVA (analysis of variance), which allows us to compare groups. Say we want to compare basketball players, volleyball players, and soccer players on their GPA. A t-test can be used to compare two groups (e.g., basketball players and volleyball players); however, an ANOVA will allow us to compare more than two groups (e.g., basketball, volleyball, and soccer players).

13   For many people, statistics seem intimidating and overwhelming. However, the importance of statistics cannot be understated. At the most basic level of statistics, there are means, medians, modes, and percentages that tell us basic descriptive information (e.g., can describe the current situation). At the more complex level of statistical analysis used by most researchers, statistics allow us to answer some very interesting questions and to make important predictions about human behaviour.

—Rachel Dean, Ph.D., and Agustin Del Vento, M.Sc.

APPENDIX B
Characteristics of Type A, Type B, and Type C Essays

Feature	Type A	Type B	Type C
Methodology	qualitative (ideas, values, qualities); may have theoretical base	usually quantitative; centred on data that are generated, observed, and recorded	qualitative: organizes studies by categories, such as approaches to subject; summarizes and analyzes them
Author	often single author	often two or more authors	varies
Abstract	sometimes	yes	sometimes
Purpose	variable: may inform, generate new knowledge, or seek to interpret knowledge in a new way	generates new knowledge	evaluates what has been written; finds gaps in the research and suggests future directions
Audience	other scholars and advanced students in the humanities	other scholars/researchers and advanced students in the social sciences and sciences	other scholars/researchers and advanced students in all disciplines, especially the social sciences; other educated and interested readers
Length	variable; tend to be longer than Type B and C; paragraphs may be lengthy due to discursive nature	variable; qualitative studies are often longer than quantitative ones	variable
Structure	may use content headings	formal, standardized headings and sections	may use content headings
Introduction	includes thesis, key question(s), or essay plan; justifies need for study and often includes literature review; claim is interpretive[1]	includes hypothesis to be tested or question to be answered; justifies need for study and includes literature review; claim is fact-based[1]	essay plan, key question(s), or thesis; justifies need for review but no special review section as the entire article reviews the literature; claim is fact-based
Primary sources	interprets/analyzes them; often uses direct quotation	generates raw (numerical) data in order to test hypothesis, arrive at conclusions; primary sources often appear in tables/charts	focuses on results/findings of secondary sources
Secondary sources	interprets/analyzes them; uses both direct quotation and summary	refers to them in literature review; uses summary	refers to/analyzes secondary sources (studies) throughout; uses summary more than direct quotation
Source treatment	uses analysis and synthesis throughout essay	uses analysis in "Results" and/or "Discussion" section; uses synthesis in literature review and in "Discussion" or "Conclusion"	uses synthesis throughout; analyzes and critically evaluates studies, often using compare and contrasting pattern; definition and division are also common

Feature	Type A	Type B	Type C
Voice	variable: may be relatively detached (humanities) or involved (some social science research involving group observation; active voice preferred	objective, detached; may use passive voice occasionally	objective
Style	variable: may be discursive and complex; longer sentences and paragraphs; sentence variety; moderate/difficult language level	straightforward, direct; simple sentence structure	variable: straightforward, direct; simple sentence structure; may at times be discursive in analyzing/evaluating studies
Terminology	specialized diction but may borrow terms from other disciplines and define their specific usage in essay; may use terms applicable to a particular theory	specialized diction; assumes reader familiarity with terms as well as experimental and statistical processes	specialized diction; may explain key terms
Ancillary material	may be included in some disciplines, such as history or Greek and Roman studies; illustrations may be used in book chapters	charts, graphs, tables, figures, photos, appendices are common	sometimes includes figures or other illustrations to summarize content
Conclusion	may summarize or focus on implications of the study's findings	indicates whether hypothesis is proved/disproved or how question has been answered; often suggests practical applications/further research directions	may summarize and/or suggest future research directions or specific ways to apply the studies reviewed; may make recommendations

[1] In an interpretive claim, the author weighs and interprets the evidence of the primary or secondary sources, using close analysis and sound reasoning. In a fact-based claim in a Type B study, the author presents his or her hypothesis and proceeds to test it under controlled conditions. An interpretive claim could use factual material as evidence; similarly, the evidence in a fact-based claim could be interpreted various ways.

Glossary

abstract   A condensed summary used in an empirical study; it is placed before the essay begins and includes at a minimum purpose, methods, and results.

academic (scholarly) journal   A type of periodical containing scholarly content (articles, reviews, and commentaries) by experts for a knowledgeable audience in related fields of study.

academic writer   A specialist in his or her subject area who is familiar with what has been written and is able to assess the strengths as well as the limitations of others' work.

active construction (active voice)   A way of constructing a sentence to show that the subject performs the action of the verb.

allusion   An indirect reference to an outside source in order to clarify a point or get the reader to look at it in a new light.

analogy   A systematic comparison between the topic item and another one that is like it in the relevant point but is otherwise unlike the first one; it can be used to make the first item more easily understood.

analysis   In analysis, you break up a whole in order to (1) closely examine each part individually and/or (2) investigate the relationships among the parts.

annotated bibliography   An expanded bibliography that includes not only the information of standard bibliographies but also highly condensed summaries of related works.

annotation (verb *annotate*)   A note that explains, expands on, or comments on a written text.

appeal to ethos   The strategic use of ethics or morality in order to help convince a reader. Intrinsic ethos demonstrates the writer's credibility, for example, through knowledge or fairness; extrinsic ethos is shown by the writer's character or abilities as perceived by others.

appeal to logos   The strategic use of reason and logic in order to help convince a reader.

appeal to pathos   The strategic use of emotion in order to help convince a reader.

audience   Whom you are writing to; includes one or more readers with common interests, knowledge level, and/or expectations.

brainstorming   A prewriting technique in which you list your associations with a subject in the order they occur to you.

case study   A carefully selected example that is analyzed in detail in order to support a writer's claim.

circular conclusion   Reinforces the thesis.

claim   An assertion about the topic appearing in the thesis statement and in topic sentences.

clustering   A prewriting technique that works spatially to generate associations with a subject and connections among them.

coherence   A principle of paragraph construction in which ideas are logically laid out with clear connections between them.

common ground   An argumentative strategy in which you show readers that you share many of their values, making you appear open and approachable.

concession   An argumentative strategy in which you concede or qualify a point, acknowledging its validity, in order to come across as fair and reasonable.

conclusion   The last paragraph or section of an essay whose main function is to summarize the thesis and/or main points in the body of the essay.

connotation (verb *connote*)   The implications or additional meanings of a word; a word's context may suggest its connotations.

conventions   Recurrent patterns that direct and organize the behaviour of specific groups of people and that, applied appropriately, help us communicate with our audience.

credibility   Along with evidence, helps support a claim. Credibility can be demonstrated by an author's knowledge, reliability, and fairness.

critical analysis   A writing activity concerned with breaking down a text to examine its structure, reasoning, rhetorical strategies, significance, and other features.

deductive reasoning   Reasoning based on a generalization, which is applied to a specific instance to draw a conclusion.

denotation (verb *denote*)   The meaning of a word, for example, as defined in a dictionary.

descriptive (content) headings   Headings usually consist of a phrase summarizing the content of the section that follows.

digital object identifier (DOI)   A number-letter sequence that begins with the number 10 often found on journal articles; serves as a persistent link for digital material.

discursive   Expansive, or covering a wide area.

documentation style   Guidelines for documenting sources put forth in style manuals and handbooks for researchers and other academic writers.

dramatic opening   A technique for creating reader interest by beginning with a question, illustration, anecdote, quotation, description, or other attention-grabbing technique.

ellipsis   Three or four spaced dots in a direct quotation, indicating that one or more words have been omitted.

empirically based study   Data or information based on an experiment or on observation; can be verified.

essay plan   A form of a thesis in which main points are outlined in the order they will occur in the essay.

focused reading   A reading strategy in which close attention is paid to sentences and words in order to extract detail, tone, style, relevance, etc.

freewriting   A prewriting technique in which you write on a subject without stopping to edit.

graph   Represents relationships between two variables.

hypothesis   A prediction about an outcome; used in essays in which an experiment is set up to prove/disprove the prediction.

inductive reasoning   Reasoning that relies on facts, details, and observations to draw a conclusion.

inference   A conclusion based on what the evidence shows or points to. More than one inference might be possible in a given situation, but the most probable one is said to be the best inference.

irony   The existence in a text of two levels of meaning, one surface and literal, the other deeper and non-literal.

jargon   Discipline-specific language used to communicate among members of the discipline.

justification   Announces reason for undertaking the study; may focus on what it will add to previous research or what gap in the research it will fill.

literature review   A condensed survey of articles on the topic arranged in a logical order, usually ending with the article most relevant to the author's study.

logical fallacies   Categories of faulty reasoning.

logical opening   A technique for creating reader interest by beginning with a generalization and narrowing to the thesis.

mixed format   A method of source integration in which you combine significant words of the source, placed in quotation marks, with your own words.

monograph   A highly specialized scholarly work or treatise in book form.

open-access journal   A kind of journal (usually scholarly) that is available online without a fee.

order of points   The way in which points are presented in an essay. Climax order is the order of points that proceeds from the weakest to the strongest; other orders include inverted climax order and mixed order.

original research   Research in which the author(s) conducts an experiment to generate raw data or uses available data to prove/disprove a hypothesis or answer a research question. Such research includes the method, results, and discussion of results.

outline   A linear or graphic representation of main and subpoints, showing an essay's structure.

paraphrase   A method of source integration in which you put someone else's ideas in your own words, keeping the length of the original.

passive construction (passive voice)   A way of constructing a sentence to show that the subject is being acted upon.

peer-reviewed journal   A type of journal in which submissions are reviewed by experts before publication; an authoritative source for scholarly research.

periodical   A kind of publication that is issued periodically, at regular or semi-regular intervals; academic journals and magazines are examples of periodicals.

policy claim   An assertion about a topic that advocates an action (e.g., to fix a problem or improve a situation).

precedent   A kind of example that refers to the way a situation was dealt with in the past in order to argue for its similar use in the present.

primary sources   Original material in a field of study; examples include literary texts, historical documents, and interviews.

process-reflective draft   A draft that emerges from a flexible engagement with what you are writing, one that reflects the connections between thinking and writing.

prompt   A word, phrase, or clause that directs readers to important content rather than containing important content itself.

purpose   Why you are writing; variables affecting purpose include your topic and your audience.

questioning   A prewriting technique in which you ask relevant questions about the topic.

reader-based prose   Clear, accessible writing designed for an intended reader.

refutation   An argumentative strategy of raising opposing points in order to counter them with your own points.

rhetorical pattern   A method for organizing and presenting information in essays and paragraphs; examples include cause–effect, classification, comparison and contrast, cost–benefit, and definition.

scanning   A form of selective reading in which you skim sections or an entire text. In a general scan, you try to determine the gist of a text—for example, by locating main ideas; in a targeted scan, you look for specific concepts or topics by keywords or phrases.

secondary sources   Commentary on or interpretation of primary material; examples include academic studies, reports, and presentations.

selective reading   A reading strategy designed to meet a specific objective, such as scanning for main points or reading for detail.

signal phrase   Introduces a reference by naming the author(s) and usually includes a "signal verb" (e.g., *states, argues, explains*).

spiral conclusion   Suggests applications or further research.

subject index   A list of important words in a text, ordered alphabetically and usually placed at the end of the text.

summarization   A broadly inclusive term for representing the ideas of a writer in a condensed form, using mostly your own words.

summary   A method of extracting the main idea (or ideas) from an original source, expressing it in your own words.

support   Evidence to help prove a claim.

syllogism   A logical three-part structure that can be used to illustrate how deductive conclusions are made.

synthesis   Writing in which elements of a work or other studies about a work are brought together, usually in order to draw a conclusion or interpret a claim you wish to assert about the work.

table   Presents detailed information in matrix format, in columns and rows that are easily scanned.

thesis statement   A statement that includes the main point of your essay or what you will attempt to prove; it is placed at the end of your introduction.

topic sentence   A sentence that states the main idea in the paragraph; usually the first sentence.

trade books   Books published by non-academic presses for general readers about topics of interest to them.

transitional words and phrases   Words and phrases that connect ideas in a sentence or paragraph, or between paragraphs.

unity   A principle of paragraph construction in which only one idea is developed throughout the paragraph.

university press   A university-affiliated publisher, usually of books or journals; authoritative source for scholarly research.

value claim   An assertion about a topic that appeals to its ethical nature (e.g., good/bad or fair/unfair).

warrant   A link between claim and evidence, showing how the evidence is relevant to or supports the claim.

Credits

Anderson, Christopher G. "The senate and the fight against the 1885 Chinese Immigration Act." *Canadian Parliamentary Review* 30 (Summer 2007), pp. 21–6.

Arbour-Nicitopoulos, Kelly P., Matthew Y.W. Kwan, David Lowe, Sara Taman, and Guy E.J. Faulkner. "Social norms of alcohol, smoking, and marijuana use within a Canadian university setting." *Journal of American College Health* 59.3 (2010), pp. 191–6. Published by Taylor & Francis Ltd. www.informaworld.com

Attaran, Amir. "The ugly Canadian." *The Literary Review of Canada* 17.5 (2009), pp. 3–6.

Cusimano, Michael D., Bhanu Sharma, David W. Lawrence, Gabriela Ilie, Sarah Silverberg, and Rochelle Jones. "Trends in North American newspaper reporting of brain injury in ice hockey." *Plos One* 8.4 (2013). DOI: 10.1371/journal.pone.0061865

Devine, John William. "Doping is a threat to sporting excellence." *British Journal of Sports Medicine* 45 (2011), pp. 637–9. Copyright 2011, with permission from BMJ Publishing Group Ltd.

Dutton, Daniel J., Norman R.C. Campbell, Charlene Elliott, and Lindsay McLaren. "A ban on marketing of foods/beverages to children: The who, why, what and how of a population health intervention." *Canadian Journal of Public Health* 103(2): 2012, pp. 100–2. Reprinted with permission of the Canadian Public Health Association.

Foote, Jeremy. "Speed that kills: The role of technology in Kate Chopin's 'The story of an hour'." *The Explicator* 71. 2 (2013), pp. 85–9. Reprinted by permission of the publisher (Taylor & Francis Ltd, wwwinformaworld.com).

Gifford, Robert. "Psychology's essential role in alleviating the impacts of climate change." *Canadian Psychology* 49.4 (2008), pp. 273–80. © 2008 Canadian Psychological Association. Reprinted by permission of the Canadian Psychological Association.

Gillam, Ken, and Shannon R. Wooden. "Post-princess models of gender: The new man in Disney/Pixar." *Journal of Popular Film & Television* 36 (2008), pp. 2–8. Published by Taylor & Francis Ltd. www.informaworld.com

Gleick, P.H. et al. Letter, "Climate change and the integrity of science." *Science* 328 (7 May 2010), 689–90. Reprinted with permission from AAAS.

Hasan, Youssef, Laurent Bègue, Michael Scharkow, and Brad J. Bushman. "The more you play, the more aggressive you become: A long-term experimental study of cumulative violent video game effects on hostile expectations and aggressive behavior." *Journal of Experimental Social Psychology* 49 (2013), pp. 224–7. Copyright 2013, with permission from Elsevier.

Healey, G.K. et al. "Community perspectives on the impact of climate change on health in Nunavut, Canada." *Arctic* 64. 1:2011, pp. 89–97. Reprinted by permission of the Arctic Institute of North America.

Hume, Stephen. "Pipeline debate shaping up as propaganda war" by Stephen Hume, Vancouver Sun, 28 December 2013. Reprinted by permission of the Vancouver Sun.

Kelman, Suanne. "Shooting the messenger: Why Canadians don't often blow the whistle on wrongdoing." *Literary Review of Canada* [19.5] (June 2011). http://reviewcanada.ca/magazine/2011/06/shooting-the-messenger/ © Suanne Kelman. Reprinted with permission. First printed in the Literary Review of Canada (LRC), June 2011.

Kingwell, Mark. "Intellectuals and democracy." *Unruly Voices: Essays on Democracy, Civility, and the Human Imagination*. Windsor, ON: Biblioasis, 2012. pp. 131–6. Published by Biblioasis and reprinted by permission of the publisher.

Krahn, Timothy. "Where are we going with preimplantation genetic diagnosis?" *CMAJ* 176.10 (2007), pp. 1445–6. © Canadian Medical Association. This work is protected by copyright and the making of this copy was with the permission of Access Copyright. Any alteration of its content or further copying in any form whatsoever is strictly prohibited unless otherwise permitted by law.

Lexchin, Joel. "Pharmaceutical innovation: Can we live forever? A commentary on Schnittker and Karandinos." Reprinted with permission from Elsevier. *Social Science & Medicine* 70 (2010), pp. 972–3.

Lightman, Bernard. "The microscopic world." *Victorian Review* 36.2 (Fall 2010), pp. 46–9. Reprinted with permission.

Maticka-Tyndale, Eleanor. "Sexuality and sexual health of Canadian adolescents: Yesterday, today and tomorrow." *The Canadian Journal of Human Sexuality* 17.3 (2008), pp. 85–95. Reprinted with permission from University of Toronto Press (www.utpjournals.com), © 2008 The Sex Information and Education Council of Canada (SIECCAN).

McMurtry, John. "University wars: The corporate administration vs. the vocation of learning." *CCPA Monitor* 16.3 (July/August 2009), pp. 16–18. © Canadian Centre for Policy Alternatives. This work is protected by copyright and the making of this copy was with the permission of Access Copyright. Any alteration of its content or further copying in any form whatsoever is strictly prohibited unless otherwise permitted by law.

Subject Index

The Subject Index includes essays in *The Active Reader* organized by 27 subject categories.

Index of Essay Types

Academic Essays

The following categories apply to the academic essays in this book. If the primary focus is on argument rather than exposition, the essay is listed under Argument.

Type A

Anderson (239), Foote (370), Gillam/Wooden (290), Lightman (363), Ouellette (284), Robidoux (300)

Type B

Arbour-Nicitopoulos et al. (180), Cusimano et al. (320), Hasan et al. (313), Healey et al. (388)

Type C

Maticka-Tyndale (257), Nord (206), Sabella/Patchin/Hinduja (337), Snow (160), Wickens/Mann/Wiesenthal (330)

Argument

Devine (358), Dutton et al. (279), Gifford (92, 376), Krahn (366), Lexchin (354), Shade (251), Young (27, 171), Zlotorzynska et al. (124)

Non-academic Essays

Attaran (192), Hume (44), Kelman (199), Kingwell (176), McMurtry (166), Miller (227), Miyagawa (231), Nikiforuk (188), Phillips (269), Saul (216), Thomas (124, 247), Toope (223), Wilson (273)

Index

Classification of Readings by Rhetorical Mode/Pattern

Most essays in *The Active Reader* employ the problem–solution rhetorical pattern; in addition, virtually all essays use some form of analysis and most use examples. However, writers use other rhetorical patterns to develop their main points. These patterns are listed below. Readings may make use of other patterns than just those listed.